Google® Business Solutions All-in-One For Dummies

Cheat Sheet

KU-675-676

Google Apps Tools

Google Apps are covered in depth in this book. Here we give quick thumbnail descriptions to guide your efforts.

- **Google Apps:** A set of software that all runs online, with the software and your data kept "in the cloud" by Google; available from any computer that's online, any time

- **Google Apps for Your Domain:** Assembles most of the Google services below into one gateway based on your domain

- **Google Docs:** Free or low-cost online word processing, spreadsheets and presentation, with collaboration support built in from the ground up

- **Gmail:** Industrial-strength free e-mail with over 1 gigabyte of free storage; much more if you pay a small fee

- **Google Talk:** A tool for instant messaging and free online phone calls

- **Google Calendar:** A multi-user tool for organizing and sharing events, accessible by everyone, all the time

- **Google Maps:** Online maps, interactive and flexible, integrated with mobile phone location-finding and Google Earth

- **Google Sites:** An easy way to create Web sites and intranet sites that host Google Docs, Google Calendars, Google Groups, Google Maps and more, all easy to interact with

- **Google Translate:** An easy way to access Web pages, including your Google Sites Web pages, in other languages

- **Google Mobile:** The #1 request from many execs is Web and intranet access from a mobile phone; that's Google Mobile.

Domain Name Rules

Here are 7 top rules for domain names:

- Getting your domain name(s) right is one of the crucial decisions you'll make, and you have to do it early and get it right. Here are some guidelines to help:

- If you're a business, try hard to find a sensible name that's available with the .com suffix. .net is a liveable second choice. Don't use .edu if you're not a legitimate university.

- Try for a "guessable" domain name. Ideally, someone who knows your business's name can figure out your business's domain name.

- If your business's name is "taken", consider including a geographical element — your home city or even street — to distinguish your name.

- Remember that domain names are used in search. Include some of your top search keywords in your domain name.

- But avoid generic terms like "shopping" and "recruiters" except if they're in your business name; these terms and their variations are heavily used and hard to "own" in the user's mind.

- More and more of your users will find you through search, especially Google Search, using the business name, product names, founders' names and/or your location. So a "good" domain name is crucial, but a "great" domain name is slightly less necessary than it used to be.

For Dummies: Bestselling Book Series for Beginners

Google® Business Solutions All-in-One For Dummies®

Cheat Sheet

Google Docs Shortcut Keys

Here is a core set of shortcut keys that work in at least two of the three Google Docs apps — Docs (word processing), Spreadsheets, and Presentations:

- **Save:** Ctrl+S
- **Bold:** Ctrl+B
- **Italics:** Ctrl+I
- **Underline:** Ctrl+U (avoid underlining on Web pages except for links)
- **Cut:** Ctrl+X
- **Copy:** Ctrl+C
- **Paste:** Ctrl+V
- **Undo:** Ctrl+Z
- **Redo:** Ctrl+Y
- **Move to cell in table or row:** Next cell — Tab; Previous cell — Shift+Tab

Shortcuts for Google Docs (the word processing application) only:

- **Select all:** Ctrl+A
- **Align left, center, right:** Ctrl+L, Ctrl+E, Ctrl+R
- **Fully justify:** Ctrl+J (not best for onscreen viewing)
- **Insert link:** Ctrl+K
- **Insert comment:** Ctrl+M
- **Bullet list:** Ctrl+Shift+L
- **Header level 1, 2, 3:** Ctrl+1,2,3

Shortcuts for Google Docs spreadsheets — moving in the spreadsheet:

- **First/last cell:** Ctrl+Home/End
- **Left- or rightmost cell:** Ctrl+←/Ctrl+→
- **Top or bottom cell:** Ctrl+↑/Ctrl+↓
- **Edit current cell:** F2
- **Move to previous cell in column:** Shift+Enter

Shortcuts for Google Docs spreadsheets — selecting in the spreadsheet:

- **Extend selection one cell:** Shift+↑, ↓, ← or →
- **Select row:** Shift+spacebar
- **Select column:** Ctrl+spacebar

Shortcuts for Google Docs presentations:

- **Insert new slide:** Ctrl+M
- **Move up/down a slide:** PgUp / PgDn
- **Next/previous slide:** → / ←
- **View full-screen:** F11
- **End show:** Esc

Google®
Business Solutions
ALL-IN-ONE
FOR
DUMMIES®

Google® Business Solutions
ALL-IN-ONE
FOR DUMMIES®

by Bud E. Smith and Ryan Williams

WILEY

Wiley Publishing, Inc.

Google® Business Solutions All-in-One For Dummies®

Published by
Wiley Publishing, Inc.
111 River Street
Hoboken, NJ 07030-5774

www.wiley.com

Copyright © 2009 by Wiley Publishing, Inc., Indianapolis, Indiana

Published by Wiley Publishing, Inc., Indianapolis, Indiana

Published simultaneously in Canada

For general information on our other products and services, please contact our Customer Care Department within the U.S. at 877-762-2974, outside the U.S. at 317-572-3993, or fax 317-572-4002.

For technical support, please visit www.wiley.com/techsupport.

Wiley also publishes its books in a variety of electronic formats. Some content that appears in print may not be available in electronic books.

Library of Congress Control Number is available from the Publisher.

ISBN: 978-0-470-38687-3

Manufactured in the United States of America

10 9 8 7 6 5 4 3 2 1

WILEY

About the Authors

Bud E. Smith is a computer book author with more than 12 years of publishing experience. *Google Business Solutions All-in-One For Dummies* is one of over a dozen books Bud has written or co-authored. His Wiley Publishing titles include *Creating Web Pages For Dummies,* now in its ninth edition, *Internet Marketing For Dummies,* and *Web Usability For Dummies.* In addition to writing books, Bud has been a computer magazine editor, product marketing manager, and project manager for online uses of video.

Bud got his start with computers in 1983, when he left a promising career as a welder for a stint as a data-entry clerk. Bud then moved to Silicon Valley to join a startup company, followed by work for Intel, IBM, Apple, HumanWare, HSBC, and others in the U. S., New Zealand, and the UK. His work and interests led him to acquire a degree in Information Systems Management from the University of San Francisco and a master's degree in Information Systems from the London School of Economics.

Ryan Williams is a writer based in Indianapolis, IN. His previous published titles include *MySpace For Dummies, Expert Podcasting Practices For Dummies, Laptops Just the Steps For Dummies, Windows XP Digital Music For Dummies,* and *Teach Yourself Visually Bass Guitar.* He also co-produces a weekly podcast on Indianapolis musical happenings and contributes low, thumpy bass sounds to various bands and musical productions in the area. He's also the most likely person in any gathering to Google any random question at any point in the discussion.

Dedication

Bud E. Smith: To Oriana — Thanks for your support through a lot of late nights and lost weekends to help bring this to life.

Ryan Williams: This book is for Jennifer, my favorite small business owner and the love of my life.

Acknowledgments

Bud E. Smith: The authors thank Amy Fandrei, acquisitions editor, and the staff that helped produce this book: project editor Christopher Morris, technical editor James Kelly, copy editor Mary Lagu, as well as the many other people responsible for page layout, proofreading, indexing, and graphic art.

The Web was initially built more for love than for money, and all the efforts going into it today are building an amazing resource that's an ever-increasing part of our daily lives. We'd like to acknowledge all those people who have invested time, talent, and care in making the Web what it is today.

Ryan Williams: Many thanks are due for the efforts and patience of the Wiley editorial staff, especially Amy Fandrei and Christopher Morris. It was wonderful to work with Floyd Smith on this book as well — never did I think I'd be collaborating on a book with a co-author from "over the pond." Finally, it'd be impossible to put this book together without the efforts of Google's staff to make their tools so freely available to developers and users alike. Thanks for making so much so open and accessible.

Publisher's Acknowledgments

We're proud of this book; please send us your comments through our online registration form located at http://dummies.custhelp.com. For other comments, please contact our Customer Care Department within the U.S. at 877-762-2974, outside the U.S. at 317-572-3993, or fax 317-572-4002.

Some of the people who helped bring this book to market include the following:

Acquisitions, Editorial

Senior Project Editor: Christopher Morris

Acquisitions Editor: Amy Fandrei

Copy Editor: Mary Lagu

Technical Editor: James Kelly

Editorial Manager: Kevin Kirschner

Editorial Assistant: Amanda Foxworth

Sr. Editorial Assistant: Cherie Case

Cartoons: Rich Tennant
(www.the5thwave.com)

Composition Services

Project Coordinator: Katherine Key

Layout and Graphics: Reuben W. Davis, Sarah Philippart, Ronald Terry

Proofreaders: Evelyn C. Gibson, John Greenough

Indexer: BIM Indexing & Proofreading Services

Publishing and Editorial for Technology Dummies

Richard Swadley, Vice President and Executive Group Publisher

Andy Cummings, Vice President and Publisher

Mary Bednarek, Executive Acquisitions Director

Mary C. Corder, Editorial Director

Publishing for Consumer Dummies

Diane Graves Steele, Vice President and Publisher

Composition Services

Gerry Fahey, Vice President of Production Services

Debbie Stailey, Director of Composition Services

Contents at a Glance

Table of Contents

Introduction

*W*hen you were starting your small business, you probably made sure that you had the basics — your brilliant idea, maybe an office or storefront, a computer, and (we hope) enough capital to get started. You're not a huge operation, so you don't have a lot of cash or resources to spend on the extras. And, you may think that this principle probably applies to your IT needs as well: If you have a computer and a network connection, you may think that's all you need.

There's more out there, though — more tools you can use to keep your records, reach your customers, and make your business thrive. These Internet-based tools can make a huge difference when it comes to your work, and they're easy to obtain. Best of all, they're available at little to no cost.

You've probably heard the name Google. The name of the company has become synonymous with looking for anything you might want on the Internet, and you can access its services from just about anywhere on the planet. What you may not know is what other services Google can offer to the small business owner. With these services, you can create your own IT department and get your business on the Internet quickly and safely.

And that's where this huge book comes in. All the information gathered here helps you get started, from setting up your own Google applications to selling your products and services online to making all your data and transactions safe. You are introduced to almost everything Google has to offer, and you see how to integrate these services to best fit your business. Really, how can you argue with better and safer services that help increase your business?

Taking a Look under the Hood

This book's size may be a little intimidating, but it's actually broken down into eight different sections that each tackles a different Google service or subject. Let's take a look at what each section contains.

Book 1: Google Apps

The first book deals with Google Apps, a comprehensive Web service that sets up your business with e-mail, calendar, online documents, and records, and many other services. This service takes your business from the file cabinet to online servers quickly and efficiently, and it helps you and you employees gain easy access to messages and information. Best of all, you can get this service for free (or get even more by paying for Google Apps Premiere).

Book II: Google Search Tools for Business

Google is best known for sifting through vast amounts of data for the information that best serves its users. This book shows you how to make your information work with Google's searches to make sure you get noticed every time. It also helps you integrate Google's search functions into your Web site to make sure your potential customers can find everything they need easily.

Book III: Highlighting Your Business

Google offers services other than just providing information through its standard search function. Services like Google Maps and Google Base provide directions, reviews, access to products and services, and even coupons online. This book shows you how to get your business listed on these services and take advantage of all they offer.

Book IV: Creating a Web Site with Google Sites

Many people have their own Web sites — why shouldn't you? Google Sites makes it simple for you to create your own Web site with a minimum of effort. This book guides you through the steps of buying a name for your site, creating your first Web page, and updating and editing your information as your business grows and thrives.

Book V: Google Tools for Your Site

Google doesn't try to keep all its services separate. Part of the usefulness of Google's Web tools is that they integrate and serve each other in extremely helpful ways. This book helps you take tools like Google Docs and Checkout to your site. Now, you can create a fully featured Web presence without spending thousands of dollars to have everything custom-made. Why reinvent the wheel?

Book VI: Google Ads and Analytics

All these Web tools are great, but how do you know how well they're working? Better yet, how can you make a little money by using them? This book introduces Google Ads and Google Analytics. With these tools, you can put ads on your site and track the amount of traffic your site receives. This is vital information if you're trying to make your site a preferred destination for users and advertisers alike.

Book VII: Securing Business Information

The Internet can be a complicated and unfamiliar place, and everybody's heard stories about the hackers and viruses that sometimes cause trouble for Web-based businesses. This book takes a look at the tools you can use to secure your information and make sure that nobody who shouldn't have access to your records gets it. You get information on securing your e-mail, your servers, and your computers.

Book VIII: Getting Noticed with Gadgets

Google Gadgets are small programs you can embed in your own Google homepage, your Google Apps accounts, and the Google desktops of other people. Not only can you use these gadgets to stay up to date on the news and your business information, but you can also write your own gadgets to spread the word about your business. Whether you're a novice or an experienced programmer, Google provides the tools to create a useful gadget.

Foolish Assumptions

Google is a large business with a vast array of services, so there's a lot of material to cover in this book. In order to get started, we had to make some assumptions about you. We didn't write this book presuming you've never turned on a computer before. Here's what we're taking for granted:

✦ You're somewhat comfortable using a computer and a Web browser.

✦ You have a steady and reliable Internet connection, whether you're at home, in the office, or at the coffee shop down the road.

✦ You have enough room on your desk or lap to handle both a computer and this rather large book.

Conventions Used in This Book

Whenever you're introduced to a term for the first time, you see that term in italics and get a brief definition of the term. This helps keep you on the same page (no pun intended) and accumulate vocabulary as you go.

Google's services can rely on using a lot of menus. If you need to navigate through a series of menu commands, you see them listed in this fashion — File⇨New⇨New Document.

This book contains a great deal of screenshots and lists of instructions. We didn't just want to tell you about what Google has to offer. Instead, we take you through the steps and show you how to make these services work inside the framework of your business.

Because this book is divided into different sections, you can feel free to skip around and read what you want to first. You find out all you need to know by going from cover to cover, but we promise you won't ruin the whole story if you skip to the end, either.

Icons Used in This Book

As you're reading, you may notice different pictures in the margins. You don't have to stop immediately and pay attention to them, but you'll find some useful information if you come back to them when you get a chance.

This gives you a little additional information or insight into the paragraph you're reading. Think of it as a bonus point.

We don't want to get you in trouble, so we're using these icons to signal what you may want to look out for. Heeding these warnings can save you from losing time, money, or your mind.

Some things are just so important that they bear repeating. If we keep bringing it up, that's because you need to know it. We just don't want to beat you over the head with this information, so that's why it goes here.

Some people are content to drive the car, and some want to look under the hood. Because you don't need to know exactly how the engine works in order to drive, you can skip over this information if you want to. If you're not satisfied with just the basics, though, read these tips to find out more.

Time to Get Started!

Now that you have some background on the book, you can begin. Feel free to jump in wherever you want, or start at the beginning and just keep reading. Either way, you'll find out what Google can do for your business and how it can make your life a lot easier.

Book I
Google Apps

"He saw your laptop and wants to know if he can check his Gmail."

Contents at a Glance

Chapter 1: Getting Started with Google Apps

In This Chapter

✔ Deciding if Google Apps works for your business

✔ Putting together the right package of applications

✔ Getting the help you need to make Google Apps work for you

Choosing the software you use for your business requires more than just selecting the easiest or the cheapest solution. You have to take into account whether the tools will actually work for you and whether your employees will be able (or willing) to use them effectively. Fortunately, Google Apps provides a formidable suite of applications that can meet your needs at a relatively low cost (maybe even for free). This chapter helps you outline your needs and determine whether Google Apps will meet them.

What Are Google Apps?

Google Apps provides the tools you need to manage your business documentation, communication, and scheduling online, and it does so in the framework of your own Web site. You don't have to worry about changing any Web sites or services you already have in place — Google Apps integrates with your domain to provide some excellent services, including e-mail, calendars, document creation and editing, and more. It's like adding a robust intranet to your Web site with little effort (and, depending on the size of your operation, little cost).

Google Apps comes in two different packages:

✦ **Google Apps Standard:** This package provides the basic level of all of these services, but you're limited in the amount and type of support you can receive from Google, and you're restricted to only 50 accounts.

✦ **Google Apps Premiere Edition:** The Premier Edition offers a great deal of personalized support and as many accounts as you're willing to pay for.

How Will This Work for Me?

Every small business is different because the people who start them are different. You may have started your own lawn-care business, a small collectables boutique, or the ever-vital dog walking service. The exact needs of each business is different — after all, the type of information you need to track differs. In one case, your clients may be buying tiny ceramic figurines of small children trapped in the rain; in the other, they may be dropping off their prized English Bulldogs for walkies. Still, no matter what your needs, your small business can use the same tools to keep everything organized and enable you to talk to the right people.

The necessary services

In order to conduct business, you must plan your activities, create and maintain records of your transactions, and communicate with your clients or customers. In the modern business world, you're most likely to perform these necessary activities using these tools:

✦ E-mail

✦ Calendar

✦ Word processor

✦ Spreadsheets

✦ Web site

For example, let's take a look at that lawn care business. Jake's Landscaping has two main employees — Jake and his business partner, James. Jake handles the bulk of the actual landscaping labor, whereas James helps out on larger jobs and manages the business paperwork and scheduling. Jake and James also sometimes have their kids and their friends help out with basic lawn-mowing jobs. So they have a core business partnership with additional temporary employees and a wide range of jobs to handle. Without the tools listed previously, it would be hard to keep track of everything. Google Apps offers some options to help.

Google Apps is a feature that's meant to work with an existing Web site with a Web hosting service. Google Apps does not provide a working Web site, although you can point the account to a Google Sites page if you must. Work with your domain registrar to make this happen, as the process can change from registrar to registrar.

What Google Apps can do for you

In this example, the partners of Jake's Landscaping are taking a look at Google Apps. They already know what they need, and they're hoping Google Apps can solve those needs in an easy and effective way. Let's take a look at Jake's Landscaping and see how Google Apps will solve some of their problems.

✦ **Your virtual file cabinet:** Jake's Landscaping had a large file cabinet full of all kinds of paperwork. Google Apps won't take the place of all this paper, but it can reduce the amount of physical space needed and give a few more options than that cabinet is able to offer.

✦ **Access anywhere:** Suppose Jake needs to look over a letter, and James isn't in the office today to send him a copy. If the letter is sent by e-mail or composed in Google Docs, James can just look up the letter on his home computer. Jake can also save important business records in a spreadsheet online and access them while on vacation if he has to (Jake is a bit of a workaholic).

The point here is that what you save online can be accessed from any online connection. In effect, this gives you instant access to your business records from wherever you are. This isn't only convenient — it's a new way of conducting business.

✦ **Security:** Putting your information on Google's servers means that your data is backed by one of the largest and most advanced Internet companies in the world today. Whereas paper can be lost or destroyed, information stored in online storage is safe.

✦ **Collaboration:** If your information is online, your partners can work with you from remote locations, so you can easily work together even when you're separated. Just attach the documents to an e-mail, share them from Google Docs, or sign into your company's site and work from there.

✦ **Search:** Imagine trying to find a single letter in an unorganized mess of a file cabinet. That gruesome task is eliminated with Google Apps. All your documents are stored and organized automatically, and you can search through your e-mails and archives using a few keywords to get what you want quickly. It's easier than organizing that cabinet and cheaper than paying somebody to do it for you.

How much will this run me?

At the basic level, Google Apps are free — that's a cost anybody can appreciate. Sure, you have to pay for an Internet connection to get to Google Apps; that can't be helped. You can also use any computer you already own. (I'm not counting that ancient Commodore 64 taking up your basement storage space right now; we're talking something that came along in the past five years or so, which is a lifetime when it comes to computers.) Whether you prefer Apple, Windows, or Linux, whether you use a laptop or a desktop, whether you travel a lot or work from home, you can use the tools you already own and avoid a huge investment in hardware.

Google does charge for services like Web hosting and support, but the costs are quite reasonable compared to other similar services, and you're getting the backing of one of the most technologically advanced companies in the market today. This full-service approach means you won't have to waste a great deal of time and money getting your business back up and running if something goes wrong. Google won't work on your computer itself, but if you can get on the Internet and sign into your account, it can help you from there.

Running Google Apps tools on your hardware

We've already talked a bit about the hardware you need to use Google Apps (and how you probably already own it). Let's take a look at some specific types of hardware and explore how you can integrate them with Google's tools:

✦ **Desktop computers:** Even Jake has one of these around the house, even though he primarily uses it to look up fantasy football statistics and exchange e-mail with his brother across the country. The point is that he can access whatever he needs in Google Apps from this desktop without having to change a thing. The hardware, the software, and the high-speed Internet connection are already in place. All he needs to do is sign into his Google account and go from there. How much easier could it get?

✦ **Laptop computers:** James is happy to use Google Apps from his laptop. He can work either from home, from a coffee shop or restaurant, or even from the job site. As long as you can connect to the Internet, the process is the same as using a desktop computer. The only difference is that you aren't stuck in your office when you work — you can move out to your couch if you want.

✦ **Public computers:** Suppose a temporary employee of Jake's Landscaping needs to check his work schedule before leaving school, so he pops into the library and uses one of the computers in the lab. He can log in from this computer and check everything he needs by using his e-mail account and calendar. Then he can clear the Web browser's settings and log out of the computer to keep his information safe and secure. If you use a few standard computer security practices, your information is accessible from anywhere (but only for you).

✦ **Mobile devices:** Even if you don't have access to a full-fledged computer, you can still work with Google Apps. Most modern cell phones (again, we're not talking about the briefcase model you bought in the last decade but just can't bear to part with) are capable of receiving and sending e-mail, so you can keep track of your e-mail on the go. Models like the iPhone and the Blackberry can also access the Internet directly, so you have full access to Google Apps from them (even if you're trying to get away). You might not feel as comfortable typing or working on documents using a small device, but it does enable you to check e-mail and calendars or read documents when you're away from work.

Coping with the switch to Google Apps

Suppose James is ready to jump on board with Google Apps from the beginning — the available applications will make his life quite a bit easier, and he sees the potential advertising benefits in using e-mail and a Web site. The temporary help is open to using Google Apps as well. E-mail is second-nature to these kids, and the calendar will help them keep their work time organized while they're attending school.

The lone holdout is Jake himself. He started the business a few years ago, and he was able to make it the success it is without using computers. Jake just doesn't see the need to complicate matters by adding additional steps to the primary job. He's also a little bit leery of putting his company's information on the Internet. Jake won't even shop online, much less keep business records on some Web site somewhere. Jake is going to be the tough sell in this case, as might be the case with your business partners or employees. That's why it's important to make the transition to Google Apps as easy and pain-free as possible.

Here are some things you can do to make the transition easier:

✦ **Emphasize the advantages:** Google Apps bring a lot of benefits to your small business, including the following:

- These relatively low-cost tools are available from many different locations at any time through a Web browser

- Google backs Google Apps with a great deal of support, and it has a high degree of reliability

- You don't have to invest a great deal in new hardware

- Even though these tools are stored online, Google backs these tools with a high degree of security

- Google Apps share quite a bit of functionality and work well together, meaning that you already have quite a robust platform in place from the beginning.

- Saving money. Part of the cost of doing business is buying and upgrading software. Depending on what platform you purchase, you could end up shelling out quite a bit of money. Google Apps won't cover every conceivable software need, but it covers the basics with ease. You also have the backing of Google when it comes to upgrading and improving your software, and you won't have to shell out a great deal of cash to make the improvements. Even somebody as distrustful of computers as Jake can appreciate a less costly solution.

✦ **Let them know how easy it is:** Google built a great deal of its reputation on the fact that its tools are so easy to use. Take a look at the Google front page — the plain white site with a simple text box doesn't confuse its users or distract them from the page's main function. That attention to simplicity and functionality runs through all Google's tools and helps new and experienced users alike become familiar with Google Apps. Typical computer users have little trouble making the transition, and newer users find a longer (but not steeper) learning curve that's easy to conquer.

Exploring the Google Apps Applications

Because the majority of Google Apps tools are available for free, you won't have to base your decisions about what you want to use on cost. Rather, you can look at each one and see if it suits your needs. You have the time to evaluate each one and make it work for you without pressure, so you can set up your Google Apps implementation to your best advantage.

Gmail

Whether used for brief chats, formal letters, or as a replacement for the fax machine, e-mail is just something businesses have to have. It makes it easy for new customers and existing clients alike to contact you, and it gives you the ability to conduct your business more quickly and efficiently. Simply put, it's a necessary tool at this point, so you might as well find a quick and easy solution for it from the beginning.

E-mail is ubiquitous at this point for small business — even Jake already has an account. Gmail is Google's version of this valuable communication tool, and it's amazingly easy to sign up and use. (See Figure 1-1.) It's also easily expandable, depending on your needs.

Because Gmail is a free service, you can sign up for as many accounts as you need. Having one for each of your business's employees is a no-brainer. You can also set up a generic account for use on your company's Web site, in the event that multiple users must check the same account (for example, to check for new business or unsolicited advertising).

It's a good idea to have separate accounts for your business and personal e-mail. Not only does it help speed up searches for important e-mails and keep your accounts cleaner, but it also helps reduce the possibility of sharing personal information with work contacts, and vice versa.

Figure 1-1:
Gmail's
simple yet
powerful
e-mail
interface.

Gmail is accessible from a variety of devices at any time in several different ways. You can access your Gmail from any Web browser by signing in at the easy-to-remember URL of `http://gmail.com`. If that isn't to your liking, you can set up your Gmail account to use several types of computer-based e-mail programs (like Microsoft Outlook or Apple's Mail) or many mobile devices. However you need to access your e-mail, your Gmail account makes it possible.

Gmail provides a huge amount of storage to its users, and it is increasing this all the time. That means you can send and receive a staggering number of files and keep just about any e-mail you receive without running out of space. It might be possible to reach your account's limits, but it's certainly a rare occurrence. This is a huge help when it comes to record-keeping and searching through correspondence.

Google Calendar

Just like e-mail, keeping an accurate calendar (or calendars) is a necessary part of any successful small business. You want to organize your appointments and employee schedules, and you also need to make them accessible to all interested parties. Google Calendars can accomplish this easily, so it's definitely an essential tool. Furthermore, it ties in directly with Gmail, so you can send invitations and centralize your activities easily.

It may not hang on your refrigerator or hold a place of honor on your wall or desk, but Google Calendar can perform tasks far above and beyond those of a traditional paper calendar (and it won't get lost in the bottom of your briefcase, duffel bag, or purse). (See Figure 1-2.)

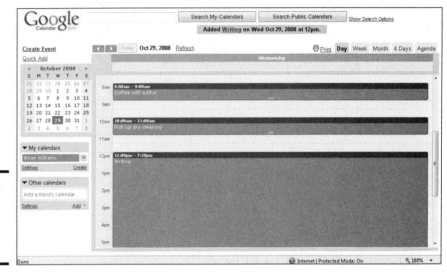

Figure 1-2:
A sample Google Calendar page.

In a business of any size, it's important to keep meetings, appointments, and jobs organized. A traditional paper calendar might get a little crowded if you have to write all your activities in a central location. Plus, if everybody keeps a personal calendar, it's hard to coordinate activities. Jake's Landscaping may need to keep one calendar for all its jobs (complete with times and details of each assignment), but all employees might want to keep their own calendars with just their own jobs tracked.

Google Calendars makes all this possible, and just as with Gmail, you can create all the calendars you need to use for free. Whether it's a number of personal calendars or a calendar designed for use by multiple employees at several different locations, you can expand Google Calendar to fit whatever needs you have. You can also color-code your entries and set up reminders and invitations to keep everybody on track.

It's possible to view these calendars from any Web browser. However, you may not want everybody to see your calendar, and Google is one of the most public services on the Internet. That's why Google Calendars provides security options that prevent unauthorized viewers from seeing your calendar. You can also limit who has access to change or modify your calendar, just to be sure that only those you want to work with your schedule can. For example, Jake may have control over all calendars relating to Jake's Landscaping, but his employees, looking at Jake's personal calendar, may only be able to see whether his time is free or busy. He may also restrict access to his calendar so that only James (or Jake's wife) can change events on his personal calendar. All these options and more are available to you.

Google Docs

Gmail takes the place of a business mail room, and Google Calendars replaces the desk blotter or pocket scheduler. Google Docs takes the place of most of the rest of your business paperwork. (See Figure 1-3.) If you're familiar with popular office suites like Microsoft Office or OpenOffice, you already know what they can do. However, if you're like Jake, you aren't familiar with such products, we now take you through the basic capabilities of Google Docs.

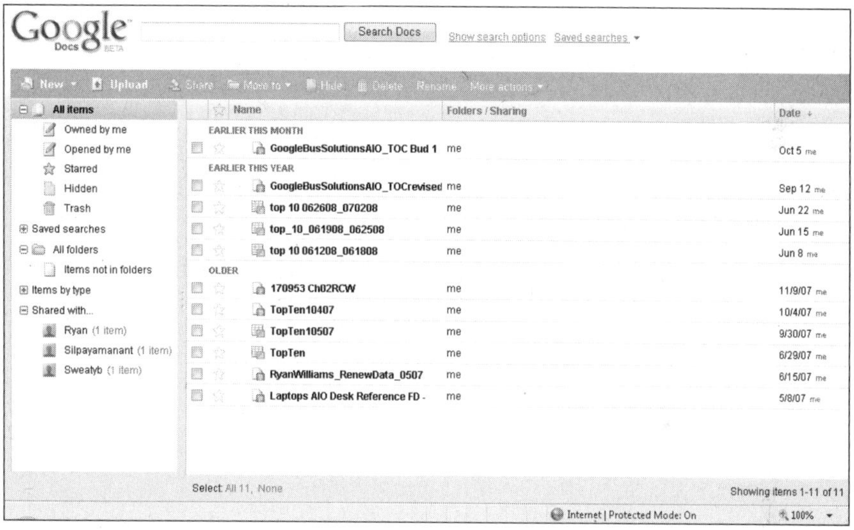

Figure 1-3: Google Docs' main page.

Google Docs can produce several types of documents — some of which may be useful to you and others that may never enter your consciousness. It all depends on your business and what you're trying to accomplish. With Google Docs, you can create the following types of documents:

✦ **Document:** The Document creates basically the same product as Microsoft Word. You use this function to create business letters or other forms of communication.

✦ **Presentation:** The Presentation is roughly the same as Microsoft PowerPoint. You use it to make sales presentations or slideshows of your work. Jake may not use this type of document from day to day, but James will find it useful when he has to sell any future clients on Jake's Landscaping services.

✦ **Spreadsheet:** If you've used Microsoft Excel before, you're familiar with the concept of a spreadsheet. This document is made up of a series of cells, each of which can contain text or numbers. The power of a spreadsheet comes to light when you use it to automatically process data (like budgets or timesheets) and to make complex calculations quickly and easily. Spreadsheets are immensely helpful in managing your finances.

✦ **Forms:** Google's forms allow you to collect feedback and other information. (See Figure 1-4.) You can customize the questions you want to ask, how you want to review the information, and use the information you get to better tailor your business to your customers.

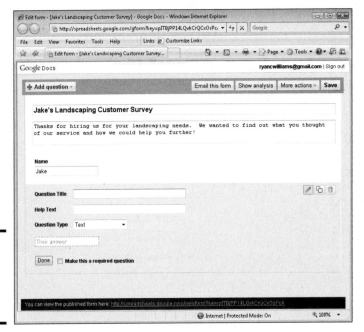

Figure 1-4:
Creating
a form in
Google
Apps.

Part of getting the information you want means asking the right questions. Be sure to try questions out on friends, family, and people you trust to make sure your questions are understood and will yield helpful results.

Google Sites

Think of Google Sites as the little brother of Google Apps. Google Sites provides very basic Web services at the free level (with a few more services at the Premier level), and it includes an `http://sites.google.com` URL along with it. Google Apps gives you much more control over the site, including more control over e-mail functions, archiving, security services, and more. Finally, it should be noted that Google Sites can be used on its own, but its features are also included in the larger Google Apps package.

Like e-mail and calendars, a Web site for your small business is an indispensible tool. Not only does it allow you to integrate all the informational aspects of your business (like the e-mail and calendar accounts), but it also acts as your introduction to your customers. These days, are you more likely to turn to an antiquated phone book or to the Internet to find out what services are available in your area? Even if your most important source of business is word-of-mouth referrals, a Web site can enable potential customers to ask any questions they might have and give them a way to contact you.

Google provides two different levels of service with Sites, so each small business has to decide what they need from their Web site. If Jake's Landscaping needs a site that explains what services it offers and how it can be contacted, the Standard service will probably handle those needs quite well. If it wants a more robust service that handles additional functions like larger e-mail accounts and collaborative services (and has the capability to keep Google's ads off your site), the Premier edition might be the way to go. (See Figure 1-5.)

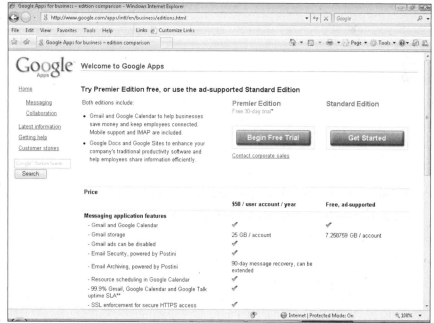

Figure 1-5:
Google even helps you compare the two different versions of their Sites.

A simple Web site is fairly easy to put together and doesn't require a whole lot of time and effort. Jake's Landscaping may just need a home page, contact information, a list of services, and a photo gallery of past work. That's three or four pages, and plenty of tools from Google can help Jake put that site together. If Jake wants to expand the services (such as adding more and more calendars and getting additional e-mail storage) or wants to get e-mail and personal support in designing the Web site, he should consider the Premier edition.

If you plan on doing any sort of financial transaction over your Web site, you need to consider the Premier edition. The secure SSL access provided by this edition is absolutely essential to processing these transactions.

Even if you have a lot of visitors to your site, you more than likely won't use a huge amount of *storage* (the amount of data stored on your portion of Google's servers) or *bandwidth* (the amount of data transmitted from Google's servers to other computers). However, if you start using some of the more advanced features of Sites, you need the bigger Premier package.

Compared to the total amount of Web traffic Google receives in a single day, your Web site will probably never present a challenge for its servers. Your big concern here is how much online storage you need and how much you're willing to pay for.

Google will put ads on your free site — there's no way around it. Advertising is a major source of revenue for Google, and that's how it is able to support your free Web site. If you're comfortable with that, then free is right for you. If you want to determine exactly what shows up on your site, however, you need to purchase the Premier edition and choose to shut off the ads. Premier Sites also gives you more customization options and allows you to do more with your Google Sites resources.

Don't be afraid to ask questions of people who use Google Sites (or other Web services) to see what they need and use. People in similar circumstances can be a great resource when you are determining what you need to do.

Personalized start page

Google's relatively simple home page belies a tremendous source of available information that can be personalized in an equally tremendous way. On Google's home page, you can add news feeds, review your e-mail and calendar, set up tabs for quick organization of information, and even play Pac-Man (just don't let the boss see you). You can also customize exactly how you want that information to be presented to you. (See Figure 1-6.)

Figure 1-6:
One humble
example
of a
personalized
Google
home page.

Google has plenty of pre-made gadgets already available for your use, and you can place them anywhere in your home page. Although these can include generic news feeds or games, you can also get personalized information like your Gmail and your calendars immediately when you log in. And all this information is attached to your larger Google Apps account, so you can view it anywhere you have access to the Internet, from your family's desktop to your mobile phone. It's like having a personal assistant deliver the newspaper, your mail, and your agenda to you whenever you want it. Unfortunately, Google does not provide coffee delivery at this point, and there's no word on when this complimentary service will be available.

Google Talk

Instant messaging is no longer just the province of teenagers and bored college students. This form of communication can be used to reach business associates, your coworkers, or anybody else on your list of contacts (yes, even your children — they're probably on there right now anyway). This service, Google Talk, is a little different from most Google services in that you have to install a program on your computer or mobile device to use it, but it's fairly lightweight in terms of system requirements and storage space, and it provides quite a few advantages. (See Figure 1-7.)

Figure 1-7:
Google Talk.

Because it can be used on both computers and mobile devices, Google Talk allows you to communicate with people just about anywhere they are, even if they don't have a phone on them. You can also keep logs of these chats (in case you need to go back and review your conversations) or turn off the logs (in case you're discussing personal matters). You can also communicate via voice or text, and there's a stripped-down Web version that you can pair up with your own Web site or your personalized Google home page. Finally, Google Talk allows you to share documents and photos, just in case you need to collaborate or review information with somebody who's out of the office at the time (and you're doing it in real-time — no more waiting on your e-mail to catch up). Google Talk is an extremely friendly and versatile communications tool, and you'll be surprised how often it will come in handy.

Setting Everything Up

After reviewing all the information, you're probably sure which version of Google Apps you want to use to set up your Web site (and you can always upgrade it later if you want). However, all Google can provide you is the Web site itself and a *URL* (otherwise known as the address of your Web site) that looks something like this: `http://sites.google.com/yourwebsite namehere`. If users type in that name, they'll get to your Web site. However, you're not making it very convenient for your potential customers (saving

them a little typing goes a long way), and you're not creating a very memorable address. And most important, you are only using a subset of what Google Apps has to offer (through the Google Sites function). To fully utilize Google Apps, you must buy a domain name. You want a domain name that's descriptive and memorable, and Google can't provide that for you (although they do partner with domain name registrars to make the process easier). You can, however, get a more memorable name and redirect that address so that it takes your customers to your Google site. For more information, contact your preferred domain name provider.

Selecting a URL

You can use any combination of letters and numbers in your URL, and you can personalize it as much as possible. You won't be able to use any punctuation or special symbols, however. Browsers interpret those characters as commands and not another symbol, so using them causes problems.

There's no real difference in using .com, .net, or .org at the end of your URL. If one version of your preferred name is taken, you can always get another version of it (if that name hasn't yet been purchased). Consequently, if you want to make sure that you control all available versions of your URL, you have to buy the rights for them individually (addresses that end with extensions like .gov, .mil, or .edu aren't usually available through commercial providers).

Just because you own three different versions of the same URL doesn't mean you have to maintain three separate Web sites. All these URLs can be pointed towards the same Web site.

If somebody already owns one version of your chosen URL (like `jakeslandscaping.com` versus `jakeslandscaping.net`), you can always buy just the address, if it's available, with no problems. However, you may want to consider a different URL (like `jakeslandscapingnyc.com`, if the business is located in New York) to avoid any confusion.

So you have your name, but you're not sure if it's already taken. There are a couple of easy ways to find out:

✦ **Type the URL you want into your Web browser and see where it takes you.** It's the quickest way to see what's going on. You might see a full Web site or a *parked domain*, where somebody has purchased the rights but hasn't developed the site yet. You could also see an error message saying no such site exists, which should be a clear sign to go buy your domain right now.

When you're performing your search, be aware of the risks of typing random addresses into your browser. You could end up seeing a site quite unlike what you had in mind when you started your search.

✦ **Search for the site name on Google.** You won't be taken directly to the site, but you will see what (if anything) exists fairly quickly. You also see what similar sites exist, so you are aware what other options exist in case you have to look elsewhere.

Some domain services perform the search for you, but some services have been known to reserve domains that were examined but not immediately purchased for themselves. If that's the case, you have to do some negotiating to get the name you want.

If somebody already owns the URL you want and you HAVE to have it, you have to contact the owners and negotiate with them. It's a lot easier to just use a different domain, however.

Establishing your domain

To get your preferred Web address, you must purchase the rights to the domain name. Basically, you're asking the powers-that-be that manage the traffic on the Internet to route those persons asking for that address to your Web site. Several providers, like `http://godaddy.com`, `http://dotster. com`, or `http://networksolutions.com`, will be more than happy to provide that service for you for a small fee, so feel free to shop around and see what's available at what price. (Godaddy.com appears in Figure 1-8.)

Figure 1-8: Godaddy.com is but one of several domain registration services available.

All you buy at this point is the right to use the URL itself. All other services, like hosting, e-mail, and the like are provided by Google, so you don't need to spend money on what you already have.

Make sure you only use reputable companies to purchase the rights to the URL. Search for positive and reputable reviews (you're already on Google, right?) to make sure you're getting what you want (and only what you want).

Each provider has different steps to sign up for an URL, so follow the instructions given to purchase your domain name. It takes a little while to reserve the name and process your account, so take it easy until you get the e-mail letting you know everything has been completed.

Pointing in the right direction

When your domain name has been purchased and you've received confirmation, it's time to claim your Google Apps site. Navigate to Google Apps at `http://www.google.com/apps/intl/en/business/index.html`, and click the button to sign up. Then follow the steps that follow. You can choose either Premier or Standard editions at this point, but we're using Premier in this example:

1. **Enter your domain name in the field shown in Figure 1-9, select whether you're an end user or an administrator, and click the Get Started button.**

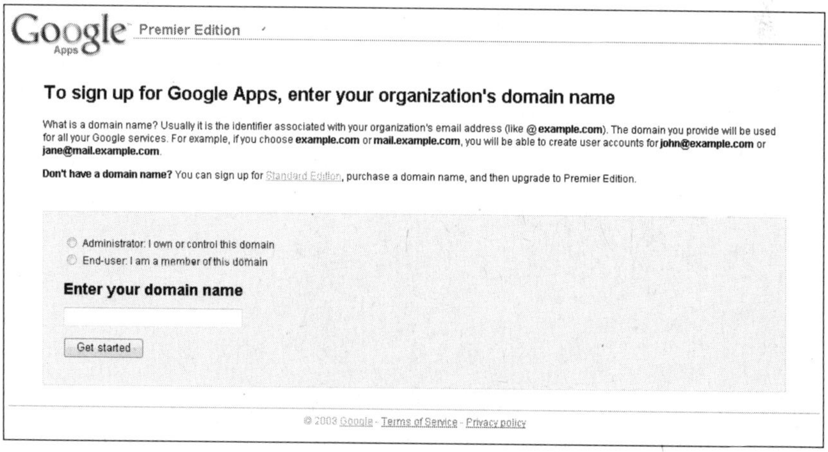

Google Apps Premier Edition

To sign up for Google Apps, enter your organization's domain name

What is a domain name? Usually it is the identifier associated with your organization's email address (like @example.com). The domain you provide will be used for all your Google services. For example, if you choose example.com or mail.example.com, you will be able to create user accounts for john@example.com or jane@mail.example.com.

Don't have a domain name? You can sign up for Standard Edition, purchase a domain name, and then upgrade to Premier Edition.

○ Administrator: I own or control this domain
○ End-user: I am a member of this domain

Enter your domain name

[Get started]

© 2003 Google - Terms of Service - Privacy policy

Figure 1-9:
Entering your domain name.

2. **Enter all the applicable information for your general site details and administrator, as shown in Figure 1-10.**

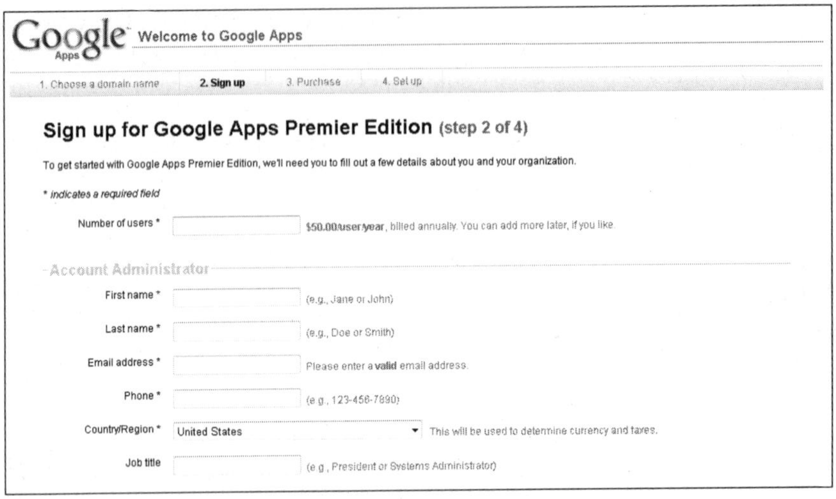

Figure 1-10:
Entering
your
general site
information.

3. **Enter all the applicable financial information and purchase the Google Apps package. Remember, you can always add more users later, but it will cost $50 per year, per user for the premium edition.**

4. **Enter all your account information (including your new e-mail address), as shown in Figure 1-11, and click the Set Up button.**

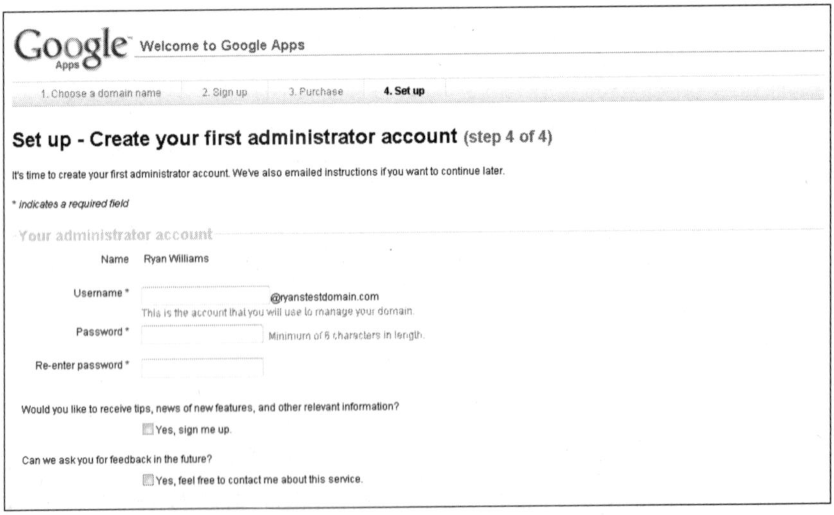

Figure 1-11:
Your new
account
information.

When all this is finished, you still have to verify the fact that you own the domain. Google gives you a couple of ways to do this — you can either add a record (known as a *CNAME*) on your domain registration account or upload a file specified by Google to your site (if you have an existing hosting account). Depending on whether you're adding Google Apps to an existing server or a new site, Google provides different sets of instructions to modify your domain settings to integrate with Google.

> **TIP**
>
> If you don't have an existing hosting service, your domain registrar likely has mail settings you can use to integrate with Google Apps. You can also use domain forwarding to point the domain name at a Google Sites page. Check with your domain registrar on how to accomplish this.

Decorating your start page

When you've arrived at the Google Apps dashboard, click Service Settings and select Start Page. Click Customize to see the available options for your Google Apps start page, as shown in Figure 1-12.

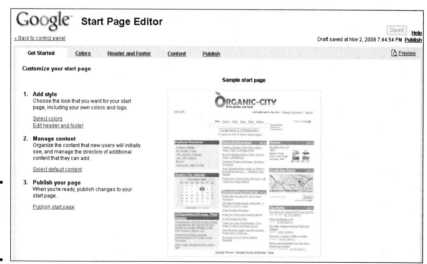

Figure 1-12: Customizing your start page.

From here, you can choose to make your start page for all the Google Apps users look more like your corporate Web site.

Change the colors of various elements of the site using the Colors tab shown in Figure 1-13.

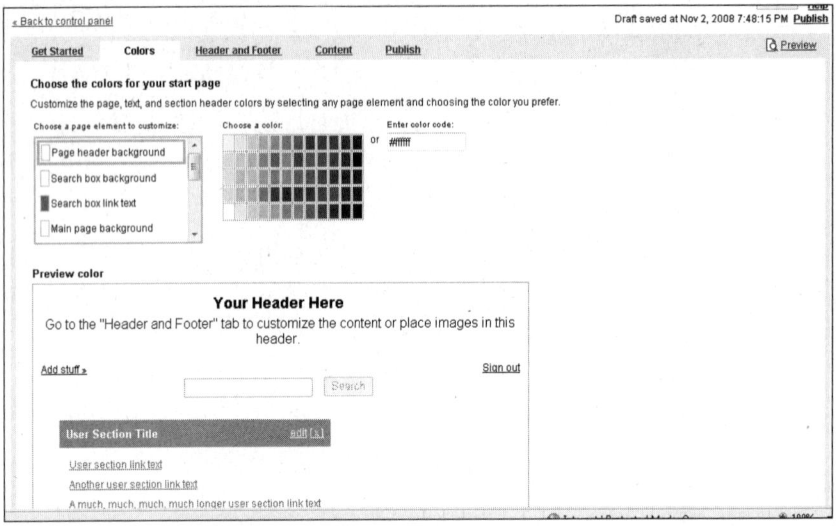

Figure 1-13:
Changing
your start
page colors.

You can change the headers and footers in the appropriately marked tab.
If you use the iGoogle function of Google's search page already, you may
notice that this layout looks remarkably similar. (See Figure 1-14.)

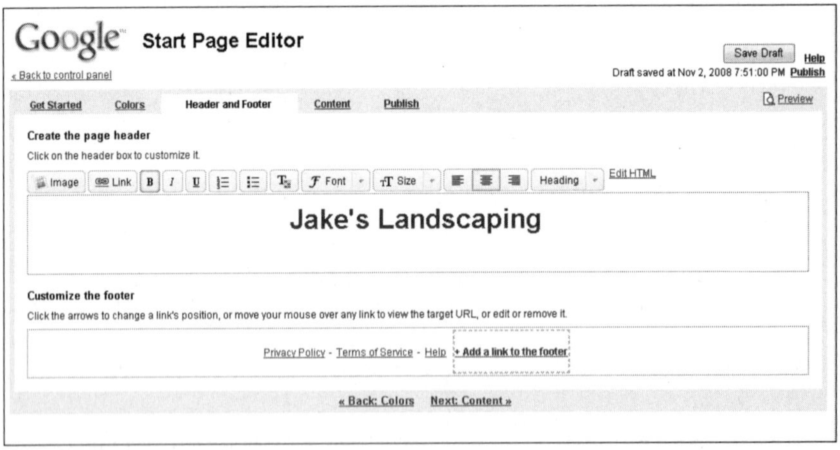

Figure 1-14:
Creating
headers and
footers for
your start
page.

Finally, you can place gadgets on the start page with the Content tab. There
are a huge number of gadgets to choose from, but you might want to start
with e-mail or calendar gadgets and move on from there. (See Figure 1-15.)

Figure 1-15:
Putting
gadgets on
your start
page.

After you've finished customizing your page, open the Publish tab and click
Publish to make the page available. Take note of the URL provided on the
Publish tab — that's the page your users have to access to see the cus-
tomized start page. It looks something like this: `http://partnerpage.`
`google.com/yourdomainnamehere.com`.

Granting access

Now that you have your start page set up, you can add accounts by return-
ing to the Google Apps dashboard and selecting User Accounts. A list of all
current accounts are displayed (as shown in Figure 1-16), and you can click
the Create A New User link to add somebody else.

Figure 1-16:
Google
Apps User
Accounts.

You are asked for the user's real name, a username, and a temporary password. You can also upload user accounts in bulk from a *CSV* (or *comma
separated value*) file you create in a text editor. This can be complicated, so
it's best to use the individual option unless you're creating a huge number of
accounts. When these accounts are created, you can contact the users and
have them log in.

Always have the users change their password after they've logged in for the first time. This is basic security protocol, but it's your responsibility as administrator to make sure it gets done.

Calling In Reinforcements

So what happens when something goes wrong? It's time to look for a little support (of the technical variety, not your basic pick-me-up or confidence booster). Two forms of support you can seek are from your peers or from the experts —, and both have their advantages and drawbacks.

Supporting your peers

Google has provided several groups to bring together those interested in solving their problems with Google Apps. Clicking the Help link in the top-right corner displays the screen shown in Figure 1-17. Not only are there several listings for common questions, but you can click the Admin Help Forum link in the bottom right corner for more assistance.

Figure 1-17:
Getting Help with Google Apps.

With the form shown in Figure 1-18, you can submit information to qualified experts and users to get assistance. There's no timetable or guarantee for these questions, but as it's free, so the price is right if you're not in too big a hurry.

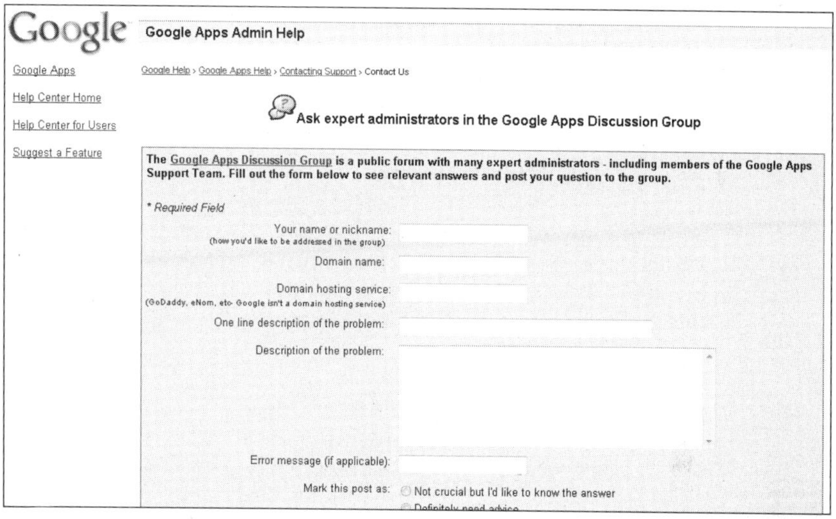

Figure 1-18:
Submitting a
question to
the forum.

Google has several groups that can be of assistance to users, so feel free to search Google Groups at `http://groups.google.com` to see what else is available. After you've joined the group, you can interact with others and find the answers to your question. Remember some basic rules about using Google Groups:

✦ **Search for your answer first.** If the question has already been asked and answered, you are saving everybody a lot of time.

✦ **Be friendly and courteous.** You're more likely to get answers if you don't give in to frustration, name calling, caps-lock abuse, and the like.

✦ **Don't post your question more than once.** It's the digital equivalent of a child pulling on a parent's clothing over and over again.

Premium assistance

If you paid for the Premier service, you have the option of contacting Google directly for assistance. From the Google Apps start page, click Domain Settings and select Account Information. You see links for contacting support via e-mail or phone. Take note that you must give them your Customer and Support PINs in order to use these services, and that the phone lines are to be used only for system critical issues (in support terms, that's a euphemistic term for "dire catastrophe"). Keep that in mind before you call. Again, be sure to keep your questions clear and concise, and try to be as complete as possible.

Chapter 2: Making Gmail Work for Your Business

In This Chapter

✓ **Making the switch to Gmail**

✓ **Configuring your Gmail system**

✓ **Importing your old e-mail system into Gmail**

✓ **Working Google Talk into your system**

*I*s there a place where you can't get your e-mail now? Such electronic communications used to be the sole domain of desktop-bound appliances and limited to a cognizant few. Now e-mail is woven into the very fabric of business, an indispensible tool in your quest to get things done. You can check your e-mail account (or accounts) from one single computer, but you're more likely to check it on your desktop computer, your laptop, your mobile device, your kid's gaming computer, and so on. Because you need a reliable e-mail service that's available from just about anywhere, Google's Gmail service is a perfect choice. And don't let the *beta* tag next to Gmail's logo fool you — it's a powerful service that keeps getting more services and more storage space.

Considerations Before You Make the Change

Before you consider the switch to Gmail and Google Apps, take a look at your current e-mail system. Maybe you're like the folks at Jake's Landscaping, who have had no cohesive e-mail system up to this point. Jake has e-mail through his ISP, whereas James uses a Web-based e-mail service. Any temporary employees have their own e-mail accounts — through school, another Web-based system, or some other e-mail service. Some may not even have e-mail yet and rely on phone-based text messaging. There's definitely room to bring in a single, unified e-mail service to simplify communications and make sure everybody has access, but you need to consider the following challenges:

✦ Coping with a loss of control

✦ Implementing a complex migration

✦ Getting adjusted to the new system

+ Training users

+ Dealing with a resistance to change

+ Managing accounts

+ Getting e-mail where it needs to go

These are all discussed in the following subsections.

Coping with a loss of control

If your small business has some IT support already, it may come as a surprise to your support staffers that you're switching to Gmail. They're used to maintaining the mail servers, and Gmail takes some of their job away and puts it in the hands of Google. This might make them feel a little uneasy. However, they still have some work to do configuring Gmail to work with your system and e-mail clients, and the relief frees up IT groups to work on other projects for your business. Still, this slight loss of control might be unsettling, so you should prepare for that possible consequence.

Google is an extremely reliable company — you don't get to be as big as it is without a good reputation for keeping up systems. However, it only guarantees 99.9% uptime for its Premier customers. That doesn't mean that you'll see significant downtime; but if problems happen, Google is going to take care of its paying customers before its free ones. Jake's Landscaping can probably handle an uptime of 99.7%, so this should be a small concern.

Depending on how you choose to set up Gmail for your company, the way you access and archive your e-mails will probably change. Depending on how you checked and saved e-mails before, this could change your workflow as well. Still, Gmail has a large enough storage capacity and a fantastically easy method of storing and accessing archives that this shouldn't be a big issue for you.

Implementing a complex migration

If you're not using a common e-mail system right now, this section is of no concern for you. Your system starts fresh — everybody gets new accounts, and you don't need to worry about moving anything off of old servers. If you do have a system in place, however, you're probably worried about getting everything from one place to the other. This kind of move isn't child's play, and you should consider your options before jumping ahead with it.

Google provides tools for migrating your e-mail from your current system to Gmail — if you're willing to pay the price. These migration tools are available only to Premier customers, so you have to decide whether the move is worth the price. If you only have a few e-mails you want to keep, print them out or forward them to the new account. If you have huge stores of vital communications, it may be time to open your wallet.

In any case, plan how you're going to stage your migration. Pick a time when you won't need access to your e-mail for a bit, and when you can afford a little downtime in case something goes wrong. You also want a backup plan (including the ever-reliable but primitive paper printout) to reduce the effect of potential catastrophe. A little bit of planning can save you a lot of trouble later.

Getting adjusted to the new system

Any new system is going to mean change, which means that you're probably going to like some new things and miss some familiar ones. It's inevitable. Planning for change now means mitigating some of those feelings. Let's determine what you should be looking for.

Google's Web site has a very distinctive look, and that look extends to Gmail. Gmail organizes e-mail into conversations, meaning that groups of messages are bundled together on the Web service instead of being organized by name or date received. If you're not used to it, this version of Webmail might throw you until you can become adjusted to it. This may not be a factor if you use a program like Microsoft Outlook to receive your e-mail and never use the Web client, but you need to know the difference between Gmail's Web client and more traditional views.

Depending on how you set up your e-mail system, you could see a whole new e-mail identity for your company. If you already have a server and a domain name, you should be okay (provided you follow the instructions and complete your migration successfully). However, if you've cobbled together a series of different Web mail services or accounts provided by your ISP, you have to change your address. If these free services allow you to forward e-mail to your new account, you can implement that feature and then notify your customers of your new address. When that's not possible, you might find yourself checking multiple accounts and forwarding e-mails until the word gets out. A good plan and plenty of advance notice goes a long way towards moving the switch forward.

Training users

If you make the change to Google Apps and you're running your own business, you may not have a huge learning curve. It's just you and your Web site, and you can rely on Google's help pages to get you going. Even with Jake's Landscaping, the only person who may need some help is Jake himself. James is already familiar with technical matters, and the temporary help is probably fairly tech savvy already. If your workers are not, however, there may be a longer transition time, and you'll have to plan for that. These are the basics to account for:

✦ Where users go for their e-mail

✦ Their new usernames and passwords

✦ How users process and archive their e-mail

✦ When and how often they need to check the e-mail

Take these factors into account and stay loose — you may have to deal with some additional factors down the road as well, depending on how your employees or coworkers react to the change.

Dealing with a resistance to change

Again, if you already have your own e-mail system, the continued use of the old e-mail system isn't going to be of much concern for you. You migrate the old system, you close it down, and everybody is on Gmail. No big deal, right? But if you're using the patched-together network of Webmail or ISP accounts, you could run into trouble. In these cases, your coworkers or employees probably control their own access to these accounts, and you're not going to be able to prevent their use.

Your staff is probably fairly attached to these accounts, as well. It's not hard to start or use a new e-mail account, but when you've gotten used to an address, it's not something you want to give up. There might be reservations about moving e-mail from one account to another or taking on another e-mail address when "everybody who knows me knows I'm at this address!" You have to encourage folks to make the transition, and you have to give them reasons that make them want to move.

Make it clear that the recipients of these new accounts don't have to close or abandon their current e-mail accounts. They just have to conduct business functions using their new e-mail addresses. Get them used to giving out the new address because it represents the company better and adds an air of professionalism to your transactions. (Would you trust tim@jakeslandscap-ingservices.com with your business more than timdude@genericWebmailser-vice.com?) If somebody sends business e-mail to the old account, just have the employee forward it along to his new account and reply from there. It may take a little time, but eventually the switch will be made.

If the Webmail or ISP service allows it, remember that you can have the old service forward e-mails to the new service so that the old account never even has to be opened again.

By moving all business e-mail duties to your new Gmail account, you also help your employees and coworkers know exactly what they're getting into when they open an account. Their personal e-mail is personal, their work e-mail is work-related, and never the twain shall meet. This helps keep workers on-task and allows them to quickly and more efficiently process their e-mails.

Another challenge you may have to deal with is the total lack of e-mail use. Those who have never used an e-mail account may not see the value in it, and they may end up ignoring the account (intentionally or otherwise) while their inbox fills up, and your business misses opportunities. You can't expect people new to the use of e-mail (rare as they may be) to immediately jump into the world of electronic communication, but you can encourage a graceful transition.

The near-instantaneous world of e-mail provides for quick access and reply — maybe too quick for the novice user. That's why it's important to start slowly. Initially, have new users sit down with patient, experienced persons who can help them get the hang of e-mail. Then, set aside one portion of the day (for Jake, it's just before he heads out for the jobs at remote locations) for new users to check their e-mail, and let that be the only time where they have to deal with e-mail each day. After they get used to e-mail and how it functions, you can start working with each individual employee or coworker about exactly when and where they have to check their e-mail and get them the devices they need to do it.

The goal here is not to force-feed e-mail to new users, but to get them comfortable with Gmail and show them how it can improve the flow of information around your business. If you make the process as easy as possible and provide a slow but persistent transition, you eventually get everybody on board with the new system.

Managing accounts

Google Apps are great because you have control over all your programs. However, it also means that somebody has to assume that control and manage the e-mail accounts. This includes creating new accounts, deleting old accounts, and helping current users keep their accounts under the 25 GB limit (which isn't a huge task). Users should also organize their e-mails into different folders and their archives (depending on your e-mail traffic, this could be a larger task).

As you might suspect, you want somebody fairly familiar with Gmail and e-mail in general to help with this transition. The candidate should also be patient and tolerant with new users, because he or she will be starting folks from the ground up in some occasions, and that can be a slow and frustrating process.

The upside is that it's pretty easy to manage e-mail accounts in the Gmail system, so you don't need to hire a full-time IT professional to get your system going. You just need somebody who's willing to tackle the task, is familiar with basic e-mail concepts, and can read a few easy instructional Google help documents (or you can skip ahead to the section in this chapter entitled "Configuring E-mail Addresses and Lists").

Getting e-mail where it needs to go

As mentioned earlier, e-mail is an almost ubiquitous service that can be received nearly anywhere. Before you institute a new service, however, you need to narrow down "nearly anywhere" a bit more. Depending on what devices you're going to be using, it's a good idea to research how Gmail interacts with the devices you are using, such as:

✦ **Desktop computers:** This is the easiest setup you have to do. Desktop computers are immobile and usually hooked up to a secure, always-on network like a wired or wireless router. In this case, you probably just turn on your e-mail program and get your messages in short order. You should have an easy series of settings to help you connect to the e-mail account, so you're ready to go with a minimum of time and effort invested.

✦ **Laptop computers:** Anymore, laptops are fairly comparable to desktop computers when they're hooked up to a network. The problem is that these are mobile devices, so they might not always be able to connect to a network, depending on their locations. It also means that your users may need access to e-mail messages even when not connected to the network, so you should take that into account when setting up your e-mail program.

Make sure that any laptop computers you own have separate password-protected user accounts for anybody who uses them. That way, in case the laptops are ever lost or stolen, you won't give strangers easy access to your data. They can still get it if they absolutely want to, but this makes the job a little more difficult. If your information is really that important, find out how to implement disk encryption on your laptops to prevent prying eyes from seeing it.

✦ **Mobile devices:** These devices present the greatest number of variables when it comes to setting up e-mail access. If you're using only standard mobile phones with the capability to receive e-mail data, you probably want to transmit the bare minimum of information — unless more is requested. That way, you avoid tying the mobile device up for too long receiving data, and you get the information you need more quickly. Full-fledged smartphones may come equipped with faster networks or WiFi access, so they can receive data more quickly. These devices might also have wizards or other helpful programs to help you check your e-mail in quick fashion.

No matter what devices you choose to use, make sure you have them all in place before making the transition. By eliminating as many variables as you can, you make the transition process that much easier.

Configuring E-mail Addresses and Lists

After you've chosen your e-mail administrators and given them access to Google Apps, they can create and administer e-mail accounts as needed. All they have to do is navigate to their link (`http://partnerpage.google.com/yourdomainname`) and sign in using the Manage This Domain link shown in Figure 2-1.

Figure 2-1:
Administer-
ing the
domain is
but a click
away.

> ryan@ryanstestdomain.com | Manage this domain | Sign out

After you've logged in, click Create New Users in the upper-left corner to add a new user (an e-mail account is automatically created for this new user). You are asked to enter the following information:

+ User's first name.

+ User's last name.

+ User's new username (the new e-mail address is username@yourdomain-here.com).

+ Optionally, you can enter a temporary password twice by clicking Enter Password. Otherwise, use the temporary password supplied by Google.

Click Create New User, and you're ready to go. You supply this information to new users either via e-mail to their old accounts or give it to them directly. When they log in at the same homepage you use to log in, they can change their passwords and sign into their new accounts.

New users can log into their e-mail accounts specifically at `http://mail.google.com/a/yourdomainnamehere.com`. This takes them directly to the e-mail account without requiring them to deal with the entire domain.

Make absolutely sure users change their passwords when they log into their accounts. Reliance on default passwords compromises your system's security.

Asking permission

After signing into the Google Apps dashboard, click User Accounts to see a list of the available user accounts. Check out Figure 2-2 for an example of what a user account looks like.

Figure 2-2:
A sample user account listing.

	Name	Username ▼	Status	Email Quota	Last signed in
☐	Ryan Williams	ryan	Administrator	▭ 0% of 25 GB	10:14 pm

Click the user's name to see the basic settings and permissions for that account, as shown in Figure 2-3. From here, you can force a password change the next time a user logs in, and you also decide whether he is able to administer the site and who can be users for your Google Apps installation.

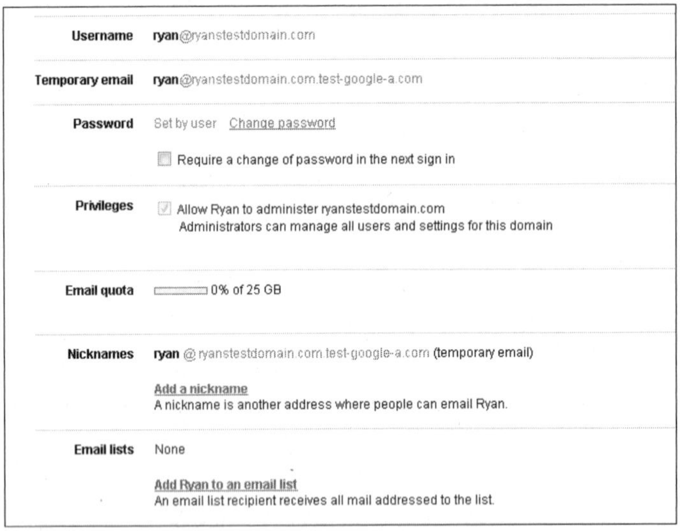

Username	ryan@ryanstestdomain.com
Temporary email	ryan@ryanstestdomain.com.test-google-a.com
Password	Set by user Change password
	☐ Require a change of password in the next sign in
Privileges	☑ Allow Ryan to administer ryanstestdomain.com
	Administrators can manage all users and settings for this domain
Email quota	▭ 0% of 25 GB
Nicknames	ryan @ ryanstestdomain.com.test-google-a.com (temporary email)
	Add a nickname
	A nickname is another address where people can email Ryan.
Email lists	None
	Add Ryan to an email list
	An email list recipient receives all mail addressed to the list.

Figure 2-3:
A sample user's account settings.

To change the password, just click Change Password and enter the new password twice. You see a small indicator below the password fields showing how strong your password us — that is, how much work hackers will have to perform to obtain or guess your password. Stronger passwords include the following elements:

✦ Using a mix of upper- and lower-case letters.

✦ Including numbers, spaces, or other symbols.

✦ Adding as many characters as you can possibly remember.

In fact, it might be more useful to think of this feature as a pass*phrase* and not a password.

You can also force the user to change his password the next time he logs in by checking the Require A Change of Password In The Next Sign In checkbox. This makes the user change his password to something more personal (and something you don't have the responsibility to remember).

If you want other users to administer your domain, check the box under Privileges to allow them access to the same rights (and responsibilities) as you have. It's best to keep to this access limited to as few accounts as necessary, for a few reasons:

✦ It increases the chance for somebody with this access to make unnecessary or harmful changes.

✦ Your domain is less secure with more people having access to your site's settings.

✦ If your site is created under the Premier package, you have to pay for additional accounts if created — you want to keep track of those accounts and who creates them.

If you can get away with it, limit your number of administrators to one or two people. The others don't need the access, and you make your life a lot easier in the process.

In this view, you can also see how full each user's mailbox is. With each account topping out around 25 GB in Premier mode and around 7.5 GB in standard mode, there's still plenty of room. This should mean you won't have to ride your users too much to keep mailboxes under quota. Still, it can be a valuable tool if necessary.

Managing e-mail settings for users

Each account carries its own e-mail account, and you should have one for everybody who will be using the system. It's best to keep everybody as separate as possible, both for the sake of security and specificity. To avoid these problems, it's good policy to make sure everybody has his own account.

However, you may have to create multiple accounts to conduct your business. For instance, you could have a general informational account for your business, such as info@yourdomainhere.com. This is the account that you post on your Web site as a general contact, just to avoid having random e-mails or spam directed at your personal accounts. Besides that, each employee could have his or her own account for more personal contact and business-related correspondence.

You can create multiple e-mail accounts inside Google Apps in two ways. First, you can always add more users from the dashboard, each with his own account. That's fine if you're using the standard mode, but it can get expensive if you're in Premier mode. At $50 a pop (at the time of this writing), you'd better be sure you want those extra accounts.

The second way is to set up *nicknames*, or e-mail aliases, that automatically redirect to the home account. You can create a nickname for your e-mail account by following these steps:

1. **Click the Add a Nickname link shown in Figure 2-3.**

2. **Type the nickname in the field shown in Figure 2-4.**

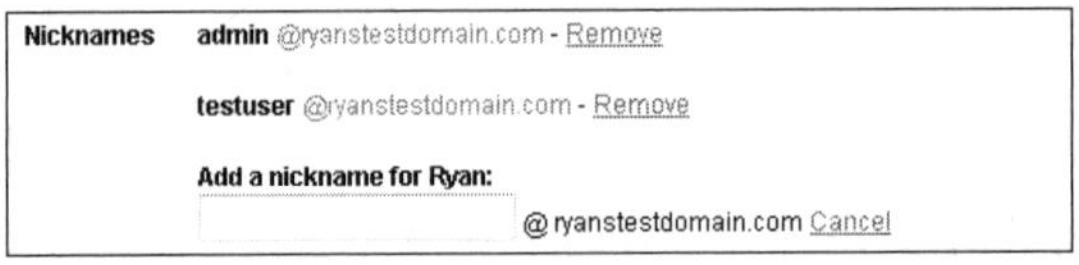

Figure 2-4:
Entering a
nickname
for your
e-mail
account.

3. **Click Save Changes at the bottom of the page to create the nickname.**

4. **Send a test e-mail to the new nickname to make sure the changes are saved correctly.**

There are advantages to this setup — you can assign as many virtual accounts to a single account as you want, change nicknames to redirect mail, or delete a nickname without having to delete an entire account. It also allows users to check their e-mails without opening multiple accounts.

However, if you do want multiple people checking the same account for various reasons (like sales leads, support requests, and the like), separate accounts may be better. You can always forward mail from one account to another by logging into the account and following these directions:

1. **Sign in to the account you want to forward and click Settings, as shown in Figure 2-5.**

2. **Click Forwarding and POP/IMAP to see the screen shown in Figure 2-6.**

Figure 2-5:
Gmail
Settings.

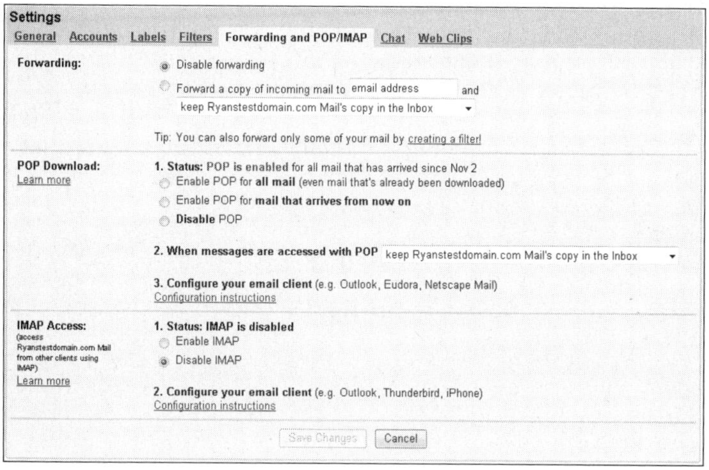

ryan@ryanstestdomain.com | Manage this domain | Settings | Older version | Help | Sign out

Settings
General   Accounts   Labels   Filters   **Forwarding and POP/IMAP**   Chat   Web Clips

Forwarding:
   ◉ Disable forwarding
   ○ Forward a copy of incoming mail to email address and
      keep Ryanstestdomain.com Mail's copy in the Inbox   ▾

   Tip: You can also forward only some of your mail by creating a filter!

POP Download:
Learn more
   1. **Status:** POP is enabled for all mail that has arrived since Nov 2
      ○ Enable POP for **all mail** (even mail that's already been downloaded)
      ○ Enable POP for **mail that arrives from now on**
      ○ **Disable POP**

   2. **When messages are accessed with POP** keep Ryanstestdomain.com Mail's copy in the Inbox   ▾

   3. **Configure your email client** (e.g. Outlook, Eudora, Netscape Mail)
      Configuration instructions

Figure 2-6:
Gmail
Forwarding
Settings.

IMAP Access:
(access
Ryanstestdomain.com Mail
from other clients using
IMAP)
Learn more
   1. **Status: IMAP is disabled**
      ○ Enable IMAP
      ◉ Disable IMAP

   2. **Configure your email client** (e.g. Outlook, Thunderbird, iPhone)
      Configuration instructions

   [Save Changes]   [Cancel]

3. **Click the second radio button and enter the receiving e-mail address
   in the field next to the button.**

4. **If you want to keep the e-mail in the original account, leave the
   Forwarding drop-down menu as is. If not, choose whether you want to
   delete or archive the e-mail by selecting that option in the drop-down
   menu.**

5. **When you're finished, click Save Changes at the bottom of the page.**

An account with an e-mail address published on a Web site and not cleared
out will reach its storage limit occasionally. Make sure you check it and clear
it out occasionally to avoid problems.

Using e-mail lists

Sending e-mail is a convenient way to address a large group of people at
one time, but it's not always convenient to type out a whole laundry list of
e-mails. It's also a challenge if you want to address only a certain portion of
your employees or coworkers as well. Creating e-mail lists makes your job
a little easier — you can make sure only specific e-mail accounts get certain
e-mails, and it saves your typing time.

For example, Jake's Landscaping has one e-mail list that includes everybody in the company, so major announcements or scheduling needs can be addressed quickly and easily. The company also has an e-mail list for Jake, James, and team supervisors for addressing administrative manners. There's also a mailing list for each team, as well as one for all temporary employees. This makes communications easy to target and manage.

Creating an e-mail list

Creating an e-mail list is easy. Just sign into your Google Apps domain, select User Accounts, and click Create E-mail List to see the page shown in Figure 2-7.

Figure 2-7:
Creating an
e-mail list.

> **Create a new email list**
>
> Choose a name for the new email list
>
> @ ryanstestdomain.com
>
> Add a recipient
>
> [Add recipient] [Add everyone in my domain]
>
> Note: You may add recipients that are outside your domain.
>
> [Cancel]

Next, perform the following steps:

1. **Enter a name for your mailing list in the first text field.**

2. **Enter an e-mail address for each recipient. It can be either somebody from your domain or another e-mail outside of your control.**

3. **Continue adding e-mail addresses for each recipient.**

4. **If you want to add everybody from your domain, click Add Everybody in My Domain.**

Now, any e-mail you send to a certain list's e-mail address goes to all the selected accounts.

Make sure to keep the names of your e-mail list short and topical. This ensures you use only the right list to communicate.

Be sure you're using the correct list — there's nothing more embarrassing than sending an e-mail to the wrong list. It's the same as accidentally using the Reply All button, because you're sending potentially damaging information to the wrong people. Giving the list a descriptive (but short) title helps prevent this potential problem.

Editing an e-mail list

You may have to add or remove names, depending on what's happening with your small business. Like most actions in Google Apps, it's an easy transition. Here's all you have to do:

1. **Log in to your domain.**

2. **Click User Accounts and select E-mail Addresses to see the screen shown in Figure 2-8.**

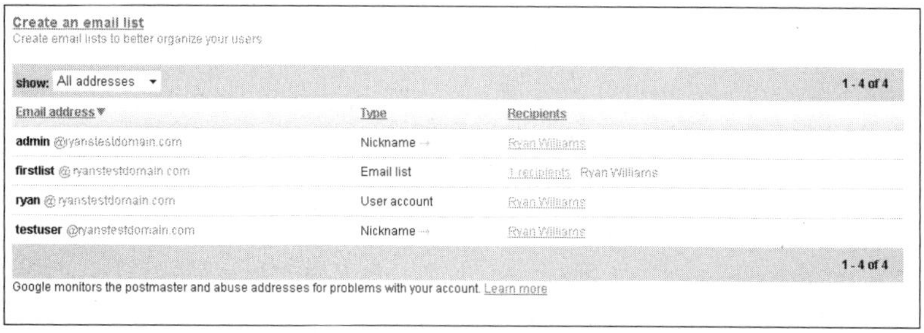

Figure 2-8: The Domain's list of e-mail addresses and lists.

Create an email list
Create email lists to better organize your users

show: All addresses ▼			1 - 4 of 4
Email address ▼	**Type**	**Recipients**	
admin @ryanstestdomain.com	Nickname →	Ryan Williams	
firstlist @ryanstestdomain.com	Email list	1 recipients Ryan Williams	
ryan @ryanstestdomain.com	User account	Ryan Williams	
testuser @ryanstestdomain.com	Nickname →	Ryan Williams	
			1 - 4 of 4

Google monitors the postmaster and abuse addresses for problems with your account. Learn more

3. **Click the recipients link to see the addresses included in the list, as shown in Figure 2-9.**

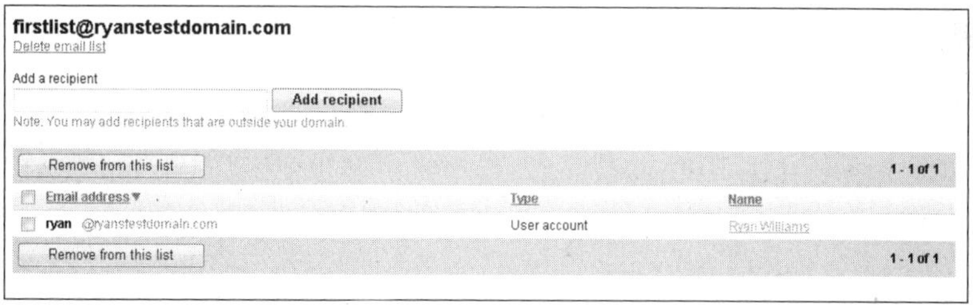

Figure 2-9: Editing your e-mail list.

firstlist@ryanstestdomain.com
Delete email list

Add a recipient
          [Add recipient]
Note: You may add recipients that are outside your domain.

[Remove from this list]   1 - 1 of 1

☐ **Email address ▼**	**Type**	**Name**
☐ **ryan** @ryanstestdomain.com	User account	Ryan Williams

[Remove from this list]   1 - 1 of 1

4. **To add a recipient, type in the address and click Add Recipient to enter the address.**

5. **To remove a current recipient, check the box next to the recipient in question and click Remove from This List.**

Deleting an e-mail list

If you think an e-mail list has served its purpose and needs to be deleted, navigate to the window shown in Figure 2-9 and select the list you want to delete. When you click that list, you see a link on the management page that says Delete E-mail List. Click that link to finish it off.

Importing Messages and Contacts from Old Accounts

If you need to move e-mail accounts over from your old system to another, Gmail can handle the transition (depending on the system you're using). The methods for moving individual accounts differ from those for bulk transfers. This can get a little complicated if you're unused to dealing with mail servers and settings, but all the information you need is available from your former e-mail service provider and Google. It's just a matter of plugging in the correct fields and going from there.

If you're using a Webmail service like Hotmail or Yahoo!, you won't be able to do a migration as outlined in this section. If there's any e-mail you need to transfer, you have to forward them manually. On the other hand, those accounts are free, so you don't need to worry about closing them and losing your information.

Bulk e-mail migration

Gmail is capable of handling a mass transfer of e-mail from one system to the other if those systems are using the IMAP protocol or a hosted system like Microsoft's Exchange. Google provides a list of all the available systems on their help pages, but before you go looking you should know a couple of things:

+ This only works for systems with several accounts, the correct protocols, and those clients who use Premier or Education versions of Google Apps.

+ You or those working for you must have some programming background in order to make this work.

If the preceding doesn't apply to you, you shouldn't consider using these services. If it does, type E-mail Migration in the search field of your Google Apps dashboard and click Search Help Center. This will give you the instructions you need to make the migration happen.

Mail fetcher

More than likely, you only have a few accounts that need to be migrated, so you'll find that Mail Fetcher is a much more useful alternative. This feature automatically grabs e-mail coming from your former account and puts it into your Google Apps Gmail account. This centralizes your e-mail accounts in one area and allows you to send and receive e-mail from one or more sources seamlessly.

Your old e-mail account must remain active in order for Mail Fetcher to work. If the account is ever closed or blocked for any reason, Google Apps will be unable to retrieve mail sent to that account.

1. **The first step is to obtain your e-mail set-up information from the old e-mail account.**

    In the case of e-mail from ISPs or similar sources, you have to check with a service representative or their help systems in order to complete this step. You need the following information:

    -   E-mail address

    -   Username for the e-mail account

    -   Password

    -   POP3 server (note that the old account MUST have POP3 access for this to work)

    -   Port number

2. **For each user migrating e-mail, sign into their Gmail account and click the Settings link. Click the Accounts tab to see the screen shown in Figure 2-10.**

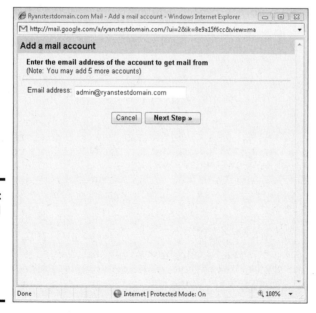

Figure 2-10:
Telling Mail Fetcher the old account's e-mail address.

3. **Click the Next Step button to see the screen shown in Figure 2-11.**

4. **Enter the appropriate information from your old account into the correct fields.**

Decide what settings you should activate on this screen. Don't leave any messages on the old account unless you're going to keep using it, so you probably don't need to activate that option. If your old account can handle an SSL connection, it's probably best to turn it on — this keeps the transmission of your e-mail secure.

5. **The other two options shown in Figure 2-11 determine how the mail is delivered to your Gmail inbox via a descriptive label and whether the e-mail is delivered to your Inbox or your mail archives. Click the options as you see fit to manage your e-mail account.**

6. **Check the Label Incoming Messages checkbox and choose the label you want to use in the drop-down menu.**

This helps you better identify where your e-mails are coming from and how you want to react to them. It also gives you an additional search option for your e-mail archives.

7. **Click the Add Account button to start the flow of e-mail to your Google Apps account.**

8. **You are asked if you want to be able to send e-mail from your old account as well. Choose Yes or No appropriately and click the Next Step button.**

You can always go back and change your settings later. If you choose to send e-mail from your old account via Google Apps, you need to verify that the account is yours via an e-mail to the old account. To do so, log into the old account and either click the link on the e-mail or enter its registration code in your new account. Click Verify, and you're ready to go.

When this process is completed, you can receive e-mail from your old account on your new account automatically. This process is seamless, and you should be able to send and receive from either the old account or your new Google Apps account without issue. The e-mail in your old account will start showing up in your new account. Just wait for a bit, and you are ready to go.

This method might take quite a bit of time, depending on your mail servers and how much information you're trying to move. It's better to schedule this process for a time when you know you're not going to be spending a lot of time on e-mail, and you are able to let the transfer move without issue.

Remember that your goal with this move is to get old e-mail over to your new account as quickly as possible so that you can stop using the old account. This feature is there to send mail from the old account if necessary, but you should cease using it as soon as possible. Thus, Jake has James move his ISP's account seamlessly, and he's ready to go with his new jake@jakeslandscapingservices.com e-mail address (just as soon as he remembers the Web address for his account). That Web address, by the way, is http://mail.google.com/a/jakeslandscapingservices.com. Yours will be much the same — just swap out the domain names and you're ready to go.

You can always have your users sign into http://partnerpage.google.com/yourdomainnamehere.com and access all services, including e-mail, from there. It's easier than having to remember more than one Web address.

Importing e-mail contacts

It's impossible to remember everybody's e-mail addresses, especially if friends or business associates have more than one. For example, it's not unusual to have a primary work e-mail account, a personal e-mail account, and a "spam" account used to sign up for online offers and the like. Multiply that by fifty or so folks (and it isn't that unusual, especially if you keep business and personal contacts in the same account), and you've got quite a few addresses to keep track of. Gmail and Google Apps make importing contacts an easy process though, depending on the capabilities of your old e-mail account.

Gmail imports contact information through a CSV (comma-separated value) file system. Basically, it's a spreadsheet that includes all your contact information with commas between every entry. Gmail reads those commas and knows when to move on to the next field to insert the information. Most e-mail systems let you export your contacts in a CSV file, so follow the instructions as provided by your e-mail service to make that happen.

After you've exported the CSV file, open your Gmail or Google Apps account and click the Contacts link in the left sidebar. You see a screen that looks like the one shown in Figure 2-12.

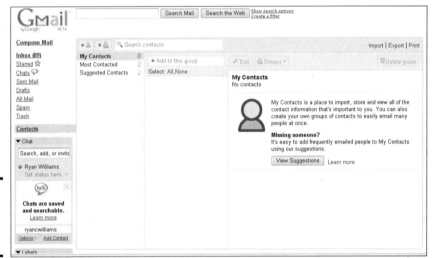

Figure 2-12: Gmail's Contacts page.

Click the Import link in the top-right corner, browse to the location of the CSV file on your computer, and click Import. The contact list is added automatically, and all your familiar addresses are included in your Gmail Contacts list as well.

If you want to create your own CSV file, use a spreadsheet program like Microsoft Excel or Google Spreadsheet (discussed more in Chapter 4) to create a table that includes a column for your contacts' names, addresses, phone numbers, and more. A simple table is shown in Figure 2-13, although you can add additional information to your contacts as well.

Figure 2-13:
Creating a
Contacts
CSV file.

	First Name	Last Name	Email Address
1			
2	John	Doe	johndoe@johndoe.com
3			
4			
5			

You have to type all this information in manually, but it's easier than adding the contacts one by one in the Webmail client or in your e-mail client program. When you're done, save the table as a CSV file and import it into your Gmail account.

Google limits you to importing up to 3000 contacts at a time. If this is going to be a difficult task for you, you're probably busy enough that you don't have time to be doing it yourself. Still, you can accomplish this task by breaking up your CSV file into two or more files and uploading them separately. When you've completed that, you can access these contacts through the Web-based Gmail client for your Google Apps domain. You are also able to export them from Google Apps into a CSV file, just in case you need to move them to another account (such as one belonging to an employee or coworker).

You can also allow members of your domain to see each others' contact information by enabling contact sharing. To set this up, follow these steps:

1. **Log in to your domain, click the User Accounts tab, and click Settings.**

2. **Click the Enable Contact Sharing radio button and click Save Changes to start the sharing.**

   This puts all the accounts in your domain in all your users' address books. Combine this with a CSV file, and you should be able to maintain your address books with a minimum of effort.

Communicate Instantly!

E-mail is a fairly quick form of communication, but sometimes you need instantaneous contact with somebody else. E-mail won't cut it, and you're away from a phone (or unable to speak because of your environment). Instant messaging comes in extremely handy on these occasions. Your messages are communicated directly to the other user as soon as you type them, and you can even share files and audio/video chats as well.

Google Apps provides IM services through two different methods. For basic text IM services, look at the left sidebar of your Web-based Gmail account. After you've added some contacts via Google Apps or Gmail (at the very least, your coworkers), you see their names listed as shown in Figure 2-14.

Figure 2-14: Gmail's Quick Chat.

Click a contact's name to open a quick chat window, as shown in Figure 2-15.

Figure 2-15: A Quick Chat window.

Simply type the message in the text field and press Enter on your keyboard. If the user on the other end is logged on, he gets the message. Otherwise, the IM will be saved as a message for the user to open later. Simply type messages back and forth to communicate. It's that simple.

Click Options in the chat window to go "off the record" (prevent a transcript of your chats from being saved, as set by default), enable a group chat by inviting more users, or popping the Quick Chat window into its own browser window. You can also choose to block users from chatting if they get a little too active or bothersome, but you don't want to remove their contact information entirely.

This service works well if the user is on Gmail and Google Apps, and all you want to do is exchange text messages. However, Google offers services above and beyond this basic chat function that you can take advantage of. Google Talk uses the same contact list as your Gmail and Google Apps account, but it also introduces the capabilities to transfer files, conduct voice chats, and receive Gmail notifications of your chats.

Open your browser and navigate to `http://google.com/talk` to explore your Google Talk options. You can access the service in one of three ways:

✦ Download and install the Google Talk program.

✦ Launch the Web-based Google Talk client.

✦ For iPhone users, download the Google Talk for iPhone app.

If you have an Internet-capable phone that's not an iPhone, you can still use Google Talk on your phone. Just access the Web address for Google Talk via your browser and use it as you would on your computer.

You can only use the voice chat function for Google Talk if you have a microphone and speakers attached to your computer. Most laptops come with these features, but you have to buy some extra equipment for your desktop. Also, make sure your computer's microphone is turned up loud enough to send a strong signal.

Choose your option from the page shown in Figure 2-16.

Figure 2-16:
The many options of Google Talk.

To use the downloadable Google Talk IM client, click Download Google Talk and follow the instructions to install the program. When the installation is complete, sign in using your Google Apps account information in the window shown in Figure 2-17.

Figure 2-17:
Signing into
Google Talk.

After you've signed in, you see a list of all your Google Talk contacts, as this only shows contacts with Gmail or Google Talk accounts. Click a contact, and click the button to Chat, Call, or Send Voicemail to the user. Chat is your text-based instant messaging service. Call is voice-based communication, just like a telephone. Send Voicemail records a message from you and sends it to the recipient as an attachment to an e-mail message.

Notice the button that looks like a downward-pointing triangle. Click that button to activate the following options:

✦ **Send Files:** Click this option to open a window for transmitting a file. Simply navigate to the location of the file on your computer, select it, and click Send. The other users can save and open the file on their computers.

✦ **E-mail:** Click this button to e-mail the selected contact. Type in your message and click Send.

✦ **View past chats:** If you've chatted with this user before and you haven't disabled the Save Chat function, you can see those past conversations.

✦ **Block:** You can block the user, if necessary. Remember that you can always unblock them later if you wish.

Click Settings at the top to change basic functions of Google Talk. Some of the more important functions in these settings include the following:

✦ **Chat:** Click Chat and select whether you want to save records of all chats or disable the function.

✦ **Blocked:** This list shows blocked contacts and allows you to unblock them if you wish.

✦ **Notifications:** These options determine if and how you're notified when friends log on, send you a message, and call or leave you a message.

✦ **Connection:** This determines how your communications pass through different servers. Unless you know what you're doing, leave it alone. Google Talk should handle this without problems.

✦ **Audio:** This setting helps you choose the microphones and speakers you want to use for Google Talk.

✦ **Appearance:** These settings help you customize how your chats appear on your screen.

To use the Web-based client, click the Launch Google Talk Gadget link on the Google Talk page. After you sign in, you can conduct text IM chats with anybody on your list. Voice chat may not be available in this window. If you absolutely need to use voice chat or voicemail, it's best to stick with the Google Talk program downloaded to your computer.

The same applies to the Google Talk app for the iPhone. You can either access it by the Apps Store via iTunes or by having it sent to your mobile number from the Google Talk Web site. Download the application, sign in, and chat away.

The best thing about Google Talk is that all these functions work across platform, so you can use these functions wherever you are on whatever computer or device you have. That makes it a valuable service. Consider the following scenario:

1. James sends a quick IM to Jake on his laptop computer asking him when a team is supposed to mow the medians on Main St.

2. Jake notices from his desktop computer (he's checking e-mail before heading out to another site) that his temporary workers are all logged into Google Talk. He sets up a group chat (a feat he's incredibly proud of) and asks when they're headed out to the site.

3. One user, on his computer at home, says he's on his way. Another one, on his phone, replies he's en route and should be there in five minutes. The last, also on his phone, says he's picking up the equipment now and will meet them all there.

4. Jake leaves a voice-mail for James (he loves using the mic now that his teenage son installed it) saying the team is on it, and he's moving on.

Many phone calls and minutes were saved in this exchange, and everybody is on his way. Great way to use technology, isn't it?

Using Gmail with Traditional E-Mail Apps

One of the great advantages of Gmail is the fact that it's accessible from anywhere you have an Internet connection, and it's also got tremendous storage and archiving capabilities. However, you may want to use a program like Microsoft Outlook or Apple Mail to view your mail as well. These programs bring e-mail into a program located on your computer, where you can store and organize mail in more traditional ways by setting up familiar folders. You can also integrate your mail into the various contacts and calendar programs offered on Windows, Apple, Linux, and other operating systems.

Which way should you go? Ultimately, it depends on which method you're most comfortable with. If you're used to working with Outlook, Mail, or another program, Gmail and Google Apps can integrate seamlessly with those programs. All you notice is a new e-mail address. If you've never used these programs, give the Web clients a try first. They're fast, they're free, and they're available worldwide.

You can also use both — check the Web client while you're on the road, and use the program you prefer at home. Depending on the protocol you use, the mail could be available in both locations without issue. Let's take a look at these protocols used to move e-mail from the Web to your program and see what works best for you.

+ **POP3:** POP stands for *post office protocol*, and the number 3 indicates the version of said protocol (that's the most recent version). Without getting too technical, this protocol moves e-mail from the server to your computer — nothing too fancy, nothing too complicated. The problem is that after the e-mail is moved, it's deleted from your server. This leaves the server clean, but it also means that if you lose the information on your computer (deleted, crashed hard drive, or errant footstep on your kevboard by a curious pet), it's gone.

+ **IMAP:** Gmail also supports Internet Message Access Protocol, or IMAP. Instead of pulling e-mail directly from the server, IMAP leaves a copy on the server and puts a copy in your mail client until you specifically delete it. This may leave a little more information on the sever, but it also means you won't accidentally lose something because there's always a backup copy somewhere. You can also access the information from your local client or the Web wherever you are. IMAP also supports the use of multiple mail folders, the capability to open your mailbox from several different locations, and the capability to read the text of an e-mail without downloading any large attachments.

So which one should you choose? Because IMAP is available through Gmail, and it's a more versatile method of receiving your e-mail, it's usually the better choice. If your client can handle it, go ahead and use the IMAP. It's not that POP3 doesn't work; it's just that IMAP works better.

Configuring IMAP access

For this example, I'll use Microsoft Outlook to access the Gmail account. It's a common and versatile client, but it's not the only choice. Gmail provides instructions for setting up other clients, such as the free, open source Thunderbird or mobile devices like the iPhone. The necessary information doesn't change — only the fields in which it's entered. Here's how you do it:

1. **Log into your Gmail account on the Web, click Setting in the upper-right corner, and select the Forwarding and POP/IMAP tab to see the screen shown in Figure 2-18.**

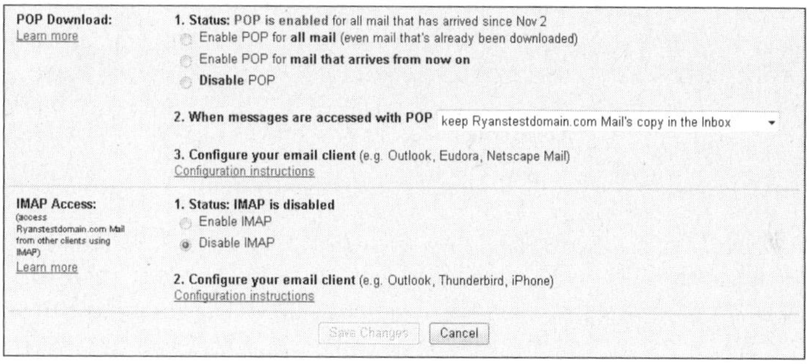

Figure 2-18:
Enabling
IMAP
access.

2. **Click the Enable IMAP radio button and then click Save Changes to allow your client to reach your account.**

3. **Open Microsoft Outlook and select Tools⇨Account Options. In the window that comes up, click New to see the screen shown in Figure 2-19.**

4. **The top radio button should be enabled automatically, but click it if it isn't.**

5. **Select Next to bring up the next window. Then select the Manually Configure check box and click Next.**

6. **Click the Internet E-mail radio button and click Next.**

7. **Enter the information as shown in Figure 2-20.**

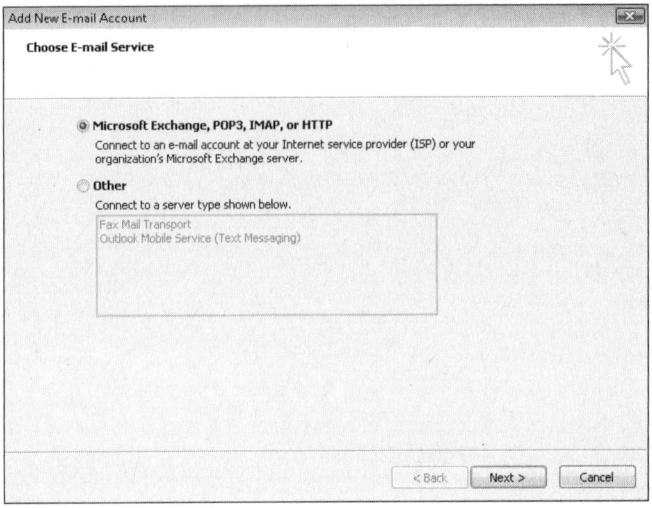

Figure 2-19:
Adding a
new IMAP
account.

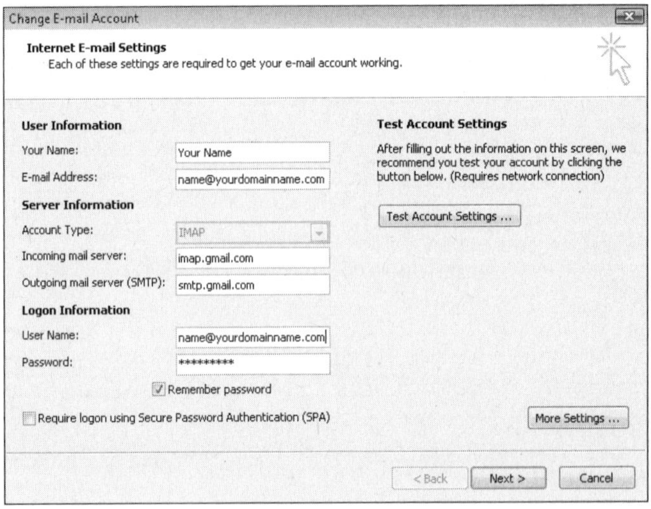

Figure 2-20:
Gmail
account
information.

8. **Click More Settings and select the Outgoing Server tab. Click the top check box and select the top radio button to require outgoing mail authentication and to use the same settings as your incoming mail.**

9. **Click the Advanced tab and enter the information shown in Figure 2-21.**

   You can verify your settings at `http://mail.google.com/support/bin/answer.py?hl=en&answer=13287`.

Figure 2-21:
Advanced
IMAP
Information.

10. **Click OK to close the window. Then select Next⇨Finish in the previous window to finish enabling your account.**

Again, the information used in this example is applicable to all other e-mail clients — only the set-up methods differ from program to program. Use it to enable your own e-mail client, or consult the Google help pages for more customized ways of adding your account to your client.

Configuring POP3 access

Configuring POP3 access is remarkably similar to configuring IMAP access. You still enable access in Gmail as shown in Figure 2-18, although you have the option to download all mail or only mail from the time you enabled your access. You also have the option in the drop-down menu to leave a copy of the message in the mailbox, leave one in the archive, or delete it entirely from the server. Otherwise, just follow the preceding instructions — all you have to change is the name of one server (imap.gmail.com becomes pop.gmail.com).

If you're on a computer you don't use that often, it's easier and safer to use the Web client to access your e-mail than to try to set up a local client. This way, you don't leave copies of your e-mail on an unfamiliar computer, and you're able to access your e-mail through an encrypted Web connection. That encryption isn't always guaranteed on a Web client (although the settings discussed earlier do use security to transmit and receive your e-mail). E-mail clients should only be used on familiar computers that you're going to have regular access to.

Common User Problems

Because an e-mail client is another step between you and your Gmail account (and because humans have to enter settings to make it work), there's the possibility that the client and Gmail won't always be able to make the correct connection. You might also have users forget their passwords for their Webmail access, too (more often than you'd like to think). Here are some common scenarios where e-mail clients have problems and what you can do to resolve them.

I can't log into my account

The first step is to make sure your user is entering the correct name and password. After you've confirmed that, take a look at the device he is using. If it's a computer keyboard, make sure that the caps or number lock keys aren't on and causing problems. If the user is working with a new mobile device, make sure that he knows how to use the keyboard properly. Blackberry, mobile phone, or other device keyboards may require a Shift or Alt key to be pressed to get a number or capital letter. Finally, if users just forget their passwords, you can reset these yourself by following these steps:

1. **Log into your Google Apps account.**

2. **In the dashboard, click the User Accounts tab and select the user you need to assist.**

3. **Click the Change Password link to see the screen in Figure 2-22.**

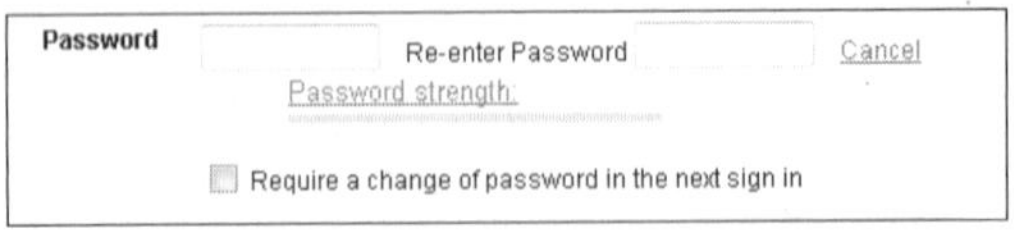

Figure 2-22:
Changing a user's password.

Password			
	Re-enter Password		Cancel
	Password strength.		
	☐ Require a change of password in the next sign in		

4. **Enter a temporary password twice and check the Require A Change Of Password box. Click Save Changes at the bottom of the page.**

5. **Have the user log in and change the password to something he or she will remember.**

6. **If he uses an e-mail client, make sure the password is changed there as well.**

It's taking too long to download messages

Slow downloading of messages usually means any of these three things:

+ There's a large attachment coming in.

+ There's other network traffic slowing the mail's arrival.

+ The Internet connection is having problems.

If there's a large attachment that's slowing e-mail coming in to the client, it's best to log in to the Webmail client and examine the message there. Either read and delete it, or let it come through and just take the hit on time. If the user is downloading large files from other sources, have him stop or delay that activity until the mail is downloaded. If the user's Internet connection is the problem, you have to check with the ISP for that location.

Mail is getting stuck in my outbox

First, make sure the user's computer is actually connected to a network. It sounds simple, but it's always the first thing you should check. If there's no network, the mail can't get through. Next, make sure the user's e-mail client settings are correct. Look at the outgoing mail server and determine whether it's set to authenticate. Refer to the IMAP instructions in the previous section entitled "Configuring IMAP Access" for the correct settings.

I'm not getting some of my mail

Make sure the e-mail is actually getting through to the Web client. If somebody tells you he is sending e-mail, but it's not getting to you or your users, be aware there's a big Internet and a host of problems that could occur between him and you. If the e-mail is being sent to the correct e-mail address, but it's not showing up in your Webmail client, refer to your domain settings and make sure they're set correctly. This varies among domain registrars, so check with them to make sure the settings are correct. If the mail is showing up in the Web client, look at the e-mail client settings. Make sure they are also correct.

Working with Google

If you've exhausted these methods and you have the Premier or Educational versions of Google Apps, you can always contact Google and work with it to solve your problems. It's far more likely, however, that your problems usually occur because of incorrect settings, so it's a good idea to recheck these before you consult Google support. Nevertheless, you are paying for the help, so feel free to contact Google if something stumps you:

1. Log into your domain and click Domain Settings.

2. Select the Account Settings tab.

3. Scroll to the bottom of the screen and decide whether you want to use online or phone support.

4. Note your customer and support PINs, and be prepared to give them when asked.

If you're stumped up to this point, Google support should be able to get you where you need to go. Be prepared to give the Google staff all the necessary information and recount all the steps you've taken up to this point. It could take a while, but having all this information available speeds up the process.

Chapter 3: Be More Productive with Google Calendar

In This Chapter

✔ Managing individual and multiple calendars

✔ Sharing calendars with multiple users

✔ Synching calendars across devices

A small paper calendar or desk blotter might be a convenient way to track appointments, but it's impossible to upload that information or share it with others. And if you lose it, everything's gone. Even if you've been keeping your appointments on a program like Microsoft Outlook or a device like a smartphone, it's difficult to share that information across several different systems or users. Google Calendar tackles all these problems not only by storing your information in a safe, central location, but also by letting you decide who has access to your calendars and by choosing what information those who have access can add, delete, or change. It's like having a giant refrigerator door calendar that you can view and change from anywhere. Sadly, there's no root beer in this virtual fridge, but you can always put an appointment on somebody's calendar to pick some up at the store.

Creating Your First Calendar

The heading above says "first" because Google Apps enables you to create more than one calendar to accomplish several different purposes. However, everybody has to start somewhere, so let's create a general calendar, such as one Jake's Landscaping might use for all its upcoming jobs. Just follow these steps:

1. **Log into your domain and click the Web link on your dashboard under Calendar. You can also access your calendar by going to the Web address** `http://www.google.com/calendar/a/yourdomain here.com` **and replacing** `yourdomainhere.com` **with your domain name.**

2. **Enter your time zone and country information as shown in Figure 3-1.**

3. **Click the Use This Time Zone button to open your new calendar in a new Web browser window.**

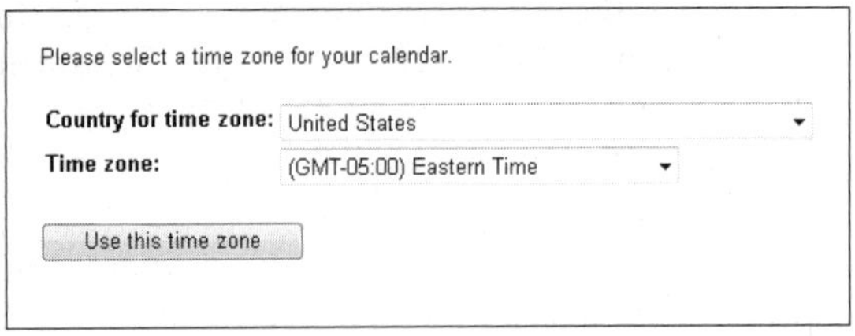

Figure 3-1:
Entering
your
calendar's
basic
information.

Please select a time zone for your calendar.

Country for time zone: United States

Time zone: (GMT-05:00) Eastern Time

Use this time zone

When you've finished performing the preceding steps, your calendar will look like the one shown in Figure 3-2. All the resources are available, so you just have to enter your upcoming appointments.

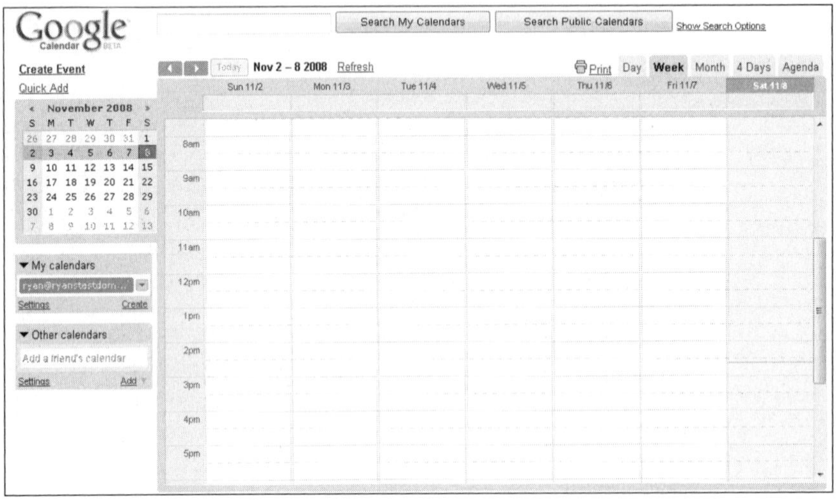

Figure 3-2:
Your first
calendar.

Adding calendar events

Click the Create Event link in the upper-left corner of your calendar to see the screen shown in Figure 3-3.

Here's where you add all the basic information for your new event. You can set the start and end times here (even if they're on different dates), set up recurring appointments, and add a location and descriptive information. For example, a recurring appointment to cut a certain lawn is set up this way:

1. **Type in** Cut Lawn **in the What field.**

2. **Enter the appropriate times in the When fields. You can leave the dates blank for this one, but you could enter them for single appointments.**

3. **Select the recurrence that you want to use in the drop-down menu under the When fields. In this case, we're selecting a weekly event that occurs every week on Monday and that never ends. You can modify each of these settings at any time.**

    You can set a range for recurring appointments, so that they end after a certain time (perfect for seasonal appointments like lawn mowing). After you select the recurrence of the appointment, enter the start and end dates for your appointment.

4. **Enter the Where and Description information in the appropriate fields.**

5. **Click Add A Reminder and choose whether you get an e-mail or pop-up window within a certain amount of time before the event.**

6. **Choose whether you want this appointment shared with others and how you want the appointments to be viewed.**

7. **Enter the e-mail addresses of guests (or coworkers, if you have a large lawn) you want to invite to the event. Separate these addresses with commas, and decide whether you let these guests invite others and whether they can view the entire guest list. If they have Google Calendar accounts, the event is added to their calendars as well.**

8. **Click Save to put the appointment on your calendar.**

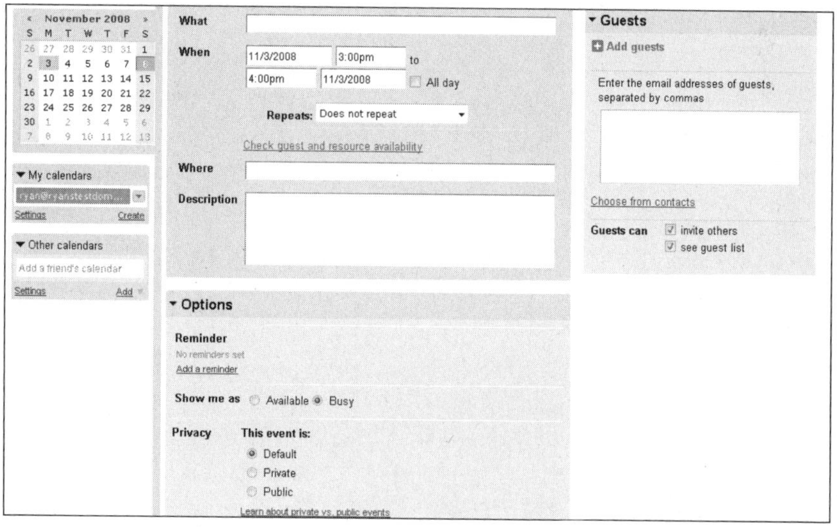

Figure 3-3:
Adding a
calendar
event.

After you've saved the appointment, you can change the ways you view the calendar by clicking the daily, weekly, monthly, or four-day spread tabs in the upper-right portion of the calendar page. You can also click the Agenda tab to see a list of upcoming appointments independent of the other views.

If you're already in the view you want to use and you just want to add an event quickly, click the point of the calendar where you want to add the event. A one-hour long event is created at that point, and you are asked to enter the What field's information to describe the event. Click Create Event, and your new event is in there. You can also click the Edit Event Info link to change more detailed aspects of your events.

Editing calendar events

Find the event you want to edit in the calendar and click it. A pop-up bubble appears with the basic event information and a link to edit or delete the event's information. Click that link to see the screen shown in Figure 3-4.

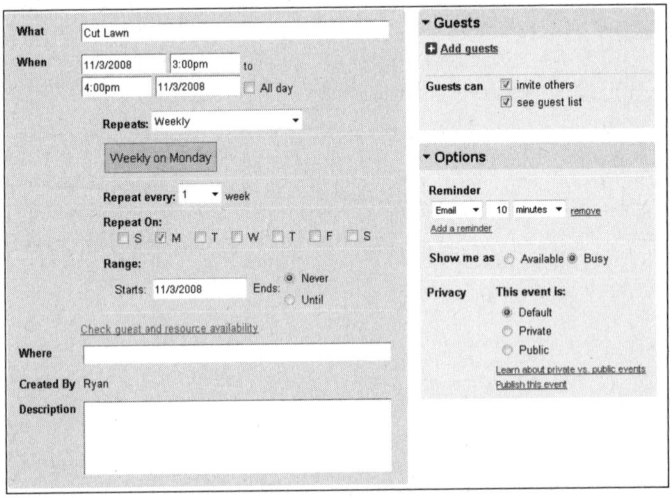

Figure 3-4:
Modifying
a calendar
event.

Change the information you want to modify and click Save when you're finished. The edited information takes the place of the old appointment, and you're ready to go.

Deleting calendar events

Click the event you want to get rid of. This brings up the pop-up bubble, and you just click the Delete link. If there's only one occurrence of the event, you are asked to confirm the decision. Click Delete to get rid of it, or click Cancel to leave it where it is.

If it's a recurring event, you are asked to delete all the events, all the events from this point on, only this event, or to cancel your deletion and leave the event as it is, as shown in Figure 3-5.

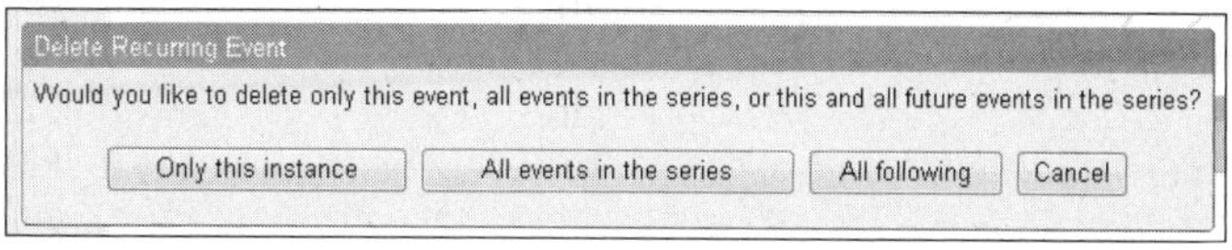

Figure 3-5:
Deleting a
recurring
event.

Make your decision, click the appropriate button, and you're ready to go

Creating multiple calendars

Adding additional calendars is a simple matter, and there are plenty of reasons why you'd want to do so. In the case of Jake's Landscaping, we already looked at the needs for individual calendars for each employee, as well as a master calendar for all their upcoming jobs and subcalendars for individual teams. Each of these calendars can be started with a single click, and you can have as many as you want.

Look at the sidebar of the calendar in Figure 3-2 and find the section called My Calendars. You see a drop-down menu featuring the first calendar you've created, along with links for Settings, for the current calendar, and Create, to create a new calendar. Click the Create link to see the screen shown in Figure 3-6.

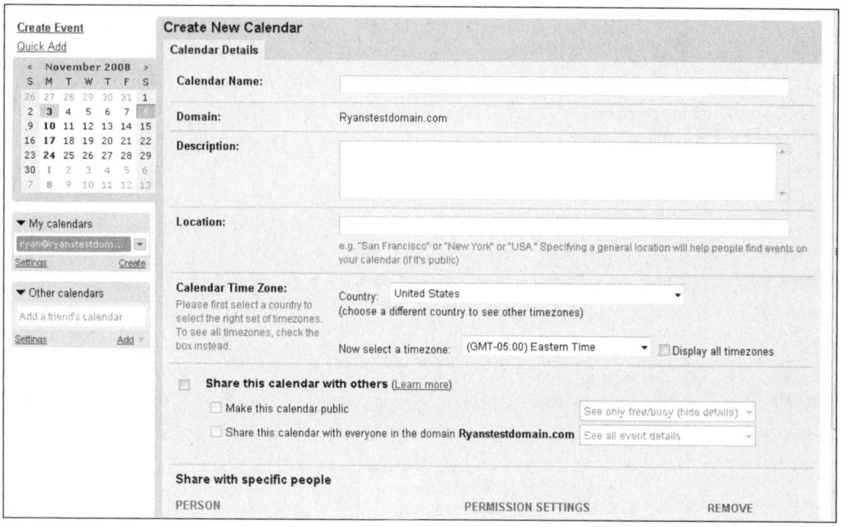

Figure 3-6:
Creating
a new
calendar.

Add the necessary information in this page, including the following fields:

+ Calendar Name, such as *Master Schedule*.

+ Calendar Description, such as *All Upcoming Jobs for Jake's Landscaping*.

+ Location, such as your hometown.

+ Calendar country and time zone, as appropriate.

+ Sharing information, which will be discussed later in this chapter in the section called "Using Shared Calendars Effectively."

When all your information has been entered, click the Create Calendar button at the bottom of the page to make it happen.

So you've created a new calendar, and you can see the name showing up in the left sidebar when you log into your account. But you see only one day in the view, and there's no sign of your new calendar. What's going on?

Google Calendar is set up so that all the calendars show up in a single view, and the appointments are differentiated from calendar to calendar by a color code. Note the information shown in Figure 3-7.

Figure 3-7:
A listing of different calendars.

Each calendar has its own color, and the appointments for that calendar show up in the main view with that color. This enables you to differentiate the appointments from one calendar to another. You can also click the downward-pointing arrow next to each calendar to bring up the menu shown in Figure 3-8.

Figure 3-8:
Calendar color and display options.

In this menu, you can customize the color of your calendar, choose whether to hide or display the calendar, create appointments, or change the settings for the calendar. It's basically a miniature control window for all your calendars functions.

Adding a subscription

Not only can you create as many calendars as you need, but you can also subscribe to external calendars provided by other people and sources. You can do this in several ways, and all of them are put on display when you click the Add link under the Other Calendars section on the left sidebar of your Calendar view. These options are

+ **Add a public calendar:** Choose Add a Public Calendar to view the available choices. You can view several different categories of calendars available for subscription, or you can search for specific information by using the text field at the top of the screen. Options include calendars for your favorite television shows (new episodes and reruns) as well as sporting events; your favorite team's schedule can be automatically added to your calendar so you never miss a game.

   Find the calendar you want to add, click the Add to Calendar button underneath it, and that information is added to your calendar view. You can change the same color and display options, just as you do on other calendars, to keep things separated and easy to identify.

+ **Add a friend's calendar:** If you have other friends or colleagues who use Google Calendars, you can subscribe to their calendars by entering their e-mail addresses and clicking Add, as shown in Figure 3-9.

   You can use either a Gmail address, a Google Apps e-mail address, or any other e-mail address you know of. However, only the first two are likely to have Google Calendar accounts set up immediately.

   If they have their calendars enabled for sharing, clicking Add gives you access to the information they've provided. If not (or if they don't have a Google Calendars account to begin with), they are sent an e-mail inviting them to share or set up an account. When that's done, you are notified and you see their calendars in your account.

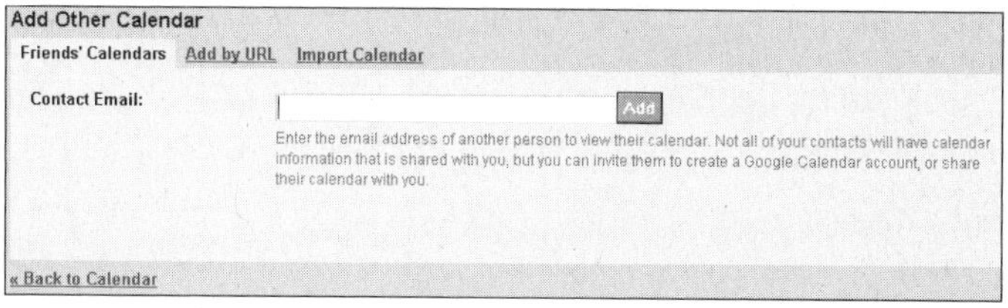

Figure 3-9:
Adding a
friend's
calendar.

Add Other Calendar

Friends' Calendars   Add by URL   Import Calendar

Contact Email: | [Add]

Enter the email address of another person to view their calendar. Not all of your contacts will have calendar information that is shared with you, but you can invite them to create a Google Calendar account, or share their calendar with you.

« Back to Calendar

✦ **Add by URL:** Some sites or organizations may have public calendars available in iCal format. To connect to one, get the URL and click the Add link to see the screen shown in Figure 3-10.

You won't need to do this for any Google Calendars, but others are available that you can connect to via this method. If you see the term *iCal* anywhere, you know you are able to use this method.

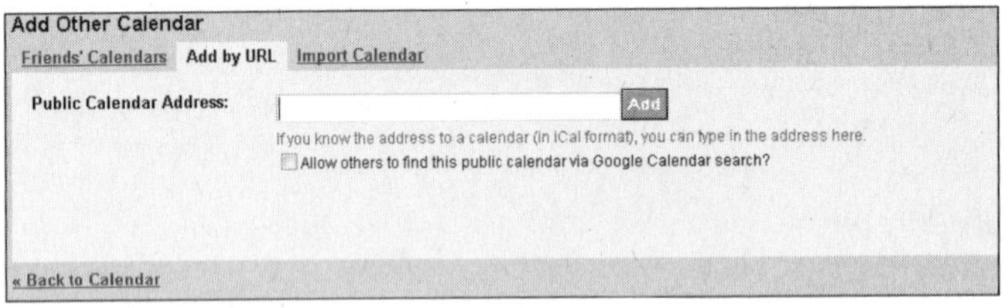

Figure 3-10:
Adding a
calendar via
URL.

Add Other Calendar

Friends' Calendars   **Add by URL**   Import Calendar

Public Calendar Address: [Add]

If you know the address to a calendar (in iCal format), you can type in the address here.

☐ Allow others to find this public calendar via Google Calendar search?

« Back to Calendar

✦ **Import calendar:** This option is best if you've been using a program like Microsoft Outlook or Sunbird to manage your calendars locally. This option lets you take .ics or .csv files and import them into Google Calendar. Here's what you do:

1. First, export the file from your old calendar. Make sure that you perform this export as one of the two file types listed here, or you won't be able to bring them in.

2. When you've saved the exported file, log into your domain and navigate to your calendar.

3. Click the Add button and select Import Calendar to see the screen shown in Figure 3-11.

4. Click the Browse button and navigate to the location of the calendar file on your computer.

5. Choose the calendar into which you want to import the new information.

6. Finally, click Import to finish the process and bring the information into Google Calendar.

If you want to put the new calendar information into a calendar of its own, not into your existing calendars, create the new calendar beforehand. Then, when you perform the upload, you can choose that calendar from the drop-down menu and move all those appointments into their new home.

```
Add Other Calendar
Friends' Calendars   Add by URL   Import Calendar

Step 1: Select File                          [ Browse... ]
Learn more              Choose the file that contains your events. Google Calendar can import event information in iCal or CSV (MS
                        Outlook) format.

Step 2: Choose Calendar    ryan@ryanstestdomain.com  ▼
                           Choose the calendar where these events should be saved.

Step 3: Complete Import    [ Import ]

« Back to Calendar
```

Figure 3-11:
Importing a
calendar.

Notifications

Google Calendars is capable of notifying you whenever several types of
events occur. You can choose to receive these notifications via either e-mail
or text messages, depending on your preferences. For example, James from
Jake's Landscaping may like getting his schedule via e-mail sent to his desktop computer, whereas Jake likes getting the updates from his cell phone
while he's out in the field.

To set up notifications, follow these steps:

1. **Log into your domain and navigate to your calendar.**

2. **Click Settings in the upper-right corner and select the Calendars tab.**

3. **Find the calendar you want to change and click the Notifications link
   next to it.**

4. **Click Add A Reminder to set default reminders for every event on
   your calendar. Choose the how long prior to the event you want to
   be reminded and whether you want to be reminded by an e-mail or a
   pop-up window on your computer.**

   Obviously, where you use your calendar is going to be the major factor
   in deciding how you receive your reminders. If you're not around a computer, a pop-up window won't help much.

5. **You can also choose to be notified about new invitations, changed
   invitations, cancelled invitations, or replies to your invitations.
   There's also an option to get your daily agenda sent to you automatically at 5 a.m. Choose how you want to receive your notification
   (e-mail or text message/SMS) and click that check box.**

You have to enable a mobile device before you can choose the SMS option.

6. **Click Save to finalize your choices.**

Now you can receive notifications when any of the chosen events occur. It's convenient and helpful — who would have thought a pop-up window could help you get to a job on time?

To get notifications on your mobile device, Google makes it easy to set up your phone via text message. All that's required is a quick verification process and you're ready to go.

1. **In Google Calendar, click Settings and select the Mobile Setup tab.**

2. **Enter your country, phone number, and phone carrier.**

3. **Click Send Verification code and wait to receive the text message with that code.**

4. **When you get that message, enter the code in the Verification Code tab and click Finish Setup.**

5. **Click Save.**

Any SMS notification options are now enabled.

Depending on how your phone provider charges for text messages, this could end up costing you some money. Make sure you know what you're getting into before you enable this option.

Using Shared Calendars Effectively

So keeping your schedule on Google Calendars helps centralize your information, lets you set up multiple calendars for different reasons, and enables you to add information from public calendars to your personal calendar. Now, take a look at how to make your own calendars public and share them interactively with different people and different layers of permissions. If we go back to the refrigerator image, you're now allowing members of your virtual family to make changes and additions from wherever they are (and the kids still can't change their scheduled bedtime on the calendar).

Adding collaborators to your calendar

To add other people to your calendar, just follow these steps:

1. **Log into your domain and navigate to your calendar.**

2. **Click the Settings link in the upper-right corner and select the Calendars tab, or you can click the Settings link under the My Calendars section in the left sidebar.**

   Either way, you are taken to the screen shown in Figure 3-12.

Figure 3-12:
Sharing
settings for
a Google
Calendar.

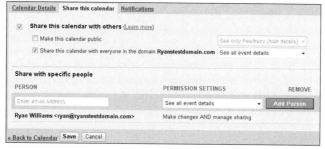

3. **Under the Sharing columns, click the Share This Calendar link (if this calendar hasn't been shared automatically) or the Shared: Edit Settings link (if the calendar was automatically shared) to see the screen shown in Figure 3-13.**

Figure 3-13:
Setting
sharing
permissions
for your
Google
Calendar.

4. **Check the top check box to allow your calendar to be shared.**

   Next, whom do you want to allow to see your information? Your next two choices determine whether the calendar is shared with everybody on the Internet or with just the people on your Google Apps domain. Unless you're trying to attract members of the public to attend the events on your calendar, you can probably leave this first check box blank. It's an easier decision to share your calendar with members of your domain.

5. **Check either of the boxes, depending on what you want people to see.**

   If you check the public box, the box allowing access to members of your domain is automatically checked as well. Because access is available to everyone with the first box, it only makes sense to check the second.

Next to each check box is a drop-down menu that sets permissions for each group. Even if public sharing is enabled, the public is only able to see whether the time is free or busy. Members of your domain are able to see event details if you let them; otherwise, they can be restricted to seeing only free and busy time as well.

6. **The preceding settings refer only to large groups of people, and they only manage whether and how the calendar can be viewed. The Share with Specific People field shown in Figure 3-13 allows greater access to individuals invited to manage your calendar. To set this setting, enter the e-mail address of the person you want to share your calendar with and click Add Person.**

7. **When that person is added, you can set permission levels for his or her interaction with your calendar. You have four options here:**

   - Manage changes and sharing

   - Manage changes only

   - See all event details

   - See only free busy time

   Some of these choices may seem repetitive, but they make sense. For instance, you might not want to make your calendar public, but you do want others outside of your domain to view it. Check the check box to have those in your domain see the calendar, and then add those outside the domain individually.

By default, those outside of the domain are only able to view free/busy time. If you log into your domain, click the Service Settings tab and select Calendar, you can see radio buttons under Sharing Options that let you set default sharing levels for those both inside and outside your domain.

8. After you've made your choices, click Save at the bottom of the page to make your decisions final (although you can go back and change them later).

Scheduling resources

Individual and group calendars aren't the only things that can be shared. Your small business may have tools or resources (like riding lawnmowers or conference rooms) that can be reserved. This ensures they aren't scheduled for use by two groups at the same time. Set up calendars for each resource you want to schedule by following these steps:

1. **Log into your domain and click Service Settings.**

2. **Select Calendar and click the Resources tab.**

3. **Click Create New Resource to see the screen shown in Figure 3-14.**

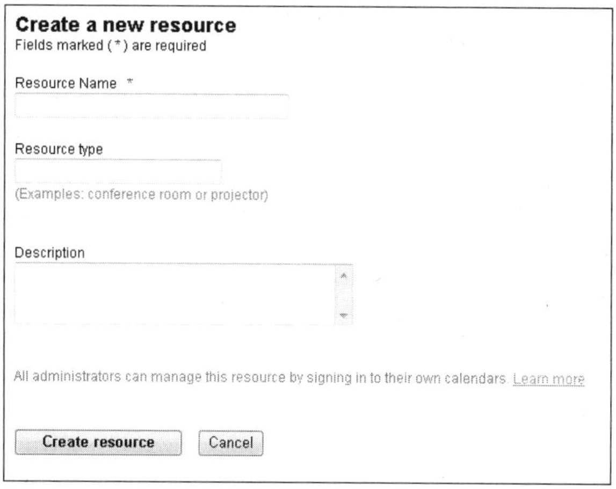

Create a new resource
Fields marked (*) are required

Resource Name *

Resource type

(Examples: conference room or projector)

Description

All administrators can manage this resource by signing in to their own calendars Learn more

[Create resource]   [Cancel]

Book I
Chapter 3

**Be More
Productive with
Google Calendar**

Figure 3-14:
Creating
a new
resource.

4. **Enter a name, a type, and a description for your resource.**

5. **Click Create Resource to create the calendar.**

6. **Google Apps give you an e-mail address. Use this address to add the resource to your calendar.**

7. **Set sharing options on the resources correctly and you're ready to share it with your coworkers and employees.**

Now they can reserve that resource and see when it's available via their own Google Calendar entries.

Adding RSS feeds for the public

Sharing and adding calendars within Google Calendars is a great option for those who already have accounts. However, you may want to try to reach as many people as possible, especially if you're running a business that schedules public events. Not everybody uses Google Calendars (maybe one day, but not now), but just about everybody does have some access to the Internet. That access makes it possible for you to make a public calendar available through several different RSS (really simple syndication) feeds. That way, everybody has a way to look at your upcoming events and see when and where they occur by using their Web browser.

To find the feeds for your calendars, log into your domain and navigate to your calendar. Follow these steps to get the links to publish your calendars publicly:

1. **Click Settings in the upper-right corner.**

2. **Click the Calendars tab in the window and find the link in the Sharing column for the calendar you want to publish. Click that link.**

3. If you aren't already sharing this calendar, click the check box to make this calendar public.

4. Now that the calendar is public, click the Calendar Details tab and scroll to the bottom.

5. Look at the icons shown in Figure 3-15. These are the links you use to publish the calendar to the public, as follows:

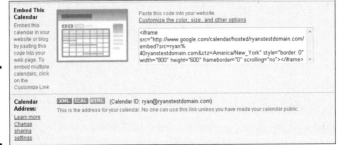

Figure 3-15:
Google
Calendar
feeds.

- *The XML button:* Click the XML button to generate a link usable in any RSS feed reader. Readers can see individual events in chronological order.

  With an RSS feed reader, people are able to keep track of any updates as you enter them. Many different feed readers are available through Web browsers, Outlook, and other programs. You can e-mail users the link or publish it in a Web page for others to put in their feed readers.

- *The ICAL button:* Click the ICAL button to generate a link usable in calendar programs like Outlook, iCal, and the like. Users can create calendars in the programs using the link and receive updates from the Web-based calendars.

- *The HTML button:* Click the HTML button to generate a link that you can place on any Webpage or e-mail. Users can click this link to open a full version of the calendar in their Web browser.

Note that all these options only allow calendar information to be viewed — nobody can edit or create entries from these feeds. Still, it's a good way for the public to view any events you want them to attend or learn when special products are arriving in your store.

Embedding your calendar

In Figure 3-17, you also see a section for embedding calendars. Embedding calendars differs from calendar feeds in that you don't have to have a special program to view embedded calendars, and you don't have to have a link that opens the calendar in a separate browser window. When the calendar is embedded in a Web page, it shows up as a portion of the page and can be viewed just by accessing that Web page.

Google Calendar automatically generates HTML code to copy and paste in your Web site with default settings, such as height, width, language, time zones, and the like. If you like the way it looks, go ahead and cut and paste that code into your Web site. If you want to make it fit into your Web site a little better by changing colors, views, and other calendar options, click the Customize the Color, Size, and Other Options link to see the screen shown in Figure 3-16.

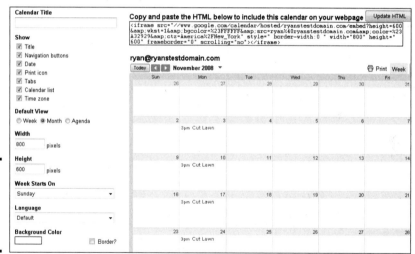

Figure 3-16: Customize your embedded calendar.

All the customization options are lined up on the left side of the screen, and the right side shows a preview of the options. Work through the options and the preview updates as you go. When you have something you're happy with, click the Update HTML button and copy the code out of the text box. You can paste that code on any Web page you want to use, and the events are dynamically updated as the calendar is changed.

Syncing Your Calendar

So far, we've seen how to share and manage calendars online and distribute these calendars via Web links and feeds. However, changing calendars requires logging into Google Calendar, and the feeds don't allow changes to be made — just viewed. Google does allow a couple of common tools to sync with Google Calendars, though. Using Google Calendar Sync, those users with Microsoft Outlook or a Blackberry are able to interact with Google Calendars and both view and change information.

Microsoft Outlook

To sync your Google Calendar account with Microsoft Outlook, download the Google Calendar Sync program from Google at `http://dl.google.com/googlecalendarsync/GoogleCalendarSync_Installer.exe`. You can also just search for Google Calendar Sync in (what else?) Google to get to the link. Download the file and install the program. After you've installed it, you see the window shown in Figure 3-17.

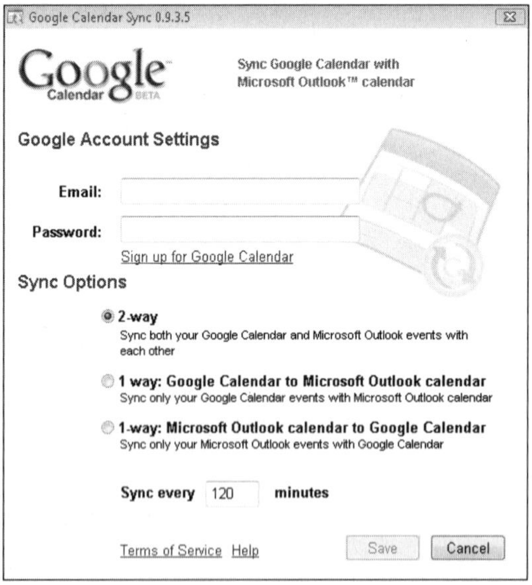

Figure 3-17: Installing Google Calendar Sync.

Enter your username and password, and select how you want to sync the events. You can either have the syncing operate both ways, or you can have Google Calendars sync to Microsoft Outlook or from Outlook to Google Calendars. Set the time for each sync, but don't set it to sync too often to keep from slowing down your system resources. After you've made your decision, click Save. Your calendar now syncs with Microsoft Outlook.

Blackberry

Blackberry devices are able to sync wirelessly with Google Calendar as well, and you don't need to install a program on a computer to make it happen — you just need to add a program to the Blackberry and go from there. Access `http://m.google.com/sync` from your Blackberry and follow the directions to download Google Sync to your Blackberry. Enter the required information, save your settings, and you are ready to go.

Chapter 4: Collaborating with Google Docs

In This Chapter

↗ Creating and altering documents in Google Docs

↗ Collaborating on Google Docs

↗ Organizing and finding documents in Google Docs

Modern business requires the use of basic office programs to create documents, track statistics on spreadsheets, or make presentations. These programs make it easy to do this work, but they also have their drawbacks. Microsoft Office, for example, comes with all the programs you need, but it's expensive to purchase and upgrade. Open Office is free, but it still requires installation on your computer, and the documents you create reside right there with the programs. To share these documents, you still have to e-mail or transfer the files to others if you want several people to see or work on them.

When this process of e-mailing or transferring documents begins, it gets hard to track all the changes and keep current copies of the documents. As a result, some copies of the documents may contain some but not all the changes, and you've got bad information going around. Even if you have a common server, it's not always possible to have multiple people work on the documents and see the changes in real time.

Google Docs presents an easy solution to these problems, and it does so in a way that allows you to control who has access to documents and how changes are made. This drastically changes the way your company does business by making your resources available wherever and whenever you need them to be.

Understanding the Power of Collaboration

Google Docs has a great amount of power, but that doesn't necessarily elevate it above computer-based office programs. In fact, programs like Microsoft Office or OpenOffice offer some things that Google Docs can't handle right now (like mail merge). What makes Google Docs so powerful, however, is that you don't have to centralize your activities around one computer or an unreliable chain of e-mail messages.

James and Jake of Jake's Landscaping may not have to work on many documents remotely, although the company could still benefit by having a central copy of any important document to which all contributors could make changes. Having only one copy available eliminates any confusion as to where the newest version of a document is located, and it prevents using outdated information to make business decisions.

Take a look at the advantages centralized collaboration offers Jake's Landscaping.

✦ **No central office:** Jake's Landscaping is run primarily from a home office and several remote locations, so having a centralized domain eliminates the need for employees to gather in one place to get work done (and James's wife is quite happy not to have a whole bunch of people running through the house at all hours). Documents can be sent and shared, employees can fill out their time sheets remotely, and customers can give their feedback without having to use mail.

✦ **Backup and security:** Because all the documents are saved online, they're safe from a hard drive crash, stolen computer, or other common disasters. James and Jake can get all the information they need, and they don't have to worry about keeping physical backups of their records (not that it's a bad idea to do so).

✦ **Cost effective:** James and Jake certainly like paying for their entire Web service rather than paying more money for Microsoft Office. All the functionality they need is ready to go without their shelling out more money.

✦ **Need some help?:** If James needs some spreadsheet help or wants his accountant to review a document, he can just send a link and get instant feedback. That kind of assistance can be invaluable.

Your small business may not need Google Docs for these reasons, or you may see additional advantages beyond those listed here. Whatever your reasons, Google Docs and the collaborative powers it offers can tremendously help your business survive and thrive.

Updating files instantly

The changes made to Google Documents are available instantly as well, meaning that you never have to wait before getting the most current information. After a document is saved, that version is immediately available to any other collaborator or viewer. This speeds up the process of creating a document because you don't have to wait for e-mail messages to be sent. Wherever you can log in, you can work.

Sharing of Google Docs also prevents having to e-mail a new copy of document each time a change is made. Each document has its own static Web location, so anybody can refer to that link at any time to see the most recent version. This can be helpful if you have documents that are referenced often but might frequently change.

Google Docs also eliminates the problems of incompatible programs. Especially with the introduction of Microsoft Office 2007 and its new default file format, people working in different versions of the available office programs often experienced problems when trading files and when opening or working on the files in different computers. With Google Docs, the files are all easily opened on any computer with a Web browser, and there's no need to buy or install software to avoid problems with compatibility.

Google Docs also allows you to upload documents to the service from office programs, so that even if you do have compatibility problems with an existing document, you don't need to recreate it in order to share. Just upload the document, and everybody can use it without issues. Google Docs is a great way to get around compatibility issues.

Sharing documents near and far

If you are working with others at a longer distance than from across town, Google Documents can be helpful in dealing with issues like different time zones or incompatible schedules. Leaving a central copy of the document in one location means that each person can work in his or her own time, whatever that may be, and you don't have to wait for inconvenient phone calls or erratic e-mails to complete the project.

Even though you don't have to be in direct contact with colleagues to work on Google Docs, direct contact with team members is easier as well. For example, an enterprising work team could use Google Talk to share voice chats while working on a Google Docs document in real time. This situation eliminates the need for transit time to meetings or gatherings, allowing you to fit more work into a smaller amount of time. It doesn't, however, take the place of a lunch meeting or getting together at the coffee shop — just make sure you plan accordingly so these meetings can fit into everybody's schedule effectively.

Understanding the different levels of sharing

Using Google Docs is easy and can lead to a huge increase in productivity, but you don't necessarily want everybody working on the same document at the same time. You may not want the information you put up to be available to everybody, or you may just want a large group of people to view the document but not make changes. That's why Google Docs has three different levels of interaction with a single document:

✦ **Owners:** The *owner*, or creator of the document, retains the highest level of permissions for the document from who gets to edit and view the document to how invitations can be dispersed and how members of your domain can interact with the document. The owner is the first person to send out invitations for the documents and can rescind permissions to edit or view whenever he or she sees fit. Finally, the owner of the document can never be booted from editing or viewing his or her own document.

✦ **Collaborators:** *Collaborators* are those invited in by the owner to edit and modify the document. They can also, depending on the permissions granted by the owners, invite others to view or modify the document. Collaborators can be blocked from the document by the owner.

✦ **Viewers:** *Viewers* are only able to look at the document — they don't have permission to make any changes to the document. They have to be invited to the document to begin with, and their rights can be revoked at any time by the owner.

Organizing and Searching for Documents

Placing documents online in Google Docs gives you the capability to search for these documents via words, document names, document type, and other attributes. If you have a huge number of documents, you have a great way to search through a lot of material quickly based on only a few key words. Imagine the amount of time you can save by searching for an important document based only on the vague recollection of the word *cucumber*, for example.

Uploading your old documents

When you're making the switch to Google Docs, a great first step is uploading all your old and essential documents to Google Docs. Not only does this provide a reliable backup for these documents on Google's servers, but it also puts your old documents into an instant search engine. Now you're able to search for not only the title of the document, but you can also search for words inside the document, specify what kinds of documents you're searching for, and more. You are also able to save types of searches to run later, in case you feel you might need this feature frequently.

To upload your files into Google Docs, follow these steps:

1. **Log into your domain and select the links for Google Docs.**

You can also access your domain's Google Docs site by entering `http://docs.google.com/a/`*yourdomainnamehere*`.com` (replacing *yourdomainnamehere*`.com` with your domain name, obviously). You see the screen shown in Figure 4-1.

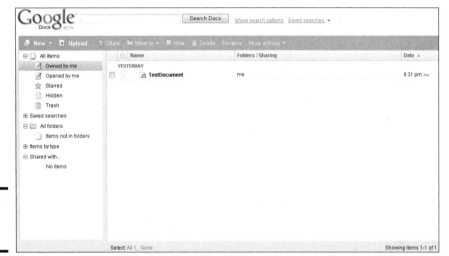

Figure 4-1:
Google
Docs.

2. **Click the Upload link in the top menu bar to view the uploading screen, shown in Figure 4-2.**

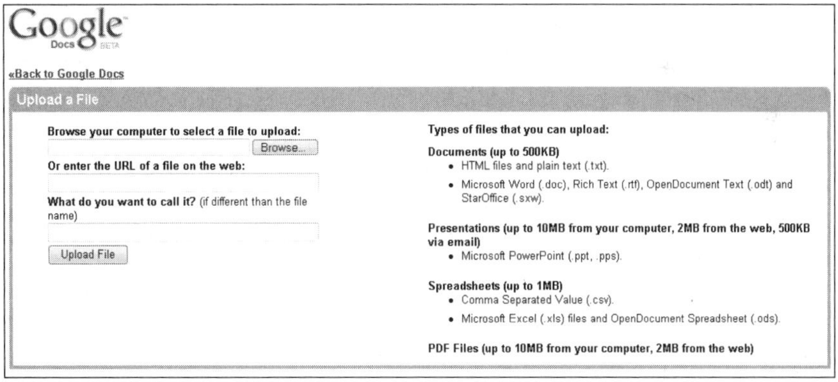

Figure 4-2:
Uploading
to Google
Docs.

Notice that you can upload files to Google Docs either from your computer (using the first text field and browsing your hard drive) or by entering the URL of an online document.

3. **Just find the file, type in any new name you want to give it, and click Upload. It's that simple.**

All right, it's not entirely that simple, as the laundry list of rules on the right-hand side of Figure 4-2 may attest. However, it does show the wide variety of file formats that can be uploaded to Google Docs, and the file size limits shouldn't be that prohibitive for most of your documents.

If you have a monster file that won't upload to Google Docs because of size requirements, consider splitting the document into two or more separate files. Simply cut and paste the material into different files, save, and upload. You can find them later, thanks to Google Docs searching capabilities.

When the document has been uploaded, you see it listed in the Google Docs window. You can log in and open that document at any time. That document opens in a separate browser window, and all the controls you'd expect from an office program are there. You're ready to go.

Google Docs translates your old documents as best it can, but there might still be differences in formatting and style after you've uploaded. Translation isn't always 100% effective, unfortunately. Be sure to check your documents after you've uploaded them and make sure that everything is still the way you want it.

Organizing your documents with folders

Google Doc's large amount of storage space and easy search functions can promote a "dump it all in" philosophy, meaning that you put all your information in one place to be searched through whenever necessary. This is acceptable, but it may not be the most efficient approach. If you want to introduce a little more organization into your files, you can add folders to your Google Docs.

For example, suppose James wants to create a folder for invoices, another for correspondence, and one for sales presentations. Here's what he needs to do:

1. **Log into Google Docs and look for the New button on the top toolbar, as shown in Figure 4-1. Click it and select Folder.**

   You see the screen shown in Figure 4-3.

   Ah, the old, reliable New Folder folder. It's descriptive, but you're going to want to do something more with the name.

2. **Click the name to add a better label and a description of the folder, as shown in Figure 4-4.**

   You can even choose a color for the folder, if you so desire.

3. **When you've entered the name and the description, click Save to finalize the folder naming.**

   Your folder appears on the left sidebar, as shown in Figure 4-5.

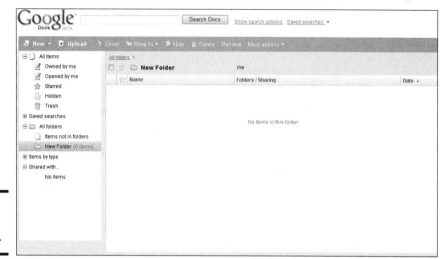

Figure 4-3:
Creating a
new folder.

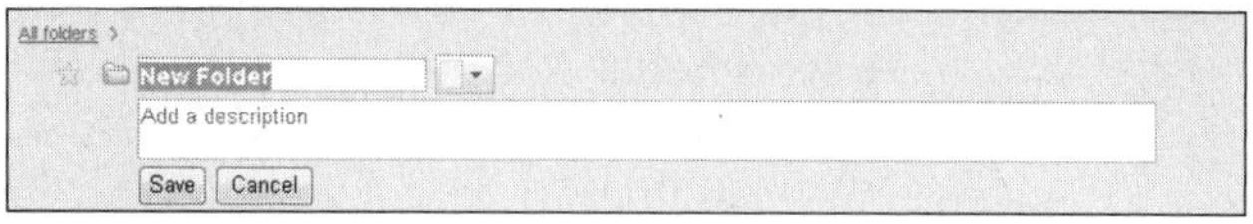

Figure 4-4:
Naming
your new
folder.

Figure 4-5:
Your list of
folders.

Note that you can create folders inside of folders, so that you can organize
the invoices by year, for instance. You can also drag and drop folders in
or out of other folders, just as you do with any other computer operating
system. With all this power, you should be able to get all your documents in
place with a minimum of effort.

Using the Search function

If you're going to stick with the "one pile fits all" philosophy in Google Docs,
you're going to get very well acquainted with the Search function. Luckily,
there's not that much work involved in using it (sort of like Google in general). The easiest way is to just type the word or words you're looking for
into the Search field shown in Figure 4-6. Click the Search Docs button, and
what you're looking for should pop up instantly.

Figure 4-6:
Basic
Google
Docs
searching.

If you want to get more technical, Google Docs allows you to specify more search terms. Click the Show Search Options link next to the search text field to display the screen shown in Figure 4-7.

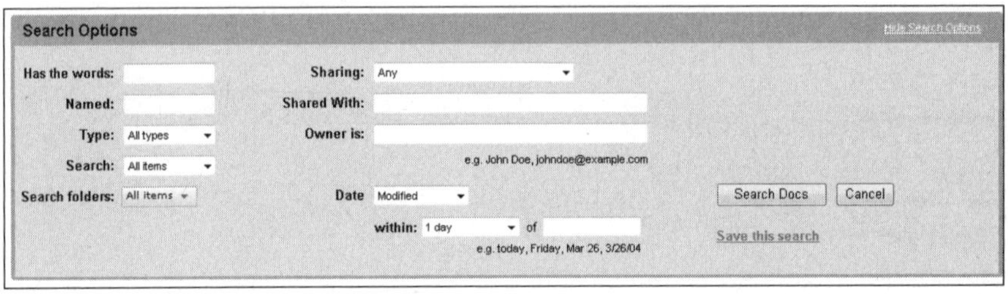

Figure 4-7:
Advanced
searching.

These options are quite helpful if you're looking for a single document in one folder or if you're looking for documents created by a specific person. Get as specific as you wish with these options — the more details you can remember, the less time you spend looking for your document.

If you're going to perform a specific search multiple times, click the Save This Search option at the bottom-right of Figure 4-7. You are able to access your saved searches from the Saved Searches link shown in Figure 4-6. Simply choose the search and execute it. Any documents that match the requirements show up, even if they were created after you saved the search.

For example, if James wants to search for any invoices he created for a specific client modified within the last six months, he just enters the client's name in the Has the Words text field, specifies spreadsheets in the Type drop-down menu, and sets the Modified information for within six months of today's date. Clicking the Search Docs button gives him the information that matches his criteria.

If you're not finding what you're looking for, try eliminating term criteria one at a time. You increase the number of documents that come up in your search, and you might have better luck paring them down from there.

Tracking changes

When you're collaborating with others, it's important to track the changes made per save. You might want to go back and review the information added by somebody else (if it's a large document, you might have some trouble finding every change). You might also want to roll back some of the changes if they were saved in error or if that person simply made a mistake with his or her edits. Google Docs retains every set of changes made between document saves so you can go back and find out what happened.

With the document in question open, click File and choose the Revision History command shown in Figure 4-8:

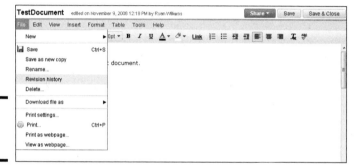

Figure 4-8:
Revision
History.

Google Docs shows you each version of the document between saves, as shown in Figure 4-9.

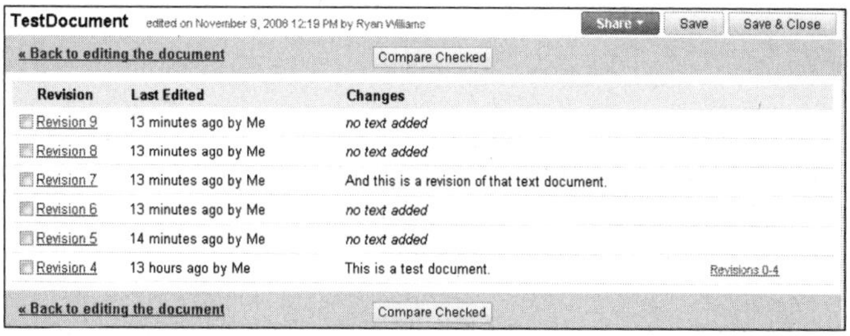

Figure 4-9:
Document
revisions.

From here, you can click each link to see the revision by itself, or you can check two revisions and compare them to each other to see which version you prefer. After you've decided which version you prefer (if it's not the most current one), click that version and click the Revert to This One button (and confirm your decision), as shown in Figure 4-10.

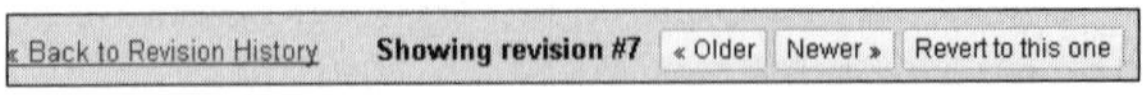

Figure 4-10:
Reverting
to an older
version.

« Back to Revision History   **Showing revision #7**   « Older   Newer »   Revert to this one

You can also make comments on changes or new additions from within the document by clicking Insert on the document's menu bar and selecting Comment, as shown in Figure 4-11.

Figure 4-11:
Adding a
comment.

This action places a comment wherever you have the cursor at the time. You can insert any text you want at that point, and it can be deleted later when the comment has been addressed. Use comments to tag your changes or address the changes of others. These stand out easily from the text, and they can be deleted or modified later.

Creating Documents Effectively

So now you know all the advantages of using Google Docs, such as

✦ It's available anywhere with a Web browser and an Internet connection.

✦ It's usable across platforms and several devices.

✦ It includes fantastic collaboration and revision tools.

✦ Its online storage and saving capabilities help you avoid disaster.

Why not jump in and start using Google Docs? This section gets you up to speed on the different types of documents available and what you can do with them.

Document

To create a new Document document, follow these steps:

1. **Log into Google Docs and click New⇨Document.**

You get a new browser window, just like the one shown in Figure 4-12.

Figure 4-12:
Your new,
untitled
Google
Document
document.

2. **Next, you should click Untitled in the top-left corner of Figure 4-12 and give your document a new name. Type in the new name and click OK.**

You might have to change your browser's pop-up window's settings to allow the window to come up.

3. **Click the Share button and determine who has access to the document.**

The Share This Document screen is displayed in Figure 4-13.

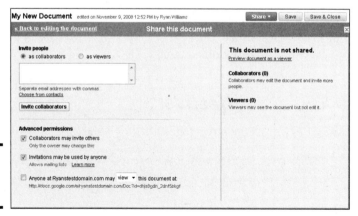

Figure 4-13:
Sharing
options.

4. **Set the permissions you want to enable and type the e-mail addresses you want to invite in the text field.**

Be sure that you make two separate lists for collaborators and viewers.

5. **Click the Invite button to send the invitations and click Save in the upper-right corner. When you've finished here, click the Back to Editing the Document link in the upper-left corner to return to your document.**

Document is a full-featured word processor, so you should be familiar with the commands shown on the top menu bar. The menu bar in Figure 4-12 displays basic actions and formatting commands, including those to save and print, determine font type and size, and set text alignment. You can use this browser as you would any other word processor program, so type away and create your document.

Save early; save often. Just because you're working on a server doesn't mean this common rule doesn't apply. The more you save, the more your revisions stay safe, and you have plenty of fall-back options in case something goes wrong.

Otherwise, the preceding commands are the same as any other word processor, including those to spell check, insert tables and special formatting, and add pictures, hyperlinks, and the like. Simply put, if you can use a word processor, you can use Google Docs without issues.

Setting default document styles

If you have a specific type of font or spacing issue that you're going to be using over and over again, click Edit⇨Document Styles to bring up the Figure 4-14.

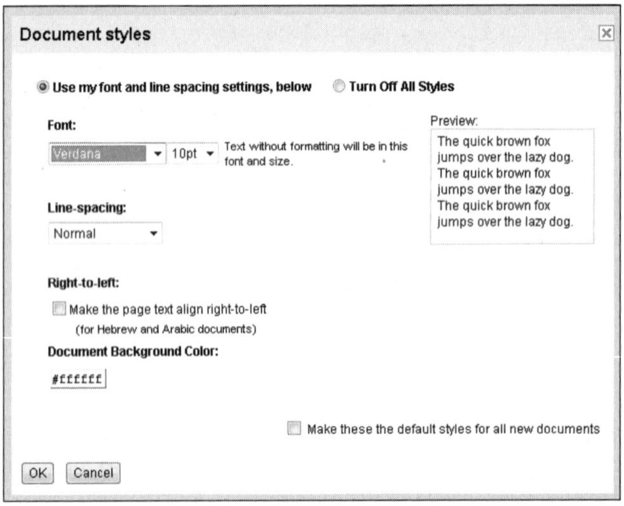

Figure 4-14:
Default
styles.

Document styles   ⊠

○ Use my font and line spacing settings, below   ○ Turn Off All Styles

Font: Preview:
[Verdana ▼] [10pt ▼] Text without formatting will be in this   The quick brown fox
                       font and size.   jumps over the lazy dog.
                                                                 The quick brown fox
                                                                 jumps over the lazy dog.
Line-spacing: The quick brown fox
[Normal   ▼]   jumps over the lazy dog.

Right-to-left:
☐ Make the page text align right-to-left
   (for Hebrew and Arabic documents)

Document Background Color:
#ffffff

                                      ☐ Make these the default styles for all new documents

[OK] [Cancel]

Set the font, spacing, and background color you want to use, and click the check box in the bottom-right corner if you want all these articles to start out this way. Click Save, and your default style is saved.

Downloading your documents

If you do have to download your document for some reason (remember, you can print and save your document from the browser), click File⇨Download File As and select the format you want the document to take. You can choose from

- ✦ HTML
- ✦ Open Office
- ✦ PDF
- ✦ RTF (real text format)
- ✦ Text
- ✦ Word

Just choose your option and click Save to bring the document onto your computer. This option is best if you're sending a final document to somebody outside of your normal circle of collaborators and viewers, such as a final bill or a final draft of a letter. The variety of formats makes sure you get the best format for your needs.

Presentation

If you're familiar with Microsoft PowerPoint or Apple's Keynote, you already know what Google Docs's presentations can do. With this program, you can crate series of slides with text and images designed to communicate your point. This program can be presented either online or in person, using a laptop with an LCD project. Log into Google Docs and choose New⇨Presentation to get started, as shown in Figure 4-15.

First, click the Untitled filename in the top-left corner and select your presentation's new name. Now set your sharing options (as we did in the Document section) and click Save to finalize your document. You're ready to start creating slides.

Adding new slides

New slides come up with two text boxes for a title and a subtitle. Click those boxes to add any text you want, or ignore them to leave them blank. You also get a plain white background to start, but you can click Edit⇨Change Theme to choose from a list of preset themes, as shown in Figure 4-16.

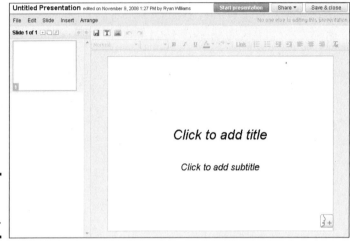

Figure 4-15:
Your new
presentation.

Figure 4-16:
Preset
presentation
themes.

Choose one of these or click the X in the top-right corner to leave it blank. You can also choose Edit➪Change Background to just change the color of your slide's background.

When you're ready for the next slide, click the plus sign at the top of the left sidebar to put a new slide after your first one. You get a list of options, as shown in Figure 4-17.

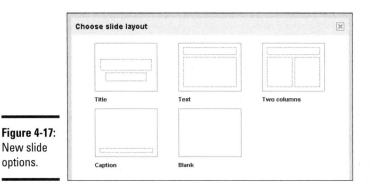

Figure 4-17:
New slide
options.

Click Insert in the top menu bar to insert elements for new slides. You can choose from

+ Text

+ Images

+ Videos

+ Shapes

If you choose text, the menu bar at the top of the screen responds the same way as the menu bar for documents. If you want to insert an image, you can choose from a picture stored on your computer or at a publically available URL. To insert a video, you must first upload it to YouTube (available at `http://youtube.com`), or you must use a video that's already been uploaded to that service. Use the search box to find your video, as shown in Figure 4-18, and click Insert Video to make it happen.

You have several choices when inserting a shape — pick one and click it to insert it into your slide. You can resize it and place it where you want after it's inserted.

Arranging your presentation

After you've created all your slides, you can re-order them in any way you wish by clicking and dragging them around into the order you want. When you're finished and clicked your final Save, click Start Presentation to see how it looks in a separate browser window. Use your keyboard to cycle through slides; you can send out the URL at the bottom of the screen via e-mail or Google Talk to invite others to view the presentation.

You must share the presentation to have remote viewers or collaborators.

Figure 4-18:
Inserting
a video
into your
presentation.

For more directions on how to create more intricate presentations (and more information on all aspects of Google Docs), check out *Google Apps For Dummies*, by Ryan Teeter and Karl Barksdale, published by Wiley.

You can save your presentation just as you do documents, although you have only the options of PDF, TXT, or PPT formats. Use PDF if you're going to hand out paper copies (who uses paper anymore?), and use PPT if you're going to download this file to use elsewhere, especially if the recipients don't have a network connection.

Live presentation tips

If you're going to present this presentation in a live environment, as opposed to over the Web or via e-mail, take these tips into account when you create your file:

✔ Use only as many slides as you need — don't weigh your presentation down with extraneous facts and figures.

✔ Don't read from your slides — hit the high-lights and let your speech take care of the rest.

✔ Don't overuse special effects — trying to be too cute obscures your message.

✔ Test your presentation — make sure you don't get any surprises the day of the pre-sentation.

✔ Multiple copies — you can avoid disaster if you keep your presentation online and on your laptop (and maybe even a flash drive).

Follow these steps, and you'll use presenta-tions to their fullest capabilities.

Spreadsheet

Users of Microsoft Excel will recognize the spreadsheet and most of the functions immediately. Spreadsheets allow users to put together documents that track numbers and perform complicated mathematical computations. All you have to do is plug in the numbers, and the spreadsheet takes care of the number-crunching. For example, James may want to use spreadsheets to track budgets and expenses for Jake's Landscaping, and any temporary employees can use a spreadsheet to track their working hours.

Staring your spreadsheet

Log into Google Docs and select New⇨Spreadsheet to start the new document, as shown in Figure 4-19.

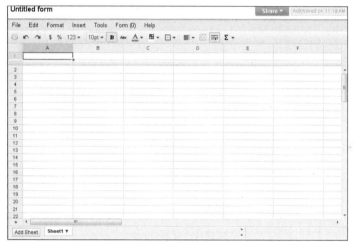

Figure 4-19:
Your new
spreadsheet.

Be sure to change the title, change your share settings, and save your document as explained in the section entitled "Documents" earlier in this chapter. Now, you're ready to start filling in your cells.

The top level of cells shown in Figure 4-19 are labels for each column. For example, a time sheet might contain the following columns:

✦ Date

✦ Time Started

✦ Time Stopped

✦ Total Hours

For each cell in the Date column, type in the date the employee worked. In the Time Started and Time Stopped column, enter the appropriate start and stop times. Put the total number of hours worked per day in the final column.

So far, the spreadsheet is doing a good job of organizing information in cells, but that's all it's doing. The next step is adding formulas to the cells to get automatic computations of your information.

Using formulas

Instead of placing actual data into a cell, formulas take other cells and produce results based on the action you specify for that cell. Let's take a look at an easy example (although it should be noted the Google Doc spreadsheets are capable of some extremely complicated processing functions).

Take a look at Figure 4-20, which shows a formula in the cells below the total daily hours column.

Figure 4-20:
A basic
formula.

Total Hours
5
6
5
=SUM(D2, D3, D4)

The SUM command tells the spreadsheet to add together the values of the cells specified in the following parentheses. You can either type in the cell names (letters specify the column, numbers specify the exact cell) or click the cells you want to add, and follow each with a comma. When you're done, type the closed parenthesis and press Return. The cell now shows the sum of the three above it, saving you from doing the (admittedly easy) math. (See Figure 4-21.)

Figure 4-21:
The results
of the basic
formula.

Total Hours
5
6
5
16

The full list of formulas available for your spreadsheet is available by clicking the Sigma icon (the last icon on the right in the top menu bar). You get a list of five common formulas, or you can click More Formulas to see the complete list shown in Figure 4-22.

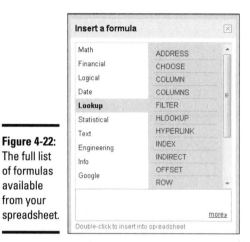

Figure 4-22:
The full list
of formulas
available
from your
spreadsheet.

Chances are you won't use a large percentage of these formulas — you
may only end up using three or four the entire time you use Google Docs.
However, this shows you the wide variety of uses for this spreadsheet, and
how you can get the same functionality from Google Docs as you would from
Microsoft Office or Open Office.

Viewing your data

Spreadsheets also gives you a chance to view your data in several types
of charts by clicking Insert⇨Chart. This displays the Create Chart page, as
shown in Figure 4-23.

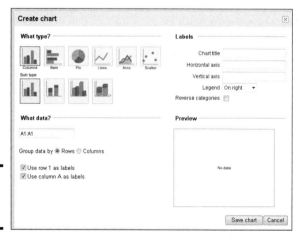

Figure 4-23:
Setting up
your chart.

To create a chart, fill in the information in the Create Chart page as follows:

1. **Place the cells you want to use to create the chart in the What Data? field (for example, D2:D4 specifies cells D2, D3, and D4).**

2. **Click the type of chart you want to use.**

3. **Type the chart labels you want to use and determine where you want the information to appear.**

4. **Examine the preview and make sure it looks like what you want to present.**

5. **Click Save Chart to place the chart on your spreadsheet.**

Not only do spreadsheets help you organize and process your information, but they can give you tools to understand and present the data to yourself and others. Spreadsheets are a powerful business tool, and it's a good idea to become familiar with their functions.

Google Apps For Dummies by Ryan Teeter and Karl Barksdale (Wiley) takes you further into spreadsheets than this book is able to — consider consulting it in case you want to make further use of spreadsheets.

Forms

Google Docs includes the capability to produce *forms* (actually, a specialized form of spreadsheet) and place them in several different locations, including online. Log into Google Docs and select New⇨Forms to view the example shown in Figure 4-24.

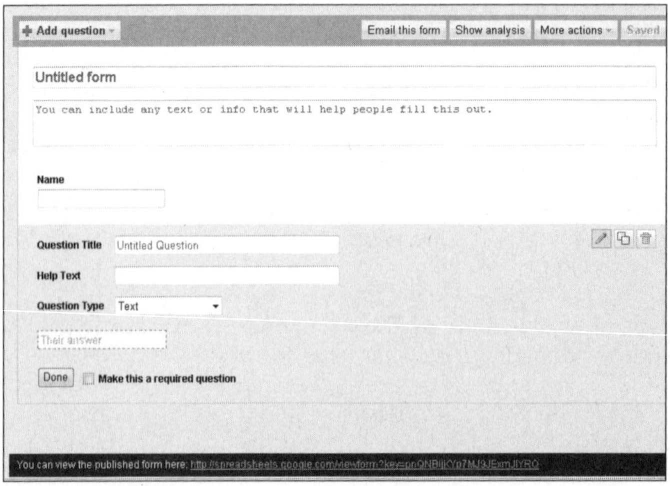

Figure 4-24:
A basic
form.

Next, follow these steps to create a form:

1. **Title and save the document as you did earlier with documents, presentations, and spreadsheets.**

2. **Next, enter a title and description for your form in the appropriate fields.**

   The rest of the fields are entered by those responding to your form.

3. **Each question has a field for a name and any help text. Choose what kind of question you want to present to your users, such as**

   - Text

   - Paragraph text for longer answers

   - Multiple choice

   - Check boxes

   - Choices in a list

   - Range, from one to your chose number

4. **For multiple choice, check boxes, or a list, you are asked to make separate entries. Enter those, decide if you want to make the question mandatory (any users must answer before they submit the form), and click Done.**

5. **Click Add Question from the top menu bar to add as many questions as you want; then click Save one final time to save the final version of your form.**

6. **Click the link at the bottom of the form to see the finished version in your Web browser, as shown in Figure 4-25.**

If you're satisfied with the form as it appears, you can place the link to this form on your Web site or e-mail the link to your intended recipients. Those recipients can enter the information you asked for and click the Submit button at the bottom of the form to send the information back to you.

To see the results, log into your form and click the Show Analysis button at the top of your form's menu bar. You see a response breakdown like the one shown in Figure 4-26.

This view breaks down all the data you've received and presents the responses depending on what question you asked. For example, you see the multiple choice questions are shown in percentages and pie charts, whereas text data is displayed sequentially. As you get more responses, you can see the changes to the data as it goes. Forms can be an invaluable tool to gather, evaluate, and act on data you receive from others.

Customer Service

Please let us know how we're doing!

Name

Were we courteous?
○ Yes
○ No

Were we on time?
○ Yes
○ No

Is there anything else we can do?

Figure 4-25:
Your final
form.

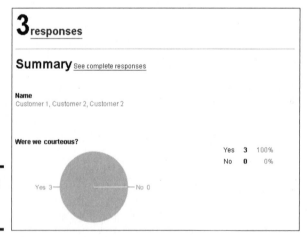

3 responses

Summary See complete responses

Name
Customer 1, Customer 2, Customer 2

Were we courteous?

	Yes	3	100%
	No	0	0%

Yes 3 —   — No 0

Figure 4-26:
Form
responses.

You can also get code to embed the form into your main Web page, just in case you want to integrate it with your current site instead of setting it up on a separate page. When you're logged into the form, click More Actions⇨Embed to get a pop-up window with the code you need. Copy and paste that code into your site to make the form appear in one of your pages instead of in a separate browser tab or window.

Chapter 5: Sharing Information with Google Sites

In This Chapter

✔ Making the Web pages you need

✔ Collaborating on your projects using Google Sites

✔ Publishing company information for yourself and the public

✔ Setting up a new site from scratch

*T*he chapter on Google Docs showed how powerful online collaboration can be. Collaboration allows you to work with others on a centralized depot of information and have the most up-to-date data at all times. You can also set up levels of permission, so you can control who has access to view or change your information. Now, apply those capabilities to Web sites, and you can track more than just a few documents — you can track entire projects. Google Sites gives you the power to create an entire information infrastructure for your small business with a little effort and time.

Google Sites is an easy tool that allows you to create collaborative Web sites for use either within your company or outside it, with the public. You can choose from several different templates, customize the color options to match corporate branding, and use several tools that allow you to maximize your collaboration options. You don't need a professional Web designer to make this happen — Google provides the tools necessary to build the sites, manage the operation of the sites, and interpret the data you receive.

What You Can Create with Google Sites

Even if you don't have the corporate needs and resources of a huge company like IBM or Apple, you can still benefit from using Google Sites to handle a great deal of your company information. This information can be made available for management only, the entire company, or the public at large, depending on your needs. Take a look at what kind of pages can be of service to you.

Company Web pages and intranets

If you don't have a central office, there's no common area for you to post information that's necessary for all employees. Even if you do, it's helpful to have all your forms, policies, and other information in one place for quick access. A great way to solve this problem is by creating a company intranet.

An *intranet* is made up of Web pages that contain information intended only for the use of those inside your company. For example, your public Web page might list basic information about your company, along with contact information, office locations, and services you provide. You'd use the company's intranet to host information like time sheets, company policies, and more.

Additionally, if you want to provide any announcements or general information about the state of your company (James loves telling the employees when Jake's Landscaping has another record quarter), a private Web page would be an excellent way to do it. This page can be used to keep people up to date on the activities of the company.

With Google Sites, you can create a company intranet that performs those functions. Not only does it store your information in one place, but each document or policy is always the latest version, so nobody is operating on outdated or wrong information.

Human resources information is exactly the kind of data you might want to have available for your employees, but you certainly don't want to make it available to the public. You can create records for each of your employees with personal information, salary history, personnel records, and more. You can gain access to this data from anywhere you need to, but the data resides on secure servers and isn't accessible to the general public.

You should access this kind of information only from computers or devices you entirely trust. Even with the information residing on a safe server, you need to make sure the computer is free of viruses, spyware, and other malware that could compromise the security of your data. Your business computer is fine, but that hotel business computer with out-of-date security programs and a thousand pop-up ads on the browser isn't a good choice.

Individual Web pages and employee profiles

Depending on your business, you may want to have your employees make a more personal connection with the public by building a site devoted to employee profiles. Jake's Landscaping may not need pages for each individual temporary lawnmower, but a business that thrives on personal connections (like a real estate agency or a salon) benefits from making better connections with the public.

Take the example of a real estate company. Having an individual page for each agent gives the company a chance to showcase the different houses it is trying to sell, letting the public know what's available, and which person to talk to in order to get more information. It's certainly more inviting than a generic e-mail address to an anonymous account. An advertising or design firm may want to highlight the individual work of its employees, giving them a place to post and display work they're proud of. Any time you want to make a personal connection, an individual Webpage is a good way to make it.

Blogs are another way to connect your company with the public. Your employees' online blogs give your customers an insight into the daily happenings at your business and gives the employees a forum to discuss matters related to their business and possibly make that information relevant and compelling to your customers. The goal for each blog should be to provide valuable information to the customers, not only about your business but about larger trends relating to your field. When updated regularly with great content, these blogs can bring a lot of interest to your business.

More than anything else, personal employee pages make your business more than a service. It allows the public to see the people behind that service and make their connection to it more than just an invoice. With these pages, you're hoping to let your customers inside the business, make them understand why you're doing what you're doing, and ultimately make them believers in your business.

Project homepages

Google Sites gives you a great resource for project management when you have to deal with multiple projects at the same time (and these days, who doesn't?). You can give each project its own site and track the progress from start to finish at one central location. Even if all your team members aren't in one location, you can centralize the project's resources and keep pushing for progress, even from multiple locations.

This central location gives you a place to list exactly what the project needs to get started, what you hope the project will achieve, the timeline the project will follow, and what actions you have to perform to get there. With these goals clearly outlined in a single location, you can keep everybody on the same page, which can be quite difficult if you're working with remote collaborators in far-flung locations.

As the work on your project progresses, you need one place to store all your work and findings. The site shows what's been done up to this point and what needs to be addressed at any given point in time. If an unexpected change occurs, you have a place to decide how you want to deal with it and where you're going to go from there. Think of this place as the newspaper for your project — all the headlines appear here, and you can react when you need to. Of course, here's hoping that all your news is good.

Above all, your project site gives you a place to store and concentrate on all your project information. There's no chance of losing documents or using outdated information when you post everything online and make all your changes on the site. Team members can always be kept in the loop regarding any progress or changes, and anybody can get a feel for the entire project just by logging into the site and reading the entire history of your efforts.

Collaborating Effectively Using Google Sites

As with many aspects of Google Apps, the real power of Google Sites lies with collaboration. The Internet is available worldwide, meaning that as long as you're connected to the Internet, you potentially have every resource available to work on your site. If you have an expert in biology willing to work on your project, for instance, and the only roadblock is that said expert resides in Turkey, it can be overcome handily using Google Sites. Just grant the expert access to the site, and you're ready to go. Anyone with access can effectively work with all the data you have online, just as easily as if they were in the office next to you.

You might also want to let the public look in on your progress, especially if that progress is something that could earn you new acclaim or business. You may just want to install a window, though, and not a door. Any public site that outsiders can view but cannot modify grants them access — maybe enough access to feel like a part of the effort, but not enough to actually affect the progress directly. You can always ask the public to submit comments or requests via e-mail or forms (that can be seen publicly or privately).

Inviting users to collaborate

The first step in the progress of your project is to ascertain whom you want to work on your project. These can be collaborators within your company, those in a similar field as yours in remote locations, or random members of the public from whom you want to solicit opinions. Divide these members into two general groups:

+ **Collaborators:** These people have permissions to change and modify any information that's present on your site.

+ **Spectators:** These people can see the site and the project's progress, but they won't be able to contribute directly to the project itself.

After the site is up, send all those interested parties an e-mail with information about the project. You want to include the following information in the e-mail:

+ The name of the project, if you have one.

+ What you hope to accomplish with the project.

+ The location of the Web site.

✦ The names of those collaborating on the project, if necessary.

✦ A quick list of the resources you're posting on the site.

✦ The next action the invitee should take.

When you know all the participants involved in the project, you can start deciding who can see and do what, especially which people should get only limited access to the material.

Defining different levels of permission

When you first set up a site, you have three choices when you set the permissions for access. You want to evaluate your needs and make your decisions based on what you're hoping to accomplish. The three levels of permissions involve the following:

✦ People inside your domain

✦ Invited participants

✦ The public at large

If everybody in your domain is going to be a part of this project, you want to enable that collaboration option. Otherwise, you have the choice to invite individual participants. Remember, you can always invite people both inside and outside your domain, if you wish.

These people are able to interact with the site and make changes to your information. Before you begin, make sure that they are able to contribute to the project in a positive way and that they can be trusted with your information. Half of the success of a project depends on the team you assemble to work on it. You can make all the resources available, but you still need to get good work from the people involved to make a project successful.

Limiting access

Just as you choose the people you want to work on the project, you may want to let them work only on specific areas of the project. For example, you may have a team working on the marketing materials for your new project, but you might not want them to have access to the technical data you're putting together with another team. You can accomplish this in a few ways:

✦ Set up pages within your project site and make sure that only certain team members have access to certain pages.

✦ Use the settings in Google Docs to grant permissions to certain team members.

✦ Be sure to tag your information appropriately so that people know what materials belong to certain team members and who should be working on that material.

It may help you to draw up a map of the site and write the names of the team members who should have access next to it. This enables you to plan permissions after the site is constructed.

It's always a good idea, even if you're not going to worry about setting permissions for pages on your site, to draw a map of the pages you're going to put up. This gives you a great visual representation of your site and gives you an idea of how you want to put up pages and how the information should be linked.

Now that you've plotted out everything, you're ready to start putting your pages together. Remember that you can always alter permissions later, but it's easier to grant additional permissions than it is to ask somebody to forget everything they've seen up to this point.

Editing pages

When you're using Google Sites, you don't have to rely on tools like Dreamweaver to alter sites, and you don't have to have an in-depth knowledge of Web design to make the pages useful for people inside and outside the country. You may not be able to make the latest and greatest cutting-edge Web pages, but Google Sites is designed to create effectively simple pages. You are able to do exactly what you need to do to create, collaborate, and further your business with a minimum of Web knowledge.

Google Sites relies on a WYSIWYG, or what-you-see-is-what-you-get Web editor. That means you get a series of controls that look like what you might see in Google Docs for a word processor or spreadsheet. You see the changes in the pages as you move along, and you are able to roll back these changes easily if you don't like them. You can also set the site to auto-save, so that you don't miss any changes if you somehow experience a disaster.

Finally, anybody to whom you give collaborative permissions is able to work and edit on this page, meaning that you don't have to have a group of Web experts to get your page up and running. Google Sites levels the playing field for everybody involved and gives them the ability to edit pages collectively.

Subscribing to page changes

Google Sites also provides notifications when changes are made to each page, so that project collaborators can keep track of what's happening at each change, including

✦ Page updates

✦ Comments

✦ Any attached files

These notifications keep the entire project team in the loop and help it track the progress of the site and the project at large.

All these features help make sure that all team members are able to participate fully in all aspects of the project. Google Sites allows you to fully control who has access to the project and how they can participate, and it also facilitates making and tracking changes in real time.

Creating a New Site from Scratch

You know the basics of what Google Sites can do now, so it's time to start actually building pages. Remember, Google Sites makes creating and uploading pages as simple as possible, so don't be afraid to leap in and make some pages. You can learn by doing here, and it's not going to cost you anything extra to learn on the job.

To create your site, follow these steps:

1. **Log into your Google Apps dashboard and select the Google Sites link.**

You can also access Google Sites at `http://sites.google.com/a/` `yourdomainnamehere.com`, again replacing `yourdomainnamehere.` `com` with your domain name. You know you're in the right place when you see the page in Figure 5-1.

Figure 5-1:
Getting
started with
Google
Sites.

2. **Click the Create Site button to start creating your first page.**

This isn't going to be the only time you see this page. This is the place you come back to whenever you need to start another page within Google Sites. Get comfortable with the big button — you may be using it a lot.

When you click the button, you see the screen in Figure 5-2. This is where you actually set the basic design for your new page.

Site name	
	Your site will be located at this URL:
	http://sites.google.com/a/ryanstestdomain.com/
	Site URLs can only use the following characters: - ,A-Z,a-z,0-9
Site categories	**(optional)** enter one or more categories separated by commas, e.g. "marketing, finance"
Site description	**(optional)** enter a short description of this site
Collaborate with	● **Everybody** at ryanstestdomain.com
	○ Only **people I specify** can view this site
	☐ Also let **anyone in the world view** this site (make it public)
Site theme	More themes...
	● Default ○ Charcoal ○ Garden

Figure 5-2:
Basic
Google Site
settings.

3. Enter the name of your site in the Site Name text box.

Give the page a basic title, preferably something to do with the subject matter of the site. For instance, if James is seeking to put together Web page to centralize Jake's Landscaping marketing project, he might want to call the project "Jake's Landscaping Marketing Efforts." Put that in the first text box and you're ready to go.

4. Create the URL for this page by entering the last part of the address.

For example, the marketing page could have the URL of `http://sites.google.com/a/jakeslandscapingservices.com/marketing effort`. Please note that you can't use any special characters in the Web address — only letters and numbers.

Web addresses can honor capital and lowercase letters, so make sure that you use capital letters only when you absolutely need to. Otherwise, stick to lowercase letters for the sake of convenience.

5. (Optional) In the Site Categories text field, enter tags that describe the page.

Be as descriptive with your tags as possible, because this helps your pages to be found more easily after they've been created and published. The more tags you have, the better the chances of locating your page.

6. (Optional) In the Site Description text field, write a short description of the work that will be done on that page.

This description helps keep collaborators on target by defining the mission of the page, and it lets others who access this page know what the page is about. Like the Site Categories field, this information is optional, but you are better able to find and categorize these pages if the information is present.

7. **Set the initial access permissions for your Google Sites page, as outlined in the "Defining Different Levels of Permission" section earlier in this chapter.**

   Remember that you can always expand permissions later, but it's more difficult to explain why you rescind permissions later on. If you've planned your project correctly, you already know exactly how you want to set permissions. Make your settings accordingly, and move on to the next step.

   Unless you want everybody in your company to be able to see the page, choose the "Only People I Specify" option at this point. You can always change it later, if necessary.

8. **Give your site a theme.**

   A *theme* is the basic look of your site, although you can tweak settings later to your satisfaction. When you first create your site, your theme is set to default, along with a couple of other popular choices. Click the More Themes link if you want to explore other options. When you've chosen a theme, click the radio button under your choice.

9. **Finish by clicking the Create Site button.**

Changing the appearance of your site

After you've created the initial site, you get a page that looks something like the one shown in Figure 5-3. The theme may change, but the initial elements look the same.

You have control over how the site looks. Click the Site Settings button and select Change Appearances to see the screen shown in Figure 5-4.

On this page are three tabs that allow you to fine-tune your site's appearance:

✦ Site Elements

✦ Colors and Fonts

✦ Themes

The next few subsections discuss these tabs in greater detail.

Site Elements

The Site Elements tab allows you to customize the basic layout of the page. Click the Change Site Layout button to see the screen in Figure 5-5.

The Change Site Layout dialog box allows you to change the width of the page itself, the header, and the sidebar. Make any changes you want and click OK. The layout of your page is changed accordingly.

Figure 5-3:
Your basic
Google Site
page.

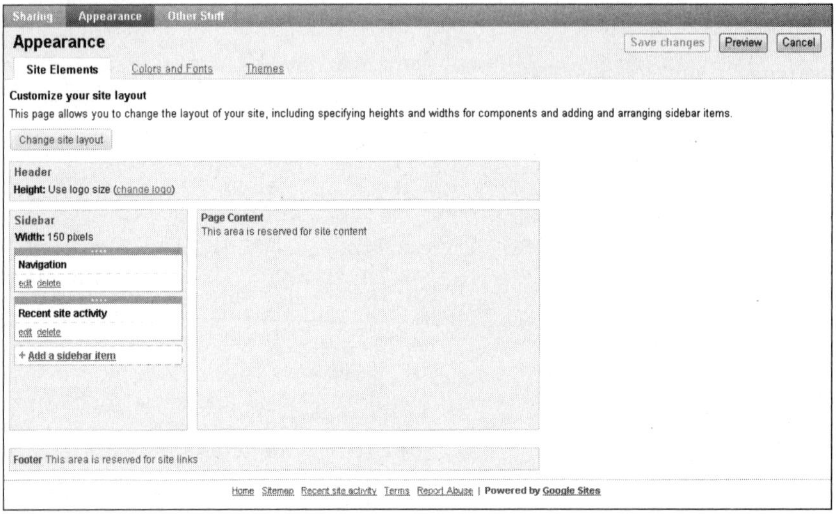

Figure 5-4:
Changing
your site's
appearance.

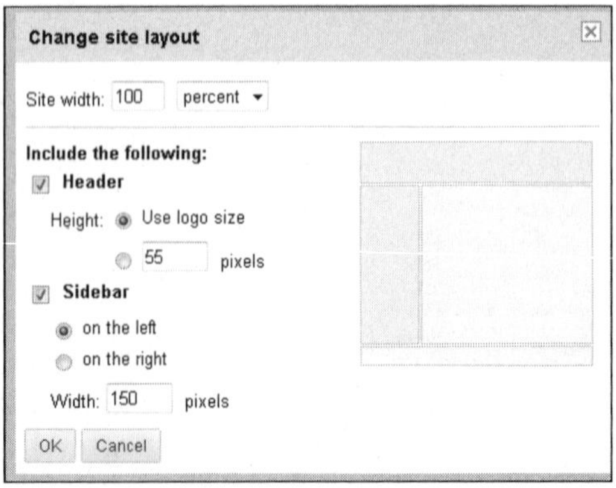

Figure 5-5:
Changing
your site's
basic layout.

Next, you can click the Change Logo link to bring up the Configure Site Logo dialog box. This box allows you to change the header or upload a custom logo to the header. Just click Browse to locate the logo on your computer that you want to upload or make another choice and click OK. (See Figure 5-6.)

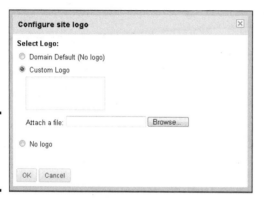

Figure 5-6:
Uploading a
logo to your
header.

Next, move on to the sidebar. On the Site Elements tab, the Navigation sidebar enables you to add links to the different pages in your site, but there's not much to do there right now. The Recent Site Activity sidebar item can be customized to show the last few actions on the site, and you can click Edit to expand the number of activities shown in the sidebar. You can also click Delete on either item to remove it from the sidebar. You can always put it back later if you want.

Finally, you can click the Add Sidebar Item to open the Choose a New Page Element dialog box. This dialog box allows you to put extra items on your page, as shown in Figure 5-7.

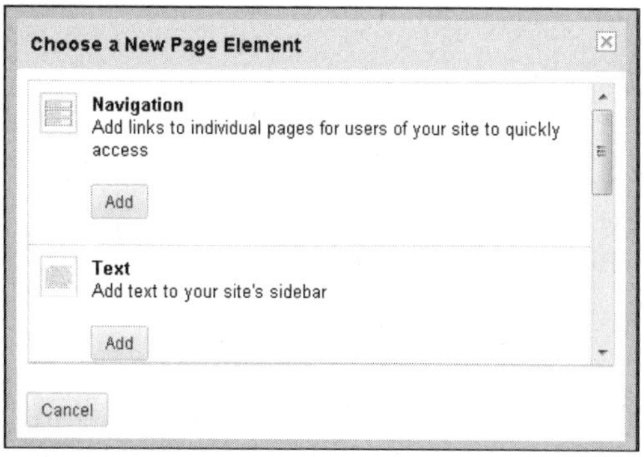

Choose a New Page Element

Navigation
Add links to individual pages for users of your site to quickly access

Add

Text
Add text to your site's sidebar

Add

Cancel

Figure 5-7:
Adding a
sidebar
item.

In addition to the Navigation and Recent Site Activity items, you can add items for tracking the signed-in user's recent activities, additional sidebar text, or a countdown to a certain date. You can have any, all, or none of these items on your page. Pick what you want or get rid of them all. When you've made your choices, click the Preview button in the upper-right corner to see how the resulting page looks, and click Save to finish your work on the page.

Colors and Fonts

Click the Colors and Fonts tab to change basic color and style elements of your page. Your choices are shown in Figure 5-8.

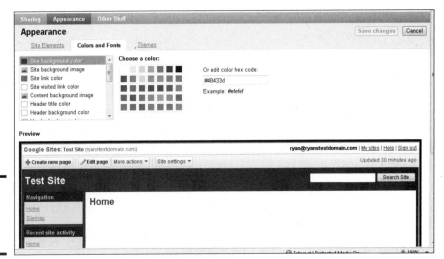

Figure 5-8:
The Colors
and Fonts
tab.

This tab gives you a huge amount of control over the color scheme and the appearance of the text on your site. Each element in the upper-left field can be altered; any element displays the available choices when you click it. For example, clicking Sidebar Font displays the available font choices for sidebars, and clicking Site Link Color displays the available color choices for site links either in visual blocks or in hex code. Clicking Background Image prompts you to upload an image from your computer. When you're done, click Save to make your changes final.

After you've decided on the colors for your page, write down the hex codes for those colors. This gives you an easy way to find exactly what you're looking for when you create a new page.

Themes

You've already seen the available themes when you first set up the page, but here's your chance to change the overall theme again. If you're comfortable with your current theme, you can leave it as is. If not, feel free to try something different. You can always change it back if you're unsatisfied. (See Figure 5-9.)

Changing themes resets all color and font options, but the site layout changes remain the same.

As you can see, there are plenty of changes you can make to your pages.

Still, keep in mind the following when making these kinds of changes:

Manage your corporate look

When choosing the look of your site, at the very least, you want to make sure your page doesn't look distracting or unprofessional. Part of the advantage of the themes Google Sites uses is that they've been professionally designed for your convenience. They may not look like a custom-designed page, but they look good, and they give you a decent-looking page to work with. Making slight changes to customize the details can be appealing, but you don't have to do a lot to the layouts if you don't want to.

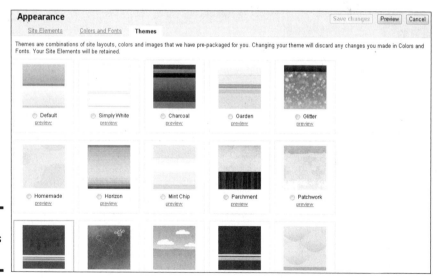

Figure 5-9:
The Themes
tab.

You may, of course, already have a corporate branding and color scheme. In that case, you can customize the color choices to match that branding scheme, and you can tweak the layouts to better resemble what your current corporate look entails. You're still working within a fixed environment, but there is enough power to change layouts and colors to match your corporate image.

Create an integrated view

There's no rule saying you have to make every page inside your site look exactly the same, but your site appears pretty disjointed if you don't keep the same look across all your pages. An integrated look is less distracting to the viewer, and it helps them remain focused on the task at hand instead of wondering why the colors just changed. It's a good idea to maintain consistency across the site. You can always change the layout from page to page, depending on the functionality of the page.

Adding pages to your site

When you created your site, you set up a home page. This is the first page your users encounter when they log into your site. However, it's unlikely that you perform all the work on your site from the home page. You can add pages to the home page or additional top-level pages, depending on your plans for the site.

This is where a good site plan comes in handy. If you've already plotted out your site map, you know exactly how many pages you want to create and where you want them to link to. It's not an easy task to move pages around after you've created them, so create them in the right place the first time around.

In the home page of your site, click the Create New Page button at the top-left corner of the page. You see the available choices in Figure 5-10.

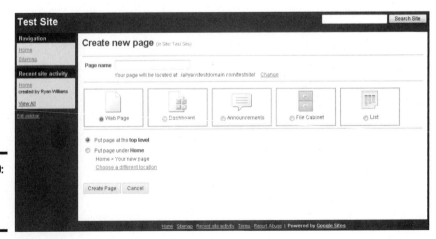

Figure 5-10:
Available
new page
choices.

Five types of pages are available here:

✦ **Web page:** A standard Web page, much like the one you've already created.

✦ **Dashboard:** The *dashboard* allows you to insert different gadgets into its four quadrants, including items from Google Docs and recent activities on your site, as shown in Figure 5-11.

Use this page to keep track of the statistics of your sites and rapidly changing elements of your project. Just like the dashboard of your car, it keeps you linked to the vital statistics of your project.

✦ **Announcements:** The announcements page tracks bulletins from all owners and collaborators — this is a great way, independent of other pages and activities, for members to let others know what's going on — as seen in Figure 5-12.

✦ **File Cabinet:** The file cabinet page acts as a repository for any documents or files uploaded to the site. Your users can subscribe to any changes made to this site by clicking the Subscribe To Changes button, as shown in Figure 5-13.

✦ **List:** The list page starts with four types of lists, including action items, issues, progress of corporate units, and a free-form option. Pick one and add items depending on your needs, as shown in Figure 5-14. Remember that you can add additional lists as you need to, depending on what your project demands.

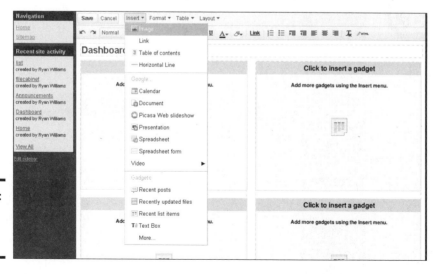

Figure 5-11: The dashboard page.

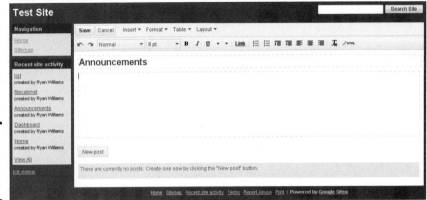

Figure 5-12:
The
announce-
ments page.

Figure 5-13:
The file
cabinet
page.

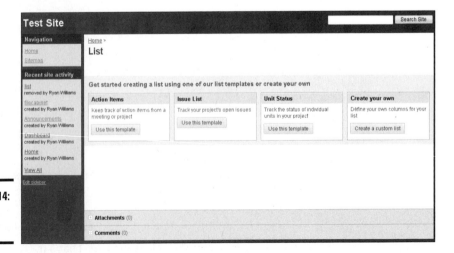

Figure 5-14:
The list
page.

Editing your pages

When you're an owner or collaborator on a Google Site, you see the Edit Page button at the top of each page you work with. Click the button to unlock the page and add or delete additional text and images. When you're done, you can click the Save button to finalize your changes. Remember that these revisions are saved so you can go back and review them later.

Organizing and sharing your pages

Now that you've created the pages you want to use, you can reorganize them and share them as you wish. Let's take a look at the list of commands available by clicking the More Actions button on the home page. You're looking at the home page in this example, but you can perform these actions on any page.

These options include the following:

✦ **Subscribe to page settings:** Setting this option means an e-mail is sent to your account when any changes are made to this specific page.

✦ **Page settings:** This command allows you to change the name of the page and show links to the page title, site navigation, attachments, and comments.

✦ **Print:** Prints a copy of the page.

✦ **Move:** Moves the page to a different location in the sitemap.

✦ **Delete:** Deletes the page.

✦ **Preview page as viewer:** Shows the page as it appears to a viewer without privileges.

✦ **Subscribe to site changes:** Sends an e-mail whenever the site is changed.

✦ **Sitemap:** Displays the map of the entire site.

Change these options to suit your preference and save the page when you're finished.

You can use this screen to set the sharing permissions for each of your pages. Click the Site Settings button on the home page to see the Sharing tab shown in Figure 5-15.

You can invite people at three different levels:

✦ **As Owners:** Owners can invite other people to the site, change the overall look and feel of the site, add attachments and comments, subscribe to changes, and create, edit, and delete any and all pages.

✦ **As Collaborators:** Collaborators can create, edit, move, and delete pages, add attachments and comments, and subscribe to changes.

✦ **As Viewers:** Viewers can only look at the site. That's it.

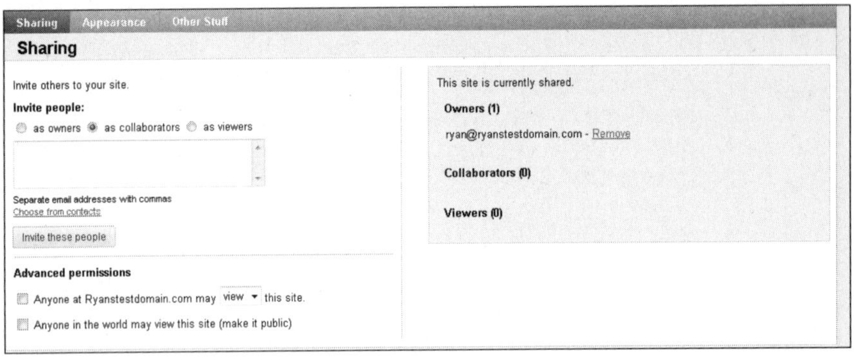

Figure 5-15:
Site sharing
settings.

You can also set global permissions for members of your domain here and make the pages viewable to the public. Finally, you can also see everybody who is attached to the site as an owner, collaborator, or viewer.

These permissions can be added, changed, or revoked at any time, but it's a good idea to plan your permissions in advance.

Adding attachments and comments

As an owner or collaborator, you are able to place attachments and add comments on certain pages. The following is a list of which pages support attachments and comments:

✦ **Home page:** Attachments and comments.

✦ **Other Web pages:** Attachments and comments.

✦ **Dashboard:** No attachments or comments.

✦ **Announcements:** No attachments or comments.

✦ **Lists:** Attachments and comments.

✦ **File cabinets:** Comments only. (Attachments can be uploaded as part of the page).

It may seem redundant to place attachments and comments on a page, but the main advantage is that these features are not viewed by casual browsers or the public. You can conduct business on the page without prying eyes. All the public sees is the final product. These notes can be extremely valuable in the creation of the pages, so feel free to use them at any time to move along your project.

Making the sidebar useful

The sidebar is an important function of the Web site, but it's up to you to customize it to make it the most useful. Think of it as a quick guide to the essentials of the site. Here are some useful customizations for your sidebar:

✦ **Navigation:** This sidebar item lays out the navigation options for your entire site. Putting this on the site gives you a quick link to any page on the site. Use this to simplify movement around your site.

✦ **Text:** Use a small amount of text to remind the users of the site of important details or add a little description about the site for everybody to read. Because readers tend to glance at this side of the page first, make sure you place only important information here.

✦ **Recent site activity:** Depending on how quickly the work on your site progresses, you might have a hard time keeping track of everything that's going on. Look at this part of the sidebar to inform yourself of what's happened since the last time you logged into the site and what you might need to do in response to the changes.

✦ **My recent changes:** This sidebar item only lists the changes you've performed recently. If you're doing a lot of work on the site, this item can remind you of what you've already done and what you need to move on to next.

✦ **Countdown:** Projects have deadlines, and this sidebar item allows you to enter a final date and tracks the amount of time before you hit that deadline. Having this information always present can help motivate your collaborators and keep your project on schedule.

Add and organize these sidebar items as necessary to be of the most use for your site. You can always go back and add, move, or delete the items later, depending on your needs.

Adding another site

Theoretically, there's no limit to the amount of sites you can create in Google Sites. Your basic Google Apps site has a limit of 10GB of storage per domain, plus the additional storage granted to Premier users. To create another site, simply click the My Sites link in the upper-right corner of your Google Sites page. You get a list of your current sites and a button to create new sites, as shown in Figure 5-16.

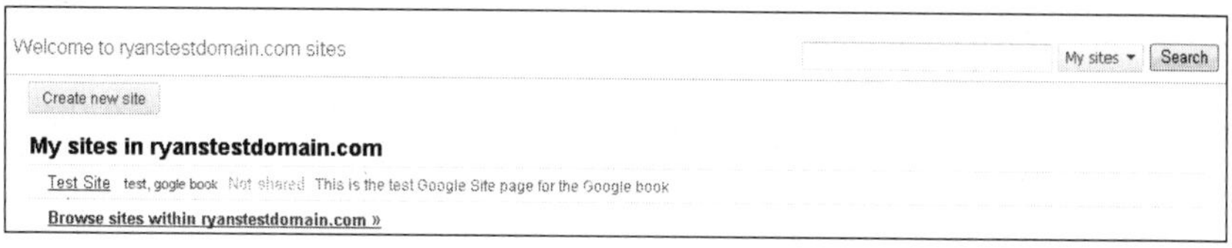

Figure 5-16: Creating a new site.

Welcome to ryanstestdomain.com sites   My sites ▾ | Search |

| Create new site |

My sites in ryanstestdomain.com

Test Site test, gogle book Not shared This is the test Google Site page for the Google book

Browse sites within ryanstestdomain.com »

Click the Create New Site button to start another site. By creating new sites, you can better organize your projects and assign permissions to the owners, collaborators, and viewers of a site. Again, plan your personnel and sitemap properly, and you should have little trouble setting up the sites you need.

Quickly Searching Google Sites

As you create more sites and pages, it might be difficult to keep track of all the information you've produced. This is where proper tagging and description text can be quite valuable, as you can use these tags and descriptions to better find the information you're looking for.

Searching through a single site

When you access a single site, look in the upper-right corner of the page. You see a text field next to a button marked Search Site. Enter the text you're looking for and click the button. Google searches though the pages of only that site, looking for the following:

✦ Text contained in the state

✦ Any tags

✦ Any descriptive text

✦ Any attachments or comments, if you're an owner or collaborator

This is why you need to be as descriptive as possible when putting together your sites. The more descriptive text and useful content you place in your pages, the more information you are able to find.

Searching through all the sites you own

If you have a large number of sites, it might be helpful for you to search through all the sites at one time. For example, James and Jake might want to search all their sites for any invoices attached to their work, or they might want to find all their timesheets. You could stop at every site and perform the same search, or you could search all the sites from one field.

Log into Google Sites and click the My Sites link in the upper-right corner of the screen shown in Figure 5-15. The search text box has a drop-down menu next to it — specify My Sites, enter the text you want to search for, and click Search. All the results for all your sites are shown in the Results page. To search all sites within the domain, change the drop-down menu to All Sites.

Again, this function is only as good as the comments and the tags contained within your sites. However, this drop-down menu gives you the tools to search through all available sites in your domain (even the ones you can only view) and find the information you need.

Chapter 6: Creating Your Corporate Start Page

In This Chapter

✔ Creating your start page

✔ Customizing what the start page includes

✔ Managing your start page's content

✔ Taking your start page online

*A*ll Web sites have a *home page*, where the browsing of a site begins and the initial information about the site is housed. A *corporate start page* is similar in function, but it's customized with information and color schemes for members of your domain. Your coworkers and employees use this page to get an instant view of what's going on in the company and also access features such as e-mail and calendar. You and your collaborators can tailor this start page to make it most useful to each individual's needs. For example, on Jake's Landscaping's corporate start page, James, Jake, and all other employees can see what's coming up in their day, their new e-mail, the weather, and any other necessary information. Let's take a look at how to set up a corporate start page.

Customizing Your Color Scheme

As owner of the domain, you establish the basic look of the page. As discussed in Chapter 5, you want to establish a look that integrates well with your corporate image. If you have a specific color scheme, this is where you implement it. This is also where you design the basic layout of the page.

Follow these steps to customize your color scheme:

1. **Log into your domain and click the Start Page link to view the screen shown in Figure 6-1.**

2. **Click the Customize link to view your options, as shown in Figure 6-2.**

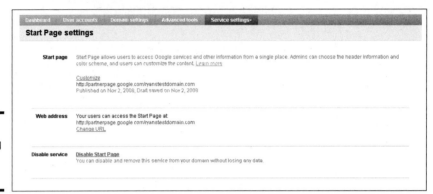

Figure 6-1:
Customizing
your start
page.

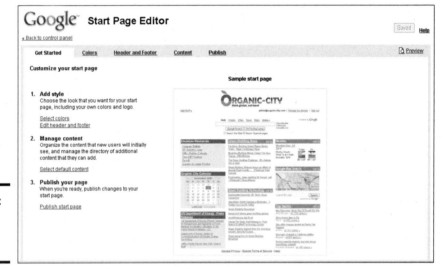

Figure 6-2:
Custom-
ization
options.

3. **Click the Colors tab to get started adjusting the colors on your page.**

4. **Figure 6-3 shows you the options you have in this customization process. Choose colors for each item on the page.**

   The preview window at the bottom of the page shows you the results of your efforts.

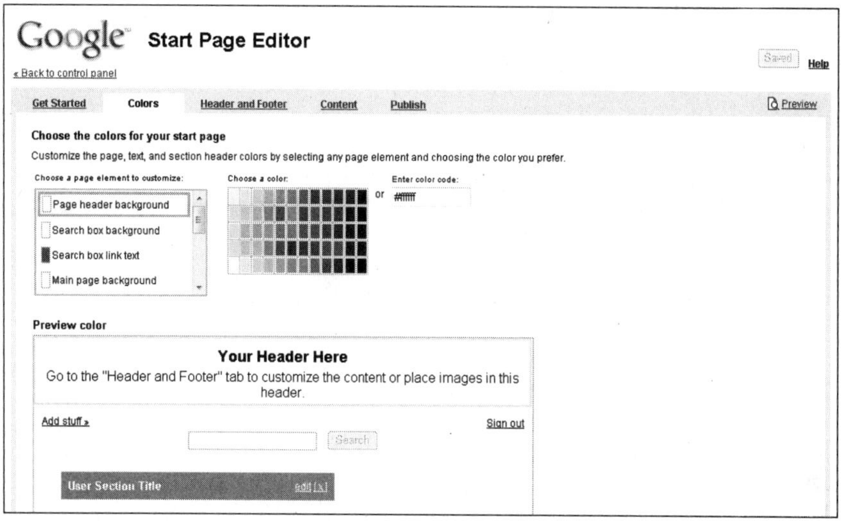

Figure 6-3:
Customizing
colors.

Keep track of these two important concepts when you're putting your color choices together:

✦ **Honor your corporate color scheme:** If you have a corporate branding scheme, make sure you use those exact colors in the scheme on your corporate start page. This helps you integrate your start page into the rest of your corporate identity and identifies the site as part of your business activities.

✦ **Don't hurt the eyes!:** If you don't have a specific corporate branding scheme, try to choose colors that complement each other and fit in with the business you're running. For example, Jake's Landscaping may choose different tones of green to design its corporate page, whereas a dating service may go with red for its page. Above all, make sure you use colors that go together. Don't make the page difficult to read (red text on a black background) or assault the viewer with loud and clashing colors.

The Internet has several sites that show you complementary color schemes — a quick search (on Google, naturally) generates tons of resources for you to consult. Find one that works for you, and enter the hex codes to make sure you get the colors you want. Honor the two preceding concepts, and you produce a site your employees and coworkers will want to use.

Creating the Header and Footer

The headers and footers are exactly what they sound like — they reside at the top and bottom of your corporate start page, and they play valuable roles in establishing the functionality and identity of the page. Click the Header and Footer tab to see the screen shown in Figure 6-4.

Notice that you have the most control over the appearance of the header. This is where you give your corporate start page its title, maybe a logo, and any other important information.

Adding images to headers

Click the Image button to add a picture in your header. (You can't add images to footers.) You can either choose a corporate logo or another important image for this section — just be sure you have the right to use it first. Browse to the location of the file on your computer or enter the Web address for the picture you want to upload, as shown in Figure 6-5.

After the photo is uploaded, you can choose a size for it and drag it to the correct location in the header.

Adding links to headers and footers

Click the Links button to place additional links inside the header. These can be links to important pages either inside or outside of your domain. For Jake's Landscaping, these could be links to timesheets or other corporate documentation. You might also include the e-mail addresses of important people in the company. Both choices are presented to you when you click the Link button, as shown in Figure 6-6.

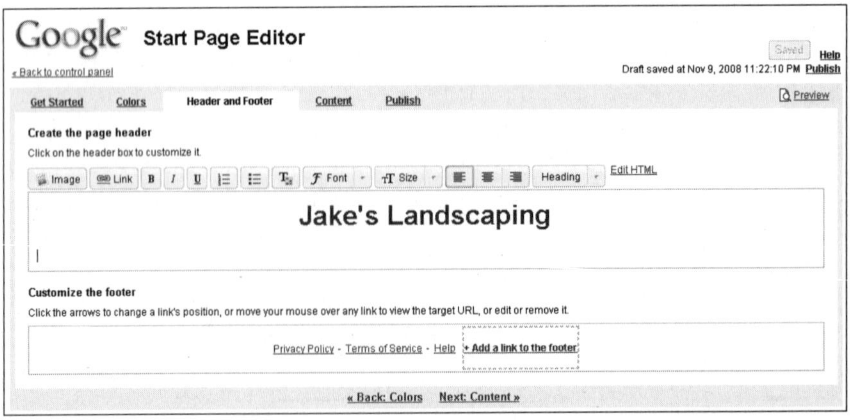

Figure 6-4: Customizing your header and footer.

You have fewer options available with the footer because there's less space for you to include items, you can't upload images, and fewer links are required because of Google's terms of service. Click the Add A Link To The Footer link to start adding hyperlinks in the footer, as shown in Figure 6-7. Again, you have the option of inserting links to other pages or to an e-mail address.

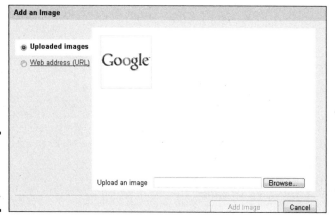

Figure 6-5:
Uploading
a photo to
your header.

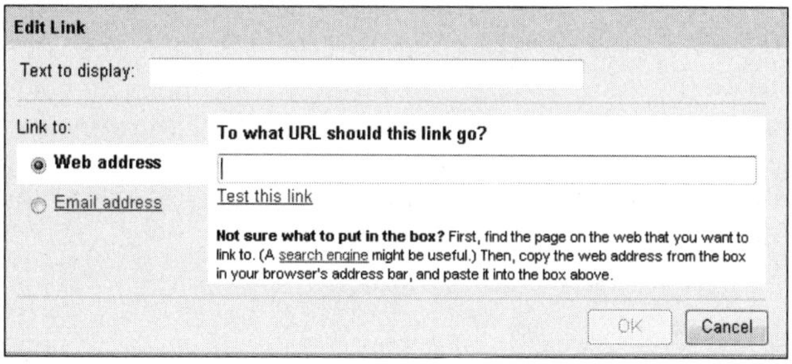

Figure 6-6:
Adding
links to your
header.

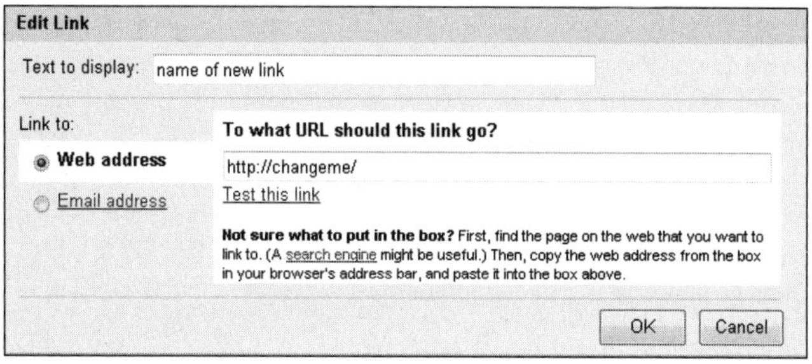

Figure 6-7:
Adding
links to your
footer.

These should aid the user to navigate around your site, so pick important pages and add links to them. These should be links that are of interest to everybody in your company, not just individual users. They should also be sites within your domain, as opposed to outside of your control. The corporate start page is intended to help your users navigate around your site, not the entire Internet.

Finally, it's okay to duplicate links from the top of the page — if a user puts together a big individual page, the links give him or her the opportunity to click to go to the next page without having to scroll all the way back to the header.

Adding text to your header or footer

You can always add more text to the header or footer. Remember that this editor treats the header like a word processing program and not a document layout program, like Pagemaker. You have to organize the information in your header as you would with a document, so take care to place the information you want to include in order of appearance and adjust your text alignment accordingly.

In any case, you want to include only the most important information in your header — you can leave the rest for the actual page of your pages within your intranet site.

Managing the Content Your Users Will See

Now that you've added the content to the top and bottom of your page, you can help your users fill up the middle of the page. Each user is able to customize the layout of his or her individual page, but you can limit the available choices. To see what's available for the start pages, click the Content tab, as shown in Figure 6-8.

You can edit out gadgets you don't want on your users' default pages by closing each gadget, and then you can organize the gadgets into a default layout. When you're ready, click Preview to see how a default page would look.

If you want to add more gadgets to your default page, click the Add Stuff link in the top-right corner to see more gadgets. You see a list of additional gadgets organized by subject in the left column, as shown in Figure 6-9.

You can add any gadgets you find here from this page. Just find the gadget you want by using the Search Content box or by browsing through the gadgets, and click the Add It Now button under the gadget to put it on the default page.

If a gadget for the information you want to include doesn't appear on the list, click the Create Custom Content link in the upper-right corner of Figure 6-9. You see the information shown in Figure 6-10.

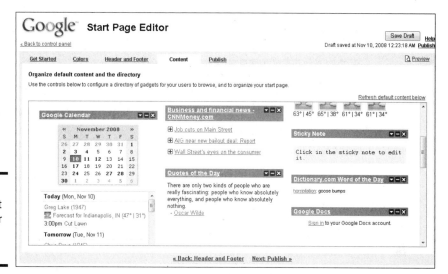

Figure 6-8:
The default
gadgets for
your start
page.

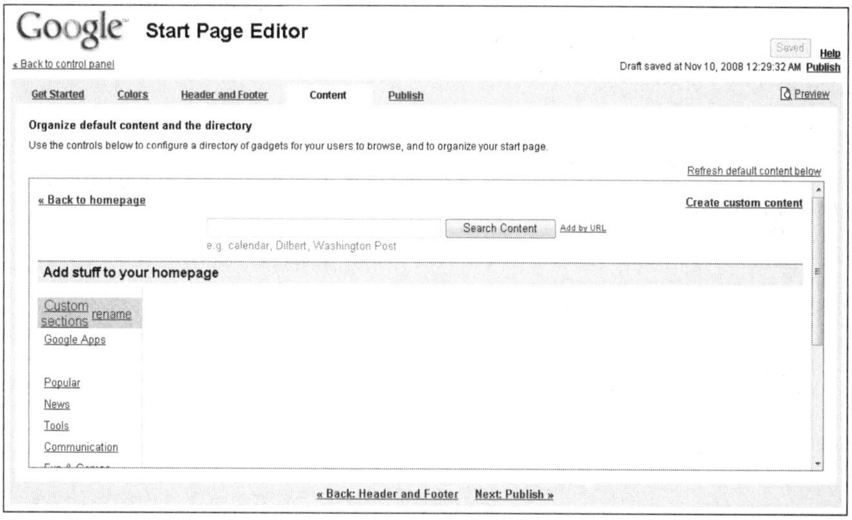

Figure 6-9:
More
available
Google
gadgets.

Figure 6-10:
Creating
custom
content.

In the dialog box shown in Figure 6-10, you have to choose what kind of section your want to add, as follows:

✦ **Static text, images, and links:** Choosing static or custom text gives you a text box. Add the information you want (like contact information or other necessary text) in that text box and click the Create Section button to add that content to the default layout.

✦ **Frequently updated content section:** If you have a news feed in RSS or Atom format, click the Frequently Updated Content Section radio button. Give it a title and place the URL for the feed in the appropriate text field. When you click the Create Section button, you add a gadget that displays the most up-to-date information from that feed. Give it a title, and place the URL for the feed in the appropriate text field. An excellent example would be the feed from your boss's or coworker's calendar or a site that carries news for your industry.

✦ **Google Gadget:** If you want a gadget that tracks a specific Web page, click the third radio button. You are asked for a title of the gadget and the URL of the page. Place them in the appropriate areas to make a gadget based on that page.

The site might not translate well to the gadget, so be sure to evaluate how it looks before you make it available on your page.

Your users can add more gadgets to their own start pages after they've signed in, but this gives them the gadgets to get started. When you have everything organized and ready to go, click Preview in the upper-right corner to open the page in a new browser window. If you don't like what you see, go back and change the page some more. Keep going until you get the page exactly the way you want it.

Making Your Start Page Live

At the end of the last section, did I mention previewing the page? Good. Now go ahead and do it again just one more time. Look at every potential detail and make sure everything is in place before you continue. When the site is published, you can go back and change the items around, but it's always good to make a positive first impression.

When you're ready to go, click the Publish tab to see the screen in Figure 6-11.

Take note of the URL and send it to all your employees and coworkers. Click the Publish Updates when you're ready, and all the changes you've made are published to your start page. Now, when your users sign in, they get the default gadgets and can add other gadgets as well.

If you need to take down your start page for any reason (such as a major overhaul), navigate back to this page and click the Unpublish button. This takes down the corporate start page until you republish it later.

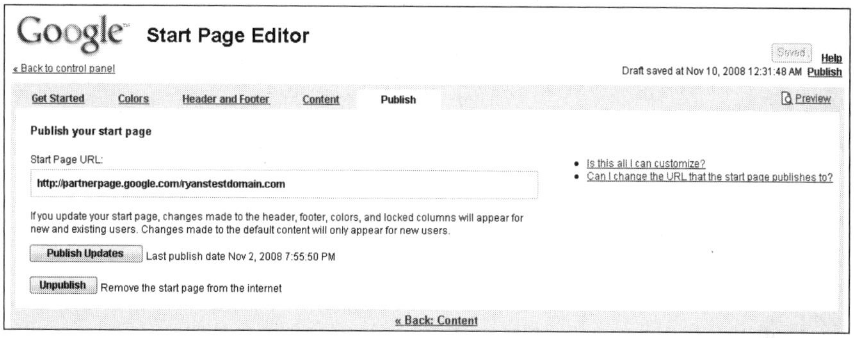

Figure 6-11:
Publishing
your start
page.

Google™ **Start Page Editor**

Saved | Help

« Back to control panel   Draft saved at Nov 10, 2008 12:31:48 AM Publish

Get Started   Colors   Header and Footer   Content   **Publish**   ⟐ Preview

Publish your start page

Start Page URL:

http://partnerpage.google.com/ryanstestdomain.com

• Is this all I can customize?
• Can I change the URL that the start page publishes to?

If you update your start page, changes made to the header, footer, colors, and locked columns will appear for new and existing users. Changes made to the default content will only appear for new users.

[Publish Updates]   Last publish date Nov 2, 2008 7:55:50 PM

[Unpublish]   Remove the start page from the internet

« Back: Content

Book II
Google Search Tools for Business

The 5th Wave   By Rich Tennant

"This is amazing. You can stop looking for Derek. According to a Google search I did, he's hiding behind the dryer in the basement."

Contents at a Glance

Chapter 1: A Smart Tour of Google Search

In This Chapter

✔ Searching with Google

✔ Exploring the free search results

✔ Fine-tuning your searches

✔ Using Advanced Search techniques

A lot of search engines are available on the Internet, but to many people, Google is the *only* search engine. About two-thirds of all searches are done through Google. The remaining search engines have survived by making themselves more and more like Google. So if you understand Google search and make it work for you, you've done just about all you need to do in the world of search.

In this chapter, we take a close look at Google search — both to make you a better Google searcher, which is important for some of the endeavors in this book, and to understand how you can make it easier for customers to find your business by using Google.

Using Google Search

The classic Google search starts at the main Google search screen, as shown in Figure 1-1. It's worth taking a close look at what users see when they use the screen.

Figure 1-1 shows Google's search screen — perhaps the most-seen screen ever on the Web!

The first thing to notice is how little there is to notice. There are 31 words on the screen in Figure 1-1, almost all of which are links.

The page, being almost all text, loads very quickly. The people at Google put tremendous effort into making things go fast. They believe that a faster response makes a difference not just of degree, but also of kind. (A search that's 10% faster might be slightly better; a search that's 40% faster might be used, say, twice as much as a slower search.)

Figure 1-1:
The Google
search
screen.

Partly because Google loads so fast, and partly because it's so useful, huge
numbers of users worldwide have their home pages set to `www.google.`
`com` or a country-specific version of Google, such as the UK version shown in
Figure 1-2. This is just another proof of how important Google has become.

The lesson here is the overarching importance of making things work fast. It
applies to your own Web presence, and perhaps even to how you run your
entire business, online and offline.

Yet even the few dozen words on the main Google screen are ignored by
most people, most of the time. Here are the key points for you to understand
about the Google search screen, from a pure search point of view:

✦ **Search term entry area:** Google uses a small amount of JavaScript to
"grab" the user's cursor and drag it into the search term entry area — as
you may have noticed if you have tried to type in a new domain name,
for instance, while Google is loading. This built-in magnetism makes it
easy for users to know just what to do when they go to Google, even
before the page finishes loading: Type in the search term(s).

✦ **Google Search / I'm Feeling Lucky buttons:** Although the I'm Feeling Lucky button is rarely used, Google has always seemed to have a soft spot for it in what, otherwise, can be a pretty cold, corporate heart. I'm Feeling Lucky takes you directly to the Web site that's the first entry in Google's search results. It's a touching statement of faith by Google in its own capability to find exactly what the user wants.

✦ **Search the Web/pages from the UK:** This option is not available within the US. Use this setting to narrow your search results to only UK-based Web pages. Additionally, UK-based businesses should note that some UK searches will narrow their focus to UK-based results, improving your ranking. If you have a US-based business, be aware that foreign users do have this option, which they can use to narrow their searches away from, well, you. If you're outside the US, it's important to take advantage of this option in your search optimization work.

Book II
Chapter 1

A Smart Tour of
Google Search

Because there is no "pages from the US" option for US users, Americans are more likely to get unwanted foreign results when they want to find something specifically American (or specifically, say, Floridian. Cutting out non-US results would be a good start in this type of search; having a state-specific option would be appreciated by many.)

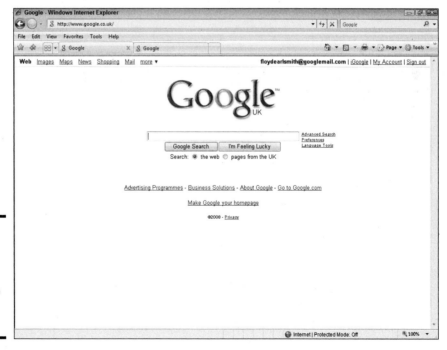

Figure 1-2:
Google in the UK can search the whole Web or just the US.

Exploring Other Ways to Start Google Search

Other ways to get to Google search are shown in Figure 1-3. These include

✦ **The Google Search toolbar:** This is a brilliant tool, as the Brits would put it, adding a lot of power to a Web browser. It's fun and puts the search capabilities of the Google home page in a convenient toolbar on every Web page, so you never lose access to Google search.

✦ **The Instant Search box:** The Instant Search box is like a mini-Google Search toolbar located in the upper-right corner of Internet Explorer 7, Firefox, or Safari browsers. However, it can be set up to use other search engines as well.

✦ **The URL area:** The box where users enter a URL can also be used, in many browsers, to enter search terms. In Internet Explorer 7, the search terms entered in the URL area use the search engine specified for the Instant Search box.

Google Search toolbar   The URL area   Instant Search box

Figure 1-3:
Search from the Google toolbar, the Instant Search box, or the URL area.

The main impact of these other ways of accessing Google search lies in the way they make Google's options available — or don't. This is most important for non-US users who like to use the "pages from the UK" option or similar ones. It's most easily available from the main Google search page; it is also available, with somewhat more work, as a pull-down in the Google Search toolbar; but it is not available from the Instant Search box or the URL area.

Understanding Free Search Results

Google has added so many ornaments around its core search results that it takes a special effort to strip them away and get back to it. Yet Google's free search results are tremendously important to many businesses.

The core promise of Google search has two aspects. The first is that, if you know a few key words about something specific, you can find it. This expectation is usually very well met, except where the key words are very general. You can compare this to looking up a word in the dictionary — you know just what you want; the only thing stopping you is spelling the word(s) right.

The other aspect of search comes into play when you have a general idea of the kind of thing you want, and Google promises to deliver suitable examples of it. This promise is much harder to fulfill, and Google doesn't always manage it. You can compare this kind of search to looking for something in an encyclopedia — some prominent terms are well-represented, but getting exactly what you want can be harder.

Most of the energy that goes into search engine optimization is focused on "winning" or featuring prominently in these more general searches. Huge amounts of money have been spent on this kind of search engine optimization, or SEO. Yet much of it is wasted, for three reasons:

✦ The first is that this kind of SEO is very expensive, using your time, money (paid to an SEO expert or company), or both. You have to be very good at converting the search engine listing into cash to pay for all the SEO work.

✦ The second reason is that other people are probably trying as hard as you are to grab that high-up Google listing, and Google is constantly tweaking its search formula to improve results for the user. This means you're likely to be in a sort of arms race with competitors in constantly changing conditions.

✦ The final reason is Google's increasing success in selling paid search listings and users' increasing dependence on them. These paid search listings, which we discuss in detail later, push free results down the page — users in a buying mood may even prefer the paid listings to the free ones. Ironically, some people pay consultants good money for top "free" search rankings — then get ignored by users clicking on directly paid-for results.

Example: A specific search

Figure 1-4 shows the search results for the name of one of the authors, Bud Smith. Unfortunately for Bud, he has the same name as a baseball player and a film director. The baseball player shows up as the first and the fourth result; the film director on the second; and our Bud, on the third.

This is a specific search in that I've entered the name of a specific person. Because Bud Smith is not that common a name, I may well find the one I'm looking for early in the results. Improving Bud Smith's own search position in these results would be difficult, and it would be hard work indeed to win the first Google search position. But it would be much harder to win the first Google search position for a more generic term such as *baseball player*, *movie director*, or *author*.

Figure 1-4:
Bud Smith
can run —
to first base,
perhaps —
but he
can't hide.

This search result shows a small example of just how good Google is. I didn't search with quotes around the name, like this: "Bud Smith." Yet I don't get a bunch of unrelated Buds and Smiths — just three Bud Smiths, in order. This is a huge advance over how search engines used to work before Google, and because of it, Google arguably has kept a small but significant lead for most searches, most of the time.

Each of the results has the words *Bud Smith, with the words right next to each other*. This is important — if people are going to be searching for *nuclear popcorn poppers*, your *nuclear-powered popcorn popper* might not make the top of the search results. It might even rank below a *nuclear-free popcorn popper*!

Also notice that I've got three different Bud Smiths in the first three results. It's quite possible, even likely, that there's a link to the Bud Smith I want right in those first few results. I don't even need to scroll down the page — so I'm never going to see search results below the first few.

The need to be near the top of the page in free search results is even more urgent when Google ads take up vital space at the very top of the page.

Also note that no ads are showing up for Bud Smith searches. That's because no one, at least on this day, wants to sell anything relating to any Bud Smith badly enough to buy a Google Ad for the term!

Note what shows up in each result. For our purposes, the most important elements are the most obvious ones: the page title of the Web page; a few words from a relevant part of the Web page; and the URL (or Web address) of the Web page.

All these are vital information. Be aware that, in your own Web site, you can control much of what shows up as the results of a Google search: the page title, the words around key words that people might search for, and the URL that appears to users.

Finally, notice that the third entry — the one that actually does mention the author of this book — that entry is from Google's own Google Books. For better or worse, it displaces the Amazon.com entry I would have expected to find in the first few results.

The Google Books search result includes some additional information, because Google knows how to index itself. Google "knows" that the search result is for a book listed on Google Books and lists the author names, date of publication, and page count. Google is using Google to advertise a Google product, something that you can expect to happen more and more.

A search for one's own name in Google is called *Googling yourself* or an "ego search." Putting a search for one's own name into a book one is writing might be called something entirely less polite!

Example: A general search

Figure 1-5 shows the search results for a broad category, *computer book author* (entered into Google without quotation marks around the term). The first few results all include the phrase *computer book author*, just as when we searched on Bud Smith.

Note that what the results *don't* have is the names of lots of computer book authors. If that's what I wanted, I'm going to be very frustrated.

This is one of the key lessons — and frustrations — of Google Search. Search doesn't find the *idea* you're looking for; it finds the *words* you use in the search. In cases like this, rather than giving you the thing you want, it gives you people talking about the thing you want.

Now imagine if we authors of this book were trying to get our names high up into these search results. Only one author's name appears, and that's because of winning an award.

Figure 1-5:
A search for computer book authors doesn't find many.

To compete, we'd probably have to win an award as well. That means we'd have to write a bunch of really good books, which sounds like a lot of effort over a long period of time. That's not how SEO is supposed to work!

But this is usually the truth of the pursuit of high search engine rankings around broad, generic terms — it doesn't work well for the searcher or the person seeking the ranking.

Let's say we did manage to get the top ranking somehow, after expending a lot of effort, time, and money. The odds are low that a searcher for *computer book author* would really want to find *us* in particular, out of all the similar people out there — or that he or she would click the link, if it appeared among the search results. It's even less likely that he or she would buy something because of the search.

The whole problem is that it's a general search. That means it's hard to "win" a high search ranking, hard to "win" a click from the Web surfer, and hard to "win" a purchase from them after they click.

You may be able to get somewhere with certain kinds of broad searches, especially if you have a strong position in the real world that you can get reflected online. If you're the world's leading vendor of Kunik the Cat dolls, you have a good shot at placing somewhere with searches on this topic. But your success is hinging on the specific word, *Kunik*, not the broader term, *cat dolls*. It's always going to be difficult to get ahead when broad terms are used.

Sponsored links and shopping results

To understand how free search results are becoming less important, let's take a quick look at sponsored links and shopping results.

Let's pick a heavily used phrase that gets a lot of hits, and figures in this book: *creating Web pages*. A lot of money in businesses and products is involved in creating Web pages, so it gets a lot of sponsored links as well as tens of millions of free search results.

Figure 1-6 shows the results of this search. Note that sponsored links crowd the crucial, initially visible part of the Web page, showing up on the right side and, frequently, above the free search results as well. In this example, if you were looking for an online service to help you host and build a Web site, you could probably find what you wanted without even looking at the free search results.

Figure 1-6:
Sponsored links can crowd free links right off the Google search page.

Google lets anyone who wants to bid on search terms using Adwords — the product that makes Google almost all its billions of dollars a year in revenues. Clearly, as the figure shows, *creating Web pages* is a highly competitive search term! We describe exactly how to use AdWords for yourself in Book 5.

But the point, for now, is that you could spend huge amounts of time and money moving your Web site up the charts of free search results — and still get crowded off the page by anyone who was willing to pay a dollar or so for a click.

In fact, it's worse than that. Because Adwords can easily be geographically targeted, you're more likely to get crowded off the page in places where people have money. (For instance, you can create an Adwords ad that displays only in London, England.) Struggling to climb the results page may pay off — and get you a spot on the search results page that's visible only in geographic areas where it's unlikely to pay off.

To add insult to injury, you can't even comprehensively test how much good your high Web page placement will do you. National targeting means that someone choosing the Pages from the UK option, for instance, may never see your non-UK-hosted Web page. And the constant ferment in the market, plus Adwords geographic targeting, means that you'll never know just where and when you get a visible placement for your otherwise top-scoring search term.

Shopping results are very similar to sponsored links, and often occur on the same types of terms. Be aware that sponsored links aren't the only thing that can crowd your hard-won free search result off the page.

Fine-Tuning Searches

Books about search often spend a great deal of time on advanced search techniques, but we're going to cover them only briefly here. You need to know how to use them for your own purposes, and to be aware that some people use them; but the vast majority of searches are done using the traditional Google interface. The whole point of Google's success is that people don't want to think about search; they just want to do it and get on with their lives.

Figure 1-7 shows Google's search preferences page. To get here, click on the Preferences link next to the search term entry box on the Google home page.

Here's a brief description of the major features and how they affect your efforts to get found by Google users:

✦ **Prefer pages written in these languages:** Arabic, Armenian, and so on: Some people do this to restrict search results to pages in English, which doesn't affect you much — though it might move your page up in the results a bit for people who choose this option. It simply moves non-English pages out of the way.

✦ **SafeSearch filtering:** This is usually set to moderate filtering, and again shouldn't affect you, unless you have a site that includes explicit sexual content — which we don't address in this book.

✦ **Display 10, 20, 30, and so on results per page:** I use this option to increase the number of results per page when doing an intensive search. This is useful, but most people won't use this option. Most people just look at the initial results that show up on their screens, click down once or very few additional times, and then move on.

✦ **Open search results in a new browser window:** Another option good for intensive search that doesn't affect you much.

The bottom line? Use these options yourself for intensive searches; consider setting the language to English, SafeSearch to restrict results per page to 100, and open search results in new browser windows. This allows you to quickly look through a lot of results and open a lot of windows to follow up.

But users so rarely take advantage of these options, and the options make little enough difference in the results, they shouldn't have much affect in how you try to use Google search to bring people to your business.

Figure 1-7:
Google
preferences
are good for
intensive
searching.

Advanced Searches

As with Preferences, Google's Advanced Search options are not that frequently used, and they don't make a big difference in getting search visitors.

Google is different from most of the search engines that preceded it in that it doesn't offer advanced search options from the home page. This confronts the user with complexity right at the beginning. Google puts the advanced options on a separate page — so those who really want these options have access, but no one has to deal with them in a particular search.

Google Advanced Search is shown in Figure 1-8. As with Preferences, you reach Advanced Search by clicking on a link next to the search term entry box on the Google home page. Advanced Search allows fine-tuning of options to do a more detailed search. You can look for exact phrases and exclude unwanted words. This is useful if you are using a term in an unusual way; for instance, if you want to search for Bud Smith, but not the baseball player, you can exclude any result with *baseball* in it from your search.

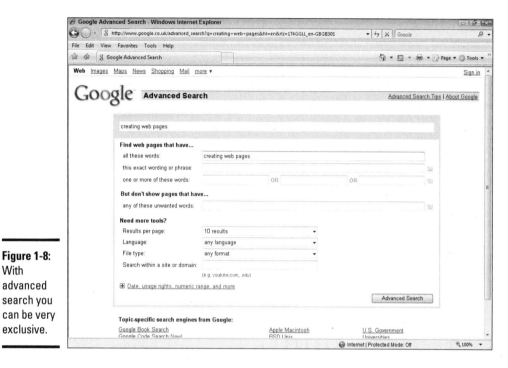

Book II
Chapter 1

A Smart Tour of
Google Search

Figure 1-8:
With
advanced
search you
can be very
exclusive.

The Advanced Search page also includes the Results Per Page option, the Language option, and choice of file type. You can also search within a site — which is a great feature. It eliminates the need to figure out a site's specific navigation or search capabilities and goes straight to what you want.

To search within a site, add "`site:`" and the site name — no `www.` needed — to your search. For instance, to search on Amazon.com for this book, type: *site:amazon.com google dummies*. This book is likely to be high up in the results.

If you click the Date, Usage Rights, Numeric Range, and More link at the bottom of the page, other options appear, as shown in Figure 1-9. Although hidden in a separate page and behind a link, this area contains an option that you may wish Google would make more prominent: date-specific search.

When you want to cut through the noise on Google and get your pages high in search results, one of the most difficult hurdles is Google's tendency to favor older results. You, of course — and, more important, users — would often prefer a focus on newer results.

The Date option, hidden as it is behind a link on the Advanced page, is a powerful capability. Many searchers would like to find results that have been updated recently; Date allows this. In fact, one could argue that this option would be used quite a bit more if it were on the Google home page — but that would also force users to think more.

People who are creating new pages certainly wish that Google tilted more toward newer pages. They also would like it if Google made it easier for searchers to specifically focus their searches.

The hidden options also allow searching within domain names or in different parts of a page. Although these options are useful, they're not commonly used.

You can also find pages similar to the page you've searched on. This is a powerful option that allows you to work around common phrases, words with multiple meanings, and so on. It's already available for regular search results if you use the option Similar Pages. This is where the option is more likely to be used.

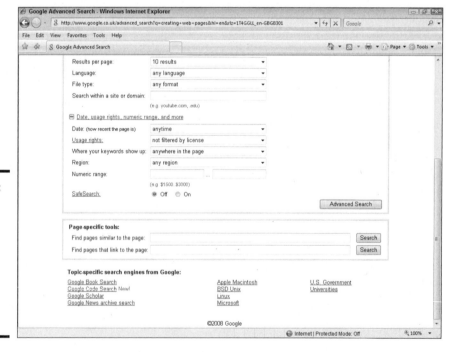

Figure 1-9:
There are hidden gems in Advanced Options, such as date-specific searches.

One option you must take advantage of is the Find Pages That Link to the Page option. This is how you find out what pages link to a given page. Google often uses links to determine how highly pages rank, as we describe in Book 3. Check the sites that are competing with you here, to see where they're getting their links.

Chapter 2: How Google Search Works

*E*ven if you're not looking to become an expert, you should understand how Google search works. That way, you know what to expect from it — and perhaps how to get it to award your site a higher ranking on key search terms.

A search engine really does just three things: looks through, or *crawls*, the Web to build an index of pages; ranks pages on various search terms; and returns search results to users.

Google keeps some details of its inner workings secret for two reasons: to protect its competitive position, and to keep search engine optimization (SEO) experts from developing tricks that get their pages higher rankings than they really deserve. Google is also constantly changing its techniques for the same reasons. So the descriptions here are likely to be generally correct, but no one can tell you what's happening specifically.

Crawling the Web

Search engines are described using terms that play off the name *World Wide Web*. A search engine starts by unleashing a *spider* — a computer program that follows links from one Web page to the next, *crawling* the Web to find pages on which someone might want to search. (Crawling the Web, in this way, makes more sense than surfing it does! Crawling is slower and more careful.)

As the search engine's spider crawls the Web, it examines each page and scores it on various criteria. It looks for terms that it determines are important — take, for example, the term *pool*. Every time the spider finds the term on a page, it gives that page a score for that term — the score is based on the number of times *pool* appears on that page, the placement of those appearances on the page, the number of appearances in headings, titles, metadata, and so on. All these elements give that page a chance to get a higher score. The whole purpose of crawling the Web is to find pages so they can be scored on various terms.

Google's spiders are very good at crawling the Web we all know and love — but it doesn't reach into databases. Most people who own databases would consider that a good thing!

Google crawls the Web in many ways — quickly, looking for newer, updated, frequently referred to Web pages, and also more slowly, trying to find every last page that fits its criteria. The slower search, which runs about once a month, is called the *deep crawl*.

The deep crawl, which happens monthly, takes a week or more to process its results and make them a part of Google search. So it may take six weeks for your site to appear in a Google search, on this basis alone.

It may take six weeks, that is, if you get indexed at all. Google may decide that your site is too unimportant to bother indexing. (Or may place it so deep in the results that neither you nor anyone else is ever likely to see it, which amounts to the same thing.) So you may have the following discouraging cycle occur: Create or update your site; wait six weeks; never see it appear or see it ranked very low; update it again; wait six weeks . . . and so on.

The same concerns that apply to your home page apply to specific pages on your Web site as well. If you have multiple products, for instance, each with its own Web page, you want them all indexed. This may not happen quickly or at all.

Google applies the same reasoning to individual pages that it applies to entire sites and home pages. This reasoning is summed up in the discussion of ranking Web pages that follows.

Ranking Pages on Search Terms

As you begin to think about how the Web looks to a search engine, you see a few limitations right off the bat. Search engines are totally dependent on words and their placement. Imagine a Web page with a giant picture of a swimming pool, but the text on that page doesn't include the word *pool*; instead, the text mostly refers to *it* or *as shown in the picture*. Any search engine, then, will have trouble giving the page a high score for the term *pool*.

This applies to some of the workarounds people use for search as well. One big problem with searching for *pool*, meaning *swimming pool*, is that you get results related to the version of billiards called pool, quotes about natural pools of water, and so on. (See Figure 2-1.) To get better results, then, you should narrow your search by searching on the term *swimming pool*.

Figure 2-1:
A search
for *pool*
gets mixed
results.

However, if you do this, your results include only pages that refer to *swimming pool*, but ignores pages that refer to the more commonly used *pool*. Searchers who try to maneuver past the search engine's limitations, then, may end up missing some pages they would really like to see.

When you've done enough searches, you soon realize that the number of times a search term appears on a page (or the various locations of that term on the page) is not necessarily indicative of the value of that page. You also want to know how "good" the page is.

(This wouldn't matter much if the Web were a centrally controlled encyclopedia of uniform quality — you would probably want the page that had used your term most often. But Web pages vary wildly in quality, and you don't want to waste time looking at the bad ones.)

Because there's no way a search engine can tell you how "good" a page would seem to a human — and because "good" could mean different things to different people, anyway — you want to know the next best thing — how popular the page is.

But because the Web is so decentralized, running on millions of servers all over the world, there's no way to determine how popular a page is when compared to all the hundreds of millions of pages out there on the Web.

So until Google came along, Web search engines tended to treat Web pages equally. A page that used a search term a lot, but was boring and useless, could get just as high a ranking as the most popular, most useful page about that term on the Web.

But Google found a way to change all that.

Understanding Google's Approach to Ranking Pages

A search engine has no way of knowing how popular a Web page is. Google found a workaround that comes pretty close to determining the popularity of a given page.

The key to Google's workings is called PageRank. Google revealed the inner workings of an early version of PageRank in its patent application, called "Method for node ranking in a linked database," filed September 4, 2001. The first page of the patent is shown in Figure 2-2.

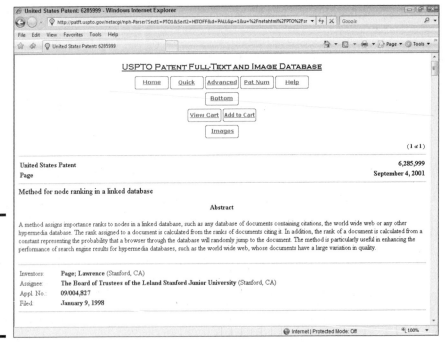

Figure 2-2: Google's patent application for its method of ranking.

The key to PageRank is that it ranks a page higher based on the number of pages that link to it. And it ranks each link higher if that link comes from another page that has lots of links.

For someone just starting out, the good news is that internal links — links within a Web site to other pages on the site — count in PageRank. The bad news is that, unless some highly-linked-to pages link to *those* pages, the internal page links don't count very highly.

Think of the Web, first, as a flat map of links. Now add a third dimension — where a page is linked to, lift it up a bit. Keep doing this as you track how many links that page has to it, and so on.

Eventually you end up with extremely high peaks — such as Google.com, Google's nation-specific home pages, Wikipedia, Amazon, and so on. There are, of course, many smaller peaks, as well as deep valleys of pages that are linked to very little, or not linked at all.

In this world of steep peaks and valleys, the key to moving up is to get higher-altitude — that is, more linked-to — pages to link to yours. This helps the pages that get the new links, and it helps strengthen your own little web of internal links as well.

One of the great tricks of business is to use one advantage to create another, new advantage — and Google has figured out a way to do just that.

We mentioned earlier that a search engine has no way of knowing how popular a Web page is, and — operating only as a search engine — it doesn't. But Google has offered the Google Toolbar, which millions of Web users have installed.

The Google Toolbar tracks the Web pages you visit, and reports summary information about your activity — with your identifying information removed — back to Google. (Users can opt out of this, as shown in Figure 2-3, but apparently most don't.)

So Google can now strengthen its algorithms with information about how popular Web pages are, which makes its usefulness that much greater. It not only knows how popular a Web page is as measured by links to it — it knows how popular a page is as measured by the number of visits to it as well.

This gives Google a huge advantage; by using its strength in search it offers a tool that gathers information to strengthen its search capabilities.

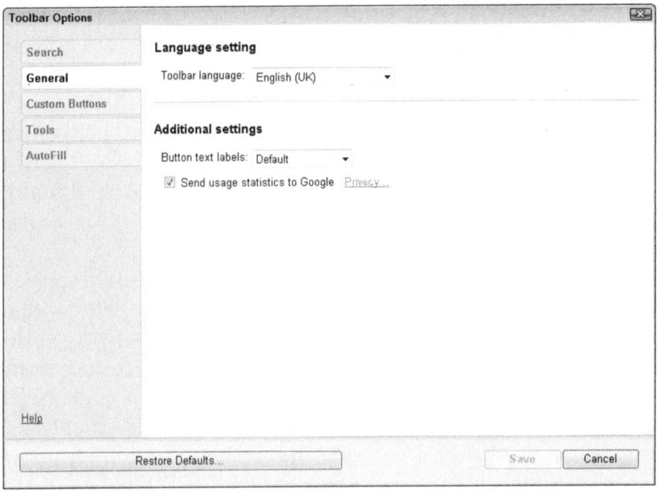

Figure 2-3:
The Google
Toolbar
lets users
opt out of
reporting.

Returning Results to Users

Users are passionate about the results they get from search engines. Even though the Web is free and search is free, users expect search engines to return fair, honest, useful results.

Google, in its early days, did a fantastic job of this. It presented nothing but a few carefully selected lines of text, easy to visit. And, with each result, Google offered a link to similar pages — so it was easy to follow up on a near miss — and a link to a cached version of the page, so the user had a fallback if the page had moved. All unpolluted by commerce.

But this left the problem of making money. How could Google make money from — *monetize*, as the awkward neologism has it — the search results?

One of the authors of this book (Smith) was working at AltaVista in the mid-1990s when that company tried to pioneer the inclusion of advertisements at the top of pages of search results. Users objected, and AltaVista quickly dropped the idea.

Google must have been watching, because it introduced the same idea a couple of years later, but much more carefully. It set up a marketplace to allow advertisers to bid on specific search terms, including a tool to actually design the ads — simple, text-based ads that loaded quickly, right along with the free search results.

Google placed paid search results only on the side of their search results. Users could easily ignore them, or get rid of them entirely simply by narrowing the browser window to exclude the ads on the side.

Google also made sure the results were useful. It carefully monitored user behavior and did research to make sure that users valued the paid results just as much as the free ones.

Google introduced this model by ensuring that only a few ads appeared at first, because it took time for search advertising to build. Now the number of ads is increasing. Gradually, Google has added paid results at the top of the page as well as on the side — the practice that so angered AltaVista users in the 1990s — and added shopping-oriented results as well.

Now, paid results can be quite obtrusive, especially for popular terms — and especially when all the paid results go in a commercial direction (such as swimming pool cleaning products when you're looking for something non-commercial, such as pool safety tips).

A search for *diamonds* shows just how far free search results can be pushed down the page — see Figure 2-4. In the first visible page of search results, eleven paid results appear — and only three free ones.

However, users continue to rate the paid results highly — at least, highly enough that the money Google makes outweighs any concerns. So Google has created a highly successful business around search, one that you can use to your own advantage, as shown in Book VI.

**Book II
Chapter 2**

**How Google
Search Works**

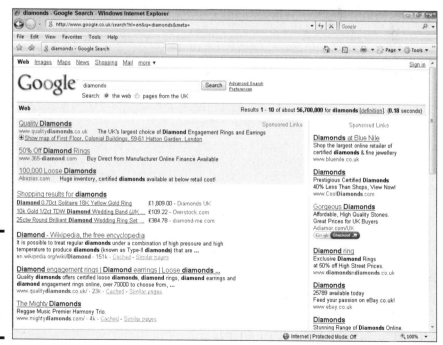

Figure 2-4:
Are
diamonds
paid
search's
best friend?

What Makes Google So Special?

Why has Google won the search wars, to become one of the most powerful companies in the world — and to be able to offer all the services described in this book?

PageRank is a big part of the reason, and Google's strengthening it with traffic information helps Google offer the best search around. Google Ads simultaneously make huge amounts of money for Google and add another dimension to Google's search option.

But what else powers Google? One thing that Google is dedicated to is *speed*. Google has always made a major priority of speed.

Google has created a combination of hardware and software that runs Web databases faster than any competing system — providing, it's estimated, 25% more work for a given amount of money. This, combined with Google's market-leading capability to make money, allows it to pour more resources into any aspect of search or related businesses than the competition.

This focus on speed is part of a more general trait of Google's: a very strong concern for users. Google's gentle introduction of paid results alongside its free results is an example of how it has been able get away with things that competitors can't — by doing them thoughtfully and carefully.

This concern permeates everything Google does. The company is far from perfect, but it tries hard to do the right thing, which has enabled its other offerings, such as Google Mail and other topics covered in this book, to start off strong — and keep improving.

What's Wrong with Google?

Google is constantly adjusting its algorithms, partly to make them work better and partly to stop people from "gaming" them. So any statement as to what's wrong with Google has to be provisional, as the reality of how Google works is changing all the time.

Still, there are some underlying concerns inherent in any search engine. Google has solved some of them, but has left others largely unaddressed. These areas are crucial to your understanding of how much work you should put into Google. These concerns include

+ **Common terms**. This is the biggest problem with any search engine — common words and words with multiple meanings. It's not fair that a businesswoman named Francesca Hargreaves should be much easier to *Google*, using the word as a verb, than a businessman named Robert Parker; but she is, and to such an extent that people might not even try with the latter name.

And terms like *pool, park,* or *polo,* to name a few, pose problems because of multiple meanings, so that, again, some searches might not even be tried. The fixes for these problems are not simple; Google avoids any that impose burdens on the user. (Google won't start asking you if a term is a noun or a verb anytime soon.)

✦ **Global focus**. Google tends to return globally useful results, but many, many searches would benefit from a local focus. If I'm sat in Manchester, as the Brits put it, searching for a tennis racket, I really don't care if a store in London is having a sale on them (unless the racket is so specialized that I'd be willing to send away for it). Even so, I'd want local options first.

Google has tried to address this need with searches based on Google Maps, but this doesn't address the needs of people who always search from the Google home page first. And neither is nearly an ideal solution.

For the best example of locally focused search we've seen yet, try `yell.com`, a search engine in the UK, which one of the authors of this book (Smith) has used to do market research. It's not perfect, but it's far simpler and easier for geographically based search of businesses than anything Google offers. If only `yell.com` would extend it's offering to America.

✦ **Oldies focus**. Google's focus on frequently linked pages is very effective, but leads to a problem. When a topic is new on the Web, dense webs of links establish themselves, and then remain relatively unchanged by newer additions. So searches tend to get results from either the beginning of the Web or from the period when a search term first burst into public consciousness.

A good example is the Web site of the Barack Obama campaign. Before the election in November 2008, it made a lot of sense for the campaign Web site to come up tops in search results. Since then, however, the campaign site persists on top, even though its real-world relevance has dropped to a much lower level. (Until 2012, at least.)

Figure 2-5 shows the results of a search for *Barack Obama* after the election.

✦ **Good beats best**. Related to the oldies focus is the fact that good, well-established links can beat newer, better ones. If you were to create a very, very good HTML Web site today, one for use by Web authors, it would probably be impossible to improve that site's search engine ranking now that it is up against older articles, stories, essays, and how-tos about Web authoring, all of which point to a "favored few" of long-established HTML sites.

Book II
Chapter 2

How Google
Search Works

Figure 2-5:
Is the
Obama
campaign
still tops?

What does all this mean to business? For very broad, or fairly broad search terms, nationally or globally available products and services that have been around for a long time tend to beat newer or locally or regionally available ones, even if the latter are better for at least some potential customers.

One of the few ways to break through is to create a strong brand image around a distinctive name and then get people to search on it — which is fine, but means you're spending a whole bunch of time and money offline before you even have a chance online.

Google Searching for Yourself

A fun way to learn about Google search and to lay the groundwork for optimizing your Web site — and perhaps even your entire business — for search, is to search for yourself, your business, your products or services, and anything related to them on the Web using Google.

Brainstorming and systematic searching take two different mindsets, so in this section we suggest ideas for brainstorming. In the next chapter, we demonstrate a structure for searching systematically and putting the results to use.

As you try the techniques below, take notes on anything that surprises you — you can follow up on it later when you do a more systematic search.

While you're searching for yourself, use the following suggestions to better understand Google search — and your own potential for using it:

✦ **Start with main search:** In Google's main search page, search for your own name (including any variations), your business name, and any product names or services that you offer.

This tells you what if any information about you and your business is already on the Web — good or bad. It also tells you how your competitors appear online; and much more.

✦ **Other Google sites:** Try the same searches on Google sites for one or more other countries you're interested in. Just search for *Google* and the country name. Leading sites that use English include Google Canada (google.ca), Google UK (google.co.uk), and Google India (google.co.in) — there is no separate US search site. Leading non-English sites include Google Mexico (google.com.mx), Google Spain (google.es), Google France (google.fr), and Google Germany (google.de).

Figure 2-6 shows search results for the term *climate change* from Google India. Note how the results are from Indian sources and have Indian references.

Book II
Chapter 2

How Google
Search Works

Figure 2-6:
Search on *climate change* from an Indian perspective.

✦ **Adding local considerations:** Again, in main search, repeat the same elements, but add one or more place names where you do business (or want to). This is a trick some of your customers may use to find you or products and services like yours.

✦ **Advanced Search:** Try more sophisticated searches in Advanced Search, seeing what it takes to get results relevant to your business. Realize that few of your customers may use Advanced Search — using it is a learning and exploratory tool for you.

✦ **Advanced search plus:** Click the Date, Usage Rights, Numeric Range, and More links in Advanced Search and look for more recently updated pages, results from various countries, and so on.

Broadening your ego search

Now that you've done a deep search on the one thing that all of us find most interesting — oneself — it's time to broaden it. Use some or all the techniques you've just tried to search on related topics:

✦ **Competitors:** Look up your competitors — global, national, regional, and local. See how easy or hard it is to get different kinds of competitors to come up near the top of a search, using local place names, for instance. See if you get different results if you search for recently updated pages.

✦ **Related types of products and services:** Look up products and services similar to the ones you're involved with. See what the commonalities and differences are among them. This helps you see what common terms get people to your general topic and what unique terms set you apart.

✦ **Professional and trade organizations:** What are the organizations related to your area of business? What terms are related to them? You can include the names of organizations you belong to in your Web pages to help them turn up in related searches.

✦ **Conferences and events:** Determine how hard it is to find conferences and events you know about from your area of business. Figure 2-7 shows a search for *product management conferences*. Again, you can include relevant conferences and events in your Web pages to improve results.

This exercise should help you think in a creative way about search, perhaps for the first time. You may just have eliminated your need for an expensive consultant to help you think through the basics of search! You may also begin to see how related terms work together to create *webs* of meaning — or something resembling meaning — that Google's spiders can identify and use. This is part of the reason that much of the energy devoted to search engine optimization is wasted — trying to trick Google's spiders merely forces you to create a Web site whose pages lack the natural interrelatedness that attracts people to value your Web site, to use it, and then to do business with you.

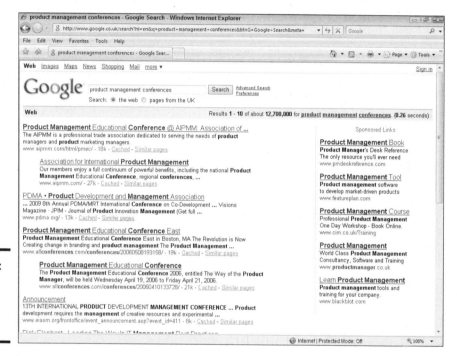

**Book II
Chapter 2**

**How Google
Search Works**

Figure 2-7:
Product management is a hot topic.

Checking domain names

Now that you've expanded your mind through a sort of disciplined approach to Google search, it's a good time to learn how to look for domain names. We talk a lot more about choosing a good domain name in Book IV, but now is a good time to experiment.

One of the key elements in attracting Google's spiders is having key search terms in the domain name of your Web site. So try some domain names that use key search terms.

Some sites do strange things in response to your searches, such as reserving names for a few days so you can register only with them. Be careful whom you use.

TIP

One site we like for trying different domain names is `123reg.com`. (See Figure 2-8.) `123reg.com` seems simple, usable, and honest. (At this writing, anyway.)

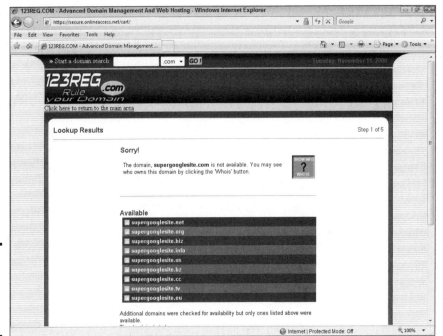

Figure 2-8:
Check for domain names on 123reg.com.

While you're experimenting, try any of the following approaches:

✦ **Your name:** Your name is, of course, the thing that people associate most strongly with you. Let's say your business is called The Cleaners. You'll never get that as a domain name, but MelloCleaners might work well for you — assuming your name is Mello.

✦ **Your business name:** Try your business name, just in case it's available as-is as a domain name. Try simple variations — but ignore the complex ones, as your customers are unlikely to remember or try them.

✦ **Words relating to your local area:** This works well, especially if you are located well within the borders of a well-known area with a convenient name. WillowParkCleaners is tough because there are a lot of Willow Parks. ScarboroughCleaners might seem tough, because Scarborough is hard to spell — but not for people who live there.

✦ **A key product or service:** You might have a branded product or service you can use. If you describe your cleaning as FuzzBusting, you could combine FuzzBustingCleaners as a domain name.

Record any good names you find — but, unless you find a perfect name, you may not want to actually reserve a name yet. It's very easy to spend quite a bit of money reserving each of the increasingly good ideas you come up with as you search — and then end up using a domain name registrar that isn't the best. See Book IV before committing.

A Note of Caution: The Google Hacking Database

Now is also a good time to learn about some of the things that Google — and other search engines — can do *to* you as well as *for* you. A good source for this is the Google Hacking Database, available at `http://johnny.ihack stuff.com/ghdb.php`.

The Google Hacking Database shows the results of Google searches that have turned up confidential or sensitive information that people put on their Web servers. Putting a Web page behind password protection or not linking to it from within your Web site doesn't guarantee that a search engine won't find it.

Some people even put passwords in files that Google can find!

The Google Hacking Database (see Figure 2-9) is no doubt embarrassing — or worse — for the many people whose confidential information ends up in it. But at least, if a site turns up in the Google Hacking Database, it's likely that the person "named and shamed" learns about it. Otherwise, the confidential information could be accessed secretly, with the owner having no way to learn he is being exposed.

Google's spiders can also be used to execute attacks on Web sites. Though Google tries hard to prevent attacks using known methods, it can't avoid every possible trick someone might pull in the future.

So be very, very careful about what machine hosts your Web site and about what information you put there. Hosting your Web site outside your own company and its network protects you from most problems; not "cleverly" — it's not clever — "hiding" — it's not hidden — confidential information on your site protects you from the rest.

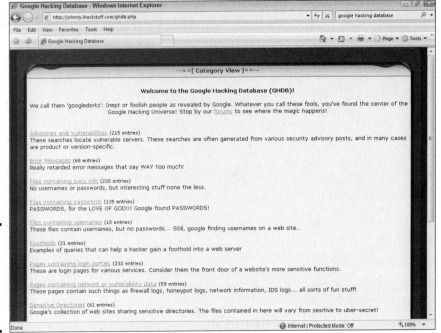

Figure 2-9:
The Google
Hacking
Database is
good as a
warning.

Chapter 3: Understanding How Your Customers Use Google

In This Chapter

✔ Examining how people really search

✔ Using the different types of searches

✔ Searching outside of Google

✔ Pinpointing your key search terms

There's an old riddle that captures some of the uncertainty of life: Which came first, the chicken or the egg? Or, in the case of your Web presence: Which is more important — your Web site or the effort to help people find your Web site?

The answer to this question can be found in another riddle: What are the three most important things in business? Location, location, location. Similarly, online, the three most important things are: Being found, being found, being found. Helping people find your Web site, then, takes precedence over the site itself. So, in this book, we describe how searching works and then investigate what this implies for your Web presence. Then, in Book IV, we describe how to create a Web site that includes search-friendliness.

Google Search is the key to the success of Google. Having watched Google from its very beginnings, we understand just how much better it has always been than anything else out there, and how much users and the entire Internet-based economy depend on Google Search.

Getting good results from Google Search can be absolutely critical for your business — or it can be merely very important.

Understanding How People Really Search

The practice of making a Web site work better with Google Search is called *search engine optimization*, or *SEO*. The common approach to SEO is based on a very outmoded idea of the way people use the Internet.

The old way of looking at SEO presupposes that people come to the Web to *surf* — that is, to look for interesting things that they might or might not do something about. In this view of the online world, the purpose of SEO is to associate your organization — usually your business — with very broad concepts, and to "win" the "battle" for good search results in broad categories like *furniture*, *beds*, or *blankets*.

This can be a winning business model for specialized businesses that can completely re-orient itself around Web search. But if you have a real business — that is, real expertise or experience, which you use to offer useful products and/or services to real people for real money — you can't just change everything you're doing to fit search engines.

Luckily, real business works well with the way that most people really search most of the time. Research shows that people come to the Web to try to get things done; usually to find very specific information or fulfill a specific task. They use any information they already have to "drill down" to the information or task they need just as fast as they can.

Also, search engines ignore the organization of a Web site as do, to a certain extent, users. To a search engine, a Web site is just a bunch of pages.

Research shows that people working their way through search results can be as oblivious to your site's organization as the search engine is. Sometimes they don't even know, or much care, what site they're on; they just view the Web one page at a time.

According to the old idea of Web search, people go online to buy. Today, this is only sometimes true, mostly for sites people already trust with their credit card details. Companies that do lots of online business either also have big offline businesses that people already trust; invest a lot of money in online and offline advertising and marketing to gain trust; or accept that they can only convert a very small percentage of unusually trusting shoppers into buyers.

People mainly search for information like the following:

+ Product or service information they can use for a purchase — often a real-world purchase

+ How-to information

+ Frequently updated information such as news

+ Real-world data such as names, addresses, and phone numbers

+ General facts and information on topics of work, educational or personal interest — such as those found at Wikipedia, the popular online encyclopedia.

Even people who are willing to buy from you online often want to call you first — or, after they have purchased from you, to call you as a follow up. So a key discipline in making the most out of online search is to make it very easy for people to find core information: your business name, personal name, address, and phone number. If you can make that information easy to find online, the rest becomes much easier. If you don't make it easy to find online, your Web presence may be pretty useless.

Defining What Google Is Best At

Google is a much better search engine than any competitor, as shown by research and validated by market response. When Google first came out, it was far better than anything else; for many searches, Google made the difference as to whether it was worthwhile to search online. Competitors have closed the gap but not erased it.

Google is absolutely amazing at helping to find specific terms that have a distinctive meaning online, such as names. And it has added options for searching within countries and languages.

Figure 3-1 shows the Google search page for Spain at www.google.es. Note that there are options for searching only in Spanish (*páginas en español*) and only within Spain (*páginas de España*).

Newer versions of popular browsers tend to allow search from within a special area of the browser or from the Web domain name line. Unfortunately, these searches don't offer the Search-in-my-Country option. Users outside the U.S. must make a difficult choice between using the convenience of the built-in options or opting for a full browser window, where they can limit their search to a country-specific one.

If you aren't based in the U.S., you have to optimize for both Web-wide and country-specific searches.

Take Google's advice

Google offers a limited amount of advice about optimizing your site for Google search. It's worth checking out; visit www.google.com/support/Webmasters/bin/ answer.py?answer=35769#1 to get the scoop. Then use the advice you find to really tie a search to the contents of your site to create the best opportunities for your business.

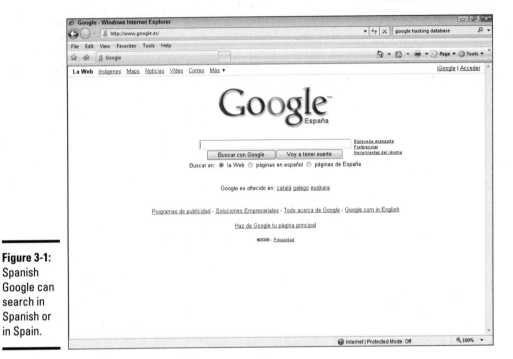

Figure 3-1:
Spanish
Google can
search in
Spanish or
in Spain.

Exploring the Different Types of Searches

Let's consider some different types of searches people might undertake and how you might make your site visible to them.

Searching by name

This is an extremely common type of search. Someone knows the name of a business, or a name related to that business, and types it into Google, hoping to find out basic information — let's focus for the moment on your phone number.

People who know the name of your business well might try to guess your Web site's domain name to get information such as your phone number. Increasingly, people use Google in preference to guessing domain names, as it's faster and more efficient in many cases.

It's critically important that potential customers can find you by a Google search on the name of your business. Many people, especially younger people, do or start to do their business online. If those people can't find you, they'll find someone else.

The main reason people stop using a supplier is a problem called *failure to supply*: The business stops meeting basic requirements for product, price, delivery time, and so on. Today, a form of "supplying" is being able to be found online. If you can't supply an easy way for online users to find you — even people who are currently your customers — they'll find another supplier.

How well can searching by name work for your business or organization? Here are some keys to successful "findability" online:

✦ **Use a name that's distinctive but not hard to spell:** It's good to have a personal, business, or other important name relating to your business that's distinctive, but not so hard to spell that it discourages people from trying to find you.

   For example, *Bud Smith* or *Ryan Williams* are just okay as search terms — none of the four words is very distinctive.

✦ **Have a distinctive type of business:** It's good to have a clearly defined type of business — and that can be used in a search.

✦ **Include a specific kind of product or service:** It's good to have products and services under recognizable names that people are able to search for — and to feature these names in your Web site.

✦ **Use a distinctive region or area:** It's good to be in a well-defined and clearly named geographical area. Many cities and towns run together, so searchers don't know just what name to use as part of a search.

If you are easy to find with a search by name you can be effective with lots and lots of searchers even if you have only a small Web design and SEO budget. It's also what your customers most want, need, and expect of you.

As an example, let's look at a search by name for Subway — imagining that the user is thinking of the sandwich shop chain rather than New York City's underground transport network. The search for Subway is shown in Figure 3-2.

Now let's look for a restaurant called Top of the Park in San Diego, as shown in Figure 3-3. Unfortunately, the search results don't place it at the very top — although it does come up in the first five search results, which is not bad. But the user would have to scan pretty carefully to find it — a quick glance might not do it.

Of course, it's more likely that the searcher would remember the exact name of Subway, which is strongly branded and advertised relentlessly. Top of the Park, which is just one local restaurant, might not come to mind as easily. (Note that a restaurant in Canada appears in the fourth search result, and the one in San Diego, in the fifth result.)

Figure 3-2:
A search for Subway sandwiches hits the jackpot.

Figure 3-3:
San Diego's Top of the Park makes the top five.

Users make successful searches relating to other businesses all the time, so if they fail when they look for you, they won't blame Google, and they certainly won't blame themselves; they'll think it's your fault.

Searching by type

This is another extremely common type of search. People search for a type of business. They know what they want — and this is how they try to get it.

Using this approach, people will search for *hardware store*, *grocery store,* and so on. In most cases, this kind of search has to be combined with a local area name to be very useful.

However, types of businesses and the products they sell can be vague in the customer's mind — and in the Web site creator's as well. For instance, drugstores in the US and newsagents in the UK are two types of businesses that sell a variety of products. People might not know to search for this type of store — or they might search for it and then become frustrated when it doesn't have the product they want.

Many of these businesses do not have a Web site — and, when they do, often these sites do not list all products. So it's easy for a user to be uncertain whether they have really found what they want.

A search for *drugstore* in the US Google site turns up an online pharmacy and several major drugstore chains, as shown in Figure 3-4. It would take quite a bit more work for someone searching for a local drugstore to find it from these results alone — and an additional effort to see if a given product was available there.

For some rare kinds of businesses, a search by business name can be sufficient by itself. For instance, tobacconists are increasingly rare. People looking for one might be willing to order online, so they do a non-local search.

For most businesses, search by type is just as important for what it won't do as what it does. It's unlikely that any given business you have or are likely to embark in is going to "win" a category of search by type results.

For instance, let's say you have an independent drugstore or are about to start one. Unless you plan to become the biggest in your country — that is, *country* as defined by the way Google splits up its national search pages, not by the way the United Nations does it — it's very unlikely you can ever "win" a search on *drugstore* in Google's free search results.

Getting "search by type" right can require a lot of creativity and research. For instance, you might have a drugstore, but why do most people searching online want to find a drugstore? You might have to conduct some research with customers to find out — and find ways to put some key product names or product types in your Web page alongside your business type and your location.

Figure 3-4:
There's
a lot of
competition
for the top
drugstore
spot.

For most of us, searches by type need to be combined with searches by name, product, or area to give the searcher a good chance to find specific businesses. So you need to get the type right — but also get the other types of searches right as well.

Searching by region or area

As mentioned earlier, Google is not really that great at local area search. Location is very important in people's lives, but the main Google search — the one so very many people use — doesn't have any direct way to narrow a search geographically.

So users are left to their own devices to figure out how to do this within a search. Often very many ways exist to describe a location. People can enter a city, town, even a street name.

This intersects poorly with the way businesses, especially small ones, tend to set up their Web sites. Very often, the only locality information on a Web site is the town or city name that's part of the address. But this often doesn't include the neighborhood area that a user might have included in his or her search.

Searching by region or area might be the most important type of search in helping customers to find you, yet it's very difficult because of how vaguely defined locations are. People can search on ZIP codes or post codes, area code prefixes, street names (spelled correctly or not), landmarks, and so on.

Again, it might be worth doing some research — a fancy way, in this case, of saying "asking some customers how they think of you." You can even ask yourself and your employees how you could describe your location to others, then turn that around and use those terms in your Web site to describe your location in a search-friendly way.

Using combined searches

It's very common for people to do combined searches, with some assortment of personal names, business names, product names, product types, and names of areas. This is often amazingly effective — but also often an opportunity for mistakes, again, by the searcher or the Web site creator.

Figure 3-5 shows the search results for *top of the park san diego*. Now the results for the Top of the Park restaurant in San Diego are much better. (They're a bit confusing because the hotel that houses the restaurant has the top spot — with a map — but useful nonetheless.)

Book II
Chapter 3

Understanding How
Your Customers
Use Google

Figure 3-5: Adding a city name gets us to the Top of the Park.

Combined searches of this type are extremely important — and very hard to guess right. It can take a lot of experimentation and work to cover most of the ways that people actually try to find you — but it's worth the effort if you can help more of them do so.

You should experiment with finding yourself and your business and contact information online. Even if you don't have a Web site, you may find yourself in a directory of some type.

Searching outside of Google

Because Google is not so great at local search, many of its remaining competitors are locally competent directories like Yahoo! Yellow Pages and Superpages.

You can use your entry in these directories as a testing ground for your search entries. And you can optimize your entries, which helps you learn even more about search.

Of course, these directories are far from perfect themselves. Figure 3-6 shows the Yahoo! Yellow Pages search results for Top of the Park in San Diego. Nothing found!

Figure 3-6: There's no Top of the Park in Yahoo! Local for San Diego, CA.

Identifying Your Key Search Terms

It takes skill — and work — to help people find you using Google search. Fill in Table 3-1 with some words relating to your business. This helps you put together or improve your Web site — and helps you select your domain name.

Table 3-1	List Terms Relating to Your Business	
	Information	*How well known?*
Your name(s)		
Business name		
Product names		
Services names		
Street name		
Neighborhood name		
Nearby landmark		
Town name		
City name		

Listing these terms is like taking an X-ray of how your business can potentially look to a search engine being driven by one of your current or potential customers.

When you've listed the terms, process the list some more. Underline the top three most important terms relating to how you're known. Circle the three that are most unique.

These are the terms to emphasize in three areas:

✦ **Your domain name:** Your domain name is very important, meaning it needs to be memorable to people — and in its effect on searches for terms reflected in the domain name.

✦ **Your Web pages:** If your local area is called Pacific Beach, but the official city name in your address is San Diego, you may not even have Pacific Beach on the Web site! Now you know to fix this.

✦ **Your marketing:** Some businesses are now using phrases like "Search for San Diego tapas" in their marketing material to reinforce their identity and at the same time help people remember how to find them online. Such a phrase can go on printed items such as menus, price lists, letterhead, business cards, and e-mail. If you do this kind of thing, you're instantly part of a hot trend — integrated online and offline marketing!

Chapter 4: Search Engine Optimization Basics

In This Chapter

✔ Optimizing your Web site organization for search

✔ Understanding SEO "tricks"

✔ Directing traffic to your home page or product page

✔ Creating content for SEO

*P*eople think search engine optimization (SEO) is difficult — and it is, especially if you try to "trick" the search engine into showing your page when it's not really a good result for the user. As Google changes its algorithms and other "tricksters" compete with you for high rankings, you are in a constant battle for top spots.

But "honest" search engine optimization is not that hard, at least from a technical point of view. Google "drills into" your Web site and finds key terms so it can offer your Web pages to searchers. If you pick key terms that relate well to what you offer and arrange your key terms so that Google can find them reasonably close to one another on your Web pages, search optimization will work for you.

A Sample Business Web Strategy

Discussing SEO in the abstract doesn't do much good. It really makes sense only in the context of a specific Web site.

Real Web sites change all the time, so let's create an imaginary one and use it as an example. Let's say we're starting a horse-related shop on the local Main Street in our suburban location, Pacific Beach, in San Diego. (We know we won't offend any real horse businesses here because PB, as locals call it, is pretty much full of people — no room for horses, stables or, as horse people call them, tack shops.)

Let's call our business Horse Emporium. We might want to expand, so we won't put the place name in the business name. But we want customers now, so we advertise the place name prominently alongside the business name.

Our main business is the store itself. Selling horse stuff online doesn't make all that much sense. Because much of it is heavy and expensive to ship, people tend to buy at real shops within driving distance. Also, people don't want to burden themselves or their horses with gear that's ugly or that doesn't fit, so they want to check stuff out in advance — that is, they want to shop, live and in person — and they want to be able to return it, get it repaired, and so on.

All this fits with the reality that few of these products are suitable for high volumes of online sales compared to total sales through real stores. Amazon's initial focus on books is so brilliant because books are extremely well suited to online sales. Yet even with this careful focus, Amazon seems to be targeting a goal of about 5% of the total book market, happily leaving the other 95% to "real" bookstores.

Amazon is using its strength in books to add other categories as well, no doubt with differing levels of expectations and plans about how well those categories will do. Figure 4-1 shows some of the many different kinds of products Amazon offers. (And with which you'll be competing if you sell in those areas.)

But don't give up hope about competing with Amazon. Their online structure and way of doing business works great for books. For electronic products, on the other hand, many customers find it much less useful.

Figure 4-1: Amazon sells all sorts of stuff.

So the first purpose of our horse store Web site is to let people find us in our local area. Including our name, address, and contact information is, therefore, crucial.

However, we also know that e-commerce does work well for some products (thanks, Amazon). We also know that e-commerce works well for repeat sales to existing customers, especially for re-orders of existing products. (We know this more subtle point from more than a decade of Web site development experience.)

We have all sorts of competitors for, say, books about horses. (Darn you, Amazon.) What do we offer our customers that's unique? Personal recommendations from us. Again, it's people who have come to know us, or know of us, that buy from us online.

So we develop an initial e-commerce capacity right away. But order-taking and credit card authorization are done — wait for it — *over the telephone*. This keeps us from having to invest the time and effort needed for full e-commerce right away, and it keeps our customers from having to worry about putting credit card information into a small site that they might not trust.

This gives us a good reason to build a Products area in our Web site that serves several purposes, including

+ **Establishing credibility:** When people see names they recognize on our site, it helps them trust us more.

+ **Encouraging "normal" sales:** If someone sees a saddle online, he or she might well come to you to inspect it further in person — and buy other things on the same trip.

+ **Encouraging Web links:** Our site has internal links to and from the page with the saddle on it. We can also hope for, or actively seek, other pages to link to our product pages, such as the one for the saddle.

+ **Bulking up your site:** We've found in our own work that Web sites get more attractive and interesting when they pass a "critical mass" of interesting and valuable content. (But stay below the "red line" at which sites become too complicated and hard to use.) Well-chosen product pages add "good" — that is, useful, relevant, and sales-generating — bulk.

So we're going to create a simple Web site structure bulked up with some product pages that serve multiple purposes. We don't expect to become the world's leading online seller of horse products overnight; we're just trying to build up a real business.

Specializing in online sales is okay, too. The key word is *specializing*. If we are selling horse stuff online, we should specialize in some area — saddles are too heavy, so perhaps we might specialize in horse blankets.

A Simple Web Site Organization

So how is this Web site organized? It should have a simple and recognizable structure. Remember, it will be accessed by busy people who are in a rush — and by computers that operate according to fixed, inflexible rules. And it will be paid for by people whose money has to stretch in a lot of directions — toward us.

You can make it easy for everyone, including yourself by creating a simple structure. Initially, most areas consist of one page, except Products:

+ **Home:** Specify that your Web site will have a home page and then create it later. The home page needs to be interesting, incorporate key search terms, and be updated regularly. So save writing it until the end.

   If you write the home page text early on, it may contain stuff that should be on other pages.

+ **Contact Us:** This is the most important page on most sites! It should contain a map, a postal name and address, and other area-related information. Be sure to include business hours.

   If you put your e-mail address on your Contact Us page, it can be read by "bots" that crawl the Web looking for e-mail addresses and then sell them to e-mail spammers. One common workaround is to list an e-mail address with words, such as "contactus <at> gmail.com". You can explain your use of *<at>* instead of @ in a note, but many people understand without being told.

+ **About Us:** It's good to have the About Us page separate from the Contact Us page. The About Us page is where you put what's described, in the French phrase, as your *raison d'etre*, your "reason for being" — what inspires you to be in business, what makes you different. Looking at it from the customer's point of view — this page states why they should shop with you.

+ **Products and Services areas:**. You should have a Products area, a Services area, or both, depending on your business. Keep this (or these) simple; start with a category home page summarizing your products or services and then add links to your most popular offerings.

+ **Press or Links pages:** If there are already press clippings about you, definitely include excerpts and links to them on your site. If not, you can get some of the same effect by linking to pages of resources for your area of business. This is also a good start for "link exchanges" with other sites.

+ **Blog entries or articles:** A big secret of SEO is to get other people to link to your site. Some links might come from directories of local sites (which you may have to pay for), newspaper articles about your business and, so on. But many other links can come if you provide interesting articles or blog entries.

Figure 4-2 shows this simple layout in graphical form, just to give you the idea.

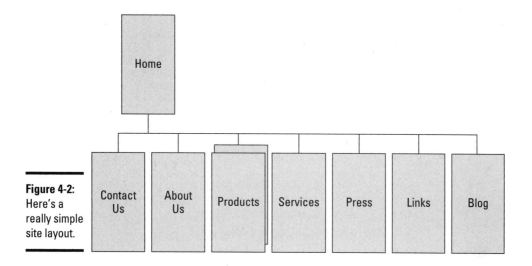

Figure 4-2:
Here's a
really simple
site layout.

Using Web Site "Tricks" for SEO

People seeking SEO for their sites are always looking for magic bullets. The trouble is that the really "tricky" approaches are the kind that get ignored whenever the search engine gurus change their ranking algorithms.

Here are some technically oriented tips you can use in your Web site that should actually make your site better for users, and which should also continue to work across reasonably anticipated changes in Web search algorithms — see Book 4 for Web site details:

✦ **Start now:** Get your search terms into key locations early. The network of links to your site that Google will use to improve your site's ranking builds up over time — the sooner you can help it get going, the better.

✦ **Put key terms in your domain name:** Work key site-related terms in your domain name. For instance, HorseEmporiumPB might just get you searchers who remember your business name — or, less usefully, remember "that horse shop in PB".

✦ **Put key terms in your `<title>` tags:** A `<title>` tag is the area of your Web page that determines the words that go in the top of the Web browser window. (In Figure 4-1, these are the words "Amazon.com: Online shopping…".) Make sure every Web page in your site has a title, and put keywords in it. If you're using a Web designer and your Web pages don't have titles, consider getting a new designer.

✦ **Put key terms in your header tags:** Header tags use the HTML codes `<H1>` and `</H1>` to surround top-level tags, `<H2>` and `</H2>` for the next level down, and so on. They appear on your Web page as headers.

✦ **Use text links between pages:** Even if you use graphics for links, supplement these with text links so Web spiders can index your site. CSS allows you to make text links look almost as snazzy as graphical ones.

✦ **Use text as a supplement to graphics:** If you have actual information in graphics, use an <ALT> tag to duplicate it in text on the same page.

✦ **Include a site map:** A site map is a catalog of links that's just as useful to a search bot as it is to your users. Figure 4-3 shows the site map for NASA, the American National Aeronautics and Space Administration. Make sure the links are text, not graphics.

✦ **Put your search terms in plain text near the top of the page:** In some early search engine algorithms, your page got a higher score if the search terms were repeated as often as possible in all these locations. But search engines now mostly discount such repetition. Just get your terms in once, in a sensible way, early on.

✦ **Add new content to your Web page regularly:** Search engines tend to "like" sites that have been recently updated. So have the new or updated pages link back to your old, unchanged pages.

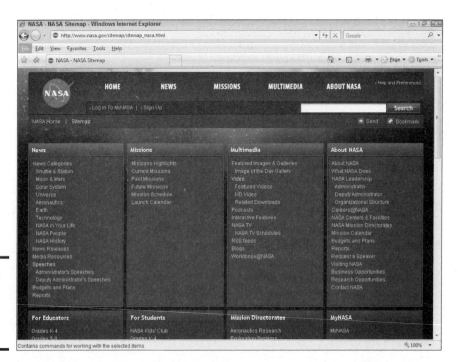

Figure 4-3:
NASA
has an
expansive
site map.

Old-style HTML didn't allow designers to control the specific look of `<H1>`, `<H2>`, and other tags, so designers ignored them and created headers using other tags, such as `<B>` for bold. This is fine for looks, but it prevents search engines from analyzing your page most effectively. Some designers even (*shudder*) made the headers into graphics, which gave complete typographical control but made the underlying words completely inaccessible to spiders. Newer CSS codes allow the best of both worlds, so make sure you or your Web designer uses them. (Make your Web designer show you how he or she is using CSS to make your Web pages search engine-friendly.)

Directing traffic to home pages or product pages

One of the key (almost philosophical) issues in search-optimizing your Web site is the question of targeting: Should you try to bring all Web site traffic to your home page, or should you try to direct specific searches to different, potentially more appropriate pages in your Web site?

Ideally, you would send people to the pages most appropriate to their searches, rather than to your Web home page. People are busy and impatient, and if you send them to the home page first, they might not make the extra effort to go to the pages in your site that they really need to see. So you and they lose the benefit of their seeing that page.

However, in the real world, as someone just starting into search engine optimization, you should almost certainly focus your energies. That means targeting most searches to the home page.

What can I expect from a site designer?

A great many Web site designers began as graphic designers for print who got asked to create Web sites. These people are originally trained to spend hours and hours creating really good-looking, high-resolution graphics, which don't work well on the Web anyway. Their skills in the many disciplines needed for successful Web sites vary wildly, and generally fall below average.

Few Web site designers operate as business people first and foremost. Be extremely careful when choosing a Web site designer, and do most of the work — site structure, writing words, and setting goals — yourself. Call in the designer specifically for design.

After you have clear goals and a limited remit for your potential site designer, start looking for one. Try to identify someone you can meet with in person and who's done work you like for people you know. If you can't find someone through contacts, ask for — and check — references.

That means your home page content should include keywords from the most important pages of your Web site. That points to it being a kind of highlights page.

This is a bit clumsy, aesthetically, but a favored strategy even from sites with tremendous resources. As shown in Figure 4-1, mighty Amazon has these words in the title of its home page: Amazon.com: Online Shopping for Electronics, Apparel, Computers, Books, DVDs & More. It hasn't divided up its big categories, but instead it has concentrated them on the home page.

Amazon would rather get more traffic to its home page — then counts on its users being clever and motivated enough to get where they need to go using a carefully designed site search and site navigation. It has not tried to direct a search to land closer to the destination page.

You can still optimize search for "direct hits" when the user enters a very specific term. The Amazon.com Grocery page, as shown in Figure 4-4, has this title: "Amazon.com Grocery: Snacks, Cookies and Candy, Coffee and Tea, Natural & Organic, Baby Care". Apparently it's looking to bring in hits for these lower-level and more specific search terms.

Figure 4-4:
Amazon Grocery "titles" its own key search terms.

You can pick some product pages to optimize for the specific product name — and suppress that product name on the home page. But direct most or all your searches to the home page to start building "critical mass" for search.

Stuffing search terms into your site

Let's see if we can construct some search-friendly text for a Web site for a horse products store. The text still has to read well — no use bringing potential customers to a Web page and then repelling them with hard-to-read text!

Many users come to your site because they know about it through shopping at your store, reading your ads, and so on. These people are probably more likely to buy from you than people who find you through a Web search, so don't put them off.

On our imaginary site, let's identify our top few products and services as horse blankets, bridles, jackets, and horse-riding lessons. Now we want to gracefully "stuff" these key terms into our site text while still keeping it readable:

✦ **Title:** The title for the Horse Emporium home page could be "Horse Emporium: Blankets, Bridles, Jackets, Lessons, and More!" Note that we depend on the context to help visitors understand that we mean horse blankets, jackets to be worn when riding horses, lessons in horseback riding, and so on.

✦ **Heading:** Because we've covered a broad range of terms in the title, we can use the heading — with the `<H1>` HTML tag — for focus. If we've done an article on the lessons we offer, it might be: "Why Lessons Help Even Experienced Riders."

✦ **First paragraph:** We can't count on a search engine looking more than 50 words into a site. Because we want to get another repetition of key terms in, we might use initial sentences like the following: "We've written a new article explaining how lessons help even the most experienced riders among us. And we have new offerings in blankets, bridles, and jackets."

   The next paragraph might go on to elaborate on the article — now that we have links to our key terms up front, we can relax a bit and be sure to finish what we've started.

SEO advice varies widely. For instance, some experts might say the preceding use of terms makes the text hard to read. Others might say too few terms are used — that we should put in more terms, used more densely.

This stuff can drive you nuts. Create the page your desired site visitors would like to read with links they'd like to visit and then concentrate on other aspects of your business.

Creating Web site content for SEO

Most of us who have spent much time — perhaps that's too much time? — surfing the Web have encountered text that seems to repeat the same terms over and over. This is an attempt to attract high rankings from search engines, or, to put it more bluntly, to trick them.

This is silly (and becoming sillier) because search engines are only part of the picture. To get the most out of your Web pages, you need only three elements:

✦ **Keywords:** Keywords need to be present — they're the vital link between the user typing in search terms and your page. But using them too densely may hurt you in terms of the other two elements — and the search engine might even discount your page if the terms are overused.

✦ **Attractiveness to readers:** If someone comes to your page, takes one look at it, and leaves, you've done no one any good. You have to be quite careful — in these days when users have been burned by keyword-overloaded pages, very careful indeed — to use keywords appropriately.

✦ **Attractiveness to linkers:** As we describe in a later section, links from other Web sites are crucial to search engine success. People who are considering linking to your Web page are even more demanding than regular users, so overuse of keywords might keep you from getting links, the very things that are most helpful of all in raising your search engine rankings!

A good approach might be to write text the way you'd write normally — then review and edit it, if necessary, to work in one natural-sounding use of your search term within the first fifty or so words.

Figure 4-5 shows an example of text from the BATCS Web page at `batcs.co.uk`. BATCS sells a book called *Get Rid of your Accent*. The title of the book has been gently worked into the first few words of text. This helps search engines find this page when one of the authors' names and part or all the title of the book are used as search terms.

Getting links

The key insight of Google when it was first developed back in the late 1990s was that the popularity and usefulness of a Web page could be approximated by identifying whether there were links — most important, *external* links — to the Web page. Google valued the Web page more highly if it attracted links — and more highly still if the linking pages also attracted a lot of highly linked-to links. And these links in were valued more highly if they themselves attracted . . . and so on.

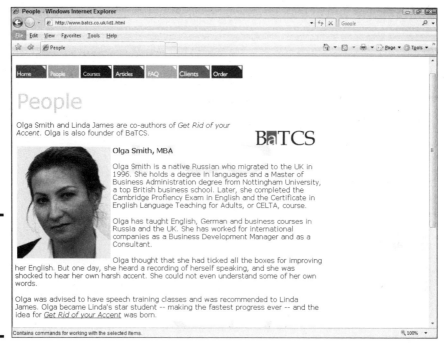

Figure 4-5:
BATCS
gets their
book title
and author
names into
text early.

This has worked out wonderfully for almost everyone involved. Earlier Web sites used only page analysis to identify search term matches; there was no way to separate popular or useful pages from others. This really annoyed people. For example, they might know that Ford Motor Company had several pages describing one of its cars, but these pages would be buried beneath obscure ones in the search results. Google enabled these pages to come up higher in the rankings because they were heavily linked to.

With Google Toolbar, Google was then able to add information about pages people actually visited. So if a new car company bought a lot of ads, it would get a lot of visits; this allowed Google to rank the popular page highly even before it attracted a lot of links.

What few people recognize is how hard this makes it for newer and smaller companies. Newer companies suffer because the Web of links on a given topic, quite possibly established years ago, excludes them. Smaller companies suffer because they lack the marketing muscle to get visits through other means and to get people updating directories, creating new links, and so on to include them.

Here are some tips for getting links — a frustrating process, but a rewarding one:

+ **Get your Web site right:** First of all, you have to create a non-embarrassing Web site. A great Web site is even better, but you're in a hurry. So ask for links early — but not until you've gotten your Web site to the point where it looks at least okay. When it does, even a "no" today might be turned into a "yes" later. But if the site isn't halfway decent, the "no" might be permanent.

+ **Decide what you're doing with content:** The best thing is to have a regularly updated Web site; that means you must keep it up. It's really embarrassing to have a site with a few "monthly updates" that abruptly ended six months ago. So make the tough call and decide what you can really sustain before you go asking for links.

+ **Link to others:** Linking to other sites helps your own rankings — only a bit, until you get some links in of your own — and helps your users. It also lays the groundwork for you to ask for links back. If you put in your links first, you're showing that your first concern is your users — and that you want links back to help users, not to play "Let's Make a Deal" with links back and forth.

+ **See who links to your competitors and other similar companies and products:** Your list of people to ask for a link should include people who have similar links already. Remember that your approach should be, "I'd like to see you help your users by including my worthwhile site," not "I've got my lawyer on the other line ready to subpoena you if you keep excluding my wonderful site from your links."

+ **Ask others:** Politely request links from people you link to, people who link to competitors, and others you've identified. When you find a suitable site, go straight to the top — track down the business's head, explain what you're after, and ask if he or she will help. After you get a couple, mention the people who already link to you in further requests for new links.

The links you get are directly useful, and they also help search engines. People looking at other sites see the link and come to your site. This not only brings you traffic that's interested in your site; if the visitor is using Google Toolbar, the visit is recorded and sent to Google, raising your site's profile as well.

Expect frustration in the short term. Many Web pages get updated occasionally or never. It's only by making people aware of good content over time that you can catch them when doing an update or creating a new page, when they're most likely to include you.

TIP

Just be steady and consistent, and realize that reaching, say, half the links you "should" have is real success.

Everything you learn and do in pursuing SEO for your site is useful in your Web advertising strategy, as discussed in Book VI.

Specializing first

To get started, identify a phrase or two that should absolutely work for your Web site — and no others.

This may be quite narrow; it doesn't matter. The goal is simply this: to be able to give people a simple phrase that finds your Web site when they use it to search in Google. When you can do this, getting good results on other search terms can be the topic for additional work.

For instance, Olga Smith, co-author of *Get Rid of Your Accent*, features her book and accent reduction courses on her Web site at `batcs.co.uk`. The site hasn't been widely advertised, but it's been up for a couple of years — long enough to get indexed appropriately. What simple phrase relating to the business can get people to the site?

Link networks

If you hire an expensive search engine optimization company, its main technique may well be to plug you, at high cost, into a network of sites that have at least some recognition in Google and that all link to each other.

There are two ways to do this:

✔ One is entirely legitimate. A company might have contacts with (or develop sites for) a lot of tourist companies in Argentina, for instance. If you have, say, a restaurant in Argentina, this is a very nice network to be a part of. You and the other companies can link to each other legitimately. What the umbrella company is doing for you is overcoming the inertia that would normally slow you from getting — and giving — links that are at least somewhat useful to real users. You benefit from the traffic your links bring as well as the improved search engine rankings that bring in Google users.

✔ The other is dodgy — not illegal, probably, but not serving user needs very well either. The network may be made up of substandard sites that offer ways to make money fast or specialized directories of sites with lots of free offers. Your site gets plugged into one or more of these sites. They get enough traffic — and you get enough clicks — to raise your search engine ranking fairly quickly. But do they bring you real, sustainable business? Probably only from your improved Google ranking rather than from the links themselves. (Unless you're offering ways to make money fast or have lots of free offers.) So you better be very good at generating business results from your expensively improved Google ranking, or you may end up losing out on the deal.

Is a UK emphasis okay?

It may seem to be a major issue that BATCS, *Get Rid of your Accent* and the accent reduction courses score more highly on UK-only searches than on global searches, but it's not an issue at all. The business, book, and courses are all focused on British-accented English; the book is sold almost entirely in the UK, and the courses are offered only in London. Customers are very likely to be in the UK and to restrict their search to UK-only Web sites. Even if they use a global search, the results are still pretty good.

Here are the candidates — you can go through a similar exercise for your own business:

✦ **Principals' names:** Olga Smith and Linda James, the co-authors' names, are not unusual enough to get a searcher straight to the site. (There's an `olgasmith.com` for a professional counselor and there's a writer named Linda James.) The principals do show up in the first few entries on Google, but it's courtesy because their book appears on Amazon rather than because of the BATCS Web site.

✦ **Product name:** The book, *Get Rid of your Accent*, does show up high in search results — but on the Web sites of various online and brick and mortar bookstores, rather than as part of the business site. (The book name does bring up the company name, but only as the eleventh-highest result.)

✦ **Service name:** BATCS offers accent-reduction courses. The phrase *accent reduction courses* brings up BATCS as the seventh result in a Web-wide search and as the fourth result in a UK-only search. The seemingly very similar phrase, *accent reduction course*, scores fourth on a Web-wide search and third in a UK-only search.

✦ **Business name:** BATCS is the winner — it's unique and heavily linked enough to be the first result in both global and UK-wide searches. (Just ahead of the Bay Area Turkish Community School in California.)

It took about two years of work, on the business and the Web site, to get to this level of results. And still there are ironies — the book name, the most recognizable phrase from the business's operations, goes to book vendors rather than directly to the Web site itself. Still, Google does the job — even for a smaller business like this one.

You should be able to build up to similar results with your own Web site. Note that, although it's nice that Google search works pretty well for BATCS and its products, the main business driver isn't free search. It's bookstore and `amazon.co.uk` placement for the book — good, old-fashioned distribution — and highly targeted Google ads for the accent-reduction course, as described in Book VI.

Chapter 5: Adding Google Search to Your Site

In This Chapter

✔ Understanding what Google site search can do for your site

✔ Testing out site search

✔ Customizing your search engine

✔ Customizing your home page

One way to gain from Google Search is to add Google Search to your own site. This is a great way to add to any site, whether large or small, the power and credibility of the best and most-recognized search engine around.

Google offers a tool called a Custom Search Engine that lets you add a Google search box to your site for free. You can even customize the look and feel. Your "price" is that Google ads appear in the search results.

If you don't want the Google ads, just upgrade to the business site search. Prices start at just $10 a year.

You can also create all sorts of fancy features like search across multiple sites. This is great stuff, but we're not here to make you a search guru, just to help you make some money (or get whatever other result you want) with your site. So use this chapter to help you create a Google search box for your site.

If you want to see the full range of Google Search features, start with the Google site on the topic at `http://www.google.com/coop/cse/`, as shown below.

Avoid the confusion

Google used to make it very easy to add a free search box to your site. Now it's made the concept more general, more powerful — and a lot more confusing.

Google now promotes its free search boxes as Custom Search Engines. It promotes Custom Search Engines as tools for searching the Web in specialized ways.

Now this is good, except it's impractical. The whole advantage of Google Search is that it's easy. There are more powerful options if you want them, but not that many people do. They just want to search from the easy, fast-loading Google Search page. And we're going to show you how to do that.

If people rarely use fancy search options from within Google's site, why would you want them doing strange, semi-customized searches from within your site?

All most people want is to search the Web and the site they're on. They know how to search the Web using Google, and now we're going to show you how to make it easy for them to search the site they're on — that is, your site.

We suggest you leave the more complex options to the experts.

Exploring the Benefits of Google Site Search

Firstly, even relatively small sites increasingly need to have site search capability. Users are increasingly accustomed to ignoring URLs and Web sites and pushing directly to the Web site they need to get the results they want.

If users arrive at your site by using a URL they've learned some other way, they'll probably at least glance at your site navigation to see if it gets them directly where they want to go. But if not, they turn to search.

If a user arrives at your site via search, the situation is even more urgent. The user no doubt saw several search results other than the one that led them to your site. If the user arrives at your site but doesn't find what she wants instantly, she'll be very tempted to go back to the search results and try something else. (Google's results listings combine results from the same site, so it's unlikely the "something else" will be another link to your site.) If you don't give users a search box for "drilling down" into your site, they may well drill down into someone else's.

So those are the "defensive" benefits — helping a user who's in a hurry to get what she wants. What are the more purely positive benefits?

Google has tremendous credibility. Unless you've built up a very strong brand of your own, or your company is a Web technology company in its own right, having the Google brand tied into your site probably enhances any user's respect for you. (Customers are aware that even a strongly branded company like an automaker includes many specialized parts in the finished car.)

Is beta okay?

Like many other Google services, Google Custom Search Engine is still labeled a beta service — meaning something that's not quite complete. Even Google's very widely used Google Mail, or Gmail, service is still in beta.

Google has a habit of leaving things in beta for a long time. It used to be cute, but now that the company is worth hundreds of billions of dollars and it expects people to count on Google for serious business purposes, this habit is a bit annoying. However, you can count on Google "beta" services to do the job; Google seems to stand behind them just as it does for non-beta products.

And Google site search works very well. Google "spiders" your site, just as it does pages on the regular Web — and then some. So your users are getting what they want — faster. In fact, there's a sort of blame transference here that works in your favor.

If you provide unbranded search and the user fails to get results, the user blames you. If you provide Google search and the user fails to get results, the user is more likely to conclude the information is missing or, at least, that the best search engine they know of can't find it.

Trying before You Buy

You can try a Google Custom Search Engine that searches a single site — preferably your own — as many times as you like before you do anything else. This is a great way to get a feel for this powerful feature.

Follow these steps to do a trial search of a single site:

1. **Visit Google's Custom Search Engine home page at** `www.google.com/ cse`**. Click Your Website, Blog, or Special Interest Group link to make the bulleted list beneath it appear.**

The Google Custom Search Engine home page appears, as shown in Figure 5-1.

2. **Click the Custom Search on the Fly link.**

The Create a Custom Search Engine on the Fly page appears, as shown in Figure 5-2. Ignore the code in the center of the page. Instead, look at the Try It Out area in the upper-right corner of the page.

3. **In the Try It Out area, enter the URL of your Web site — or another small-sized Web site that you know — in the box next to the prompt.**

There's no need to enter `www.` at the beginning of the URL; Google finds the site without it.

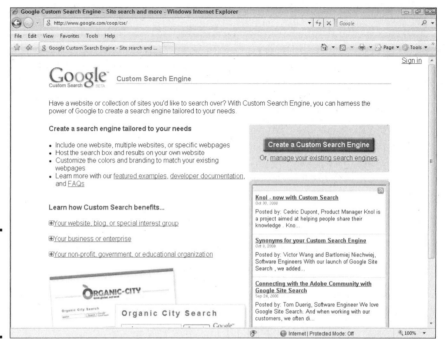

Figure 5-1:
Google
Custom
Search
Engines are
still in beta.

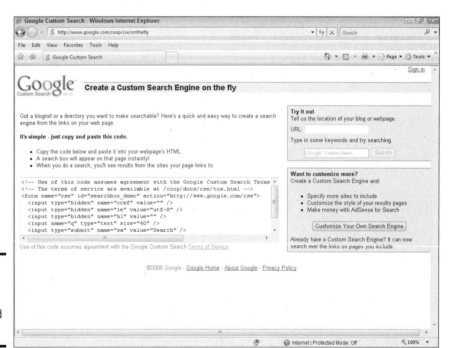

Figure 5-2:
Ignore the
code and
play around
instead.

4. **Now type in a keyword or short phrase that you expect appears on the site. Click the Search button.**

   Custom search results appear, as shown in Figure 5-3. Note the sponsored link that appears in the results. Also note familiar Google options like the Search Within Results link. And note that the user has the option to continue to search the designated Web site or to search the Web.

5. **Click the Back button to return to the Create a Custom Search Engine on the Fly page.**

Note the Google ads that appear on the results page. If you pay for Google Site Search, you can get rid of these.

But they're really not a big deal. In fact, part of the rationale for Google's ads is that they actually ad value to search. For the Web site shown in the figures, some of the search results include sites that sell the authors' books. So in this case, at least, having sponsored links in the results is not a bad thing.

TIP

You can make money from ads on your site as well. You might as well get paid if people are leaving your site! Unless your site is very high-volume, however, this is not going to be a big money-maker for you.

Book II
Chapter 5

Adding Google
Search to Your Site

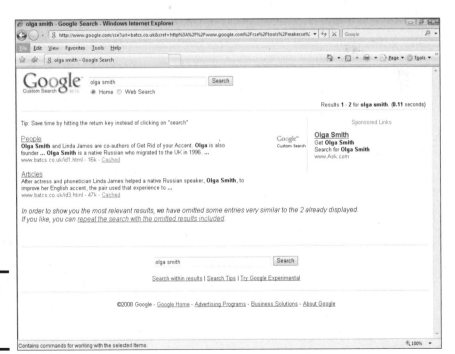

Figure 5-3:
Try your custom search.

The ad that appears in this figure, allowing you to search for Olga Smith on `ask.com` — a search that's nearly random and unlikely to yield worthwhile results — is not a very good example of a relevant ad.

Creating Google ads that don't make a lot of sense can actually make your site look bad instead of good, so keep your ads relevant and useful — just like your Web page content.

Customizing Your Custom Search Engine

Now's the time to create your own Custom Search Engine — keeping it simple all along the way:

1. **On the Custom Search Engine home page at `www.google.com/cse`, click the button Customize Your Own Search Engine.**

   Page 1 of the Create a Custom Search Engine form appears, as shown in Figure 5-4.

2. **At the Search Engine Name prompt, enter a name for your search engine.**

   Keep it simple; for instance, we've called the search engine for the BATCS site by the clever name `BATCS Search`.

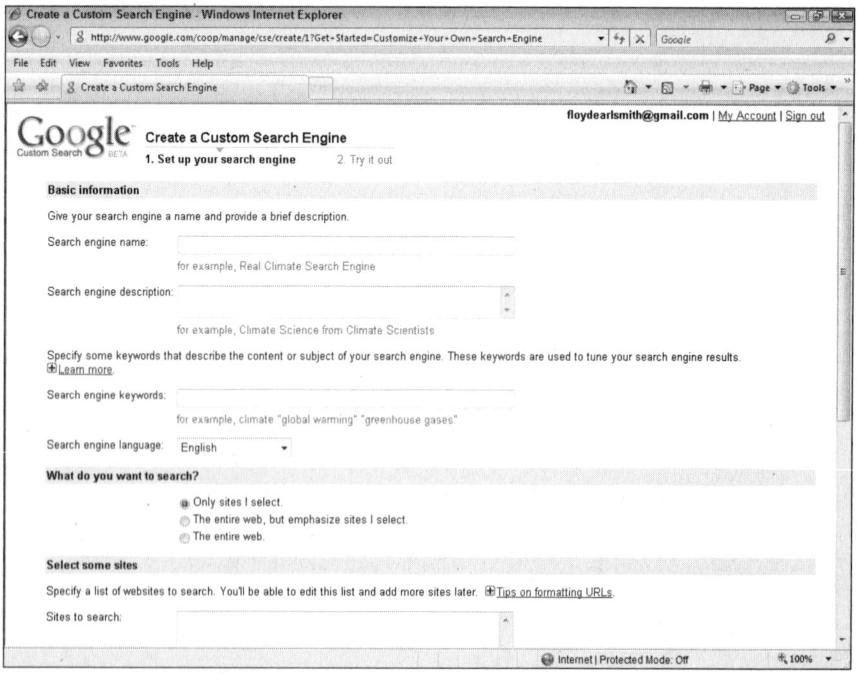

Figure 5-4: Now it's time to set up your site search engine.

3. **Next to the Search Engine Description prompt, enter a description for your search engine.**

   You don't have the option of leaving this blank, so keep it simple; something like `Search batcs.co.uk`.

4. **Enter search engine keywords to "prime" the search engine for the topic it's focused on.**

   For site-specific search, you want an unbiased search based on the words the user enters, so consider leaving this field blank.

5. **Choose the language for the search engine to use from the scrolling list.**

   Google has always been quick to add language options, and this is a good example.

6. **Specify which kinds of sites to search from the available options:**

   - Only Sites I Select
   - The Entire Web, but Emphasize Sites I Select
   - The Entire Web.

   For site-specific search, the right choice is Only Sites I Select.

7. **Enter the URLs of the sites to search in the box next to the Sites to Search prompt, as shown in Figure 5-5.**

   For site-specific search, just enter the name of your site; you can leave out the www.

   If you need a more specific search — for instance, if your site is in one area of a broader site — click the Tips on Formatting URLs link and follow the instructions.

8. **Select the edition you'd like to create:**

   - *Standard edition,* which includes ads.
   - *Business edition,* which has no ads but costs a minimum of $100 per year.

   Always choose Standard edition first so you can try it out, even if you think you might want to pay for an ad-less version later. It's good to "try before you buy."

9. **If you have a nonprofit, university or government site — usually with a domain name ending in `.org`, `.edu`, or `.gov`, respectively — click the box to eliminate ads on results pages.**

   The fact that these sites usually have specialized domain name endings makes it easy for Google to make an initial check on whether you're being honest.

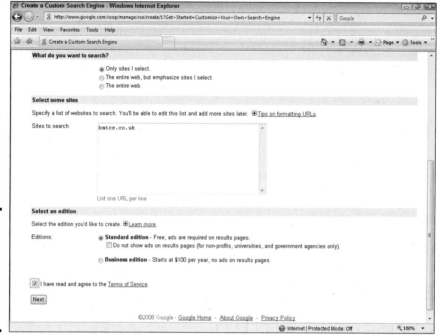

10. **Click the Terms of Service link to view the Google Terms of Service. Click Back when you're finished.**

The Terms of Service page appears. You won't lose any of the information you've entered so far when you return to the page.

11. **Click the check box to indicate that you've read and agreed to the Terms of Service.**

12. **Click Next.**

The second step of the process appears, including a trial version of your custom search engine, as shown in Figure 5-6.

13. **Try different search terms in your search engine.**

Take this opportunity to see how your site looks to other people; note missing titles on Web pages, odd-looking text in results, and so on.

14. **Click the check box to send a confirmation e-mail to yourself. Then click Finish.**

The My Search Engines page appears, as shown in the figure in the next section. This is your control panel for the search engine you just created and any others you create going forward.

Figure 5-6:
Now your
search
engine
appears.
Try it!

Customize Your Home Page

Google gives you lots of options to customize your home page from your
control panel on the My Search Engines page, as shown in Figure 5-7.

Among the options available through the links on this screen:

✦ **Add your search engine to your Web page:** The Homepage option lets
you specify the look and feel of your search engine on your Web page.

✦ **Make money from Google ads, change the look and feel, and more:**
The control panel option allows you to specify a business account for
money — probably not a lot of money — that you make from Google
ads, change the look and feel of your site, and much more.

✦ **Track statistics on your site search:** With the statistics option you
can use Google analytics, which we discuss in Book VI, to analyze the
results.

✦ **Delete:** You can even get rid of the whole thing with the Delete option.

Figure 5-7:
Google
lets you do
even more
with your
new search
engine.

We go into all these options about how to create a Web site in Book IV, because this is where you align your custom search engine with the purposes of your site.

One of the more knowledgeable and, yes, personable personalities in computing is Dave Taylor. His Web site, Ask Dave Taylor!, is not only useful for its content — it's also a good example of using Google ads to make money.

Dave has an answer on his site about Google search boxes that you may find worth a look. You can get to it by going to his home page, at www.askdave taylor.com, and searching for most of the words from the following question: How can I add a Google search box to my site?

Book III

Highlighting Your Business

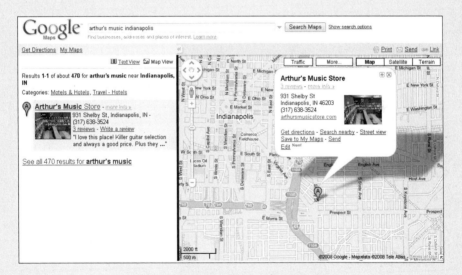

Position your business on Google Maps

Contents at a Glance

Chapter 1: Standing Out on Google Maps

In This Chapter

✓ Exploring the features of Google Maps

✓ Using Street View

✓ Searching with Google Maps and with GOOG-411

✓ Using Google Maps to promote your business

✓ Sweetening your deal with Google Map coupons

✓ Embedding Google Maps in your Web site

*W*hen you first open Google Maps, you see a huge layout of the entire United States, a simple search field, and some basic choices for how you want to view the map. Like most things Google, this simple presentation belies the vast amount of information and potential that lies beneath. With this seemingly simple tool, you can show your potential customers the way to your product or service, entice them with offers, and generally enhance your presence on the Internet.

In this chapter, we discuss the ins and outs of Google Maps and show you how best to use it to benefit your business. At its heart, it may just look like a collection of maps. However, the features that Google uses to enhance these maps make them so much more. It's not just the map that makes Google Maps so useful — it's everything that Google allows you to do with those maps.

The Basics of Google Maps

To get started, point your browser to `http://maps.google.com` and examine the screen shown in Figure 1-1.

The search box at the top allows you to search for specific locations, and how specific you make the search is totally up to you. Type in *San Francisco*, and you may choose between San Francisco in Argentina and San Francisco in California. Specify an actual country or state, and you get a more specific map. Start adding street addresses or ZIP codes, and you get pinpoint accuracy.

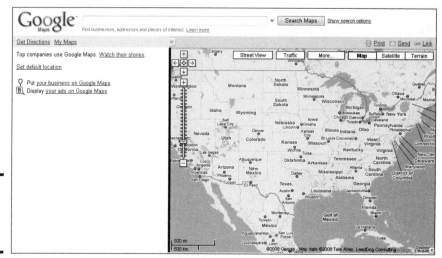

Figure 1-1:
The basic
Google
Maps view.

We're going to stick with San Francisco, CA, for this search, as shown in Figure 1-2. Google thoughtfully provides you with a few choice options on the left of the page, including photographs and popular searches. On the right, you get the basic map of the entire city with a few simple controls and buttons. On the left, you have the manual controls you can use to move around the map. At the top of the map, you see buttons you can use to control how you view that map.

Move the slider at the left closer to the plus sign to see the close-up view shown in Figure 1-3. You can either click the Plus or Minus signs or click and hold the slider and move it up and down. If you draw it all the way back, you get a vision of the world in general. It's probably best if you find the happy medium somewhere, but Google Maps lets you decide where that point is located.

When you zoom in on Google Maps, you'll get more than street names and addresses. Depending on the location, you may see everything from highway exit numbers to bus and trolley routes. Pay attention to the details, and you'll be rewarded.

The arrows just above the slider let you move around the maps in north, south, east, and west directions. If you get lost somehow, just click the button in the middle and you are taken back to the location of your first search

TIP

These controls help you if you don't have a specific address or destination in mind when you first start your search. You can ask for a general location, look over the area, and survey from there.

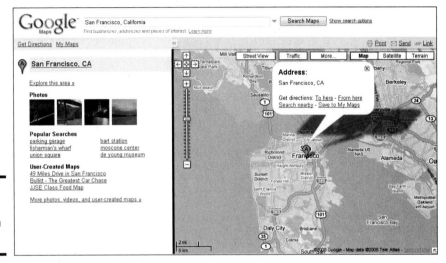

Figure 1-2:
A Google
Map of San
Francisco.

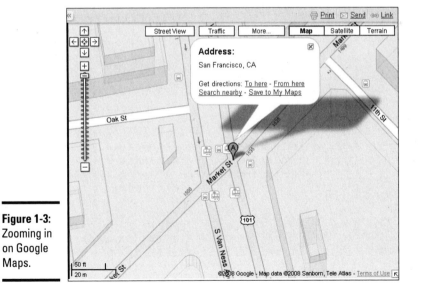

Figure 1-3:
Zooming in
on Google
Maps.

**Book III
Chapter 1**

**Standing Out on
Google Maps**

Changing the map view

Google Maps starts with a default map that has no data overlaid, and you can choose what displays you want to view from there. The following are the three basic types of map views:

+ **Map:** This view is the one displayed in Figure 1-3. You get streets, 3-D representations of buildings, and general landmarks in standard colors. That's pretty much it. With the map view, you get an interactive version of your standard atlas or roadmap.

+ **Satellite:** In Satellite view, you see actual photos taken from space in the place of the standard map. This gives you a better, more realistic view of what you're looking for. Figure 1-4 shows an example of Satellite view.

+ **Terrain:** The Terrain view is a topographical display of your location. It may not be much help in getting general directions, but imagine how useful this view would be if you were planning a biking expedition or a cross-country road trip during the winter. (See Figure 1-5.)

Choose whichever view makes the most sense for you and click that button. Now you can choose whether you want to add more data to your view.

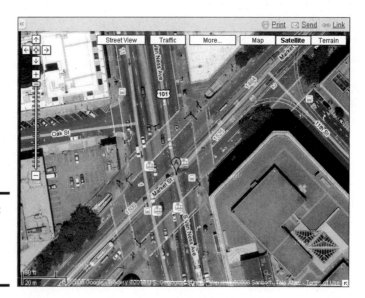

Figure 1-4:
Satellite
view in
Google
Maps.

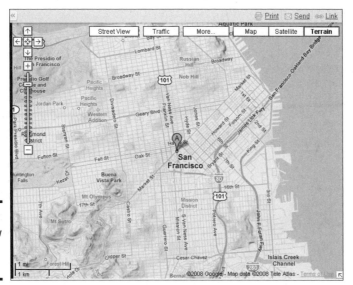

Figure 1-5:
Terrain view
in Google
Maps.

Adding more information

The Satellite view gives you a bird's-eye view of your map, but it's not that useful if you're cruising along the streets at a decidedly lower altitude. And it doesn't necessarily point out the traffic along the way or tell you what others might have said about the location. That's why Google Maps allows you to overlay other forms of data on the map to get the most from your search. The three buttons you can use to see this data are

✦ **Street View:** Google's Street view uses the pictures taken by Google's researchers, armed with cars and special 360-degree cameras. These intrepid persons drove the streets of some major metropolitan areas to piece together views of Google's maps from the road. Click the Street View button to see the screen shown in Figure 1-6.

Streets where photographs are available are outlined in blue, and you can click any location with that blue outline to activate Street View.

Google hasn't managed to get every square inch of the United States (or the world, for that matter), so Google Street View isn't available in all locations. However, if you find that Google Street View is available for the location you're looking for, just click anywhere on the map to bring up the screen shown in Figure 1-7.

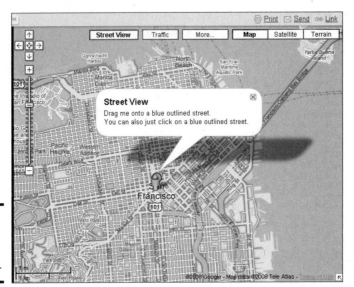

Figure 1-6:
What's
available In
Street View.

Figure 1-7:
Google
Street View.

We look more at Street View in the section later in this chapter titled, "Hitting the Streets."

✦ **Traffic:** Google Maps can also give you traffic information along major highways, which can be helpful if you're travelling when local radio stations don't have their traffic helicopters in the air (or if you don't want to put up with annoying morning DJs). Click the Traffic button to see the screen shown in Figure 1-8. You get a legend in the upper-right corner with the colors that indicate an average traffic speed, and the map shows the colors and icons that indicate any accidents along the main roads.

✦ **More:** When you click the More button at the top of the Google Maps screen, you get a choice of two check boxes — Photos and Wikipedia. When you check one or both, you see a series of icons overlaid on the map view you've chosen, as shown in Figure 1-9.

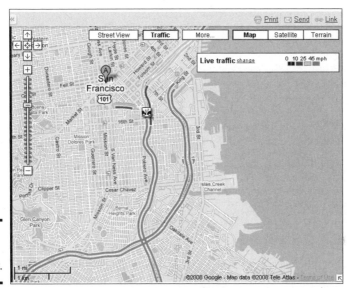

Figure 1-8: Google Traffic View.

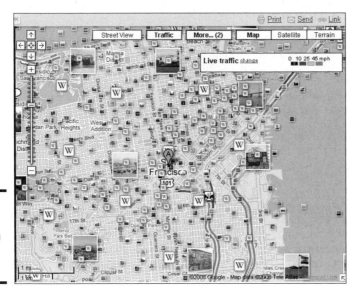

Figure 1-9: Overlaid information in Google Maps.

The Photos check box merges Google Maps with images that have been uploaded to Panoramio, a service also owned by the good folks at Google. These photographs have been tagged with specific locations, so they show up at the precise location on the map that they were taken. Click a photo to open that image in a separate window, so you can get a view of that map location.

Any W icons you see are linked to specific entries in Wikipedia linked to that location. Click the icon to view the entry, as shown in Figure 1-10.

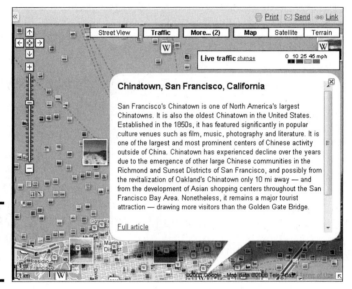

Figure 1-10:
Google
Maps and
Wikipedia.

This can be a handy resource if you're looking for more information on places of interest near your destination.

Wikipedia is a handy resource, but remember that anybody can edit the entries on that Web site. That means that anybody can enter valuable information, but it also means that anybody can enter . . . *anything*, really, whether it's true or not. False information will probably get taken down eventually, but there's no guarantee. Take anything you read there with a grain of salt.

Starting Your Search

As mentioned before, you can start your search of Google Maps with a specific destination in mind, or you can start on a large map and narrow it down from there. The choices are yours, and Google can accommodate either type of search with ease. You can even get directions to your destination from just about any location. Here are the general approaches to searching on Google Maps:

✦ **Searching by name:** If you have a specific name, just type that name in the search field at the top of the Google Maps page to get the information you're looking for. For example, the results in Figure 1-11 came from a search for *Arthur's Music*.

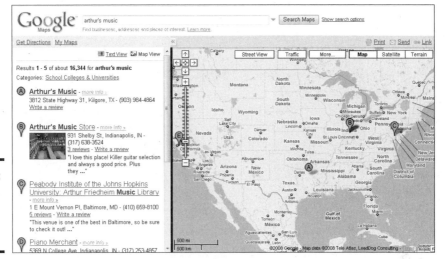

Figure 1-11: Searching for a name in Google Maps.

Book III
Chapter 1

Standing Out on
Google Maps

Unless you're confused about general geography, you should be able to choose between the Arthur's Music in Indianapolis, IN, and the Arthur's Music in Kilgore, TX. Just in case, Google Maps also provides additional information like addresses, phone numbers, and even pictures and reviews when available.

✦ **Searching by location:** Suppose that you want to try a different approach to your search. You know you're looking for a music store, but you forget the name. You do, however, remember the address. Type that address into Google Maps and click Search Maps to see your location, as shown in Figure 1-12.

This search turns up the address on the map, as well as a photo of the location from Google Street View. Again, depending on what you're looking for, more information may be available for you to review.

✦ **Searching by type:** Now, what if you're looking for a business in a specific location, but you've totally forgotten the name and street address? Google Maps can narrow that down for you and have you on the right track quickly. Let's stick with the music store example and choose the location in Indianapolis. Figure 1-13 shows the results when you type *music store Indianapolis* into the search field at the top of Google Maps and click Search Maps.

TIP

Searching for general terms means you get a lot of results — Google has a lot of information to wade through. Be as specific as you can when you're searching for information, and you'll find what you're looking for quickly, as opposed to slogging through hundreds or thousands of somewhat similar results.

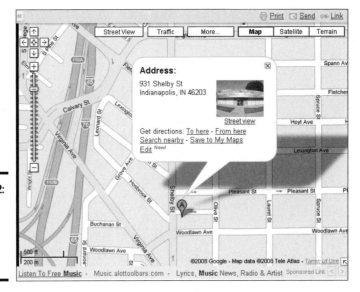

Figure 1-12: Searching for an address in Google Maps.

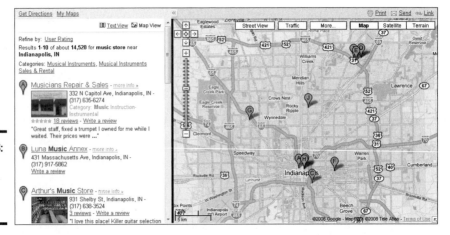

Figure 1-13: Searching by type in Google Maps.

In any of these searches, you can get directions or save maps for later, which can be a huge help for both you and your customers. Take a look at the two links in the top-left corner of Figure 1-13:

✦ **Get Directions:** Clicking the Get Directions link brings up a dialog box in which you can enter addresses for where you are and where you're going, as shown in Figure 1-14.

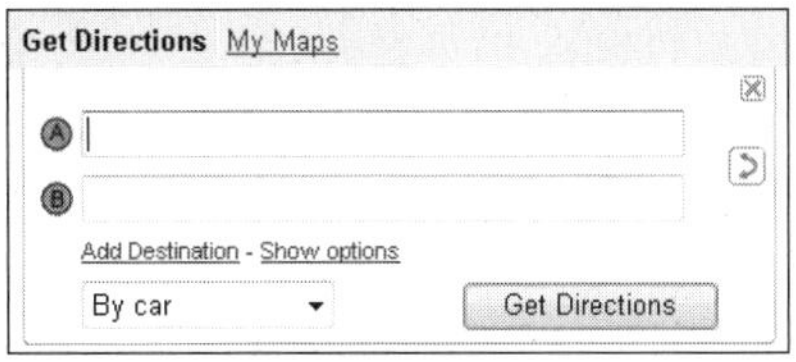

Figure 1-14:
Getting
directions
from Google
Maps.

> Get Directions · My Maps
>
> Ⓐ [   ]
> Ⓑ [   ]
>
> Add Destination - Show options
> [By car ▾]   [Get Directions]

Within the Get Directions dialog box, click the Add Destination link to add additional stops on your tour, or click Show Options to specify if you want to avoid toll roads or major highways. You can even alter your map to view directions by car, walking, or public transit. That's flexibility. Click the Get Directions button to have Google prepare a customized and printable set of travel plans for you.

The Get Directions command is also available from a specific address in the Map view. Just type in a specific address and click Get Directions in the pop-up balloon. You are asked to specify whether the address is the beginning or end point of your journey and to enter another address (for your origin or your destination, depending on your needs). Click Get Directions, and your trip is planned.

✦ **My Maps:** If this is a map you plan to access frequently, save the map for later and you don't have to search for it again. Click My Maps to see the screen in Figure 1-15.

Give your map a name, a description, and decide whether you want other Google users to have access to your directions. When you're finished, click Save to keep that map on hand whenever you sign into Google Maps.

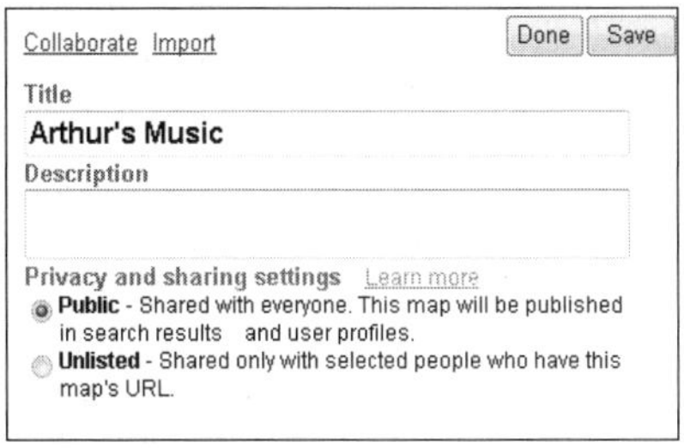

**Book III
Chapter 1**

**Standing Out on
Google Maps**

Figure 1-15:
Saving
a map.

> Collaborate Import   [Done] [Save]
> Title
> **Arthur's Music**
> Description
> [   ]
>
> Privacy and sharing settings   Learn more
> ● **Public** - Shared with everyone. This map will be published
>   in search results   and user profiles.
> ○ **Unlisted** - Shared only with selected people who have this
>   map's URL.

All of these customized and saved searches are dependent on you signing into Google with your account.

Hitting the Streets

Google's Street View takes a simple map and makes it a more useful visual resource than just a normal map. It enables you and your customers to get turn-by-turn directions, and, even better, to find exactly what your neighborhood looks like and see where your business is located. This can be extremely helpful for home-based businesses or for locations that are tucked away in larger buildings. Street View shows you exactly where you're going — no more guessing or wrong turns.

Refer back to Figure 1-7 earlier in this chapter to see a typical Google Street View. Notice the controls on the left side of the picture. The two arrows at the top-left of the picture let you spin the picture in a 360-degree view, giving you a full picture of your location. Use the slider below those arrows to zoom in on a specific part of the photo (like the address or to see how many spots the parking lot has). In case you're just a little off on your address or you want to tour the general location, click the arrows overlaid on the street to move up and down to different addresses. Google has taken panoramic pictures of all the locations in Street View, so you can go as far as you want in any direction by clicking those arrows.

These aren't live views, and Google has a lot of territory to cover, so these pictures aren't likely to change soon. Have a look at your address and make sure you are comfortable with the photo before you integrate it into your business materials.

Have fun searching around Google Street View. In some cases, people knew ahead of time when the Google cameras were coming around, so they staged some wacky and entertaining scenes.

Google Street View is the difference between giving customers a set of directions and sending them exact photographs of your location. It's almost like giving them a guided tour to your business. Posting these photos on your Web page or sending your customers these directions gets them familiar with your location and lets them feel confident in finding your location. Whether they're walking or driving, Google Street View takes them to the neighborhood before they actually get there.

Searching Locally with GOOG-411

Google can even help you when you're isolated from your computer or the Internet (which is admittedly difficult to achieve in today's modern world). All you need is a telephone (even harder to get away from these days) and the number 1-800-GOOG-411. Dial it, and you've got access to Google Map's resources from wherever you're calling.

When you dial, you are asked for a business name or category and a location (either city and state or ZIP code). The handy feature here is that you can add the information from your keypad or by speaking into your phone. That applies to ZIP codes and other numeric information or by spelling a name out by using the keys.

After you receive the results, you can ask for more details simply by saying "Details." If you're on a mobile phone, say "Text Message" to get directions and information sent to you by SMS. You can also get a link to a map by saying "Map it." When you're using a smartphone, this command gives you a ready-made map to your destination.

At the time of writing, GOOG-411 is available only in English to users inside the United States and Canada. No word is available on when and how this service will be expanded.

One way or another, Google Maps gets you or your customers to their destination in the fastest and most convenient way possible. All you have to do is choose how and where you want to integrate this information into your business's Web site.

**Book III
Chapter 1**

**Standing Out on
Google Maps**

Promoting Your Business on Google Maps

It's obvious how useful Google Maps will be to you and your customers for finding all sorts of things around town (or getting out of town for a little bit). Now's the time to figure out how you can make Google Maps work to your advantage. The options you have to consider take into account every facet of using Google Maps, from bringing your business to the attention of potential customers to enticing them to visit. Google leads the league when it comes to Internet-based advertising and searching, so make sure your presence is felt by those who use their services.

The next few subsections discuss some of the ways you can use Google Maps to give your business a leg up.

Displaying your AdWords ad on Google Maps

AdWords is Google's name for its advertising branch, and it places your advertisement in several different locations around the Internet, including but not limited to

+ Google's Internet searches

+ Google services, like Gmail

+ Other Google-owned sites, like Blogger

Basically, an AdWords ad can appear on just about any Web page Google owns. It can also appear on sites where the owners have included AdWords in order to earn some referral income and further Google's advertising reach. The power of Google's advertising lies in the fact that it's targeted directly at the user viewing the page at that time. People searching for water skis won't see an ad for theater make-up — they get a link that directs them to the largest online retailer for waterskiing accessories.

AdWords are discussed in far more detail in Book VI of this book, but here we can take a look at how those ads are worked into Google Maps. After all, if somebody is looking up the best pizza in Marietta, GA, wouldn't you want your Marietta, GA-based pizza restaurant on those search results, front and center?

Google's ads usually take the form of an attention-grabbing headline, a few words describing the product or service being advertised, and the all-important hyperlink taking the user to your Web site. These are tailored to appear in several different locations across the Google universe, and they show up depending on the keywords you've chosen to include as part of your AdWords advertisement. This is the most basic form of Google's advertising, but it has a dramatic reach, which includes Google Maps.

Depending on what you have chosen for your keywords, your AdWords advertisement shows up when somebody conducts a search that's right up your alley. Thus, for that Marietta, GA-based pizza place to improve its position in the search results, it should include the name of the place, the location, and the keywords of *pizza*, *breadsticks*, or any other menu items. When those keywords come up, so does your advertisement (depending on your AdWords settings, of course).

You learn much more about Google's AdWords service in Book VI.

Back when the old physical phonebook was a necessary part of finding business information, people had choices regarding their listings. You could either find yourself with a simple line in the appropriate section (like "Restaurants, Pizza" for our friends in Marietta, GA), or you could pay a little more and stand out amongst the others with a larger ad, a photo, or different colored text.

That's the same basic philosophy behind adding a local business ad to Google Maps. When users search on Google Maps, they get some basic text ads on the side of the view, just as they would on any other search. However, if you've upgraded to a local business ad, the Google user sees something a little different for your business. Your upgraded ad includes

✦ An icon placed on the Google Map being searched.

✦ An image you use to display your business location or other facet of your business.

✦ Additional information about your business displayed when the user clicks your ad or your map icon.

Letting your users know exactly what you do and exactly where you are is a big help in drawing customers to your business. It's the difference between "Let's find a pizza place" and "Let's go to the corner of 5th and Main where there's a Chicago-style pizza joint that's open until midnight."

Before you can place an enhanced ad on Google Maps, you have to have a registered AdWords account and have your business listed on Google Map's Local Business Center. We discuss creating your AdWords account in Book VI, and we look at putting your business in the Local Business Center in Chapter 2 of this minibook. When you've taken care of these small business details, follow these steps to make a local business ad:

1. **Log into your AdWords accounts.**

2. **Select your campaign and ad group.**

3. **Under the Create New Ad section, click Local Business Ad.**

4. **Select the business you want to advertise from your list of available businesses.**

   List multiple locations of your businesses separately to make sure you get listed in multiple map locations.

5. **Upload the map icon and the business image you want to use.**

   Images must be 125x125 pixels in size, and icons need to be 16x16 pixels. You can only use JPG, PNG, or GIF files no larger than 20 Kb.

6. **Enter your business's description in the provided text field.**

   Be as descriptive as you want, including your chosen keywords in a well-written paragraph. Don't include your basic business information — this is your time to sell your business.

7. **Click the Save Ad link, and you're ready to go.**

   The ad may not show up immediately, but it shouldn't be long before users will be able to access your ad. You can check it by searching for your business in a few hours.

Getting better results with Universal Search

Without getting too far into the world of search engine optimization right here (we leave that to the information contained in Book II), it's safe to say that the more Google knows about you, the more likely you are to show up in its searches. And, because Google has the capability to search and index all types of information, make sure that everything you have ends up in Google's listings — including your Google Maps entry.

Google also has an interest in knowing your information and using your contributions on their sites (like Google Maps) in searches conducted by Google users. Simply put, Google wants users to stay on its sites as long as possible because that increases the likelihood that advertisements will be clicked and followed.

That's where Universal Search comes in. *Universal Search* is the term Google applies to its efforts to showcase everything on its site, and not just what it assumes are the most relevant text links. Let's say you were running that Marietta, GA pizza parlor we discussed earlier. Universal Search means that a search for *pizza Marietta GA* won't just return a series of links to Web sites with those terms used (we hope that includes your Web site). Instead, Google presents some AdWords ads (we hope that includes yours), a few relevant Web sites (we hope that includes yours), a PDF menu from your restaurant, your Google Maps listing, and maybe a funny YouTube video put up by you and your employees.

By maximizing your presence on Google's associated sites, you increase the possibility of being seen by potential customers. At this point, you're offering your information in a way that benefits both you and Google, making it more likely that you'll be seen. To take advantage of this, take as many of the following steps as you can:

✦ Enter your information in Google Maps' Local Business Center.

✦ If it's in your budget, place AdWords for your business.

✦ Include Google Maps links and information on your Web site.

✦ Put up information on other Google sites, like YouTube and Blogger.

By increasing your presence on Google's services, you give Google the information necessary to present you to the public in the fullest, most complete way possible.

Fine-tuning your business location

Until you've entered more information for Google Maps to use, users looking for your business get only a simple address, if you're lucky. You may have your photo shown if your location has already been mapped for Google Street View, but at this point, that service covers only major metropolitan areas. Unless you give it more, Google won't have the information to distribute.

That's where the Google Local Business Center comes in. If you enter your information in this service (for free, it should be added), Google draws an exact bead on your business and is ready to distribute it when the appropriate search arises. Look ahead to Chapter 2 of this minibook for more information on getting your business listed.

Attracting customers with coupons

Even if you've provided your potential customers with your name, your location (with a convenient icon on Google Maps), a quick photograph of your business, and all the sales text you could fit into your ad or description, you may need a little more enticement to bring them in to your store. Google took the opportunity to provide that enticement with a more traditional marketing idea — the coupon. There's nothing that brings people in like saving a little money.

Associating coupons with your Google Maps entry means that you're giving a personal invitation to Google users to get them to use your business. This goes beyond pointing the direction to your business — it gives them a compelling reason to visit. They're already interested in what you provide, or else they wouldn't have been searching for it to begin with. Giving them the coupon may just seal the deal for a long-lasting relationship.

Look ahead to Chapter 3 in this minibook to find out how to best use these coupons to help your business.

Adding Google Maps to Your Web Site

So far, you've learned how to use Google Maps and integrate your business into the Google Maps system. This isn't an entirely one-way relationship, though. Google is more than willing to provide tools for you to integrate Google Maps into your existing Web site to help get your customers where they need to be. As you integrate these tools into your business materials, keep the following steps in mind.

Creating your map

The first step is actually creating the map for your business, and it's an easy step. Just go to `http://maps.google.com` and search for your business address. Use Arthur's Music from earlier in this chapter as an example, as shown in Figure 1-16.

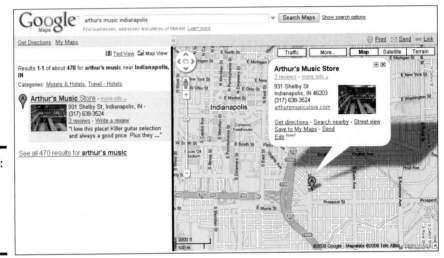

Figure 1-16:
Locating
your
business
on Google
Maps.

This map includes the location of the business (as well as the enhanced local business information) as well as nearby major forms of transportation and clearly labeled roads. This looks like a good candidate for the Web site, and you can even save the map if you want for future use. To save your map, follow these steps:

1. **In the pop-up balloon on the map, click Save to My Maps link.**

2. **In the resulting drop-down menu, choose whether you want to save the map to your My Saved Places location or whether you want to create a new map. Click the Save button.**

The map is saved to your chosen location, and you can modify how the map looks from here, as shown in Figure 1-17.

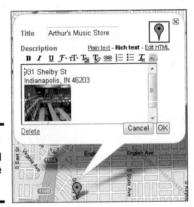

Figure 1-17:
Customizing
your Google
Map.

3. **Click the icon in the upper-right corner of the balloon to choose from custom icons for your location, as shown in Figure 1-18.**

   You can choose from the default icons shown or click Add an Icon to upload from your computer.

   Your new icon has to be uploaded to a Web server, it has to be 64x64 pixels in size, and it has to be in JPG, GIF, BMP, or PNG formats.

Figure 1-18:
Adding an icon to your Google Map.

Book III
Chapter 1

Standing Out on
Google Maps

4. **Change the title of the map in the text box at the top of the pop-up bubble, if you wish.**

   A descriptive custom title helps users find your business.

5. **Use the additional text field to customize your map's information.**

   This field includes familiar word processing functions, and you can also include pictures and links to help your customers along.

6. **Click Delete if you want to remove the place marker and start over.**

7. **Click Cancel if you want to erase your changed information and start over with the current place marker.**

8. **Click OK if you're good with the changes and you want to save your map as is.**

   In the left column of the Google Maps screen, you see the screen shown in Figure 1-19.

9. **Enter the title and description of your map and make sure the Public radio button is clicked.**

   Saving your map as Public means that users searching for your business can find your custom-made map as part of Google's Universal Search, even if they don't have your address or location as part of their search. Think of it as leaving a trail of bread crumbs for your potential customers before they even think of looking for them.

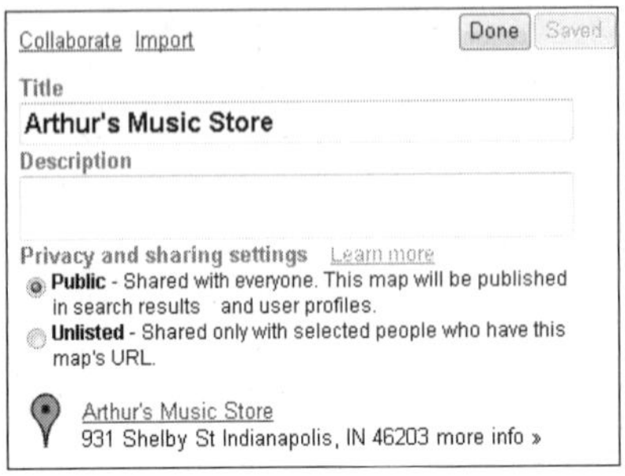

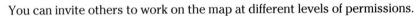

Figure 1-19:
Saving your
Google Map
information.

10. **Click Done to save your information.**

You can always select the map in the left column of Google Maps and click Edit to change the information later.

11. **If you want others to work on the map with you (such as entering information or descriptions to your text), select the map in the left column of Google Maps and click the Collaborate link to bring up the screen shown in Figure 1-20.**

You can invite others to work on the map at different levels of permissions.

This feature is helpful if you want others to add landmarks or other features to the map, or if you just want the advice of a remote collaborator on your work.

The maps you save are listed in the left column of Google Maps, and you can always refer back to them for edits or sharing later. Make as many as you want, depending on the needs you have. For example, you can create one map with all your business locations, or you can make a separate map for each separate location. Make as many as you want — you can always choose which ones you want to share later, and you never know when these maps will come in handy.

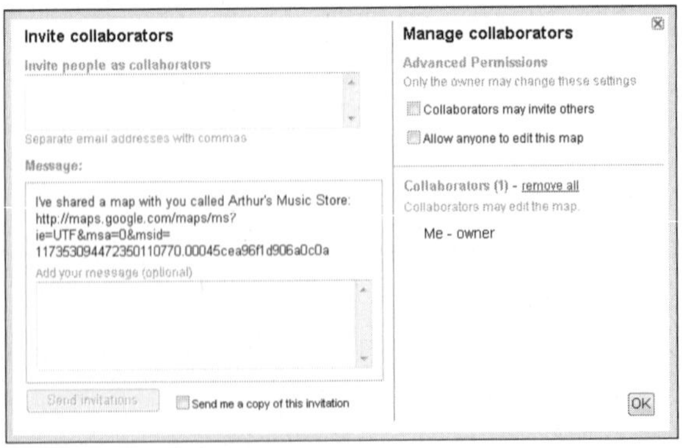

Figure 1-20:
Collabor-
ating on
Google
Maps.

The preceding steps help you create the map you want to share, but the following section gives you some ideas to keep in mind when you're putting your final product together.

Understanding your customer's point of view

Unless you live at the end of a very long dead-end road, it's a fair guess that your customers come from all directions. Make sure that when you use Google Maps, your directions and maps are customized to allow all customers to take advantage of them. Keep these points in mind as you go:

✦ Include directions from all major highways or lines of transportation.

✦ Use landmarks if you can.

✦ Keep directions short, clear, and precise.

Try to be as inclusive as possible, and you'll find that more customers are able to make their way to your location.

Additionally, a full map of the United States is not going to help anyone find your particular location. On the other hand, a close-up view of your street location may not be too helpful if nobody knows how to get to that street. Your goal in using Google Maps should be to offer your customers exactly the information they need to get from wherever they are to your location. Make sure to center the map on your location, and then expand the detail from there. Again, include all major transportation routes or landmarks in the map to make sure your customers have a fighting chance to get there.

**Book III
Chapter 1**

**Standing Out on
Google Maps**

Putting a simple map on your Web site

If your customers have found your Web site, you're already doing pretty well. They know who you are, they know what you do, and they're looking for a way to get to your business. This is where Google Maps makes it easy for you. You can present them with the map you've already made, right there on your Web site and you're ready to go.

You have a few different options to include the map you created earlier (in the section "Creating your map"). So let's take a look at what's available.

Adding a link to your map

Putting a link on your Web site is probably the easiest way to go, because it doesn't take up a lot of room, and you can place that link under any text you want. Take a look at the map shown in Figure 1-16 and notice the link named Link (it's repetitive, but still descriptive) in the upper-right corner. Click that link to see the screen shown in Figure 1-21.

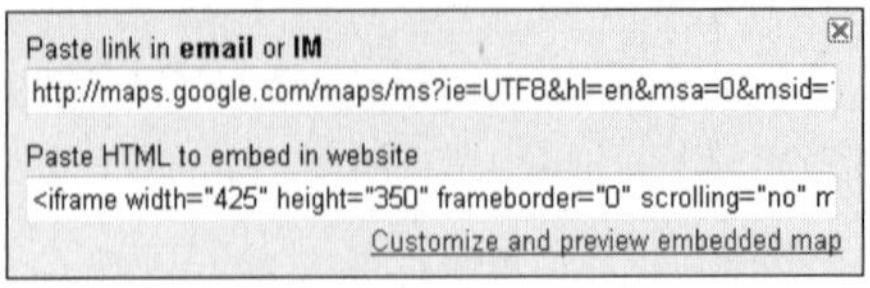

Figure 1-21:
Linking your
Google Map.

The top field of the screen is a hyperlink that takes anybody who clicks it to the map you've saved. You can present this link in one of two ways:

✦ Simply cut and paste the link into your Web site and tell the users what happens when they click the big link under your text, as shown in the code example that follows:

```
Click the link below for a map to my business!

http://maps.google.com/maps/ms?ie=UTF8&hl=en&msa=0&m
    sid=117353094472350110770.00045cea96f1d906a0c0a&l
    l=39.763092,-86.148777&spn=0.031405,0.054932&z=14
```

✦ Attach the link to text that's already on your Web page (such as "Click Here For Directions to My Business"), as shown in the following code. You can paste code like this directly on your Web site, and the users see only the text — not the link. Users click the text to pull up the map.

```
<a href="http://maps.google.com/maps/ms?ie=UTF8&hl=en&m
    sa=0&msid=117353094472350110770.00045cea96f1d906a0c0
    a&ll=39.763092,-86.148777&spn=0.031405,0.054932&z=14
    ">Click Here For Directions To My Business!</a>
```

Embedding your map in your Web site

There's a second field in Figure 1-22 that goes beyond a simple text link. Embedding the map in your Web site means that customers see the Google Map in all of its visual glory without having to leave your Web site. Think of it as putting a window in your Web site that looks out to Google Maps — your customers can see what they need, but they don't need to go anywhere to get the information they need.

Your first step is making sure the map you show meets your exact specifications. Click the Customize and Preview Embedded Map to see the screen shown in Figure 1-22.

All the options that modify your map are included in the embedding code, so this is your chance to put in your options and get the map looking the way you want it.

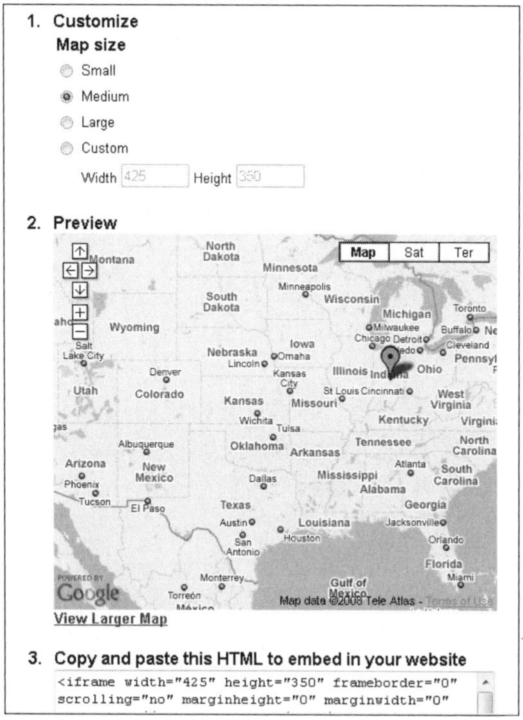

1. **Customize**
   Map size
   - ○ Small
   - ◉ Medium
   - ○ Large
   - ○ Custom

   Width `425` Height `350`

2. **Preview**

3. **Copy and paste this HTML to embed in your website**
   ```
   <iframe width="425" height="350" frameborder="0"
   scrolling="no" marginheight="0" marginwidth="0"
   ```

Figure 1-22: Customizing your embedded map.

The first step is to customize the size of the map. Google provides three basic options, appropriately titled Small, Medium, and Large. When making your decision, click each option to see how the maps will appear. You can also click the Custom radio button to specify a size of your choosing, and the map below changes to show you how your changes will look.

If you have others putting together your Web site, this is a good time to bring them in and get their opinions on how big the map should be. If you do it yourself, just play around with it until you get something you like. It's a good idea to get some outside input from a knowledgeable source, though, just for some perspective.

The second step lets you interact directly with the preview window, either using the zoom and direction controls at the left of the map or clicking and dragging the map directly to get the location you want to highlight. For example, by using the zoom slider on the left of the map and dragging the map to the appropriate location, you get the more useful map shown in Figure 1-23.

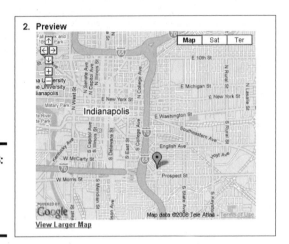

Figure 1-23:
Moving
around
in Google
Maps.

Three buttons are located at the top-right of the map that allow you to choose how you want the map to appear:

✦ **The Map button:** Click the Map button to show your map in a normal roadmap view. This is the most helpful view for those trying to find road directions because it shows all the roads with names. It's also helpful for those wanting to print out the map because it takes less time and looks better on paper used in most common printers.

✦ **The Sat button:** To make your map stand out a little more, click the Sat button. This brings up Google Maps' satellite view, overlaying road names on actual pictures of the location you're giving directions to. This map won't mean much unless you zoom in closely to show as much detail as possible.

✦ **The Ter button:** Click the Ter button to see the terrain view. You still get street names, but you also see elevations on the map. This probably isn't the most useful view, unless of course your business involves mountain climbing or skiing.

When you've got your map up to speed, your last step is to select and copy the code in the third window shown in Figure 1-23. This is the code you paste into your Web site. After you do that, the map shows up directly on your site.

Make sure that you copy EVERY character in the embedded code, in order, exactly as it is presented to you. If you don't, you end up with a bunch of incoherent babble on your site. Everything has to be in place in order for the embedded code to work.

The embedded code shows up on your page as an *iframe*, or an embedded frame linked to an external Web page. You can customize the location where this iframe appears on your page using some basic Web design skills, either by hand-coding it or by using an HTML editor like Adobe's Dreamweaver.

Positioning your map

Where should you place your Google Map on your site? Because each Web page is different, there's no one answer to this question. There are a few rules to take into account, though:

✦ **Don't hide it.** You want the map to be easily viewed, so don't hide it or draw attention away from it. Wherever you locate the map, make sure it's shown front and center on that page.

✦ **Use your contact page.** If you have a contact information or an "About My Business" page, people probably look there for directions or location information. That's a logical place to put your map.

✦ **Fit the map in with your general Web design.** Make sure you integrate it onto the layout of your Web site and don't just stick it on as an afterthought.

✦ **Don't be afraid to put multiple links on your site.** For example, you can put a small link at the bottom of your main page and embed a map on your contact page. It doesn't distract potential customers too much, and it gives them multiple avenues to your location.

✦ **If you need Web design help, don't be afraid to ask.** A little advice on placement can give you some ideas you might not have considered before.

Making it work the best way you can

No matter where you put it or how you display it, you want to maximize the effect of your map to your customer. Always take into account what your customers need. Let's take a look at a few examples:

✦ **If you're going to have customers coming in from long distances, it may be a good idea to have more than one Google Map available.** For example, you could have a map that's drawn back enough to show all the available highways coming into your area. You could then include a more detailed map showing more streets.

✦ **Call attention to the maps, either by placement or reminding your customers that the maps are there.** Don't make them look for the information; give it to them up front.

✦ **ALWAYS make sure that your location is centered on the map.** It may seem like an easy thing to do, and Google centers the location by default. However, make sure that everything is still in line after you've clicked and dragged your options.

**Book III
Chapter 1**

**Standing Out on
Google Maps**

Give your embedded map the once over when you're done, and you should be fine.

Letting customers interact with your map

Embedded maps help direct your customers to your location and keep them on your site, but Google Maps provides so much more functionality beyond a simple map. Let's take a look at how customers can interact with the map you've placed on your Web page or saved through Google Maps:

✦ **Map controls:** The very same map controls you can use on Google Maps works with your embedded map as well. Customers can choose to zoom in or out of your map or move to the north, south, east, and west. They can also view the map in Map, Terrain, or Satellite view. You can start them out however you want, but they can change the maps to make them more useful to their individual needs.

✦ **View Larger Map:** Each embedded map includes a View Larger Map link near the bottom of the map. Encourage your customers to use this link if they want a little more help in using Google Maps. When clicked, this link takes users to the full Google Maps edition of your map, giving them more options.

✦ **Print Map:** If your customers want to take the map on the road and away from their computer, the good old standby of the Print command is available at the top of all Google Maps. Print out the map, and you're ready to go (even if you don't have a smartphone or other similar device).

✦ **Send Map:** Right next to the Print link shown in Figure 1-16 is the Send link. This command sends an e-mail with a link to the map to whomever you choose. This is a great way to address potential customers directly — you can send them a link to your standard map, or you can customize a map specifically for them and send it directly to them.

✦ **Get Directions:** When you look up a specific address in Google Maps, you get a pop-up balloon similar to the one shown in Figure 1-16. Let's take a closer look at the three choices at the bottom of that balloon.

You have three choices in this screen:

• **To here:** By clicking the To Here link, you get the opportunity to enter a starting address in a text field.

• **From here:** If you click the From Here link, you use the current map as a starting point and get directions to another location.

In either case, after you've entered the address and clicked Go, you get a map outlining your trip route and turn-by-turn directions. That's convenience.

- **Search nearby:** The third choice is the Search Nearby link, which allows users to look for locations near you by keyword. Type in a search term and click Go to see any locations (like restaurants) around your central location, as shown in Figure 1-24.

  This can be valuable if you're encouraging people to come and stay in your area for an extended period of time. For example, somebody operating a bed-and-breakfast may want to put together a map that shows restaurants, tourist destinations, and other points of interest around the location. This is an easy way for business owners and customers alike to find what they're looking for.

Figure 1-24:
Finding
locations
around your
business.

- ✦ **Reviews:** You may also notice in the pop-up balloon an area that shows reviews of a business. This is a great way for customers to let others know how they feel about your business. Click the link that specifies the number of reviews (or asking users to write a review) to see what others have said and to contribute your own views. It's an easy way to hear what your customers are saying (you hope, good things) and let others know about those comments.

- ✦ **RSS Feed:** The RSS feed at the top of the screen in Figure 1-16 lets you and your customers know that anybody can subscribe to this page and be notified when changes are made to this map. It may not seem like a big deal at first glance; after all, how often are you planning on moving or changing business locations? Still, there is some value to this RSS feed. If you operate a business like a bed-and-breakfast or a tourist destination, you want to keep enticing people to come to the area. Adding in new and exciting attractions to your maps could make those subscribed to your feed want to make a return visit.

You may also have different locations you want to direct your customers to. For instance, if you're running an art business and are exhibiting your works in several different areas, you may want to show each location where your products are available. Likewise, if you run a home repair or improvement business and want to display examples of your work, this is a good way to keep potential customers up-to-date. Google Maps makes this a snap through their RSS feed.

If you're working on private residences, make sure the owners of these homes know what you want to do with Google Maps. They might not appreciate having strangers driving or stopping by their house uninvited, and they may not want their address highlighted on the Internet.

Adding items to a map

If you want to make your map a little more helpful, you have the option of adding features to your saved map to help your customers along. Your first step is to create and save your custom map, as detailed in the "Creating Your Map" section earlier in this chapter. From there, click the Edit button in the left column of Google Maps to see the screen shown in Figure 1-25.

This screen is where you go to add locations and other items to your map directly, instead of leaving it up to user searches.

If the map itself and your selected locations aren't enough to communicate your message, Google Maps gives you the option to add additional components to your map. Whether it's a marker to show a potential spot of interest or highlighting a particularly enticing shopping district, you can easily illustrate any point you want to make.

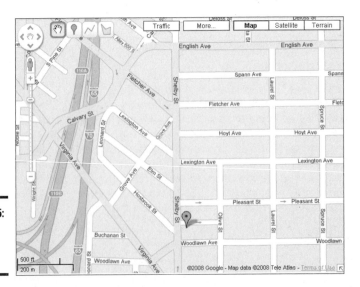

Figure 1-25:
Adding
items to
your map.

As useful as these tools are, it's best to use them only when necessary. A map full of shapes, points, and lines could end up confusing a customer and making the map useless. Include only what you need, and don't be afraid to ask for outside help in reviewing your map and making sure it accomplishes the purpose you intend. Sometimes what you leave out is just as helpful as what you put in.

Adding multiple locations

If your business has multiple locations, you can include them all on one map. Follow these steps to create your master map:

1. **In Google Maps, click Create a New Map at the top-left of the screen.**

2. **Give your map a title and description in the bottom-left corner of the screen and make sure the Public radio button is clicked.**

3. **Search for your main location in the text field at the top of the screen.**

4. **Click the location you want to use in the left column to bring up a pop-up balloon for that location on the map.**

5. **Click the Save to My Maps link in the pop-up balloon.**

6. **Select the map you want to save and click Save.**

7. **Continue to search for your locations in the text field at the top of the screen. Conduct a search for each location you want to include.**

8. **For each location, click the Save to My Maps link, select the map, and click Save.**

9. **When you're finished, click the Done button in the bottom-left of the screen to finalize your map.**

If you have subscribers or an embedded map, each new entry shows up automatically, so you don't have to worry about manually changing any code on your Web site. Everything is taken care of for you.

Adding points of interest

In a saved map, click the Edit button near the bottom of the left column to bring up the screen shown in Figure 1-25. Look at the buttons highlighted in Figure 1-26.

Figure 1-26:
Pointer,
Line, and
Shape
Buttons
in Google
Maps.

The second button from the left allows you to place additional points of interest on your map aside from locations you may have found through Google. For example, you may just want to point out a particularly interesting piece of street art or show your customers where additional parking is available. Click the Pointer button and then click a point on the map to bring up the screen shown in Figure 1-27.

Figure 1-27:
Placing a
point on
the map.

You can add as much information here as you want, from the title of your point of interest to information photos, text, and links. This function enables you to direct your customers to wherever they need to be, even if that point isn't easily searchable through Google.

Adding lines

Click the third button from the left to enable the Line tool in Google Maps. When you've enabled this tool, click anywhere to start your line. Move your cursor to the endpoint of the line and click there to stop the line. You can either double-click that point to make the line complete there, or you can move to another point and click to put another line there. The solid line shown in Figure 1-28 indicates a line that's been finalized, whereas the dotted line indicates a line still in progress.

You can use this line to draw a walking tour route or show the best route from one place to another.

Adding shapes

The button at the right of Figure 1-26 allows you to draw a shape on the map in a similar manner to the line tool. The only difference is that you click the points of the shape and end on the point where you began. After you've done this, you get a highlighted shape similar to the one shown in Figure 1-29.

Figure 1-28:
Drawing
a line on
the map.

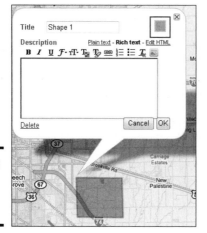

Figure 1-29:
Putting a
shape on
the map.

You can enter the same information for this shape as you can for a point or a line, meaning that it's a great tool to use for highlighting a range of territory.

Showing Street View of locations

If the location you're highlighting has been mapped out by Google Street View, you see a Street View link in the pop-up balloon for that location. Click it to see the screen like the one shown in Figure 1-30.

Again, Street View works in the same manner as outlined earlier in this chapter in the section called "Adding More Information." You can navigate and spin the view as needed by clicking and holding on the picture and moving the cursor in the direction you want to go. You can also click the arrows shown on the bottom of the screen to go up and down the street as desired.

Figure 1-30:
A sample
Street View
in Google
Maps.

Google Street View is important for those wanting to get an exact look at their destination before they head out. It's also useful for those who want to explore the neighborhood and see what's around their destination before they leave.

Not all areas are available in Google Street View. Only select metropolitan areas can be viewed at this time.

Chapter 2: Listing in Google Maps Local Business Center

In This Chapter

✔ **Putting your business on the map with Local Business Center**

✔ **Making it easy to find your business**

✔ **Uploading photos and videos into your listing**

✔ **Finding your business's unique attributes**

Google is global in scope, so sometimes it's hard to think of such a large service being concerned with information that drills down to the most local of levels. Although Google is big, it still pays attention to details. Google uses the Local Business Center to centralize information about businesses in any given area and make that information available on Google Maps. The best part? You can submit your business's information to this vast service and get what amounts to advertising to the entire world . . . for *free*. That's a great deal.

Adding Your Business to the Local Business Center

To start the process of adding your business info to the Local Business Center, point your browser to `http://google.com/local/add`. This brings up the screen shown in Figure 2-1.

From here, you can either enter your business information or use a data file to upload information from several locations at one time. If you click the Add New Business button, you can enter your basic business information as shown in Figure 2-2.

If you choose to add several locations at one time, you have to create a *feed file*. A feed file is a special kind of text file that contains information about your business. Each piece of information is separated, or *delimited*, by a tab. You can create a feed file with a text editor or a spreadsheet program like Microsoft Excel. In addition to adding business information, you can use a feed file to edit or delete information about your businesses. Google provides instructions on how to do this, as shown in Figure 2-3. If you're familiar with using spreadsheets and you have several business locations, this is a good option for you. Otherwise, it's best to stick to adding your business locations separately.

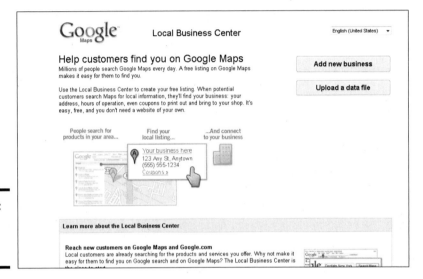

Figure 2-1:
The Local Business Center.

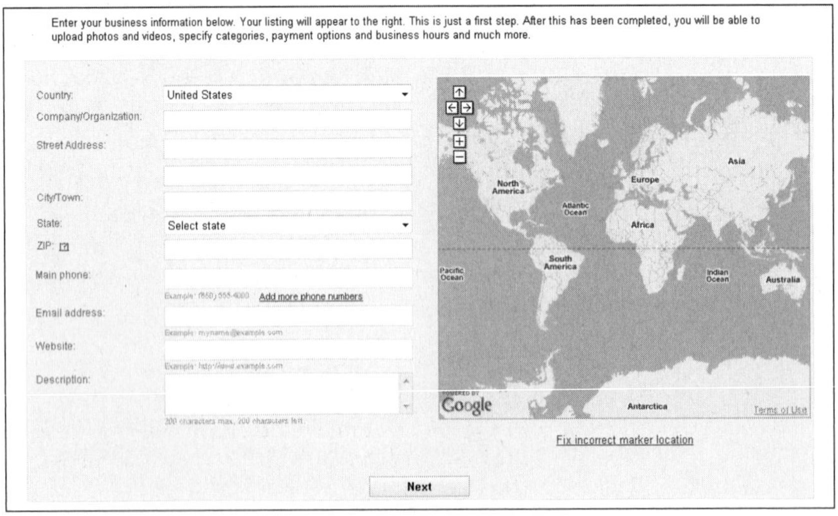

Figure 2-2:
Adding your business information.

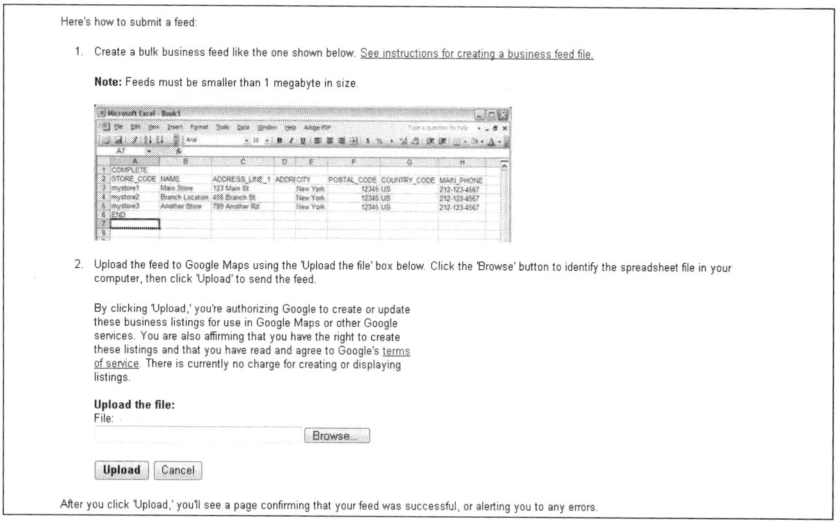

Here's how to submit a feed:

1. Create a bulk business feed like the one shown below. <u>See instructions for creating a business feed file.</u>

   Note: Feeds must be smaller than 1 megabyte in size.

2. Upload the feed to Google Maps using the 'Upload the file' box below. Click the 'Browse' button to identify the spreadsheet file in your computer, then click 'Upload' to send the feed.

   By clicking 'Upload,' you're authorizing Google to create or update these business listings for use in Google Maps or other Google services. You are also affirming that you have the right to create these listings and that you have read and agree to Google's <u>terms of service</u>. There is currently no charge for creating or displaying listings.

   Upload the file:
   File:

   [Browse...]

   [Upload]   [Cancel]

After you click 'Upload,' you'll see a page confirming that your feed was successful, or alerting you to any errors.

Figure 2-3:
Uploading a
data file.

All these screens assume you've signed in using your Google account. If you're getting screens different from those seen here, you may need to sign in to proceed. All this information is added to your account anyway, so go ahead and sign in now.

Look back at Figure 2-2 to see the kind of information you must enter to get started. Everything should be self-explanatory, but here's some advice on how to fill in your information.

✦ **Make sure you use your street address and not your mailing address.** A post office box does no good for those trying to find your location on a Google Maps search.

✦ **Be careful when adding phone numbers.** You can add additional phone numbers by clicking the Add More Phone Numbers link underneath the main phone number field, but be sure you're ready to get all your primary business calls on the number you enter first. It's probably best to start with business land lines and move on to mobile or personal numbers.

✦ **Be as brief and descriptive as possible in describing your business.** You have 200 characters to use in describing your business, but you don't have to use all of them. Include only what you have to — it helps those trying to find your business if you give the message succinctly without cluttering it up.

Google updates your map location and business information as you type, so, when you're finished, your final page should look something like the one shown in Figure 2-4.

Review your business information and make sure everything is correct. When you're satisfied, click Next to move on. Google checks to see if your listing matches any existing entries. If it does, you can click Claim Listing to make that entry your own. If not, click the Add Listing button next to the information you entered to put a new listing on the Local Business Center.

Assuming you're adding a new business, the screen shown in Figure 2-5 is where you can add some additional information.

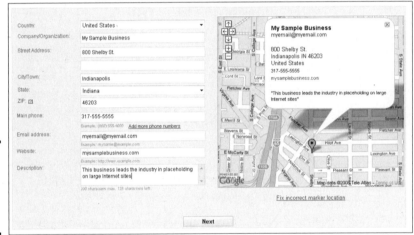

Figure 2-4: Your finished business information.

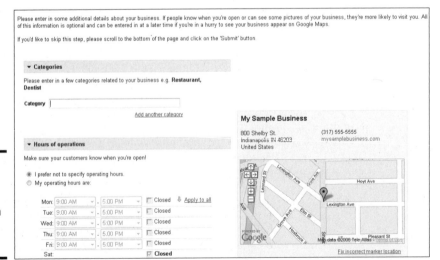

Figure 2-5: Adding additional information about your business.

Some of the information requested in this area is fairly self-explanatory, but some requires more attention. Let's look at the easy stuff first:

✦ **Hours of Operation:** Google assumes you'd rather not specify information right now, but you can click the radio button under this section to enable hours and fill out the information from there.

✦ **Payment Options:** Click whatever check boxes describe the way you accept payment.

✦ **Additional Details:** If you want to specify that you have on-street parking or public restrooms, fill in these categories by specifying the subject in the first blank and describing what's available in the second blank. If you do offer public restrooms, you'd enter "Public Restrooms" in the first blank and "Yes" in the second. Then, just stand back and watch the desperate and thankful customers roll in.

That takes care of the easy business, so to speak. The next few categories require some additional attention because they have a direct effect on how your business can be found using Google Maps.

Using Business Categories for Search

The Categories field shown in Figure 2-5 is at the top for a reason. Business categories are at the top of the details Google looks at when a user conducts a search. That's why it's important to make your categories as specific as possible.

The best way to categorize your business is to imagine you're explaining your business to a stranger in as few words as possible. Don't say, "I make thin-crust, New York-style pizzas on a well-seasoned pizza stove." That's just too much — you're looking for simple terminology here. "Pizza restaurant" will do just fine.

As you type in your key words in the category field, available category choices come up. If you see a category that fits what you do, click it. Don't try to create a new category unless it's absolutely necessary. Google gives more weight to commonly used categories, and you don't want to be left out.

Use the most common terms available to describe your business, and don't try to get fancy at this point. Again, Google and users alike gravitate towards using the most common and accepted terms, and you want to make sure you're included on that list.

You might be enticed to put in several different categories for your business in the hopes of getting more attention and more customers. It's not a good idea, though. Google monitors this kind of activity and tends to rank down those people who engage in it. It's best to just stick to the truth and run with that. It makes your listing easier to find and keeps it from cluttering up other searches. For example, a pizza restaurant might want to just stick to the two categories shown in Figure 2-6 (and the second category would only work if the restaurant serves more than just pizza).

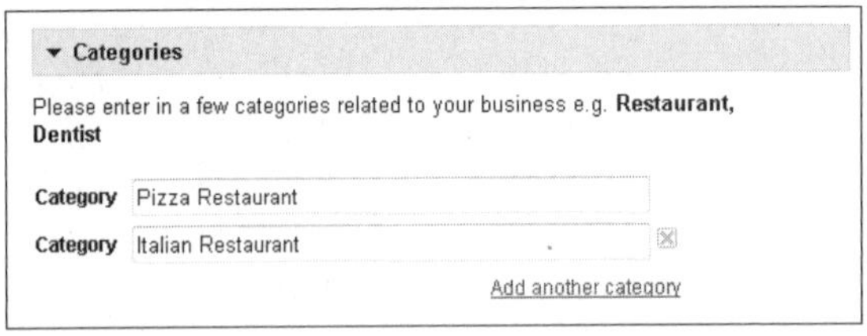

Figure 2-6: Putting categories in for your business.

Using Photos and Videos in Your Business Listing

You can help your business listing pop out from just a simple text entry to something more enticing by uploading photos and videos to your Local Business Center entry. Google even hosts the files for you, making sure that your Web site is kept free for all the hits and orders you should be receiving.

Any photos or videos you can provide should help by giving another view of your business. You're looking to show your potential customers things you can't express through text, such as

+ Photos of your storefront

+ Interior shots of your business

+ Shots of specialized products you make

+ Videos of you and any employees in action

These kinds of photos and videos can be helpful, but you need to be sure they accurately reflect what you're trying to communicate or sell. Take these steps to make sure you get the most out of your photos and videos:

+ **Get a professional:** Getting the right picture may mean bringing in people who know what they're doing, both when they take the photo and when they optimize it for Web use.

+ **Choose the right time:** If you're a restaurant, take a picture before you open when everything is clean and presentable, not after the night is done and you're still bussing tables.

+ **Don't overload the system:** Take good photos and put only those on your listing. Too many photos overload your users.

+ **Make sure you own your photos:** Google will pull any photos that violate or infringe copyright protections.

After you have your photos picked out, you can either upload photos from your computer or link to online photos. Just click the appropriate radio button and either browse to the location on your computer or add the hyperlink to the photo. When you're finished, click Add Photo to link it to your business listing. (See Figure 2-7.)

Videos must first be uploaded to Google's YouTube site. When you've uploaded your video to that site, just paste the link to that video in the text field for videos and click Add Video. Remember to use the hyperlink listed for your YouTube video, as shown in Figure 2-8. You don't need the embedded code, however.

Photos must be less than 1 MB in size, be fewer than 1024x1024 pixels in height and width, and be in JPG, GIF, PNG, TIFF, or BMP formats. Videos must be less than 10 minutes long, under 1 GB in size, and come in AVI, MOV, MPG, or WMV formats.

Figure 2-7:
Uploading
photos and
videos.

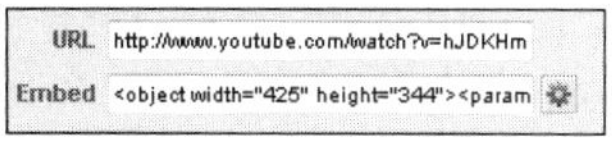

Figure 2-8:
The
hyperlink
code from
a YouTube
video.

Your Unique Business May Require Unique Attributes

When you've added all your categories and the special attributes for your business, go back and search again for your business. Remember, Google uses these categories to efficiently search through all of the available businesses and return as many correct results as possible. You want your business to stand out, but you also want to make sure it can be easily found.

So just do another search. Make sure you're not reinventing the wheel, and use an available category when it fits.

Chances are that your business is not absolutely unique — this is a big world, and you don't come by entirely new ideas that often. Your business probably fits into a broad category that can be easily searched. You may be branching out by trying to start an all-toaster-oven-pizza restaurant, but it still fits under a broad category. Start with overarching descriptions, narrow it down as far as you can, and then go with that category.

However, if you really do have a new attribute, just type it in the category field and click Add. There's nothing wrong with using a custom attribute. Google indexes the category and makes it available for others to use. Who knows? You may just be blazing a new trail.

Finishing Your Local Business Center Listing

When you've inserted all the necessary information, click the Submit button at the bottom of the page. You see a screen like the one shown in Figure 2-9.

Google needs to verify your entry, and it does so either by your choice of a phone call or a postcard. Follow the instructions you receive, and your information will show up in Google's Local Business Center as soon as possible.

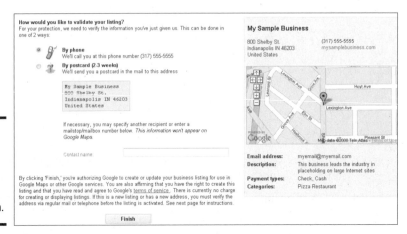

Figure 2-9: Finishing your Local Business Center Submission.

Chapter 3: Attracting Customers with Google Coupons

In This Chapter

✔ Deciding whether your business should use coupons

✔ Making your coupons attractive and useful

✔ Creating your coupons and putting them online

✔ Using your coupons with Google Checkout

Sometimes, a little incentive is necessary to get your customers inside your doors, whether those doors are brick-and-mortar or the more metaphorical doors found on the Internet. Luckily, a good, old-fashioned solution works well in both arenas: the *coupon*. The coupon is a time-tested way to bring customers into your business and to get them to try your product or service. This chapter takes a look at how you should create coupons that are beneficial for all involved.

The Art of Using Coupons

Before you put just any discounted offer up on the Internet, you should take a look at what coupons can do for your business. You need to analyze whether discounting your product or service will help your business and whether you are able to take the brief financial hit in order to set up long-term business relationships. Read through the following points and make sure coupons are the right step for you.

Should my business use coupons?

In certain situations, issuing a coupon could help your business:

✦ You're starting a new business and you need to get customers to try you out.

✦ You're launching a new product or service as part of your existing business and you want to attract attention to it.

✦ You're trying to rid yourself of some excess product, and you want to offer some incentive to potential buyers.

✦ You're looking to bring in new clientele to your business overall.

Whatever your reason, you must decide how much you can afford to give away via a coupon and whether that small hit will bring you a larger return in the long run.

You also need to make sure that the coupon is enough incentive to actually bring customers in to your business. Giving somebody fifty cents off your large pizza probably won't be a huge draw, but an order of breadsticks might do the trick.

Finally, make sure that you clearly outline all the requirements of your coupon. You don't want to accidentally give away your whole store, and you don't want to end up with a bunch of angry customers either.

Where do people find my coupons?

By creating coupons through Google Maps, you can locate your offer on a few different locations, including the following:

✦ **Google Maps:** Obviously, any coupons attached to your Google Map site shows up when users click your location. The coupon appears in the pop-up balloon when users click More Info. Users can find the coupon by following the link shown in Figure 3-1.

 Users can also search for coupons directly by pointing your browser to http://maps.google.com/coupons and searching for coupons in your location. For example, a search for "paper" in Indianapolis provided the results shown in Figure 3-2.

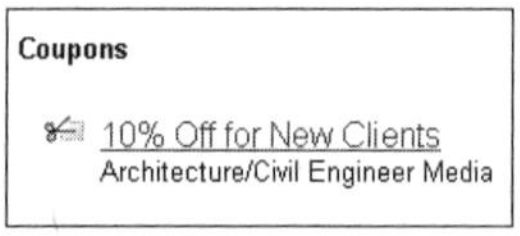

Figure 3-1: A coupon link from Google Maps.

Coupons

✂ 10% Off for New Clients
Architecture/Civil Engineer Media

✦ **Coupon Subscriptions:** If they have a Google account, customers can subscribe to your coupon feed to see all the available details. On each coupon page, they see a list of buttons shown at the top right in Figure 3-2:

 • *Subscribe:* If the users click the Subscribe button, they get a link automatically placed on the Subscribed Links page, available at http://www.google.com/coop/sl. When these users search for terms that match your coupons, the results show up automatically. This gives your coupons a direct link to your customers' Google searches.

- *Link to This Page:* By clicking the Link to This Page link as shown in Figure 3-2, you get a link you can paste onto your Web site to refer customers directly to the coupon. That way, even if they don't use Google Maps, they can take advantage of your offer.

- *Send to Friend:* The Send to Friend link allows users to forward the coupon on to other potential customers. Referrals are a great way to get additional business, but be careful that your coupon doesn't spiral out of control. Remember, these coupons are available to anybody with Internet access.

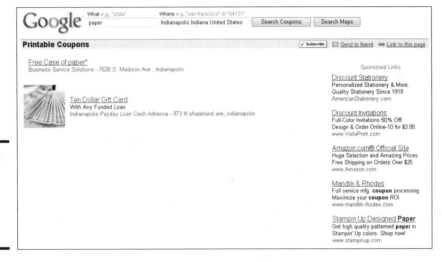

Figure 3-2:
A sample search in Google Maps' Coupons.

Creating a Printable Coupon

Even though these coupons are based on Google Maps, you still have to make them available to those who want to print them out and use them. You must control how the coupons are used, keeping track of who turns them in and when. Because you're probably trying to drive traffic into your physical location, you have to allow physical copies of your coupons.

First, you have to decide what you want to offer and what you can afford to let go as part of the coupon offer. Be sure you consider your options carefully and make sure you can honor the offer you're about to make. Also, be sure that you include an expiration date if you just want the coupon to be a short-term business incentive.

Google provides an autogenerated layout for your coupon, so you don't have to worry about making a coupon from scratch. As you enter information, Google shows your updates as you go. After you've entered everything, your coupon is ready to print and use.

Here's all you have to do to create your coupon:

1. **Sign in to your Local Business Center account at `http://google.com/local/add`.**

2. **Click the Coupon tab to see the screen shown in Figure 3-3.**

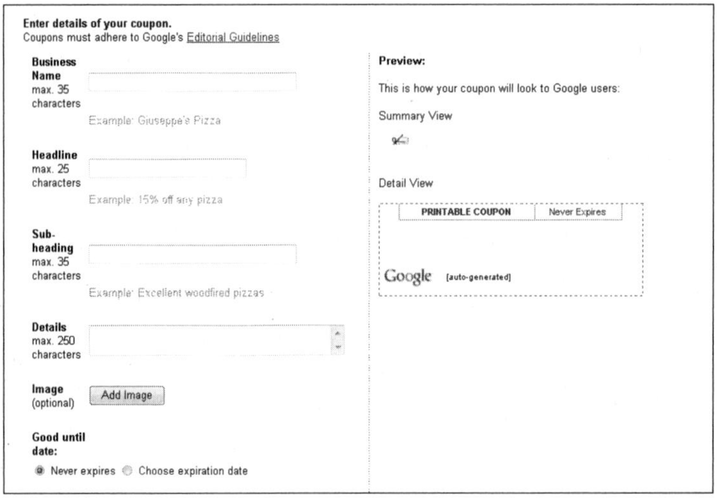

Figure 3-3: Starting your Google Coupon.

3. **Enter the requested information.**

    As you enter information, you see your coupon take shape in the Detail View section on the right.

4. **When you've inserted all your information, click Continue to add the coupon to your Google Maps account.**

Keep these things in mind as you create your coupon:

+ **Keep your coupon attractive:** Make sure that any photos or logos you upload to your coupons look good and present your business in a positive light. You don't want an ugly product to distract from your business and its offer.

+ **Make your coupon useful:** If the coupon isn't going to bring anybody in, there's really no use in putting it online. Make sure that your offer is compelling before you put it up, or else you're wasting your time.

✦ **Include ALL terms and conditions:** Lay out all the terms of your deal in the coupon to make sure your transactions go smoothly. If everything isn't clear from the beginning, you're liable to lose a lot more than you bargained for, and you risk alienating your potential customers as well. Be specific and precise with your coupon, and you save a lot of hassle later. Think of the common requirements you see on other coupons:

- One per customer

- One per visit

- Not valid with other offers

- A specific expiration date

Use these to bring the customers in without losing your shirt in the process.

Using Coupons with Google Maps

It won't be an instantaneous process, but eventually every coupon you create and attach to a specific business location will show up on the details page of your Google Maps entries. These coupons show up automatically at the bottom of your details page with a quick link and a small summary of your offer.

Remember that you have the option to assign coupons only to certain locations of your business. Click only those locations when creating your coupons, and they only show up on those locations.

If you're going to make coupons applicable to only certain locations, it's a good idea to include those terms in the description section of the coupon. Make it as precise as possible, just so everybody's clear.

Coupons and Google Checkout

If you're conducting a great deal of online business, it's possible you're using Google Checkout already to handle your online order processing. Google Checkout is a powerful and convenient way to smooth your online business transactions, and it allows you to process a great variety of payments. As it turns out, it also means you can offer online coupons.

Just because your coupons are available online doesn't mean that you can ignore the rules outlined throughout this chapter. Be sure you can back the offer you're making, and make sure that all the terms are outlined clearly and precisely to keep everybody honest.

If you're going to offer the same coupon in both physical and online forms (and if you want to track the effectiveness of the offer alone), give them the same coupon code. That way, no matter where it comes from, you can track the coupon's results. However, if you're interested in tracking where your business is coming from, you might want to make the physical and online coupons different. That way, you can see what channel is bringing you the most business.

Google Checkout has a method of processing coupons different from that used by Google Maps. To create an offer through Google Checkout, log into your Google Checkouts account and follow these steps:

1. **Click the Tools tab.**

2. **Click Coupons and select Create a New Coupon.**

3. **Enter the information for your new coupon.**

4. **Click Create to finalize your coupon.**

You can use these coupons to duplicate physical coupon offers or make special online-only details. This can be helpful if you want to expand your online business or make deals available only to the online folks.

For more information on setting up a Google Checkout account, refer to Book V in this minibook.

Chapter 4: Showcasing Your Stuff with Google Base

In This Chapter

✔ Using Google Base to find products and services

✔ Putting your own information on Google Base

✔ Keeping your Google Base data up to date

*W*hen you conduct a search with Google, you're looking through a worldwide index of information. Google crawls the entire Internet, looking for the information to provide what you're looking for. However, a relatively new service — Google Base — makes Google as much a database as an index. Google Base is a repository for all kinds of information, all of it searchable from a simple series of text fields. It enables you to make your work known to the entire world without having to put up a Web site of your own.

Finding Products and Services

As with many of Google's powerful services, your first step to using Google Base is deceptively simple. When you point your browser to `http://base.google.com`, you see the very simple screen shown in Figure 4-1.

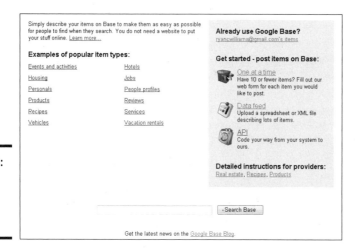

Figure 4-1: Your first view of Google Base.

Google provides a popular sample of the things you can find on Google Base, as well as the ways you can post items on Google Base. Finally, there's a simple text field where you can enter search terms and start looking through Google's vast repository of knowledge.

Searching on Google Base

Because you can search for practically everything on Google, let's start with a tool many people use as part of their small business: a laptop computer. Type the word *laptop* in the text field at the bottom of the screen shown in Figure 4-1 and click the Search Base button.

Take at look at the top of the screen in Figure 4-2. This is the first part of your search results, and by default, you're looking through the items entered in Google Base. You could also switch and search the entire World Wide Web by clicking the Search the Web button, but stick with Google Base for now.

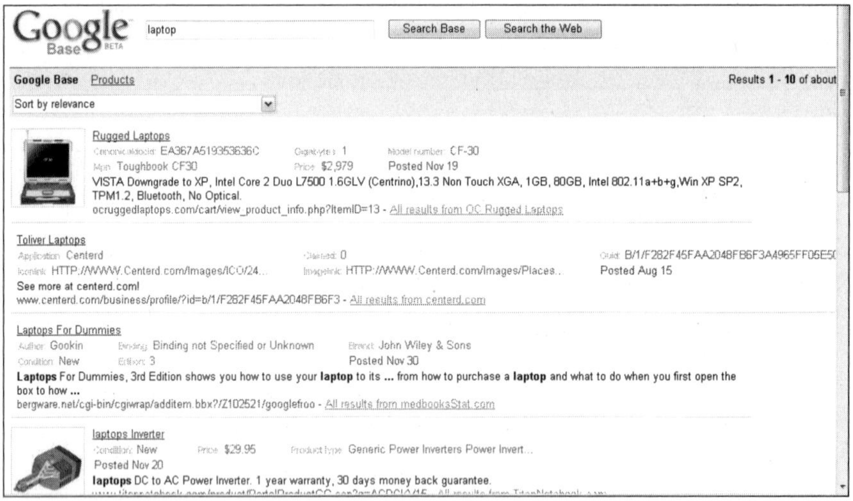

Figure 4-2:
The initial
Google
Base
search.

Google displays a list of relevant items based on your search in a standard format. With most entries, you can look at images for each entry, as well as standardized information fields and a brief description of the item. As opposed to a standard Web search, which returns all manner of information in a variety of formats, Google Base takes the information you've requested from its records and puts it in a format that can be easily and quickly reviewed. Think of it like a card catalog for one of the world's largest databases.

The drop-down menu shown at the top of the screen in Figure 4-2 lets you sort the results by Google's assigned relevance or by the date the items were posted on Google Base. This helps you choose between the item that most closely matches your search terms or a matched item with the most recent entry. Depending on how time-sensitive your search is (nobody wants year-old goat's milk, for example), this can be a big help.

When you find the Google Base item you're looking for, you can click any available links to take you to the relevant site. In some cases, this could be an external page or Web site. Many businesses and services post items from their own sites on Google Base and then direct potential customers to their own sites. However, Google Base hosts information for users as well, so you could end up on a Google page when your search is completed. What you do with the information from there is up to you.

Finding products and services on Google Base

Take a look again at the top of Figure 4-2. Right next to the Google Base link is a link for Products. This space could contain any number of links, depending on what the results for your search term returned. That's because Google has customized Google Base to tailor itself to several different types of information. In this case, Google also found information in a related service called Google Product Search on *laptop* and presented it as an additional search option. If you click that link, you get an entirely different view of the information, as shown in Figure 4-3.

Book III
Chapter 4

Showcasing Your
Stuff with
Google Base

Figure 4-3:
An initial
look at
Google
Product
Search.

You've got a more specific way to search for information here because you've told Google that you're looking specifically at items being sold via the Web. Now you can narrow down your searches even more and target what you want precisely. This is a powerful tool, and we cover it in Chapter 5 of this minibook.

Just to see what else is available from Google Base, go back to the screen shown in Figure 4-1 and click the Services link. Services are another type of information that might interest a small-business owner like you. When you click that link, you get a screen like the one shown in Figure 4-4.

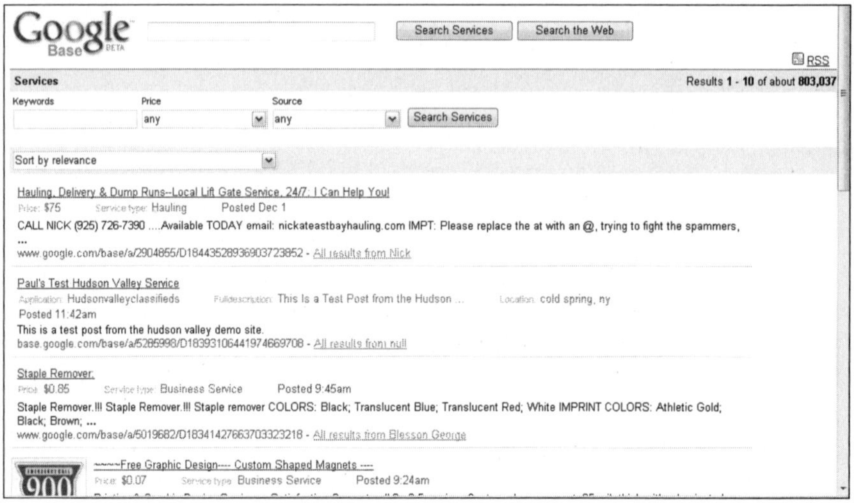

Figure 4-4: An example of services listed in Google Base.

Notice how the search fields have changed yet again — you see fewer fields than in Google Product Search, but these fields are tailored specifically to find those services entered in Google Base. Enter the search term *lawn care* in the keywords field and set the drop-down menus to whatever you might choose. Click the Search Services button to see a screen like the one shown in Figure 4-5.

The results you see have been dramatically filtered by Google Base, and you're much closer to finding what you want (which is a bonus for those who might hate mowing their lawn and want to find relief). Each of the links shown in Figure 4-1 has its own unique search fields and capabilities, so it's up to you to look for what you want.

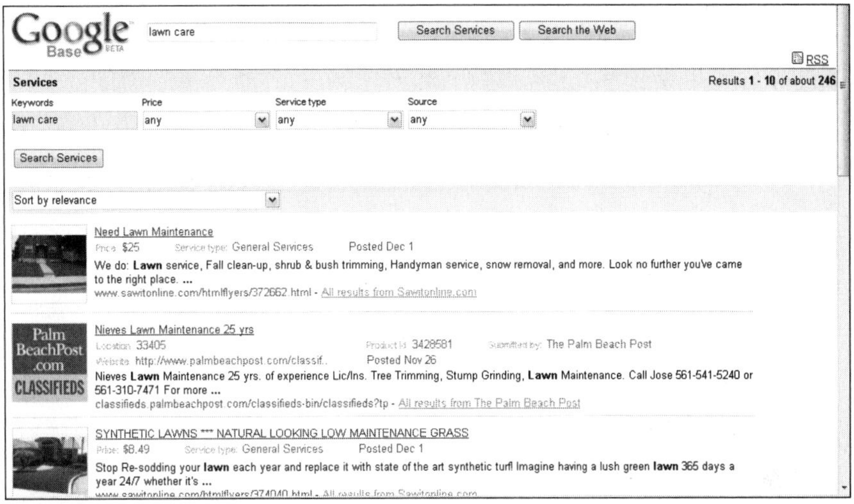

Figure 4-5:
Searching
for lawn
care
services
on Google
Base.

Narrowing your search

With just a few clicks, you should be able to find a great deal of information on what you're searching for. Google greatly reduces the amount of time you spend searching for what you want. If you're more interested in a vast wealth of general knowledge on a topic, you should stick with the Google Base text field shown in Figure 4-1. For example, if you're looking to buy a laptop, searching across the entire Google Base gives you access to product listings, reviews of those available products, and maybe some information on accessories or instructional materials you might want to get as well. When you're ready to buy, you can switch over to Google Product Search and find exactly the computer you're looking for. And, should that laptop computer ever fail for any reason, you can search Google Base's listing of services to see who can help you fix your laptop and potentially recover any data you may have lost.

Adding Products and Services to Google Base

Now that you've seen what's available on Google Base, it's time to add your products or services to the mix as well. Even if you've never heard of Google Base before this book came along, you may have already interacted with it, simply through your normal interaction with Google. Making the world's largest search engine aware of your products can't be a bad thing.

When you make your entries into Google Base, you make your products and services available worldwide. That may be a little hard to grasp, given that just a few short years ago, worldwide access to a global market wasn't possible. With Google Base, however, you have a pipeline to anybody who might want to hire or buy from you (whether you're willing to travel to Thailand with your lawn care service is another matter).

Your goods and services are also put into the same pool as those from other online services, like eBay. Google Base takes feeds and information from these services and places them on Google Base. You can check Google Base, to get information from all those sources as well. It's the ultimate source of one-stop shopping.

Google Base usually sorts entries based on their relevance to your search — what most closely matches your search terms is what pops up at the top. However, as shown in Figure 4-2, you can reorder this item in terms of the most recently posted items. This helps you keep track of the newest, freshest items on Google Base.

Beyond that, Google Base allows you to make your products available to the public in the quickest manner possible to the world's largest potential consumer base. After you post something on Google Base, it's ready to go. Anybody can access it, anybody can contact you about it, and you can make a sale at any time. You don't have to wait for other stores to update their Web sites or expand their inventories. You're up and running from the first click.

What can you add? The short answer is that you can add just about anything to Google Base. Obviously, you're not going to be able to sell any illegal products and services on the service, but there are categories for just about everything else on Google Base, and you can add custom categories if you need to. Note that products and services are just a few of the kinds of items you can add to Google Base. You can also add any of the following:

- ✦ **Events and Activities:** These are upcoming public events that you may want to inform the public about.

- ✦ **Housing:** Trying to sell a house or rent an apartment? This is where you'd go.

- ✦ **Jobs:** Whether you're trying to hire or get hired, make your entry here.

- ✦ **Personals:** This is where you go if you're trying your luck with love.

- ✦ **Products:** If you're trying to sell something, this is where you want to go.

◆ **Recipes:** You might want to check with your grandmother before posting the family secret, but post it here if you want to risk it.

◆ **Reviews:** This is a huge source of information and opinions on all kinds of products and services.

◆ **Travel Packages:** Sell your tickets and lodging here.

◆ **Vehicles:** I wonder who will still pay for an AMC Gremlin? I can find out here.

Google Base enables you to define custom categories if you want (and in case your product or service is that unique). More than likely, though, your product fits under one of these headings, and it's a good idea to keep your entries in one of the more established categories. After all, that's where most people searching Google Base are looking, and you want to make sure the largest number of eyeballs see your Google Base items.

When your entries have been made, they end up on Google Base under the larger category you defined for them. You can also specify which countries you want the items to be targeted to as well, if you have travel or shipping concerns. Your item comes up when somebody searches for the keywords and categories you specified in your entry.

Adding Items One at a Time

The screen shown in Figure 4-6 shows you the options you have for uploading your information to Google Base. If you only have a few items, Google provides a service that allows you to add them individually through a Web interface.

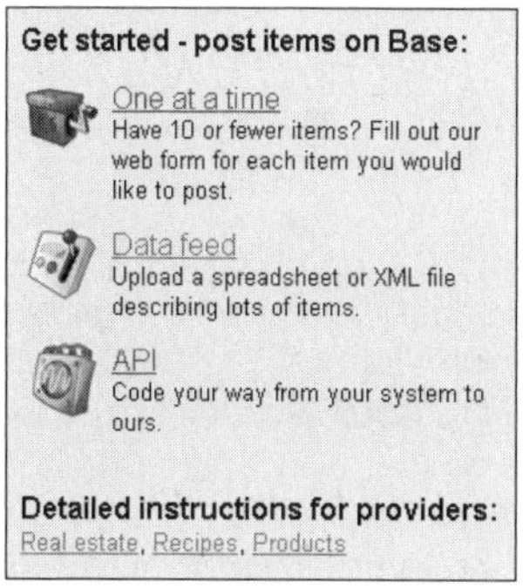

Figure 4-6:
Entering
items into
Google
Base.

Get started - post items on Base:

One at a time
Have 10 or fewer items? Fill out our
web form for each item you would
like to post.

Data feed
Upload a spreadsheet or XML file
describing lots of items.

API
Code your way from your system to
ours.

Detailed instructions for providers:
Real estate, Recipes, Products

Real Estate listings, recipes, and products have some additional instructions you may want to check out. They're nothing dramatic, but you might want to click the links at the bottom of the screen shown in Figure 4-6 for more information.

Follow these steps to upload your information:

1. **Click the One at a Time link shown in Figure 4-6 and sign into your Google account (if you haven't done so already) to continue.**

2. **If you've never uploaded items to Google Base before, you have to agree to its terms of service. Notice the slider at the right of the page — you want to review the lengthy text to make sure Google Base is what you want to use. Read it and click the Accept button at the bottom of the screen to continue.**

   At this point, Google Base wants to know what you're adding. Here's where you choose the categories you reviewed earlier or create a custom category for your item. Based on your response, Google gives you sets of questions to answer in order to list your information.

3. **Pick your category from the drop-down menu in Figure 4-7 or click the radio button next to the custom text field and enter your category there.**

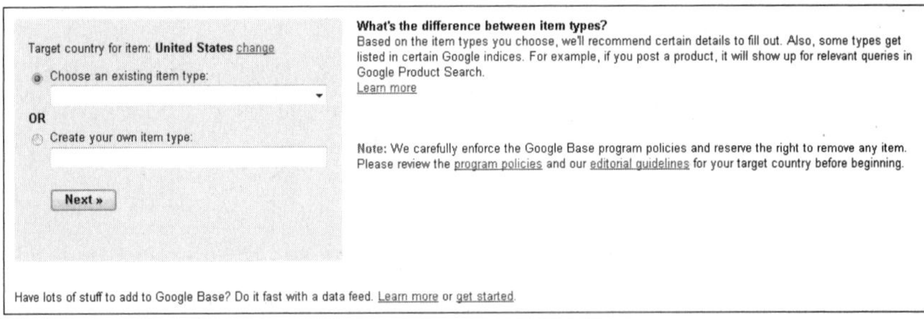

Figure 4-7: Choosing your Google Base category.

Target country for item: **United States** change

○ Choose an existing item type:

OR

○ Create your own item type:

[Next »]

What's the difference between item types?
Based on the item types you choose, we'll recommend certain details to fill out. Also, some types get listed in certain Google indices. For example, if you post a product, it will show up for relevant queries in Google Product Search.
Learn more

Note: We carefully enforce the Google Base program policies and reserve the right to remove any item. Please review the program policies and our editorial guidelines for your target country before beginning.

Have lots of stuff to add to Google Base? Do it fast with a data feed. Learn more or get started.

For example, if you're listing an ad for a product, such as a car, change the drop-down menu to the appropriate category (vehicles) and click Continue to see the screen shown in Figure 4-8. In addition to the items shown in that figure, you are asked to upload a photo or attach one from the Web, add contact, payment, and location information, and an expiration date. Google Base automatically moves all items to an inactive list after a maximum of 30 days to make sure its records remain current and vital.

On the other hand, if you're advertising a service, you see a screen that looks like the one in Figure 4-9.

Notice how the fields change to apply to the category chosen. You can also add additional fields by clicking the Create Your Own link at the right of Figure 4-9. This gives you the option shown in Figure 4-10.

Again, put the name of the field in the first text box and put the information in the second text box. You can add as many as you want, but make sure they are as descriptive as possible.

Figure 4-8: Choosing item types in Google Base.

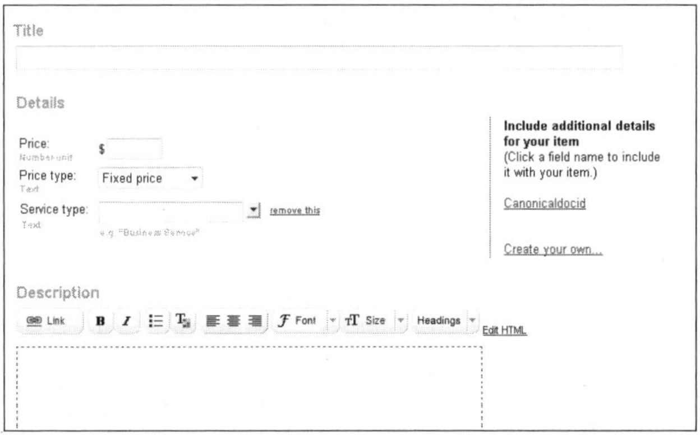

Figure 4-9: Putting a service ad on Google Base.

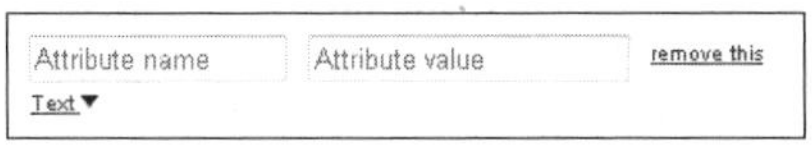

Figure 4-10: Adding fields to a Google Base entry.

If you don't need them, it's best if you leave out additional attribute fields. Include specific description information in the description text field.

Fill out as much information as possible in order to make your product easy to find.

4. **When you're finished, you have four choices for your ad:**

   • Click the Preview button at the bottom of the screen to inspect your ad.

   • Click Publish to put your ad on Google Base without further delay.

   • Click Save Draft to put your ad away and come back to it later.

   • Click Cancel to start over or leave the page.

These fields change depending on the category you choose. To clarify matters, then, examine the following example of a product.

Take a look at how a product listing is added to Google Base. In the screen shown in Figure 4-11, we chose to add a product listing and enter the information in the fields provided.

The custom fields at the right of Figure 4-11 can be added as well, should they be applicable. If you have a picture to add, scroll down and choose whether your photo is located on your computer or already on the net, such as a picture hosted on Flickr or MySpace. You also add location, payment, and contact information as well as the expiration date of your ad, as shown in Figure 4-12.

When you're finished, click the Publish button to put your ad online. You see a screen like the one shown in Figure 4-13.

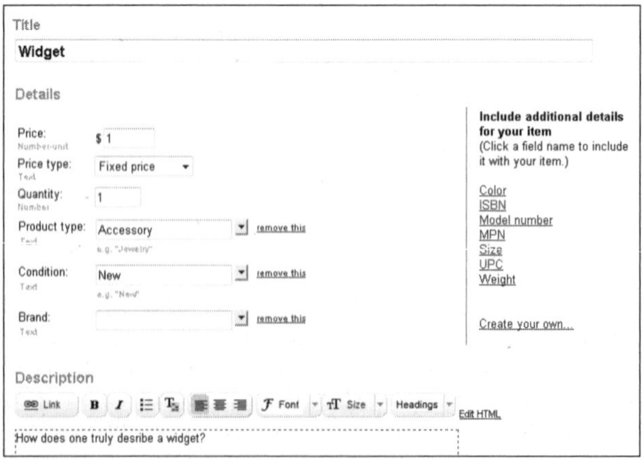

Figure 4-11: Adding a product to Google Base.

Book III
Chapter 4

**Showcasing Your
Stuff with
Google Base**

Figure 4-12:
Adding
more
information
to your
Google
Base ad.

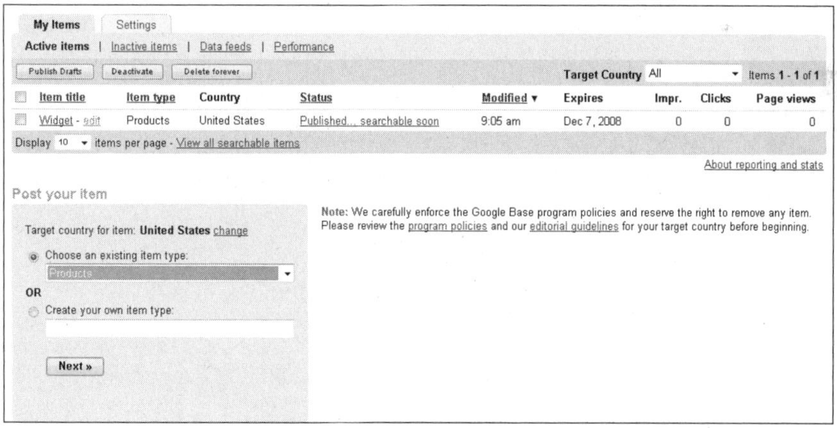

Figure 4-13:
Your
published
Google
Base entry.

Notice the new ad is shown in the Active Items tab. After it expires, the ad
moves over to the Inactive Items tab, where you are asked to renew it if you
want to post it again. There are also links for data feeds and performance,
which you see in the next section entitled "Creating a Data Feed to Add
Multiple Items at Once," later in this chapter. If you click the Settings tab,
you are prompted to enter more complete contact information, as shown

in Figure 4-14. This allows you to update the public information attached to your Google Base entries as well as private information only Google can use to contact you.

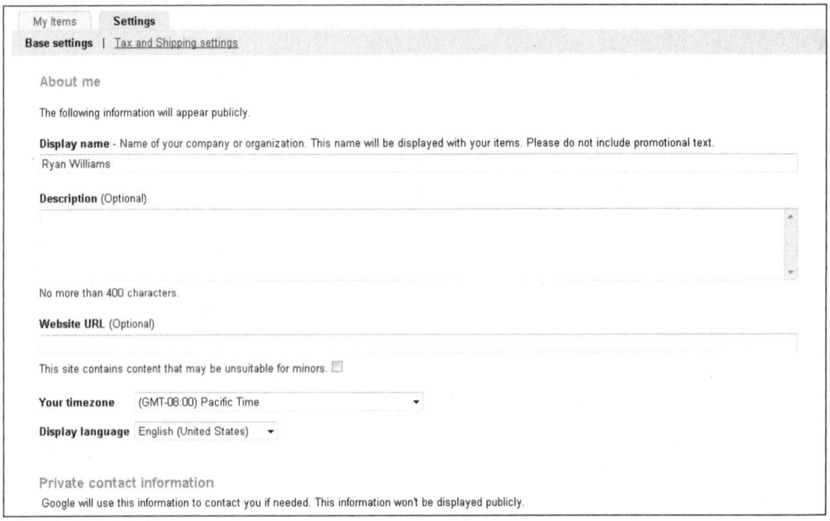

Figure 4-14:
Changing your Google Base settings.

My Items	**Settings**

Base settings | Tax and Shipping settings

About me

The following information will appear publicly.

Display name - Name of your company or organization. This name will be displayed with your items. Please do not include promotional text.

Ryan Williams

Description (Optional)

No more than 400 characters.

Website URL (Optional)

This site contains content that may be unsuitable for minors.

Your timezone (GMT-08:00) Pacific Time

Display language English (United States)

Private contact information

Google will use this information to contact you if needed. This information won't be displayed publicly.

Make sure your contact information is always up to date. If you're trying to sell something, you want to make sure people can get in touch with you.

You can have multiple Google accounts — for example, you can have one private account for e-mail and one for business. Be sure your information is correct for the account that you're using.

Take a look at the bottom of the screen shown in Figure 4-13. It looks just like the screen you saw at the beginning of this process. Here's where you can continue to add items to your Google Base entries. Just choose the category for the next item and click Next. You repeat the process for each item, as many times as you want. It may seem a little tedious, but this method makes sure that all the information needed to successfully locate your product or service makes it on to Google Base.

Creating a Data Feed to Add Multiple Items at Once

The steps we just went over are great if you're only putting a few items up on Google Base, but that process could get a little tedious if you have a large inventory of items or services to advertise online. The repetition is a time-waster for some, and Google has provided a way to avoid that problem. Using a simple text file, you can let Google Base know everything that has to be uploaded in a few simple steps.

Setting up your feed

Google Base accepts two different types of text files as input for uploaded entries. You can create these files by hand in a program like Notepad for Windows or TextEdit for Mac. You can also use Microsoft Excel to create the file and then save it as a text file.

Google Base does not accept files in Microsoft Word or Excel formats. They have to be saved specifically as text files or it just won't work.

The first type of text file is a tab-delimited file, where the information contained in the file is separated by tabs. The easiest way to create a tab-delimited file is to use a program like Microsoft Excel, enter all the information in the sheet, and export it as a tab-delimited file.

Google Base provides a list of the common data types for each category at `http://base.google.com/support/bin/answer.py?answer=59451&hl=en`, and you should check that list when you're putting your information together.

The more information you include, the easier it is find your item or service on Google Base.

In this case, let's add a service to Google Base. Google requires the following fields to add a service to Google Base:

- ✦ Description
- ✦ Link
- ✦ Service_type
- ✦ Price
- ✦ Title

That means that every feed for submitting a service must have these fields in order to be accepted by Google. If you're putting a text file together with Microsoft Excel, it might look something like the screen shown in Figure 4-15. You can also use the spreadsheet in Google Docs to create your text file. To save it as a text file, go to File➪Export➪.txt Sheet Only and save the file from the new browser window or tab that contains the document. Be sure to save it with the `.txt` file extension.

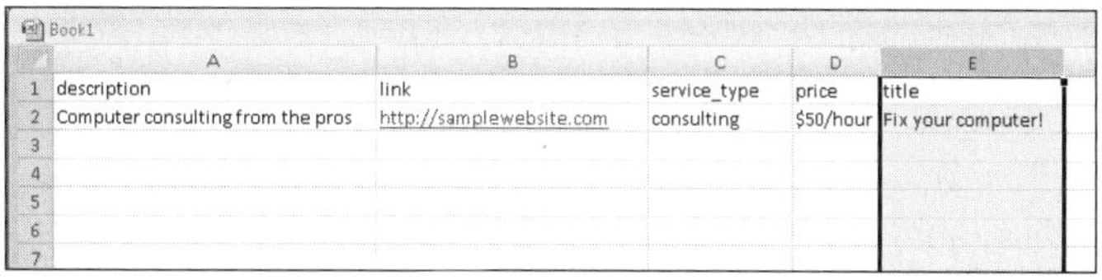

Figure 4-15: Creating your upload file

	A	B	C	D	E
1	description	link	service_type	price	title
2	Computer consulting from the pros	http://samplewebsite.com	consulting	$50/hour	Fix your computer!
3					
4					
5					
6					
7					

Google also provides a list of optional fields you can enter. For example, you can also add images and links to your items, as well as unique IDs. It all depends on exactly what you're uploading. After you've placed all the items you want to include in your data feed, follow these steps to create a tab-delimited text file.

1. **In Microsoft Excel, click the Office button and select Save As⇨Other Formats.**

2. **Click the drop-down menu of the Save window that comes up and select Text (Tab delimited).**

3. **Enter the name of your file and choose the save location through the save window.**

4. **Click Save when you're finished.**

In the other instance, you can set up an XML file to upload. You won't need any spreadsheet program to put this together, but it could be a little complicated if you've never had any experience with tags and mark-up languages. If you're used to HTML and XML, however, this is a snap.

In your text editor of choice, enter the following example:

```
<?xml version="1.0" encoding="UTF-8" ?>
<rss version ="2.0" xmlns:g="http://base.google.com/ns/1.0">
<channel>
<title>My Data Feed</title>
<description>The services offered by my company</description>
<link>http://www.sampleWeb site.com</link>
<item>
    <title>Fix Your Computer!</title>
    <description>Computer consulting from the pros</
    description>
    <link>http://www.samplewebsite.com/computerinfo.html</
    link>
    <g:price>50</g:price>
    <g:service_type>consulting</g:service_type>
</item>
</channel>
</rss>
```

Everything in this code has to be typed exactly as it appears in order for it to work, but there are parts you can customize. Although the tags (the information inside the brackets) can be customized for your specific purposes, the rest of the code must stay exactly the same. For example, in the code that precedes the <item> tag, everything has to stay the same except for the information inside the `title` and `description` tags. You can change `My Data Feed` to anything you want. You can also change the information inside the description tags to anything you want.

The item tags include the information for all the services you include in this feed. All the tags have to stay the same in this section as well, but you can change the information inside the tags to fit your product. Notice how the information inside the code is the same as the information in the spreadsheet shown in Figure 4-15. You recreate this section of code for each item in your feed.

TIP

There are additional tags you can use, as provided by Google. Tags that adhere to XML and RSS universal standards appear normally, whereas tags with a "g" before them are specific to Google.

If it seems like a lot to digest, just remember this: You don't have to write all this out. Google has already created the examples for you, and specific instances of the code are listed for each type of service available on Google Base. That means it has already done all the work for you. All you have to do is copy the information from the examples on Google, paste it into your text editor, make the changes, and upload the file. There's no need to reinvent the wheel here — copy and paste works just fine.

When your file is completed, save it with the file extension `.xml` and place it wherever you can find it easily. Now it's time to register your feed. Just follow these steps:

**Book III
Chapter 4**

**Showcasing Your
Stuff with
Google Base**

1. **Navigate to `http://base.google.com` and click the Data Feed link to see the screen shown in Figure 4-16.**

Figure 4-16:
Uploading a
data feed.

2. **Click the New Data Feed to start the process.**

3. **You need to add some general information, as seen in Figure 4-17. Enter what you need to add and click Next.**

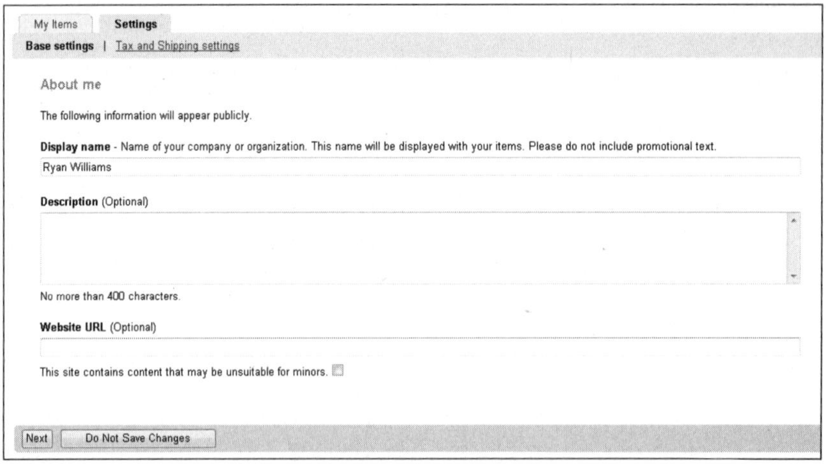

My Items | **Settings**
Base settings | Tax and Shipping settings

About me

The following information will appear publicly.

Display name - Name of your company or organization. This name will be displayed with your items. Please do not include promotional text.

Ryan Williams

Description (Optional)

No more than 400 characters.

Website URL (Optional)

This site contains content that may be unsuitable for minors. ☐

[Next] [Do Not Save Changes]

Figure 4-17:
Entering
your new
data feed
information.

4. Now, you enter specific information regarding your feed, including the country you're targeting, the type of information you're uploading, and the name of the file, as shown in Figure 4-18.

5. Click Register Data Feed and your feed is listed on your profile, as shown in Figure 4-19.

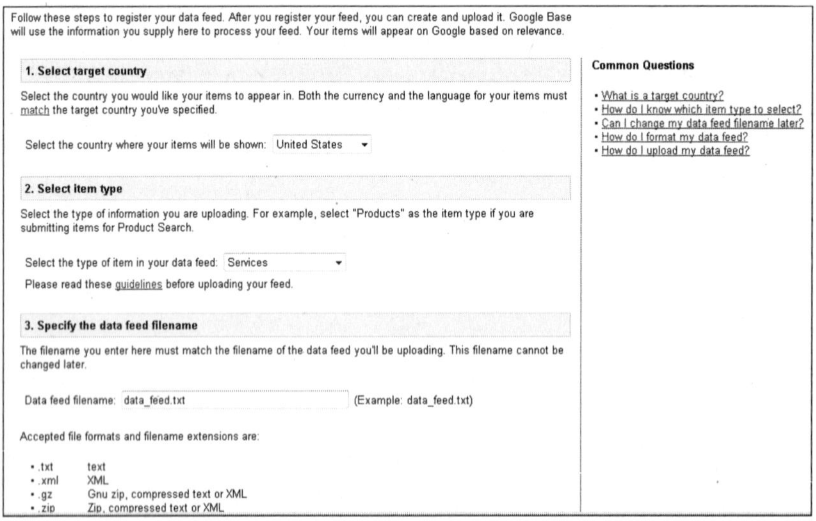

Follow these steps to register your data feed. After you register your feed, you can create and upload it. Google Base will use the information you supply here to process your feed. Your items will appear on Google based on relevance.

1. Select target country

Select the country you would like your items to appear in. Both the currency and the language for your items must match the target country you've specified.

Select the country where your items will be shown: United States ▼

Common Questions

- What is a target country?
- How do I know which item type to select?
- Can I change my data feed filename later?
- How do I format my data feed?
- How do I upload my data feed?

2. Select item type

Select the type of information you are uploading. For example, select "Products" as the item type if you are submitting items for Product Search.

Select the type of item in your data feed: Services ▼

Please read these guidelines before uploading your feed.

3. Specify the data feed filename

The filename you enter here must match the filename of the data feed you'll be uploading. This filename cannot be changed later.

Data feed filename: data_feed.txt   (Example: data_feed.txt)

Accepted file formats and filename extensions are:

- .txt   text
- .xml   XML
- .gz   Gnu zip, compressed text or XML
- .zip   Zip, compressed text or XML

Figure 4-18:
Registering
your data
feed.

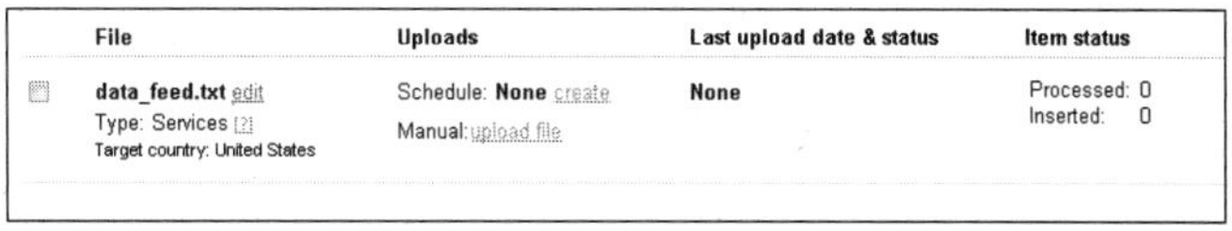

Figure 4-19:
Your new
data feed.

File	Uploads	Last upload date & status	Item status
data_feed.txt edit Type: Services [?] Target country: United States	Schedule: **None** create Manual: upload file	**None**	Processed: 0 Inserted: 0

Now that Google has reserved your data feed, you can upload the text file. You can either do this manually by clicking the Upload File link or create a regular upload by clicking the Create link. If you choose to schedule an upload, you have to put a file on your Web site and put the link in your Google Base feed.

Whenever you want to make changes, just edit the file on your own computer and either upload it to Google or your site for a scheduled update. You can also delete a feed by clicking the check box next to the feed and clicking the Delete button. You can also add as many data feeds as you need to — just repeat the preceding process as many times as it takes. You have to make a new data feed for each type of service, product, or other category you put on Google Base.

Testing your XML file

If you choose to create an XML file and want to be sure it works before you upload it, use a feed validation site like the one located at `http://validator.w3.org/feed/`. Either give the site the URL of the file or copy and paste the entire file into the site and click the Check button. If there's something wrong, it shows you where the problem is. If everything is fine, you get a message saying so. Don't be afraid if the Google tags (the ones with a "g" in the tag) do not validate. They work for Google's purposes, and you can leave them in there.

Chapter 5: Feeding Your Products to Google Product Search

In this chapter

✔ **Getting your products on Google Product Search**

✔ **Managing your Google Product Search inventory**

✔ **Working with Google Product Search data feeds**

C hapter 4 introduced you to Google Base, a vast repository of knowledge with several different categories for all kinds of data. It's easy to get lost in this huge repository of information, and it could get a little frustrating if you're shopping for a certain item. Think of heading out for a light bulb and ending up in the Wal-Mart the size of North America. That's why Google narrowed down the search a bit and gave the shoppers more options with Google Product Search. Although Base can hold all kinds of different information, Product Search focuses specifically on goods for sale.

Google Product Search is a combination of the Mall of America and a DIY flea market where everybody is invited to set up a booth and sell his wares. Instead of wandering through booth upon booth, however, you can go directly to what you want by using a quick product search and clicking a few times. Just go to `http://google.com/products` to view the screen shown in Figure 5-1.

Figure 5-1:
The opening
screen of
Google
Product
Search.

In addition to the simple text box, Google provides links to recently sought items, just in case you want to take a look at one of those entries. If not, just go ahead and type in what you want. Click Search Products, and you're off.

Using Google Product Search's Advanced Search Options

Because the Google Product Search database draws on a tremendous amount of data, you may want to click the Advanced Product Search link next to the Search Products button. You'll find more ways to narrow down the scope of your search and find exactly what you're looking for. Look at the screen shown in Figure 5-2 to see those options.

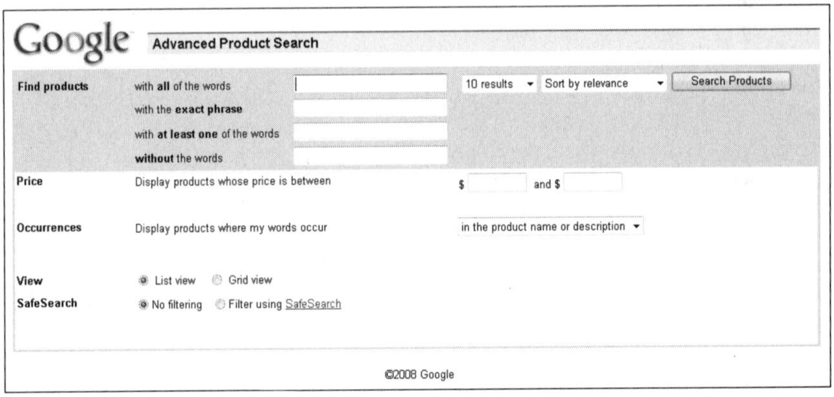

Figure 5-2: Advanced Search Options for Google Product Search.

The first set of text fields lets you define the search terms for your product:

✦ **With all of the words:** The entry has to include every word in this field; all others are discarded.

✦ **With the exact phrase:** Only those entries with these words in the exact order listed are considered.

✦ **With at least one of the words:** You cast a wide net when you consider every entry with at least one of the words in this field.

✦ **Without the words:** Any entry with the words in this field is discarded.

You can further reduce the scope of your search by choosing to display between 10 and 100 items and sort them based on relevancy, price, product rating, and seller rating. Additional text fields shown, in Figure 5-2, let you set a price range and search for your terms in the product title, description, or both. Finally, you can choose to display your items in grid or list view and choose to have your results filtered through SafeSearch, which removes any graphic sexual content.

Let's conduct a search for a type of camera using the search terms shown in Figure 5-3.

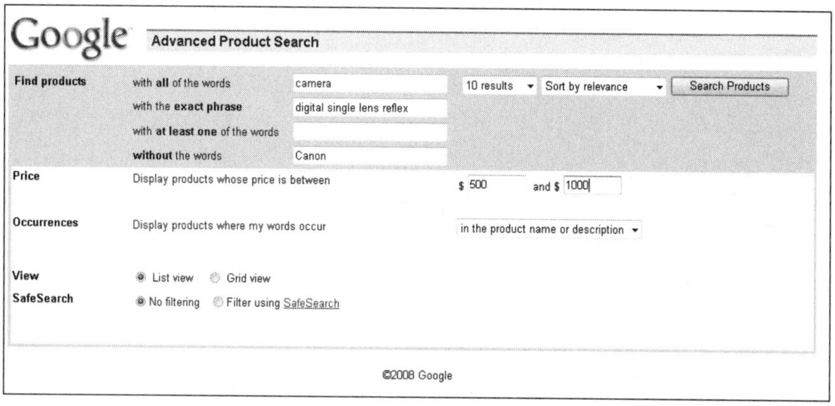

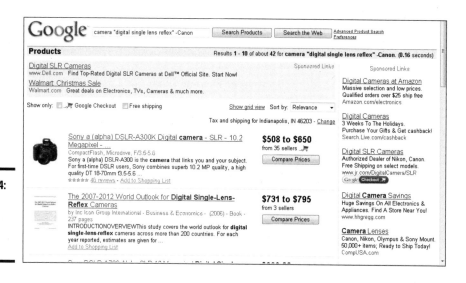

Figure 5-3:
Searching through Google Product Search.

Running these search terms gets the results shown in Figure 5-4. Notice how Google lists paid ads at the top and relevant results in the main section of the page. More sponsored links are shown in the sidebar.

Figure 5-4:
Google Product Search results.

This is a small, small portion of what you can find using Google Product Search, so be prepared to do a lot of searching. Precise search terms and filtered results should speed along your search, however.

Adding Products to Google Product Search

Like most of the services provided by Google, Google Product Search allows anybody to add items for free. After all, Google is in the business of collecting and indexing the largest amount of data possible — your data brings users to Google's sites, and that's what Google wants. Navigate to `http://www.google.com/base/help/sellongoogle.html` to start putting your products on Google. This Web address brings up the screen shown in Figure 5-5.

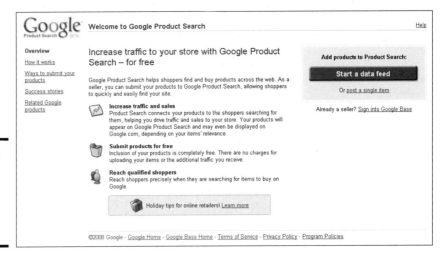

Figure 5-5: The initial screen for Google Product Search.

Google Product Search is a part of the larger Google Base database, so this process might seem familiar to those who reviewed Chapter 4 of this book or worked with Google Base before. The two options for entering items into Google Product Search are shown in Figure 5-5. Let's start with the simplest way — entering items individually.

Submitting your products

Click the Post a Single Item link shown in Figure 5-5, and you see the screen shown in Figure 5-6.

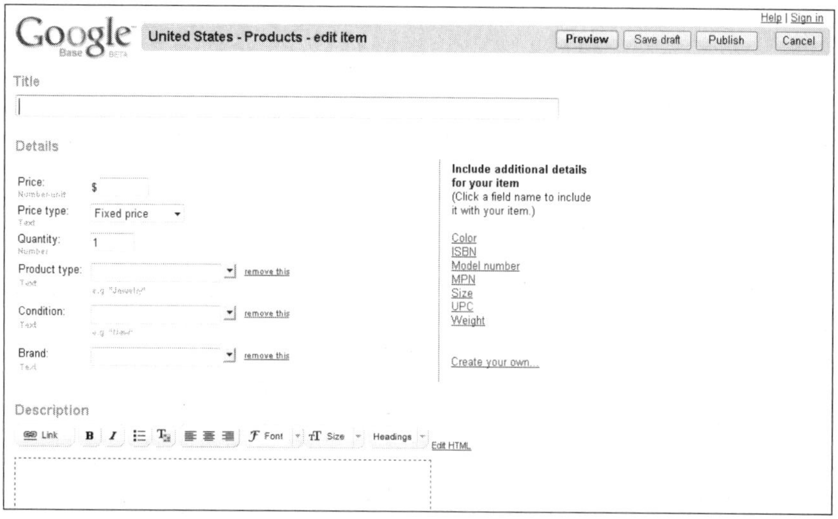

Figure 5-6:
Submitting
your
product
to Google
Product
Search.

Google Product Search gives you some default fields to talk about your project:

✦ **Title:** The introduction to your product.

✦ **Price:** How much you want for your product.

✦ **Price Type:** Choose between Fixed, Negotiable, and Minimum.

✦ **Quantity:** Provide the number of the items available.

✦ **Product Type:** Either choose from the drop-down menu choices or create your own.

✦ **Condition:** Select New, Refurbished, or Used.

✦ **Brand:** Again, choose the brand name of your product from the drop-down menu or enter your own.

If you want to remove the Product type, Condition, or Brand name text fields, just click Remove This link next to them. You can also click the links at the side of Figure 5-6 to add any fields you want to include in your product listing. As shown in Figure 5-7, you can also add images, either from the Web or your computer. You can also edit your contact information, payment information, and location information.

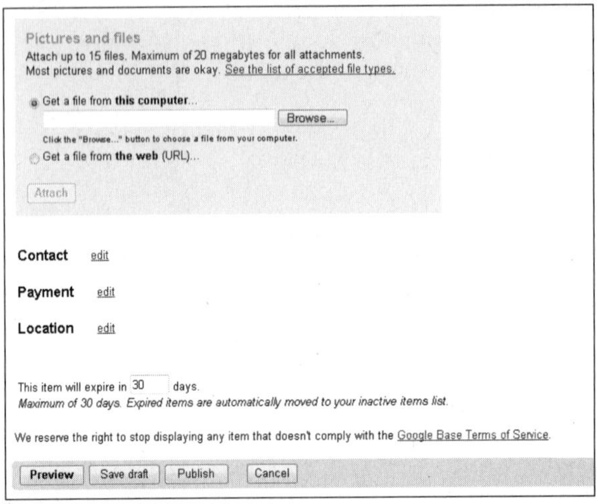

Pictures and files
Attach up to 15 files. Maximum of 20 megabytes for all attachments. Most pictures and documents are okay. See the list of accepted file types.

● Get a file from **this computer**...

[   ] [Browse...]

Click the "Browse..." button to choose a file from your computer.

○ Get a file from **the web** (URL)...

[Attach]

Contact   edit

Payment   edit

Location   edit

This item will expire in 30 days.
Maximum of 30 days. Expired items are automatically moved to your inactive items list.

We reserve the right to stop displaying any item that doesn't comply with the Google Base Terms of Service.

[**Preview**] [Save draft] [Publish] [Cancel]

Figure 5-7:
Adding more information to your Google Product Search listing.

If you choose to edit your contact information, click Edit to the side of the Contact heading and enter your name and phone number. Click Edit beside the Payment heading to specify what forms of payment (such as Google Checkout, Visa, and so on) you accept for the product. Finally, click Edit next to location to enter the physical location of the product. This can be your home address or a place of business.

Make sure you want your home address to be attached to this product before you post it. You don't have to enter this information if you don't want to.

When you're finished, you can click one of the four buttons shown at the bottom of Figure 5-7:

+ **Preview** displays your ad as it would appear on Google Product Search, but it doesn't create the entry.

+ **Publish** submits your information as is to Google Product Search.

+ **Save Draft** saves your information for later modification or publishing.

+ **Cancel** cleans the slate and lets you start from the beginning.

Like all the items on Google Base, your active listing has a maximum expiration date of 30 days. Beyond that, you have to reactivate the listing or let it go inactive and unseen.

When you click Publish, your item is added to your inventory, available for viewing every time you sign into Google Product Search with your Google account. Each listing appears like the example shown in Figure 5-8.

Note the information at the right of Figure 5-8. Google Product Search shows you information about how your listing is used by others. The columns are as follows:

✦ **Impr.:** Short for impressions, this shows the amount of times your listing comes up in a search.

✦ **Clicks:** This statistic shows how many times your listing was clicked during a search.

✦ **Page views:** This statistic measures numbers of visits to your overall `base.google.com` page.

Additional controls are available near the tabs at the top of Figure 5-8. They include

✦ **Active items** show products that are currently available to the general public.

✦ **Inactive items** show product listings that have expired. You can reactivate them later.

✦ **Data feeds** show automated feeds of your product listings.

✦ **Performance** shows you charts of how many products you've added and how many clicks you've received.

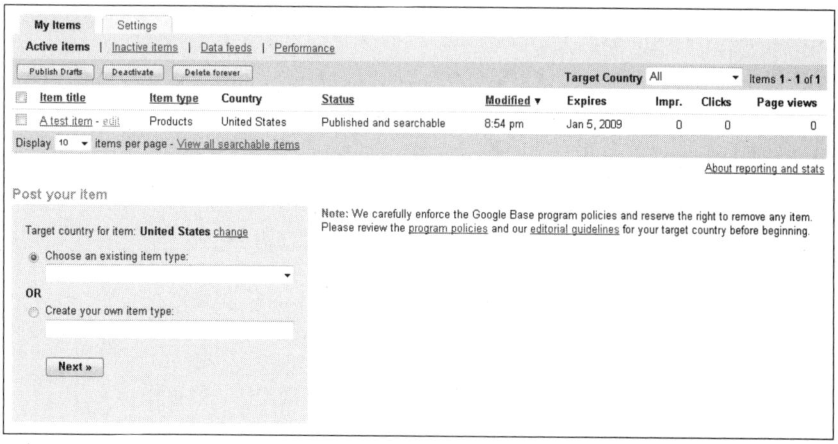

Figure 5-8:
A Google Product Search listing.

The buttons beneath those links control individual items. Just click the check box next to the items you want to modify and click the button to perform your chosen action. These buttons perform the following tasks:

- ✦ **Publish Drafts** takes any drafts you've saved and makes them active listings.
- ✦ **Activate Item** moves inactive items back to the active list.
- ✦ **Deactivate Item** moves the listing to the inactive list.
- ✦ **Delete Forever** removes the listing entirely from Google Product Search.

Where is my product?

It sometimes takes some time for your listing to show up on Google Product Search. Be patient — it will get up there soon enough. If it doesn't show up, check the Inactive list. Google Product Search may have disapproved the ad if it doesn't meet Google's standards, and you may have to modify some information. Google always tells you why it didn't approve the listing, and you have the opportunity to revise and resubmit the listing immediately.

Google's Terms of Service and usage requirements are available as links on the Google Product Search page. Review them before submitting to avoid headaches and delays with your Google Product Search listings.

Managing My Products

If you routinely change products or revise your prices, you may have to change the listings of your products. As with most Google-based functions, it's an easy process. Just click the Edit link next to the product listing shown in Figure 5-9.

Editing your product listing

Just as when you created the product listing, you can modify the included fields or change the information, as shown in Figure 5-10.

Edit link

Figure 5-9: Editing your Google Product Search listing.

Title

Widget

Details

Price: $ 1.00
Number, unit

Price type: Fixed price
Text

Quantity: 1
Number

Product type: Accessory   remove this
Text   e.g. "Jewelry"

Condition: New   remove this
Text   e.g. "New"

Include additional details for your item
(Click a field name to include it with your item.)

Brand
Color
Model number
MPN
Size
UPC
Weight

Create your own...

Description

Link   **B** *I* ≔ T₃ ▤ ▤ ▤   𝓕 Font ▾ ᴛT Size ▾ Headings ▾   Edit HTML

The only difference between the initial listing and the edited listing is the lack of a Save Draft button. You can preview your new listing, publish it, or cancel your changes and leave it the way it is.

Removing your product listing

You have two options when you want to take your product down from Google Product Search. You can either deactivate the listing or remove it entirely from Google Product Search.

To deactivate the listing, click the check box next to each item you want to remove and click the Deactivate button shown in Figure 5-9. These listings are still available for your examination or listing later, but nobody can view the product until you reactivate it.

If you want to remove the product entirely from Google Product Search, repeat the same process for deactivating a product, but click the Delete Forever button instead of the Deactivate button.

Delete Forever is just as final as it sounds. The information is permanently removed from Google Product Search, and you have to complete the entire listing process again to get the information back up. If you're not sure that you want to totally stop selling the product, it's better to just deactivate it and wait until you are sure.

Promoting your product

Just because your product is listed on Google Product Search doesn't mean that the buyers will be flocking to your door in seconds. You need to get the word out that your products are available. Google Product Search takes care of those searching the database, but you can send out links to specific items through a variety of outlets.

First, in the screen shown in Figure 5-9, click the View All Searchable Items link. This brings up the screen shown in Figure 5-11. All the items you have placed on Google Product Search are listed in this view.

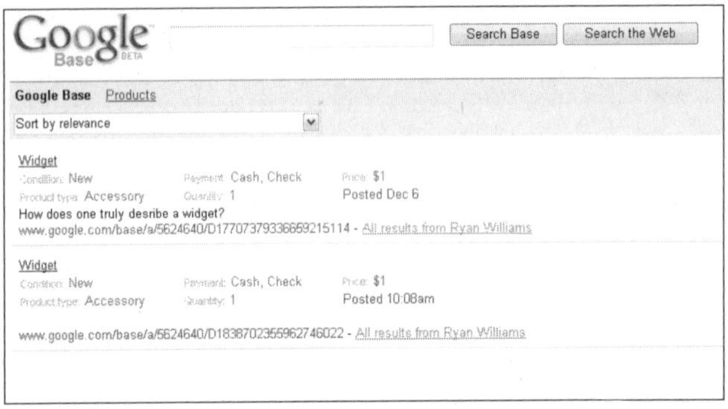

Figure 5-11: A full listing of Google Product Search items.

Each item has a direct link to that product printed below the name of the product. When clicked, that link takes a user directly to the product listing. When you have that link, you can place it in several locations to bring customers to your products. Those locations include

✦ **Web sites:** This is an obvious way to promote your products. Just post the links on your Web site and have your customers click there.

✦ **Blogs:** If you manage a blog for your company, post the link in a blog entry and let your readers discover what you have to offer.

✦ **E-mail lists:** If your company publishes e-mail newsletters for your customers, you can include the links to your new product in those e-mail newsletters.

Be sure you only send e-mail to those who have actively agreed to be part of your e-mail newsletter list. Not only do you risk annoying potential customers with your unwanted messages, but some areas may ban the use of spam.

✦ **Other social media:** If you use MySpace, Facebook, Twitter, or other similar social media services, you can post notes or bulletins with those links and let your friends find your products.

No matter how you choose to promote your products, these links always lead directly to your products. You can also click the All Products By link (my name appears in the example shown in Figure 5-11, but it'll be your name in the actual screen), copy that URL out of your browser window, and paste it in whatever location you desire. That way, your customers can see your entire inventory in one screen.

Introducing Product Search Feeds

Google Product Search Feeds are similar to the Google Base feeds shown in Chapter 4, but all the listings have the same basic fields and are listed in one large service, as opposed to being spread out over several different categories. Product search feeds also offer several convenient features over entering items individually, including the following:

+ **Convenient uploads of multiple items:** Using data feeds, you can upload several products at one time without the hassle of repeating the individual process. By entering all the information in one document and then performing one upload procedure, all your products are listed at one time.

+ **Central location for change:** All your product records are kept in one place, so you can make sure that all your modifications are made on one single document. This ensures that everything stays current and up-to-date, with no worries about out-of-sync product entries.

+ **Make changes anywhere:** Even if you don't have access to a network at the time, you can make changes to the data feed and upload it. Take the information you need to add or modify, alter your feed, and upload it when you get the chance.

+ **Convenient formats:** If you're comfortable with Microsoft Excel or Google Docs Spreadsheet, you can use that program to create your data feed. If you're more comfortable using a text file with tags to upload your data feed, you can use that as well. There are many ways to create your data feed, so you can use whichever one appeals to you more.

Creating a Product Search Feed

When you start your data feed, no matter whether you're creating an XML or tab-delimited text file, you must include five required fields:

+ **Title:** This is the overall name for your item.

+ **ID:** This is a unique ID for your product, taken from your records. You can make it whatever you want, but it can't change after you've entered it.

✦ **Description:** This information describes the product itself.

✦ **Link:** This hyperlink points to a Web page associated with the product, like your company's home page or a specific page for the product on your site.

✦ **Price:** This listing sets the price for the product, usually in U.S. dollars.

Google Product Search also has other fields you can include in your product feed. These are not required fields, but you can use them to expand the details about your product. This is helpful because the additional search terms give users more options. These fields include

✦ **Brand:** This is the name of the manufacturer of the product.

✦ **Condition:** You can specify new, used, or refurbished.

✦ **Image_link:** This includes a hyperlink to an image of the product.

✦ **ISBN:** This is a unique identifying number used for books.

✦ **MPN:** This is a manufacturer part number assigned by the manufacturer.

✦ **UPC:** If your product has a universal product code, enter it here.

✦ **Weight:** Enter the weight of your item. This defaults to pounds, but you can specify other units.

✦ **Color:** Specify the color of your product.

✦ **Expiration_date:** Put in the date your listing expires in the format YYYY/MM/DD (year/month/day).

✦ **Height:** Enter the number and unit of measure for height.

✦ **Length:** Enter the number and unit of measure for length.

✦ **Model_number:** If your product has a model number, enter it in this field.

✦ **Payment_accepted:** Google lets you specify Cash, Check, Visa, MasterCard, AmericanExpress, Discover, and WireTransfer. Each payment option has to have its own entry.

✦ **Payment_notes:** Place any payment policies in this field.

✦ **Price_type:** If the price is negotiable or a starting point, enter that information here.

✦ **Product_type:** Enter the keywords for your product here.

✦ **Quantity:** Enter the number of items you're selling here.

✦ **Shipping:** If your shipping prices differ from region to region, you can specify that here.

✦ **size:** Add values like small, medium, and large here.

✦ **Tax:** Enter any sales tax information here.

✦ **Width:** Enter the number and unit for width here.

✦ **Year:** Enter the year the product was produced here.

Choose the fields you want to use in addition to the required fields and choose how you want to create your data feed. You have two options:

✦ **Tab-delimited text files:** These are the text files created using text editors or spreadsheet programs that contain your business and product information.

✦ **XML files:** If you're comfortable creating and using XML files, you can use these files to outline your business and product information.

Each of these is discussed in greater detail in the next two subsections.

Tab-delimited text files

To create a tab-delimited text file, open up Microsoft Excel and enter the required fields as shown in Figure 5-12.

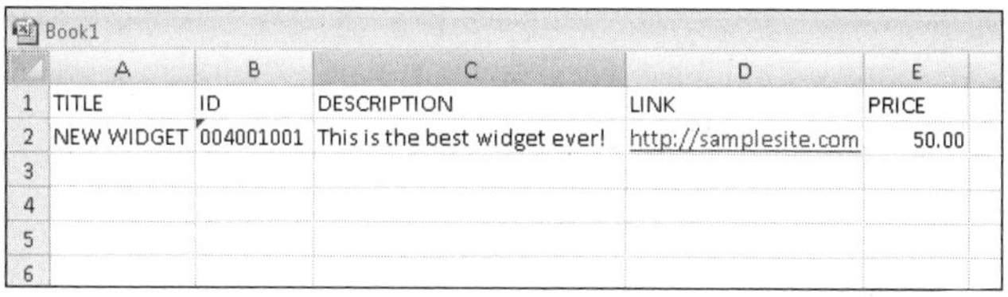

**Book III
Chapter 5**

**Feeding Your
Products to Google
Product Search**

Figure 5-12:
Creating a tab-delimited text file in Microsoft Excel.

	A	B	C	D	E
1	TITLE	ID	DESCRIPTION	LINK	PRICE
2	NEW WIDGET	004001001	This is the best widget ever!	http://samplesite.com	50.00
3					
4					
5					
6					

When you've made all your entries, click the Office button in the top-left corner and select Save As➪Other Formats. In the drop-down menu at the bottom of the Save window, select Text (Tab-Delimited). Type in the name of the file and select the location. Save it, and you're ready to go.

Keep this file around and change it as necessary. You'll find it takes less time to make your edits than it does to recreate the file.

XML files

With a text editor like Notepad for Windows or TextEdit for Macs, you can create an XML file that will be posted on the Internet and used to publish your data feed. Creating an XML file is an easy task if you're used to dealing with markup languages and tags, and you can always copy and paste the examples from Google's help section. In this case, a sample feed for a product data feed would look like this:

```
<?xml version="1.0"?>
<rss version="2.0">
<channel>
<title>My Data Feed</title>
<link>http://www.samplesite.com</link>
<description>This feed lists products from my
   company.<description>
  <item>
  <title>My Widget</title>
  <link>http://samplesite.com/myproduct.html</link>
  <description>This is the best widget ever!</description>
  <g:price>25.00</g:price>
  <g:id>W1</g:id>
  </item>
  <item>
  <title>My Second Widget</title>
  <link>http://samplesite.com/myproduct2.html</link>
  <description>This is the best widget ever! Even better than
   the last one!</description>
  <g:price>50.00</g:price>
  <g:id>W2</g:id>
  </item>
</channel>
</rss>
```

All the tags, or the text inside the brackets, have to be included in your feed in the order they're listed. Each item (that is, all the information between `<item>` and `</item>`) has to have its own entry as well. Just copy that text, change the information for the next item, and add it after the last item, as shown in the above code example. Note the g included in some of the tags — this means that they're specific to Google and not part of the larger XML standard. Don't worry about it. Google honors the tags without a problem, and other XML services ignore them. When you're done, save the file with the file extension of `.xml`, and you're ready to go.

The good thing about XML files is that you can edit and upload them whenever you want, and you can specify as much information as you want.

Google may require different attributes for some of these XML values, so be sure to check your tags with the Google help section to make sure they're current. Markup languages are always changing and evolving, so you may see different values past the time of this book's printing.

Registering and Submitting Your Data Feed

When you've saved your product feed, no matter what format you used, it's time to make Google aware of your product feed. Here's all you have to do:

1. **Point your browser to** http://base.google.com/base/dashboard **and click the Data Feeds link to see the screen shown in Figure 5-13.**

2. **Click the New Data Feed button and enter the information required in the fields shown in Figure 5-14.**

3. **Click Next when you're finished.**

4. **Enter the specific information about your feed. Click Register Data Feed when you're done.**

   Enter the information in the fields shown in Figure 5-15. Make sure the name of your data feed exactly matches the name of the text file you created.

This may seem very much like the instructions for adding a new feed to Google Base (in Chapter 4 of this minibook), but by following these instructions, your product automatically moves to Google Product Search.

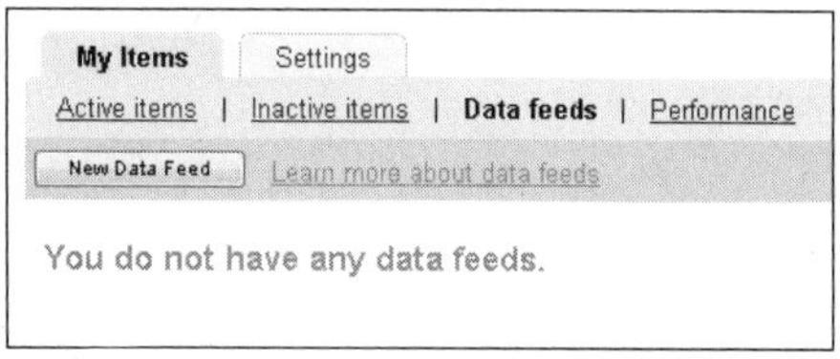

Figure 5-13:
Adding
a new
data feed.

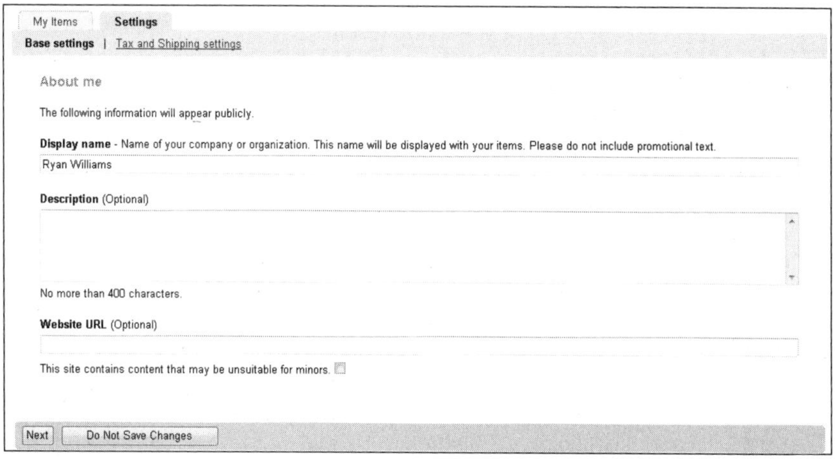

My Items	Settings
Active items	Inactive items	**Data feeds**	Performance

New Data Feed   Learn more about data feeds

You do not have any data feeds.

Figure 5-14:
Basic
data feed
information.

My Items   **Settings**
Base settings | Tax and Shipping settings

About me

The following information will appear publicly.

Display name - Name of your company or organization. This name will be displayed with your items. Please do not include promotional text.
Ryan Williams

Description (Optional)

No more than 400 characters.

Website URL (Optional)

This site contains content that may be unsuitable for minors. ☐

Next   Do Not Save Changes

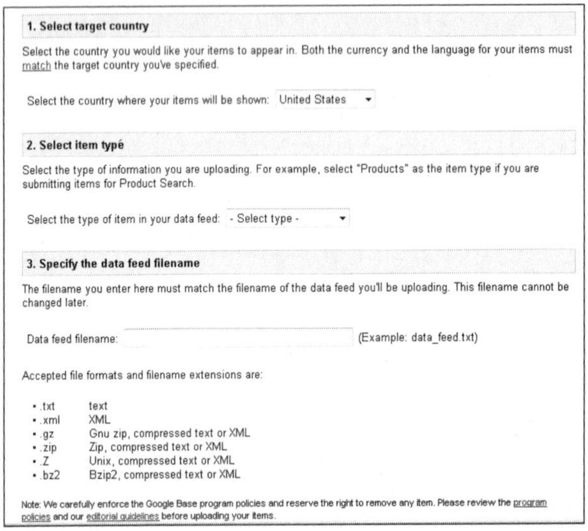

Figure 5-15:
Naming and
targeting
your data
feed.

5. **Click the appropriate Upload File link in the screen shown in Figure 5-16, as follows:**

   - *For uploading tab-delimited text files:* If you want to upload a text file, click the Upload File link and locate your text file on your computer. When you've uploaded the file, your data feed is ready.

   - *For uploading XML files:* If you're using an XML file, you have to upload the XML file to your Web site via an FTP program. Then, click the Create link next to the Schedule heading to force Google to check your XML file. When you've created a schedule, you can change and upload your XML file whenever you want, and the file will be updated on Google as scheduled.

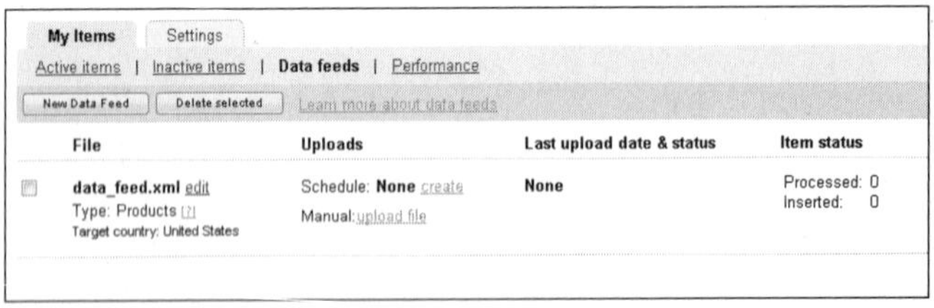

Figure 5-16:
Uploading
your data
feed.

Book IV

Creating a Web Site with Google Sites

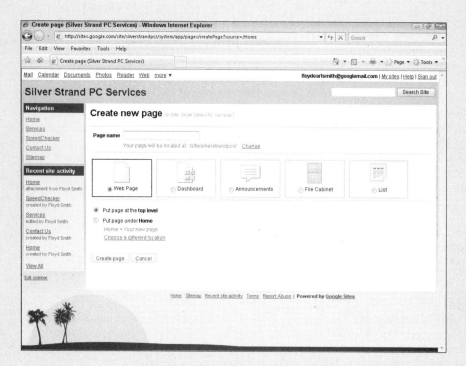

Creating a new page with Google Sites

Contents at a Glance

Chapter 1: Domain Names for Existing Businesses

In This Chapter

✔ Understanding how domain names affect Google search results

✔ Examining domain name endings

✔ Determining your site's ideal domain name and length

*N*o matter how you create your Web site — whether you use Google Sites, some other tool, or a combination — you need a domain name. Domain names, today, are absolutely crucial to your business.

In this chapter, we concentrate on creating the domain names for existing businesses — the most common-case scenario. The information in this chapter is just a starting point. In the next chapter, we explore choosing a new domain name for a new business.

The right domain name makes you and your business look serious and sensible. And it helps customers find you easily online, either by someone typing in your URL or by using Google Search.

Your domain name is also part of your — and your employees' — e-mail address. Again, this is further reason why your domain name should be serious, appropriate, and memorable.

The US Government has a guide to setting up a Web site for businesses that want to export to other countries. (This isn't just for export businesses, however; most of the advice seems to hold for any business.) It puts selecting a domain name first, as shown in Figure 1-1. (For the full guide, visit `http://www.export.gov/sellingonline`.)

Figure 1-1:
Get
government
help with
the naming
process.

Improving Google Search Results with Domain Names

Our key focus in this book is, of course, using Google tools, with Google's search capability having pride of place. How does your domain name make a difference with Google Search?

It apparently makes a big difference. There is a continuing game of cat and mouse between Google and search engine optimization (SEO) practitioners, authors, and consultants. Google tries to deliver the most accurate and useful results; SEO practitioners, authors, and consultants try to gain or sell high Google placements while expending the least possible effort. (And, in many cases, whether or not the high placement meets user needs.)

Google advertisements are one legitimate avenue for this, but people understandably still want to get high placements in Google's unpaid search. Google is always looking for indicators of a site's value and purpose that can't be easily manipulated. It's easy and inexpensive to manipulate the content of a Web page. A domain name costs a fair amount of money and takes effort to register and maintain. Therefore, it's more likely that a domain name is part of the legitimate representation of a legitimate page. Also, the length of domain names is restricted. This means the name has to represent one or, at most, a very few concepts, product types, and so on. Some short domain names with an obvious purpose sell for very high prices. Here are seven of the top-priced domain names ever (and the prices paid for them):

- ✦ **poker.com:** $27 million
- ✦ **beer.com:** $7 million
- ✦ **diamond.com:** $6 million
- ✦ **casino.com:** $5.5 million
- ✦ **asseenontv.com:** $5 million
- ✦ **wine.com:** $3.3 million
- ✦ **vodka.com:** $3 million.

What is a domain name, really?

The Internet is based on the Internet Protocol, a set of rules for how computers can communicate with each other over a network. The fundamental principle of the Internet Protocol is that each machine on the Internet has a unique Internet Protocol address (IP address).

IP addresses are a lot like home addresses — your house number, street, city name, and ZIP code or post code (and, for international mail, the name of your country) give you an address separate from anyone else on the planet. Because of this information, all the mail sent to you gets to you.

An IP address is made up of four blocks of numbers, each between 0 and 255. A typical IP address is 192.9.205.21. The first three blocks, 192.9.205, identify a particular network; the last block identifies a particular machine.

People have a hard time remembering IP addresses, and they're never very easy to tie to a particular company name or person's name. Because of this, domain names were invented.

A *domain name* is simply a set of characters that is assigned as the name for a specific IP address. The only purpose of this is to make an IP address easier to remember.

Domain names must be no longer than 63 characters; the only characters allowed are a-z, 0-9, and hyphens; no spaces.

Domain names are supported by Domain Name Servers, also called DNS servers (which is repetitive, we know). These servers map the words to the numbers. When you create a new domain name, it takes a certain amount of time for the new pair of name and IP address to be copied to all the DNS servers worldwide. It's claimed this can take up to two days, but we've never seen it take more than a few minutes.

Although we rarely recommend buying multiple domain names for your business, you should consider doing so if you create a name with one or more hyphens in it. (Hyphenating a name can help Google and other search engines find the individual words in the domain name.) Consider also buying the same name with no hyphens, such as both `fun-fish-finders.com` and `funfishfinders.com`.

Set up the unhyphenated domain name, during registration, to direct all traffic to the hyphenated version. This ensures that people who know your domain name but forget to type the hyphens — or who guess your domain name except for the hyphens — still end up at your Web site.

**Book IV
Chapter 1**

**Domain Names for
Existing Businesses**

The terms you expect people to use when they search for you are legitimate contenders to include in your domain name. You can then decide on other search terms using the content of your pages. Google is likely to respect the keywords in your domain name on an ongoing basis.

Typing Domain Names Directly

Domain names are also crucial to a type of search that's almost the opposite of Google Search: People remember or guess your domain name and type it in directly. (Remembering and guessing are not mutually exclusive because people use the two processes in combination when deciding what to type.)

To help people who want to type in your domain name directly, your domain name should have three main characteristics:

+ **It should be guessable:** People should be able to guess your domain name from what they know about your business. This usually means that your domain name is the same as your business name.

+ **It should be memorable:** Businesses and organizations have found, over and over, that it's difficult to get people to remember the name of your business or organization. Trying to get them to also remember a domain name that's different from your business name is just about impossible; the business and domain names should be the same, or as similar as possible.

+ **It should be spellable:** Your domain name should be easily spelled out by anyone who hears it. It should present no difficulty in spelling or in getting the right version of a word. (Words that sound the same but are spelled differently are called *homonyms*; avoid such words, or phrases that act in the same way, if at all possible.)

For example, let's say you own a tanning salon called Pallor Lifter, because it lifts the whitish tone, or *pallor*, that many people take on if they don't get enough sun. The name is clever, but if you were to say it to people, they would probably misremember it as something else, like *parlor, palor, paller*, and so on. If you had already invested in this business name, and the domain name were available, it would be the right name to use — but it's not an ideal choice.

Plurals, possessives, and hyphenated terms are particularly subject to confusion. For instance, *Floyd's Flowers* is harder to render as a domain name than *Flowers by Floyd*. If `flowersbyfloyd.com` is taken, you may be tempted to adopt the domain name `flowers-by-floyd.com` — but that's probably not a good idea. People will have trouble remembering the hyphens and will go to the already-taken domain name instead.

Especially avoid "clever" variations on an existing name in an attempt to "own" a variant, as with the "flowers-by-floyd" example; you'll lose too much traffic to the existing name.

A good test for a possible domain name is to say it to people and have them write down what they think they hear. You'd be amazed how often people can misunderstand what seems like a perfectly simple domain name.

Choosing Appropriate Domain Name Endings

In addition to the main part of the domain name, there are a lot of domain name endings besides the most common one, .com. These other options include .edu, .org, and .net at the global level. At the national level, there are national-specific names such as .co.uk or .fr.

It used to be that in order to use a domain name ending, you were required to follow rules that specified its meaning:

+ .com — A business, not necessarily registered or "official," but still out there to make money.

+ .edu — An educational institution, usually meaning a university or four-year college. (That's *college* in the American sense of the term, a generally slightly less prestigious version of a university, rather than the usage in many other countries — a school for pre-university study).

+ .gov — A governmental organization.

+ .net — An organization making up part of the fabric of the Web, such as an Internet Service Provider.

+ .org — A non-profit organization not fitting one of the previous categories.

The formal restrictions on types of domain names were lifted several years ago — they were never very enforceable — and now, supposedly, all bets are off. However, violating the rules just confuses people, so stick to .com for business, .edu for education, and so on.

If you have a business in the United States, .com is easily your first choice — almost your only choice because Americans are so accustomed to using .com for business domain names. And if you have a business with operations in several countries, you almost certainly need .com as the domain name ending for your overall corporate site — which might be your only site. But if your business exists entirely in a single, non-US country, or if it is spread among several countries, you might want to consider using — or also using — a country-specific domain name or names, as described in the next section.

.mobi and more

Many, many domain name alternatives are now used in addition to the original set described here. Two of the better-known ones are `.biz`, `.tv`, and `.mobi`.

You should consider these only if they are in some way a great fit for your business or purpose — and almost always as a second choice after `.com`. Even `.mobi`, which has a clear and admirable purpose — mobile-phone–specific sites, or mobile-phone–specific versions of existing sites — doesn't seem to get used much.

People instead expect to be able to use the `.com` site from their mobile phones, an expectation that is well met only by sites that are capable of detecting a mobile phone connection and can serve up a different, mobile-phone–specific site. Google's Gmail, for instance, has a specific version for the Blackberry that makes excellent use of the device's screen space and manages the amount of information downloaded in reasonable ways. But only a big company like Google can easily afford to offer specific versions of a free service such as Gmail for various kinds of devices.

The bottom line is: If at all possible, start with `.com` — or the national equivalent in non-US countries — stick with it, and consider alternatives only as supplementary options.

`.net` is probably the closest thing to an exception to our advice to stick with the rules. Not many people used or understood them back when the rules were more actively enforced. All Web sites are online, so `.net` sounds kind of sensible for any Web site. Consider using `.net` if you really must have an alternative to `.com`.

Nation-Specific Alternatives

Countries have their own versions of the top-level domains described in the previous section. Unfortunately, these aren't uniform:

✦ `.fr` — Added to any of the traditional domain name endings, the French version of it.

✦ `.co.uk` — A British business.

✦ `.ca` — A Canadian (not Californian!) site.

The list goes on; each country can differ somewhat.

The general rule regarding these is simple: Always use `.com` for business. However, when it comes to internationally based businesses, the best approach is a bit more complicated than that.

If your business is entirely in a single, non-US country, it can actually be to your advantage to use that country's name. Users are accustomed to typing in the country's *TLD — top-level domain*, such as `.co.uk` — for some sites and the more general TLD, `.com`, for others. Having a country-specific TLD such as `.co.uk` may actually fit your image as in the following case, a particularly British business.

Having a `.com` business name is basically fine, but it might imply ambitions beyond the country the user is in — and a lack of complete focus on that user's country. Foyles, a London-based bookseller, proudly uses `foyles.co.uk` as its Web address, and advertises this broadly, even though it also owns `foyles.com`. (It's redirected to `foyles.co.uk`.)

Similar logic applies to companies that operate in multiple countries. `Lastminute.com` is an Internet-based company that uses its brand name in several countries, and the `.com` TLD is part of the branding. So if you type `lastminute.co.uk`, you're simply redirected to `lastminute.com`. (Whichever URL you type, however, the site detects which country you're coming from and gives you appropriate options for that country.)

Orange, on the other hand, is a European telecommunications company based in France that competes against more broadly based companies — Vodafone, for instance, is fully global — and more narrowly focused companies. If you go to `orange.com`, you get the global Orange site, with a pull-down menu to take you to different country sites; but if you go to `orange.co.uk`, you get a UK-specific site.

You should pick a domain name for which you can control all the variations you need. For instance, if you would like to choose `SashasDanceStudios.com` today, but are planning to expand to the UK soon, then you ensure that you can acquire `SashasDanceStudios.co.uk` as well. A dance studio, essentially a local business, is more likely to function well as two national presences than a single, multinational one.

Choosing the Ideal Length

Common advice for domain names is to make them easy to remember, easy to type, and short. However, it is hard to find a name which satisfies all these requirements.

Most Web users are at least somewhat capable touch typists, so the harder thing is remembering a domain name, not actually typing a few more letters. Shorter names are not actually a good thing if they interfere with users' ability to remember them.

Why domain names are so contentious

Any time a new area of "land" is made available — even if the "land" is in the form of domain names, each occupying a tiny piece of cyberspace — speculators try to buy the good bits, hoping to "flip" them on to someone who can actually make productive use of them.

Domain names are very inexpensive — as little as a few dollars each — and potentially very valuable. The domain name `shopping.com` sold for $3 million back in the 1990s, for just one example.

So speculators buy all kinds of domain names in the hope of being able to make a killing on a resale.

Speculators aren't the only problem. Your business, Sarah's Pizza Parlor, may be huge, employ hundreds, be known around the world, and so on. But from a domain name point of view, it may have no more right to `sarahspizza parlor.com` than the smallest such business anywhere in the world. So if the little guys got "your" domain name first, there may not be much you can do about it. (But see Chapter 2 of this minibook for alternatives.)

If you have a real business with a specific name, and speculators have "your" name, there's a chance you can get it back — perhaps even without going to court. But you may still wish to check with a lawyer before making any decisions.

Web browsers now tend to remember formerly entered domain names, so it's quite possible that a user only has to fully type your complete domain name once on a given computer. The user may also choose to use search — most likely, Google Search — to find the business, so the role of the domain name in supporting search is just as important as whether it's easy to type in full. (Both are important, but never forget the role of search, which is becoming ever more important with time.)

So if your business name is Sasha's Dance Studios, you're better off with the Web site name `sashasdancestudios.com` than coming up with a shorter, but harder-to–remember name. Now if `sashasdancestudios.com` is taken, you may want to look for something shorter rather than longer as an alternative. But don't be scared of using an ideal domain name 25 characters long or so, if it's guessable, memorable, and easy to spell.

The most popular domain name length is about 11 characters long, not counting the top-level domain (`.com`, `.org`, and so on), as shown in the graph in Figure 1-2.

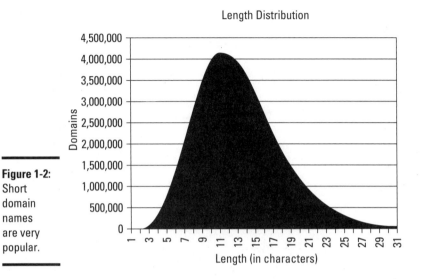

Length Distribution

Figure 1-2:
Short
domain
names
are very
popular.

Determining Your Ideal Domain Name

People expect to see your business name as your domain name, preferably ending in .com. They don't expect to see any punctuation, misspellings, odd domain names, or other "tricks."

The ideal domain name for a business called Lunar Toys for You is simply: lunartoysforyou.com.

So the first choice for a domain name for your business is simply your business name, with any punctuation removed, plus the .com ending. Follow the steps for how to check available domain names (in this chapter) to see if that name is available.

If your ideal domain name is available, we recommend you register it right away, using the additional steps we give in Chapter 3 on how to do just that — even if you don't plan to create a Web site right away.

In fact, it's possible that not registering your ideal domain name could be taken, in a trademark infringement case, as evidence that you're not serious about protecting your company's business name in the real world. If you're not willing to spend an hour and less than $20 to protect your trademark in cyberspace, a court somewhere may look askance at your seriousness in protecting it in the real world.

There may be additional concerns, though, even if your ideal domain name is available. So work through the ideas that follow to see if you should register other domain names as well.

If your ideal domain name isn't available, it becomes more important to get the strongest possible alternative. Customers and potential customers might be confused or frustrated that your ideal domain name is not, in fact, yours. You should identify and use the strongest alternative you can.

If your ideal domain name isn't available, go through the pointers in this chapter for finding a good domain name — then consider re-naming your business to match your domain name. This may seem like a huge effort to expend, but it eliminates what will otherwise be a persistent problem. Also, re-naming can be a good hook for a marketing push, off-line as well as online.

Selecting Keywords for Domain Names

Whether your ideal domain name is taken or not, you should identify other strong candidates, consider registering the best of them, and then redirect them to the one domain name you actually use.

The trick is to first identify keywords that can be used as components of your domain name. Contenders include

✦ **The business name:** Your ideal domain name is your business name; but even if that's taken, your business name (or words in it) still needs to be considered as part of your domain name.

✦ **Name(s) of the owner(s):** The more closely identified you or others are with the business, the more useful it is to use your name(s) as part of your domain name.

✦ **Product names:** Many companies, even big ones, end up re-naming themselves after their most successful product or product line. Seriously consider product names as keywords for your domain name.

✦ **Words that describe the business's location:** Location words are great for creating a domain name that includes your business name but is different from existing names. If you don't have a strong association with a place or part of town — if you aren't already known as "the one on the South Side" or wherever — then consider using the name of the street you're on.

✦ **Words that describe the type of business:** If your business name isn't strongly identified with a type of business, these can differentiate you from similarly named businesses. You can also use this strategy if your ideal domain name is owned by someone else.

Use the preceding words to help identify domain name candidates. Bounce candidate names off others to get their response.

Figure 1-3 shows Nameboy, an online service to help you try different combinations of keywords in domain names. You can use it with the keywords you generate.

See Book II, Chapter 3 for a worksheet to use in identifying key search terms.

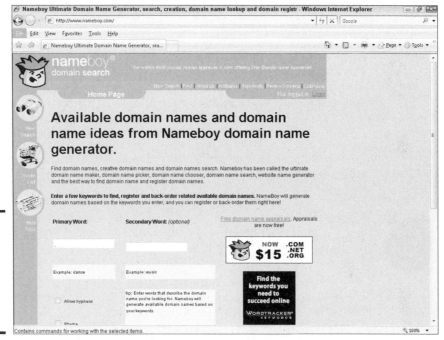

Figure 1-3:
Boy, can this service help you find a domain name!

Avoid the temptation to use categorical and conceptual names, such as verybestmattresses.com, unless you really are the worldwide leader in that category. Even if you are the worldwide leader, consider buying the category name and then pointing it to your branded business. With a few exceptions, category names such as shopping.com have proven surprisingly weak as Web site names.

Check for Trademark Infringement

Any advice on legal matters you read in a book like this one is, of course, general, and not a replacement for speaking to a lawyer who is an expert in applicable law in the jurisdiction(s) in which you wish to operate.

Trademark infringement is a tricky matter. There's no global register of protected names and their applicability that you can check in advance before registering a domain name.

**Book IV
Chapter 1**

**Domain Names for
Existing Businesses**

Most small- to medium-sized businesses never have to worry about the applicability of their trademarks outside their industry and outside the geographic areas in which they operate. But Web sites are inherently global, so it's easy to get into trouble in places, and with organizations, you've never heard of.

Use Google to search for business names similar to yours. In general, different geographic areas and different areas of business are protections against trademark infringement. So is the fact that someone has not registered a given domain name. But if they've registered a country-specific version of a name, and you're considering operating in their country with the `.com` version of the same name — or vice versa — watch out. (For instance, it doesn't seem smart to name a company `lastminute` anything, unless you like to collect letters from lawyers.)

You also run into the difference between being right and being sued. It's not unheard of that a business with, say, a particularly clever name sues to try to protect it, even if it is likely to lose. The lawsuit itself may scare off potential claimants to the name, and the lawsuit buys time and proves to investors that the company has done its best to protect its assets.

For the US, `copyright.gov` is a good resource; see Figure 1-4. Even if you aren't planning to operate in the US, it's good to avoid problems there. Many American companies are well-funded, and Americans are considered by people in other countries to be litigious.

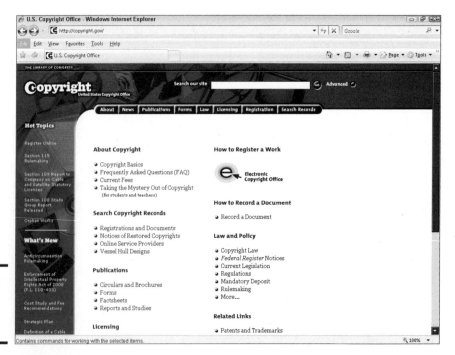

Figure 1-4: http:// copyright. gov/.

Chapter 2: Domain Names for New Companies and More

In This Chapter

✔ Choosing a domain name for your developing business

✔ Creating your site's appearance and determining its size

✔ Making a good impression

*T*he previous chapter described creating a domain name for an existing business. Your choice of a name in this situation is quite constrained by what already exists in the real world. If you have a new business, creating a domain name is much harder as the possibilities can seem endless.

It's easy to find yourself cycling among possible businesses you could be in, products and services you could offer, locations where you could be based, and domain names that are — or aren't — available.

It's no crime to register a few domain names that you end up not using. But if you reserve many more than that, you are probably wasting time and money you need for building your business.

This chapter briefly describes how to narrow your choices to a realistic handful, make a choice you can live with, and then focus your online effort. If you want to take an existing business to the next level or if you are considering a strong Internet extension of your business, this chapter is for you.

Designing an Internet Business

Because it's new, the Internet seems to offer nothing but possibilities. But actually, one of the most important factors for real-world businesses is what *is not* available on the Web.

In the real world, you start a business of a given type — say, a pet store or a hair salon — that happens to meet the needs of a group of proximate customers. In fact, a huge problem for many real-world businesses is not being realistic about the number of nearby potential customers necessary to make a business practical.

On the Internet, however, your competitors and customers are always a click away. If you are primarily an Internet-based business, people don't care much whether you're based 10, 100, or 1,000 miles away.

People *do* care if you're in the same country. Don't expect strong sales in a given country unless you've established a solid presence there, including a Web presence with the right kind of URL, excellent translation into the local language, an appropriate mailing address, and a customer-support phone number.

So there's no geographic protection for your business, and if you're just starting out now, you're rather late to the Web world. If you're a *pure play* Web business — an online-only business without a strong presence in a specific location — what kind of protection can you have?

The main advantage for a new Web business today is *specialization,* a narrow focus on a specific type of product or service and a unique way of offering it. That is, you don't just want to be the best site for teddy bears; you want to be the best site for antique, expensive, or yellow teddy bears. You have to be the best — preferably the *only* — online source for a given type of product.

(*Only* is a little tricky. Even if someone can buy one or two antique teddy bears on, say, eBay; you may win their business if you provide scores of antique teddy bears, useful information about them, and expert customer service. Of course, in such a business you'd probably use eBay as one of your sales outlets.)

Another advantage for a Web business is an association with a person or organization that's a proven name in a given field. For instance, if you buy insurance from a bank, the insurance is probably really provided by a separate company that operates under the bank's name as part of its customer relationships. (This applies both to online banking and doing business in a physical bank.) This is a variation on taking an established business into cyberspace, and it takes real creativity to pull off — but can be very rewarding if handled well.

Picking a Novel Domain Name

Picking a domain name for a truly new Internet business is in some ways the opposite of picking a name for an existing company. Truly new Internet businesses benefit from unique and interesting names that stick in the Web surfer's mind.

For such a business, trying to own a generic title is still not a good way to go. The name `antiqueteddybears.com` might or might not work. (It's very hard to trademark commonplace descriptive words; if someone comes up with a very similar name, you might have no recourse.)

It's probably better to come up with a novel name that you can "own" in the user's mind and then brand yourself around it. It's very hard and expensive to build up a nationwide or worldwide brand, but Amazon took on this challenge rather than choosing a name like SuperOnlineShopz or some other generic name — which, back when Amazon started out, was a real option.

A good example of a distinctive name is Zanzara, a real-world usability business that works with many technology companies. (The Zanzara Web site is shown in Figure 2-1). The online presence of Zanzara is tremendously important. Zanzara doesn't necessarily have anything to do with usability — but, like Amazon, it isn't burdened by other strong business associations, either. (*Zanzara* means *mosquito* in Italian.)

Zanzara is also, like other good, novel domain names, personally meaningful to the business owners. (One of the owners was nicknamed Zanzara as a child by her Italian grandmother, who thought she was always buzzing around.) Having a story behind a name creates positive associations and makes a name more memorable.

With a novel business, picking the domain name is only half the battle. Hammering it into your potential customers' heads is the other half. Being strongly focused is a huge help in identifying early target customers and in creating a distinctive image of your business in their minds.

Figure 2-1:
www.
zanzara.
com.

Sizing Your Online Effort

Deciding how much of an investment to make in your online effort is a big decision, and not an easy one. It's also works somewhat the opposite of what you might expect.

If you have an existing business — which probably means you actually have sales and profits to invest — you can get away with a fairly simple site. Your main presence is in the real world, so your site has to be good enough to be non-embarrassing, but not fantastic — just enough not to disappoint those who know you from the real world.

Also, as an existing business you are likely to have *content* — the annoying Internet word that you just have to get used to — that you can *repurpose* — another Internet word — for your Web site. Existing ads, brochures, and catalogs are all grist for your Web site. For some well-established businesses, the issue is more what to leave out rather than what to keep in.

Even where you don't already have content, it's easy to create. The Zanzara site is a good example. It was easy for Zanzara to have case studies created for its site because it had done a lot of good work (see Figure 2-2).

Figure 2-2:
www.
zanzara.
com/
casestudies.
html.

As an existing business, you can also gradually add to your site with a mix of repurposed content from your real-world marketing efforts — every new advertisement you run can be featured on a new Web page — with specifically created Web-site content.

For new businesses, especially those that plan a strong online effort from day one — and especially for businesses that exist primarily online, the pressure is on to create an excellent Web site right from the start.

Figure 2-3 shows a list of venture capital-funded companies for 2007 in Orange County, California. You can guess some of the companies that are primarily Web-oriented just by looking at the list.

Despite the fact that you don't have sales or profits yet, you are expected to have a slick, professional-looking, easy– to–use Web site. And you'll be depending on expert application of Web sales and marketing tools, in particular the Google tools described in this book, to get things moving quickly.

At the same time, as a new business, you're unlikely to have much existing material to put on your Web site. Even if you create a nice-looking site that works well, it's hard to have content that creates the right impression when you don't have much reality to talk about yet.

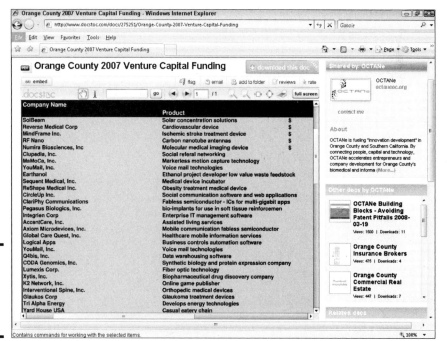

Figure 2-3: Venture capital loves Web companies.

It's hard to achieve balance between not saying enough and saying too much, between having a sparse site and one that makes big claims without a lot to back them up.

The solution is to be straightforward — although that tends to leave your site on the sparse side at first. The trick is to steadily add content to your site as your business develops.

It's hard to believe, but soon — in most cases, in just a few months — your site will reach a critical mass and it will no longer border on being sparse. And the content that fills it out will be genuine and really related to the real business you're developing. When you see this happening, it is a proud moment.

For the Web site `batcs.co.uk`, that tipping point was reached when a couple of British newspapers wrote about the business. Adding the reviews to the site tipped the balance making a site that was a bit empty into an interesting one, and it's been getting good feedback ever since.

 It might seem that one can do anything on the Web, but usually successful sites are based on strong interests and deep experience of the people behind them. Inside knowledge, connections, and passion all matter in separating the sites that almost make it from the real winners. So if you're building a truly new site online, seriously consider doing it in an area in which you have experience and that you really care about.

Defining Your Site's Appearance

The toughest issue for companies creating a Web site that works well is the appearance of a site. It's like dressing to work in a big corporation — if you're not used to it, it's easy to fall short of the slick, professional look you need. In fact, if you lack experience, it might be a good idea to get professional help before your first day at work.

Let's make a comparison of two sites, one which demonstrates the state of the art and a site that just barely makes the grade.

The `apple.com` site (see Figure 2-4) is truly advanced — not only is it the online face of a multibillion-dollar corporation, but one whose products are used by a preponderance of professional Web site designers, and one that hosts one of the bigger online stores around.

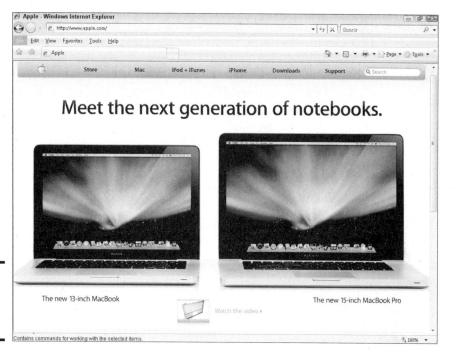

Figure 2-4:
Apple gets
the Jobs
done.

Yet it's deceptively simple. The *graphical navigation bar* at the top is really text in a table with fonts and coloring used to make it look like graphics. (Because it consists of text, it works well with, among other things, search engines.)

The Apple site has just eight categories (called *tabs* in the trade, whether they look like notebook tabs or not), including Search. The site has large images of products and, lower on the page, carefully designed buttons. The site even breaks basic Web design rules — the crucial top navigation bar is too wide for many monitors and much wider than the 700 or so pixels many authorities recommend.

Compare this to the BATCS site (see Figure 2-5). You can see the seams — the buttons made of separate graphics (you can see them download separately if you watch carefully). There are seven categories for this small site — the seeming simplicity of the Apple site takes a great deal of work. Branding is via an image of a business card — reusing existing materials, as described earlier.

Figure 2-5:
BATCS
borrows
credibility
from clients.

To make a point about how "cool" its clients are, the site uses the logos and the flags of the countries they come from — "borrowing credibility" through a simple yet, we hope, effective device.

There is money spent here — the BATCS logo, the business card, and the buttons were designed by a professional, and the site was put together by a semiprofessional using an online tool offered by the hosts of the Web site. The total cost would be the equivalent of a couple of thousand dollars US, plus quite a few hours of work by the owners.

The site is not a "wow." But the site design is solid and, together with content built up over a couple of years, it makes a good impression on customers.

Making the Right Impression

It's very tricky for owners of an existing business with a new online presence, and even more so for owners of a brand new business, to know just when they have the pieces right — the domain name and a sufficiently attractive and polished Web site.

You have to put the pieces together as best you can and keep checking with friends, colleagues, and customers to get their opinions and suggestions. Expect for the process to take a while — but, when you get it right, the site will become an important part of your business, whether or not you actually sell through your site.

What not to wear

A lot of things banned in other processes are not necessarily banned in domain names or Web content, but you should avoid certain things anyway. You won't get stopped when you're choosing or registering your domain name or when you post content to your Web page, but you may get sued or even arrested for some content. (And if not in your home country, you may be served with papers or even arrested while travelling abroad. It happened to some European gambling Web site moguls who had the bright idea of changing planes in America, where gambling Web sites are in some circumstances illegal.)

So what's illegal or likely to get you sued? Child pornography is a huge problem area, and there are large differences in its definition across jurisdictions, so don't even joke about this online. If you're doing anything relating to children online, consider getting legal advice in advance. Defaming, abusing, threatening, or harassing people (because of race, gender, or for other reasons), being involved in hate crimes, or threatening terrorism are among the dangerous areas, as, of course, is gambling.

Not many of us can be on top of the requirements in all jurisdictions, and it's unlikely that you'll have problems with some content that might be borderline — unless you're successful, in which case you might get a lot closer scrutiny.

If you use a private registrar, as described in the next chapter, that person actually registers the name for you, so any hint of these kinds of things are eliminated — because the private registrar is taking on the responsibility for the name. Actually, what is banned is not the "wrong" kind of domain name — that's subjective — but *the private registrar's interpretation of it*. The same goes with hosts and your Web site — your site could suddenly be dropped to avoid what the host views as dodgy content. Whether you register the name yourself or through others, and whatever kind of Web site host you use, be squeaky clean in order to avoid problems at any stage of the process.

Chapter 3: Buying a Domain Name

In This Chapter

✔ **Researching available domain names**

✔ **Registering and purchasing a domain name**

✔ **Registering a name privately**

✔ **Buying multiple domain names**

*B*uying a domain name, which is both inexpensive and easy, can have a surprising number of pitfalls. It's hard to learn about the pitfalls without going through the process — and making some mistakes — a few times. Having done this, we can share our experiences with you.

The key things we recommend are

✦ Avoiding mistakes during the sign-up process.

✦ Registering only names you need.

✦ Locking up "your" name — the one that seems ideal to you — with a domain name registrar.

✦ Guarding against spam, identity theft, and fraud.

In this chapter, we first describe where to register, depending on who's going to host your site; then we take you through the domain-name purchasing process. Next, we address the major possible pitfalls and show you how to avoid them.

Why Are Some Domain Names Unavailable?

It's a lot of fun to check different domain names and dream of what you might do if you find a good one.

Many of the domain names you might want are already tied up, for several possible reasons, including

✦ **Legitimate use for a "real" Web site:** This is the obvious one. Someone has registered the domain name for legitimate uses and has already or is about to put up a Web site behind the domain name.

✦ **Domain name speculation:** Someone has registered the domain name hoping to sell it at a profit. If a speculator has your domain name, you may be able to buy it from him, but it's rarely worth it; or you can wait for the speculator to allow it to expire when the current registration period for that domain name ends.

✦ **Domain name parking:** The domain name is being used to make money through relatively random or general content. Let's say yellow conkers, a new species derived from regular conkers — which are, of course, the nut of a horse-chestnut tree — are discovered and get some news coverage. Someone might register `www.yellowconkers.com` and variations. He then puts more or less relevant content on it that relates to yellow conkers but links to sites that pay for traffic. This pays enough to block folks who wants to create a truly marvelous yellow conkers site — that might eventually be worth millions or help mankind somehow — unless they can raise the money to buy the modestly profitable site based around the "parked" domain name.

A typical price for a profitable asset is ten times its annual profits. That can be a rather high number — and there's also the potential for additional profits if a domain name happens to become really popular. That could increase the price that the holder of an even slightly profitable domain name can ask.

✦ **Domain name tasting:** A domain name can be registered for free for five days, during which time it can be parked to see if it generates any revenue. This is called *tasting*. Even worse, a domain name registrar can note that you are checking a given name and then park it for the five-day period so you can't buy it from a different registrar. No one tells you this, so you may think that, between one session and the next, someone has bought your preferred domain name, taken it off the market for at least the full two-year registration period, and killed your dream!

This last point is the most dangerous; you have to be careful when you test a domain name. Anyone who knows you are interested can "taste" the name out from under you if you don't complete the initial registration for any reason.

Bob Parsons, the CEO and founder of GoDaddy, has strong opinions that he isn't afraid to share with the world. On his blog at `www.bobparsons.tv` — on which he hosts a lot of video, thus the use of the `.tv` suffix — he's gone after domain name tasting, which he calls *domain name kiting*. Visit the page on the topic at `www.bobparsons.tv/DomainKiting.html` to learn more. Note the sample in Figure 3-1.

Figure 3-1:
Domain
name kiting
is not a
favorite
of Bob
Parsons.

ICANN, I cried

In his song I Am, I Said, the famous Neil Diamond sang that "no one heard at all, not even the chair." ICANN will stay in better touch with you than that, if you let them.

ICANN is the Internet Corporation for Assigned Names and Numbers, a non-profit organization that manages domain names. ICANN's procedures were created before identity theft and spam became such problems. They are weighted toward openness, possibly at the expense of privacy. It's very important that ICANN be able to reach you, especially by e-mail. Yet you need to be aware that information you enter during the domain name registration process may become more public than you'd prefer.

ICANN is a serious part of the Internet infrastructure and gets attention from all kinds of companies and government agencies internationally. The figure shows the first part of a Web site showing a hearing on ICANN's processes in the US House of Representatives.

ICANN collects about $5 per domain name registered, so GoDaddy and other registrars are trying to provide registration services using the difference between ICANN's $5 and what they charge you. Saving a few pennies to get the very cheapest registrar may not be your best investment decision because any mistakes or hassles now or down the road can create very big problems indeed.

Checking for Available Domain Names

GoDaddy is a registrar that doesn't practice domain name tasting on their customers or potential customers — and, GoDaddy is one of the domain name registrars currently recommended by Google.

So let's use GoDaddy to check the availability of some domain names. Just follow these steps:

1. **Visit the GoDaddy site at www.godaddy.com.**

The GoDaddy Web site appears, as shown in Figure 3-2.

There's an option on the GoDaddy home page to try a domain name search, but it's better to use the Smart Domain Search feature described in the following steps.

2. **Choose Domains⇨Register Domain.**

The initial Domain Name Search page appears.

3. **Choose SmartSearch. (Ignore the Internationalized Domain Names option for now, even if you need it; check the non-specialized options first.)**

The SmartSearch page appears, as shown in Figure 3-3.

Figure 3-2: GoDaddy is a very popular Web host.

Figure 3-3: GoDaddy's Smart-Search makes an anxiety-causing process fun.

4. **Click to check the boxes for the domain extensions you want to look for.**

   We recommend checking all the traditional extensions available: `.com`, `.net`, and `.org`. You may want to register all three to protect yourself. The other options on offer — `.info`, `.biz`, and `.us` — are newer, less frequently used, and probably, like other newer domain name options, not needed.

   On the other hand, if you have a site that fits one of these options — for instance, a specifically American business that might fit the `.us` option well, include it.

5. **Click to check the boxes for the intelligent search options you want to use.**

   Intelligent search options add to your results by trying variations on the name or keyword you enter — popular prefixes in front of the name or keywords you enter, popular suffixes on the end, dashes in the middle, or related keywords. We recommend that you try all of them at first and then eliminate the ones you don't find useful.

6. **Enter the domain name you want to check and then click the Search button to try the search.**

   Results appear, as shown in Figure 3-4. The available names, based on the keyword and extension combination, can be purchased right away. Keyword and extension combinations that are in use can be *backordered,* which means that, if the combination becomes available — usually by not being renewed at the end of the two-year registration period — GoDaddy will buy it for you.

If the domain or domains you want are available, write down the names so you can give them some thought. This far into the Web site revolution, it's unlikely someone will snag your name within a day or two, and it's worth giving it some thought before committing even a small amount of money.

If the name you want relates to a newly hot topic, you may want to take the plunge and register it right away. See the following sections for how to do it.

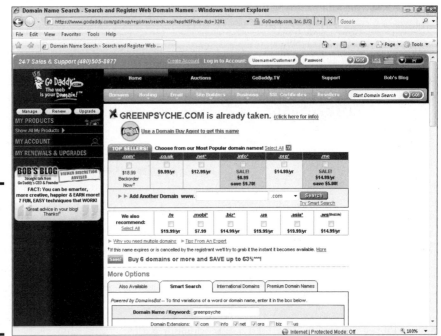

Figure 3-4:
Enjoy the ecstasy — and agony — of domain name search results.

7. Check the Results page for related options, as shown in Figure 3-5.

GoDaddy generates other options for you to consider. It adds popular words like *new, free, best, hot,* and so on to the front of your domain name or keywords, and variations such as *foryou, store* and *online* to the end.

Marketing people say *new* and *free* are the two best words for marketing, so these words are worth considering. Other options may be worthwhile or give you some new thoughts of your own.

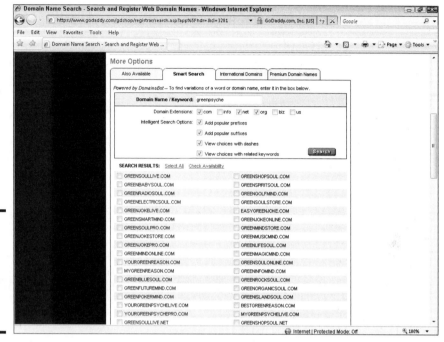

Figure 3-5:
GoDaddy's
Smart-
Search
generates
options
for you.

8. **Keep trying different names, writing down the ones that work — and the ones that don't. (This saves you hours of checking the same names several times over.)**

9. **Check other tabs in the More Options area of the search results as needed — including Also Available, Previously Searched Domains, International Domain Names, and Premium Domain Names.**

   There's a lot to look at here, so just skim these areas for ideas. The exception is International Domains for the US and UK. These are both very active Web markets with a great many businesses in one that also do business in the other. If your main need is for the .com site or the .co.uk site, seriously consider getting both; otherwise, your ability to grow may be limited, and a competitor could use the other site type to confuse your customers.

Talk to friends and colleagues about your options. Use Google to search on different terms to see what sites already exist and what ads appear along with the search results. Write down what you find — it's very easy to get confused after trying several similar names and getting slightly varying results. You might be surprised what you discover.

Do you need a .mobi domain?

.mobi domain names are specifically for mobile phones. There are actually four ways for a Web site to handle mobile phone access:

- Expect people to come in through the main .com site and do the best they can with your Web page just as it appears.

- Keep only a .com site, but use style sheets to serve the same content with different formatting for mobile phones. This is the approved way of doing it within the ideals of Web design, but it seems unrealistic to us that the same content and overall screen design can be used on such different platforms.

- Still only have a .com site, but serve different content to mobile phones. This seems the preferred option for companies that

really want to do a lot with their sites on both PCs and mobile phones.

- Have a .mobi site and expect mobile phone users to come into your Web site using that. This is the purpose of .mobi, but we haven't seen a lot of publicity for .mobi sites; it seems that .mobi is supported by some, but certainly not all sites, even major ones. At this writing, for instance, neither Microsoft nor Apple have .mobi sites, although Google does.

We recommend that you begin by creating the best possible PC site you can and, after your site is successful, considering options for mobile phones. You may never need the .mobi extension, even if you add mobile phone support.

Registering with GoDaddy

Registering as a user with GoDaddy, or with another domain name registrar if you choose to use a different one, is different from registering at most sites. That's because your information may be used as part of registering a domain name, which can result in your personal information being widely available on the Web. So a bit of extra care is needed.

If you're concerned about exposing your information to the world, you can be completely honest and accurate in registering with GoDaddy — then use the GoDaddy-owned service, Domains by Proxy, to have your domain registered in a way that protects your privacy. Register with GoDaddy as described here and then use Registering a Domain Name Privately, as shown in the following steps.

Follow these steps to register with GoDaddy:

1. **Visit the GoDaddy site at www.godaddy.com.**

   The GoDaddy Web site appears. (Refer to Figure 3-2).

2. **Click the link Create Account near the top of the Web page.**

   The Create a New Customer Account Web page appears, as shown in Figure 3-6.

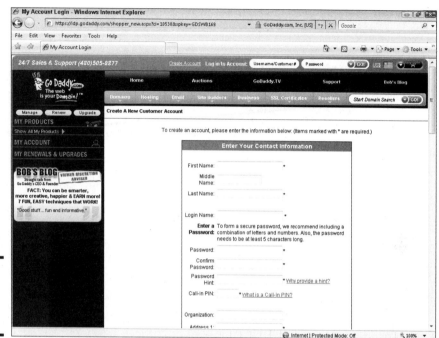

Figure 3-6:
Tell
GoDaddy
everything.

3. **Enter the descriptive information about yourself carefully and accurately. Be aware that this information is used to contact you for renewing your domain name in two years, when it expires, and possibly for other important messages as well.**

   The typical American, for example, moves every seven years, so the odds of your moving during the time you own a domain are pretty high. Be sure to use a permanent address and an e-mail address that you're sure to keep for a long time to come.

   ICANN requires that you receive one e-mail per year to verify and update your contact information, so again, be sure to use a permanent e-mail address — and watch out that a spam filter doesn't block you from receiving this e-mail message.

   You may want to set up an annual reminder for yourself to check in with GoDaddy about maintaining your information.

   As far as the bodies that register domain names are concerned, the e-mail address you enter is the main proof of who you are, so you have to do a lot of work if you lose access to it — and even more so if you also lose track of your password and PIN.

   Choose your password and PIN carefully and note them someplace secure but accessible. You may not use them much — yet they are very important when you do need them. Keep them secure because it's a major hassle to fix things if the wrong people gain the ability to edit your Web site.

4. Choose options in the Stay Informed! area.

Enter the Stay Informed! information carefully as well. We recommend you say Yes to the first two choices — the monthly product update and non-promotional notices about your account, and so on. (Saying Yes to the latter is a necessity.)

The GoDaddy podcast and offers from GoDaddy are optional. You may want to say No to text message notices, Yes to US Mail contacts — this is expensive enough for the sender that it's unlikely to be abused.

Note the following disclaimer from GoDaddy that appears when you mouse over the question, "Include your registrant information in third party Bulk Whois requests?": "We are contractually required by ICANN to provide your registrant information to third parties who request to purchase this information unless you select "NO", directing us to not provide this data to third parties". That means GoDaddy has no choice in the matter; only you can protect yourself from this kind of access to your information — which may not always be for entirely legitimate or desirable purposes — by saying No.

5. Review all your choices and responses.

Consider printing out the page and reviewing it to make sure everything you've entered is accurate and what you've intended.

6. When you're happy with all your choices, click the button Create a New Account.

Your account is created.

Purchasing a Domain Name

We recommend that you separate the processes of choosing a domain name from the process of actually purchasing one, so you don't buy impulsively and then regret it later. Use the steps in the previous section to help decide on your name — especially try to talk to others about your options — and then follow the steps in this section to actually buy it.

You can also buy a domain name as part of the process of setting up your Google Sites site, but if you're in a hurry, do it separately, as described here.

Follow these steps to buy a domain name:

1. Visit the GoDaddy site at `www.godaddy.com`.

The GoDaddy Web site appears. (Refer to Figure 3-2.)

2. **Enter the domain name you want and select the extension from the pull-down menu. Click Go.**

The results appear. (Refer to Figure 3-3.) Ideally, the name you've chosen is still available!

3. **Scroll down the page and click Proceed to Checkout.**

A page with STOP at the top appears. (See Figure 3-7.) This page offers you discounts on combinations of variants of your domain name. There's a Standard option with core variants, `.net`, `.org`, and `.info`, if `.com` is your main choice and a Premium option with additional variants, `.mobi` and `.us`.

Consider the Standard option to protect your core name; consider the Premium option only if you specifically need the additional names or are extra-concerned about protecting your core name.

Read the tips under the tab, "Why buy more than one domain name?" shown in Figure 3-7, to see the main arguments for purchasing additional domain names.

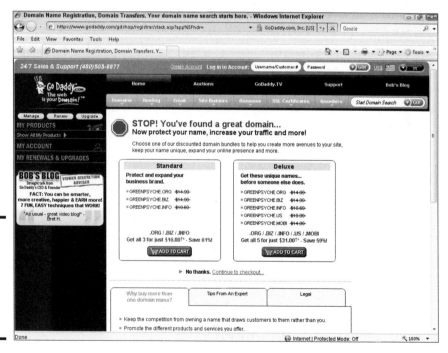

Figure 3-7: GoDaddy makes the case for buying variant names.

Book IV Chapter 3

Buying a Domain Name

4. **Click the button Continue to Checkout.**

   The Domain Registration Information page appears.

5. **Enter the information to create your account.**

   If you haven't done so already, enter your name, address, e-mail address, and so on, as described in the section "Registering with GoDaddy," earlier in this chapter.

6. **Click the link "Important information about email accounts," to see a pop-up window about what type of account to use.**

7. **Enter your name, address, e-mail address, and so on.**

   Be sure to use an e-mail address you're highly likely to keep for the long term because e-mail is the primary means used to contact you about your account. This is important for many reasons. First, you will receive a reminder to renew your domain name at the end of the two-year registration period. If you miss reminders, your domain name could lapse, and you could lose it to someone else — who might want big money to sell it back to you, or might not even sell it at all. It's also highly embarrassing to have your Web site fail because of neglecting to renew your domain name. All too many companies and other organizations — including some very large ones — have found this out. You may also be contacted about security threats and similar problems that can be important.

Registering a Domain Name Privately

The early days of the Web were a lot of fun, and it seemed that all things were possible. But as it's become a big part of the real world, many of the problems of the real world have come to the Web as well — along with some new ones.

The personal details you enter when you create a Web site are published online, available to anyone who cares to look. This makes sense, when you think of it from a normal person's point of view — for instance, you might want to contact a domain owner to offer to buy his domain.

But from a crook's or spammer's point of view, the publication of personal details is an invitation to cause trouble. Identity theft and fraud are rife online, and fraudsters can create a fake version of "you" given even less information than is available from a domain name registration.

Making the situation even worse is that the information in your domain name registration can be combined with information on your Web site to get quite a complete picture of you — your work, your family, and more.

Also, publishing any valid e-mail address makes you a target for spam. As with fraud, the more information a spammer has handy, the more trouble he can cause you.

Having this information public also makes it easy for bosses and others to know about side businesses, moonlighting, and so on — or reveal to the customers of your online business that it's only a part-time venture.

Domain name registration requirements strictly require that the contact information of the actual registrant be disclosed. In most cases, that means you.

But there are a few special domain name registrars that can act as intermediaries. You register with them; then they register your Web site for you. They're the owners of the site — so you have to trust them highly. It would be easy for a scammer to set up such a site and use it to steal money and/or the very personal information you're trying to protect.

GoDaddy is one of the relatively few reputable companies that handle private domain name registrations through a separate company called Domains by Proxy, hosted on the GoDaddy Web site. Be aware of a few things before starting:

✦ With Domains by Proxy, registering privately costs extra — about double the cost of a normal domain name registration;

✦ The extra charge for private domain name registration is waived if five or more domain names are registered;

✦ Existing domains can be transferred to Domains by Proxy and made private from that point forward;

✦ Domains by Proxy can't be used for many types of domains, including .us, .ca, .co.uk, and other important domain name endings;

See the comparison shown in Figure 3-8 for an example of how a Domain by Proxy registration differs from a typical one.

Other private domain name registrars are likely to have similar pricing and policies. You should definitely shop before you buy, but Domains by Proxy is one of the original and larger of such services, so include it in any comparison list.

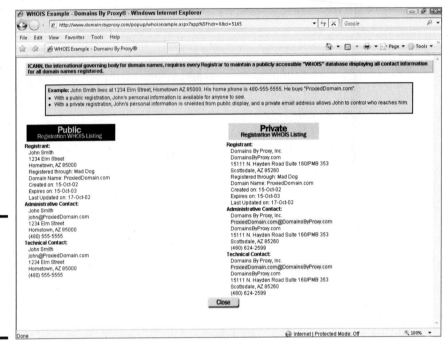

Figure 3-8:
GoDaddy makes the case for buying variant names.

The process for registering a domain name by proxy is very similar to registering a domain name directly in your own name (and with your own contact details):

1. **Check for the domain name you want using the steps given previously in the section "Checking for Available Domain Names."**

2. **Create an account as described in "Registering with GoDaddy," earlier in this chapter.**

3. **From the tabs near the top of the page, choose Domains⇨Private Registration.**

    Be careful to mouse over the words Private Registration so they change color, or you won't go to the right page. (Menus within a Web page aren't always as robust as menus in programs hosted on your computer.) The result should look like Figure 3-9.

4. **Enter the domain name you want to register.**

    The results of a check for the availability of your domain name appear — if you've checked on it recently, the name should still be available.

5. **Follow the steps listed in the section, "Purchasing a Domain Name," earlier in this chapter.**

Figure 3-9:
Privacy is
nice to have
on the Web.

Purchasing Multiple Domain Names

Purchasing domain names is a habit that's hard to stop, once you've started. Although they aren't very expensive, it's a waste of time, money, energy, and effort to register domain names you don't need.

However, you can have several domain names in use at once; they can be for separate sites, or you can have several names "pointing to" the same site. This is an option available when you buy a domain name: You specify that traffic to the domain name you're buying is redirected to a different domain name.

It's not unusual for a business or organization, perfectly legitimately, to have several domain names registered. There's the one you actually use, and then there are additional names that you buy for very good reasons. These additional names tend to fall into three central categories:

✦ **"Instead of" names.** An "instead of" name is a domain name that people might try instead of your actual domain name. "Instead of" names are good to use for handling misspellings and misunderstandings. In one famous example, the photo site Flickr.com is well-known to Web users — but when you ask your elderly aunt to look at a photo on Flickr, she's quite likely to try flicker.com instead. The Flickr people should buy `flicker.com` and point it to their own site just to reduce confusion. (Without this, you may find yourself explaining over and over "That's f, l, i, c, k, r .com — no *e* in *flickr.*")

+ **Names you buy to protect trademarks and traffic.** If you have a trademark on your cool toy, Fred's Lunar Rover, you don't want anyone else using the name. So as part of your trademark protection you might buy `fredslunarrover.com`, even if you don't intend to use it. (Or, you can use it as an "instead of" name pointing to your site, as explained earlier.)

  Even if you don't have a trademark, you certainly don't want anyone else registering a name associated with your product — then directing traffic to their competing or simply different product. You might win a court case on this one, but that's a lot more expensive and difficult than simply buying the domain name.

+ **Names you buy to build your search engine position.** Having several reputable sites — reputable, that is, in Google's eyes, which includes being linked to by well-regarded "outside" sites — pointing to each other is a very good way to build the search engine rankings of all the sites involved. Doing this in a manipulative way is a trick, which Google may eventually catch onto — and punish the sites with lower rankings. But you do it in a way that genuinely helps people seeking information, it's a good thing that benefits users as well as the sites' search engine position.

Chapter 4: A Tour of Google Sites

In This Chapter

✔ Exploring the origins of Google Sites

✔ Understanding the advantages and drawbacks of Google Sites

✔ Creating a Google Site

✔ Changing your site's appearance

*G*oogle Sites is a good choice for creating Web pages because it supports several different approaches to the Web. The traditional approach — I create and publish a site; you visit it — is supported. But so are newer approaches.

Google Sites is a tool for creating Web sites that is considered part of Google Apps. Google Sites serves as a content management system (CMS) for creators. That means people separated in space and time can work together on content, both editing and contributing. This is a great strength for Google Sites as a Web-site creation tool; usually, a CMS costs money and takes time and trouble to learn. Google Sites is both free and easy to use.

In addition to serving as a CMS for the site itself, Google Sites lets you create sites that host Google Apps documents such as word processing documents, spreadsheets, presentations, and calendars. All of these documents can be shared. Though other Web sites can host Google Apps documents, the ease with which you can do this is unique to Google Sites.

So Google Sites is a powerful tool. The only drawback some people see to it is the complement of its strengths — as hosted software, both the software itself and your data are in "the cloud," protected only by Google's security and not physically within any company's or organization's buildings. Although this is a wave of the future, it still causes insecurity to some.

In this chapter we concentrate on the traditional aspects of Web publishing. This is the core need for small businesses. But by using Google Sites, you're also laying the groundwork for the additional functionality that Google Sites makes possible, for colleagues, collaborators, and customers.

What Is Web 2.0?

Google Sites is both an example of a Web 2.0 site and a tool for creating your own. But just what is Web 2.0?

Web 2.0 fulfills part of the original purpose of the Web. When Tim Berners-Lee invented the Web at the European physics laboratory, CERN, in 1989, he intended that it be almost as easy to create a Web page as to visit one. And he intended Web sites to be extended through collaboration.

The Web took off quickly. Millions of people created Web pages, and many millions more used them. But there was still a sharp division in roles. You were either creating a Web page, with sole control of how it looked and worked, or you were visiting one. You might do both on a single day or even in a given work session, but you were still either accessing or creating, not both.

Web 2.0 blurs these distinctions. Bloggers (and people commenting), users of Facebook and mySpace, YouTube, LinkedIn, Flickr, and many, many more are creating the Web sites at the same time as they're visiting them.

There are even tools that allow you to create sites that people can use for collaboration. Google Sites is just such a tool.

Ironically, Web 2.0 was not created by the Web that Tim Berners-Lee originally invented. Instead, it results from large amounts of back-end data processing — not excluded from the original Web definition, but not included in it either — and front-end flexibility.

Front-end flexibility means a real user interface that can respond quickly to user input, without waiting for data to be exchanged with the server supporting the Web page. JavaScript, XML (a superset of HTML), Flash, and Java are all tools used — separately or in combination — to provide this end-user flexibility.

Google Apps is based on Web 2.0. The capability to offer, for example, a spreadsheet program online, as Google Apps does, pushes some of the technologies that support Web 2.0 to their limits.

As you set out to create your Web page in Google Sites, it's important to understand that terms like *Web*, *Web page*, and *Web site* now mean different things to different people, or sometimes have different meaning for the same people at different points within a given conversation.

The static, command-and-control Web pages are still most commonly used by business to present itself to the public. And then there's the growing interactive Web that's used by the public, within companies and, in a few cases, by companies interacting with — not just presenting information to — the public. By using Google Sites, you position yourself to do all of the above.

How Google Sites Started

Google Sites is an example of Google growing by acquisition. Google acquired a company called JotSpot, a company that developed tools for corporations to build wikis.

The most famous example of a wiki is Wikipedia (shown in Figure 4-1). Note that the Wikipedia site is at www.wikipedia.org, not .com — but if you type www.wikipedia.com, you're redirected to .org.

Wikipedia is owned and run, amazingly, by a not-for-profit organization. This tool that has largely made traditional encyclopedias obsolete and made it much easier for users to be well-informed and up to date is one of the best examples of Web 2.0 in action.

Figure 4-1: Wikipedia is a deservedly famous success.

A *wiki* is a database of content that can be edited by many different people. It's good for corporations because it's a very easy way to achieve knowledge management — to build up a body of knowledge independent of the comings and goings of people in and out of different jobs and the company.

JotSpot was a very early tool for wikis — it was pretty brilliant of its creators to be able to build a strong offering when there wasn't much else out there. It included templates that made getting a wiki up fast and easy and provided functionality for project management, spreadsheets, and more. Beyond the templates, however, JotSpot was said to be hard to use.

So when competitors began to catch up with its features, JotSpot faced the classic dilemma of software innovators: Find the time and money for a total rewrite without angering your current customers and without making any mistakes — or keep falling behind.

Instead, Google acquired JotSpot. It made the interface much simpler, trading off features for ease of use. It even abandoned the wiki focus for general Web site building.

Plusses and Minuses of Google Sites

When choosing a tool to start your Web site, the question that arises breaks down into two parts:

✦ Is this the best tool to get started with?

✦ Can I stick with this tool for a long time, or will I have to switch?

Let's look at each part of it as it applies to Google Sites.

Is Google Sites the best tool to get started with? For most people who are using any other parts of Google Sites, it probably is. That's because it's integrated with your Google account, with Google Apps, Google Docs, and Spreadsheets, which can be hosted on your Google Site. It also is connected with Google Analytics that can help you understand how much and what kind of traffic you're getting.

Google Sites is definitely easy enough to use for getting started — especially with a guide like this book to take you through the potentially confusing early parts (and lots of other support from online sites, magazine articles, consultants, and so on). And it's free, which is a huge advantage. You might waste a bit of time with Google Sites, but you won't waste any money.

Not only is Google Sites free, it offers amazing amounts of storage — 100MB of storage for free accounts and an incredible 100GB for Google Apps users.

The incredible amount of free storage makes Google Sites particularly attractive for users who wish to host a lot of video — something Google is good at.

You can also limit your site to up to 20 named users. This is a big advantage when you're building your site or if you have a small business intranet site.

Each page gets an entry in the Navigation pane — creating navigation yourself is a major pain, if you'll excuse the pun — and the capability to attach files as well as support for user comments. You can turn these off, but for many sites these are nice features indeed.

Crucially, Google Sites include free gadgets, allowing you to build up your site's capabilities very quickly.

The collaboration features are awesome, if you need them even a little bit. You can let others change the site's template, add or remove pages, and so on. Believe me, it's no fun to be the go-fer for updating a Web site — the only person who can make changes that others would like made. The collaboration features in Google Sites not only get you out of the line of fire for simple changes, they allow the site to grow in ways you might never have imagined.

A popular site, `c4lpt.co.uk` — the UK's Centre for Learning & Performance Technologies — ranks Google Sites quite high. It was recently ranked the 59th best site for learning and performance support.

So you may be about to decide that Google Sites is the tool for you. What's wrong with it?

✦ **Google Sites is limited.** You can't add your own HTML to a site; you have to use the HTML editor in Google Sites. This is a big restriction.

✦ **Customization is limited.** You have to choose from among roughly two dozen site themes and use the structure provided. You can change colors, font sizes, and so on, but you can't add Cascading Style Sheets (CSS) or other advanced HTML or edit your content in a Web editor.

✦ **Other tools have different advantages.** Yahoo!'s GeoCities Pagebuilder tool, for example, is more flexible; FreeWebs and Wetpaint have some powerful options.

All this says, however, is that Google Sites is a great place to start, but you may want to upgrade eventually. You may even feel the need to spend some money at that point, which is fine. Even then, you can use your Google Sites site as a starting point for the new site's design and features, saving you huge amounts of time and money. And you can continue to use your Google Sites skills for prototypes of your new main site, for collaboration, for an intranet, or for lesser sites — again, a great way to build search engine rankings — and on and on.

Understanding What Google Sites Can Do for You

Because Google Sites is so easy to use, it can be the main tool for creating your site. However, the Web is tremendously varied today, so you can use Google Sites in many ways.

Web sites created with Google Sites are less easily customized and "slick" than hand-designed Web sites. They're also not database-driven in the same sense as many larger sites. (You can recognize database-driven sites because the Web page addresses — the URLs — are database calls rather than hierarchical folder and page names. An example is the URL of a Web page about Google Sites on the PC Magazine Web site: `http://www.pcmag.com/article2/0,2817,2317341,00.asp`.)

You can also use Google Sites to create a test, alternative, or experimental site. This kink of site is quick and easy to update, either for one person or two or more working together.

You can also take advantage of the capabilities and use Google Sites to build an *intranet site* — a site for internal organizational use only. Intranet sites are very much about collaboration — in a company, you can trust people not to abuse the privilege, because if they do you can discipline them. And the slight lack of slickness of Google Sites is fine for many intranet sites, on which the additional functionality far outweighs a slight lack of "cool."

But you can also take advantage of the capabilities of Google Sites in a "real," non-intranet, public-facing Web site, offering collaboration features to regular end users. This may increasingly become the norm as the Web changes — but we can't be sure. For every long-term winner in technology, several contenders bite the dust. (Remember push technology? I didn't think so.)

The bottom line is that your efforts in learning to use Google Sites are likely to pay off many times over. You'll be learning a lot about the traditional capabilities that have made the Web a worldwide success and also about the new ones that are beginning to transform it. Given its status as an important offering from one of the world's most successful companies, Google Sites itself is likely to grow and change as a tool, giving you more and more capabilities.

Creating Your First Google Site

It's worth going through the process of creating a Google Site just to get a feel for it, even before you do anything serious.

We're going to use content about Web pages from the For Dummies site at www.dummies.com to create a simple Web site, so you can follow along if you'd like. Just don't publish a site with For Dummies or anyone else's content on it without permission.

You may want to decide on your desired domain name before you start. Use the earlier chapters in this book to help identify the domain name you want to buy.

Follow these steps to create your initial Google Site:

1. **Go to the main Google site at www.google.com and sign in.**

2. **Go to sites.google.com.**

   The screen shown in Figure 4-2 appears.

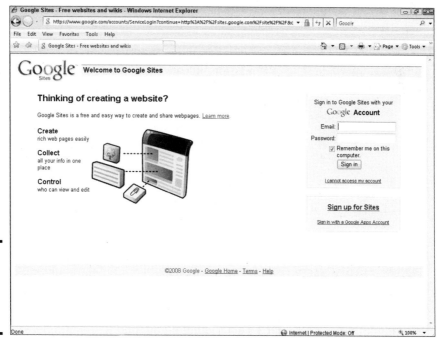

Figure 4-2: Your own Web presence is in site.

3. **Click the Create site button.**

   The Welcome to Google Sites screen , shown in Figure 4-3, appears.

4. **Enter the site name and press the Tab key.**

   The site name you enter must stripped of any spaces or special characters — anything except a-z, 0-9, or the hyphen (-) — and made into part of a URL.

   You may want to make the site name the same as the core part of the custom Web domain name you want to buy and use for your site. If so, follow the steps in the earlier chapters in this book before proceeding.

5. **Enter the Site Description and click the check box if you want to mark the site as having mature content for adults only.**

   Though entering a description is optional, it's worth doing. The site description will show up as the title of your page — that is, as the words that appear in the top of the Web browser when you visit a Web page.

6. **Choose a radio button to specify whether *Everyone* in the world can view your site, or *Only people you specify*.**

   This is where you decide whether you're creating a classic World Wide Web site — clearly meaning one for all to see — or an intranet site limited to a few. The great thing about Google Sites is that you can limit access during development and then go public.

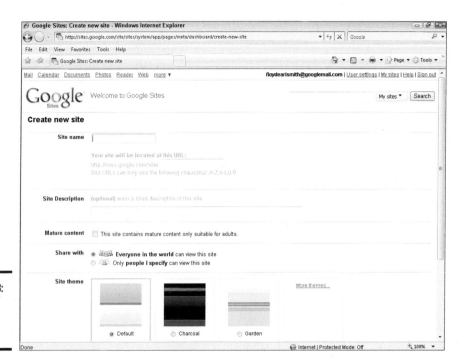

Figure 4-3:
Proceed
with
caution.

7. **Now it's time to choose a graphical theme for your site. Begin by clicking the More Themes link to expand the themes available.**

   The area showing the available themes expands, as shown in Figure 4-4.

   You can always change the theme — but you only get one chance to make a first impression with viewers. So give your choice some thought and change it right away if you decide you don't like it.

8. **Enter the security code.**

   Having to enter a code is annoying; but without it, hackers would abuse the system: Specially written computer pages could come along and create Web pages on Google Sites and then use them to host all sorts of malicious software. (When someone tried to shut down the offending domain, they would find out it's run by the otherwise trustworthy provider, Google.)

9. **Click Create Site.**

   Your initial site appears, as shown in Figure 4-5. The site's name, greenpsychesite, appears in the upper-left corner of the Web page and as part of the title; the site description, Home, is the other part.

The remaining sections of this chapter describe what you can do with your site; Chapter 5 takes you through, in detail, how to create a Search-friendly site.

Book IV Chapter 4

A Tour of Google Sites

Figure 4-4:
Give yourself a wide choice among site themes.

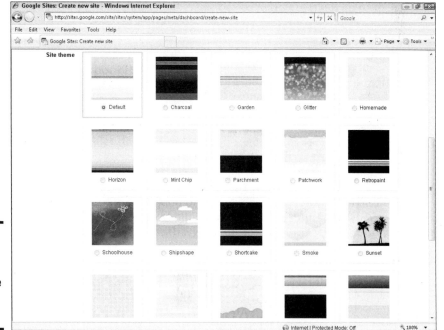

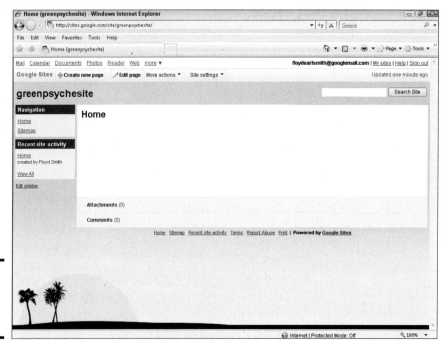

Figure 4-5:
Getting
started is
half the fun.

Adjusting your Google Site's appearance

The words in the heading are chosen carefully — you can *adjust* your Google Site's appearance; you can't *change* it in big ways. That is, there are limits to what you can do.

There are three sets of interactive elements you can adjust:

✦ The theme, which you chose in the previous section

✦ Site elements

✦ Colors and fonts

These options are accessed by choosing Site settings⇨Change appearance. This brings up the Appearance page, which has three parts — Site Elements (see Figure 4-6); Colors and Fonts; and Themes, which you already chose initially as explained in the previous section.

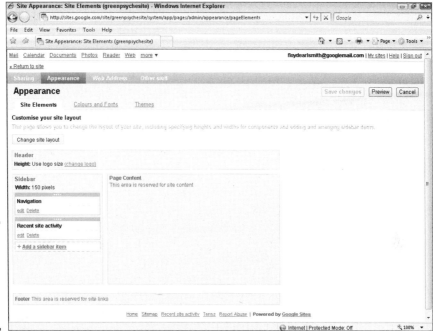

Figure 4-6:
You can change your site's appearance here.

Changing site elements

Elements you can change in the Site Elements tab of the Appearance page include

✦ **Change site layout:** You can make major changes to your site here, as shown in Figure 4-7. Options include the Site width — in percent of the window size or pixels; whether to use a Header, and its height (logo size, or a set number of pixels); whether to use a Sidebar, and its width (in pixels) and location (left or right).

You'll never have an easier way to try different configurations for a Web site. Use the site layout to make adjustments as you build your site and try different options.

Keep track of changes so you can always go back to a previous look. Google Sites includes a robust Undo option, and changes aren't recorded until you click the Save changes button, but it's easy to forget what the site looked like the last time you really liked it.

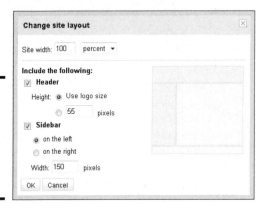

Figure 4-7:
Make the
layout one
you — and
users —
can live
with.

✦ **Header:** This is the top area of the page, determined by the height of your logo. Note that the logo is the only thing on the top of the page, so you lose the entire horizontal area not occupied by the logo.

 Use a short graphic for the header, or create a short version of any logo or other graphic you already have and want to use.

✦ **Sidebar — Navigation:** The Navigation area automatically fills in as you add pages. You can edit the navigation area or delete it.

 Editing the Navigation area is shown in Figure 4-8. You can change the name of the Navigation area; shift pages up and down; remove pages from the Navigation area, or add pages to it.

Figure 4-8:
You can
configure
the
navigation
easily.

Configuring the Navigation area may seem a bit complicated, but there's no truly easy way to create and manage the navigation for a site. The way Google Sites does it is about as good as it gets.

You can also delete the Navigation area, but then you have to replace it — probably with something harder to manage.

Don't delete the Navigation area while you're building and intensively editing your site because the Navigation area gives you — and, potentially, others who are editing your site — an easy way to manage site navigation while the site is changing quickly. If you want to replace the Navigation area, do so when your site starts to settle down.

✦ **Sidebar — Recent site activity:** The Recent site activity area shows what's happened on the site. You can change the number of actions shown in the list by clicking the Edit button and then changing the setting from the default, 5, to what you need.

Those of us who are old-fashioned about these kinds of things think that each and every edit to your site is not the typical user's business. (You can put a *What's New* area on your site, which gives you a more controlled way to show change than showing every edit.) However, the *Recent site activity* area is great way to keep track of additions during site construction and editing — and change them if the effect isn't what you want.

Keep the Recent site activity area when building up your site; consider deleting it when the site goes public or settles down.

✦ **Add a sidebar item:** The Add a Sidebar item lets you add a variety of different kinds of elements to your sidebar, including Navigation — to augment or replace the original navigation panel; Recent site activity or My site activity, replacement or additional panels showing activity (My site activity is only for activity by the currently signed-in user); Text, for a text box; or Countdown, showing the name of an event and the number of days until it happens.

The Countdown is great when you're building up your site and want to keep track of a deadline for launching it.

✦ **Text:** The Text Box is an option in Add a sidebar item. Figure 4-9 shows where you choose to add a Text Box, and Figure 4-10 shows a Text Box and the Configure Text Box panel. This includes all the options for configuring text — a title, links, tables, headings, and more.

The capabilities of a Text Box are great, but build it up gradually. Space in the sidebar is limited, and if you try to do too much with a Text Box, you may spend a lot of time — and then end up deleting it.

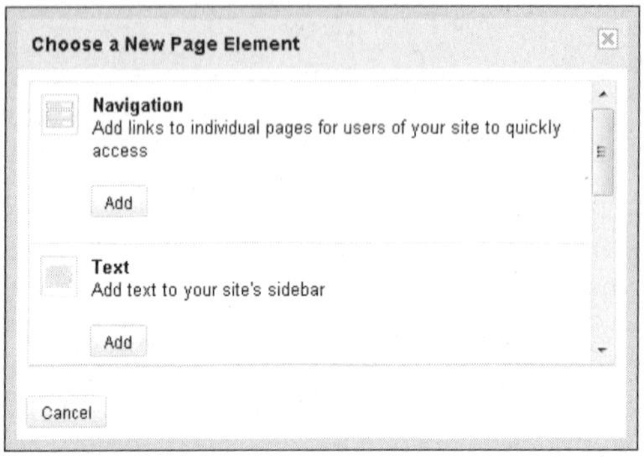

Choose a New Page Element ☒

Navigation
Add links to individual pages for users of your site to quickly access

Add

Text
Add text to your site's sidebar

Add

Cancel

Figure 4-9:
Get creative
with your
own new
elements.

Configure Text Box ☒

Title:

Content:

Insert ▾   Format ▾   Table ▾

↶ ↷ Normal   ▾ 8 pt   ▾ **B** *I* U̲ A̲▾ ✂▾

Link ⅛≣ ⅛≣ ⇥≣ ⇤≣ ≡ ≡ ≡ 𝐓 ⁄HTML

OK   Cancel

Figure 4-10:
You can
text up your
sidebar.

Changing Colors and Fonts

You can make a lot of changes to the look of your site here. Whether you *should* is discussed in the Chapter 5.

If you and others working on your site aren't experts, keep your site colors and fonts very simple. Otherwise you can waste a lot of time and effort. Consider doing the rest of the site yourself — then getting expert help for fine-tuning the look.

The Colors and Fonts area shows a version of your site with the current settings, as shown in Figure 4-11, and updates the version of your site with your choices.

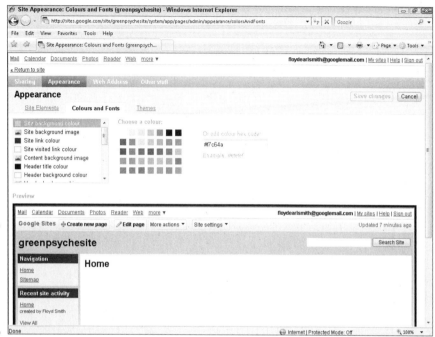

Figure 4-11:
Give
yourself a
wide choice
among site
themes.

Begin by familiarizing yourself with the options, some of which are buried in
the interface:

✦ **Page font** and **Sidebar font:** The font options are buried among a variety of different options for background images, colors, and so on; but
consider choosing the fonts first. Also, consider using the same font
for both the main page and the sidebar unless you're sure that varying
them is an improvement. The fonts you choose are critical to the look of
your site. Google Sites gives you a limited number of font options, which
reflects the fact that the number of fonts that you can count on across
different kinds of computers and operating systems is limited. (See
Figure 4-12.)

The fonts you choose may appear somewhat differently on Mac, PC, or
Unix machines, on different browsers, and so on. As your site settles
down, try to view your site on various systems to see how it looks.

✦ **Background image: Site, Content, Header, Page, and Sidebar title
background image** (see Figure 4-13). It takes creativity to design and
use background images in a way that enhances, rather than detracts
from, the appearance of your site.

Leave background images, alone unless you're a pro, until you've made
most of the key content and appearance decisions for your site. Then
you can try different options — always keeping in mind that few serious
sites use site background images any more.

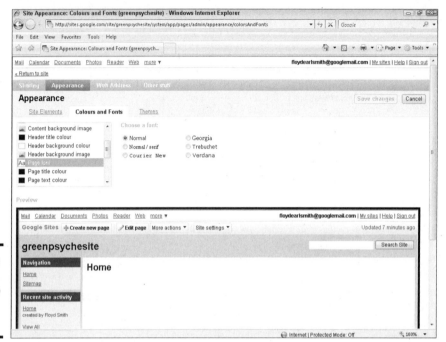

Figure 4-12:
Fonts are
important to
the look of
your site.

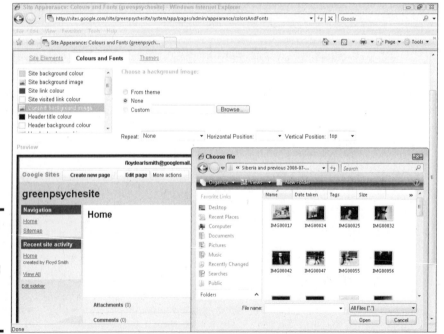

Figure 4-13:
You can do
a lot with
background
images
in Google
Sites.

The BATCS site that one of the authors works on, at `batcs.co.uk`, uses a background image fairly effectively.

✦ **Background, title, and text colors: Site, Header, Page, Sidebar title, Sidebar background and so on.** (See Figure 4-14). You can choose a whole variety of background, title, and text colors, but it's all too easy to create an impossible-to-read mess.

You can choose from a palette of 35 pre-defined colors or enter a hexadecimal code — see the sidebar.

Most books and magazines and Web pages are printed with black (or near-black) text on a white (or near-white) background for a reason — high contrast makes things easier to read, and black on white is the highest-contrast and easiest-to-read of all the options. Stick with this tried and trusted combination for your site unless you can identify a model or get help that will make you sure of choosing something better.

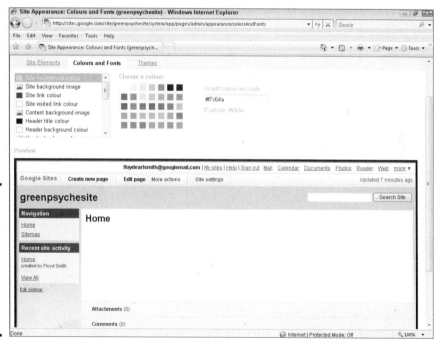

Figure 4-14: Be careful not to get into color trouble when designing Google sites.

Going further

It's helpful to work on your site's look before you put much content in it. That way you can get some of the key elements settled before you go on.

In the next chapter we delve into designing and creating a several-page site — something that puts you well on the way to becoming a competent Web site designer without even having to learn HTML or any tool more complicated than the Google Sites editor.

Hexadecimal colors

You can find good explanations of hexadecimal colors in many books and on many Web sites. Here's a very brief explanation.

A hexadecimal color such as #373b3d is two characters each for three colors: red (37, in this instance); green (3b), and blue (3d).

Each two-digit number is made up of the normal digits, 0-9, and the letters a-f. The higher up the digit or letter, the higher the number is represented. The first digit is most important by far. 00 is the lowest, or none of the color; ff is the highest, or all of the color.

Here are some simple hexadecimal colors:

- #00FF00 — No red, full green, no blue — green.

- #CCFF00 — Nearly full red, full green, no blue — a greenish yellow.

- #000000 — No red, no green, no blue — white.

- #FFFFFF — Full red, full green, full blue — black.

- #666666 — Part red, part green, part blue — light grey.

You can get a feel for different hex colors by clicking on the 35 preset colors shown in the Colors and Fonts area and observing the hex codes that show up; interpret them in terms of the amount of red, green, and blue they include, and you'll learn something about color as well as about hex codes.

Chapter 5: Creating a Search-Friendly Site

In This Chapter

⮑ Selecting the best, most effective keywords for your site

⮑ Distributing keywords on your site

⮑ Understanding how these keywords affect your site's structure

⮑ Creating a working draft of your site

*T*he advantages of publishing a site on the Web fall into certain categories: flexibility, the ability to make changes easily, and the opportunity to equalize the presence of little guys versus the established Goliaths.

Making your Web site search-friendly somewhat goes against these advantages. Search-friendliness is about stability, consistency, and building up a place in the Web's system of links over time.

Why is this? In online and in real business, the hardest thing to fake is authenticity. And putting in the time and effort to garner a lot of links to your site from other, well-trafficked sites gives you the surest sign of authenticity out there. ("Putting in time and effort" is exactly what the get-rich–quick types who try to trick Google and other search engines don't want to do, which is why Google always looks for signs of real time and effort at the expense of technical tricks.)

Unfortunately, there's only one opportunity to be first. The Web has developed in layers, and sites that got there early all seem to link to each other, and many of them attract a great deal of traffic. It's extremely difficult for recent sites trying to win significant link traffic on well-established topics — especially technology topics relating to the Web itself, computers, and so on.

But one of the best brief formulas for making money has always been, "Find a need and fill it." If you can do this with your Web site, you have a good chance of building up a strong search position over time.

Creating a search-friendly site is not easy, but it's important. Like much else having to do with Google (or with business in general), early, seemingly minor decisions can affect you for a long time to come. So take the time to understand the points in this chapter and be ready to put them into practice.

Selecting Your Dirty Half-Dozen

The Dirty Dozen was a classic World War II movie about a special mission in enemy territory. "The Dirty Dozen" were specially selected soldiers who fit Wellington's famous statement about his troops on the eve of battle — that he didn't know what effect they would have on the enemy, but "they frighten me."

You need to choose a group of keywords that will win battles for you in Google Search — augmented, as described in Book VI, by Google Ads. Because you need to focus these efforts, and because the typical person can retain a list of five to seven things in short-term memory, I recommend you initially focus on half a dozen.

You can add additional terms later, but you're much more likely to achieve early success and positive momentum by starting with a short list.

Here are possible sources of your first half-dozen terms:

+ **Your name:** (Or the name of the founders of your business, other senior people in the business, even endorsers.) A distinctive personal name is a huge asset on the Web (say the authors knowingly, neither being blessed with such).

+ **Your business's name:** Again, a distinctive yet easy-to-remember and easy-to-spell business name is worth its weight in gold on the Web.

+ **Your business's location:** There are several possible relevant locations — the area in which you are the only business of your type, the area in which you're the largest business of your type, the town you're in, and the major urban area you're in or nearest to.

+ **The type of product or service you provide**. Terms such as *printers* and *groceries* are the most valuable and most difficult kind of keyword to own. But more people are combining such terms with town names and so on. Google Ads helps you attract locally targeted searches even on broad keywords, so don't give up.

+ **Any descriptive terms about how you do business, your customers, and so on.** For instance, if you provide products largely to architects, *architects* is a term you should consider focusing on. If you're *green*, *friendly*, and so on, consider including one or two such terms.

+ **The specific names of the products or services you provide**. These should be distinctive and memorable; if not, consider creating names that meet these criteria.

As with most Web site and search optimization work, this is not just about taking something that's already perfect and building on it. You're likely to find yourself changing some underlying aspects of how you do business as well.

For instance, trying to identify your search-friendly terms may lead you to think about your business in a whole new way. After you do your search optimization work, you may begin describing your business as, say, "Connecticut's #1 environmentally friendly printer" — something you hadn't realized was true until you started looking into search terms.

It's important to use laymen's terms — terms that your customers and other stakeholders use about your business — and not insider or expert terms. For instance, you may run a dry-cleaning business that uses a specific chemical for cleaning. Unless people know the name of that chemical, however, you need to focus on a benefit of your process (cleaner cleaning? cheaper cleaning?) instead.

After you've identified potential search-friendly terms, test them in Google and other search engines. Primarily test them in Google, however. Google has most of the searches in most markets, and it's Google where you'll be following up with Google ads, analytics, and so on; so it's the right place to focus. Yahoo! (www.yahoo.com) and, to a lesser extent, Windows Live Search (at www.live.com) are also worth checking.

This should enable you to identify search terms that you can potentially "own" — that is, use to get a good search engine result — either on an absolute, global basis, or in combination with other words or with narrowing by locality (which can be accomplished roughly by the user, as part of a search, or more precisely with the targeting capability of Google Ads).

Table 5-1 is a worksheet to help you focus on search terms. Consider creating a worksheet like this as part of the process of creating or upgrading your Web site.

Table 5-1	Search Terms Worksheet		
	Potential terms	*Terms after search test*	*Final term(s)*
Your name			
Business name			
Location			
Product/service type(s)			
Descriptive terms			
Product/service name(s)			
Other			

Search terms for BATCS

As a case study, look at the search terms exercise for a business that one of the authors (Smith) is associated with, Business and Technical Communications Services (BATCS) in London, UK.

Here's the short list of terms the business's principals have identified for search:

✦ **Personal name:** The main, publicly known principal of the business is Olga Smith. Her coauthor for BATCS's one and only book (so far) is Linda James. Neither name is hugely distinctive, but each has possibilities.

✦ **Business name:** BATCS markets itself by its acronym, which is not quite a word but fairly easy to remember.

✦ **Location:** BATCS advertises itself as a London business, as it's one of very few businesses of its type in London.

✦ **The type of product or service you provide:** The general area in which BATCS operates is *accent reduction*. However, this is not a great keyword — key phrase, technically — to own, because many sites of long standing from various countries focus on it heavily.

✦ **Any descriptive terms about how you do business, your customers, and so on.** For BATCS, the type of business is uncommon enough in London that there hasn't been a need to be the *friendly, green, high-end,* or *low-cost* provider, although these are good terms to focus on in more crowded markets.

✦ **The specific names of the products or services you provide.** For BATCS, the sole book that the company publishes, *Get Rid of Your Accent*, is a strong product name; the accent-reduction courses aren't branded except under the BATCS banner and by association with the book.

All these wording and naming choices have evolved over time, tested in Google and other search engines.

For instance, BATCS — which wants to appear as a solid company — doesn't provide detailed descriptive information about the founders and staff on its Web site. This avoids possibly appearing to be a "one-(wo)man-band" or small company. Yet the main principal is also one of the book coauthors, so a description of her background fits nicely on the site's People page, which describes the coauthors, as shown in Figure 5-1.

This provides an easy target for anyone searching on the names of either of the book's coauthors.

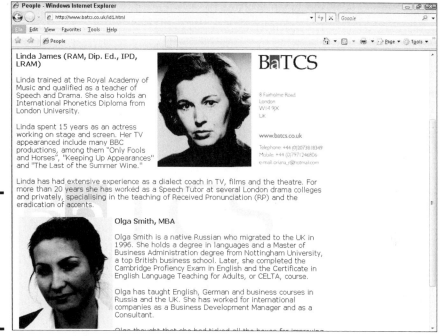

Figure 5-1:
BATCS has
principals
and
co-authors
on its
People
page.

The content shown in the browser window:

Linda James (RAM, Dip. Ed., IPD, LRAM)

Linda trained at the Royal Academy of Music and qualified as a teacher of Speech and Drama. She also holds an International Phonetics Diploma from London University.

Linda spent 15 years as an actress working on stage and screen. Her TV appearance include many BBC productions, among them "Only Fools and Horses", "Keeping Up Appearances" and "The Last of the Summer Wine."

Linda has had extensive experience as a dialect coach in TV, films and the theatre. For more than 20 years she has worked as a Speech Tutor at several London drama colleges and privately, specialising in the teaching of Received Pronunciation (RP) and the eradication of accents.

BATCS

8 Fairholme Road
London
W14 9JX
UK

www.batcs.co.uk

Telephone: +44 (0)2073818349
Mobile: +44 (0)7971246806
e-mail: oriana_r@hotmail.com

Olga Smith, MBA

Olga Smith is a native Russian who migrated to the UK in 1996. She holds a degree in languages and a Master of Business Administration degree from Nottingham University, a top British business school. Later, she completed the Cambridge Profiency Exam in English and the Certificate in English Language Teaching for Adults, or CELTA, course.

Olga has taught English, German and business courses in Russia and the UK. She has worked for international companies as a Business Development Manager and as a Consultant.

One term that turns out to be important to BATCS is *elocution*. Many people slightly misuse this term — which is mostly about speech optimization for native speakers — when looking for something slightly different, accent reduction for (mostly) foreigners. Rather than try to explain all this on the Web site — which might even come across as a bit insulting — BATCS uses *elocution* as a search term for Google Ads.

Competitive surfing

A much overlooked way to get ideas for keywords for your Web site is to look at competitors' sites.

Pick any three to five competitors. Include a mix of smaller and larger competitors, and "bricks and mortar" versus online-only competitors, if that applies to your business.

Now follow these steps to identify effective keywords for your site:

1. **Search using a variety of keywords you've already generated, plus new ones that you think of as you go along. (Write them down, or you'll forget them.)**

Which of your competitors come up? Which ones would you, as a surfer, want to go to first? Are there any competitors you didn't know you had until you tried this?

2. **Search using combinations of keywords to narrow down your search locally or by product type.**

   Which combinations occur naturally? Which ones work best for finding what you're looking for?

3. **Finally, search using inside information, such as the name of a business, its principals, its products, or parts of an address.**

   How well does this search work?

Figure 5-2 shows search results for pizza parlors in and around Hammersmith in West London. Note that Google is providing local search results, and there are also many sponsored links. Global chains have several of the local results, and Wikipedia has the top spot in the non-local organic search results. It's going to be tough to crack a list like this!

In each case, note the use of Google text ads within your search results. Which of your competitors are using these ads? (We use this information in Book VI.)

Figure 5-2:
Get a pizza the action in Hammersmith.

Use the information you gather to further hone your own list of keywords. Also use it to set realistic expectations about what results you'll get from organic search — not a lot, you may find — as opposed to text ads, which can do much more for you, much more quickly.

Distributing keywords on your Web site

One of the key debates in Web site design today — seriously — is how to distribute top keywords on a Web site.

There are two approaches, which can be described as the *strong site* and *strong page* approaches. One is to cluster keywords on the home page, hoping to make it as strong as possible. The other is to distribute keywords across the site, hoping to make lightning strike where it's most appropriate — that is, hoping to have different Web pages from within your site come up in response to searches on specific terms.

Web site creators tend to favor the strong site approach. "If only we can get people to our site," Web site authors think, "we can get them to see not just what they want — but learn other things about us as well."

Unfortunately, people have a surprisingly strong tendency to see the Web not as a collection of sites but as a collection of Web pages. They're just trying to get things done, and they use sites more as reference points or accelerators rather than as destinations. (Consider, for instance, someone who researches a car purchase online before completing the sale at a car dealer.)

Even the US military has come to understand this. The military offers a custom search engine, as shown in Figure 5-3, that allows users to search a variety of site options, including the following:

✦ All Military Web Sites

✦ U.S. Army Only

✦ U.S. Air Force Only

✦ U.S. NAVY Only

✦ U.S. Marine Corps Only

✦ National Guard Only

✦ All Government Web sites

Note that the Department of Defense is not trying to educate people on the right *site* to use; it's trying to help them find the right *page* within a specified site or range of sites.

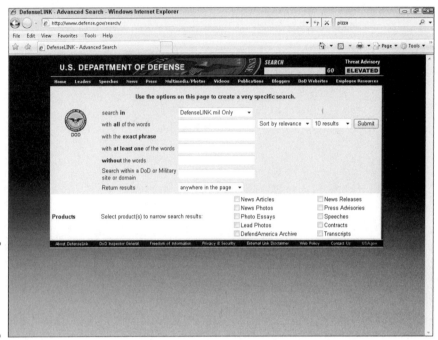

Figure 5-3:
Paging
the US
Department
of Defense.

So we tend to lean toward the site-based approach. People use the Web to get things done; a Web search should lead them to a Web page that helps them complete their task. This argues for bringing searchers to pages that actually help them finish that task.

However, the former approach has its place. Where there are keywords that aren't associated with a specific piece of information or task, such as general terms describing the business, you should place them so that they point toward the home page, along with the business name.

The description of the company that normally goes in an About Us page can be used to build up another page of the site. For instance, BATCS — which wants to keep its site small and have strong search engine impact — put its "about the company" information on the home page, as shown in Figure 5-4. Search engine users who search for BATCS by the company's name are thus brought to the main page of the site — which also contains the latest course information — rather than to a dry interior page.

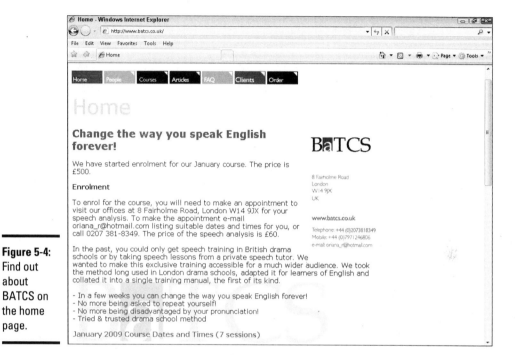

Figure 5-4:
Find out about BATCS on the home page.

Using Keywords to Create Your Site Map

Because search engine terms are so important, you should design your site around them, right?

Well, not exactly. The best overall design of your site is largely fixed before you even start on it!

How can this be? It turns out that users have a fixed idea of what should be on a Web site, especially a small company Web site.

Think of your Web site as a grocery store. Users instantly guesstimate the size of the site and form expectations about what it should contain and where things should be. Although they've never been at your site (or a specific grocery store) before, they stride forth confidently, sure that things are in reasonably predictable places.

**Book IV
Chapter 5**

Creating a Search-
Friendly Site

A simple Web site map from the US Federal Government is shown in Figure 5-5. This depicts part of the site for the US Fish and Wildlife Service Endangered Species site. Note how specific program names are mapped to specific pages.

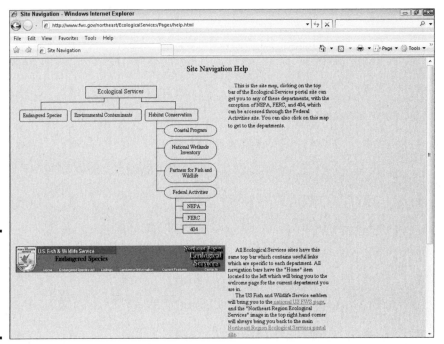

Figure 5-5: Get straight to the endangered species info you need.

The site reflected in the site map shown in Figure 5-5 is both simple and search-engine-friendly, if you know the specific name you're looking for. If not, you may never get there, unless you're pretty lucky with your keywords. (NEPA stands for the National Environmental Policy Act, and FERC for the Federal Energy Regulatory Commission, in case you were wondering.)

Now, you can also mix things up a bit. For instance, shoppers go to a store's checkout counter when they're done buying. But clever store designers put a last few small items at the counter, to encourage impulse purchases in addition to the key, most desired items.

Or, think of your Web site as a Christmas tree — and your key search terms as bright, shiny ornaments. You can use the search terms to lead them to the core of the tree — or to the specific branch that might also contain the information (such as your phone number) or functionality (such as the ability to buy a product) that they want.

Here are the key navigational elements that a typical user expects to find on a company Web site:

✦ **Home page:** The hardest page to get right, this can be introductory to the site, contain some information that might otherwise go elsewhere (as with BATCS, above), or even contain the whole site on one page. As hard as it is to define a "good" home page, if you get this wrong, users will leave very quickly indeed.

✦ **Contact us:** The second most important page of the site. A friend recently described the ideal visit to his company's Web site: "They find us on Google; come to the home page to find out what we do; click to the Contact Us page; then call us and arrange a salesman's visit."

✦ **Products or Services:** What you sell. These can be named for major products/services or product/service lines, grouped into one, or divided among strongly branded products or services and other items.

✦ **Buying/Where to buy:** Products and services descriptions should include or link to a way to buy, but this information should also be in a separate tab for those who know exactly what they want. This area can allow people to buy directly or point them to where they can do so.

✦ **About Us/People:** A description of your company and key people in it. It is intended to be reassuring — and, if you're brave, to attract the customers you want most and subtly deter the ones you want least. Also it usually includes press information and job offers.

✦ **Service and support:** It's amazing how much time, energy, and money can be saved by even a relatively basic service and support area in your Web site. Unless you want your customers to call you with each and every question about your products — which is a plausible strategy early on — a service and support area is a must.

✦ **Validators:** A catch-all name for one or more tabs with information that supports your company's or products' reputation and value. This page can include information about suppliers, links to or excerpts from press articles, key customers, and more. Some of this can be at the top level and some can be included in About Us or elsewhere.

✦ **Subsites:** Even small companies should consider having a separate subsite about their most popular product or service. This can combine product information, how to buy, and "fan" information, possibly including message boards. It's fine for the content to strongly overlap the main site, but you'll probably need professional involvement to help manage the overlap and tie the navigation of one to the other.

There are two opposing forces operating here. You want each page to do one thing, and do it very well. Yet you want each page to be easy to find in navigation or search. And you want no more than five to seven tabs to make it easy for users to keep the site navigation in mind as they move around your site.

These conflicting needs are relatively easy to meet on a small site. As you work on a larger site, you need to consider secondary navigation for core functions, second-level navigation (not the same thing at all), combining some functions, and extending others across multiple pages or levels of navigation.

An example is shown in the site for the US Department of Health and Human Services' 2005 Conference on Aging (see Figure 5-6). Even a site focused on a single conference has main navigation, local navigation, and footer/utilities around the page content. You can bet a lot of work went into an overall template from which this specific site's navigation was derived.

Navigation for even moderately complex sites is not easy. In this book we focus on simple examples, but as your needs get more complex, you may have to develop expertise of your own — or hire in experts to help. The more you do right from the beginning, the less help you'll need. (And the less of your money and, very importantly, time, you'll need to invest in outsiders.)

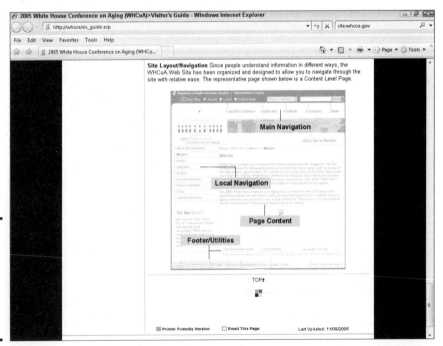

Figure 5-6:
Even a single conference can have complex navigation.

Case study: The BATCS site map

BATCS is a relatively small business, but it's complex enough. BATCS offers a product — *Get Rid of your Accent* — a service — accent-reduction courses — and has distributors, suppliers, newspaper articles, and prominent customers. How does it fit all these elements within the five to seven tabs, with no second-level navigation, while remaining a desirable small company Web site?

Here we examine how the major site components described in the previous section are handled on the BATCS site:

✦ **Home page.** This page includes current course information and information about the company that usually goes in the About Us area, as well as introductory information about the key product, the book *Get Rid of your Accent*. It is potentially confusing, but by including immediately useful information, it makes itself useful and communicates confidence.

✦ **Contact us.** One of the graphics that holds the site together visually is a scanned graphic of a business card, containing all the address, phone number, and contact information for the company. This is another confident and useful approach. (It would be more sophisticated to use clever HTML to make this text rather than a graphic, but this would require a bit of expensive outside help and possibly make the site harder to edit.)

✦ **Products or Services.** The BATCS site has an Order page for its main product, the book *Get Rid of your Accent*, and includes a brief description of the book on the home page. The main service is courses offered, described on the home page and under a Courses tab.

✦ **Buying/Where to buy.** The Order page takes care of orders for the book. The Home page and Courses page both urge visitors to contact BATCS using the contact information on every page. The Order page also lends credibility through the listing of name partners such as amazon.co.uk.

✦ **About Us/People.** This is handled under the People tab, which describes the two authors of the book — both of whom have taught courses for BATCS as well.

✦ **Service and support.** With no explicit support page but plenty of contact information, the site invites anyone with problems to contact the company directly.

✦ **Validators.** Having a published book is in itself a validator, and two tabs are explicitly for validation: Articles includes published articles from UK newspapers such as the *London Times*, the *Sun,* and others; and Clients, as shown in Figure 5-7, includes the flags of countries whose ambassadors and other diplomatic staff have participated in the courses.

✦ **Subsites.** BATCS does not run any custom-made subsites, but the book page on amazon.co.uk for Get Rid of your Accent serves as a subsite for the book, as well as a powerful validator.

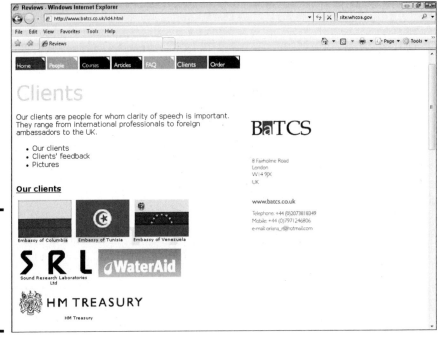

Figure 5-7:
National flags provide powerful validation for BATCS.

Creating a draft of your site

People get very concerned about the technical part of creating a Web page — but really, the hard part is getting the site design and the content right.

Only you can create the content. You can get help with the site design and the technical bit, but no one else can decide what needs to go on your Web pages except you.

The best way to get the toughest and most important problem — content — solved first is to create a draft of your site. Then you can get advice or help from others on the content, the side design, and the technical chore of making a Web page.

You can create a draft of your site using tools you're familiar with — and then "cleanse" the text to make sure it loads into Google Sites without problems.

The steps that follow are for Microsoft Word running on a Windows PC. On a different kind of computer or a different word processor, the steps may be slightly different. The important thing is to try to save the file as a single Web page document (.htm).

It's possible to do all your Web page creation work in Word, but Word inserts a lot of extra coding, and it's very difficult to tell what Word functionality is supported by HTML and what functionality isn't. We recommend that you use Word, if you're comfortable with it, for mock-ups, but use Google Sites or another Web-specific tool for creating the actual site.

On a Windows PC running Microsoft Word, follow these steps:

1. **In Windows, create a new folder.**

   This folder will hold the Windows draft of your site.

2. **Start Microsoft Word. Choose File⇨New.**

   The New Document pane appears, as shown in Figure 5-8.

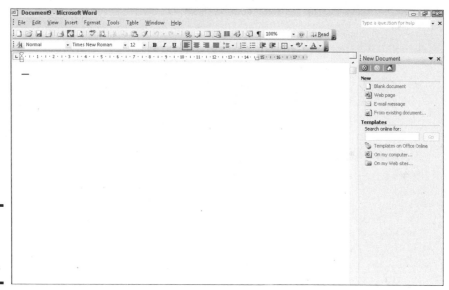

Figure 5-8: Word lets you create Web pages.

3. **Click the second option under New, Web page.**

   A new document appears.

4. **Save the file as a Web page. Choose File⇨Save As Web Page.**

   The Save As dialog appears.

5. **Next to the prompt, Save as Type, select the option Single File Web Page. Use the pull-down menu to change the option to simply Web Page, as shown in Figure 5-9. Use the navigation in the upper part of the dialog box to save the file in the folder you've reserved for your site. Use the Change Title button to change the page title to what you want the user to see at the top of the browser window. (Unlike words** in the navigation, this should include a moderate use of search terms.) Click the Save button to save the file.

That's a lot to do in one dialog box!

The document is saved with the `.htm` extension.

A Single File Web Page — the default option, for some reason — doesn't mean a Web page saved one character at a time, all lined up in single file. It means all the files that make up a Web page are included in a single file on disk. It combines the text *and* graphics for a Web page in a single file whose filename ends in the file suffix `.mht`, rather than the usual `.doc` (for Word documents) or `.htm` or `.html` (for Web pages). The Single File Web Page option is nice for keeping your Web text and graphics in one place, but is not usable by most Web tools. Keep your Web pages as separate `.htm` and graphics files for more flexibility.

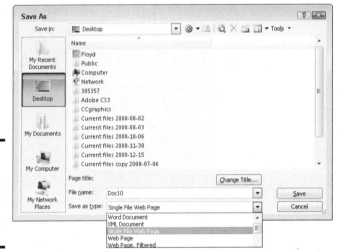

Figure 5-9:
Save as a
Web Page
instead of a
Single File
Web Page.

6. **Repeat, creating additional documents for the additional pages you need. Save all the files in the same folder.**

Don't overuse keywords in navigation. Users expect functional words (like *Books* rather than specific book titles), with the exception of strongly branded product and service names. Get opinions from friends and colleagues if you're not sure.

7. **Create simple navigation for your pages. Create a list of words representing the names of your Web pages. Separate the names with spaces and vertical bar characters. Then highlight the first word (usually Home) and choose Insert⇨Hyperlink.**

The Insert Hyperlink dialog box appears.

8. **Choose the file for the Home page. (Yes, you're linking the page to itself.) Repeat to link to all other pages.**

The result will be similar to the list shown in Figure 5-10.

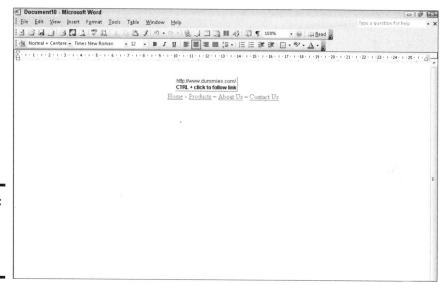

Figure 5-10:
Create a linked list for simple navigation.

9. **Copy the list of links to all the pages and save them.**

10. **Add content and images to the pages. Discuss with others. Make changes.**

Use keywords liberally in your Web pages, with some focus on the first 100 words of each page. But don't overstuff your content with keywords — users won't like it, Google may actually penalize use of too may keywords.

Using this draft version of your Web site allows you to experiment flexibly.

Check your site when you're done to make sure that the keywords cluster the way you want them to — either pulling users toward the home page, or toward a specific, relevant page within your site.

Chapter 6: Creating a Google Site

In This Chapter

✔ **Making initial site decisions**

✔ **Creating your first pages**

✔ **Adjusting the page navigation**

✔ **Changing themes, colors, and fonts**

✔ **Dealing with collaboration**

*T*his chapter shows you how to create a useful and search-friendly site. In this chapter we use Google Sites as our tool, but the lessons here apply to any Web site you create and any tool you use to create it — or even sites created for you by an expert.

Creating a search-friendly site is not easy, but it's important. Like much else having to do with Google (or with business in general), seemingly minor early decisions can affect your site for a long time. So take the time to understand the points in this chapter and be ready to put them into practice.

Initial Site Decisions

To better demonstrate some of the concepts in this chapter, we use an example business site. In this site, we advertise a small business with a single service — computer repair in your home or office — and a single product — a tool called SpeedChecker that ensures that your computer is running up to specifications. A lot of businesses start as a service and then develop products out of tools they use, so this is a common situation.

Our small business is based in Coronado, California. The main road through Coronado is called the Silver Strand, so we call the business Silver Strand PC Services.

Note that we're careful to avoid calling the business Coronado PC Services. That's because Coronado is a very specific place, and if we eventually sell SpeedChecker more broadly, we don't want to sound too local. Silver Strand has local meaning, but it is a bit less specific so it should scale well when we try to reach a larger audience. We might discuss the "silver strand of performance" running through an organization's PC setup, for instance.

Use useit.com

It's famously said that there are lies, damned lies, and statistics. This is nowhere more true than in Web page design, which is a new discipline that's operating across a constantly changing base of hardware and software — with millions and even billions of dollars at stake.

Such an environment lends itself to dramatic headlines, often featuring a researcher or company doing a quick study and announcing results that soon become a sort of online urban legend, even if the realities that helped produce the results change in the meantime.

A welcome antidote to all this is the world-famous Jakob Nielsen and his very simple and easy-to–use Web site of roughly fifteen years'

standing, `useit.com`. This is the one and only top site for consistent, repeatedly updated information about Web site usability.

You can find out about Nielsen by reading his publications and attending his conferences, but you can get a great education just by reading his top columns from over the years, helpfully gathered together at `http://www.useit.com/alertbox/`.

Even the design of Nielsen's site, as shown in the figure, is meant to educate you about what's possible in terms of easy-to–use, fast-loading pages. (You can bet the people at Google were up to speed on Nielsen and Alertbox before launching their famously sparse site in the late 1990s.)

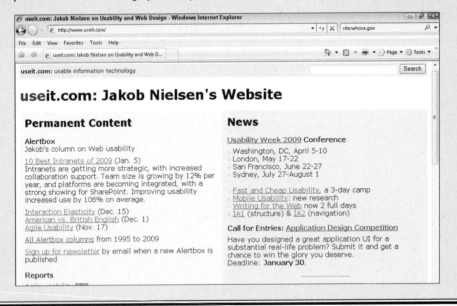

The goal of Silver Strand PC Services is to get a big share of computer repair work in Coronado and then put more time and effort into the SpeedChecker product and perhaps follow-on products.

Our domain name is `www.silverstrandpcs.com`. We include the following pages in our simple site:

+ **Home page:** A brief introduction to the business and a call to action for browsers to contact Silver Strand if they have the kinds of problems the business solves.

+ **Contact us:** All the contact details, including directions to our office in Coronado.

+ **Services:** What Silver Strand does for local businesses.

+ **SpeedChecker:** Product information for the testing product.

Because Silver Strand PC Services is quite small, we leave out detailed people information. Our services and product are new, and we want to know all about any problems, so we won't put explicit service and support information on the site yet. And we don't have many validators — no reviews and so on, just some favorable comments we've solicited from early users. These go on the products page.

Even this type of basic early planning saves you a tremendous amount of time and effort. It's amazing how many people just fire up a tool like Google Sites and start writing text and adding graphics, tacking on pages as the need seems to arise — then wonder why their site is, well, a mess. Spend a little time up front to avoid this kind of problem yourself.

Creating a Site

Now it's time to actually create a site. This is a lot of work, but should also be a lot of fun. Google Sites takes a lot of the pain out of the process and makes it possible for you to follow the old tech company motto: "We only do what only we can do."

We toured Google Sites in Chapter 4. In this chapter, the steps are a bit abbreviated, focusing on the practical decisions you must make as you create your initial site.

Follow these steps to create an initial site:

1. **Go to `sites.google.com` and sign into your Google account.**

The Welcome to Google Sites screen appears.

2. **Click the Create Site button.**

The Welcome to Google Sites screen appears.

3. **Enter the site name, URL, and description. Specify if the site contains mature content.**

   The site name should include your business name, and the description is a welcome message to the site. Change the URL to the one you intend to use as your domain name for the live site.

4. **Choose whether to let everyone view the site (good for getting comments from a broad range of your contacts) or just people you specify. Choose a site theme, enter the verification code shown, and click the Create button.**

   The site appears. For Silver Strand PC Services, the Sunset theme actually works quite well (for now, that is; as we grow, we'll hire a graphics person to help us develop a custom visual identity.)

You can change these items using the Other Stuff tab, in Google Sites. We use this tab in our coverage of Google Analytics in Book VI.

Creating initial pages

Google Sites lets you create pages and then decide whether to put them into the top-level navigation. This is nice, but it's also an easy way to get confused about what goes where. We favor setting up your site structure and navigation before putting in content, so you have a framework to work in.

Having an established framework is also a plus if you have other people working with you on the site. Usually, you want one person to decide things like the site structure, with others restricting themselves to editing content or adding pages in agreed-on areas lower in the structure.

So here's how to use Google Sites to set up the initial navigation for a simple site:

1. **Click Create New Page.**

   The Create new page screen appears, as shown in Figure 6-1.

2. **Enter the Page name — in this case, Contact Us.**

   Google Sites uses this to auto-create the URL for the page. If you want a different URL, click the Change link and edit the page name, as shown in Figure 6-2.

   This is a bit tricky. You have to separate what looks good in the navigation area (the page name) from what looks good in the page URL that Google Sites generates automatically. When in doubt, change the URL to something you're sure is suitable.

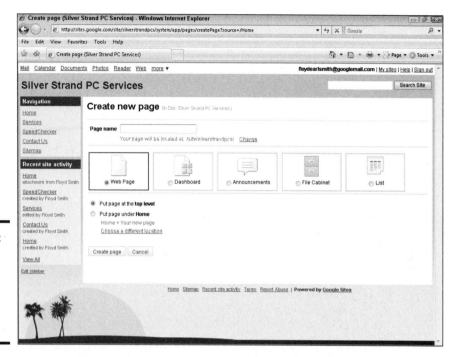

Figure 6-1:
Creating a
new page
gives you
several
linked
options.

Figure 6-2:
You can
edit the
page name
directly.

In the case of Silver Strand PC Services, we want the navigation to read
Contact Us, but this causes Google Sites to generate the URL: /site/silver
strandpcs/contact-us. This looks a little goofy, so we clicked the Change
button and changed the URL to: /site/silverstrandpcs/contact. A small
change, but an important one: It takes into account what users expect as
they navigate the site or if they save the Web page to their hard disks.

Avoid capital letters in URLs. Many Web site servers don't handle them
well, so most Web sites avoid them. Although capital letters work okay
in Google Sites, they look odd to users, who are used to seeing only lowercase letters in most URLs.

Book IV
Chapter 6

Creating a
Google Site

3. **Click the radio button to choose Web Page as the type of page.**

   You have a choice of four page types. Most of them are optimized for creating an intranet. The page types are as follows:

   - *Dashboard* allows you to use Google gadgets, which are fun but not the type of thing you'd use a lot in a typical company Web site

   - *Announcements*, for new information

   - *File cabinet*, for sharing files

   - *Lists*, a kind of project management tool.

   For Silver Strand PC Services, we're not using any of the specialized page types initially. Eventually, we could use them in lower-level pages, in protected areas accessible by partners or customers (called an extranet), or in an intranet for employees. But they're not usually the kind of thing customers expect to see prominently placed on a company Web site.

4. **Click the Put Page at Top Level radio button.**

   You might also want to try the alternative, Put Page under Another Page, and watch the file location, described in Step 2, change to show where the page is in the site hierarchy.

   This is how Google Sites allows you to manage the hierarchy of pages in your site. It's simple and powerful, but gets confusing as the extent and depth of your site grows. For Silver Strand PC Services, we're keeping everything at the top level.

5. **Click Create Page.**

   The new, empty page is created. We're not going to put anything in it yet.

   The new page is *not* automatically added to the site's navigation, as you might have expected. That doesn't happen until you explicitly add it, which we describe how to do in the next section.

6. **Repeat Steps 2 through 5 for your additional top-level pages: Enter the page name; change the URL if you wish; specify the page type; specify the page's level in the hierarchy.**

   For Silver Strand PC Services, we've added the Services and SpeedChecker pages.

7. **Check the site map to see your progress so far. Under the Navigation area, click Sitemap to see the site map. (See Figure 6-3 and Figure 6-4.)**

While in the Site Map, you lose access to many of your controls for editing pages or changing site settings. Simply click Home to return to a page which gives you access to these controls.

The Hierarchy View in the Site Map, as shown in Figure 6-3, displays how the pages relate to each other. This is useful for watching the development of the site.

The List View, as shown in Figure 6-4, displays who did what to each page, and when they did it. This is useful for keeping track when several people are working on a site as a joint project.

Both the Hierarchy View and the List View show pages in alphabetical order, not the order in the navigation (better for the Hierarchy View), nor the order in which pages are created or modified (better for the List View). You can't change the sort order or drag and drop pages into any order you want; it's always alphabetical, which is at least predictable. This makes the built-in Sitemap less attractive as something to keep in the site's final navigation, which you can do if you like.

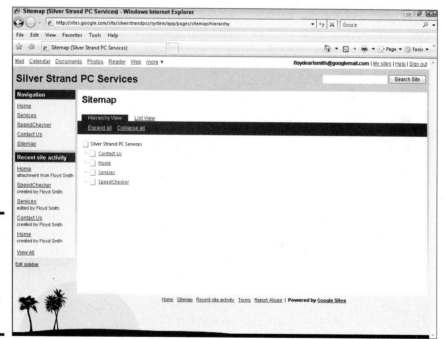

Figure 6-3: The Hierarchy View shows the structure of your site.

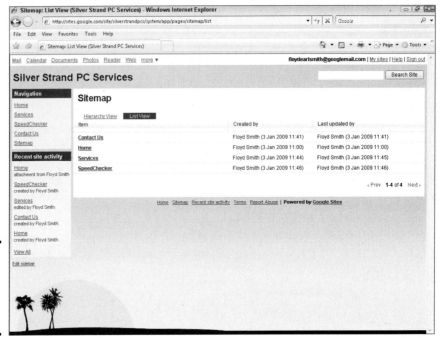

Figure 6-4:
The List
View shows
who did
what, when.

Note that both views shown in Figures 6-3 and 6-4 also show recent activity on the site. This is another useful tool when multiple people are working on a site.

Click the link, Recent Site Activity, at the bottom of the screen to see a comprehensive list of all activity that has occurred on the site, most recent first.

Changing navigation

Google Sites lets you explicitly change site navigation in a way that doesn't necessarily reflect the actual structure of the site. This gives you useful flexibility but can lead to problems, for instance, people editing the site may not be able to figure out how things are really arranged, versus how they show up in the site navigation.

For this reason it's a good idea to have the site navigation match the actual file structure of the site's pages — also, to keep things simple, reducing the chance of problems.

Follow these steps to modify the site's navigation:

1. **Click the link in the lower-left corner of the page, Edit sidebar.**

The Appearance screen appears.

2. **In the Navigation box, click the link *edit*.**

The Configure Navigation dialog box appears.

3. **In the Configure Navigation dialog box, click the link, *Add page to sidebar navigation*.**

The Select Page to Add dialog box appears, as shown in Figure 6-5.

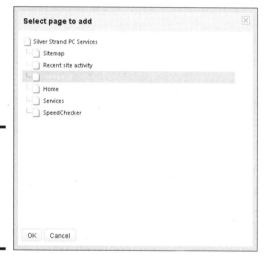

Figure 6-5:
You can
structure
the
navigation
any way
you want.

You can move both of the dialog boxes while the second one is open. Move the dialog boxes so you can see which pages are already in the navigation.

4. **For each of the pages you want to add, click the page to highlight it and then click OK.**

The page is added to the Navigation box.

5. **Repeat Steps 3 and 4 to add all the pages you want to the Navigation box.**

Don't worry about the order of the pages; you'll be changing that next.

6. **To order the navigation items, highlight one and then click the Up or Down arrow to move it. To delete it from navigation, click the X in the dialog box.**

   The link in the Navigation box moves or disappears as appropriate.

7. **Click Save to save your changes.**

   Your changes are saved; you won't go to a new screen.

8. **Click Preview to view your changes.**

   A new window with your changes reflected appears. It's somewhat confusing that this window is fully editable, but the Site Appearance window you had been working in is still open as well.

Changing colors, fonts, themes, and so on

As also described in Book IV, Chapter 4, you can change the site layout, colors, and fonts used in your site, themes, and so on.

Among the items you can change are the contents of the sidebar and its width. You should make the width of the sidebar just wide enough to hold the navigation links in a sensible way — without breaking onto a second line if at all possible.

As for colors and fonts, you can create a coherent design if you're good at it. But part of the purpose of themes is to make these choices for you in a coherent way so you don't need to worry about them.

It's very easy to "uglify" a site with ill-considered choices of colors and fonts. We recommend that you stick with the theme choices while you work on the content and structure of your site. Then, set aside some time — and get the help of a person competent with computer graphics, if needed — to experiment with design choices and get the look you want.

One sensible approach is to have a logo and printed stationery designed for you by a graphics person and then use that design to guide your Web site. This gives your business a coherent look, online and off.

It's easy to waste endless amounts of time and money on your site's look and still not get anywhere. Set modest goals for what you're trying to accomplish and limit the time and money you spend.

Managing collaboration

With Google Sites you can specify exactly who can work on your site — even who can view it.

Although Google Sites can make the process easy, it can be a hassle to manage the various people editing and viewing your site. The easiest choices are the default ones — you own the site and are the only one who can edit it; anyone who has the URL (or finds the site by online search) can visit. If you decide to widen the number of people who can edit your site or limit the number of people who can view it, be prepared for some extra work and hassle.

In order to be included in Google's collaboration management, a person must have a Google account. This is easy, but it's a hassle factor for potential users who don't already have such an account. If they do have an account, be sure to use the e-mail addresses tied to their Google accounts. In these days of multiple e-mail accounts, you may have to ask the people if they have Google accounts and what e-mail address it's tied to.

Here are the different levels allowed for a site on Google Sites:

✦ **Owners:** Owners can do everything; manage who can own, collaborate on, or view the site; change the theme and layout; change the name; delete the site (this is unrecoverable); and do everything collaborators and, of course, viewers can do.

✦ **Collaborators:** Collaborators are more limited in their capabilities, but they can still cause trouble if not careful. Collaborators can create, edit, delete, and move pages, change the sidebar navigation, and add attachments and comments.

✦ **Viewers:** Viewers can only view pages. The main problem with specifying viewers is that there's always one more person who needs to see the site, and that someone may be frustrated by the hassle of having to set up a Google account if she doesn't already have one.

To invite someone to be an owner, collaborator, or viewer, follow these steps:

1. **In Google Sites, click the Sharing tab.**

   The Sharing page appears, as shown in Figure 6-6.

2. **Use the radio button to choose whether to invite people as owners, collaborators, or viewers.**

   Before the "as viewers" permissions settings have any effect, you must first clear the Anyone in the World May View This Site check box. This check box is on the Sharing page.

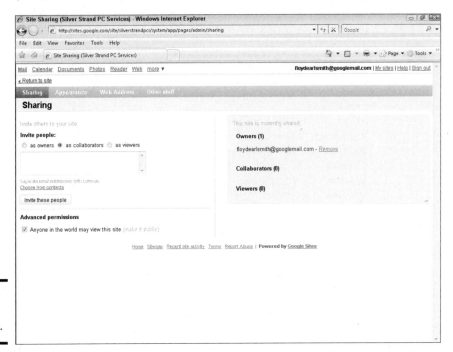

Figure 6-6:
Share and
share alike.

3. **If you use Google Mail and if one or more of your invitees is likely to be on the list, click the link, Choose from contacts.**

   A list of contacts appears. Use the pull-down menu to choose My Contacts, Most Contacted, Friends, Family, Colleagues, Titles, or Suggested Contacts — you can manage these categories in Google Mail. Click names to add them to the list and then click Done to move the selected names into the list on the Sharing page.

4. **Add additional e-mail addresses to the list. When complete, click the Invite These People button.**

   A dialog box appears allowing you to change the subject and enter a message, as shown in Figure 6-7.

5. **Change the subject, if you wish, and enter a message to accompany the invitation. Click the CC Me check box if you want a copy. Click the Send button to send the invitation.**

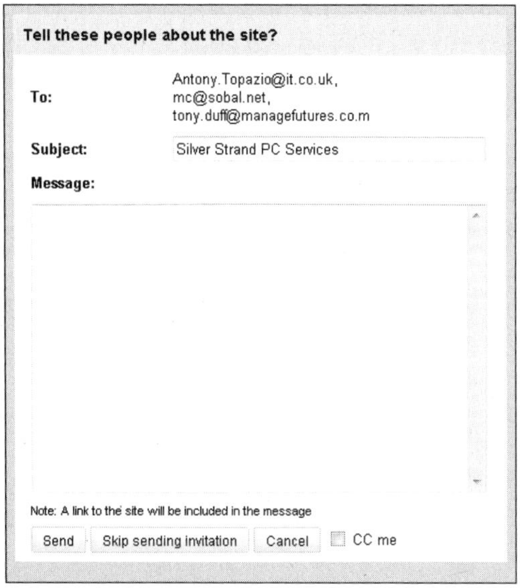

Tell these people about the site?

To:	Antony.Topazio@it.co.uk, mc@sobal.net, tony.duff@managefutures.co.m
Subject:	Silver Strand PC Services
Message:	

Note: A link to the site will be included in the message

Send | Skip sending invitation | Cancel | ☐ CC me

Figure 6-7:
Get your
invites out.

Here's what appears in the e-mail before the custom message you enter:

```
I have invited you to share a Google Site:
Silver Strand PC Services
http://sites.google.com/site/silverstrandpcs/
```

Here's what appears after:

```
Google Sites are websites where people can view, share
    and edit information. To learn more, visit http://
    sites.google.com/
```

Your e-mail should describe the level to which the person is being invited, what permissions you're giving him, and why you're doing it.

6. **Repeat to invite additional owners, collaborators, and viewers.**

Each person receives an e-mail inviting him or her to join the site at the level of capability — owner, collaborator, or viewer — you specify when sending the invitation.

Chapter 7: Editing a Google Site

In This Chapter

✔ Understanding the best ways to present text on your site

✔ Editing pages with the Format menu and with HTML

✔ Using horizontal rules

✔ Linking within your page and outside your page

✔ Dealing with images

*A*fter you've created your Google site and set up the initial structure — pages, navigation, and sharing — it's time to actually put something on the pages. This takes a little getting used to.

Increasingly, Web sites are the public face of a business. Whereas people used to judge you from your reputation, your advertisements, and their initial experience of your customer service, they can now thoroughly investigate you via the Web. If you look solid and professional online, they're more likely to do business with you; if not, they may well call someone else.

Mostly, you learn by experimentation, but it's good to know what is and isn't possible before you start. You need some guidance as you prepare content for the first time. So this chapter takes you through the basics.

Editing Pages — Text Options

Although the Web is getting more and more media-friendly and interactive, text is still the most important element of most Web sites, especially company sites.

Reading onscreen is physically difficult because the screen has lower resolution than a page and is very bright from emitted rather than reflected light. Site visitors often tend to skim text rather than read it closely. Use smaller chunks of text with high readability realizing that users are likely to surf away as soon as possible.

Formatting, used appropriately, helps make text easier to read. The most important single formatting options in HTML, in my opinion, is the list. Lists break up text and make it easier to scan rather than read closely but still give readers the gist of the meaning. Also, when you convert your text into lists, you tend to shorten it, giving a double benefit to your site visitor.

HTML is not a strict formatting language, but is interpreted differently by different browsers. The Cascading Style Sheets (CSS) tool — invented after HTML was well established — allows more control. Still, Google Sites doesn't allow you access to every possible CSS option, and you don't have total control in any event.

Therefore, don't count on strong page layout capabilities in Web pages in general and in Google Sites in particular. Keep your text short and your formatting simple.

It's good to have the text prewritten in a word processor document or even prepare a draft version of the whole site, as described previously. But you may find yourself writing some or all the text in Google Sites.

Note that if you cut and paste text in, your pasted text loses all its formatting. This is good, in a way — no odd formatting codes get pasted to cause trouble — but also bad, in that you may lose a lot of the work that went into making the text look just so. Bullet points, larger fonts, bold, and italics are among the things that disappear.

It's easy to simply reproduce the formatting of the text after pasting it if you have the original in view. It's much harder if you have to read the text carefully and decide all over again how it should be formatted.

When you are cutting and pasting text from existing copy into your Web site, if you have a wide screen (such as with most modern laptops) or a two-monitor setup, have the formatted document onscreen next to the Web version so you can quickly reproduce the formatting. Or, if you have only one small screen, print out the original and use the printout as a guide.

Start by taking a look at Figure 7-1, which shows Google Sites' Editing window (rather subtly indicated by the words "Currently editing" near the top of the screen). The buttons near the top of the page include the most common HTML editing options; you may recognize one or more of them from previous word processing or Web editing work. Read on, however, because there are some subtleties about how formatting works on the Web.

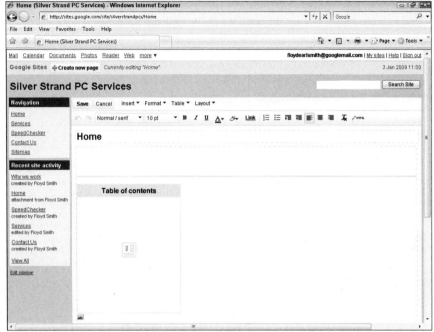

Figure 7-1:
Editing in
HTML is not
all that hard
with Google
Sites.

Google Sites allows all the editing capabilities of HTML, which have more limitations than strengths. The options supported by button controls are as follows:

✦ **Undo and Redo buttons:** Google Sites has excellent, theoretically unlimited undo and redo capabilities. Don't count on them too much, though; it's easy to end up losing work over too many levels of undo and redo.

✦ **Font choice:** Google Sites gives you a choice among Normal/serif (a *serif* font, like the one you're looking at, has little features at the end of letters such as f's and l's, making the letters easier to distinguish), and four *sans serif* fonts: Courier New, Georgia, Trebuchet, and Verdana.

The choice is limited to fonts that are nearly certain to be available on any computer that might display your Web page, or to have a near equivalent.

✦ **Font size:** Google Sites gives you a choice of font sizes from 8pt to 24pt.

However, the font size you choose may not always be respected, for instance on older browsers that don't support CSS or when a font substitution occurs.

**Book IV
Chapter 7**

**Editing a
Google Site**

+ **Bold, italic, and underline:** These standard formatting capabilities mean something a bit different on the Web. **Bold** is quite useful, though best applied sparingly. *Italic* works better in print, where it also makes words stand out, than onscreen, where the lower resolution of the screen means that words in italic are hard to read. Underline is almost a no-no onscreen, as it usually indicates a Web link; using underline simply for emphasis is likely to confuse your Web site visitors.

+ **Text color** and **text background color:** This is a flexible and powerful capability, but you should use it sparingly. Magazines and reports rarely use these capabilities just for emphasis; you should do the same.

+ **Link:** Linking text causes it to be underlined and appear in blue, by default. This is a powerful formatting option because many users skip from link to link in a page, looking for something interesting before deciding whether to read the page more closely or surf on. We cover the mechanics of linking separately later in this chapter.

+ **Numbered list:** Lists, as mentioned earlier, are a very important formatting option in HTML. The numbered list is appropriate only when a list has strict ordering, but you should look for those occasions and use numbered lists as much as possible.

+ **Bulleted list:** Lists, as mentioned above are a very important formatting option in HTML. The numbered list is appropriate when a list does not require strict ordering.

+ **Indent right and left:** Indenting is a clever way to make text stand out, but the usual implementation in HTML leaves a lot of space around the text. Also, in a narrow window, indented text can become very narrow indeed. So use indenting, but sparingly.

+ **Left-justified, centered, and right-justified text:** Like indentation, justification is a good way to make text stand out, but use sparingly to avoid confusion.

+ **Undo formatting:** This option clears all the formatting from text. You can undo this with the Undo button.

Google Sites and HTML

The options available for formatting text in a Google Sites page are the same options HTML supports, which means your Web page can be used on a very wide range of computer systems that access the Web.

Google Sites' main capability for editing text is what is known in the trade as a WYSIWYG editor — a What You See Is What You Get editor, which hides HTML behind an easy-to-use interface.

Google Sites does not allow you to easily or reliably enter HTML directly, which means you have to format your text directly in Google Sites, and you can't directly use Cascading Style Sheets (CSS), the newer and more efficient way of managing Web page display.

You can paste HTML-tagged text into the HTML window, as described in the following section, but it's unlikely to match Google Sites' HTML standards, and therefore causes problems.

Follow these steps, if you're brave, to edit HTML in Google Sites:

1. In Google Sites, click the HTML button.

The Edit HTML window appears, as shown in Figure 7-2.

As you can see in the figure, Google Sites repeats the same HTML tags over and over — each little block of text is surrounded by tags specifying the letter spacing, for instance, even if it's unchanged. These can make your Web pages heavy and slow to download and update if left in, but they makes editing easier. The extra tags are removed when you publish your page.

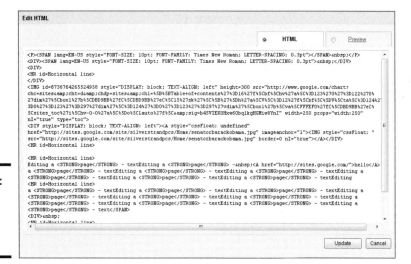

Figure 7-2:
What the HTML is going on here?

2. If you're brave, edit the HTML directly.

There's a Find capability, but no Find and Replace.

You can paste HTML-tagged text in here from another program. Or you can copy the HTML-tagged text generated by Google Sites into a text editor or word processor, edit it, and then paste the edited text.

Be careful to match the HTML tags Google Sites uses; for instance, the <B> (for Bold) tag won't work because Google Sites uses <STRONG> instead.

If you mess up the HTML-tagged text too much, it won't work, and the Undo capability may or may not save you.

3. **Click the Update button to implement your changes, or the Cancel button to return to the WYSIWYG editor without saving your changes. (A safer choice.)**

Editing with the Format Menu

The Format menu, shown in Figure 7-3, includes several options also available on buttons, plus a few that aren't found elsewhere. Here's how to use the unique ones:

✦ **Heading (H2, H3, and H4)**. Use the heading options for top-level (H2), intermediate (H3), and lower-level (H4) headers.

Google Sites supports only three of the six heading levels available in HTML. This should be enough for most purposes — even a full book such as this one doesn't use six levels of headings — but it's sad not to have all the options.

If you're brave and patient, you can go into the HTML, as described in the previous section, and change an H2, H3, or H4 header into an H1 (the true highest level), H5, or H6 header. Just so you can see what you're getting into, Figure 7-4 shows all the header levels.

Figure 7-3:
Format gives you some of the same choices — plus new ones.

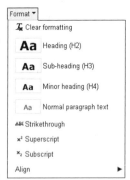

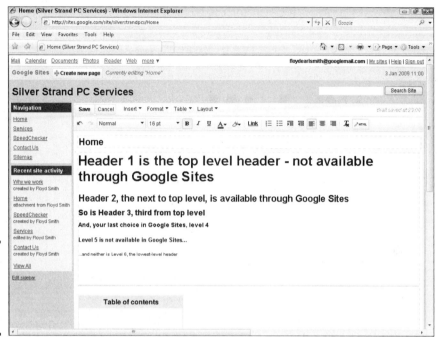

Figure 7-4:
Get your
header
around H1
through H6.

✦ **Normal paragraph text:** Similar to the Clear formatting option, this option takes text that had been a header, for instance, and returns it to normal text.

✦ **Strikethrough:** Another formatting option, like bold, italic, and underline. The most common uses of strikethrough are two. The first use is for editing when working on a document with another person. An editor can recommend deletions by marking the text in strikethrough. The second is to indicate crossed-out material, especially in blogs. The idea is to suggest, that you had second thoughts, often to make a joke by saying what you really think, putting that in strikethrough and then using a more broadly acceptable construction. ("The teachers here at High School High are ~~cruel~~ `strict` attentive to detail.")

✦ **Superscript and subscript:** Additional formatting options that are useful for mathematical expressions and chemical formulas.

✦ **Align:** The Align options are left, center and right — all useful for making your Web page look the way you want. There is no fully justified option, but full justification doesn't work very well on the lower resolution of a Web page (compared to a printed page) anyway.

**Book IV
Chapter 7**

**Editing a
Google Site**

Where to go for more guidance

Although we have included some key high-lights, this book is not a Web design guide. You can find several good books about this. We like *Web Design For Dummies, 2nd Edition* by Lisa Lopuck (Wiley, 2006). There is also an over-whelming amount of information online, much of it contradictory.

The figure shows what we think is a good refer-ence: Web guidelines for the state of Virginia's

employee education system, which you can find at the following Web address:

```
http://www.section508.va.gov/
    docs/Style_Gd_EES.pdf
```

A lot of Web guidelines are out there, but we like ones like Virginia's, which reflect patient and consistent work over a period of time. They are constructed for practical rather than commercial purposes and are kept up to date, as well.

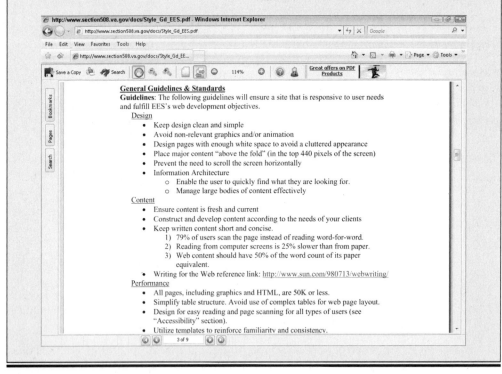

Inserting a Horizontal Rule

Of the many design elements you can use to format your Web page, horizon-tal lines — called *horizontal rules* — are the best and easiest to use. Why?

There are a few reasons. First, horizontal rules are built into HTML. A single, brief command — <HR> — in your HTML code causes a nice, gray horizontal line to appear in your Web page.

This horizontal line automatically gets wider or less wide as the user resizes the Web page. Because it is interactive, it acts as a gray separator line would within a printed page — while staying up to date with the dynamic environment of a Web page.

A number of HTML characters are required to include a graphic. When the graphic is downloaded to the user's browser, however, it won't resize to fit ever-changing browser window widths. Horizontal rules are superior to graphics in that they resize automatically and don't take up much space in your HTML code.

In the early days of the Web, horizontal rules were sometimes overused. Then Web designers became so afraid of overusing them that they stopped using them completely. So if you use one now, it won't make your page look like all the other pages out there.

By default — that is, if you don't specify otherwise — horizontal rules are centered, 1-pixel tall, and extend the entire width of the Web page. You can align horizontal rules to the left or right, make the line more solid, and set its height or width. Here are a few examples:

✦ <HR ALIGN=LEFT>: A left-aligned horizontal rule

✦ <HR NOSHADE>: A solid line with no shading; in some browsers, thick horizontal rules appear shaded unless you use the NOSHADE option

✦ <HR SIZE=5>: A 5-pixel-thick line

✦ <HR WIDTH=50>: A 50-pixel-wide line

✦ <HR WIDTH=80%>: A line running 80% of the window width

The main part of an HTML tag, such as HR, is called, well, the *tag* — whereas modifiers, such as ALIGN or SIZE, are called *attributes*. You can combine attributes in any way that makes sense.

The rule within HTML is that a browser ignores anything it doesn't recognize. So if you create a tag and attribute combination such as, say, <HR HEIGHT=5>, your Web page shows a horizontal rule, but with the normal 1-pixel size. This can drive you nuts. When you quickly scan your code, you see the attribute where you expected it. What you don't realize is that the browser is ignoring the incorrect attribute, HEIGHT. To correct, you must replace it with the attribute SIZE. Google Sites shields you from most of this, but as soon as you start editing HTML directly, you're plunged into it.

Inserting a horizontal rule in your Web page is simplicity itself; you can then add attributes to make it special, which is trickier:

1. **In Google Sites, click Insert⇨Horizontal line.**

A horizontal line appears in your Web page, as shown in Figure 7-5.

Horizontal Line

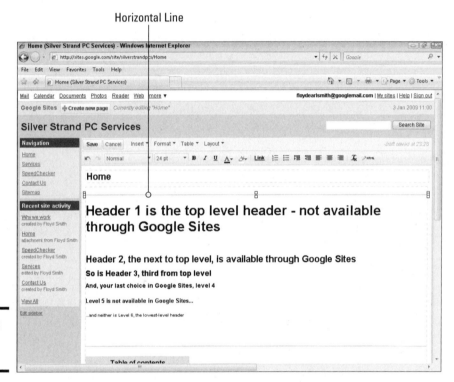

Figure 7-5:
Horizontal
rules rule!

You might find the internal menus in Google Sites a bit touchy. Click and hold to keep the menu open. (This is different from Windows. In Windows, you can click the menu and release, and the menu stays open until you click elsewhere.)

2. **To change the attributes for your horizontal rule, save the page — this may clean up the HTML. Then click the HTML button.**

The HTML for your Web page appears in a separate window.

3. **Choose Edit⇨Find from the browser window controls.**

The Find dialog box appears.

4. **Find the `<HR>` tag within the HTML code.**

   The HTML for your Web page appears in a separate window.

5. **Add attributes as needed.**

   See the text preceding these instructions for examples.

6. **Click the Preview tab to view the results.**

   This allows you to make further changes if you don't like what you see, or to cancel the changes made in the HTML editing window if you've really messed up.

7. **When finished, click Update in the bottom of the window to accept the changes, or Cancel to reject them.**

   You are returned to the editing window.

For more about using HTML, the book *HTML, XHTML, and CSS For Dummies, 6th Edition* by Ed Tittel and Jeff Noble (Wiley, 2008) is a good resource. There are also many online resources; just look up a tag like `<HR>` in a good search engine (like, say, Google) to learn more.

In most of these resources, "good old" HTML tends to be pushed aside in favor of more modern CSS code. But there's still a lot of life left in traditional HTML; don't be afraid to use it for quick fixes like horizontal lines.

Create a routine way of using horizontal rules within your pages. For instance, consider using a horizontal rule at the bottom of your page's content, with a copyright notice below. Such repeated use of simple elements is reassuring and creates a feeling of familiarity for your users. (It is similar to the way you can recognize a page from your favorite newspaper or magazine even before you see the name.)

You can "brand" your site more strongly if you make the line a bit distinctive. For instance, you can make the line a bit thicker, or always use a standard width, or left- or right-align it in a way that looks sensible. These little tricks can help postpone the day that you have to call in a graphic designer to improve the look of your site!

1 Think, Therefore 1 Link

Hypertext links, to give them their full name, are the secret of the Web. Links are what give "Web surfing" its name, making it instinctively easy to move from one page to another.

Links are an excellent example of making a computer capability — in this case, a Web page — easy to use. But sometimes, you have to work hard to make that happen. (The comparison that's often made is that users should feel that they are walking on water, even if you have to work very hard underwater to keep them from falling in.)

Google Sites makes linking easy, but makes it harder to use one important linking capability: links within a page. We briefly describe how to do this, but you may find that, despite your best efforts, the code for the internal link are removed when you edit or save your site.

Here are the main types of links:

✦ **Links to another Web site:** These are the most exotic kinds of links because they can reach easily to sites right around the world, yet these are the easiest to create. As a Web page author using Google Sites, you just select the text that serves as your end of the link, plug in the URL for the Web page at the other end, and away you go.

✦ **Links to another page in the same site:** These links are very much needed to make your site useful, both for formal navigation and when the content on one page refers to another. They also help with search ratings, as each page contributes slightly to the rank of the ones it links to.

   These links are often tricky to construct because it can be hard to specify exactly where the page to link to is on your machine — in a way that survives the transition when your site is transferred to a Web host. But Google Sites handles all this for you. It's also made easier by the fact that your site is being initially created on its Web host.

✦ **Links to a location within a page:** This is the type that Google Sites makes difficult. Links to another Web site or another page in your site go to the top of the page by default. But to link to a spot within a Web page, you have to construct a destination anchor with a name to link to and then create a link that goes to that named spot.

Follow these steps to create a link in Google Sites:

1. **While editing a page in Google Sites, highlight some text that you want to make into a hyperlink.**

   Make sure the text is appropriate for a link. Some people really like links in special phrases — such as "for directions to the library, click here"; others like to work them in more naturally, as in "you can drive, take the bus, or walk to the library".

2. Click the Link button.

The Create Link dialog box appears, as shown in Figure 7-6.

What you do next depends on whether you want to link to a page within your site or a page outside your site.

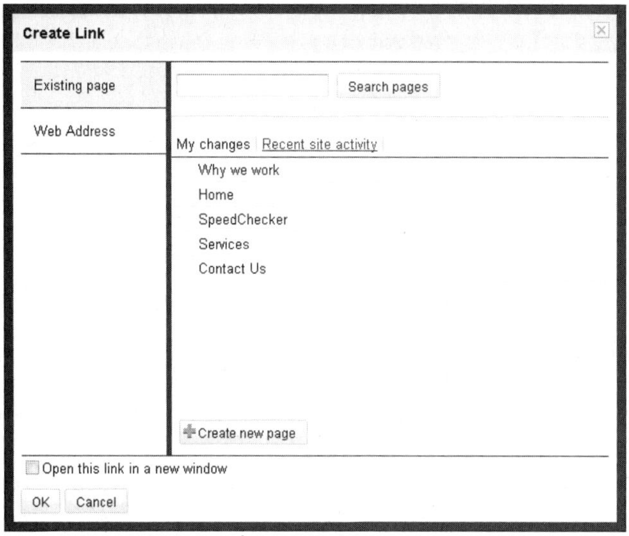

Create Link ⊠

Existing page	[_____] Search pages
Web Address	

My changes Recent site activity

Why we work
Home
SpeedChecker
Services
Contact Us

✚ Create new page

☐ Open this link in a new window

OK Cancel

Figure 7-6:
Link it to me, baby.

3a. To link to a page within your site, click the Existing Page button in the Create Link dialog box. Click the page you want to link to. If you want the link to open in a new window — rare for an internal link — click the check box, Open this link in a new window. Then click OK. Skip Step 3b and go to Step 4.

TIP

The link is created.

You can also choose the option, Create New Page, to create a new page and link to that. For more about this option, see Chapter 2 in this book.

3b. To link to a page on the World Wide Web, first find the URL of the page you want to link to by surfing to that page in a separate Web browser window. Then click the Web Address button in the Create Link dialog box, as shown in Figure 7-7. Enter (or, to avoid mistakes, copy and paste) the Web address. If you want the link to open in a new window — common enough for an external link — click the check box, Open This Link in a New Window. Then click OK.

**Book IV
Chapter 7**

Editing a
Google Site

The link is created.

It's common for links to change, but some links — such as links to news stories or blog entries on certain sites — are just about guaranteed to change. Look for a permanent link, often called a *permalink,* to your destination, and check the links on your site regularly to be sure they work. (It's very easy for a site to have *broken links,* as they're called. These are very frustrating for users.)

4. **Check the link. In the editing window, click the link. A small box appears with the link destination and the options Change and Remove. Confirm that the destination is the one you want; if not, click Change to modify the link or Remove to eliminate it. Click X to cause the small box to disappear.**

   If the text you've linked to is incorrect, you can change the text or move it elsewhere; the link will persist.

5. **Test the link. Click the link to make the small box with the link destination appear. Then, click the link to bring up the destination in a new window, as shown in Figure 7-8. (The destination appears in a new window because you're in editing mode, even if you didn't check the Open This Link in a New Window check box, in Step 3a or Step 3b.)**

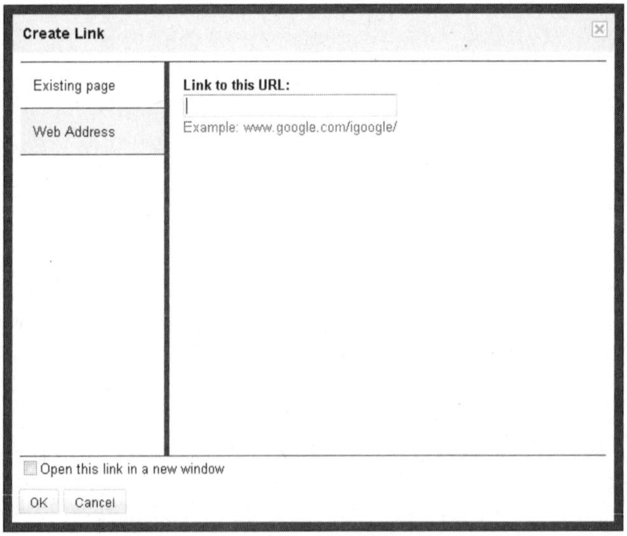

Create Link ☒

Existing page	**Link to this URL:**
Web Address	Example: www.google.com/igoogle/

☐ Open this link in a new window

OK   Cancel

Figure 7-7:
Link to the
world.

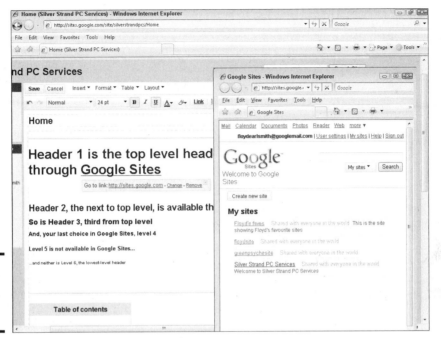

Figure 7-8:
Test that
your links
are strong.

Linking within a Page

One of the great advantages of Web pages over print pages is that you can scroll up and down on Web pages. As a Web author, you can have the psychological advantage of putting a bunch of related content in a single page without strict limits as to how much content you add. You can "stretch" the page with confidence that, if your content is necessary — or at least interesting enough — users are likely to scroll down to get to more of it.

But with long pages, you may need to provide links to specific spots within a page. You may even want to design pages that use internal links to help the user navigate up and down within the page.

Internal links are a helpful tool for making the most of a long Web page. An example is a long Frequently Asked Questions, or FAQ, page. Such pages often have all the questions in a short list at the top and internal links to the answers within the page. Each answer finishes with a link back to the list at the top.

Such pages are very helpful to anxious users who want to quickly find answers to their questions. They can use the question list for navigation, scroll the page themselves, or even use the Find capability in their browser windows to search the page for a specific word or phrase.

Consider establishing an FAQ page on your own site. It's a great way to handle seemingly random topics and to generate traffic within your site, which helps build search engine rankings. Then, if the FAQ gets popular among your site visitors, you can split it among multiple pages, which generates even more traffic to help build your search engine rankings.

You can see an example of a good FAQ page on the US Government's copyright site at `www.copyright.gov/help/faq/`, as shown in Figure 7-9.

That's great, you may say, but how do you actually do it?

Here's where things get interesting. Tools (like Google Sites' Web page creation tool) always break down at some point. You reach a point where there's something you can't do with the tool and you're suddenly thrown into the full complexity of the system that the tool is trying to help you with.

This is the case with internal links and Google Sites. The tool doesn't include a direct way to work with internal links. You have to put them in yourself, either by a workaround within the tool or by entering the HTML directly.

Not only does Google Sites somewhat abandon you when it comes to creating internal links; it can actively undermine your efforts. If you enter HTML directly and it's not formatted in exactly the way Google Sites wants to see it, Google Sites may simply remove your code, leaving you with work to redo and unanswered questions about just what you did wrong. So be careful!

There are two ways to create internal links within Google Sites: by "tricking" the tool into generating them for you and by inserting them directly in HTML. Here's how to generate internal links within Google Sites' Web page authoring tool:

We find the internal menus in Google Sites to be a bit "tetchy." as the Brits put it — a bit tricky to use. For instance, when using the Insert function, it's very easy to accidentally choose the Horizontal Rule option, even if what you want is something else in the list. Be ready to use Undo to remove an unwanted horizontal rule or other option, and practice until you get good at selecting what you really want.

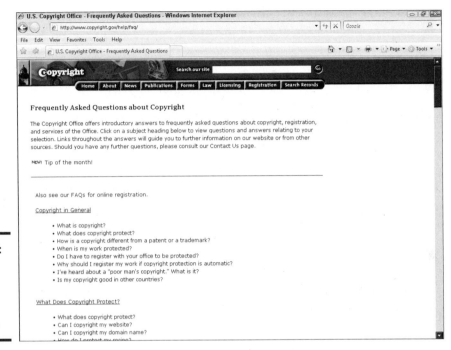

Figure 7-9:
Just the
FAQs,
ma'am,
about
copyright.

Follow these steps to have Google Sites create link destinations for you:

1. **While editing a page in Google Sites, break up the text by including several headers.**

   Using headers to break up your text is a good idea even if you don't use internal links.

2. **Insert a Table of Contents: Within Google Sites' page editing capability, choose Insert⇨Table of Contents.**

   The Insert table of contents dialog box appears, as shown in Figure 7-10.

3. **Enter the width to use, in pixels.**

Figure 7-10:
Make
your users
content with
contents.

Insert Table of contents

Tables of contents are created from text headers on the page. For a basic page index use a narrow width (250 px with wrapping text) and for a FAQ-style index try 100% width.

Width: 250 px (leave empty for 100% width)

Save Cancel

**Book IV
Chapter 7**

Editing a
Google Site

Google Sites recommends 250 pixels width for a basic Table of Contents, and 100% width for an FAQ-style list that's integrated with the rest of the Web page.

Leave the box empty to get 100% width.

You can't enter a percentage width — only a width in pixels — except by leaving the box blank, which gives you 100% width.

4. Click Save to create the Table of Contents.

The Table of Contents appears in your Web page.

5. You can get links to the destinations — which are headers — by right-clicking on each entry in the Table of Contents and then using the link destination as the destination of a new link. The destination appears in a pop-up window in this form:

```
https://sites.google.com/a/google.com/SITENAME/
Home#TOC-PAGENAME
```

6. Record the link destinations, either by using them in a new way within your site or by saving them in a separate document.

After you record the destinations, you can delete the Table of Contents if you wish.

You can't delete the headers that you use as the destinations for your links or the destination tags, as described in the next set of steps, also disappear.

You may want to create destinations and links to them without headers or without a Table of Contents. Or, you may want to get started with the preceding approach and then lose the headers that serve as link destinations. Follow these steps to create link destinations directly:

1. While editing a page in Google Sites, save it.

This often causes Google Sites to clean up the HTML somewhat.

2. Click the HTML button.

The page's HTML appears in a window.

3. At the appropriate point in the HTML, insert the anchor in the following form (where `text to be linked` is the text that forms the destination of the link):

```
<A NAME="anchorname">text to be linked</A>
```

4. You can now create a link to the new anchor in the following form:

```
https://sites.google.com/a/google.com/SITENAME/
pagename#anchorname
```

The psychology of Web page size

Research shows that users really like it when all the content of a Web page fits entirely on the screen when the user first arrives at the page. The area that appears first is called the area *above the fold* and gets extra attention, because users are reluctant to scroll downward. (Advertisers and sponsors often pay extra for placement above the fold.)

Of course, the fold is an elastic concept, as its exact location depends on the users' monitor resolution and the size they've set the browser windows to. However, the fold is usually considered to be within the first 600 pixels or so of the page, measured vertically in a relatively narrow browser window. (To get more content above the fold, many sites are now going to a very wide minimum browser window size, even though this excludes some users with small monitors from being able to use the site easily.)

You can certainly break through the fold and create long Web pages — see Wikipedia at www.wikipedia.org for an example of a site that does this consistently and well. (Sites with long columns of junk down the left-hand navigation bar and little in the content column are examples of sites that do this inconsistently and poorly.)

Both these methods are tricky. Consider setting up test pages and trying them several times to work out any problems before using them in real pages that you've put work into. Build up pages by creating the links first, then adding content, and finally testing as you go. (HTML is not a full programming language, but the techniques you use to make it work the way you want it to are often the same ones used in computer programming.)

Inserting Images

There were a lot of Internet applications before the Web. Text-only e-mail, ARCHIE, VERONICA (seriously), and Gopher were among early Internet applications. Images gradually got used more and more, but as file attachments that took extra work to view.

The real key to the success of the Web is the capability to insert images alongside text in a natural-looking way. This allows Web pages to be dressed up much like magazine pages. (Not with the same pinpoint control, mind you, at least not until recently — and not within Google Sites.)

There are two different uses for images in Web pages, as there are on magazine pages:

**Book IV
Chapter 7**

Editing a
Google Site

✦ **For formatting and page design:** Little images, lines, and colored areas combine with consistent navigation and layout to create a common look and feel for every page in a site. The BATCS business card on every page of the site, shown in earlier chapters, is an example of this kind of use of images.

A big part of the reason for Google Sites' themes is to provide a ready-made look for your site, so you don't have to worry about most of these aspects in the early days of your site. We won't spend much time on this here. You can tackle the topic yourself after your site is well established, get expert help, or use a combination.

✦ **To communicate actual information:** This is the "picture is worth a thousand words" bit. For example, a picture of a Hollywood star catches the attention of readers far more than any words could. And graphics can convey a great deal of information.

Figure 7-11 shows an iconic use of images. (Yes, we know *icon* means *image*, smarty) — to compare the settings used in taking two different photographs. The words above each photo describing the photo settings are, rather cleverly, made part of each image — so there's no layout hassle with getting these words, which serve as captions, to line up with the photos. However, this also makes it impossible, for instance, to select the words as text and copy them to an e-mail message because the words are really part of their respective images. This is just one of many text-image trade-offs you may find yourself making in Web pages.

Figure 7-12 shows another use of images, more typical to a business Web site. The author of the blog has her photo on the site. Appropriate, given the topic.

Photos add life to a site. More specifically, photos of managers and workers in a business give a feeling of trust, comfort, and familiarity — a bit like actually meeting a person. When you're asking someone to trust you, this kind of bridge-building can go a long way. Many business Web sites that are otherwise quite buttoned-down in their overall look include photos of important people in the business for just this reason.

These two brief examples should give you a feel for good ways to use pictures in your site. In the next section, we describe how to get images ready for use on your site — a very important topic.

Image size on disk and in display

You must understand the basics of images to avoid two complementary problems: really ugly images on your site; and good-looking images on your site that are very large in terms of disk space, so they take a long time to download for people with slower Web connections. (This describes most Americans, whose broadband connections tend to be slower than those in other parts of the world.)

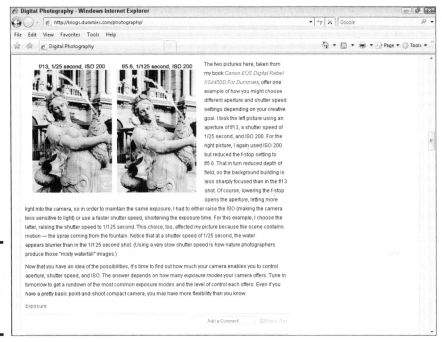

Figure 7-11:
Sometimes
only images
get the job
done.

Figure 7-12:
Principal
photography
for a
Dummies
blog.

When you access a Web page, several files are actually copied from a Web server to temporary storage on your own computer. The first file is the Web page text and layout information — the HTML file that we call a Web page. This is usually only about 2KB in size.

Other text files can also be requested and sent. JavaScript programs can be stored in one or more separate text files, as can Cascading Style Sheet (CSS) files.

The images that are shown in a Web page are also kept in separate files from the HTML file, and can come from the same server as the HTML file or any-where on the Web. Graphics files are anywhere from 1KB or less up to many megabytes. So what we call a Web page can include many different files and be many megabytes in size.

(You can sometimes see this process in action as the text for a Web page appears, then shifts alarmingly as graphics files arrive and are displayed. A tightly designed Web page includes pre-defined space for the graphics files, preventing this visible shifting.)

The back and forth required to get files covered by a type of US Government security called P3P, which requires at least one additional file transfer, is shown in Figure 7-13. However, this figure combines several requests and responses into each arrow; the back and forth for even a seemingly simple Web page can actually require a dozen or more file transfers for each page, totaling anywhere from a few kilobytes (KB) to many megabytes.

The trick is that it's particularly easy to put a good-looking photograph on your site and downsize it in your Web page to fit in a particular spot — without realizing that the photo that gets downloaded is still many mega-bytes in file size and, therefore, in download size, despite the fact that the displayed image is quite small.

Here's an example using an official US Government photo of then-Senator Barack Obama standing in front of the US Capitol, shown in Figure 7-14. The photo is actually very high resolution, and, therefore, very large in display size onscreen and in disk space (2MB) — but the Internet Explorer browser automatically downsizes the image displayed to fit in the window.

The photo is over 2MB in size (and many pictures you get from, say, a digi-tal camera are much larger) — but, by looking at the version displayed in Internet Explorer, you wouldn't realize that.

You can also make part of the photo display in, say, a 70-pixel–wide by 100-pixel–tall window in a Web page. It would still be a 2MB photo — but only provide about one-fiftieth of the visually displayed area of your Web page.

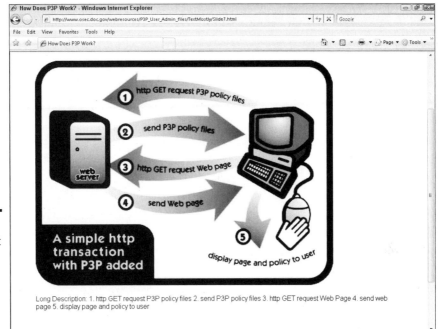

Figure 7-13:
There's a lot of to- and fro-ing for each Web page you see.

Figure 7-14:
Obama gets right-sized auto-matically.

So to use the image in your Web page, you have to actually downsize the image — which means using a graphics program to reduce the size at which it displays. This is different than compressing the image, which makes the image take up less space on disk (and, therefore, in download time) without changing the displayed image size.

Typically, to use an image in a Web page properly, you have to downsize it *and* compress it. You should downsize it to the exact image size you need for your Web page — which may also involve selecting only part of the image to get the proportions right — and only then compress it so you get the smallest file size you can while sacrificing as little as possible of the visual quality.

Table 7-1 shows the image size and download time for several different sizes of the Obama image over a dial-up connection.

Table 7-1	Downloading time for uncompressed images	
File size:	*Uncompressed (approximate)*	*Download time (56Kbps)*
Full-size image (4800 pixels wide x 6000 high)	28,800,000 bytes (28MB)	70 minutes
Quarter-size image (1200 x 1500)	7MB	18 minutes
Sixteenth-size image (300 x 375)	1.8MB	5 minutes
Web-size image (100 x 125)	600KB	2 minutes

Why consider dial-up connection speeds when most people have broadband? First of all, you want to consider the experience of users with slow connections. Just as important, even broadband speeds experience various slowdowns that can lead broadband users to have connection times nearly as slow as dial-up users.

Also, why consider uncompressed images when just about all photos used on the Web are JPEG-compressed? Because JPEG compression has various settings, from light to heavy, that give you more compression at the expense of image quality. Even light JPEG compression entails some costs to image quality. You need to consider the full-size file before deciding just how strongly to compress the image.

Always resize and clip an image to the size you need it in your Web page before compressing it. If it's already JPEG-compressed, resize it before considering whether to compress it further.

Never stretch an image or shrink it disproportionately when resizing it; this makes the image look very odd. Only shrink the image, and then only in its original proportions. If you need different proportions, clip the image — select part of it, leaving the rest behind.

GIF, JPEG, and PNG images

People who create Web pages for a living spend a lot of time learning about the different types of images available and when to use each. We give a short introduction to these topics here to help you avoid mistakes that can cause you to waste a great deal of time.

To begin with, you need to understand something about how colors work. When you look at a solid green wall, for instance, you tend to think there's one color there — and in a way, you're right, in that only one color of paint was used on the wall. But the truth is, you actually see many different shades of green as influenced by reflected light, shadows, and so on. For each original color in an object or scene, hundreds or thousands of variations of that color appear, depending on patterns of reflected light or shadow.

A person's face is a good example. Our skin tones are slightly uneven, but the patterns of light and shadow falling on a person's face, with its many shapes and curves, generate thousands or millions of different shades. To recognize the face, you need to be able to see most of the subtly different shades. Even a little bit of compromise looks strange indeed, as the human visual system and brain are very alert to anything that seems odd in the appearance of a face.

When you create an image in a computer graphics program, it's likely to be made up of just a few colors, with no variations due to reflections or shadows. Such images — any image with fewer than 256 colors — can be handled in a simple, highly compressed file formatted called Graphics Interchange Format, or GIF (pronounced to rhyme with "gift"). So you should compress images in GIF format whenever possible.

However, some carefully created computer-generated images, as well as most color photos of real-world scenes, use many thousands of colors. These images look terrible when compressed in GIF format; the loss of subtle shadings makes them look blocky and odd, even unrecognizable. Faces are particularly vulnerable to GIF compression.

For these images, you need to create JPEG images (pronounced "jay-peg") — that is, images compressed using the Joint Photographic Experts Group (JPEG) standard. This standard is a brilliant creation that takes advantage of the strengths and weaknesses of the human visual system to compress an image greatly, by reducing the number of colors in the image, while leaving it highly recognizable.

**Book IV
Chapter 7**

Editing a
Google Site

For images larger than about 100 x 100 pixels, you can usually decide from looking at the original image whether GIF or JPEG is more suitable. For images smaller than 100 x 100, you need to try both and see which is better.

So far we have GIF for most images and JPEG for photos. Figure 7-15 shows the Obama image with both JPEG and GIF compression — at the larger size, GIF has bad effects, but at smaller sizes the difference is nearly invisible, in grayscale (as shown here) or in color.

Figure 7-15: Obama looks odd in a large GIF image.

But some images with many colors don't work well with either JPEG or GIF. A good example is a screenshot of a computer desktop showing windows with text in them.

GIF compression of such images tends to be clumsy and leave the image visibly odd-looking. JPEG compression tends to blur text and other fine features and surround them with fuzzy or blobby areas.

For these images, a third option called *PNG* compression (for Portable Network Graphics) is best. There are a small number of Web browsers out there that don't display PNG images, which is pretty awful for users of those browsers, but not as bad as having all your users see an image that looks bad with either GIF or JPEG compression.

Resizing images

Many people get help from a graphics expert for relatively simple image tasks. Many others try fixing the image themselves — but risk making mistakes.

Here we show you how to resize and then how to compress an image using a free program available on all Windows PCs, Microsoft Paint.

Follow these steps to downsize an image:

1. **Start Microsoft Paint; choose Start➪Programs➪Accessories➪Paint.**

   Microsoft Paint appears.

2. **Make a copy of the image. Choose File➪Save as, and rename the file. Save the copy in the same file format but with the new name.**

   This helps keep you from regretting any mistakes you make while resizing the image.

3. **Choose File➪Open to open an image; select an image using the Open dialog box.**

   The image opens in Microsoft Paint.

4. **Resize the image: choose Image➪Resize/Skew; the Resize and Skew dialog box appears, as shown in Figure 7-16. Enter a percentage in the Horizontal and Vertical dialog boxes and click OK.**

   For the example, we've used a high-resolution image of Secretary of State Hillary Rodham Clinton — her old Senate photo. This gives you a feel for downsizing, clipping, and compressing large images such as you might get from a commonly available high-resolution digital camera.

   We usually downsize an image 50% or 25% at a time, still keeping it much larger than needed, before deciding just how to clip it by selecting part of the image.

   Always enter the same percentage in the Horizontal and Vertical boxes, or the image looks quite odd. And don't use the Skew options unless you want the image to look truly strange.

5. **Clip the image: Pick out the part of the image you need and copy it. Open a new window by choosing File➪New.**

   For the Web, a relatively large image of a person is 100 pixels wide, 100 to 150 pixels tall. Such an image should contain just the person's face, neck, and a few inches below the neckline of a shirt — both shoulders should be cropped out, not just one or the other. If you include all of both shoulders, the head will look too small.

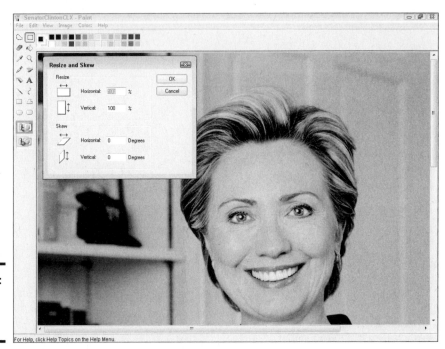

Figure 7-16:
Paint can
do a lot for
you.

A small image of a person is typically 70 or even 50 pixels wide and a few pixels longer than wide. Such an image should include just the person's head and the top of her neck.

6. **Now downsize the image the rest of the way. Choose Image⇨Resize/ Skew and use the percentage that gets you the proportions you need. (This might require a bit of time with a calculator.)**

To identify the current display size of an image, move the mouse pointer to the lower-right corner. The current location of the mouse pointer — and therefore the current display size of an image — appears in the lower-right corner of the window, as shown in Figure 7-17.

7. **Save the image.**

Always save the image after you downsize it and before you compress it. Otherwise you risk losing all your downsizing work if you make a mistake in compression.

You may want to check that the image, in its current size, fits in your Web page before proceeding further.

Figure 7-17:
You can see
the current
image size
(299 pixels
wide, 374
pixels tall) in
the lower-
right.

Compressing images

After you've resized an image to make its disk size smaller along with its image size, it's time to compress the image. This make its disk size smaller without making the image size smaller.

So, where does the savings come from? GIF makes files smaller by noticing runs of several pixels in a row of the same color. It stores a code for the color and the number of pixels in a row with that color. If the image is mostly made up of blocks of the same color, this saves a lot of space. But GIF never loses any data, unless the number of colors in the file is more than the 256 that GIF can handle. That usually happens only with photos, which have many hundreds or thousands of subtle shades of color.

JPEG is more clever. It looks at a block of pixels and assigns a code to it that reproduces a pattern similar to the block, but that can be stored in a small amount of space. In creating a similar pattern, the JPEG algorithm uses facts such as the human eye's inability to distinguish between very many shades of blue. JPEG almost always loses data, but it can easily compress many photographs by 80% to 90% with hardly any visible change; the visible changes tend to come about when you are trying to squeeze the file more than 90%.

**Book IV
Chapter 7**

**Editing a
Google Site**

In compressing images, it's worth remembering that even a 50KB file — quite large by JPEG standards — takes only about 10 seconds to download on a dial-up connection. So as you squeeze the file down below 25KB, you're only saving a second here and there, risking a possibly significant loss in image quality.

Table 7-2 shows the download time for various file sizes usually associated with compressed images. Note that, below 32KB — which is where most JPEG files end up — shaving a few KB off the file size barely affects download times.

Table 7-2	Download times for image files
File size	*Download time (56Kbps)*
1MB	2 minutes 30 seconds
512KB	1 minute 15 seconds
256KB	37 seconds
128KB	18 seconds
64KB	9 seconds
32KB	5 seconds*
16KB	3 seconds*
8KB	2 seconds*
4KB	2 seconds*

* For small files, handshaking — communications overhead between your PC and the host computer — slightly increases transfer times

In the steps that follow, we use Paint, which automatically highly compresses files, to do compression. But in other programs you might use, you have a choice of how strongly to compress the file. Don't wreck the visual quality of the image just for the sake of a few kilobytes.

1. **Start Microsoft Paint; choose Start⇨Programs⇨Accessories⇨Paint.**

   Microsoft Paint appears.

2. **Make a copy of the image. Choose File⇨Save as, and rename the file. Save the copy in the same file format but with the new name.**

   This helps keep you from regretting any mistakes you make while compressing the image.

3. **Choose File⇨Open to open an image; select an image using the Open dialog box.**

   The image opens in Microsoft Paint.

4. Choose File⇨Save as to save the image.

The Save As dialog box appears.

5. From the pull-down menu, Save As Type, choose a file type from among the types used for compression: JPEG, GIF, or PNG. Click Save.

The file is saved with the extension .jpg, .gif, or .png, respectively. For JPEG, Paint automatically selects a fairly strong degree of compression.

6. If you wish to compare the appearance and file size of several versions of the file, repeat Steps 3 through 5 for one or both of the other two file types.

The file is saved with the appropriate extension from among .jpg, .gif, or .png.

7. Open the files and compare their appearance and file size. For your Web page, choose the one that offers the best tradeoff for your purposes between appearance and file size.

Inserting an image in Google Sites

After you've selected your image, resized it, and compressed it, actually putting it in your Google Sites Web page is not hard at all. Just follow these steps (see the next section to use an image hosted on the Web):

1. In the Google Sites editing area, choose Insert⇨Image.

The Add an Image dialog box appears.

2. Choose the radio button Uploaded images, not the button Web address (URL). (To use an image hosted on the Web, see the next section.) Then click the Browse button.

The Choose File dialog appears, as shown (together with the Add an Image dialog box) in Figure 7-18.

Book IV
Chapter 7

Editing a Google Site

Figure 7-18: Upload to Google Sites.

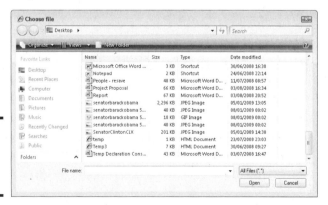

3. **To narrow the files you can view to image files — GIFs, JPEGs, and PNG files — use the pull-down menu to choose Pictures. Then navigate to the file you want and select it. Click Open to upload it.**

   The file is uploaded to Google Sites' servers.

4. **To add the image to your Web page, click Add Image.**

   The image appears on your Web page.

Using a Web-based image in Google Sites

If you want to use an image that already exists on the Web in your site, Google makes it easy — but warns you against doing it in most circumstances. (For our warning, see the sidebar, Using an image from the Web.)

But if this is what you want to do, here's how to do it:

1. **In the Google Sites editing area, choose Insert⇨Image.**

   The Add an Image dialog box appears.

2. **Choose a radio button — Uploaded images or Web address (URL).**

   Uploaded images are copied to Google's servers and downloaded each time your page is visited. Images from a Web address are downloaded into your Web page from their home on someone else's Web server each time your page is visited. (See the sidebar, Using an image from the Web, for details.)

3. **For Uploaded images, click the Browse button. For a Web address, skip to Step 6.**

   The Choose File dialog appears, as shown (together with the Add an Image dialog box) in Figure 7-19.

4. **To narrow the files you can view to image files — GIFs, JPEGs, and PNG files — use the pull-down menu to choose Pictures. Then navigate to the file you want and select it. Click Open to upload it.**

   The file is uploaded to Google Sites' servers.

5. **To add the image to your Web page, click Add Image.**

   The image appears on your Web page.

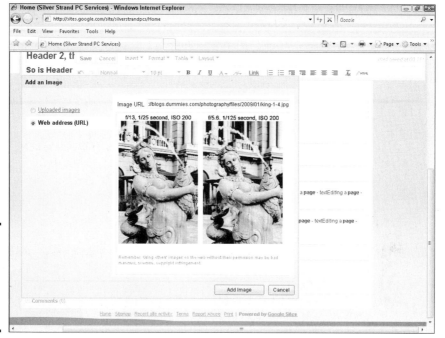

Figure 7-19:
Upload to
Google
Sites, or
borrow
bandwidth?

Using an image from the Web

You can, theoretically, use an image from the Web in your own Web page. You simply provide the URL of the image you want when inserting the image. Google Sites creates the HTML code to retrieve this "foreign" image every time your page appears. Your site has a cool additional graphical element — and the image is downloaded from someone else's Web server!

That's the problem. When you do this, you have not gotten permission — either for the copyrights on the image nor for "borrowing" someone else's bandwidth for use by your users.

So this is one of those capabilities that's technically possible but not necessarily a good idea. Think carefully before you include a "foreign" image in your own Web site. The exception is sites like Flickr, which advertise themselves as hosts for your images, or images on Web sites you control.

Book V
Google Tools for Your Site

"It's web-based, on-demand, and customizable. Still, I think I'm going to miss our old sales incentive methods."

Contents at a Glance

Chapter 1: Adding Google Documents to Your Web Site

In This Chapter

✔ Inserting Google documents

✔ Using Google Calendar on your site

✔ Using Google Presentations on your site

✔ Using Google Spreadsheets on your site

✔ Embedding Google spreadsheet forms on your site

*O*ne of the key advantages of Google documents — really *Google Docs documents*, but let's use the shorter version — is that you can host them on your Web site.

Google Documents are described in Book I, Chapter 4, and at length in the book, *Google Apps For Dummies* by Ryan Teeter and Karl Barksdale (Wiley, 2008). They have many advantages, a few of which are highlighted in the following chapter.

To open diverse types of documents, the user often has to have the same software as was used to create the document — in a recent-enough version. The user also has to be careful to save and send the document in the right version for others to use it — and someone has to manage all this, avoiding "versionitis" problems.

These problems have been exacerbated in the last few years with the arrival of Windows Vista. Corporations have tended to stay with Windows XP and Office 2003; consumers have received Windows Vista and, where they've purchased Office, Office 2007 on their new PCs. So "versionitis" problems have multiplied, with the so-called amateurs — consumers — ahead of the pros working in large organizations.

With a Google document, the live document actually "lives" on the Web site. People can review and edit it, using permissions set by the owner. The software is hosted online and free to all — no worries about incompatibilities, changes, and versions of the document, or the software getting out of sync.

This chapter introduces Google Docs, one application at a time, and shows how to incorporate these applications in a Google Sites Web site. This helps you make full use of all Google's business solutions.

This chapter, though, covers only Office-type applications — Calendar, the (word processing-type) Document, Presentation, Spreadsheet, and Google's innovative Spreadsheet forms. These are all designed for shared, interactive use. Picasa Web slideshows and videos, multimedia content that often tends to be controlled by a single author, are covered in the next chapter.

Using Google Documents on Your Site

It's easy to misunderstand the purpose of Google documents on your site and create, frankly, a mess that confuses people and puts them off. But if you do it right, you can use Google documents to create a powerful, capable site that helps you run your business better.

One of the key advantages of the Web is its simplicity. You should compromise that simplicity only in order to offer powerful advantages to people who are already interested, to a greater or lesser degree, in what you have to offer.

Even with the simplest Web site, there's a problem with getting people's time and attention. If you ask the casual Web site visitors to work hard to get at information or to enter information, they're far more likely to leave than to do what you ask.

Table 1-1 shows guidelines for what you can ask of your Web site visitors, depending on their relationship to you and their needs.

Table 1-1	Using Google Documents with Web Site Visitors	
Visitor type	*Need*	*Recommended approach*
Web surfer	Getting information or shopping	Plain Web pages, animations, videos, downloadable documents
New customer	Buying on an occasional basis	Web pages with forms — only request "must-have" information
New or existing customer	Becoming a member or subscriber	All the preceding plus optional use of contributions to online document such as a spreadsheet
Regular customer	Make it easier to work with you	Regular contributions to online documents; make benefit clear, offer other options such as phone calls

Visitor type	Need	Recommended approach
Selling partner or supplier (extranet)	Build up relationship with you	Regular contributions to online documents, less need to offer other options
Employee (intranet)	Handling employment matters	Regular reference to and contributions to online documents, little need to offer other options
Employee (intranet)	Getting work done	Refer to, update, and create online documents
Investors	Increase or manage their investment	Plain Web pages, animations, videos, downloadable documents

The trick is to make things very easy and to only ask much effort from people who already have a strong investment in their relationship with you. With customers, everything must be for their benefit, and you always have to give them additional options that fit the way they want to work. You're *asking*, not *demanding*.

You also have to adjust to customers' habits and expectations. If none of your competitors is asking customers to, for example, open a Google Docs spreadsheet and enter information into it, you shouldn't either. The only exception is for a very clear benefit such as managing regular purchases or a standing order; even in these cases, you need to offer the option of calling or sending an e-mail with the required information (which one of your employees will, assumedly, enter into the Google document).

With customers, you always have to make things very easy, realizing that many things that seem reasonable to you might seem like an unwarranted hassle to them. Anything that might require additional time, work, or complexity has to be offered, rather than demanded, and additional options have to be included.

The For Dummies site at www.dummies.com offers a good example of this. The For Dummies people wanted to make it richer and easier to use — taking the For Dummies concept further within the Web site. They people wanted to do all they could to make the changes to the site easier for people.

Many people developing a new system might assume there are two choices: either make the new system very, very easy; or make it relatively easy, but offer additional support and documentation to smooth over the rough spots.

The state of the art when dealing with customers, however, is to do both — to make the new system very, very easy *and* to offer additional support or documentation.

You still need databases

More and more of the core capabilities of companies are being captured in and driven by databases. Web sites of various types end up being database interfaces, driving the knowledge management that is increasingly at the core of companies.

An example of this is shown in Figure 1-1. This Highlights site has a database call as its URL. It's not as user-friendly as it could be, but it's certainly functional for database interactions.

Google Docs does not eliminate the need to have database support for more and more of what you do in a company. Instead, Google Docs gives people more and better ways to work together — which often results in data that's entered into those very databases. In many cases, the Google Docs approach ends up being a forerunner of what later becomes a database-driven application.

Figure 1-1 shows a typical store page on the For Dummies Web site. It's low-key and functional — kind of like the Dummies titles themselves.

Figure 1-1:
The For Dummies site.

It's worth looking at the bottom of the page separately because this area is below the fold (that is, not included on the initial screenful of information) on many screens, especially on ever-more-popular laptops. Figure 1-2 shows that, at the bottom, the store page includes a link, Explore the New Dummies.com. (Also, note how a partner has been integrated into the site.)

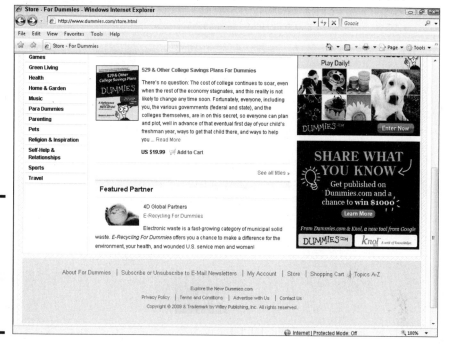

Figure 1-2:
The For
Dummies
site shows
partners
and new
feature
support.

Figure 1-3 shows the destination of this link, a "how to" for the changes on the site. It includes a video section — a capability included in Google Docs. The "how to" accomplishes several internal and external purposes:

✦ It makes the site developers clarify what they're doing in terms of how it benefits the user.

✦ It gives users, including end users, business partners, the press, and anyone else, a chance to see and comment on the changes before they're introduced.

✦ It trains users in how to get the most out of the new capabilities.

Figure 1-3:
Highlights of
the new For
Dummies
site include
video.

The balance is different when you're the customer. Depending on how important you are to your suppliers, you can put them through all sorts of rigmarole to earn your business. (Big companies and government departments, for example, make suppliers register, fill out large numbers of forms, and so on.) You don't want to take this to extremes, but it's not too much to ask to have suppliers, for instance, add to a spreadsheet as a way of letting you know about orders.

Business partner relationships depend on the nature of the relationship. If you're providing the Web site support, you're probably the lead partner, and can ask others to do things your way. Or the partnership can agree to work together to create a special-purpose Web site to support shared work — kind of an intranet/extranet hybrid.

Employee support is tricky, and there's a continuum of approaches depending on just what the employee is using the site for. For routine employment matters such as holiday requests, travel arrangements, and expenses reimbursement, you can ask the employee to use online forms and documents. Because employees use these capabilities over and over, it's worth it for everyone involved to take the time to learn to use them initially.

It's in doing real work, though, that the capabilities of Google Docs really shine. Employees often work in teams including people around the world, with different skill sets, in different companies and other types of organizations.

Getting the best of both worlds

Transitions are always difficult because people have to keep up their skills in the old way of doing things and at the same time learn the new one. For many companies, this means keeping up Windows and Office skills — on Windows XP and Office 2003, Windows Vista and Office 2007, or various combinations — while embracing the brave new world of Google Docs and Google sites.

In order to make this a positive for people, you need to make clear the benefits of the new approach. Explain to people why you're offering the new approach and what the benefits to them are. Even where the benefits are, in the first instance, mostly to you, find the benefit for your customer, supplier, or employee. ("Using this new approach significantly reduces our costs, which enables us to offer a better service.

" Or, "faster turnaround on requests," or whatever other benefit is applicable.)

Fortunately, people's skills in the Windows and Office environments are highly transferable to the Google Docs world. Although there are fewer features in some areas, the enhanced collaboration and Web-friendliness of Google Docs is evident to everyone. And fewer features can sometimes mean getting work done faster and more easily. This will be more of a positive as Google adds any crucial missing pieces that are still required for people to get their work done, most of the time. Traditional Office applications can be used as specialized tools for external audiences or highly demanding internal ones — the use of Office word processing applications in your publications department, for instance, or the use of spreadsheets in finance.

Having shared documents that people can contribute to all around the clock is really the only way to work — and this capability just isn't as available in other solutions as it is in Google Docs.

Hosting shared documents on a Web site that's easily updated by designated people is also the only way to go, and Google Sites majors in this. It has less room for the finer points of graphic design, but a lot more built-in capability to support shared work.

So here's how to deploy Google documents on various kinds of Web sites:

+ **Customer-facing Web sites:** Use Google documents on the "leaves" of the site, not in the core. Have them play an optional or supporting role. The exception is video, which is easy to use and highly attractive to some users. (And, as we describe later on, highly unattractive to others.)

+ **Partner or supplier Web sites (extranets):** Use Google documents as needed, but keep it simple — don't make people learn much to get things done.

+ **Employee Web sites (intranets):** For employment support, use Google documents with a light touch, not requiring much learning. For real work, take full advantage of all the capabilities of Google documents and Google sites.

Google Documents — Word Processing in Your Web Site

A few specifics make Google Documents particularly suitable for use as a Web site.

First, be reassured that the core features you're used to in a word processor are all there, but some of the more advanced features are not. For example:

+ **Formatting:** Fonts, bullet points, and simple tables are there; page headers and footers are lacking, but table of contents generation and footnotes have recently been added.

+ **Document checks:** Find and replace, auto-saving, spell checking, and word count are all available, including readability assessments.

+ **Interoperability:** You can easily bring in and export Word, OpenOffice, RTF, PDF, and HTML documents — although you can expect occasional lost formatting or missing features with any kind of document interchange.

But of course, what really sets Google Documents apart is the way it handles sharing. As with Google Sites, you can specify collaborators and viewers. A revisions tab lets you find changes and see who made them and when.

This isn't really for the most demanding work — like, say, writing (or at least finishing) a book, or designing an advertisement for print. There are some slight delays when working online, and all those "little" features that are left out are just the ones needed for sophisticated documents or getting the look just right.

But at the same time, traditional word processors aren't really suitable for use in collaboration. For collaboration, you need people to work and share freely. You don't want people walking all over your precise line spacing settings, so better to keep those out of the shared document.

Inserting a Google document

For most Google documents you want to insert in your Google Sites Web site, the process is basically the same. Here are the options you have:

+ **Calendar:** A shared calendar showing who's where when.

+ **Document:** A word processing document.

+ **Picasa Web slideshow:** For either a series of images or a simple presentation.

+ **Presentation:** For more fully-featured presentations.

+ **Spreadsheet:** For financial or other numeric information.

✦ **Spreadsheet form:** An easy to use workaround to traditional database-driven forms.

✦ **Video:** More like traditional multimedia than the others. This is a way to easily get YouTube or Google Video clips on your site.

In the example that follows, we use a document because it's the most likely piece to share, especially as you're learning.

The semantics — the exact mouse clicks to manage, say, a menu — in Google Sites and Google Docs are a bit different than those used in desktop applications such as Microsoft Office. Consider offering informal training sessions in using Google online applications, especially because many people will need to work in both worlds for a good long while to come.

Follow these steps to insert a Google document in your Google Sites Web page:

1. **Create or open a Web page in your Google site.**

   The Web page appears, along with menus for modifying it.

2. **Click the Insert menu and look at the options under Google.**

   The options appears, as shown in Figure 1-4: Calendar, Document, Picasa Web slideshow, Presentation, Spreadsheet, Spreadsheet Form, and Video, with two suboptions: Google Video and YouTube.

   Unlike in a typical Microsoft application, if you move the mouse carefully, the menu remains "pinned" open even while you move the mouse cursor to another window. This is a popular approach in Unix-based applications, from which Google Docs in part descends.

3. **Choose the option you need from the menu.**

   The Insert dialog appears, as shown in Figure 1-5. For this example, we've chosen Document, so Document is selected first. However, you can, in effect, change your mind at this point and choose Presentations, Spreadsheets, (spreadsheet) Forms, or Folders in which any of the preceding might be located.

   After you make a choice, a list of documents available in your account appears.

   The Recently selected option produces a shortlist of documents you've recently used.

4. **Find the Google document you need.**

   Finding the Google document you need is more than a notion. You are presented with documents available in your Google account. You can Search among the documents or paste in a Web address — which implies that you might open a separate Web browser window, search for the document you need, and thus generate a Web address to paste into the Insert dialog box.

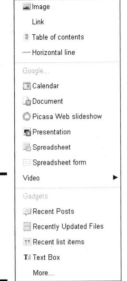

Figure 1-4:
You have
lots of
Google
Docs
options.

Figure 1-5:
Inserting
your Google
document,
dialog 1.

Insert...

All items		
Documents		
Presentations		
Spreadsheets		
Forms		
Folders		
Recently selected		

Search

Marketing Assistant Manager	9/23/08
SCB - Business Development Support- Marketing	9/23/08
Note on using Google Docs instead of ...	7/10/08
Copy of Note on using Google Docs instead of ...	7/10/08
02_ANTHEM_30_Oct_07	6/10/08
Floyd Enfield demo addendum	6/4/08
Gabe,	4/7/08
Sales calls 1	4/7/08
Sales calls 2	4/7/08
Sales calls 1	4/7/08
LSVT notes	4/7/08
Why Obama Matters CLP	4/7/08
Spanish and UK printers	4/7/08

Or paste a web address here:

Select   Cancel

5. **Select the document by highlighting it and clicking Select — or, if the document appears in a list or as a search result (but not as a Web address), by double-clicking on the document name.**

Using Google Documents on Your Site **419**

Book V
Chapter 1

Adding Google
Documents to Your
Web Site

The Insert Google Document dialog appears, as shown in Figure 1-6. This dialog is for formatting the appearance of your document in your Google Sites Web page.

6. **First make the appropriate choices using the check boxes — whether to have a border; whether to include the title; and the height and width of the area in which the document will appear.**

   In most cases you want to include both a border and the title, to make it clear that this is an embedded document. However, if the document is not intended to be edited apart from the Web page in which it's embedded, you may leave these options out.

7. **Next, make the appropriate choices using the Height and Width fields — the size of the window in which the document will appear. If you leave the Width area empty, the document takes up 100% of the available Web page width.**

   When in doubt — that is, not constrained by a design standard for the Web page, and if the document is not particularly narrow — consider setting the Height to a moderate value such as 300 or 400 pixels. Take advantage of the option of leaving the Width field empty to have the document use 100% of the available Web page width. This not only gives a good experience across a wide range of users' screen sizes, it also gives users both the feeling and the reality of control, which they value as they try to juggle precious screen real estate.

   The document appears within a Web site with navigation, header and footer, so the overall Web page will be much larger than the height and width you enter here. Don't overdo it.

8. **Click Save to finish inserting the document.**

   A graphic representing the document appears in the Web page, as shown in Figure 1-7. If you click the graphic, a dialog with options for the embedded document also appears.

Figure 1-6:
Inserting
your Google
document,
dialog 2.

Insert Google document ☒

🗋Sales calls 1   Change

Display:

☑ Include border around Google Document

☑ Include title: Sales calls 1

Height: 600   px

Width: px (leave empty for 100% width)

Save   Cancel

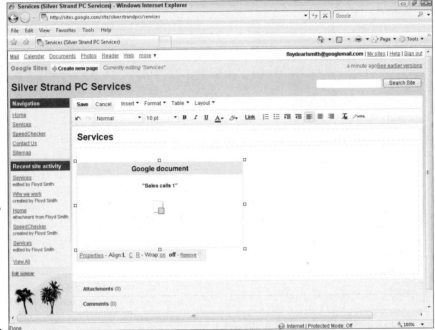

Figure 1-7:
An ugly
placeholder
shows
where your
document
will go.

9. **Change the options as needed: Click Properties to revise the options in the Google document Properties dialog box, which are the ones described in Steps 6 and 7; click L (the default), C, or R to align the contents left, center, or right; and turn Wrap on or off (Off being the default). Click Remove to remove the inserted document.**

Different choices may be appropriate for different documents, but for most documents consider leaving the contents left-aligned, but changing the Wrap setting to On. This allows more display flexibility for the contents, which works well unless the document is highly formatted.

10. **Click Save to save the document and see the live content, as shown in Figure 1-8.**

The preceding paragraphs give you a lot to think about; but you'll find, as with most other software programs, that most of the steps and choices become routine, with only a few demanding real focus each time you embed a document.

The choices for embedding documents have implications for your Web page designs. However intranets — where you are most likely to embed a lot of documents — are sometimes less tightly designed than customer-facing Web pages. Expect to learn as you go along.

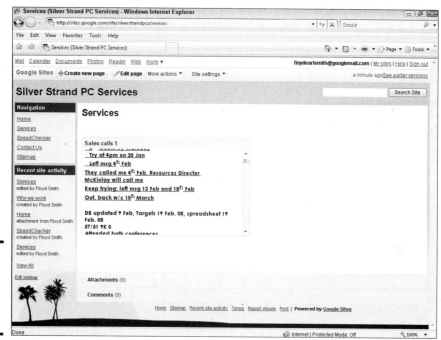

Figure 1-8:
Saving
brings the
live content
to life.

Understanding screen size issues

As the Web becomes ever more useful, it also splinters in many directions. One axis of differentiation, discussed briefly here, is the target audience — the world as a whole (the customer-facing World Wide Web), a strictly internal audience (intranets), or a limited audience of stakeholders in your organization (extranets).

Another axis of differentiation is the type of device your page is viewed on, with three main targets of interest:

✦ **Desktop setups with big screens or multiple screens:** Whether a given computer is a desktop or laptop, it can be part of a desktop setup with a big screen — perhaps a large, high-resolution screen on a laptop or attached to a desktop, sometimes in combination with additional screens. This is often the setup used by those creating Web pages because it is great during the design process. But it tends to make designers forget the more limited environments in which users may be working.

✦ **Laptops or other medium-screen environments:** For a Web page with embedded documents, the old mainstream standard design target of an 800 x 600 screen may be unrealistically small. Depending on your target audience, you may want to count on the common laptop resolution of 1280 by 800 or more. (Note that this is quite wide and quite short, in contrast to many corporate documents, which tend to be narrow and long.)

✦ **Blackberrys, iPhones, and other mobile devices:** Corporate employees are increasingly dependent on mobile devices and increasingly demanding access to corporate databases. A typical Blackberry screen is 320 x 240 pixels, and other mobile device screens may be even smaller.

You can see the problem here. A Web site designed on a system with multiple large screens is unlikely to work well — perhaps not at all — on a Blackberry. Though Google Sites and Google Docs are designed for flexibility, you have to think quite carefully about how your work will be used, and be cautious about what you commit to. I was recently involved in a project in which the corporate executive sponsoring the project made Blackberry access the key "must" for Day One of a new tool — and almost broke the project, which became impossible to achieve in a reasonable timeframe. (So therefore the project ended up being completed in an unreasonable timeframe.) Set easy initial targets; then add additional features.

Collaborating with Google Calendar

One of the most obvious applications for collaboration is a calendar. In fact, individual calendars are pretty useless; trying to keep them in sync or to keep track of someone else's calendar is cumbersome to the point of being just about impossible. Shared, computer-based calendars are the way to go, and an easy sell in any work or group environment.

The business world is largely divided among people who use Microsoft Outlook and Lotus Notes. These two huge software empires each have their own, incompatible ways to manage lists of users, which is the basis for calendar management, e-mail communications, and more. Getting these to work properly as separate "islands" and also to talk to one another are tasks that generate many employment opportunities in technology.

So Google's accomplishment in making a highly interactive collaborative application (such as an online calendar) work at all is nothing to be sneezed at. And integrating it into Google Sites, where it can be hosted online and shared among numerous people, is impressive indeed.

Best of all is making the basic version free. Although you get more features with the Premier Edition or Education Edition, the ad-supported Standard Edition has more than enough to get you started.

A view of Google Calendar is shown in Figure 1-9. It's almost as graphically sophisticated as Outlook's calendar and doesn't have the old-fashioned look of the calendar in Lotus Notes.

Figure 1-9:
Google
Calendar
— high
powered,
low priced.

Getting people on your Calendar

Having cited its numerous advantages, there's still a big issue with Google Calendar: getting people to use it. Most of your potential users have spent a good deal of time with Microsoft Outlook or Lotus Notes calendar functions and are fairly attached to them.

The main selling points are collaboration and price. It's quite difficult, using either Outlook or Notes, to schedule meetings with people outside your organization or with people who use a different tool. Yet that's the norm these days. As the world gets more ~~overcomplicated~~ interesting, this kind of interoperability is indispensable.

After collaboration, the other benefit is price. The cost of running the servers and employing the people to support Outlook or Notes far exceeds the low price of Google Apps Premier Edition — $50 per user at this writing — let alone the free price of the ad-supported Standard Edition. (The price for Education Edition varies.) If you make clear to your employees the benefits of this lower price for your organization — and therefore, in the big picture, for them — along with the collaboration benefits, they're likely to put up with the annoyances that any such change is bound to bring.

Key points of Google Calendar

As you decide when and how to use Google Calendar with your Web site, it's worth keeping in mind some of its key points — and using these points to sell it to your colleagues:

✦ **Keyed to e-mail addresses:** The simplest way to bring the interoperability of Google Calendar to life is to point out how it's keyed to simple e-mail addresses, not to complicated user definitions. You don't have to know where someone lives (from an Outlook or Lotus Domino server point of view) to include them; you just need his or her e-mail address.

✦ **Integrated with Gmail:** You can use a Gmail message to set up an event, as shown in Figure 1-10. So Gmail users get integration within two of their key tools.

Figure 1-10: Gmail taps into Calendar.

✦ **Going mobile:** Google is doing an impressive job of making many of its capabilities work with smart phones; one of the authors (Smith) almost prefers using Gmail on his Blackberry to using it on a PC. Google Calendar also works well on mobiles. Google keeps optimizing its applications for all the different screen sizes out there, making it easy to use for all kinds of people. And you can schedule events by text message.

✦ **Tiered sharing options:** You can customize how much information about your calendar you share with the world at large, with people in your same Internet domain (the domain in `budsmith@dummies.com` is `dummies.com`), or with specific people. This allows you to share very little — yet designate one or a few people to have full access to view and even change your calendar. You can also freeze out everyone you don't specifically name (both in the world at large and in your own domain). You can hide anything except whether you're free or busy; or you can let people see what it is you're busy doing.

✦ **Outlook Exchange-ability:** (That's a minor pun on Microsoft Exchange, the data management service that supports Microsoft Outlook; sorry.) It's easy to get information from Microsoft Outlook into Google Calendar — and sort of easy to get it back. This is great for working with all kinds of people. (Lotus Notes interoperability is provided by some free, third-party utilities at this writing.)

✦ **Extra capabilities for Google Apps:** When using Google Calendar in Google Apps, you can coordinate other people's schedules — finding their free times before inviting them to a meeting, for instance. And if you use Premier Edition or Education Edition, you can schedule resources such as rooms. These editions have a Room Finder, an impressive capability for a low-cost system.

Google Calendar in your Web site

The real joy of Google Calendar, though, comes when you use it in your Web site, as we're describing here, or in your blog. That's because it makes it easy to share calendars with a large group with more ease and greater interactivity than ever before.

The "beauty" part, as Canadian slang would put it, is that this works, not just in Google Sites but for any Web site. This is not a disadvantage if you're a Google Sites user — it means that you and others can deploy Google Calendars in lots of places, which means more people get more experience using them. Having more Google Calendars out there makes each new one more powerful because of the format's increasing popularity.

Usually, you create a new calendar for your Web site to show the events relevant to the purpose of the site. However, if you already have a calendar for, say, a team of people whom you're creating a site for, you can use that calendar.

If you don't already have a Google calendar to put in your Web site, you need to create one. Here's how to do it:

1. **From within Google Sites, right-click the Calendar link at the top left of the Web page and choose Open in New Window from the context-sensitive menu that appears. Or, open a new Web browser window and enter `calendar.google.com` in the address area. Sign in if you need to.**

   The Sign up for Google Calendar Web page appears, as shown in Figure 1-11.

Figure 1-11: Get in the zone with Google Calendar.

Why a separate window? Tabs are great, but this is one time you may want to use a separate window because it allows you to go back and forth between the calendar and Google Sites.

2. **Enter your name, location, and time zone. (If your time zone is not available in the pull-down menu, click the Display All Timezones check box and then select your time zone.) Click Continue.**

   If you choose Display All Timezones, a list of hundreds of locations appears. Choose the right one.

   Click Continue and a calendar appears.

3. **Experiment with the calendar.**

To add an event covering a whole day, click just under that day's date; to add a time-specific event, click at the appropriate spot in the calendar grid. You can choose settings for your Calendar, export it, combine it with other calendars, and more. Your calendar can show the weather and you can integrate it with your mobile phone. (It takes a couple of steps back and forth with your phone, but we don't remember this option in Lotus Notes or Microsoft Outlook!)

The overall Settings for the calendar are shown in Figure 1-12. For more details on these options, see *Google Apps For Dummies* by Ryan Teeter and Karl Barksdale (Wiley, 2008).

Don't forget two of the most powerful features of Google Calendar: its search functionality. This becomes invaluable as you accumulate months and years of information. You have the capability to access the full calendar from anywhere, not only via cell phone but also from any PC with Web access.

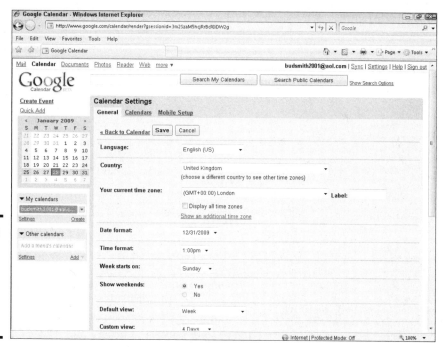

Figure 1-12:
All the settings you might expect are in Google Calendar.

4. **Exit the calendar by signing out of your account — click the Sign out link.**

Your calendar is created.

Some options — including the important option to get its address (see the next set of steps) — aren't made available until you exit and return to the calendar. Logging out makes these options available.

Take some time to experiment with Google Calendar so you can think through how to use it, not only for yourself but in a Web sites context. You'll see some things that match or even exceed the competition:

✦ Customizable views of the number of days and weeks you want to view.

✦ Agendas that list upcoming events by day.

✦ The ability to create multiple calendars for, say, work and time off, and then flexibly combine and separate them.

✦ The option to subscribe to public calendars for work events, holidays, and so on.

✦ The option to add events flexibly — if you enter "Lunch at Gino's with the boss, January 10, 12:30," there's a good chance Google will put the right data in the date, time, and location fields.

✦ Easy ways to invite others.

✦ Extensive reminder options, including pop-up messages onscreen, e-mail messages, and text messages to your phone.

✦ Great sharing options — sharing with Google Calendar users, embedding on your Web page, and of course embedding in a Web page.

After you have a calendar, follow these steps to put it in your Web site:

1. **Create or open a Web page in your Google site.**

The Web page appears, along with menus for modifying it.

2. Click the Insert menu and look at the options under Google.

The options appear: Calendar, Document, Picasa Web Slideshow, Presentation, Spreadsheet, Spreadsheet Form, and Video.

3. **Choose Calendar from the menu.**

The Insert Google Calendar dialog appears, as shown in Figure 1-13.

To use an existing Google calendar, open the calendar. Choose Calendar settings⟳calendars⟳(click link to specific calendar)⟳calendar address@->HTML; the address appears. Copy the address and paste it in the text entry field. For a new calendar, leave this field blank.

The Google Calendar also offers HTML code for use with non-Google Sites Web sites.

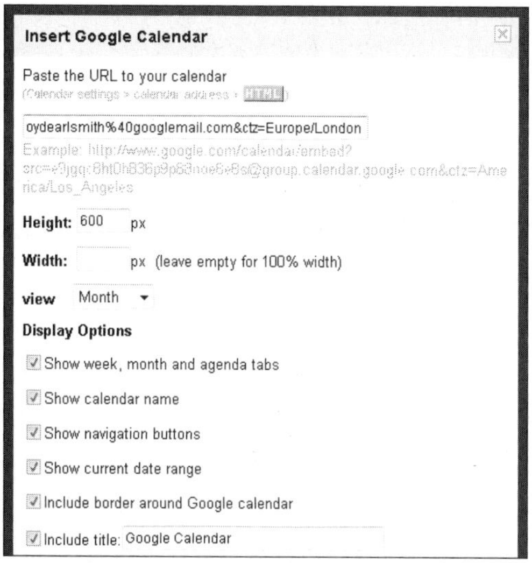

Insert Google Calendar   ☒

Paste the URL to your calendar
(Calendar settings > calendar access > [HTML])

oydearlsmith%40googlemail.com&ctz=Europe/London

Example: http://www.google.com/calendar/embed?
src=e9jgqc6ht0h836p9p63ncc6i-8s@group.calendar.google.com&ctz=Ame
rica/Los_Angeles

Height: 600   px

Width: px   (leave empty for 100% width)

view   Month   ▼

Display Options

☑ Show week, month and agenda tabs

☑ Show calendar name

☑ Show navigation buttons

☑ Show current date range

☑ Include border around Google calendar

☑ Include title: Google Calendar

Figure 1-13:
Get control
of your
calendar.

5. **Enter values for the Height and Width of your calendar as these fields appear in the Web page.**

   As noted earlier in the section, "Inserting a Google Document," if you leave the Width area empty, the document takes 100% of the available Web page width. Also see that section for tips on sizing.

6. **Choose whether to show the week, month, and agenda tabs.**

   In most cases you want to show all these tabs, both for the capability they offer and for consistency with other Google and non-Google calendars which typically have these options, or similar options, available.

7. **Choose whether to show the calendar name.**

   Because you can add a custom title (see the following steps) that you can customize to match the location in which this calendar appears, it may be better not to show the name that the calendar has when you import it.

8. **Choose whether to show navigation buttons.**

   This may seem like an automatic yes, but you may not want to do it if, for instance, you only want to show the current month.

9. **Choose whether to include a border.**

   Try this both ways, but it might be good to leave it out if you can; screen space is at a premium anyway, and calendars are pretty distinctive without a border.

10. **Include title.**

You may have a header or other surrounding content that makes the calendar's purpose clear enough without the need for a title.

11. **Click Save to insert the calendar.**

A graphic representing the calendar appears in the Web page, as shown in Figure 1-14. If you click the graphic, a dialog box with options for the embedded document also appears.

12. **Change the options as needed: Click Properties to revise the options in the Google Calendar Properties dialog box, which are the ones described in Steps 4–10 earlier; click L (the default), C, or R to align the contents left, center, or right; and turn Wrap on or off (off being the default). Click Remove to remove the inserted document.**

Different choices may be appropriate for different Calendar setups, but for most calendars consider centering the contents and leaving the Wrap setting off because calendars are expected to have a specific look.

13. **Click Save to save the document and see the live content, as shown in Figure 1-15.**

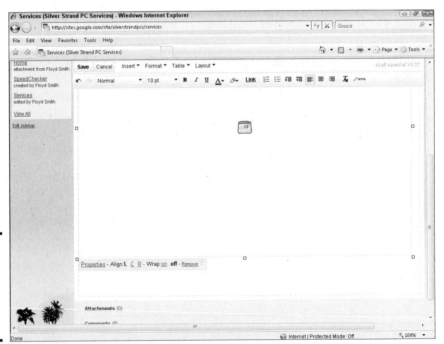

Figure 1-14:
Control
time itself
with the
Calendar on
your site.

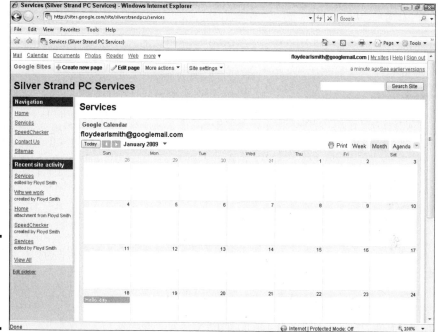

Figure 1-15:
Saving
brings the
live content
to life.

Embedding Google Presentations

Time was, we might not have realized the usefulness of including presentations in a book like this — either as a standalone application or as something to share in a Web page. Presentations seemed boring and ordinary.

Then one of us (Smith) took a job at AOL a few years back. As a place to work, it had plusses and minuses, but wow, did they use slideshows! No idea could be successfully communicated until you had created a *deck* — an interactive, multimedia Microsoft PowerPoint presentation — about it. Even marketing geeks — as opposed to the plain old geeks who wrote the code — with no other discernible computer skills were whizzes at creating these fancy presentations.

People were perfectly happy to modify one another's presentations, too. Instead of making suggestions in an e-mail, different respondents would change slides in the presentation and add new ones with additional details. Eventually, the slides would actually get presented to real people in a real meeting — usually as fast as the participants could read the slides and the presenter could run through all the animations and sound and video clips that adorned the (by now, very large) PowerPoint file.

Google Docs pluses — and minuses

One of the pluses of Google Docs is the way they can be constantly updated and improved by Google. It's exciting to be a Google Docs user and see a new blog entry that adds a cool new feature or announces a fix for a major problem. (Google Docs spreadsheet forms, described in a later section — a major feature if there ever was one — were introduced in just this way.)

But as you put increasing amounts of your business on Google Docs, the patch, mend, and extend model can get a bit frustrating. There's no single release point in which everything is brought together — and around which structured learning, books, magazine articles, and training courses can focus, confident that

nothing major will change for a couple of years. Instead, everything just builds by accretion — and if you take your eye off the ball for a while, you may miss something important.

Consider designating someone in your office to stay on top of Google Docs, to evaluate new features, and to take responsibility for letting the rest of the team know about them. You might even task that person with producing some (gasp) documentation pertinent to the way your organization uses Google Docs. Otherwise you might miss out on, or not get the most from, some good and worthwhile features.

If there had been a one-button technique for converting PowerPoint presentations, after the project was approved, into Web pages, productivity in the team would have rocketed upward.

So a presentation — like a Google Docs presentation — really can be a valid means of human expression, and many hands really can make light work, even in presentation mode.

There's more on Google Docs presentations in *Google Apps For Dummies* by Ryan Teeter and Karl Barksdale (Wiley, 2008).

What Google presentations can do

Google Docs presentations have one double-edged advantage and one that's almost entirely positive.

The double-edged advantage is that Google Docs presentations are simpler than other existing types of presentations. There are fewer features and less complexity. This is great for most people, most of the time — but is a bit of a downer when you need that one additional feature that isn't there in Google Docs presentations, but is present in the competition.

The other advantage is freedom from huge presentation files. Even simple presentations tend to be many megabytes in size. Including photos, animations, and videos can make files truly gigantic. (This is made worse by the tendency, familiar to Web page authors, to include a multi-megabyte high-resolution photograph, for instance, even though only a tiny piece of it appears in a slide.)

With a Google Docs presentation, all you need is an Internet connection and your presentation is easily available — and it can be accompanied by YouTube video and other online resources without the need to generate a huge file.

There's an occasional nightmare here too, of course. Even in these seemingly enlightened times, it's all too possible to end up in a spot where you don't have easy Internet access. You can still work, but it's less convenient.

But for most purposes, most of the time, Google presentations are great. Here are some of the key features you can count on:

✦ **Integration with other Google Docs applications:** Google Docs documents (the word processing type), presentations, and spreadsheets are very similar in their layout and commands, reducing your learning curve.

✦ **Presentation management functions:** Familiar functions, if you've used a presentation package before, are present: inserting, duplicating, re-ordering, and deleting slides. Not only are these functions available to the experienced, they're easy enough to learn that the less experienced can get up and running quickly.

✦ **Themes:** Just as it's easy to create an ugly — or even unreadable — Web page by choosing mismatched colors and fonts, so it's easy to create an ugly — or even unreadable — presentation in a similar manner. Google's solution in both cases is the same: themes, which combine relatively complementary choices into packages that can be chosen with a single mouse click. (And still modified as needed.) Figure 1-16 shows some of the themes offered in Google Docs presentations.

✦ **Shapes:** Google Docs presentations include a wide range of canned shapes that are easy to drop into a slide. (Yes, there is an art to using them in a way that doesn't look like you just dropped canned shapes into a slide; this comes with either talent, which only some of us have, or experience, which all of us can get.)

✦ **Text in boxes:** You can put one or more text boxes in a slide, giving you a lot of control over text. (Yes, we're with you if it seems strange not to be able to just click somewhere and start typing, as you can in a word processing document or spreadsheet, but you get more control this way.)

✦ **Images:** Images bring presentations to life, just as they do for Web pages — so be ready to add lots of images to your slides. Be careful not to include small pieces of big images, though, or there might be pauses while the image downloads during editing, or worse, during presentation.

✦ **Interoperability:** As with other Google Docs document types, you can easily import, and somewhat less easily export, Google Docs presentation to and from other formats.

The old saying, "Experience is what you get when you don't get what you want," was nowhere more true than in learning how to use computer programs — whether traditional software or based "in the cloud" (available directly online), like Google Docs applications. Be prepared to put in the time to get used to any new technology.

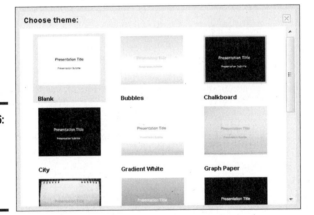

Figure 1-16:
Google
Docs
presents
you with
themes.

Sharing Google Docs presentations

It's always unfair — but just human nature — that we tend to harp on the negatives of a new product before the positives. For Google Docs presentations, the positives are pretty great. They relate directly to the evolving way people really want to use presentations today rather than to the old, command-and-control model of traditional desktop applications.

Here's a brief list of the most important examples:

✦ **Multi-user support with revision control:** Google Docs presentations give you a handy list of changes made, who made them, and links to previous versions of the presentation — so you can always get back to where you (or your presentation, at least) once belonged.

✦ **Online sharing for development:** The ability for multiple people to edit a presentation in real time is especially valuable in a type of document that's so often used in pressure-filled situations, often hours before a meeting (off-line, on-line, or combined) in which the presentation may be the main focus.

✦ **Online sharing for presentation:** Being able to let multiple people access a presentation — not as some kind of special function but as the way the presentation inherently works — is tremendous for on-line meetings, training, sales, and so on. It avoids much hassle, expense, and opportunities for failure. Using Skype, the tool for (mostly) free online phone calls, as a way to make the requisite phone calls for free makes it even better.

✦ **Discussing a presentation live:** The Audience panel in a presentation is a kind of chat window you can use during a presentation. (See Figure 1-17 for an example.) This may seem like a substitute for a shared voice connection, but actually it's a complement; as an audience member, for instance, you can let the presenter keep talking while you type your comment. Then it can be quickly answered by another attendee (verbally or by typing) or addressed by the presenter. This democratizes meetings without making them chaotic.

✦ **E-mailing presentations:** You can, of course, e-mail links to a presentation, secure in the knowledge that edits made by the recipients will be available to everyone — and can easily be reversed.

Audience panel

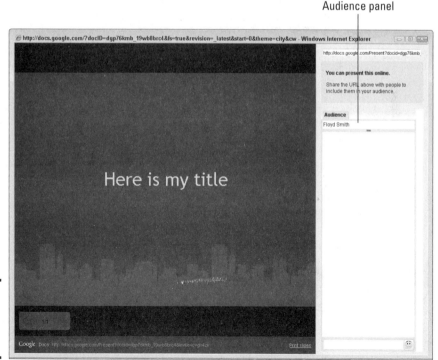

Figure 1-17:
Get the
Audience in
on the act.

Google Docs presentations in your Web site

Putting a Google Docs presentation in your Web site then becomes just another way of collaborating on it and presenting it. You can use the Web site itself to hold comments, revised or modified versions, and so on. Unlike spreadsheets — as described in the next section — everything in a presentation is right in front of you.

The Web site can also be a place to integrate various pieces that you may not want to make part of the presentation itself. Let's say you have a video clip that you plan to show only if there is time and interest. This is easily done with a Google Sites Web site that holds pieces of content that users can return to after the presentation to see more.

If you don't already have a Google Docs presentation to put in your Web site, you need to create one. Here's how to do it:

1. **Open Google Docs at `docs.google.com`. Sign in if you need to.**

   Google Docs opens.

2. **Choose New⇨Presentation.**

   A new presentation appears.

3. **Set up the presentation.**

   There could be a whole book about this. (Now there's an idea.) But we leave it to you to experiment with all you can do.

4. **Click Save.**

   A dialog box allowing you to name and save the presentation appears, as shown in Figure 1-18.

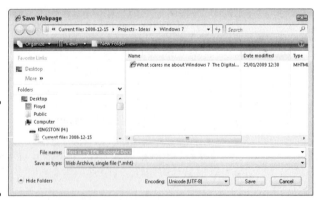

Figure 1-18: Present yourself with Google Docs.

5. **Enter a name for the presentation and then click OK.**

After you've created a presentation, follow these steps to put it in your Web site:

1. **Create or open a Web page in your Google site.**

   The Web page appears, along with menus for modifying it.

2. **Click the Insert menu and look at the options under Google.**

   The options appear: Calendar, Document, Picasa Web Slideshow, Presentation, Spreadsheet, Spreadsheet Form, and Video.

3. **Choose Presentation from the menu.**

   The Insert Google Presentation dialog appears, as shown in Figure 1-19.

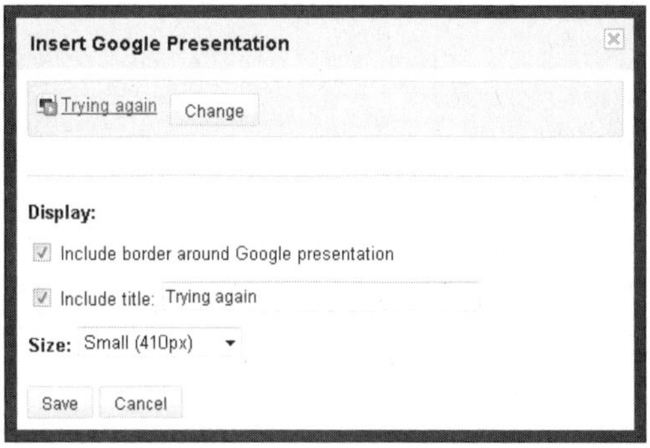

Figure 1-19:
All present
and
accounted
for.

4. **Specify whether to include a border around the presentation and whether to include the title.**

   Presentations are all about appearances, so you need to decide whether to use a border on the rather shallow basis of what looks better. This varies depending on the details of the graphical layout of the presentation and what's around it in the Web page in which it's embedded.

   Including the title is usually a good idea for presentations because they're so likely to be re-used. Leave it out only if you're fairly certain the presentation will live only in the Web site(s) in which you embed it.

5. **Enter a size for the presentation's appearance — small (410px), medium (555px), or large (700px). This is the width of the spreadsheet (410, 555, or 700 pixels); the height is fixed, and is about 80 percent of the width.**

Size matters a great deal with presentations, and they don't benefit visually from the extra "stuff" surrounding them on a Web page. Consider giving the presentation outside the confines of the Web page even if it otherwise lives well within it.

6. Click Save to insert the presentation.

A graphic representing the presentation appears in the Web page. If you click the graphic, a dialog box with options for the embedded document also appears.

7. Change the options as needed: Click Properties to revise the options in the Google Presentation Properties dialog, which are the ones described in Steps 4 and 5; click L (the default), C, or R to align the contents left, center, or right; and turn Wrap On or Off (Off being the default). Click Remove to remove the inserted document.

8. Click Save in the upper-left corner to save the document and see the live presentation content, as shown in Figure 1-20.

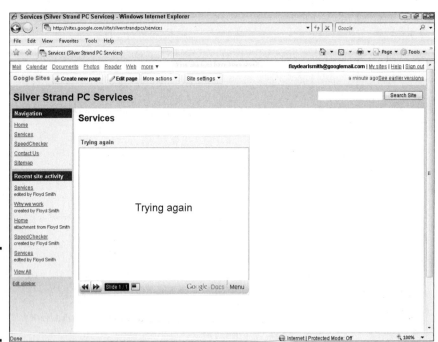

Figure 1-20: Presentations live well in Web pages.

Sharing Google Spreadsheets

Way back in the late 1970s, when PCs were first introduced — back when the Internet was still called Arpanet and few people had any kind of a modem — it was spreadsheets that really made PCs popular. First Lotus 1-2-3 and then Microsoft Excel became indispensable tools for all sorts of people.

The spreadsheet, then and now, is not limited to financial uses. Spreadsheets are used to crunch numbers for all sorts of people. But more than that, they're used for organizing information. It's amazing how many spreadsheets hold text — names, addresses, phone numbers, employment information, schedules, and just about everything you can think of.

So sharing spreadsheets is really important, and people spend a great deal of time updating and sharing them — and cursing when changes and versions get out of sync with each other, leading to all sorts of problems. It's quite difficult to fix word processing documents after they get out of sync, but spreadsheets — in which a single, well-hidden change in a formula can totally change a result — can be nearly impossible to repair.

In fact, Microsoft has made a good business out of the limitations of spreadsheets by introducing the Microsoft Access database, and charging a pretty penny for it on top of the usual cost of Microsoft Office. People pay for Microsoft Office, including their spreadsheet program — then have to fork out the additional money for Access. Database design and programming are a whole different world compared to the relative ease and simplicity of using a spreadsheet where all your data — though not your formulas — are right in front of you. We've even been involved in long discussions with people insisting on one over the other for different purposes.

So a truly sharable spreadsheet is, in fact, a really big deal, and the spreadsheets that are part of Google Docs are a big contribution to how people use computers. With Google Sites, you can host such a spreadsheet on your site.

This makes a further difference in how people work. After a spreadsheet is up on a site, no one really owns it, and it doesn't really have a home — it's just in "the cloud" of data and computing power available on the Internet. This is really a different way of working with the world than the old model provided, and for those of us who have spent way too much time messing around with sharing spreadsheets, it's a bit of a revolution.

What Google spreadsheets can do

People are so used to their existing way of using spreadsheets that getting them to change is very difficult. There are two main camps here:

✦ The people who don't much like using spreadsheets: The knowledge these users have is hard-won. For them, using a different spreadsheet, even if it's quite similar, is going to be frustrating.

What is nice for these people — really, for everyone involved — is that Google Docs spreadsheets work much like a Google Document. The menus are similar and have similar entries. So what you learn in one carries over readily to the other.

✦ The power users: These are people who have gotten a lot done, and in some cases even made a decent living, out of their mastery of the complexities of a particular kind of spreadsheet. These people may easily adjust to small differences — they'll probably enjoy the learning process — but they are quick to point out anything that a Google Docs spreadsheet can't do that their accustomed spreadsheet can.

The list of things Google Docs spreadsheets can do, however, is long:

✦ Google spreadsheets are made up of cells, arranged neatly in rows and columns.

✦ Cells can be formatted with various fonts, bold, italic, underlines, colors, currency symbols, alignments, wrapping settings, and so on.

✦ Cells can be merged into larger cells, cutting across the row-column grid.

✦ Cells can hold numbers, text, and labels.

✦ Cells can hold formulas with hundreds of functions defined.

✦ Charts of several kinds can be created based on the data in your spreadsheet — and are automatically updated as you change the underlying numbers.

✦ All this can be converted and exported to and from other formats, most important of these are Microsoft Excel and OpenOffice. The spreadsheet can also go into HTML, text, or a PDF for publishing. (In a format that doesn't let anyone alter your precious work!)

Because charts are so important, Figure 1-21 shows the range of chart options available in a Google Docs spreadsheet. You can see at a glance that many common features are there — but also that there's a little less functionality than in the competition. For most purposes, however, it is fine.

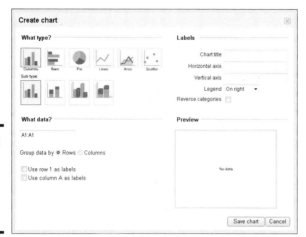

Figure 1-21:
Charting
your future
is easy in
Google
Docs.

This is a far too brief introduction to the tremendous power of Google Docs spreadsheets. For some additional details, see *Google Apps For Dummies* by Ryan Teeter and Karl Barksdale (Wiley, 2008), and be prepared to spend a lot of time experimenting to get things right until you learn the program thoroughly.

An important feature of Google Docs spreadsheets is multiple spreadsheets in the same document. This is not only a good way to handle complicated models, it's also a good place to put a "known good" version of a spreadsheet before sharing it with people. That way you can review changes people make in the tab that's intended for sharing and compare them to your earlier version.

Sharing Google spreadsheets

Although some people are very accustomed to the way their non-Google spreadsheet package works, the power of sharing built into Google spreadsheets is so powerful it will generate its own fans.

In Google Docs spreadsheets, several people can update the same spreadsheet at the same time. The names of current collaborators are shown across the bottom of the screen, and you can always retrace what changes were made by whom.

You can invite people to share the spreadsheet. You can also open viewing or even editing up to anyone who shares your domain. You can even chat with people about what you're doing on the spreadsheet while you're doing it.

Figure 1-22 shows the sharing options built into a spreadsheet.

Share with others ☒

| Invite people | People with access | Advanced permissions |

Invite: (Any email address will work)

Subject:

Shareable spreadsheet

Message:

⦿ To edit   ○ To view

Choose from contacts

Privacy
⦿ Always require sign-in
○ Let people **view** without signing in
○ Let people **edit** without signing in

☐ Send a copy to myself

[Send]   Add without sending invitation

Figure 1-22:
Share and
share alike.

Google Docs spreadsheets in your Web site

Putting a Google Docs spreadsheet in your Web site extends the power of collaboration by exposing it to all the people who come visit your site. They can use it for reference; add entries to it, treat it as a simple database; or really go to town, adding new formulas, charts, and graphs.

The strengths of Google Docs and one of the key weaknesses of spreadsheets intersect here. Even in a carefully controlled system with individual responsibility for spreadsheets, it's very difficult to audit spreadsheets — to be sure that they're doing what they're intended to do. With shared responsibility, it may be impossible. So be careful how much you rely on results from a spreadsheet that a number of people have had access to.

With a little care, though, a Google Docs spreadsheet in a Web site is a great thing, giving you a lot of power and flexibility.

If you don't already have a Google spreadsheet to put in your Web site, you need to create one. Here's how to do it:

1. **Open Google Docs at `docs.google.com`. Sign in if you need to.**

Google Docs opens.

2. **Choose New⇨Spreadsheet.**

A new spreadsheet appears.

3. **Set up the spreadsheet.**

Think like a publisher and a computer programmer in doing this. You want to create a small system that other people can get something out of. So make it useful and interesting to them, as a publisher would; and try to direct people toward entering data where you want them to and away from unnecessarily changing underlying formulas, as a programmer would.

4. **Click Save.**

A dialog box allowing you to name and save the spreadsheet appears, as shown in Figure 1-23.

Figure 1-23: Carefully create your Google Docs spreadsheet.

5. **Enter a name for the spreadsheet and then click OK.**

Think carefully about what you name spreadsheets — or anything else — in Google Docs. Each item you create is a reusable resource of potentially great value. Consider creating a list of files and their purposes — perhaps in a Google Docs spreadsheet!

After you've created a spreadsheet, follow these steps to put it in your Web site:

1. **Create or open a Web page in your Google site.**

The Web page appears, along with menus for modifying it.

2. **Click the Insert menu and look at the options under Google.**

The options appears: Calendar, Document, Picasa Web Slideshow, Presentation, Spreadsheet, Spreadsheet Form, and Video.

3. **Choose Spreadsheet from the menu.**

The Insert Google Spreadsheet dialog appears, as shown in Figure 1-24.

4. **Specify whether to include a border around the spreadsheet and whether to include the title.**

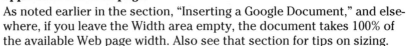

Spreadsheets are both visually distinctive and screen space hogs — early spreadsheet users were always after the latest and greatest large screens. (One of us, Smith, fondly remembers going from 640 x 480 VGA resolution up to a stunning 800 x 600 Super VGA screen — and sitting in a standards committee meeting to help settle the details.) So no need to waste precious screen space on a border around something that will stand out anyway.

Including the title is a different kind of decision. Include the title if some or all your users may need to re-use this spreadsheet elsewhere. Leave it out if the spreadsheet will, for most people's purposes, live entirely in the Web site(s) you embed it in.

5. **Enter values for the Height and Width of your spreadsheet as it appears in the Web page.**

    As noted earlier in the section, "Inserting a Google Document," and elsewhere, if you leave the Width area empty, the document takes 100% of the available Web page width. Also see that section for tips on sizing.

6. **Click Save to insert the spreadsheet.**

    A graphic representing the spreadsheet appears in the Web page. If you click the graphic, a dialog with options for the embedded document also appears.

7. **Change the options as needed: Click Properties to revise the options in the Google Spreadsheet Properties dialog, which are the ones described in Steps 4 and 5 earlier; click L (the default), C, or R to align the contents left, center, or right; turn Wrap On or Off (Off being the default). Click Remove to remove the inserted document.**

    As with calendars, different choices may be appropriate for different spreadsheet setups, but for most spreadsheets consider centering the contents and leaving the Wrap setting Off because spreadsheets are expected to have a specific look.

8. **Click Save in the upper-left corner to save the document and see the live content, as shown in Figure 1-25.**

Figure 1-25:
Saving
makes the
spreadsheet
"real."

Using Google Docs Spreadsheet Forms

Google Docs spreadsheet forms are, frankly, strange hybrids that end up working rather well. However, they're hard to understand unless you have a fairly broad background in Web page creation and even programming — or unless you have a helpful resource like this book.

What too few people realize is that one of the most valuable things a Web site can do is gather information from visitors. This is partly because Web site visitors are quite reluctant — and getting ever more so — to enter any information. It's also because it usually takes a lot of technical expertise to do anything useful with the information after it's gathered.

As soon as you have users enter data into a Web page, it goes from a nice, easy-to–create, easy-to–manage online brochure to a giant and hard-to–manage computer program. A Web page that gathers data has to provide a user interface that makes sense and reassures the user; it has to check the data the user enters and, you hope, give the user useful feedback; and it has to store the data somewhere for processing. All the attributes of a real computer program.

You are probably aware that when you enter data into a Web page, you're using a *form*. Forms are defined in HTML, rather clumsily, but the data has to be handled by a combination of JavaScript running in the Web page (to give feedback to the user if you so choose) and "real" computer or database programming on the back end to store and perhaps process the data. Again, this is a lot of complexity for someone who was previously fooling around in, say, Google Sites using templates to create Web pages.

Google Docs spreadsheet forms, introduced early in 2008, are a fairly magnificent hack. They use the underlying capability of a Google Docs spreadsheet to allow users to enter data; and they support sending the data to anyone you choose via e-mail, to work around the need to have it processed. (Actually, they push the need to process it onto the poor sap who gets the e-mail — which may well be you.) The form data is also saved in a spreadsheet, where you can do with it what you will. (If you're getting a lot of data, this might just be a nice way of saying "good luck" with the data management task this implies.)

Google Docs spreadsheet forms have such staggering implications that we're going to leave them aside for now because it would take several chapters to fully explore them — in fact, maybe we've just figured out the topic for our next book! Instead, we just show you how to use them in your Google Sites Web site and let you find the best use for them yourself, at least until we or someone writes that book about them.

What Google spreadsheet forms can do

Google spreadsheet forms are amazing. They take care, in an easy-to-manage way, of scores of questions people face when creating form interfaces in Web pages. (Often these people pay front-end and back-end programmers to help them get and manage the data.)

They push a lot of work onto you as the site owner, though. This is fine for small sites and small volumes of data, and that's very much in the spirit of the Web and Web tools — you can get started easily. But if your site is going to be used by a lot of people and generates a lot of data, don't be surprised if you end up hiring some of those previously mentioned programmers to set up things properly for you.

Don't worry, you still win. The things you discover from your experience with Google Docs spreadsheet forms and users' feedback vastly simplifies the task of telling the programmers what their job is, saving you a great deal of time and money.

The beginning interface for a Google Docs spreadsheet form is shown in Figure 1-26. Remember, this is just a beginning point; you build up your form by using and repeating these elements until you're done.

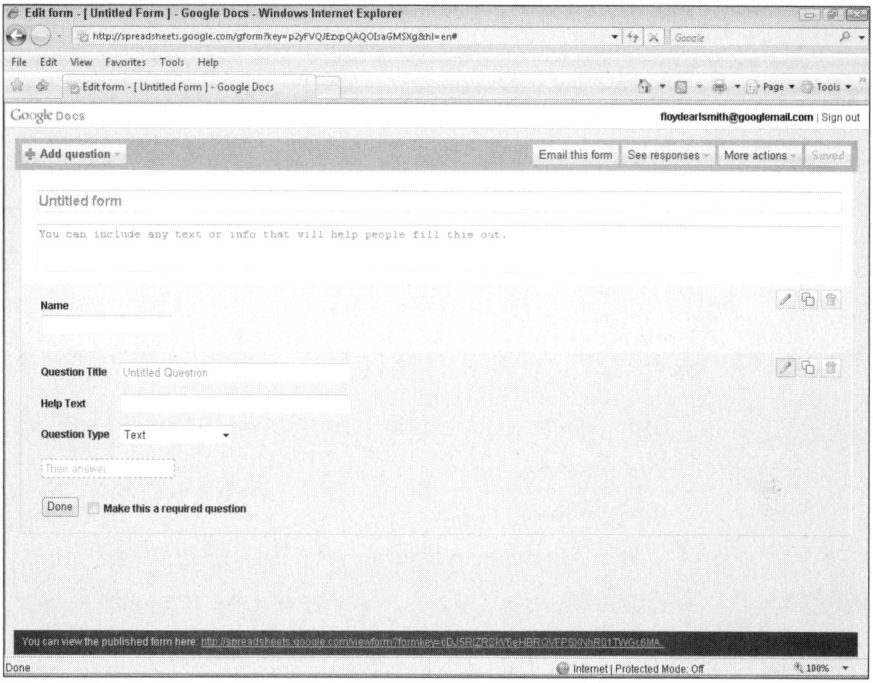

Figure 1-26:
Introducing questions of good form.

To begin with, you have to think in terms of an entire form. The form is made up of several elements, some of which you only need enter once, others have to be repeated several times to fill out your form. These elements include

✦ **Title:** Your form should have a title that helps you manage it and helps users know what to do with the form. Insert this in the area called Untitled Form.

✦ **Introductory text:** Appearing under the title, this text introduces the purpose of the form, guiding people in how to use it.

✦ **Name:** This is the name of the field that the user enters data into. You can delete this if needed.

✦ **Question title:** The prompt for the data entry field.

✦ **Help text:** Supporting text for the data entry exercise.

✦ **Question type:** Here you have initially confusing options including paragraph text, multiple choice, check boxes, choices on a list, or choices on a scale value from 1 to n, with n being a number you choose.

✦ **Make this a required question:** This is a check box that prevents users from completing the form until they've answered a certain question.

The question types above are the ones supported by HTML with some fields that are sensible in a form, some contribution from the Google people about arrangement, and some extras such as the ability to make a question required.

This is a far too brief introduction to all you can do with spreadsheet forms in Google Docs. And, unlike other Google Docs capabilities, spreadsheet forms are so new that they aren't covered in any existing books. If you want to do very much with them, be prepared to spend some time experimenting and looking for answers online.

Here's how to create a Google Docs spreadsheet form to put in your Web site:

1. **Open Google Docs at docs.google.com. Sign in if you need to.**

   Google Docs opens.

2. **Choose New⇨Form.**

   A new spreadsheet from appears, as shown in Figure 1-26.

3. **Enter the title and introductory text for the form.**

   Consider creating the entire form in a word processing document or even on paper first. It's hard to think about the overall design and flow of the form when you're caught up in using the Google Docs interface to create the individual fields.

4. **For a given question, enter the name of the area of the form, if any, or delete the name field by clicking the trash can icon. Then do the same for the question title and help text, entering or deleting these fields. Choose the question type and then the specific fields for that type — for instance, for a question type of Checkboxes, enter the text for each check box option. Then click the check box if you want the question to be required. Finally, click Done.**

   The new form question and its accompanying fields appear in your form. You can click the form question to edit it further.

5. **Repeat Step 4 for each of the fields in your form.**

   Build up the form one field at a time. Be prepared for this to take a while as new ideas come to you.

6. **Choose More actions⇨Edit confirmation.**

   The Edit Confirmation dialog appears, as shown in Figure 1-27 (which also shows a couple of entry fields). Enter the confirmation text.

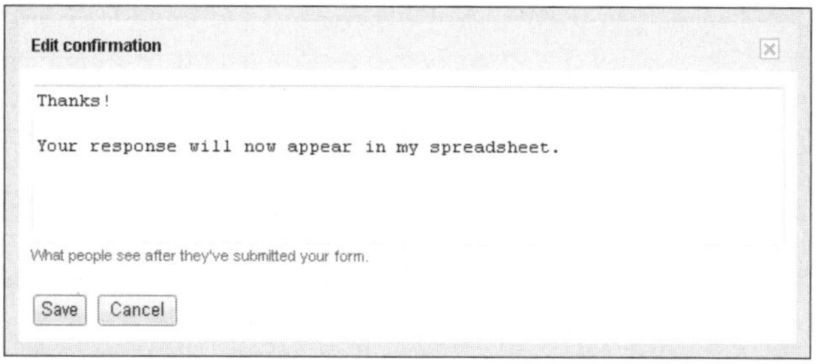

Figure 1-27:
Reassure
your users
with a well-
crafted
confirm-
ation.

> **Edit confirmation** ⊠
>
> Thanks !
>
> Your response will now appear in my spreadsheet.
>
> What people see after they've submitted your form.
>
> Save   Cancel

Sharing Google spreadsheet forms

Unlike other elements of Google Docs, the entire and only point of Google
Docs spreadsheet forms is to be shared. There's no reason for you to create
a form and keep it to yourself — it exists entirely to get information from
other people for you to do something with.

After you've created a spreadsheet form, follow these steps to put it in your
Web site:

1. **Create or open a Web page in your Google site.**

   The Web page appears, along with menus for modifying it.

2. **Click the Insert menu and look at the options under Google.**

   The options appears: Calendar, Document, Picasa Web Slideshow,
   Presentation, Spreadsheet, Spreadsheet Form, and Video.

3. **Choose Spreadsheet form from the menu.**

   The Insert Google Spreadsheet Form dialog box appears, with the same
   options as for a full spreadsheet, shown in Figure 1-27.

4. **Specify whether to include a border around the spreadsheet and
   whether to include the title.**

   Spreadsheet forms are visually distinctive enough that you don't usually
   want a border around them, and few Web forms have borders.

   As for including the title, probably best to leave this out. Users don't
   care if it's a re-usable element; they're more likely to depend on the page
   title and other text to make sense of the form.

5. **Enter values for the Height and Width of your spreadsheet as it
   appears in the Web page.**

   Unlike other elements of a Google Sites page, you want the height to be
   just right for your content. Experiment with this until you get it right.

As noted earlier in the section, "Inserting a Google Document," and elsewhere, if you leave the Width area empty, the document takes up 100% of the available Web page width. Also see that section for tips on sizing.

6. Click Save to insert the spreadsheet form.

A graphic representing the spreadsheet form appears in the Web page. If you click the graphic, a dialog box with options for the embedded document also appears.

7. Change the options as needed: Click Properties to revise the options in the Google Spreadsheet Properties dialog, which are the ones described in Steps 4 and 5 earlier; click L (the default), C, or R to align the contents left, center, or right; and turn Wrap On or Off (Off being the default). Click Remove to remove the inserted document.

As with calendars, different choices may be appropriate for different spreadsheet setups, but for most spreadsheets consider left-aligning the contents and leaving the Wrap setting Off because forms are expected to look like a normal part of the Web page.

8. Click Save in the upper-left corner to save the document and see the live content, as shown in Figure 1-28.

Figure 1-28: Saving makes the form real.

Chapter 2: Adding Google Media to Your Web Site

In This Chapter

✔ Understanding what Picasa Web Albums and YouTube can offer your site

✔ Choosing a resolution

✔ Embedding multimedia

✔ Creating and inserting a Picasa Web Albums slideshow

✔ Creating and inserting a YouTube video

*U*sing your Web site to host traditional Office-style documents is a wonderful capability — as described in the previous chapter. Using Google multimedia in your Web site has many similarities to using Google documents, but there are key differences as well.

The two main channels for multimedia in Google Sites are based on Web properties that Google owns, one for photos, the other for videos. These are Picasa Web Albums, which is fairly well-known, and YouTube, which is a Web and cultural phenomenon, and one of the top few sites on the Web — along with Google itself.

What both have in common is that they import data from fairly complex Web sites. These sites incorporate a tremendous amount of functionality and are used to manage data that's hard to create — and hard to change, especially by anyone except the creator.

Embedding Picasa Web Albums presentations of images — usually photos — and YouTube videos in your Web site is, in a sense, more traditional and less truly collaborative than embedding Office-type applications. This is simply because of the difficulty of collaboratively changing the data that's being presented in the Web site.

With Office-type documents, individual chunks of data — words in a word processing document, slides in a presentation, formulas or rows and columns of data in a spreadsheet — can easily be updated by different users. The same idea is a bit of a stretch for a group of photos, because it's hard to relate a new photo thematically to existing ones, and strange indeed for a video. (Are different users going to edit or add new frames?)

However, the story of the Web's growth over the last 20 years or so is the story of the impossible becoming first possible and then common. So in this chapter, we present Picasa Web Albums images and YouTube videos as mostly fixed data that's embedded in a Google site.

It may not be too long, however, before at least some users treat this kind of data as fully collaborative and updateable. The slide show of images that results from full collaboration, we imagine, may be a bit odd — and video that results from full collaboration on individual frames may be strange indeed!

A Brief Description of Picasa Web Albums

The two major photo hosting Web sites are Picasa Web Albums, which we focus on here, and Flickr. It's quite possible that you and your friends and coworkers use either or both.

The great thing about a photo sharing site is that it's an online version of an old-fashioned photo album, but one that can easily be shared around the world. Both Picasa Web Albums and Flickr do this very well. Picasa Web Albums is a fun and easy-to-use site. (See Figure 2-1.)

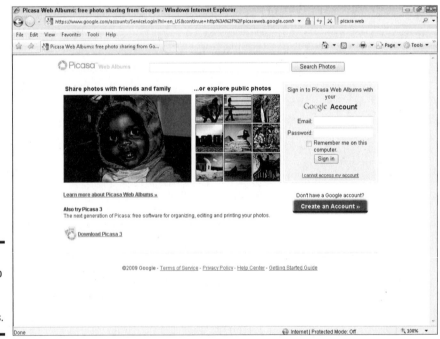

Figure 2-1:
Picasa Web
Albums is a
fun site for
your photos.

For many people, the main difference between these two sites is that Picasa Web Albums is owned by Google and Flickr by Yahoo!, each of which has its own e-mail service, its own strengths and weaknesses, and its own fans. Flickr, shown in Figure 2-2, is also the older service and is somewhat better known.

Figure 2-2:
Flickr your
way to fun.

When we looked online for information about Picasa Web Albums and Flickr, we didn't find much rabid advocacy of one over the other; it's not a Mac-versus-Windows-type rivalry. In fact, we found information about how to use both services in combination to get complex photo processing tasks done. (Each site has add-ins, compatible third-party sites, books, and articles — a whole ecosystem around it.)

The key advantage of Picasa Web Albums is that it's paired with a free photo-editing application, Picasa — shown in Figure 2-3 — that serves as a front end to Picasa Web Albums. This makes a great deal of sense if you're planning to put your individual photos and photo albums into a Web site. (Flickr users are perhaps more likely to do the opposite and have their photos on Flickr serve as their overall Web home.)

Figure 2-3:
Picasa is an application that works with Picasa Web Albums.

If you already use Flickr, you'll find it easy to use Picasa Web Albums to store photos and create photo albums that you can then integrate into your Google Sites Web site. If you already use Picasa Web Albums and Picasa, or if you don't yet have an online home for your photos, the integration with Google Sites is a real joy.

A Brief Description of YouTube

Before we get into the nitty-gritty of using Picasa Web Albums photos and slideshows in your Google Sites pages, we first discuss YouTube.

Why? For a few reasons. One is that the way you use Picasa Web Albums photos and YouTube videos may be quite similar. In fact, there may be times when you have a creative, aesthetic, and technical choice to make between creating a Picasa Web slideshow instead of a YouTube video. So it's good to know about both before you decide to use either.

YouTube is a huge hit — but many people who have heard of it haven't necessarily used it. The visible side of YouTube is a site that people use to upload and view videos. But there's also a hidden side — people upload their videos, then publish them within Web pages. YouTube hosts the video, but it appears to the user, and is played, from within another site.

Video is unreasonably popular on the Web right now, and on corporate intranets as well. One of the authors (Smith) recently had a consulting assignment setting up part of a global network for sharing videos inside a company. There he saw the popularity of video rising rapidly in companies worldwide. You may find yourself pressed to use video, even when a slide-show of photos might do the job better — in particular, if the photos have a better image quality.

Solving the Hosting Problem

Just why are photo-sharing sites — and, to an even greater extent, the leading video-sharing site, YouTube — so very, very popular?

The main reason is that they've each found a business model that allows them to offer lots of very large files for free. A typical small- or medium-sized Web company or hosting provider simply has to put limits on what an individual can upload, as well as on the total number of images or video clips hosted. Otherwise, the company would go broke, leaving behind big bills for bandwidth. YouTube does all this hosting for free, with very few limits, solving a big problem for you: where to host your media files without having to pay for the privilege.

Note that part of the secret is hosting not just one or a few people's photos or video clips. It's hosting so much content that the site itself becomes an interesting destination for all sorts of people, not just those who want to see a particular photo or clip.

In fact, to many people, YouTube is a destination — where they go to see videos. But huge numbers of videos that look like they're part of various Web sites are, in fact, hosted on YouTube behind the scenes. (They usually have the YouTube logo stamped on them just to make it clear.)

Photo- and video-sharing sites have three different uses:

✦ Hosting photos and video clips that are published on different Web sites — as you're about to do here, using your Google Sites Web site.

✦ Hosting specific photos and video clips that people go to the site to see.

✦ Hosting enough photos and video clips to make browsing the site interesting, whether the users visit the site to browse or to upload their own content or to view someone else's.

Each of these uses feeds off the other, building enough traffic to make the site as a whole worth the costs of running it.

You Say You Want a Resolution?

Why do photos look so great on the Web and videos look so ugly? The reason for the difference involves image resolution, optics, physics, and bandwidth.

In terms of *resolution* — the number of dots of color that make up an image — online photos are awful. A typical screen has anywhere from 72dpi — dots per inch — to a couple hundred. A photograph has many hundreds or thousands of dots per inch. The process that produces the photograph is also likely to be well-calibrated, unlike your typical video card and (probably dirty) laptop screen or separate monitor. Those new, "cool" LCD screens actually have worse image quality than the CRT (Cathode Ray Tube) displays they replace.

But, luckily for online photos, backlit images (with the light coming from behind and through the image, as on a monitor) look great. And a lightly compressed video, using the JPEG standard, still keeps very good image quality. So still images online can, and often do, look great.

One of the best regularly recurring displays of images online is the Big Picture feature on the *Boston Herald*'s Web site at `www.boston.com/bigpicture`. The large images look so great that they tend to make anyone depicted look like a hero or a star. See Figure 2-4 for an example.

Figure 2-4:
The *Boston Herald* has the Big Picture.

Videos, though, involve movement as well as images, with up to 30 frames shown every second, so video files tend to be huge. To work at all online, they have to be compressed quite harshly. The eye can construct a pretty good moving image from pretty poor individual frames, but online video tends to be compressed so harshly it doesn't look very good.

YouTube, which is amazing as a free service supporting this disk- and-bandwidth-hogging medium, crunches files pretty darn hard. So videos tend to look muddy and low in quality, especially if you haven't done everything right.

Figure 2-5 shows a video with above-average quality. You can see the black background, which greatly helps compression; what you can't see are the professional director and student assistants who got the most one can get out of YouTube. To see more typical YouTube results, just pay a visit to the site and look at any randomly selected group of video clips.

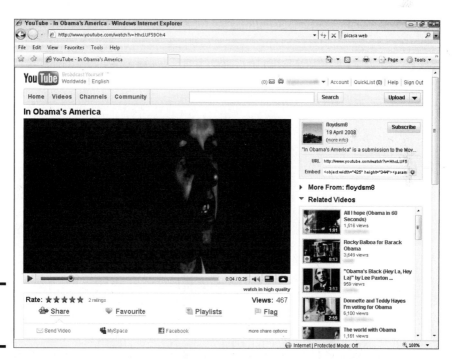

Figure 2-5:
Smith is on YouTube.

So don't be surprised if you get better image quality with stills than with video, especially if both are shot by amateurs. But video clips are still particularly effective in many contexts, so be ready to use both kinds of media in your Web site.

Embedding Multimedia in Your Web Pages

Embedding multimedia in your Web page is not usually easy — but Google makes it easy.

Slide shows of images are very popular in Web sites, but they've been very hard to create and manage — until now. With the Picasa software application editing your images, Picasa Web Albums hosting slideshows of your images, and Google Sites displaying the slideshow in context, things that used to be difficult and expensive have become easy and free.

There's more than one way to skin a cat, as people who don't much like cats say — there's also no reason you can't use a Picasa Web Albums slideshow for a presentation. You can make it all Google Docs presentation slides or intermix photos and put video alongside. This can make your presentations more varied and interesting and may help you avoid the terrible affliction jokingly referred to as "Death by PowerPoint."

Video integration with Google is even more impressive. Most of the difficult and expensive steps of video integration — uploading the video, compressing it, getting it hosted, worrying about paying every time the video is downloaded during viewing, and presenting a Web link for you to use — are handled easily and inexpensively by YouTube. Google Sites handles the final problem — making it easy to embed the video in an actual Web page.

Creating a Picasa Web Albums Slideshow

There are a thousand different possible ways to upload images to Picasa Web Album and create a slideshow.

Don't get confused; the Picasa desktop software, Picasa Web Albums, and Google Sites all use the terms *slideshow* and *Web album* pretty much interchangeably. The Web album is where a group of photos are stored; a slideshow is a way of presenting them, which you can activate within Picasa, Picasa Web Albums, or Google Sites.

In fact, the Google Sites option shows all the photos in a Picasa Web Albums album, even if you want only one. So plan your Picasa Web Albums photo storage filing system around what you might need in your Google Sites slideshows.

Consider uploading any photos you might want to use before starting with Picasa. The Picasa software scans your system for photos, and you might as well have them all available.

These steps are truly the For Dummies version, assuming you already have photos edited and ready to upload:

1. **Visit the Picasa Web site at `picasaweb.google.com`. Sign in if needed, using your Google account. Click I accept to accept the terms.**

The Web site appears, as shown in Figure 2-6.

Figure 2-6:
The Picasa
Web site
offers you
software.

2. **Click the button to download the Picasa software. Follow the instructions to install the software and begin running it.**

The software downloads; the file is relatively small for an application, about 10MB. (Some image software programs are 100MB in size or even much larger.)

3. **The Picasa software opens and offers you the opportunity to scan your system for pictures. Choose the option you want and click Continue.**

The Picasa software scans your system, finding pictures.

4. **From among the photos displayed, select several that you want to make into a Web Album.**

All your photos are displayed in a scrolling window. You can use Shift+click to select and deselect a range of photos, and Control+click to select and deselect individual photos.

5. **Click the Upload button along the bottom edge of the Picasa application.**

   You are asked to sign into your account.

6. **Sign into your account, as shown in Figure 2-8. If you're using a non-shared computer, click the check box, Remember Me on This Computer. Then click the Sign In button.**

   You are signed into your account. Then the Upload to Web Albums dialog appears, as shown in Figure 2-7.

Figure 2-7: You can upload your photos in the size you choose.

7. **Choose a size for the images from the pull-down menu.**

   See the sidebar, "Size matters," later in this chapter, for details. When in doubt, choose the Small size option; you can always re-upload larger images later if needed.

8. **Choose a visibility for the album.**

   See the sidebar, "Security matters," later in this chapter, for details. Everyone has his own comfort level, but there are millions of photos up on the Web with no security.

9. **Click the Upload button. Click the Conserve Bandwidth check box if you want to restrict the amount of bandwidth used during the upload process. (If, for instance, your housemate is watching TV online.)**

The Upload Manager appears and the photos upload.

10. **Click the View Online button to view the photos online.**

If you click this button, your photos appear online, as shown in Figure 2-8.

11. **Click the button (to the right of your photos), Link to This Album, to get a URL.**

The URL appears, along with a line of HTML code, as shown in Figure 2-8. For Google Sites, it's the URL that you want. (You can also get a URL for a specific photo to insert into your Web page outside of any slideshows.)

Figure 2-8:
Kunik from
Mars can
has cheez-
burger.

Even if you're careful about what you upload, you probably want to reorganize your photos online for use in Google Sites. From within your Picasa Web Albums album, choose Edit⇨Organize and Reorder to get started.

Picasa and Picasa Web Albums have a huge array of options and capabilities beyond what we've described here. Just for one example, you can use Google Earth to geocode your photo to a specific location. And there are compatible tools, companion sites, and Flickr to explore as well. But the information here is, we believe and hope, all you need to work with photos, Picasa, Picasa Web Albums, and Google Sites.

Inserting a Picasa Web Albums Slideshow

After you've put your photos in a Picasa Web album, it's easy to create a Picasa Web Albums slideshow. This puts a nice, interactive, multimedia feature in your Web site. Such slideshows can be useful for everything from sharing with friends to selling your house — or your business's products. Or your business.

It's all up to your imagination — which is not always good, because there aren't a lot of existing models out there for you to learn from. Expect to go through some trial and error as you learn to make the best use of Picasa Web Albums slideshows in your site.

Follow these steps to insert a Picasa Web Albums slideshow in your Google site:

1. **Follow the steps in the previous section to create a Picasa Web Albums album with only the desired photos in it and expose the URL of the album.**

   The Web site appears, as shown in Figure 2-6.

2. **Open a separate Web browser window and open your Google Sites Web site in it.**

3. **Click Edit Page to edit the page.**

4. **Click Insert⇨Picasa Web Slideshow.**

   The Insert Picasa Web Slideshow dialog box appears, as shown in Figure 2-9.

5. **Copy the URL (not the HTML) from your Picasa Web Albums slideshow and paste it into the field, Paste the URL of your Picasa Web Albums album in the dialog box.**

6. **Choose a slideshow size — Small 144px, Medium 288px, Large 400px, Extra-large 600px. or Extra-extra-large 800px.**

   Smaller is usually better, especially as larger images may cause problems with browser window management on the user's potentially crowded screen as well as possible pauses while images download or update.

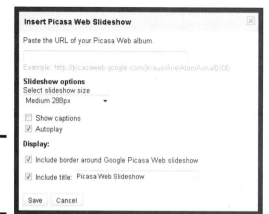

Figure 2-9:
Time to
insert your
slideshow.

7. Specify whether to show captions.

Captions are likely to be enlightening once and annoying after that, so when in doubt, leave them out.

8. Specify whether to Autoplay the images.

Many users prefer control, so consider leaving this off.

9. Specify whether to include a border.

A border may be visual overkill — try it both ways and decide.

10. Specify whether to include a title, and enter one if you want.

This is a nice option and telegraphs to users whether they want to wait or click — depending on whether you have Autoplay turned on — to view the remaining photos. If you do have a title, consider including the number of pictures in it.

11. Click Save to finish inserting the slideshow.

As with other embedded documents (see previous chapter), a graphic representing the slideshow appears in the Web page. If you click the graphic, a dialog with options for the embedded document also appears.

12. Change the options as needed: Click Properties to revise the options in the Google document Properties dialog box, which are the ones described in Steps 6 and 7 earlier; click L (the default), C, or R to align the contents left, center, or right; and turn Wrap On or Off (Off being the default). Click Remove to remove the inserted document.

The alignment and wrap choices don't affect Picasa Web Albums slideshows much.

13. Click Save to save the document and see the live content, as shown in Figure 2-10.

Figure 2-10:
At last! A
slideshow
in your Web
page.

You see that you've actually done quite a bit to get a slideshow into your Web page; but this is the easiest way to do it in any mainstream Web tool we're aware of because of the solid integration among Picasa software, Picasa Web Albums, and Google Sites. Although this can seem like a bit of a toy at first, the increasing prevalence of slideshows online both demonstrates how valuable they are and gets your Web site visitors used to them. You may well find Picasa Web Albums slideshows worth using in your own site(s), whether for fun or for serious business purposes.

Size matters

What size should you use when uploading videos to a Picasa Web Albums album?

It matters a lot because you have a 1GB (one gigabyte) limit on your free photo space. That's 1,000 super-sized, 1MB photos. That may sound like a lot, but you'll be surprised how fast you fill it up — and how disinclined you'll be to go

back and delete or downsize 1,000 or so photos to claw back space within the limit.

So use the smallest size you think you can get away with. The best option is called Small — 640 pixels (for blogs and Web pages). This is half the width of a typical widescreen laptop and plenty for giving people a good idea of what something looks like — in fact, it is, if anything, a bit wide to fit comfortably in a typical Web browser window.

In terms of storage consumption, these images are about 50KB each — or about 20,000 per gigabyte.

Note that the largest size available in Google Sites is extra-extra large, 800 pixels; the next size down is extra large, 600 pixels. So any size except Small that you choose for Picasa Web Albums is wasted in Google Sites.

The other choices are only needed if people are really, really interested in what you're showing. The next larger choice is Medium: 1024 pixels (for sharing). The image size is larger than a typical laptop screen, so the people you're sharing with are more likely to be annoyed than appreciative of the extra bandwidth and online storage space you're taking up.

The really big sizes are Recommended: 1600 pixels (for prints, screensavers, and sharing). Actually, this size is "no man's land" — too big

for onscreen use, but not really good enough for printing (especially because many people now own, or have access to, proper photo printers that will make a high-resolution image look good and a lower-resolution image such as this look cheap). These images are about 250KB each, about five times the size of a small image.

The right choice for printing — and only for printing — is Original size (slowest upload). Use this only for your best images and for people who are likely to obsess about details, such as someone considering the purchase of a new car or a grandparent looking at a photo of their grandchild. (If the latter, 1GB is not likely to be enough storage . . .)

Note that these are Picasa options, not necessarily exactly what you want. For instance, many high-resolution digital cameras and the software used with them have a raw mode that captures and stores all the pixels from an image plus associated data. Raw files can be 10MB or more each, and yes, some people prefer to upload and store these online.

Security matters

What level of security should you use when uploading photos to a Picasa Web Albums album?

The Public option means anyone who knows the URL of the gallery your photos are in can view them, and they'll appear in Public Search (which includes searching within Picasa Web Albums, Google, and other services). This option imposes the fewest hassles when you publish your Web slideshow to your Google Sites Web site. Remember, people can only search on your photos by the text

associated with them, so if you restrict that text, you restrict search success.

The Unlisted option also generates a Web address, but it's intended to be very hard to guess — and the photos don't appear in Public Search. Not perfect protection, but not bad.

The final option is called Sign-In Required to View. Users have to sign in — and you have to add them to a "Shared with" access list. This list cuts through the security levels and allows specified people access to the photos.

Creating a YouTube Video

Creating a video and getting it uploaded to YouTube can be a very complicated or a very simple process. For instance, professional-quality video, like the one shown in Figure 2-5, can take many hours of scripting, planning, setup, capture, and processing. The result is a polished, professional-looking video that gets the most out of YouTube.

YouTube also hosts music videos, for instance, which often cost hundreds of thousands, even millions of dollars, to produce. The versions on YouTube can be anything from crude copies off videotape to lovingly crafted, digital-to-digital transfers.

Yet YouTube videos are, as often as not, low-resolution Webcam captures shot from an angle that's halfway looking up the nose of some bored-looking collegian who should be studying for exams instead of video blogging on YouTube.

So how much effort should you put into creating a Web video? If you're a bored college student who doesn't mind coming across as one, not much. But if you're putting video onto YouTube and, by extension, your Google site for business purposes, or you are concerned about communicating a certain level of competence even with something that's clearly personal, you might be worried about, frankly, embarrassing yourself.

Having had pretty solid experience with corporate use of online video, we have a few recommendations for avoiding regrets, including the following:

✦ **Make a sincere effort:** Be careful and attentive about what you're doing. Start early. Don't do something rushed — pressure removes options and worsens decisions. Time pressure is just about the only thing that will make you create and post something you really regret later. (That's "really regret" as opposed to "being mildly embarrassed by," which is common and often endearing.)

✦ **Just do it:** In corporate video, all that matters is having the person with knowledge or news conveying it into the camera with sincerity and their own inherent dignity. The person may be stiff, boring, poorly dressed, standing at an odd angle, in front of a weird background, and so on. It doesn't matter all that much. Get the "doer" talking and you're golden.

✦ **Everyone gets better with practice:** Production people, cameramen and women, the people doing compression and uploading, onscreen "talent" — everyone involved gets better with practice. Which means the initial efforts are likely to be fairly bad in one way or another. Don't worry; just give the effort a bit of time, be sincere, and get on the learning curve.

Finding free content

The best place to look for free content is US Government Web sites. The government takes the view that everything it creates is paid for by the US taxpayer, so most things that aren't secret are released without copyright. (This is itself a bit brave because, as the open software people have found out, in today's world there's no such thing as "no copyright," and offering things for free can expose you to liability.)

So if you're looking for clip art — or, in this case, clip video — US Government Web sites are a good place to look. You can use a Google restricted search to help. For instance, to find a Windows Media movie file, we type the following into Google's search box:

```
.wmv site:*gov
```

This searches for a Windows movie file — a file with the file extension .wmv, which isn't readily displayed in recent versions of Windows — on sites whose URL ends in .gov, which is supposed to mean a US Government site. (The people who provide you the domain name don't check, so you could get a .gov site tomorrow if you wanted — but don't. Why confuse people?)

You can even focus your search by adding qualifiers to it. Try adding terms like NASA, dolphin, or skiing to your search. You'll be amazed by what turns up. (Did you know that groupers — a kind of fish — and Moray eels hunt together? Neither did we!)

We've seen very ordinary corporate executives become quite compelling performers through effort and practice. Even those who don't improve much get a strong reception just by saying what they know and believe with clarity and sincerity. The same applies to you, whether you're inside or outside the corporate world. Just say something you believe into the camera, and give yourself time to learn a bit as you go through the technical steps of editing, uploading, and deploying your video.

In the early days of technology, it was easy to laugh at the low standards and poor quality of, say, broadcast-quality video compared to the wonders that would soon be unleashed by digital technology. But those broadcast engineers were actually coaxing some pretty good quality out of their admittedly poor equipment and delivery channels.

As mentioned previously, YouTube, in order to host millions of videos for free without losing vast amounts of money, "steps on" its videos quite hard in the process of compressing them during upload. Most YouTube videos look pretty ugly.

This lowers the bar for you. People don't expect great quality in online video. Just make a sincere effort and give yourself time to redo things that really don't work, don't post a video that really turns out badly, and try to do a better job next time.

With practice, you may find that you and the people you work with can start to raise that low bar by creating ever-improving videos.

Consider uploading any video clip you can find — even any old WMV file, in the case of Windows, lying around on your computer — and publishing it in a practice Web page just to get a feel for the process. This lowers the learning curve so you're more ready when you have real video that you need to get up in a hurry.

Follow these steps to upload a video to YouTube:

1. **Identify a video file that you can use for experimentation or that you actually want to publish.**

   See the sidebar, "Finding free content," for tips.

2. **Save the file to your hard disk.**

3. **Visit YouTube at www.youtube.com.**

4. **Sign in using your Google account.**

   The screen changes slightly to include more options, including an Upload button in the upper-right corner.

5. **Click Upload⇨Video File.**

   The other option besides Video File, Quick Capture, is for using a Web cam; if you have one. You should experiment with that as well.

   The Video File Upload screen appears, as shown in Figure 2-11.

6. **Click Browse.**

   The Choose file dialog appears.

7. **Navigate to your video file and click the Upload Video button.**

   The file is uploaded to YouTube while the Video File Upload dialog appears, as shown in Figure 2-12. You now enter text associated with your video file — called *metadata*, data that accompanies the video.

A key purpose for metadata is to support search, a key focus, of course, for anything Google does. Keep in mind that Google has no way of knowing the names, places, dates of filming, colors of clothing worn, or anything else about your video, even things any three-year-old would instantly know; you have to tell Google these things in the metadata.

8. **Enter a Description for the video.**

   The Description appears in YouTube. Enter a brief description that accurately represents the video. Include keywords that someone might use to search for the video.

9. **Enter Tags for the video.**

   Enter any keywords that don't appear in the Description.

Figure 2-11:
YouTube
helps you
find a video
file.

Figure 2-12:
Get the
metadata
right for
your video.

10. **Enter a Category for the video.**

    This may matter, but we haven't observed much use of video categories on YouTube.

11. **Choose a Privacy level.**

    Sharing your video with the world is the easier option and means you don't have to manage access, but you also have the choice of making it Private, restricted to 25 named people.

12. **Click Save.**

    The data will be saved.

13. **Click Sharing Options.**

    The URL and embedding code for the video appears.

14. **Keep the window open for embedding your video in a Google Sites Web page.**

There are many, many things you can do with a YouTube video besides embed it in a Google Sites Web page, and hundreds of things to know about creating, uploading, and organizing your videos. We encourage you to do all of these things, but in this chapter is just the bare minimum you need to know to use YouTube with Google Sites.

Embedding YouTube Videos in Your Web Page

It sometimes seems everyone wants to use video on the Web. As a Google Sites user, you have it very easy.

Follow these steps to embed your YouTube video in your Google Sites Web page:

1. **Follow the steps in the previous section to upload a video to YouTube.**

2. **Open a separate Web browser window and open your Google Sites Web site in it.**

3. **Click Edit Page to edit the page.**

4. **Click Insert➪Video➪YouTube.**

    The Insert YouTube Video dialog appears, as shown in Figure 2-13.

5. **Copy the URL (not the HTML) from your YouTube video and paste it into the Paste the URL of Your YouTube Video field.**

6. **Specify whether to include a border.**

Figure 2-13:
Bring the
power of
YouTube to
your site.

Videos are graphically distinctive enough that you probably only need a border if there's a lot of white space in the video. (That's rare, but a very good trick for conserving bandwidth.)

7. **Specify whether to include a title, and enter one if you want.**

   A title can help the user decide whether to play the video.

8. **Click Save to finish inserting the video.**

   As with other embedded documents (see previous chapter), a graphic representing the video appears in the Web page. If you click the graphic, a dialog with options for the embedded document also appears.

9. **Change the options as needed: Click Properties to revise the options in the Google document Properties dialog box, which are the ones described in Steps 6 and 7 earlier; click L (the default), C, or R to align the contents left, center, or right; and turn Wrap On or Off (Off being the default). Click Remove to remove the inserted document.**

   The alignment and wrap choices don't affect videos much.

10. **Click Save to save the document and see the live content, as shown in Figure 2-14.**

The simplicity of these steps might obscure the power of the process. Google has made something very easy that, until quite recently, was very difficult, time-consuming, and expensive: compressing video, uploading it to the Web, hosting it there, and letting people access it without paying big download charges — indeed, with no download charges at all. Then it enables you to easily embed it in a Web page for playback.

Sensible use of video in your Web pages can make a tremendous difference in the usefulness and interest offered by your Web page. The bare mechanics described here are only part of the process. Take advantage of the ease of use and power offered by YouTube and Google Sites to start using video as soon as you can.

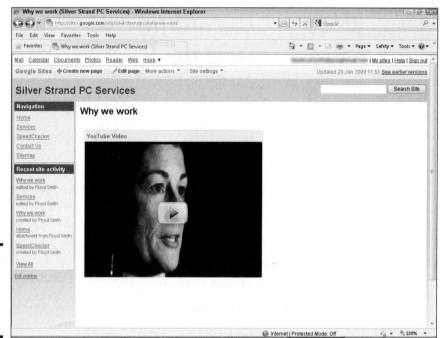

Figure 2-14:
Bring video
to life in
your Web
page.

What about Google Video?

One of the options for inserting video in a Google Sites Web page is Google Video. (The other, of course, is YouTube.) Why don't we say more — okay, why don't we say anything — about Google Video?

Early in 2009, Google decided to stop accepting new videos on Google Video (a service Google had launched before it acquired YouTube). Clearly, YouTube is the winner over Google Video, not only on the World Wide Web as a whole but within Google as well.

Chapter 3: Adding Google Gadgets to Your Web Site

In This Chapter

✔ Understanding what Google Gadgets offer your Web site

✔ Using Gadgets for fun and for work

✔ Finding Google Gadgets

✔ Making Google Gadgets

✔ Adding Google Gadgets to your Web page

The dream of being able to add real programming code to your Web site has long been an elusive one. Programming would give you all the advantages of software running on a standalone PC, combined with all the flexibility, collaboration, and communication made possible by the Internet and the Web.

But there have been almost as many challenges as successes. In the early days of the Web, Java was touted as the cure to all Web programming problems — until it was finally realized that Java is better for programming across networks than on actual Web pages. So the name JavaScript was invented for a scripting language that's basically unrelated to Java.

In recent years, JavaScript has been combined with an advanced coding standard called XML, for eXtended Markup Language — a cousin of HTML — to form Ajax, or Asynchronous JavaScript and XML. (JavaScript is always asynchronous — that is, it runs in your Web page separately from any code running on the back-end server — so the word was apparently added just to create a good acronym.)

If you want to know more about both Java and JavaScript, visit java.net, "The Source for Java Technology Collaboration." The diagram in Figure 3-1 is a simplified version of the interaction among JavaScript, XML, and a few other "players" for making Web applications work.

Sorry to have gotten all technical on you here — the point is that there's finally a useful, highly functional way for experts to program Web pages. Ajax is at the heart of what's called Web 2.0, with Web-based programs such as Google Apps and Picasa Web Albums, described in the last chapter. (We find it pretty amazing that Picasa Web Albums allows you to drag and drop files in a Web page!)

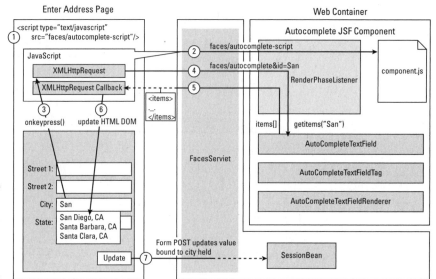

Figure 3-1:
If you squint, this diagram explains it all.

All this new technology is used to make Google Gadgets, pre-built small applications, and support your ability to drop them into the Web site you're creating. Not only are Google Gadgets available for your Web page, you can put them on your desktop, in your personalized iGoogle page (see the following sections), in your Blogger blog, and so on. So you and your users have the opportunity to put Google Gadgets to work wherever you need them.

In this chapter we discuss using Google Gadgets in your Web site.

Using Google Gadgets

For a while, the "easy" way to get programming into your Web page was to learn at least a bit of JavaScript. Then you could search various online libraries of scripts that would, when pasted into your Web page, run as small programs. But you had to know at least some HTML and some JavaScript to position the code in your Web page and to make minor but crucial changes to customize the script. If you got stuck, you had to either give up or keep learning more JavaScript until you solved the problem.

Many of the most interesting things you could do with JavaScript required Java or other code running on the Web server. This was not easy for Web hosts to offer. Having code run on their servers caused all kinds of problems. And it was nearly impossible for many Web publishers, who were now being required to learn and use two different programming languages to get even simple programs to run within their Web pages. Many became expert — experiencing all sorts of problems along the learning curve(s) — but most simply never bothered to try.

Today, though, an increasing number of online Web site construction tools offer drop-in Web applications that you just drag and drop into your Web page. Google's Gadgets are perhaps the best example, and they are constantly being added to and improved on by Google and others.

These drop-in Web applications are actually much better than any alternative because with them the code that runs on your Web page can be easily synchronized with any code running on the server; the online Web site construction tool has control of both the Web page and the back end. So everything can work easily and smoothly, giving you a tremendous amount of capability.

Figure 3-2 shows a Web page of Google's Gadgets. At current count there are over 50,000 on Google's site alone. That's because Google develops only some of them — developers and users create the rest. Finding the right one is tough, but it's great to have so many great resources out there.

Figure 3-2:
Google
Gadgets are
proliferating.

Using Gadgets in a "Proper" Web Site

Unfortunately, Google Gadgets and other drop-in Web applications aren't often used on customer-facing company sites or other organizational Web sites. Both the look of the applications and their functionality can seem too playful and fun to fit in the serious environment of a customer-facing Web site.

The look of such applications is improving. The applications that make up Google Apps, for instance, are obviously quite professional-looking. (Whereas the look of Google Earth shows some of that playfulness I was mentioning.)

The Ajax programming community is looking to up its game. You can find a great article on Ajax design issues at `www.dummies.com/how-to/content/addressing-ajax-design-issues.html`.

Still, progress is gradual. Bigger companies have the resources to create their own applications with what is usually a tasteful and restrained onscreen appearance, well integrated with the carefully designed page they fit into. The somewhat more garish look of a drop-in Web application, combined with the less carefully designed look of the surrounding Web page, doesn't stand up very well against a corporate site.

But with Google Sites and Google Gadgets, you have a reasonable chance of coming up with a good-looking and smoothly functioning mix of Web page and drop-in Web application. And site visitors, experienced with Facebook and online tools such as Picasa Web Albums, are becoming more tolerant of interfaces that may be a bit rough around the edges but allow them to get lots of great things done.

So do try using drop-in applications in a customer-facing Web site. But if you have a personal site, hobby site, intranet site, or so on, the sky's the limit. These sites can set aside branding in favor of getting things done and even — whisper it, now — having fun.

Just to show how serious Google Gadgets are getting, Lotus now supports the use of Google Gadgets as Lotus Notes plug-ins. Notes is considered a very serious corporate data processing tool, so for Notes to host Google Gadgets is amazing — and a big step forward toward having them taken seriously.

The interface for searching for Google Gadgets at the Google Gadgets directory page (refer to Figure 3-2) is not very good; use the lists and instructions here to identify Google Gadgets separately so you can quickly insert the right ones into your Web page.

Is there any competition?

Yes, Google Gadgets face stiff competition from Lotus Widgets, which are based on a tool called Konfabulator originally developed for the Macintosh. Lotus Widgets are often quite visually appealing. Also, having been around longer, there are a lot of them. However, Google Gadgets have more underlying power, with all the capability of Google Search available, and more momentum. So you won't go far wrong with Google Gadgets — but if you are really interested in Lotus Widgets, you might try them, too.

Official Google Gadgets for work

Google Gadgets do all kinds of things. In this section we include our list of the ten best "serious" Google Gadgets, developed by Google itself, which you might want to consider for a customer-facing site or intranet.

Why do you want Google Gadgets developed by Google? There are several reasons worth giving some thought to:

✦ The design of Google's Gadgets has a crisp, clean look suitable for business.

✦ If you're starting out with Google Gadgets, the implication that they are reliable is reassuring.

✦ Many of the most popular gadgets are from Google.

✦ As a Google Sites user, you want to get the most out of your investment by learning all things Google.

To find these gadgets, just search for the gadget by name while creating your Google Sites Web page.

Here is our list of the ten best official Google Gadgets that are on the more serious side:

✦ **Google Search:** This might seem old hat to you, because you may already have the Google Toolbar or use the Google Chrome browser, both of which allow you to search from within your Web browser. But it's a big hassle to get to Google Search from within a Web page. So consider offering Google Search.

✦ **Google Blog Search:** Google Blog Search can be useful in many ways, but particularly for users of Google Apps. Blogs are a major support tool for Google Apps, so having a way to search only within blogs is very powerful.

✦ **Google Map Search:** Travel is part of business, and Google Map Search can help support travel. For an intranet, consider creating a travel page with Google Map Search, local transit and traffic information, and so on. (Also available: the Driving Directions Google Gadget.)

✦ **Translate my page:** This is a very popular tool for letting non-English-speakers use your English-language Web page — for example. The translations are good enough to get most of the meaning of any page, although subtleties are likely to be lost.

✦ **Google Talk:** Another official Google Gadget, this instant messaging tool may seem more like fun, but people are finally realizing that collaboration is very powerful for business as well. This is almost a necessity for a Google Site, which tends to emphasize collaboration anyway. How can you not want a quick, easy, free way for users who have a Google account — which tend to be most of your users — to collaborate by instant messaging?

✦ **Google Calendar:** Just another way to get your public Google Calendar on your site — or to take the calendar that's on your site already and put it more places. Managing time is a crucial business concern.

✦ **Google Reader:** Google Reader is one of the best of many available RSS feed readers — tools for accessing news and other updates from right across the Web. There's so much going on with RSS feeds that a feed reader is an important tool. With the right feeds, Google Reader can become an important part of your Web site.

✦ **To-Do List:** This is a useful tool that can be shared among teams as well.

✦ **Sticky notes:** This surprisingly powerful tool gives you reminders, important Web content, and so on.

✦ **Google Docs:** This is a list of active Google documents, especially valuable for teams.

Figure 3-3 shows a few Google Gadgets in use in iGoogle just so you can get a feel for them. Note their crisp, clean — and work-friendly — appearance. You should definitely try these before deploying them in a Web site.

Google and non-Google Gadgets for fun

Now, here are six official Google Gadgets that are more fun-oriented (see Figure 3-4):

✦ **Google News:** People love to keep up, and this is a customizable gadget that allows you to choose exactly what news is shown.

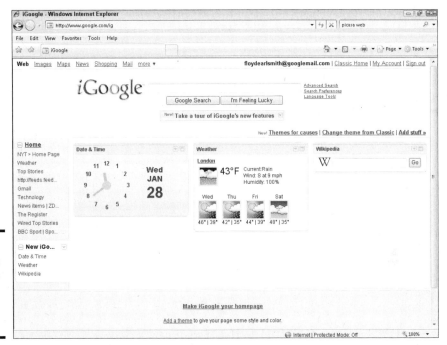

Figure 3-3:
iGoogle is a
great place
to preview
Google
Gadgets.

✦ **Google Finance Portfolios:** This great tool for investors or just the financially literate is also a possible candidate for work use in companies with stock listed on the exchanges.

✦ **YouTube Gadget:** This gadget shows the top YouTube videos at any given time. Users can also browse YouTube and play videos they find, all without leaving your site. Although there is useful, work-related stuff on YouTube, there's also enough silliness and, sometimes, obscenity to disqualify a YouTube Gadget from most "serious" Web sites, but it's great on a fun site.

✦ **Sports Scores:** This update is great for sports fans. If you use it as a substitute for visiting sports sites, it's a time-saver. If you use it as an alert that makes you go visit sport sites, it's a time sink.

✦ **Color Junction:** A puzzle game from Google? Those of us who think Google leaves some of their offerings in beta for too long might wish they weren't fooling around creating puzzles. . . .

✦ **Eyes:** An early hit, this Google Gadget features eyes that follow your cursor around the screen. You might put this on a separate "fun" page, as it could prove distracting on a page where one was trying to do work.

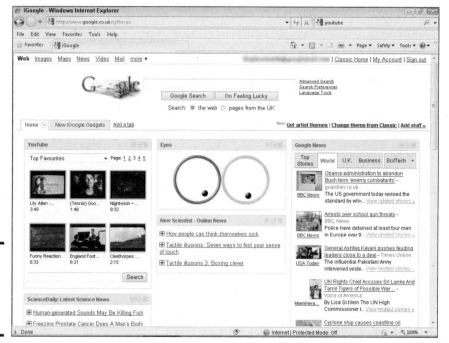

Figure 3-4:
Fun Google
Gadgets
liven up
your page.

Here are a few third-party Google Gadgets that are especially suitable for fun — and even possibly usable on a business site:

✦ **Quotes of the Day:** These are humorous quotations — a way to have fun with a bit of learning tossed in as well.

✦ **Joke of the Day:** Comedy Central has a Google Gadget with a joke of the day — again, one of the more acceptable fun sites for the workplace.

✦ **Dilbert:** It's been proven that people learn more when they're having fun, and Dilbert is a good way to do it — and the most acceptable comic strip in most workplaces as well. (Except the ones where the boss is really touchy or has two peaks of pointy hair.)

✦ **Amazon Top Sellers:** This is a fun and useful Gadget that shows the top-selling books in 35 categories of Amazon.com. Because the list changes all the time, this is not only useful, it's lively. And you can click an item to get pricing, ratings, and availability information. We find this useful not just for finding a book, but for quickly knowing what people are talking, thinking, and writing about.

Most popular categories

The most popular categories for Google Gadgets, according to blogger Niall Kennedy, are:

✔ Tools — for productivity

✔ Fun and Games, such as Tetris

✔ Lifestyle, such as photo of the day or YouTube videos

These three categories total 80% of tools. The remainder fall into News, Technology, Communication, Finance, and Sports.

Check out his findings at: www.niall kennedy.com/blog/2007/03/ google-gadgets-statistics.html.

Finding Google Gadgets

Most of us want to know what the most popular Google Gadgets are as a starting point. Luckily, Google keeps just such a list handy.

Follow these instructions to reach the Google Gadgets Most Users list:

1. **Visit the iGoogle Web site at www.igoogle.com. Sign in if needed, using your Google account.**

   The Web site appears.

2. **Click the Add Stuff link.**

   The iGoogle Gadgets home page appears, as shown in Figure 3-5.

3. **Click the Most Users link.**

   A list of Google Gadgets appears, beginning with the ones with the most users on down.

In addition to the Most Users category, definitely check out Hottest; Newest; Editor's Picks; and the specific categories you're interested in. But starting with Most Users means you won't miss things that millions of other people are already benefitting from, and it gives you a standard of comparison for other Google Gadgets you may find.

Figure 3-5:
iGoogle
presents
the latest
Google
Gadgets.

There are some other places you might check as you pursue useful Gadgets:

✦ **Top 7 Google Gadgets for Productivity:** About.com's take on which Google Gadgets help you get things done. It's just as useful for the commentary as for the list — which includes a few paid-for gadgets and, oddly, a calorie counter. See the list at:

```
http://google.about.com/od/toolsfortheoffice/tp/gadgett
picks.htm
```

✦ **10 Best Google Gadgets For Your Blog:** Worth looking at for the Countdown Gadget alone. A great list for bloggers, but also for anyone. This list represents one well-informed person's opinion. Visit it at:

```
www.quickonlinetips.com/archives/2008/03/10-best-
google-gadgets-for-blogs/
```

✦ **2006 Google Gadget Awards (for university students):** It seems that Google did this only once — unless the Google search engine is letting us down. But it's worth looking at what was chosen and reading the descriptions to get an idea as to what's possible. See the best of the students' work at:

```
www.google.com/intl/en/events/gadgetawards/winners.html
```

Making Your Own Google Gadgets

There are two ways to create a Google Gadget. One way is to use a simple form interface to customize an existing Gadget with your own content.

To get started, go to the Make Your Own Gadget page, as shown in Figure 3-6, on Google:

```
http://www.google.com/ig/gmchoices
```

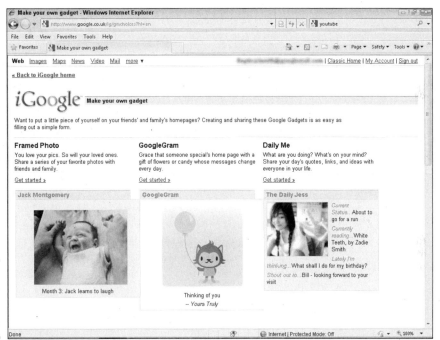

Figure 3-6:
Making your
own Gadget
can be easy.

Customize one or more of the following to make your own gadget:

✦ **Framed Photo:** Put your name and stream of photos into a Gadget. Fantastic for grandparents, other family members, and friends. Also useful for team-building in a work environment.

✦ **Daily Me:** An update of messages from you — a really nice alternative to Facebook, Twitter, and other ways of staying in touch. Also a great way to send project updates!

✦ **Free Form:** Combine text and images in interesting ways. Another possibility for project updates.

✦ **YouTube Channel:** Now this is where you can put YouTube to work. Create your own YouTube channel of relevant videos, avoiding all the distracting stuff on YouTube.

✦ **Personal List:** Publish a To Do list — perfect for project management.

✦ **Countdown:** This is an easy way to customize the popular Countdown Google Gadget.

If you're brave, you can make a "real" Google Gadget from the ground up. Start with the Gadgets page on Google, as shown in Figure 3-7, or visit:

```
http://code.google.com/intl/en/apis/gadgets/index.html
```

Figure 3-7: Google offers many ways to make a Gadget.

You have a choice of three methods:

✦ **The easy-to-customize Gadgets:** These are the Gadgets described in the Make Your Own Gadget page.

✦ **The Google Gadgets Editor:** This editor uses an older, "legacy" Application Programming Interface, or API, and offers an interactive tool for creating some very capable Gadgets.

This is not necessarily easy, however. If you easily understand the phrase, "The legacy gadgets API has been "renamespaced" into the gadgets.* JavaScript namespace," then the Google Gadgets Editor may be a cakewalk.

✦ **The new, more capable Gadgets API:.** This API also supports something called the OpenSocial API.

The important thing for most readers of this book is not to learn to use either of the APIs — though using the legacy API in the Google Gadgets Editor is tempting. The point is to understand what you might be able to get a technically oriented person on your team, or a developer you hire in, to do. It looks like the answer is: Quite a bit!

Inserting Google Gadgets in Your Web Page

Now that you've seen many of the most popular Gadgets — only a tiny fraction of all those you can find — you have a pretty good idea what they can do for you. It's time to try one or more on your site.

We say *try* in deference to the old Latin phrase, *de gustibus non disputandum* — in matters of taste there's no argument, or, as many people put it, there's no accounting for taste.

Google Gadgets are likely to produce strong reactions from people — to be regarded as tools by some and toys by others. So put one or more Google Gadgets in your site and then try them out on people; give yourself time to find a different way to do things if the Google Gadgets answer isn't acceptable.

Don't wait until you're in the middle of editing your Web page to go looking for the Google Gadget you want. Use the lists and tips above to identify the Google Gadget you want before you need it.

Follow these steps to insert a Google Gadget:

1. **Follow the steps described previously in this chapter to identify or even create the Google Gadget you want. Open a Web browser window showing the Google Gadget you want — its name or its URL.**

2. **Open a separate Web browser window and open your Google Sites Web site in it.**

3. **Click Edit Page to edit the page.**

4. **Click Insert⇨Recent Posts. You can also select one of the other choices there: Recently Updated Files, Recent list items, Text Box, or More, as shown in Figure 3-8.**

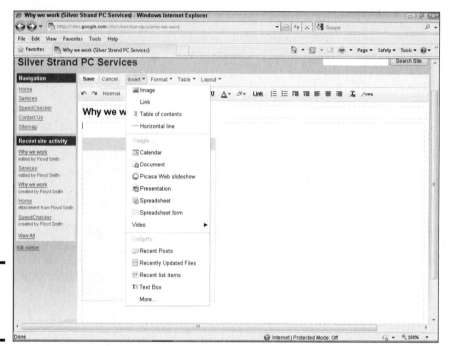

Figure 3-8:
Time to
insert your
slideshow.

Choose one of the convenient items listed, which draw from an existing announcements page (Recent Posts), file cabinet (Recently Updated
Files), or list page (Recent list items); or choose More to insert an item
from the wide list of available Google Gadgets described earlier.

The "canned" choices, in most cases, draw on resources within Google
Sites that are best suited to shared files and information in an intranet.
The More option gives you a choice from Google Gadgets that are more
likely to be pertinent to a publicly facing Web site.

5. **(For this example, we show what happens if you choose More.) A list
   of Gadgets appears, as shown in Figure 3-9.**

6. **Rather than clicking links, enter the name of a Google Gadget you've
   found in a separate browser window — see Step 1 in this list — and
   click Search. Alternatively, enter the URL of the Google Gadget if you
   have it.**

   Select your Google Gadget and the Set Up Your Gadget dialog box
   appears. Or, if you've entered a URL, the dialog box appears directly.

   An example, for the Official YouTube Gadget, is shown in Figure 3-10.

Figure 3-9:
Here's
where you
search for
a Google
Gadget.

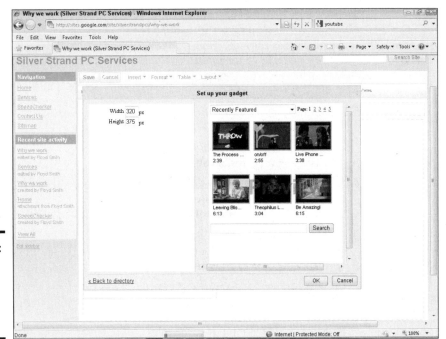

Figure 3-10:
Here's
where you
forest up
a Google
Gadget.

7. **Enter the Width and Height of the window.**

   When in doubt, use the recommended values because they are likely to have been chosen to be as small as reasonably popular for the content. You can always resize the Google Gadget later.

8. **Click Save to finish inserting the Google Gadget.**

   As with other embedded documents (see previous chapter), a graphic representing the Google Gadget appears in the Web page. If you click the graphic, a dialog with options for the embedded document also appears.

9. **Change the options as needed: Click Properties to revise the options in the Google document Properties dialog box, which are the ones described in Step 6; click L (the default), C, or R to align the contents left, center, or right; and turn Wrap On or Off (Off being the default). Click Remove to remove the inserted document.**

   The alignment and wrap choices don't affect many Google Gadgets much.

10. **Click Save to save the document and see the live Gadget, as shown in Figure 3-11.**

Now show the new page around, and get people's opinions on the Gadget. Be open-minded, but do your best to make sure that your Web site ends up with the functionality you chose the Gadget for.

Figure 3-11: YouTube — or another Gadget — in your site.

Chapter 4: E-Commerce with Google Checkout

In This Chapter

✔ Understanding e-commerce and Google Checkout

✔ Determining whether you should use Google Checkout

✔ Exploring Google Checkout's features

✔ Signing up for Google Checkout

✔ Adding a Buy Now button to your Web site

With Google Gadgets, as described in the previous chapter, you can achieve the dream of adding programs — even customized ones — to your Web site. Google Checkout helps you pursue an even bigger dream, one that's been even more out of reach: adding e-commerce.

E-commerce has a rich and checkered history. Amazon.com is the archetypal example of a successful e-commerce site — and has, in fact, helped a lot of other, smaller e-commerce businesses through its Amazon Marketplace partnerships.

But for every Amazon.com, there are several examples like Pets.com. Pets.com was intended to be an online store for pet food. It never took off; somehow the expense of paying perhaps $20 for shipping a $20 bag of dog food didn't appeal to many people.

Dreams of e-commerce riches can make success seem so easy; yet it can be so hard.

The stopping point for many of those dreams was that people didn't have the time, money, or expertise to build an e-commerce system for their site — an expenditure that, in the early days of the Web, could reach or exceed $1 million. Now, with Google Checkout, you can get an even better, more trusted capability nearly free.

The sad tale of Shopping.com

In our discussion of domain names (see Book IV), we describe how attractive generic domain names were to entrepreneurs — names such as Pets.com, Furniture.com, and of course Shopping.com. Consider the case of Compaq Computer — who in 1999 bought Shopping.com for the incredible sum of $220 million.

It was a private deal, so details were not revealed publicly, but Shopping.com was not very well run, and it had poor sales and little visible profits. In many ways, the purchase of Shopping.com was the most expensive domain name sale in history.

At the time, Shopping.com sold more than two million products and had more than 1,000 merchandising partners. Sounds good — but customers were complaining of inaccuracies on credit card statements, difficulties connecting to the site, and checkout delays.

Compaq, who at the time also owned search-engine giant AltaVista, was determined to combine their resources to turn the company around. The head of AltaVista said that AltaVista and Shopping.com would "fully combine these two capabilities" — search and shopping — "into one synergistic user experience." Nice use of a buzzword there.

No one came out of this well. If a magician had wanted to make billions of dollars disappear the deals around Shopping.com would have been the way to do it. Eventually Compaq sold off AltaVista, which then had to cancel an Initial Public Offering (IPO) of stock a year later, just as the dot-com boom was bursting. AltaVista ended up being sold for less than it paid for Shopping.com.

And Shopping.com still exists, with separate online stores for the US, the UK, Germany, France, and Australia.

Trust, Sales, and E-Commerce

Before you spend time and effort adding Google Checkout or any other e-commerce capability to your site, it's worth spending a bit of time thinking about trust. Frankly, some people still don't trust most online shopping. They're very concerned that the purchase itself is somehow a ripoff, that receiving customer service will be difficult or impossible, that receiving the goods at home (while they're at work) will be too hard, and — most importantly — they fear that their precious credit card details will be lost, stolen, or misused.

There are tiers of trust in the online world. Companies that are well-respected names in the non-online world and that offer nice-looking and easy-to-use shops online, can do well with e-commerce. A relatively small number of online companies have become such big brands that they're highly trusted as well — Dell Computer and, of course, Amazon.com are among the most successful examples.

Sites that are less well-known often find it tough to get started. It can work —
but you need to keep at it, slowly building up confidence and your offering
over time.

In order for your site to use e-commerce successfully, people have to trust
it — a lot. Even then, most people won't buy from your site simply because
they distrust any online shopping, particularly online shopping at smaller
sites — especially if it's obvious from looking at your site that you're new
at it.

Google Checkout is actually a big help in building trust. Because it is a
trusted name, users assume that Google has a lot to lose if people abuse
its checkout system to deliver poor products or poor customer service, let
alone to operate any kind of scam. Sites that use Google Checkout never see
the customer's credit card number. The site can also lose the right to use
Google Checkout if they abuse it (or their customers), and customers can
get a refund from Google in case of fraud. So people seeing Google Checkout
on your site will be more likely to buy from you.

You still need to build up a relationship with customers in order to get them
to trust you enough to get involved in e-commerce. If people regularly visit
your site, receive a newsletter from you, know you or know of you in the off-
line world — all these are starting points for building up online sales.

There's one indicator that can help you know that it's time to "do" e-commerce: People who already visit your site are asking you to add e-commerce
to your site. They like your site and trust it (and, therefore, you) and they
know you have expertise or access to products that they want to buy from
you online.

Google has several success stories on its Web site that give good examples
of successful use of Google Checkout to build up e-commerce — and you
can visit the sites involved to see how they do it! The products represented
range from the top of the line — Diamondgeezer.com, which sells "a girl's
best friend" — to the humble, at Dustbag.co.uk — to the seemingly silly —
Bedworld.net sells beds online. (Shades of dog food sales from Pets.com —
but it is successful.)

The success stories page is shown in Figure 4-1. To learn more, and to check
out the sites themselves, visit `https://checkout.google.com/seller/quotes.html`.

We rarely offer our readers strictly business-related tips, because you know
what you're trying to do online better than any book can tell you. But there
is one business-related tip for e-commerce that can make you a lot of money.
The best place for many businesses and organizations to start with online
sales is with resales or follow-on sales of products to existing customers.

Figure 4-1:
Google
Checkout
has success
stories.

These are people who trust you, who want to deal with you. Like you, they are interested in making the selling/buying process easy. And you know it's worth investing in your relationship with them because they're already customers and, if you do things right, are highly likely to continue to be.

Mentioning these concerns and tips is not to discourage you from doing e-commerce; it's to help you understand that it's not a get rich quick scheme, but instead is an important area of your business, one you're likely to need to build up slowly and carefully. Even today, people may be envious when they hear that you've gotten started in e-commerce, thinking the money will just roll in. But, as you now understand, it's the start of a steady stream of work.

This, and other small starting points for e-commerce, is where Google Checkout is so great. It used to be that you had to "go big or don't go at all". That is, you had to spend perhaps a million dollars up front — which meant you had to spend many more millions to try to make your site a success from day one. Unless you quickly generated tens of millions in sales, you could never pay back the initial investment, let alone keep paying all the employees to build and run the site.

With Google Checkout, your initial investment is so very low — a few hours of your time being the bulk of it — that you really can start small and build. Online resales to your existing customers is probably not, today, a multimillion-dollar business — but with Google Checkout you don't need it to be, you just want a useful and growing one.

How many buyers will you have?

Before you engage in e-commerce — and we're encouraging you, really — it's good to look at all the factors that go into building up your e-commerce business.

For every such business, there's a "sales funnel" that leads to a certain number of online sales. It's similar to the "recruiting funnel" shown in Figure 4-2 — though in the case of a recruiting funnel you're buying, rather than selling, so the process is a little easier on you!

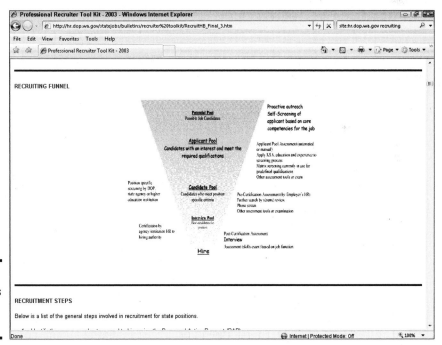

Figure 4-2:
Recruiting is
like selling,
only easier.

Though the details are different for every business, in general the sales funnel for e-commerce goes something like this:

✦ **All potential buyers.** This is the total number of people who might ever buy your product. If you're selling men's shoes in Hawaii, your potential market might be all male Hawaiians over 18.

✦ **Potential buyers who you can reach.** How many of these potential buyers can you get your name in front of? This is where people start making big ad buys — or dreaming up PR stunts. Sacrificing a pair of your best shoes to the volcano at Mauna Loa, perhaps?

✦ **Potential buyers who you can bring to your Web site.** Now, how many of the people you can reach will come to your Web site? Having the right domain name helps, but it can take a lot of offline advertising and promotion — or a very special, and therefore probably loss-making, promotional offer — to drive an online visit. Online advertising is so popular because it drives site visits very effectively.

✦ **Potential buyers who will consider buying online from you.** Many Web site visitors are very much "just looking" and rarely or ever consider e-commerce or they reserve their buying for a few sites they already trust. (Google Checkout will actually increase some people's trust because Google is a well-known and well-liked brand.) The ones who consider buying online from you are a fraction of your site visitors.

✦ **Potential buyers who buy that day.** The potential buyers who are on your site and consider buying, then need to be "converted" into customers by an offer that brings them through the checkout process — which is always a hassle, although Google Checkout makes it as easy as possible.

An example sales funnel

So let's say we, the authors, have written a book about Mauna Loa and want to sell it ourselves, in Hawaii, through our Web site, named `maunaloafire. com`. (Yes, it's available, at least at this writing — see Figure 4-3.) Here's a fanciful example of the sales funnel:

✦ **All potential buyers:** Every adult or teenager in Hawaii, including visitors — let's say 1.5 million people.

✦ **Potential buyers we can reach:** We buy a newspaper ad for the local section of two newspapers, running on three different days across a week, where sales reps assure us that a total of 100,000 people will see our ad. And we buy a Google text ad for searches on the term Mauna Loa, which the Google ad tools tell us 10,000 people will see.

✦ **Potential buyers we can bring to our Web site:** Now the numbers converge. Taking what the ad reps tell us, and cutting their estimates in half just to be safe, we figure 1 in 100 of the people who see our ad will visit our Web site (with its easy-to-remember name, especially so for people in Hawaii). That's 1,000 people. And we figure that 1 in 20 of the people who see our Google ad will click it — that's an additional 500 people. (Yes, we'll be checking to see who buys and who doesn't.)

✦ **Potential buyers who will consider buying online from us:** A book is an inherently credible product, not too expensive nor potentially harmful, and many people have bought books online. Not from us, true, but the cool name of our book — or perhaps we should say, the hot name of our book — and our use of Google Checkout will help. So we figure that, of our 1,500 visitors, 500 will consider buying the book from us.

✦ **Potential buyers who buy that day:** We decide to include a free slice of Mauna Loa obsidian with every book during our advertising/promotion week, which costs us $2 a book. We also give free shipping, so people don't worry about the cost of shipping the obsidian chunk. (Having some kind of time-limited offer greatly increases sales.)

We figure that, if we cheat and include people who come back to the site two or three times before purchase as "buying that day," and quietly extend our one-week offer to two weeks to accommodate slow trigger fingers, about 100 will actually purchase.

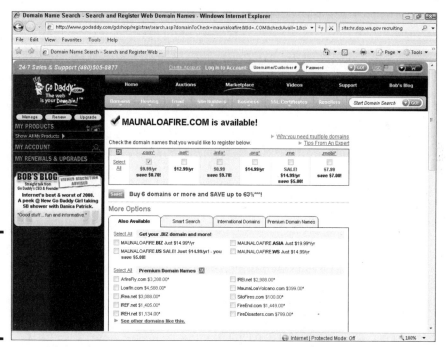

Figure 4-3:
We didn't start the fire — but we can buy the name.

Now when we actually do all this, we can test, test, test. We can see how many people come from the front page of the site — probably from our advertisement — and how many come in through the page that our Google ad links to. We can send them each to a slightly different buying page so we can see our sales success from each approach. And, of course, we can see how many people actually buy, because we have to send them each a book and a rock.

What might our financial results be? Let's leave out our time and costs of writing the book, getting the jacket done, and so on, for the moment — as well as the time and costs of building the site — and just count the per-copy cost of each book. Here are some made-up, but not totally unrealistic numbers:

Newspaper ad:	$250
Cost of 500 Google ad clicks at 10¢ per click:	$50
Cost of 100 books:	$300
Cost of 100 rocks:	$100
Cost of shipping 100 books + rocks:	$200
Google checkout costs at 2%+20¢ each:	$60
Total cost:	$960
Sales at $20/book:	$2,000
Profit:	$1,040

So this initial promotion looks like a pretty good deal for us, going some way toward repaying the cost of writing the book and setting up the site — if our numbers hold up. Using Google tools and careful setup of our site, we can track each path and decide if, for instance, newspaper ads or Google ads are better. They reach largely different audiences, so if each is profitable, we'll do both.

An e-commerce example from BATCS

The BATCS site doesn't sell the book/CD package *Get Rid of your Accent* directly. The book is well-distributed in its target market, the UK, and sales would be quite small compared to the many sales through real and online shops. Figure 4-4 shows the many links to online sales on the BATCS Web site.

Also, BATCS gets a commission through the Amazon.com partners program for sales through Amazon, on top of the selling price of the book. And, finally, there's the risk of diminishing retailer enthusiasm for the book if the other sellers feel the online site is competing with them. (We would need to offer free shipping, signed copies, or other promotions to drive online sales, which would make retailers feel disadvantaged.)

But BATCS does sell courses online. Every month or so, several aspiring speakers of better, less-accented English gather to take courses from the authors.

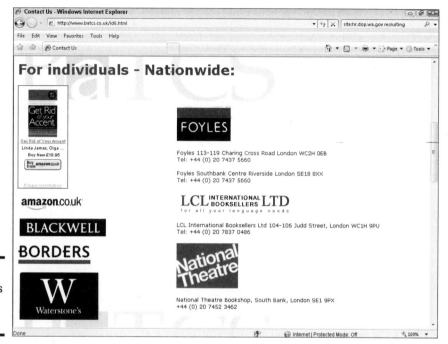

Figure 4-4:
BATCS links
to online
shops.

BATCS advertises through three methods:

✦ **Ads in a local free newspaper, Metro, given away by the hundreds of thousands of copies every weekday morning on the London Underground:** Although the newspaper is free, advertising in it isn't; a small, back-of-the-book display ad, albeit in color, costs a couple of hundred British pounds.

✦ **Google ads:** If a Google user types in *accent reduction*, say, he'll see an ad for BATCS — but only in the UK, where the book and the courses are offered.

✦ **Ads for the course inserted in the book.** This kind of cross-promotion is quite effective — someone has already decided you're credible enough to buy a book from, so they might buy a course from you, too.

The BATCS.co.uk home page lists the upcoming course information right up front. And the Courses page (see Figure 4-5) lists the current course — for current students who want to double-check the course dates and times — and the upcoming one, for prospective students.

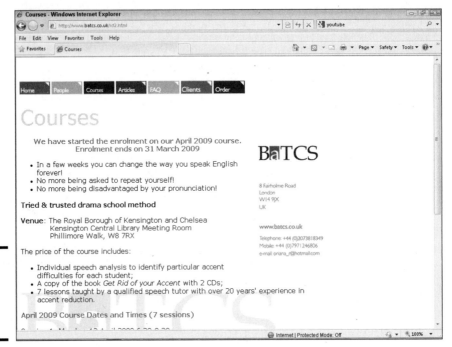

Figure 4-5:
BATCS
mentions
trust right
up front.

Payment is not taken online, but in person. And although BATCS.co.uk, does not take payments directly, it is in a very real sense an e-commerce site.

Your site may be similar. If you do go ahead with e-commerce, you should have similar information leading to buying decisions for your site visitors. The decision as to whether to "do" e-commerce, in one form or another, is different for every site.

Google Checkout Features

Google Checkout offers several key advantages:

✦ **For shoppers:** A single log-in that works for Google services as well as across all the sites that use Google checkout; fraud protection; confidentiality for credit card numbers (even from the merchants the shopper buys from); the ability to hide one's e-mail address throughout the process; and an easy checkout process.

✦ **For merchants (that's you):** All the shopper advantages are good for merchants too, and Google offers fraud protection to merchants; also, AdWords users can use the Google Checkout badge on their ads and receive ten times their Adwords expenditures worth of free processing, after which the cost is 2% plus 20¢ per transaction. (For UK merchants, it's 1.5% plus 15p per transaction.)

Google Checkout also has a type of flexibility that makes a lot of sense for you as a vendor. You can add a Buy Now button to your Web site in about 20 minutes. This takes your customer to the Google Checkout site to complete the transaction. Not very integrated, but very easy — and reassuring to many customers.

You can also use other e-commerce partners in league with Google Checkout. But an even more powerful feature is Google Checkout's Application Programming Interface, or API. This means you, or someone you hire, can completely integrate Google Checkout into your own Web site. Not something you're likely to need on Day One — but a necessity if your online business grows into a real going concern.

Now that you've decided to go ahead with e-commerce, you want to know whether Google Checkout is the best option out there.

The main direct competition to Google Checkout is PayPal, a venerable payment processing service owned by eBay and used by thousands of retailers. (See the home page of PayPal in Figure 4-6.)

Figure 4-6:
PayPal offers convenience — and ties to eBay.

PayPal is not just for credit or debit card processing; it also supports transfers direct from bank accounts and transfers among users, and allows you to store funds with PayPal for use in shopping. (This also gives PayPal a nice pile of money, called a *float*, to earn interest on.) And PayPal works all over the world, not just in the US and UK, as does Google Checkout at this writing. (Buyers using Google Checkout can be from anywhere, whereas merchants must be based in the US or UK. Credit card companies will usually handle any currency conversions needed.)

All this makes PayPal very popular with many people — the company claims over 150 million accounts worldwide — who value its flexibility. But PayPal has its detractors, too — people who find a different method of payment, let alone one that wants to hold onto some of their money, to be, well, weird.

So the correct answer to the question, "Google Checkout or PayPal?" is: Yes. That is, you should eventually consider using both because each has its own fans. (Users have to register to use either service — and, once registered, they'd prefer to keep using that service.)

But Google Checkout does what it says it does and is easier for you and for users. Also, the Google name is better known and trusted outside the somewhat narrow world of e-commerce. So it's the better service to start out with.

If the customers of your growing online business — or people who want to be your customers, but prefer PayPal — start asking for it, you can offer PayPal, too.

Signing Up to Use Google Checkout

If you're going to be offering Google Checkout as a merchant, you want to know what it's like to use it as a customer as well.

Follow these steps to sign up for Google Checkout:

1. **Sign into your Google account at www.google.com.**

   Your Google Account page appears, as shown in Figure 4-7. One of the options is Edit payment method.

   Google doesn't really call attention to Google Checkout for users. It simply treats it as a container for a payment method that can be used for several things, such as paying for AdWords. This is kind of confusing.

2. **Click the Edit Payment Method link.**

   Now you see Google Checkout! The Google Checkout introductory page appears, as shown in Figure 4-8.

Figure 4-7:
Your
purchasing
capabilities
are subtly
shown in
your Google
Account.

Figure 4-8:
Check out
Google
Checkout.

3. **To verify your identity, enter your password and click Sign in.**

   The Welcome to Google Checkout! Page appears, as shown in Figure 4-9.

4. **Enter your credit card, address, phone number, and other needed information.**

   The process is quite streamlined; your users are not going to have a hard time signing up for Google Checkout if they need to do so to buy from you.

5. **Click the Create My Account button. Time to shop!**

Figure 4-9: Welcome to Google Checkout.

Signing Up for Your Account

Now that you've seen the few steps that buyers go through, it's time to do the seller's bit. In this section, we show you how to create a customized Buy Now button for a single product to place on your Web site.

Follow these steps to sign up as a merchant on Google Checkout and create a Buy Now button:

1. **Sign into your Google account at `www.google.com`.**

2. **Go to `checkout.google.com`.**

   The main Google Checkout page appears.

3. **Don't sign in to Google Checkout. Instead, scroll down to the bottom of the Web page, keeping your eye on the middle, Sell with Google Checkout column. Click the link in the middle, *Sign Up Now*, as shown in Figure 4-10. (Note the link of the same name to the left of it, which applies to buying with Google Checkout, not selling.)**

    The Start Selling! page appears, as shown in Figure 4-10. You're asked: Does your business have a Google Account for services like AdWords or Google Mail?

Figure 4-10:
You have to
Account for
yourself to
Google.

4. **Click the button for Yes because you already have a Google Account from other Google services mentioned in this book. (If not, open another Web browser window, sign up for a Google Account, close the window, and return to this window; then click Yes.)**

    You may think you want to create a new account for this service to keep things separate, but Google is about to give you the option of creating a separate account just for Google Checkout. (If you go on holiday, you can use Google Mail to arrange for e-mails relating to Google Checkout to be forwarded to someone who can respond.)

5. **If you want to use your existing account for Google Checkout — the most likely scenario for smaller organizations — click the Yes, We'd Like to Use Our Existing Google Account for Google Checkout radio**

button. (See Figure 4-11.) Sign in as indicated, then go to Step 7. Otherwise, go to the next step.

Note that Google gives you the option of signing in as a different user.

After you sign in, the Tell Us about Your Business screen appears, as shown in Figure 4-13.

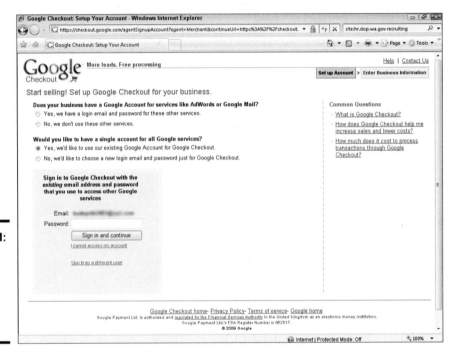

Figure 4-11: Google lets you use your existing sign-in details . . .

6. **If you want to create a new account for Google Checkout — the most likely scenario for smaller organizations — click the No, We'd Like to Choose a New Login E-Mail and Password Just for Google Checkout check box. (See Figure 4-12.) Fill in the blank fields and click Create Account.**

Note that Google gives you the option of reading the Terms of Service and Privacy Policy. Because you will be handling confidential information and money through this account, you may want to give this information extra attention.

After you sign in, the Tell Us about Your Business screen appears, as shown in Figure 4-13.

7. **Enter the information in the Private Contact Information section.**

This is how Google contacts you. Make sure to keep this information updated if you move or change e-mail addresses or phone numbers.

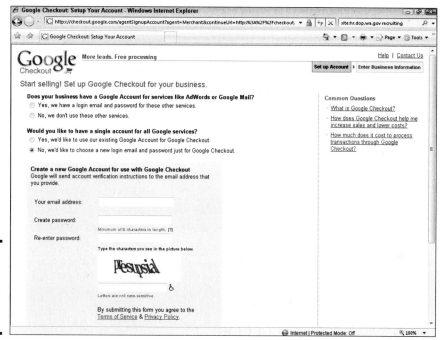

Figure 4-12:
. . . or helps
you create
a new
account.

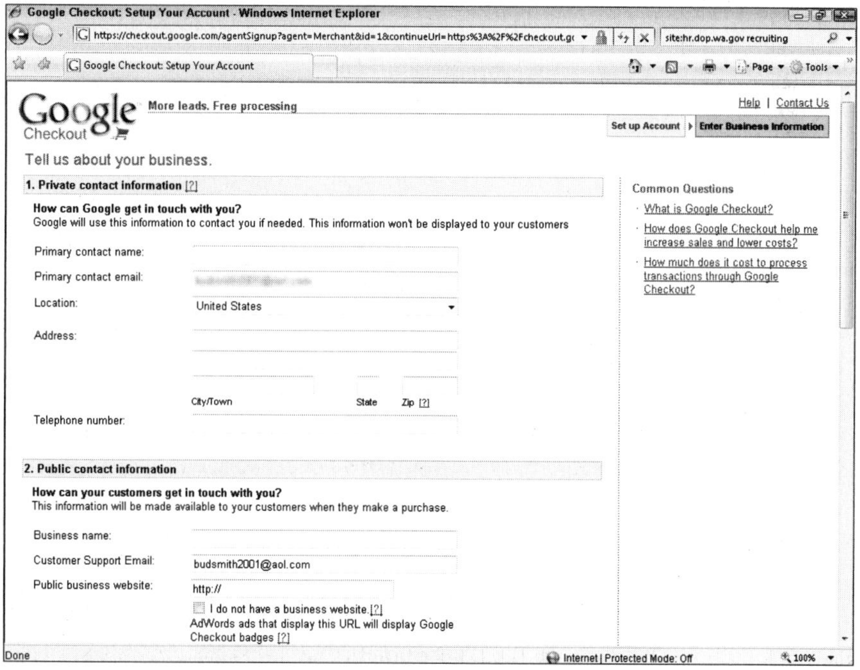

Figure 4-13:
Tell Google
a little
bit about
yourself.

8. **Enter the information in the Public Contact Information section.**

   This is information Google shows to customers to contact you. The most important parts of it are your customer support e-mail address and your Web site address. You also need to specify whether to use the same address as for your private contact information. It may be tempting to use a post office box or other non-personal address, and this is fine as long as you don't introduce unsustainable delays or costs in your interactions with customers. (Also remember that some shipping firms don't ship to PO Box addresses.)

   In the What Do You Want To Be Called on Your Customers' Credit Card Statements? field, use a name that can be used to find your Web site via Google search; this helps your customers keep their business expense reports and taxes straight.

9. **Enter the information in the Financial Information section.**

   This includes your current — not hoped-for! — sales volume, as well as tax-related information. This is information Google shows to customers to contact you. The most important parts of it are your customer support e-mail address and your Web site address. You also need to specify whether to use the same address as for your private contact information. The same cautions that are given in the step above relating to what kind of address and name to use apply.

10. **Review the information in the Terms of Service section.**

    Look at the Terms of Service for your market — United Kingdom or United States. (If you do business in both, you may need to review both.) Also look at the Privacy Policy and Google Checkout Content policies. If you have, or are planning to have, substantial business, consider having your attorney review these before agreeing to them. Also consider both saving these on your hard disk and printing these out and keeping them with other important business papers — if terms change, you are not bound by the new terms, only by the ones you agreed to, unless Google officially notifies you otherwise.

Consider checking the check box to receive newsletters and surveys. Newsletters not only provide potentially important information on a current topic, they also remind you to keep on top of your Google Checkout account.

11. **Click the I Agree to the Terms of Service check box. Then click the Complete Sign Up button.**

Adding the Buy Now Button to Your Web Page

It's been a lot of work to get to this point — but note that the work has been administrative, which any business person can handle, rather than technical, which only a few people can manage.

Now you need to insert the HTML for the Buy Now button into your Web page. This small amount of code causes the graphic for the button to appear and take the soon-to-be-customers to the Google Checkout page to complete their transactions.

Most of your work in Google Sites is done in what's called WYSIWYG mode — What You See Is What You Get. That means you don't see the underlying HTML. But to insert your Buy Now button, you need to get into the underlying HTML for a minute.

Follow these steps carefully to avoid problems when inserting the HTML code:

1. **Keep the window with the HTML code for your Buy Now button open. Select the HTML code and choose Ctrl+C to copy it into the clipboard.**

   You can always recopy the code if you do something else that causes it to be cleared from the clipboard.

2. **Open a separate Web browser window and open your Google Sites Web site in it.**

3. **Click Edit Page to edit the page.**

4. **Put the cursor at the location in the page where you want the Buy Now button to appear.**

5. **Click the HTML button.**

   The HTML for your Web page appears.

6. **Click Ctrl+V to paste the Buy Now button's HTML code into the existing HTML code for your Web page.**

   The button's code appears in the existing page's code.

7. **Click Update to finish inserting the HTML.**

   You return to WYSIWYG mode, but now with the Buy Now button.

8. **Change the options as needed: Click Properties to revise the options in the Google document Properties dialog box, which are the ones described in Steps 6 and 7 earlier; click L (the default), C, or R to align the contents left, center, or right; and turn Wrap On or Off (Off being the default). Click Remove to remove the inserted document.**

   The alignment and wrap choices don't affect videos much.

9. **Click Save to save the document and see the live content.**

Despite the technical step of inserting HTML, this the easiest possible way to integrate e-commerce into your site. Your users now have the ability to buy a product from you, safely and securely. Congratulations!

Chapter 5: Adding a Blog with Blogger

*B*logging is one of the most widely used words relating to creating content for the Web — and one of the most poorly understood.

Blogging relates closely to the original purpose of the Web. When Tim Berners-Lee first designed HTML — HyperText Markup Language — while working at the CERN physics laboratories in the late 1980s, he intended for users not only to visit Web sites but to be publishers as well.

It turned out, however, that even using HTML — as simple as it is — plus the hassles of getting a domain name, securing Web hosting space, and paying for these extra costs were all too much for most people. As Web use exploded, Web publishing seemed to be limited to a smaller and smaller percentage of the audience.

Blogs should be viewed as both a precursor to and part of the same social networking phenomenon as Facebook, MySpace, Flickr, Picasa Web, LinkedIn, and other social networking sites largely built on a Web 2.0 technical foundation. (Blogs, however, predate Web 2.0 by a bit.) Tim Berners-Lee was right to think that people very much wanted to express themselves on the Web, as individuals and as groups; however, the Web needed specialized sites that removed some of the complexity to help them do it.

Now blogs have evolved a bit, not only for personal use but also for business. Some general guidelines can now be offered to help you use them successfully — and, given that Google owns one of the leading blogging tools, Blogger, detailed steps for actually using them can be offered as well.

This chapter is a quick take, with a business focus, on a huge topic. For more information see *Google Blogger For Dummies* by Susan Gunelius (Wiley, 2009).

Where does that ugly word come from?

The word *blog* is a contraction of *Web log*. A *log* is like a captain's log — a set of entries of important or interesting events. With technology, though, it's easy to put the new entries first; the blog reads like a newest-first series of snapshots rather than like a traditional story.

The word *blog* sounds ugly, but it's spawned a whole host of neologia (new words, that is). Bloggers, like other writers, like to try to be verbally clever. Emphasize the word *try* there. For example, *Photoblog*'s meaning is obvious. A *vlog* is a video blog — perhaps that means a blog of sound recordings should be a *slog*? Sorry . . . .

A *microblog* is a blog made up of very frequent, very short entries; Twitter is the leading site for microblogging. Yes, "at the store for milk" is a typical microblog entry, as well as all sorts of far more personal updates that many of us would really prefer not to know about. There have even been recent newspaper columns concerning exactly which personal activities it might, and might not, be appropriate to commemorate with a microblog entry.

Many people use Twitter in a more traditional way, however — to send more important news and updates. The Obama campaign alerted the world to his Vice Presidential choice by text message in just this fashion.

The *blogosphere* is the collective community of all blogs. (Are traditional newspapers and magazines and their contributors now first part of the blogosphere? Discuss . . .)

Taxonomy of a Blog

Figure 5-1 shows a blog for the Phoenix Mars Mission at `http://phoenix.lpl.arizona.edu/blogs.php`. It's shared among different authors and updated irregularly, but the posts that do get made are pretty good.

The Phoenix Mars Mission blog shows some of the main parts of a typical blog:

✦ **Header:** In this case, a photo of Mars, a logo, and title, along with a very brief introduction. ("Researchers and students take on the mission and the world of space exploration," is a rather clumsy way to describe something that occurs between and across worlds . . . There's that blogger attitude again!)

✦ **Entries:** On this blog, entries appear as "teasers" — the title, author name, date, and a few lines on the home page, continuing internally via a "Read More" link. This is a little different from a classic blog, in which the entire current entry resides on the home page. The teaser approach is increasingly popular, but to me is a step away from a true blog and more toward a regular Web site, encouraging selectivity rather than immersion.

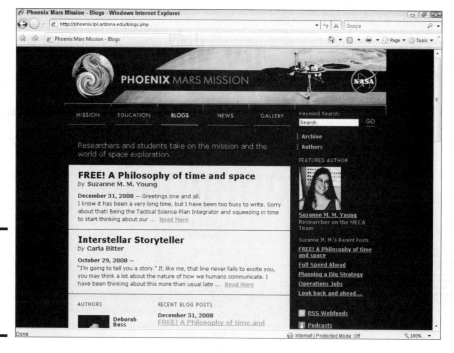

Figure 5-1:
Where no
man — or
woman —
has gone
before.

✦ **Archives:** These are lists of previous posts. In this case, an archive of a specific author's previous posts is right there above the fold, and shown on the right side of the figure; other contributors to this blog and their posts are linked further down the page.

✦ **Comments:** These are almost always found at the end of a blog entry, often requiring the user to sign in and a wait while the comment is reviewed before posting.

✦ **Categories:** The posts on this blog are only characterized by author, but many other categorizations could be used. Be guided by what's useful to site visitors, and don't overdo it.

✦ **Permalink:** In a classic blog, a posting starts out at the top of the home page, then migrates down the page before being pushed out to the archives. So if someone links to a blog posting that's on the home page today, the link becomes outdated as the intended target migrates away. A permalink is a pointer to the long-term home of a post deep within the archives, its permanent location — rendering the link permanently valid. Thus the name.

Why Blogs Are So Popular

Blogs are used to capture people's thoughts and experiences, whether in work or in student or personal life. A *crossover* blog covering a major Antarctic research project led by Bill Hanshumaker of Oregon State University is shown in Figure 5-2; note that he just happens to use Blogger, and that his blog offers lots of interesting photos.

Figure 5-2: Breaking the ice on Blogger.

The key points that make blogs distinctive and popular are

✦ **Little setup hassle:** The domain name, hosting, and so on are easily set up; as a blogger, you pay nothing (for Google Blogger, for instance) or a small monthly fee.

✦ **Little design work:** At least when starting out, you don't need to do much design or arrangement of information when creating your blog. You use a template in which most of these decisions are made once, in choosing the template; then you largely just fill in the blanks.

✦ **Always fresh:** The key innovation of blogs is putting the newest, freshest content right on the home page, and pushing the older postings down the navigation hierarchy. This breaks the tyranny of the home page and saves the user from having to scour a site for new content.

✦ **Personal comments:** Blogs have evolved to be very personal, especially compared to a lot of the marketing fluff on business sites. Blogs that aren't at least somewhat personal seem boring and off-putting to people and quickly lose comments and readers.

✦ **Controlled interactivity:** Commenting on blogs — both in comments that hang off the end of the blog and in whole new blog articles — has proven a powerful way to hold people's interest and build community.

✦ **Journalistic contribution:** Blogs have become part of "real" journalism as well. Reputable newspapers post articles from their print editions online and allow readers to comment; journalists create blogs alongside their print articles; bloggers quote from newspapers and write entire blog entries around the excerpts.

✦ **Technological and social infrastructure:** Blogging matters. People can blog from e-mail, mobile phones, and telephones. Photo blogging, video blogging, and microblogging — short messages via services like Twitter — are all popular. Bloggers are courted by marketers and political campaigns. Even the newest and most unseasoned bloggers know that they're starting something that might become important.

✦ **Good for search engine rankings:** All the fresh, regularly updated content, use of keywords, and interlinking among blogs is mother's milk to search engines — not least Google — which tend to look for these things when adding up search engine rankings.

Personal blogging and work

Blogging is good for your job — but you have to be careful what you do where, and how you do it.

Many companies expressly prohibit using company resources for personal work. It still happens all the time, but it's a convenient hook for disciplinary action — even firing — if one of your blogging entries is considered embarrassing to the company. So don't update your personal blog at work.

Similarly, don't reveal confidential work information on your personal blog. Be careful what you say about colleagues; things you say on your personal blog could be considered harassment at work. Consider not revealing the name of your employer on your personal blog at all. That way no one can assume you're speaking for them.

Do consider letting your boss know about your blog, even if that seems difficult. Letting your boss be sandbagged on it when a concern arises could be worse than telling him yourself.

These are general guidelines; your workplace may have specific rules for blogging. Find out what they are — and also consider rules on e-mail and electronic communications that may apply.

Along with their technical and communications characteristics, there's a certain attitude common among blogs that's hard to define but, if you've spent much time reading blogs, easy to recognize. Fans might call it *empowered*; critics might call it *entitled*. Fans might call it *educated* or *articulate*; critics might call it *elitist*. And on and on.

You can't really criticize bloggers — because in doing so you're just making them feel even more important, and giving them something else to write, speak, video themselves, and otherwise comment about.

Blogs seem to be created to allow people to bring their personality to the online world — but they should not bring personal information as well. It's hard to blog usefully without revealing your name and job title, but leave out information a fraudster could use for identity theft, including: your Social Security, driver's license, passport, or bank account numbers; your birth date, specific birthplace; children's and parent's names; and personal phone numbers (yours and others').

What's Different with Business Blogs

Business blogs are now an entire phenomenon on their own. Given that this book is all about using Google for business, we describe how to use blogs for business and then how to actually begin a blog using Google's Blogger. (From whence it can always be republished on other sites, on your company's Web site, on an intranet, or elsewhere.)

A good online source for information about blogs, including Google Blogger and business blogs, is the For Dummies Web site at `www.dummies.com`. Go to the site and enter *blogs* in the in-site search engine. You'll find a number of useful resources with a nice mix of general information and useful specifics.

What's different with business blogs? Here are some key desiderata we've observed:

+ **Have the right person speaking:** If the intent is an overview of the entire company, the chief executive must be the blogger, not a marketing person who works for him or her; if it's recent technical advances, a key technical contributor must blog, not the person who writes the department's press releases.

+ **Keep it real . . . :** Because blogs are so personal, a business blog must show the personality, interests, and concerns of the person blogging. This goes hand in hand with having the right person blogging; blog visitors have to be able to discern the personality of the blogger.

+ **. . . but keep a bit of control:** Businesses must operate under a thousand constraints. So either the bloggers themselves, or someone assisting them must remove anything truly objectionable or problematic, such as comments that might be libelous or early release of not-yet-announced financial information. But the touch must be very light, or the blog becomes bland, uninteresting, and, all too soon, unvisited.

✦ **Keep it interactive:** The most important element of blogs is the opportunity for readers of the blog to comment at the end. Many people carry out a good part of their social lives in interactions within these comments across a variety of blogging and traditional sites.

✦ **Keep it updated:** Blogs lose all interest when they're not updated. When personal bloggers stops updating their blogs they are, in effect, saying to whatever audience they've built up, "I don't care enough about you anymore to keep doing this." When a chief executive stops updating his blog, he is, in essence, saying exactly that to all the organization's employees!

One of the most popular blogs around, in the technology world anyway, is the Scobleizer blog by Robert Scoble of Microsoft, shown in Figure 5-3. It's largely focused on blogging itself. Scoble's main blog is largely a video blog, but the point isn't great video; it's to record ongoing comments on technology from someone who works in it day in and day out. Scoble also uses Twitter, just to show that the medium is not the whole message here.

Figure 5-3:
Scobleizer uses tech to comment on tech.

Playing defense with blogs

As much as having your own blog(s) can help you, other people's blogs and other social networking comments can hurt you even more. In fact, one of the key reasons for having your own blog is that it provides a great first line of defense when others go after you, your company, or your products.

The classic example is the Intel Pentium bug of the mid 1990s. It was found and first mentioned in online message board comments that millions of Intel Pentium chips had a minor — in engineering terms — bug that would cause certain unlikely but possible mathematical operations to yield incorrect results. By first ignoring and then trying to downplay the problem, Intel inflated it, causing a major drop in its stock price and creating the need for a recall of the affected Pentium chips.

Major corporations now have high-level executives with large teams who do nothing but scan for and respond to online comments about their business. The goal is to respond early, calmly, and with facts, defusing wild rumors and half-truths before they have a chance to spread — and answering real issues substantively before they have a chance to become public relations problems.

An established blog is the perfect place to handle small issues in their entirety and get out an early response on those that later require a larger effort. If you're not already established in the social networking world, you're likely to under-respond at first and then over-respond. With a blog in place, you have the perfect, credible forum for an early and appropriate first response. Online firestorms are like real-world fires — every one is different, and it takes patience, expertise, and experience to manage them down to a successful conclusion.

Planning a Blog

One of the biggest advantages of blogs is their spontaneity and loosely structured nature — loosely structured, that is, in terms of content. The overall format of new daily entries pushing earlier ones down into the blog archives is quite well established. But having a plan for a business blog is actually a good idea.

A plan can help eliminate two of the biggest problems of blogs in general and business blogs in particular: the tendencies of entries to stop for no apparent reason and for the blog to be over-edited and thus bland and boring. (Bland and boring content leads to a lack of feedback, which leads to a lack of willingness to post, which leads entries to stop; so these are related problems.)

So here's a suggested plan for a business blog — based on, for the most part, treating it like any other project:

✦ **Set a main goal for the project:** What's the overall goal of the blog? For a manager, right on up to and including the chief executive, it's usually some variation on: Make the employees in this team/division/company feel more involved. Well then, you'd better keep censorship to a minimum, right?

✦ **Specify measurements toward the goal:** This is where pageviews, number of comments, and so on come in. Remember, pageviews are not usually the goal; they're a measurement of the goal. So don't obsess about the numbers.

✦ **Consider doing measurements before and after:** The employee engagement surveys that are all the rage in companies now are great to take before and after a high-level blog. Although there isn't any way to measure percentages, comments about the blog can be solicited and associated with changes in the numbers.

✦ **Specify a frequency:** Set an intended frequency and a minimum frequency that will be met no matter what.

✦ **Set a start and end date:** The blogosphere seems to collectively believe that blogs should all start several years ago, be updated daily or more, have new features added frequently, and go on forever. But business projects work best with start and, particularly, end dates. Even if you renew the blog after the end date, the ending gives you a chance to take stock, implement changes, and set new goals.

You don't have to take our word for it; an article on the excellent Problogger site (shown in Figure 5-4) makes many of the same points we would — perhaps better. (Another article on the site says you should do something only if it's likely to succeed — or make up a good story if it fails.)

Figure 5-4:
ProBlogger
speaks up
on planning
and more.

Is Blogger right for your project?

Blogger isn't some last-ditch corporate catch-up effort by Google. Blogger was started by Pyra Labs in the late 1990s and was one of the first widely available blogging tools. Free and easy to use from the beginning, it's widely credited for playing a major role in making blogging popular. The business plan was also successful — the famous Silicon Valley "grow like crazy then sell it, and let the acquirer figure out how to make a profit" approach.

Blogger — seemingly, unlike some of the company's projects — is also a strategic part of Google. Owning Blogger seems to have helped make Google better at searching fast-changing blog entries and at supporting its products — support which is now significantly provided in blog form.

So is Blogger right for your project? If you're just getting started, quite likely. Its ease of use and integration with other Google services give it a big leg up. You might decide later that a different tool is better for other projects, but that's just part of your learning curve with any new kind of software, service, or product. Blogger will do the job for any but the most sophisticated needs and won't cause you unnecessary grief.

Here's a brief mock plan for a chief executive's business blog, directed internally:

> Hi team,
>
> Thanks to all of you involved in setting up the new blog for employees and convincing me to do it. As we discussed, our goal will be to make everyone in the company more aware of our business goals for this year and more involved in meeting them.
>
> We've just done the "before" survey, which I'm afraid showed widespread ignorance of and uninterest in the plan. So we've planned quarterly follow-ups to track the improvement we hope to see, and we hope that pageviews for each entry will represent about 10% of the employee population (enough that points from the blog get mentioned in meetings, and so on). We set a rather arbitrary goal of about ten comments per blog entry, knowing that we can't predict what will or won't set off comments.
>
> I've committed to try to add entries as I participate in or learn of events and news that affect meeting or not meeting the plan. This will subtly demonstrate something important I've learned over the years, which is that opportunities to really affect meeting the plan are rare and important. I'll do a catch-up post on Fridays or a "let's go" post on the following Monday.

You've committed to keep review comments to matters of potentially serious legal or financial impact and otherwise "let me be me." The same is true for the comments made by employees. We won't get employees feeling involved if my blog entries — or their comments — read like a press release.

The blog will be launched along with the annual plan — I've already drafted the first entry. It will end in a year, with a wrap-up entry shortly after annual results are announced. I'll then give myself a break from blogging for a good long while — and give all of you a break from reading my blog entries!

Thanks . . .

If I were this chief executive, I'd do my best to meet all of the goals — and then definitely take a break after my year, to increase my focus during the project, to make it more special, and to set the stage for doing it better if I undertook a new project somewhere down the road.

Getting started with Blogger

A blog can be a very important part of, or beginning to, your online presence. We're covering it more briefly in this All-in-One because a Web site is even more important — you can't, for example, use Google Adwords without it. But the brief coverage here is intended only to be a business-oriented introduction. Follow up with the aforementioned *Google Blogger For Dummies* by Susan Gunelius (Wiley, 2009), the For Dummies and Blogger Web sites, and of course all the good information you can find in a Google search.

Actually getting your first blog up is easy — as many people have found, it's the subsequent entries that are hard. Follow these steps to get started:

1. **Visit Blogger at `www.blogger.com`.**

The Blogger home page appears, as shown in Figure 5-5.

2. **Sign into your Google account on the home page.**

The screen labeled 1. Sign up for Blogger appears.

3. **Click the Terms of Service link to view them. (They appear in a separate window.) Then enter your display name and click the check box to indicate that you accept the terms of service. Click the Continue button.**

Figure 5-5:
Blogger's
home page
shows some
of what you
can do.

Your display name is used for your blog posts. You need to choose a name distinctive enough that it's not likely to already be taken and serious enough that you won't be embarrassed about it when you want to point coworkers, friends, and family to one of your blog posts. Also keep in mind you don't want to reveal your employer, place of birth, full name, and so on.

So GiantsFan28 is likely to be something you can live with; DancingQueen42, perhaps not so much.

After you click Continue, the screen labeled 2. Name Your Blog appears.

4. **Enter the title for your blog; this is a headline that appears above your blog. Then enter the blog address; use the Check Availability link to try different options before committing. We suggest you ignore the Advanced Options area for now; if you agree, click Continue.**

As with your display name, the address for your blog needs to be distinctive, not too silly, and not too revealing — kind of like dressing for "casual day" at work. You may want to consider running it by friends, family members, or colleagues, depending on what tone you want the blog to strike.

After you click Continue, the Choose a Template screen appears, as shown in Figure 5-6.

Figure 5-6:
Choosing
a template
can put
angst in
your plans.

5. **Choose from among the dozen templates using the vertical scrollbar to view more templates and the Preview Template link to see what each template looks like. Click the radio button for the template you like and click Continue.**

   It's hard not to spend a lot of time on this screen, but you can indeed always change it. Keep in mind that a black background may be a tiny bit more energy-efficient but is harder to read than a white one; otherwise, just choose the setup you're comfortable with. Not only can you change the template later, you can create a custom template later as well; so you're not stuck with the choice you make here.

   After you click Continue, the Your Blog Has Been Created page appears!

6. **Click the link, Start Blogging, to start using your new blog.**

   The Posting page appears, as shown in Figure 5-7.

   Whether you're writing your first novel or your first blog post, and whether you're using a quill pen on vellum or a fast new laptop, looking at that blank first page is always alarming.

7. **Create your first entry by adding a title in the Title area and text in the main window.**

Figure 5-7:
The
infamous
blank page,
digital
version.

TIP

You can write whatever you like, and you can always edit it later. But we suggest that, for your first post, you try to avoid writing an introduction and statement of intent. Everyone does it — we know we have — and they all tend to sound alike. You can put one in later when you have a better feel for what you want to do.

Instead, try to write a "normal" blog post. That means an entry about recent events or thoughts that fit into the developing theme of your blog. Get right into the swing of things.

8. **Click Save Now to save your precious text. Then try adding a link within your posting: highlight a word or phrase (you can also do this with an image), and then click the Link button. The Hyperlink dialog box appears. Enter the URL of the Web page you want to link to and then click OK.**

The text appears in blue and underlined with a blue line to indicate that it's a link. When your user moves his mouse over the text, the destination URL appears; when the user clicks on it, the Web page corresponding to the destination URL replaces the current window.

Book V
Chapter 5

Adding a Blog
with Blogger

9. **Try the other options on copies of your text: Font name, font size, bolding, italics, text color, alignment (left, center, right, and fully justified), numbered lists, bulleted lists, blockquotes, inserting images, and videos. Click the Edit HTML tab to see the HTML — as shown in Figure 5-8 — and then click the Compose tab to return to the normal view.**

   Your post, of course, changes as you make these changes. You can remove them by deleting the affected text, if it was a copy, or by selecting the affected text and clicking the eraser icon, which removes formatting from selected text.

10. **Click Publish Post to publish your post on the Web. Visit your post, as shown in Figure 5-9, and see if it looks and works as you expect.**

   You will probably see a number of things you want to change. Years of experience with Web sites has taught us to write these ideas down quickly, but completely, or you lose track of them — until they bother you again some time later, at which point you'd better seize the opportunity to write them down.

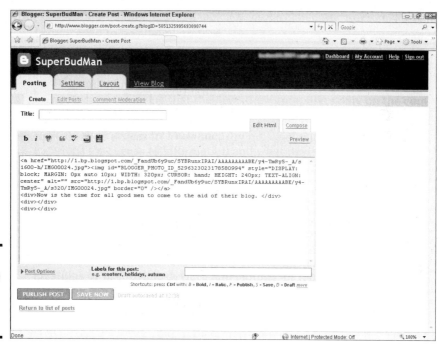

Figure 5-8:
You can see and change HTML even in Blogger.

Figure 5-9:
Even cats
can blog.

Changing settings in Blogger

Although you can learn most of what you need to know about Blogger by trying things, some options may be hard to make sense of without a little explanation — or some changes may be urgent, but require some explanation first.

Many of these high-impact options are on the Comments page, shown in Figure 5-10.

Admirably, the default options put comments at the bottom of your post and allow comments to be made on new posts — which, as a new user, are all your posts. But we recommend you change a couple of other settings relating to comments.

There are three basic strategies for comments to your Blogger posts:

✦ Allow comments to be made and displayed freely.

✦ Allow lots of comments but review and approve them before publication.

✦ Restrict comments to the point where you don't need to manage them.

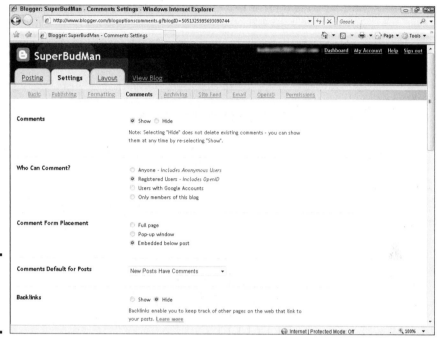

Figure 5-10:
Comments
are key in
Blogger.

The default settings for comments in Blogger tend toward the third option.
Only registered users — those with Google accounts or some others who are
part of something called OpenID — can comment. But comments are unmod-
erated, presumably because having a Google account, or something similar,
somehow imposes some discipline.

This is a restriction that could frustrate you. It would cut you off from commenting unless you signed up for an ID that you may not otherwise need.
And it cuts out just the kind of less-frequent Web users who might have
more interesting comments than those of us who are online all the time. But
if you're overwhelmed with spam — or even genuine comments — this is a
good way to stay on top of it.

The first option — allowing comments to be made and displayed freely —
is, unfortunately, risky in two ways. Not only can people make dodgy
comments — which will tarnish you by association — but spam programs
and other sources can automatically generate junk and put it on your site.

So I recommend the second option — allowing lots of comments, but reviewing and approving them before publication.

To change this, visit the Settings tab in Blogger and choose the Comments area. Then change Who Can Comment to Anyone and Comment Moderation to Always.

This obligates you to visit Blogger regularly to review comments that pile up in your Dashboard — but if you don't review, you have to check even more often to make sure no one (and no machine) has put garbage in your comments area.

Book VI
Google Ads and Analytics

Contents at a Glance

Chapter 1: Introducing Google Ads

In This Chapter

✔ **Exploring what Google ads can offer you**

✔ **Defining an AdWords ad**

✔ **Understanding what makes a good AdWords ad**

✔ **Researching keywords**

✔ **Targeting your ads to your customers**

*A*lthough we tend to forget it now, nearly ten years after its introduction, Google Search is a revolution in the use of the Web. But from its early days, Google, like other search engines, faced the question of how to make money from providing Web search.

Before Google came along, AltaVista was the search engine company that quickly rose to lead the market. It tried a controversial answer to the money-making dilemma: placing paid ads in with search results.

The introduction was rushed, and the paid ads came first — listed before the unpaid, organic search results. It's easy to forget that commerce of any kind had long been banned on the Internet, and even after the ban was lifted, many users frowned on paid ads. When "real" information was displaced by paid information, enough people complained to cause consternation, and the experiment was quickly killed.

Google always claims to put the customer first. So when it introduced paid ads a few years later, it was done more carefully. The first AdWords ads showed up only to the right of the organic search engine listings — so far to the right that, if you narrowed your browser window a bit, you didn't even see them. They were interesting rather than intrusive.

Google also worked very hard on the advertiser experience. It created a tool that made it very easy to create and place ads, and to control the total amount one spent. No need for nasty surprises from unexpectedly large bills.

Google measured the success of AdWords not only by how much money was made, but by whether users liked the ads. It realized that, handled properly, AdWords ads could be an additional source of information for users, not just an intrusion of commerce into the purity of the Web.

Since then, Google has carefully experimented with the use of AdWords ads. For some types of searches, the ads remain off to the right. For others, the ads appear at the top of the search listings as well as to the right — forming an inverted L of commercial results that displaces most of the organic search results.

It's all driven by keywords — the words and phrases the user types in as part of his search. Advertisers bid to associate their ads with specific keywords, with the high bidders getting the best placement — giving their ads the best chance to attract interest, the most clicks, and the greatest chance to make money.

The result is another revolution, this time in making money from the Web. AdWords ads are *pay per click*, meaning the advertiser pays only if the user clicks the ad. A typical payment is just a few pennies. But the Google AdWords machinery, from creating the ad to delivering it to acting on that precious user click, is so strong that those pennies now add up — no pun intended — to many billions of dollars a year.

And people are building useful, interesting, and successful businesses using the traffic they get on their Web sites from AdWords. Enterprises from the local vet to the largest international companies are using AdWords to increase their business.

AdWords has grown fast, but it still isn't used by many businesses that really should be using it. (To see some examples in your area, try some searches on different types of businesses in your area and see which ones there are Google ads for.) Getting in now, while some good keywords are still under-used, is a huge opportunity.

And although AdWords is still a bit of a secret, there's another secret even within AdWords — one that's a potential goldmine for many small- and medium-sized businesses. This secret is the capability to localize ads.

With localized ads, if you're based in the south side of Chicago, you need to pay only for ads to appear in the south side of Chicago — no need to show your ad, and potentially pay for wasted clicks, in the rest of the world.

We go into this in more detail later, because you don't get the chance to localize your ad until you've done a lot of other work. But we have to raise the issue here because, although it's absolutely crucial, it's very easy to lose this seemingly small detail in the mass of other things you need to do to get AdWords working for you. We've even seen entire books on AdWords that don't mention it at all. Not this one!

What Is an AdWords Ad?

It's easy to talk about AdWords ads in a vague way and to make all sorts of high-sounding pronouncements about it. Yet to be successful with AdWords requires a sharp focus on the details.

Figure 1-1 shows an AdWords ad for BATCS, which is, as you have probably noticed in the rest of the book, a business in which one of the authors (Smith) is involved — and for which he's designed and maintained a successful AdWords campaign, learning as he went along.

BATCS ad

Figure 1-1:
Putting the
accent on
AdWords.

Let's look at every element of the ad to understand how AdWords ads work for users. This is the perspective that you need to keep in mind while creating and testing the ad — you can't get so lost among the trees that you lose sight of the forest.

Here are the components of the BATCS ad — or any AdWords text ad:

✦ **Placement:** The BATCS ad shows up first among the Sponsored Links. The user will judge an ad, and respond to it or not, based on what surrounds it. BATCS wants to attract people who will pay for its book or courses in London. When the user searches using the keyword *accent*, the top few organic links are to Wikipedia — a great resource, but not one that offers courses — and Accent Group, a socially aware business. No competition there, then — none of them sells anything relating to accents. Note that a competing ad does show up just under BATCS's ad.

✦ **Title:** For the BATCS ad, the title is Get Rid of Your Accent — which also happens to be the title of the one book the company publishes. This is the most visible part of the ad. It's a link, which takes advantage of the fact that users love links, and the eye is naturally drawn to them. Also links are what people are looking for from a Google search. The title needs to be somewhat eye-catching — but not alarming — and must make sense as a link.

✦ **Title link:** The hidden part of the title is the destination it links to. For BATCS, the title links to the site's home page — which has been redesigned just to "catch" people coming from this link. After a user's click — which is the part that costs you money — he goes to the page the title links to, so what happens from there is crucial.

You can use an existing page on your Web site or create a special *landing page* designed specifically to help a visitor coming from an AdWords ad. Whether an existing page or a special one, the landing page is crucial to whether you get any return on your AdWords investment.

✦ **Ad text:** For BATCS's ad, the first line of the ad text is: "Accent reduction course from 17 Feb." The second line is: "Tried & trusted drama school method." The ad text is two lines of 35 characters each. Shorter text is more likely to get read, so this is good for you — but it can be a real challenge to say what you need to in 35 characters times two lines!

✦ **Displayed URL:** For the BATCS ad, as with almost any ad, the displayed URL is the home page URL — www.batcs.co.uk. This is the Web address that you want people to type in if they decide to type, or cut and paste, your URL rather than clicking the link. It should almost always be your home page URL, which is the simplest, easiest to remember URL you've got. (If your ad is for a very specialized product within your company, you may want to point to a subpage instead.)

✦ **Location:** For the BATCS ad, the location is London. Google ads that are targeted by location show the location they're targeted for below the result — which helps users know that the ad is directed toward them, to "see themselves in the ad."

✦ **Highlighting:** Note that the search term — *accent*, in this case — is highlighted in the ad results, just as it is in the organic search results. This is an additional factor that connects the word in the user's mind that he just typed into Google search to the results that appear. Note that, for the BATCS ad, the search term is highlighted in the title — and is also highlighted as the first word of the ad text.

Just to really get a handle on this, let's see what happens if the user searches on what BATCS customers really want: Accent reduction. Figure 1-2 shows the result. There are different organic search results — and a lot more paid search results as well.

Figure 1-2:
Accent
reduction
gets the
nod.

The first organic search result is for a competing training course, which is a very good result for them. Although an organic search result is inherently more credible — and has excellent placement, in the upper-left corner of the page — note also that the organic search result is not as visually appealing as the more "designed" paid search result. The long URL is particularly off-putting.

The long list of paid search results shows that "accent reduction" has gotten a lot of attention from people wanting to make money. Why *accent reduction* and not *accent*, for most of the advertisers? They want the more targeted mindset that goes with the more focused term — and they don't want to pay for clicks from just-looking types who are less likely to buy. But the geographic targeting of the ads that appeared on the *accent* search helps reduce this factor.

With careful testing — including asking callers what term they had searched on, for those who remembered it — the value of each term can be determined and the AdWords campaign rejigged accordingly. For instance, the term *accent*, by itself, may truly not be pulling its weight. BATCS's competitors sure seem to think so!

Although the focus on details we've indulged in here might seem maniacal in its intensity, this is just the beginning — those who are most successful with AdWords spend hours poring over these details.

If you enjoy this stuff, you'll love AdWords. If not, consider having someone you work with do it for you, or hiring someone to do it. The secret of success with AdWords lies in relentless examination of details and endless tinkering, and you might as well have someone on the job who's well-suited to it.

Marketing win-win-wins

One of our favorite marketing remarks of all time came from a product manager at Apple Computer when the company was introducing QuickTime 1.1.1. Now it's rare for a company to make a big deal of a "dot release", such as a 1.1 version, let alone a "double dot release", such as a 1.1.1 version. But Version 1.1.0 had experienced some problems, so Apple wanted lots of people to know about Version 1.1.1.

In introducing the product, this product manager breathlessly exclaimed: "I'm here to tell you why one-one-one is a win-win-win!" The engineers rolled their eyes, but the assembled journalists paid attention.

Marketing is like this. It's a psychological process, not a strictly logical one. Repetition, reassurance, and reinforcement are critical.

In ad testing for a (different) Silicon Valley company, we found that intent to purchase didn't begin rising until an ad had been viewed three times — then rose steadily for the fourth, fifth, and sixth viewings. This drove the more nerdy members of the product team nuts. There was no new information in the subsequent viewings. How could they be viewed as positive, rather than as an annoying negative?

It's the same thing with your Google Ads. You want your prospects to have heard of you in all sorts of advertisements, news stories, conversations with friends, and so on. Then your Google ad only has to tip the user into action — not carry the entire burden of selling the product or service itself.

A nice sidelight to this is that Google doesn't charge you for showing your Google ad when no one clicks on it — but every such showing has the chance of building your brand a little bit in the Web surfer's mind. When he sees the ad several times, we hope on top of previous mentions from other sources, he becomes more likely to click — and more likely to buy after he does.

See, Click, Convert

Building your AdWords success depends on understanding the idea of funnels as it relates to sales, just as we describe in Book V.

The big-picture AdWords funnel depends on three cut-off points, which we can summarize as *see, click, convert*:

+ **Who *sees* your ad:** You want to get your ad in front of the right people. This depends entirely on what keywords you associate your ad with and what locations you run the ad in.

+ **Who *clicks* on your ad:** Your ad can only accomplish anything if people click it. So your ad must be designed, it would seem, to get as many clicks as possible.

+ **Who *converts* from a looker into a customer:** But getting clicks is not really accomplishing anything — in fact, you start by losing money on every click. The trick is to make money out of the clicks. This is where your Web site, and the business offer presented in it, make all the difference.

**Book VI
Chapter 1**

Introducing
Google Ads

Let's return to our example from Book V of a self-published book called *Mauna Loa Fire*, about how cool — oops, that's how hot — Hawaii's Mauna Loa volcano is. This illustrates some of the pleasures and perils of AdWords advertising.

See, Part 1: Choosing keywords

Who do we want to get our ad in front of — and what keywords will tie these people to our ad?

You can't do the main work of choosing keywords when you're in the AdWords control panel setting up your ad; you have to start with a bit of spare time and a blank screen or blank sheet of paper. You have to share ideas with people, make phone calls, engage in e-mail exchanges, do Google searches, and more.

Then, when you're in the Google AdWords control panel, you can use the built-in tools to estimate the costs associated with your ideas and generate new ones.

You can start with an initial set of keyword ideas you generate yourself. Carry a piece of paper around for a few days and make notes as ideas occur to you. You'll find that conversations, TV shows, and songs on the radio can all help jog your thinking process to help you come up with new possibilities.

But, while you should start off on your own, you should definitely get help as well. A fairly efficient process for expanding your initial set of keywords can be likened to the hit TV show, *Who Wants to be a Millionaire*? The game show also features in the hit book, *Q&A* by Vikas Swarup (Scribner, 2005), which is the basis for the hit movie *Slumdog Millionaire*.

When a contestant on *Who Wants to be a Millionaire*? isn't sure of an answer, he or she can turn to three "lifelines."

- ✦ **Phone a friend:** On the *Millionaire* show, people often get crucial answers from a friend — and equally often don't. You should do this, too, but you're under less pressure and can do it more broadly. Phone several friends, not just one. Or meet with them in person, or send e-mail. Emphasize how much work this is, and how only with your help is it likely to pay off at all — so they don't think *their* ideas are going to instantly make *you* rich. Then keep your ears open and listen to their ideas.

- ✦ **Ask the audience:** The principle of the "wisdom of crowds" is demonstrated when *Millionaire* contestants poll the audience for an answer. Often, the audience is nearly unanimous. But, more interestingly, even if 90% of the audience doesn't know the answer, the few who do often tip the balance and make the right answer the highest-ranked one in the poll.

  Assuming you've already e-mailed all your friends, you can get the "wisdom of crowds" going for you by looking on three sources that reflect popular wisdom: Google, Wikipedia, and Amazon.com. Google shows you Web sites associated with your initial keywords; Wikipedia — which is all user-generated content, remember — shows you articles; and Amazon shows you books.

  You can also get "official" information relating to dictionary definitions by using an online thesaurus. There's one in Microsoft Word that we find quite useful, though experts criticize it a lot. The Merriam Webster dictionary Web site has a thesaurus as well. There are also paid thesauri, but it's probably not worth paying for them. Figure 1-3 shows a thesaurus search for *speech* on the Merriam Webster Web site.

- ✦ **50:50:** Your own thinking, plus "phoning a friend," and "asking the audience" will get you a lot of ideas. On the *Millionaire* show, the remaining lifeline allows contestants to remove half of the four possible answers, leaving only two to choose between — and improving their odds to 50:50. You can get the same effect with *split testing*, which allows you to compare keywords or ads to one another and pick the more successful one. We explain split testing in Chapter 2.

Generating keywords is a brainstorming process, which means being open to new ideas and gathering all kinds of data. When someone brings up a keyword that you'd already generated, don't say "I already have that one." Say "Thanks" and note that another person has suggested that word. Or reply, "Good one. Can you think of other words related to that one?" in order to get more ideas.

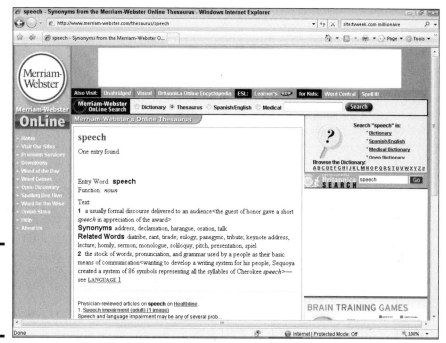

Figure 1-3:
Synonyms
for *speech*
help with
keywords.

You can also think outside the box. For instance, Mauna Loa brings to mind powerful images of an erupting volcano — so why not do an image search in Google and see if that generates some ideas? Or a map search to see what's on the mountain and nearby?

The process of generating keywords, like much else about AdWords, may seem to be somewhere between excessive and obsessive. But keywords matter. The most successful keyword is often the one your competition hasn't thought of yet. So keep thinking!

As you pull your list together, also consider misspellings and alternative spellings and versions of words. The keywords you finally use could easily end up costing you, say, $100 a month each, so it's worth getting the most out of everything you have.

For *Mauna Loa Fire*, here's a list of top keywords generated by the previously described process — not all of them obvious at first glance — grouped together conceptually:

✦ **Name:** Mauna; mona; Loa; Mauna Loa; mona loa; Mauna Kea (the other famous "Mauna"); mona kea.

✦ **Location:** Hawai'i; Hawaii (even people who know about the apostrophe may not bother to type it into Google); Big Island (a popular nickname for the island itself); island; isle.

✦ **Category:** Volcano; lava; magma (the scientific word for lava), mountain (Mauna Loa is the biggest mountain in Hawaii and, compared to its surroundings, in the world); flow (what lava does); crater.

✦ **Adjectives:** Large; largest; fiery; fire.

✦ **Related events:** Eruption (Mauna Loa had three eruptions in the last century, two causing fatalities).

✦ **Other related words:** Observatory (Mauna Loa hosts a famous observatory); astronomy; macadamia (Hawaii is famous for its macadamia nuts; they are known to grow on Mauna Loa, and The Mauna Loa Macadamia Nut Corporation is a leading maker, quoth Wikipedia).

See, Part II: Targeting locations

The keyword search is great for conceptual breadth. But we're going to be paying for every click, so we want depth as well — specifically, people whose pockets are deep when it comes to our product or services.

Not localizing your ads can easily double your AdWords costs or more, as you pay for clicks around the world that you have little hope of selling to or supporting, with little or no increase in sales. Without localization, your AdWords work can run out of money before it properly begins.

For our book, *Mauna Loa Fire*, we know that lots of people around the world have heard of Mauna Loa volcano, and many of them have even visited. But we also know that if we put our Google AdWords ad on screens all over the planet, lots of people who only have a passing interest will click our little ad, costing us money — with little prospect of return.

Particularly in the beginning, when our book is little-known, our brand is weak, our distribution poor — shipping long distances costs money — and our resources short, how can we target our ad to the very highest rate of return? (Always with the ability to expand selectively when things go well.)

For a book called *Mauna Loa Fire*, we know that the state of Hawaii will have a much higher proportion of interested people than anywhere else on Earth — including locals and tourists who are in Hawaii at the time.

In fact, just to be really harsh, we can exclude the other islands and, if AdWords will let us, just focus on the Big Island, Hawaii — where we can expect a warm reception (no pun intended). The Hawaiian Islands are shown in Google Earth in Figure 1-4, just to help us get our bearings (and plan the next steps in our campaign).

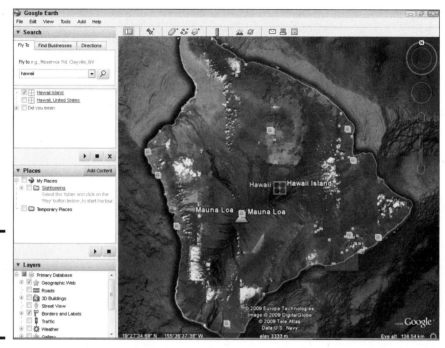

Figure 1-4:
Google
Earth can
help us
target our
AdWords.

Google Earth is very helpful for ad targeting when driving distance is an issue. For our *Mauna Loa Fire* campaign, driving distance on an island is a big concern; driving distance between islands isn't a factor.

People on the Big Island are likely to be in sight of the volcano at least part of the time, to have visited it, to mention it, and navigate by reference to it in their daily lives. If they don't want our book — locally focused, locally written, locally available — no one will. So we geo-target our initial ad just to the Big Island itself.

Of course, any problems are probably not with our book per se. But in the early days we're going to be discovering problems with our ad, our keyword targeting, the amount we're paying per click, how well our Web site converts visitors into customers and on and on. So we have leakage in our pipeline — we want the most motivated buyers who will overcome obstacles to get to our product.

It may take us quite of investment of time, energy, and money to get the pipeline in shape. Then we can turn our geo-targeting around. Instead of looking for the slam-dunk locations — the small list of places where we are almost guaranteed to be able to sell our product — we'll be looking for good and even marginal locations — any place on Earth where it's worth paying to run our Google Ad, which may eventually extend to the entire planet. In the meantime, we'll be finding, and advertising to, every pocket of Mauna Loa-philes we can find!

Click — Targeted content

For text ads — and there are other kinds, which we mention in Chapter 2, but for now text ads make up the vast majority — the words you use and their arrangement determine whether you get clicks.

And you can forget about using fancy formatting or lots of exclamation points to gain attention; Google does a good job of keeping eye-catching "tricks" out of text content. Potentially problematic ads are even reviewed by an editor before being approved or kicked back to you.

So it's all a matter of choosing the words and arrangement that will get the most attention, right?

Well, no. You don't want the *most* attention, you want the *right* attention. You don't just want clicks — you want clicks from people who are the most likely to buy from you.

Part of the problem that AdWords both suffers from, and helps solve, is that words commonly have many different meanings. *Vacuum*, as a verb, will help us sell vacuum cleaners; *vacuum*, as a noun, on the other hand, will help us sell spacesuits. And on and on. Figure 1-5 shows a Google search on the word *vacuum*. The first organic search result relates to space — but all the text ads are for vacuum cleaners.

Your AdWords ad text has to attract the housewives and househusbands looking for a vacuum cleaner, and deter the astronauts — or vice versa, depending on what you're trying to sell.

A good example is our made-up endeavor *Mauna Loa Fire*. A lot of people searching on *Mauna Loa* are looking to visit the volcano and perhaps that day are not interested in a book; people searching on *fire* may be looking to build a fire, or fire an employee, not to read a book about a volcano.

So our ad needs to be clear about what we're selling — a book — and at least strongly imply that we want anyone who clicks to be willing to — buy it.

You have four or five lines in which to do it — three lines you actually write: 25 characters in the title; 35 characters in the first line of copy; 25 more characters in the second line of copy; a display URL; and, if you've locally targeted the ad, the name of the target area that the searcher resides in.

Figure 1-5:
You can find a lot of meaning in a vacuum.

Here's an example of an ad written off the top of our heads — a first cut:

Hot new book on Mauna Loa (25 characters)

Mauna Loa Fire is "best new book" (33 characters)

The world's most famous volcano (31 characters)

www.maunaloafire.com

Hawaii

This ad accomplishes most of our purposes. It makes quite clear what the product is and includes many of the keywords we've identified — *Mauna Loa*, *fire*, *volcano*. The only obvious gap is that we haven't included the word *buy* in it; someone might think this is a link only to a review of the book. If the viewer visits wanting to read the review and not to buy, there's our 5¢ or so down the drain!

An ancient marketing dictum says that the two best words to attract customers are *new* and *free*. We have the word *new* right there in the title of our ad; and although *free* is missing, at least the ad's viewer, knowing it's a book, has a reasonable expectation as to the price.

Part of the reason this ad is easy to read and not off-putting is that it's quite low-key and doesn't sound too much like an ad. That's largely because, while giving a nod to the *new*-and-*free* rule, it breaks some of the key rules of advertising.

Now let's rewrite the ad following a recommended approach that does follow the rules. Here's a formulaic — and counterintuitive, as long as we're throwing around big words — approach to building a Google ad. Here's the formula:

✦ **Title:** State the main customer benefit

✦ **First line of copy:** Aspects of the product that meet reader's needs — "qualifiers"

✦ **Second line of copy:** A call to action to inspire buying now

So let's rewrite our ad to follow these rules. Here's the revised ad:

Why Mauna Loa matters (25 characters)

Mauna Loa Fire is "best new book" (33 characters)

Free volcano stone if you buy today (35 characters)

www.maunaloafire.com

Hawaii

This meets the rules, as shown in Table 1-1.

Table 1-1	Deconstructing the Rewritten *Mauna Loa Fire* Ad.		
Line / Function	Old	New	Notes
Title / Main customer benefit	Hot new book on Mauna Loa (25 characters)	Why Mauna Loa matters (25 characters)	The missing word, cut for length, is *learn* or *know*. Neither of these is very strong, especially when implied rather than stated — but it's often hard to state a clear-cut benefit for a book, which meets many disparate needs.

Line / Function	Old	New	Notes
Line 1 / Qualifiers — meeting reader's needs	Mauna Loa Fire is "best new book" (33 characters)	Unchanged (33 characters)	Buyers want the newest book, the best book, or both. The potential customer may expect this to be spelled out on the site. Note this didn't need to be changed from the "top of the head" original.
Line 2 / Call to action	The world's most famous volcano (35 characters)	Free volcano stone if you buy today (35 characters)	Here we get in the crucial word *free* and introduce a sense of urgency. Customers may understand that this is not today only, but will expect it to end soon.

What's changed most between the first and second ad?

The biggest change is going from a flat and boring statement of fact — "The world's most famous volcano" — to a call to action (and one that will cost us money to meet) — "Free volcano stone if you buy today."

We can promise you that a group of product developers, engineers, or journalists will much prefer the first statement — they deal in facts. Marketers and PR people will prefer the second — they deal in wishes, hopes, and dreams. If you're in the former group, as most small- and medium-sized businesspeople (or their employees in charge of setting up an AdWords account) are, you have to get the latter involved and give their approach an even chance.

Now with this work, we have a lot of grist for our mill when it comes to AdWords ads. We can test versions against each other to see which ones drive the most traffic. Of course, this just tells us which ones cost us the most! We need to set up ad and site analysis to see which ones result in the most sales, which is often quite different. Which brings us to the last point: converting clicks into business.

Convert

This is the hardest part of running a business — and the farthest one from the mechanics of online marketing, until you set up a full e-commerce site and run a lot of your business through it. So we touch only briefly on conversion.

Conversion is turning the potential customer's attention into a sale.

Now if we were perfect businessmen and businesswomen, we would always be aware of profit: what brings us the most money with the least effort. But we actually tend to focus on activity. In most businesses, sales, customer visits (in person), site visits, and buzz all get a lot more attention than the bottom line.

An interesting exception is the banking industry — which, admittedly, hasn't gotten a lot of good press lately. One of the world's largest banks — one which has done better than most in the recent downturn — gives very little attention to revenues, assets, numbers of accounts, and so on. All report-ing relates to profits. If a division of the company can make a billion dollars by having one, and only one, customer, great; if a division has 100 million customers, with each having $10,000 on deposit, but only makes a dollar in profit from each of them, it may get shut down.

You have to think like a banker, or like a banker's supposed to think. You have to know which of your products, services, and activities makes the most profit, and put all your efforts into building those up and cutting the rest.

The key to conversion is deciding which of the potential customers' actions lead to sales and encouraging those actions. Conversely, actions that help you can "turn off" a potential customer are good ones to identify, too.

For a very large number of businesses, that key action is nothing to do with the online world — what's wanted is a phone call. People are too busy to pursue various paths across a Web site to try to figure out if they should go to yet another Web page to start a long and involved path to purchase.

Often what you want is as simple as 1, 2, 3 — get their attention; give them with a brief description of your product or service; and, if they're interested, have them give you a call.

Blogger, described in Chapter 5 of Book V, uses this approach in signup. It's 1 — Sign in. 2 — Set up. 3 — Create your first post. At each step, you can bail out — but if you really should be a blogger on Blogger, it's made as easy as humanly possible.

Amazon.com is another good example. In fact, you may have noticed that the front page of Amazon reconfigures itself based on your past visits and purchases, as shown in Figure 1-6. (This can be a bit embarrassing just after you buy a book on underarm odor, even if you bought the book for someone else.) This is all to work Step 1: Get your attention. The book descriptions naturally qualify you, which is Step 2, and every one is strongly linked to an opportunity to buy — which is Step 3.

Figure 1-6:
Amazon
starts the
old 1, 2, 3.

But until you make your Web site as slick as Amazon's, phone calls are also great when you're trying out new marketing techniques, as you are very much doing here. You can get a feel for the customer's level of interest and quickly complete the sale — or find out that your offer is not for him or her, and why. If you gently work a couple of questions into each such conversation and record the answers, you're actually doing a survey — one that will strongly guide your next steps.

Chapter 2: Creating Your First Google Ads

In This Chapter

✔ Comparing pay-for-placement to pay-per-click

✔ Signing up for an AdWords account

✔ Viewing your campaign

Creating your first Google ads is a lot of fun — but potentially hazardous to your wallet.

Google ads represent a wonderful opportunity to build your business. Like eBay before them, Google ads are building up an entire new business environment, with millions of people making relatively small amounts of money — and a few people making millions of dollars.

A Google ad charges you a small fee — usually just a few cents — for each potential customer it brings to your Web site. As these fees add up, you need to be making enough profit from these potential customers to pay the fees, with some left over to give you a reason to spend time on Google ads instead of on other ways of building your business.

It's all too easy to "fire and forget" — to launch a couple of ads, with a seemingly small daily budget, then lose a surprising amount of money as the money goes out each day without bringing in much business.

That's why it is so valuable to read a book like this one — and to think and plan about what you're doing. You discover how to shorten the time it takes to make Google Ads profitable and lessen the amount of money you spend while you're figuring out what you're doing.

To get started, you need to experiment and learn from your mistakes — but you need to experiment inexpensively and learn fast.

Understanding the Data-Driven Business Model

Increasingly, business, government, and even charities are data-driven. They prosper by amassing mountains of data about their current and potential customers (or citizens or beneficiaries) and carefully crafting products and services that are more and more customized, sometimes down to the individual level.

This trend has hit politics, where the presidential campaign of Barack Obama used social networking and data mining to build a fund-raising and volunteer-enrolling machine that seemed to generate money — and votes — out of thin air. First Hillary Clinton and then, to an even greater extent, John McCain, never knew what hit them.

It's also greatly affecting sports. Successful baseball teams are increasingly run by what's called *sabremetrics* — the use of statistics to analyze situations during a game and make the best call to leverage one team's strengths against the other team's weaknesses. Figure 2-1 shows an analysis of baseball scores in Mathematica, a truly serious mathematics processing program. (It is described by some as "easy" — if you have a doctorate in physical or social sciences, perhaps.)

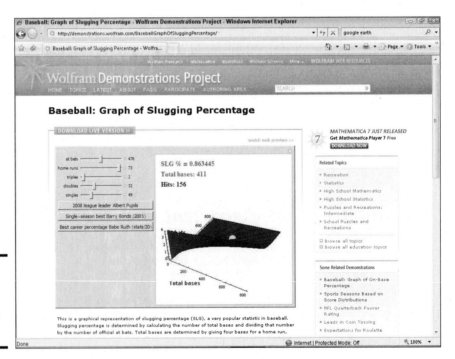

Figure 2-1: Rocket science, meet Babe Ruth.

Even the social sciences are affected. Departments of psychology, sociology, and so on are increasingly driven by dissension between qualitative approaches — based on, say, talking to people and thinking carefully about what you hear — and quantitative ones based on data analysis.

What has this got to do with you and AdWords? It's tough to realize if you're in a small- or medium-sized business, but this trend is sweeping through the entire economy. On the one hand, you're competing against huge companies that can refine large amounts of data and cost-effectively craft ever more individualized offers to their — and your — customers. On the other hand, you're competing with a million Mom and Pops — or former Moms and Pops who have grown large — who use eBay or, increasingly, AdWords to reach your customers online. Not all of them do a good job of it, but there are a lot of them.

Your traditional customers, who use a variety of media, are steadily being replaced by younger customers who do a lot — or seemingly everything — online. You need to be there too to reach them.

Google ads may seem like just another tool in your business arsenal. But actually, they are opportunities for businesses — especially small- and medium-sized ones — to take advantage of trends toward the use of statistics and targeting.

Over the years to come, these trends will become everyday elements of running a business. We're reminded of a harsh phrase that was once popular in Silicon Valley relating to one's willingness to embrace the latest new technology breakthrough or management approach: "Get on the train or die."

A very cruel way to say it, perhaps, but this is what millions of small- and medium-sized businesses face. AdWords presents an opportunity today. AdWords, or something like it, will be a necessity tomorrow; after that, those who don't embrace the new way of doing things will steadily lose market share to those who do.

Comparing Pay for Placement to Pay-per-Click

Traditional advertising is "pay for placement." You pay hundreds of dollars to put your ad on, say, the back page of your local paper's sports section. Then you wait for the phone to ring.

If it rings off the hook, you don't pay more; if it doesn't ring at all, you don't pay less. It's an expensive and difficult way to learn what works and what doesn't.

Even worse, if you're running several ads, doing promotions, listing your business in phone directories, and so on, you don't know what is and isn't driving the calls. This is what inspires the old marketing adage: "I know half my advertising dollars are wasted. I just don't know which half!"

Initial efforts in online advertising mostly used the pay-for-placement model as well; it's much better, in the short run, for the seller. Advertisers, of course, wanted pay-per-click. Some sellers were brave enough to offer a smattering of pay-per-click as a kind of reward for a commitment to buy on a pay-for-placement basis.

Google was the first big — by the scale of online business at the time — vendor to offer pay-per-click — through AdWords. What it recognized was that, over time, pay-per-click could be as good for the seller as for the buyer.

Well, almost as good. Pay-per-click is a volume business; It's not the *Mad Men*-type world of sharp-suited advertising executives convincing clients to make multimillion-dollar ad buys over martinis. (Traditional advertising salespeople are paid as a percentage of the size of the ad buy, not the sales or profits that do or don't result!)

When you have a volume business, you have to cut costs. So both Google and its customers relentlessly track their respective bottom lines, looking for tiny advantages that, over thousands or millions of interactions, become major ones. Just for one example, Google has developed cheap custom Web servers that can process searches — and serve AdWords ads — at a cost estimated to be a third lower than any competitor.

All a bit boring — except when the money comes rolling in. Google and its AdWords customers make money together; and together, they're making more and more of it.

Signing Up for AdWords

Signing up is not a quick process for most people. Unless you're very well-prepared, set aside a couple of hours — yes, *hours* — to complete it. During the process you may wish to search online, review Chapter 1, click links to helpful information from Google, interact live with a Google AdWords Specialist, and be in touch with friends, colleagues, and advisers.

So are you fired up and ready to go? Follow these steps to get started by signing up for an AdWords account:

1. **Visit AdWords at `adwords.google.com`.**

The AdWords home page appears, as shown in Figure 2-2. Take a minute — or several minutes — to read the useful tutorial on the lower half of the page and then go to Step 2.

Depending on the day and time, it's quite possible an AdWords Specialist is available to chat live online. Consider using this service if available. Pointing the AdWords Specialist to your Web site quickly gives him or her an idea of how best to help you.

2. **Don't sign in unless you already have a valid AdWords account attached to your Google account. Otherwise, click the Start Now link.**

   You're given the opportunity to choose the Starter Edition or Standard Edition, as shown in Figure 2-3.

3. **Choose Starter Edition.**

   Starter Edition is simplified in useful ways — it has an easier signup process, it supports only one product or service at a time, and it limits you to text ads only. Reporting is basic, targeting is to one region only, and cost controls, planning tools, and placement targeting by Web site are all limited or absent.

   Having used both, we can say it's easier to get up to speed more quickly — and to conserve your precious funds — by using the Starter Edition first, figuring out the basics, and then upgrading to the Standard Edition, rather than by diving straight into the Standard Edition.

Book VI Chapter 2

Creating Your First Google Ads

Figure 2-2: The AdWords home page shows the 1-2-3 of reaching your customers.

Figure 2-3:
Dip your toe
in the water
with Starter
Edition — or
plunge into
Standard
Edition.

If you are working with partners or colleagues, the Starter Edition is an even better idea because it's easier to explain and demonstrate to them what you're doing as you go along.

4. **Choose between the options: "I have a Webpage" or "I don't have a Webpage. Help me create one."**

   These steps assume you already have a Web page, perhaps using Google Sites, as described in Book 4. If you don't have a Web page, you can either leave Google AdWords now and go create one — taking your time and doing it right — or create one quickly within the Google AdWords.

   There are arguments both ways. A Web site you create in a few minutes is not going to be robust enough to support much in the way of sales, so it will need a lot of work; but a Web site created from the beginning with Google AdWords in mind may end up as a better sales tool than a more traditional Web site. These steps do not describe how to create a Web site within the Google AdWords sign-up process, but the process is similar to the Google Sites how-to in Book IV.

5. **Optionally, lower on the same page, enter the country, phone number, and location of your business. Google uses this information to look up your business in their directory and pre-fill in fields for you.**

Many commentators have expressed concern about just how much data Google can accumulate about people. If you're a bit concerned that Google has your business in a directory you didn't know about, you aren't alone!

6. **Click Continue.**

The Set up Your Ad page appears, as shown in Figure 2-4.

7. **In area 1 of the page Location and Language, choose where your customers are located.**

You can use either the radio buttons offered — representing Google's guesses as the areas you might want to target — or click one of the links: Select a Different Country or Territory brings up a pull-down list of countries and territories and Select a Different Area in This Country or Territory allows you to search among major metro areas.

A smaller region reduces your impression count, but choosing the right region has the potential to improve your click-through rates while reducing the number of clicks that don't result in profitable business for you. If you want to limit your ads to, say, Boston and Baltimore, you need to move to the Standard Edition. (And if you want to use Google Earth to interactively choose various finely-tuned areas, you also need to move to the Standard Edition.)

Figure 2-4:
Start setting
up your ad.

Choose a small region based on factors that include: an area where you might already be known, where your current customers and best prospects are located, and where delivery, service, and support of customers are easy.

Although it may be your intention to do business remotely, it can be very valuable in the early days to be able to visit a customer easily — so choosing a region local to you may be very helpful.

If you choose a specific metro area, its name appears at the bottom of your AdWords ad, as mentioned in Chapter 1 of this minibook. This may serve as a valuable additional part of the advertisement, showing your focus on and commitment to the area named.

 8. **Still in area 1, choose the language your ad will be written in.**

Depending on what product or service you offer, and the specific country, you may be surprised how many prospects will be willing to click on an English-language ad — and buy the product or service advertised — in areas where the first language isn't English. Also, such English-speakers tend to be more highly educated and more highly paid, which may be part of your early market targeting anyway.

 9. **Scroll down to area 2 and write Your Ad. In the text box, enter the specific URL of the Web page your link will send visitors to.**

The search terms users enter, the ad they click, the landing page they arrive on, and the remaining steps to purchase form a funnel that leaks prospects — whose clicks you've paid for — at each point along the way. Choose or create a page that closely connects clickers with the remaining steps to become customers; if you don't have the Web content and functionality yet to support this, give basic information and then encourage customers to call or e-mail you, both by giving contact information prominently and by specifically urging them to contact you at specific points in your Web page text.

 10. **Now enter the text for your first ad — an exciting moment! Enter a headline (up to 25 characters, including spaces), the first line and the second line (up to 35 characters each). Edit the displayed URL, usually to the main URL for the home page.**

For guidelines on writing a good ad, see Chapter 1. A brief reminder of the recommendations there: Consider having the headline offer a benefit, use the second line to reassure the users about qualifiers they might be looking for in your product or service, and in the final line include an offer with time urgency or a price break.

For more information, click and read the Five Keys to Powerful Ads link and, especially, the Editorial Guidelines link found on this page.

You are prevented from using excessive capitalization, clever punctuation or symbols, and some specific phrases. You are also prohibited from making competitive claims, claiming to be tied to a company you're not associated with, and using inappropriate or offensive language. Ads for many types of products and services are prohibited as well. For details, see the guidelines.

11. **Scroll down to area 3, Choose Keywords. Enter keywords or keyword phrases directly in the large text entry area, one per line.**

Google AdWords may also offer you additional choices based on a scan of your site; to include these choices, click the Add link. To generate alternatives, in the small text box, enter one keyword or keyword phrase at a time; click Return, and a list of related keywords and phrases appears. Click Add to add each one to your keyword list, as shown in Figure 2-5.

Keep in mind the recommendations in Chapter 1 and Google's suggestion that you restrict yourself to about 20 keywords or keyword phrases.

Be aware that Google's recommendations can be a bit off-target; for BATCS, for instance, the recommendations include *accent* but don't include *pronunciation*, a term which is clearly useful. See Figure 2-5 for examples.

Book VI
Chapter 2

Creating Your First Google Ads

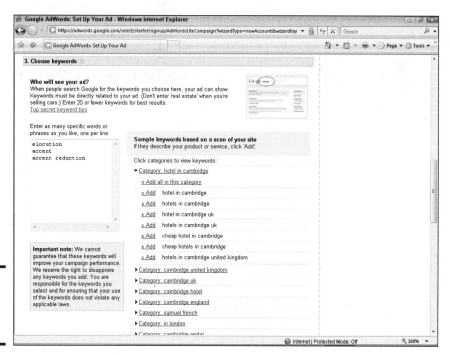

Figure 2-5:
Now for
the fun:
keywords.

For a broad match, which may include plurals, among other things, just enter the word; for a precise match, surround the word in quotes; for a precise match of a term, surround it in square brackets; to exclude a term, put a dash directly in front of it.

TIP

For more valuable tips directly from Google, click the Top Secret Keyword Tips link.

Consider using just a few, highly specialized keywords at the very start so you can use them to test whether your AdWords ad appears when you enter the search term.

12. **Scroll down to area 4, Choose Your Currency, as shown in Figure 2-6. Choose your currency from the scrolling list.**

This doesn't affect how people pay you, just how you pay Google. If you do all your banking and business in one currency, choose that currency for simplicity's sake. If this is not a simple choice for you — if you have the ability to pay in different currencies, for instance — click the link, Payment Options, to review the options for each currency before deciding.

13. **In area 5, Set Your Budget (refer to Figure 2-6), choose your monthly budget from the choices offered, or (preferably) enter the budget that fits your needs exactly.**

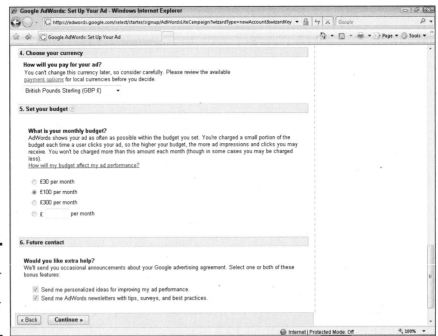

Figure 2-6:
Choose your
currency
and set your
budget.

Don't be afraid to set a small amount, even less than you're prepared to spend in a month; this will force your ad campaign to stop while you re-evaluate, make any changes needed, and then add more money. Google warns you if you enter an amount it thinks is too small, but at this writing it allows you to enter a figure as small as $20.

14. **Scroll down to area 6, Future Contact. (Refer to Figure 2-6.) Choose whether to receive personalized ideas from Google — which is a good idea — and whether to receive standardized AdWords newsletters — another good idea.**

These contacts not only teach you things but remind you to stay on top of your AdWords account.

15. **Click Continue.**

The Setup menu appears, asking if you have a Google account.

16. **Click the appropriate radio button — for most readers of this book that is the second one, indicating that you do have a Google account.**

You are asked if you want to use your existing account or create a new account just for AdWords, as shown in Figure 2-7.

Book VI
Chapter 2

Creating Your First
Google Ads

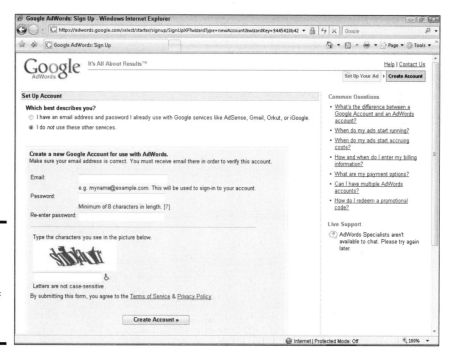

Figure 2-7:
Figure out how to account for yourself with AdWords.

In most cases, we recommend that you create a new account just for AdWords. You can still receive e-mail about your ads in your existing Google or other e-mail account, but if you separate AdWords, you can allow other people to help manage and report on your campaign without giving them your Google account details.

17. **Enter your e-mail address and password and then enter the characters you see in the graphic.**

18. **Click Create Account.**

    Your account is created and you see the Congratulations screen, as shown in Figure 2-8. Note that you have to verify your account and enter billing information before your ads start running. See the next section to do this.

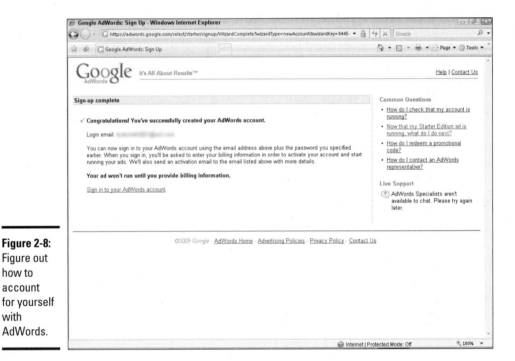

Figure 2-8:
Figure out how to account for yourself with AdWords.

Book VI
Chapter 2

Creating Your First
Google Ads

Don't be content with the Content Network

As soon as you start your account — which you do in the steps that follow — it starts running in the Content network of Google partner sites as well as in Google search results. We recommend that you turn off your ad's appearance in the Content network, at least at first.

The Content Network is a group of sites that run Google ads alongside their content. This is a wonderful and very cool capability that's making a lot of great Web sites viable. However, the response an ad gets in the content network can be much different from one it gets in search — *different* meaning mostly worse. Our limited experience is that the Content Network costs us as much as Google Search but provides many fewer sales.

Not that it was easy to tell. Unlike ads in Google Search, you don't get a detailed, keyword breakdown of Content Network clicks, impressions, and costs, just a grand total.

A Google Search user is actively hunting for information. Google has done such a good job with AdWords ads that they fit, for many Google Search users, as just a slightly different type of information. If your ad meets the user's needs, it has a good chance of getting a click from a motivated searcher who may become a buyer.

In the Content Network, users may be more passively reading or even — heaven forbid — relaxing. The sites vary, so it's hard for you to get a feel for what they look like for a "typical" user. Also, Content Network site managers can "tone down" your ads so they don't stand out too much visually. All of these factors mitigate against the click-through rates or conversion rates that you might hope for from Google Search.

You may need to use the Standard Edition, rather than the Starter Edition described here, to manage Content Network ads effectively. That's because the Standard Edition enables you to create separate campaigns with one or a few keywords per campaign, improving your understanding of just what is and isn't working in the Content Network.

The Content Network may turn out to be quite cost-effective for your kind of ad and product, and you really should experiment with it. But we recommend that you turn it off for a while — until you have a baseline of success in Google Search — before taking on the extra complexity and uncertainty involved in advertising in the Content Network.

Viewing Your Ad Campaign

It's become typical that you have to do some to-ing and fro-ing between the Web and e-mail to verify a new online account, and Google AdWords is no different. Follow these steps to launch your new account and to set up payment and then start managing your campaign:

1. **Go to your e-mail account and look for a recent e-mail from `adwords-noreply`. Open the e-mail and click the verification link.**

    A page appears from Google Accounts stating that your e-mail address is verified and your account is activated.

2. **Click the Click Here to Continue link in the Google Accounts page.**

    You are taken to the Advertise Your Business on Google page. (Refer to Figure 2-2.)

3. **Sign in to Google Adwords with the new account you just created.**

    The Welcome to Adwords — Starter Edition page appears, as shown in Figure 2-9.

4. **Click the Enter Billing Information and Activate Ad link.**

    The Billing Preferences screen within the My Account tab appears.

5. **Choose your country and time zone. Click Continue. Follow the prompts to choose your form of payment, agree to terms, and provide billing details.**

    These steps are similar to what you may have done for online purchases.

    After you've entered all the information, the My Ad Campaign tab appears, as shown in Figure 2-10.

Figure 2-9:
Time to set
up billing in
AdWords.

Figure 2-10:
You're now
in control
of your
campaign.

6. **To edit your ad, click the Edit Your Ad link. A screen very similar** to area 2, Write Your Ad appears. (Refer to Figure 2-7.) Enter the new text or link and click Save Changes.

    Don't just make changes for the sake of making them without tracking the results. You may just be throwing out a potentially successful baby along with the bathwater. Because of the delay of several hours while changes propagate, it's easy to be unsure how many clicks a given ad version generated if you changed a lot. Use split testing, described in the next chapter, to improve your ads in a managed way.

7. **To pause your campaign, click the Pause link. To restart it, click the Resume link.**

    Your campaign is paused, then resumed — although possibly with a delay of several hours or more each time you do this.

8. **To change your keywords, use the Add More Keywords link. A screen very similar to area 3, Choose Keywords (refer to Figure 2-5) appears. Use this to add keywords. To delete keywords, click the Delete link next to each keyword.**

    It's common to start with a very small set of keywords just to ensure things are working.

9. **To turn off the Content Network, as described in the sidebar, click the Turn Off link, next to the Content A Network label in the row near the bottom of the table.**

The Are You Sure? screen appears, as shown in Figure 2-11.

10. **Read the contents of the Are You Sure? screen carefully.**

This screen makes the case for keeping the Content Network, and in the longer term that's probably a good thing to do. But if you're controlling your costs while building up your capabilities, consider turning it off.

11. **To turn off the Content Network, click the Turn Off Content button. To retain it, click the Keep Content button.**

Whichever button you click, you are returned to the My Ad Campaign tab. The current status of the Content Network, Off or On, will be displayed next to the Content network label — along with a link that allows you to reverse it.

Figure 2-11:
The Are you sure? Screen explains the content network.

And that's it for the basic functions of the Starter Edition. Wait for clicks to show up in the My Ad Campaign screen Keywords tab. Also, try your search terms in Google Search — assuming you're in the area you've targeted — to make sure they work.

In the next chapter, we show you how to get more information out of Starter Edition, how to understand what it's showing you, and how to start optimizing your campaign and your Web site.

You won't always see your ad in search results, even on targeted keywords, unless you set a pretty high budget that doesn't run out. If you set a lower budget, Google rations your ads, running or not running them at seemingly random intervals. This is pretty frustrating when you're testing your results or trying to show a friend, family member, or colleague your cool new Google ads. The only way to resolve the problem is to use narrowly targeted keywords and a big budget, which is not necessarily what you want to do — especially early on.

Chapter 3: Selling More with Google Analysis Tools

In This Chapter

✔ Increasing sales by making adjustments to your Web site

✔ Understanding and implementing split tests

✔ Exploring AdWords graphs

✔ Introducing Google Analytics

*P*eople talk a lot about how much the Web does for business — and a lot of success stories back that up. Google Apps and all the related Google tools are a great opportunity for you to create your own success story.

Google Ads represent a new, attractive technique for bringing in business. But to get the most business possible at the lowest price and with the greatest results takes analysis.

There's an old saying about how too much thinking and studying can prevent action: "paralysis by analysis." But these days, acting without having the data to back up your choices is often just not good enough.

Selling is increasingly data-driven, with hard information replacing guesstimates and intuition or laying the groundwork for intuition to be used on a higher level.

Salespeople have a famous differentiation: Real potential customers are *prospects*, but people who are just gathering information and wasting time are *suspects*.

By using a data-driven approach, you can find more prospects and avoid suspects before they even begin to waste your time. In fact, with Google Ads, you can let prospects find you — the suspects just find other things to do.

Then, intuition and analysis can combine to help you get the most out of the opportunities in front of you.

Does your Web site make AdSense?

AdSense is a marvelous tool from Google that helps you make money from a Web site by allowing Google to run ads on it. Yes — your site becomes one of those Content Network sites we mentioned in the previous chapter.

Notice, though, that we said AdSense helps you make money from *a* Web site, not *your* Web site. That's because AdSense doesn't make sense for the kind of Web sites we've discussed in this book: Web sites that represent an organization to the world.

Putting other peoples' ads on your Web site usually looks kind of cheap. You almost cheapen your brand, and it's certainly unlikely that it will make much money for you.

Where AdSense is great is in creating a follow-up or separate devotee's Web site about a topic you or your organization care about. The specialist site can do e-commerce, tie into offline sales, and use Google Ads and AdSense as well. And everything you know about using Google Ads and other Google Apps tools helps you do a better job of it.

For details, see *Google AdSense For Dummies* by Jerri Ledford (Wiley, 2008).

Modifying Your Web Site to Increase Sales

Most Web sites suffer from the need to be many things to many people. The site has to give a good impression of your company, host news and other interesting information, show people how to get information on product support, and also serve as the front end for one or more different kinds of selling processes. No wonder most Web sites are so busy and, frankly, ineffective.

Google AdWords neatly solves this problem for you — at least for the traffic that comes in through Google Ads. Your Google Ads text is sales-oriented. People who come into your site are, in large part, ready to buy.

Here are the seven steps of a traditional sales cycle and how they relate to Google AdWords:

1. **Prospecting:** *Prospecting* means finding potential buyers. Your Google Ad and the user themselves have done this for you. You can assume those who come to your site through the Google Ad are potential buyers — and they should arrive at a page that leads them through the rest of the buying process. (The Google Ads-sourced visitors who aren't potential buyers can easily click away to other parts of your site.)

2. **Contact:** In a sense, you have your original contact through AdWords, but you don't have the flexibility of a person-to-person interaction yet. So AdWords and your Web site, by themselves, provide a form of contact, but a limited one.

3. **Qualification:** This means determining if the contact needs your product or service and can afford it. Google Ads, your Web site, and the users themselves can do a lot of this for you. Either give a price online or find ways to communicate whether you're a low-, medium-, or high-price brand. Then, customers who are interested in your price range tend to be the ones who contact you.

4. **Presentation:** This is telling prospects about your product or service. Again, the users can do much of this for themselves on your Web site.

5. **Removing objections:** Your Web site can do some of this, but it's much easier to do on the phone or in person. Skilled salespeople can read someone's body language (or tone of voice) and identify when he or she is still asking questions versus being ready to buy.

6. **Closing the sale:** This is getting the order, which you can do through e-commerce, on the phone, or in person. Everything else you do is a step in this direction.

7. **Getting referrals:** This is where you get references to other people you can sell to. The strongest referrals are to the customers themselves, who in most cases should be ready to buy from you again and again! But also give the customer ways to "share the wealth" and invite friends, family, and work colleagues to buy from you.

**Book VI
Chapter 3**

Selling More with Google Analysis Tools

You can see the steps of the sales cycle showing through as you use Google AdWords and Google Analytics. Every number you see relates to part of it.

Now this process is far from complete — and far from perfect. For instance, it ignores *positioning* — the value of branding in the customer's mind. As an example, if a customer is convinced your product is the best, all objections but price melt away; if the customer thinks your product is low-quality, you have to set a very low price indeed to close many sales.

But let's focus for the moment on the core of the process, dealing with a user who comes to your site through AdWords. Here are the remaining steps. You can handle these entirely on your Web site through information pages and e-commerce or entirely interactively by having someone call to complete the sale or by arranging an in-person meeting:

✦ **Presentation:** For the prospect to learn more about the product, its price or price range, and so on. This is where prospects can be separated most painlessly from suspects, so try to arrange for a lot of this to happen on the Web.

✦ **Removing objections:** Objections vary widely, so address the most common ones on the Web, but expect to handle some common and some uncommon objections live — on the phone or in person.

✦ **Closing the sale:** This is getting commitment from the buyer. It can be handled through e-commerce, but until that's up and running, it's best handled live — on the phone or in person.

✦ **Taking the order:** Again, eventually you can handle this through e-commerce, but until then you need to do it live. Many salespeople close the sale and then hand it off to an assistant to take the order.

Although some sales can be handled entirely through your Web site, usually it requires personal involvement for some or all of your sales. Fill in Table 3-1 to see what you should try to do in your Web site and what you should leave to live approaches — in person or on the phone.

Table 3-1 Figure Out What to Do on the Web and What to Do Live

	Web				Phone/In person			
	Always	Often	Some-times	Rarely	Rarely	Some-times	Often	Always
Presentation								
Removing objections								
Closing the sale								
Taking the order								

Table 3-1 helps you determine at what point you want to start encouraging people to call you or e-mail you to call them.

BATCS: A case study

For many products and services, the Web cycle is very short: Tell them a bit about the product or service and then encourage them to call or e-mail you.

BATCS is a good example. For book sales, the entire sales cycle takes place online — but the last step or two (closing the sale in some cases; taking the order in all cases) takes place on a partner site such as Amazon or in a book-store — like a top salesperson handing the customer off to an assistant to take the order!

For in-person courses, which cost hundreds of pounds, the sales cycle is quite different. Presentation of basic information takes place on the Web, as does part of the job of removing objections. The BATCS Web site includes a favorable review of the company's book. The very existence of the book and good notices remove objections to the course.

But, because the course is a substantial commitment of time and money for the student, the next step is always a phone call, usually concerned with removing more objections before closing the sale.

In fact, BATCS has a two-part sales cycle for courses. The first part is a speech analysis, which costs only £60 (about $90 US). The potential customer is only committing to spend this amount in an initial meeting.

The second part is the course itself, which costs £500 (about $750 US). The customer only has to agree to this after getting the chance to meet the teacher in the speech analysis.

BATCS has, over time, modified its entire sales cycle around AdWords. If sales were being made in person, there might not be the same need to split the speech analysis and the course; but because the initial contact for the courses is online, commitment has to be built up:

+ **User clicks the AdWords ad.** Commitment: low. Cost to company: about 10p (about 15¢ US).

+ **User visits Web site, learns about book and courses.** Commitment: moderate. Cost to company: none.

+ **User phones or sends e-mail (which leads to a call) to learn more and set up an appointment.** Commitment: higher — people are often nervous when they call — and quite high if they agree to pay £60 (about $90 US) and come to the office for a speech analysis. Cost to company: about 15 minutes of time for the call or e-mail interaction; the speech analysis, if it happens, is a sale.

  Note: BATCS gets much positive feedback for responding quickly to potential customers. No sense letting enthusiasm fade at this delicate point.

+ **User visits for speech analysis.** Commitment: high; the person's paying £60 and considering spending £500 (about $750 US) more. Cost to company: none; customer is paying for the visit — which usually also results in a course sign-up.

+ **User signs up for course.** Commitment: highest, £500 and 14 hours of classroom time. Cost to company: none; customer is paying for the course.

Notice how the commitment gradually escalates, from a 10p cost to the company, through a £60 speech analysis, to a £500 course commitment.

Changing your site

One can make a thousand adjustments to a site in response to the changes AdWord brings. But for most products and services, you need just a few crucial changes:

✦ **Consider product and service pages to be landing pages.** (You may later make customized versions for various purposes, but even these can be based on product and service pages.) Think of visitors to these pages as potential buyers — but don't change to urgent, sales-oriented language.

✦ **Look at the rest of your site as supporting information for sales.** Pages on your site should meet objections, provide supporting information, and so on. You still need to provide other information for other stake-holders, such as the press; in fact, AdWords-inspired visitors consider this reassuring.

✦ **Make it very easy for people to contact you.** Every site should have a Contact Us or similar link on every page; Wiley, an extremely reputable company, has a contact link at the top and bottom of every page. For smaller sites, being easy to contact means putting an e-mail address and phone number on every page. BATCS achieves this by using an image of a business card as a graphical element on every page, including the vital phone number and e-mail address.

✦ **Make sure everything on your site is correct — spelled right, for-matted correctly.** This is far more important than fancy graphics or advanced multimedia features. With AdWords, you can be sure that you're meeting potential customers on your site. Getting these details right is like dressing well for a meeting; getting them wrong is like arriving with torn trousers and ketchup stains on your grimy t-shirt.

Do you need professional help?

Google offers the option of getting professional help with starting your AdWords campaign. If you commit to spend a few hundred dollars a month on AdWords, a Google pro will help you get started.

This is certainly an attractive option for larger businesses that can devote a lot of time to acting on the pro's suggestions. For medium-sized and small businesses, though, the commitment may outweigh the benefit. You may get clicks and traffic — and pay for it — before you're ready to turn it into a profitable business.

Consider getting started with the steps in this chapter, getting a couple of months of results, and making a few sales through your AdWords efforts before jumping on the Jumpstart bandwagon. Then, when you're ready, visit www.google.com/jutart.

Using AdWords for a Split Test

One of the most sophisticated marketing techniques ever invented (and that usually costs at least thousands of dollars to implement) is just a few clicks away in AdWords: the *split test*.

The idea with split tests is that you run two versions of an ad (or sell a product in two different boxes, for two different prices, and so on) and see which one does better. The difficulty is in the numbers.

You not only need to get thousands of people to see the two versions; you need to get hundreds to act on them. You can imagine the expenditures in ad placements, dummy boxes, and so on, needed to get any kind of meaningful results. You spend weeks of time and make payments to people who think up, set up, execute, and analyze the whole process.

You can do the same thing for just a few dollars in AdWords. And get results in hours or days. And try variations as fast as you can think of them.

Now, as with any AdWords work you do, we're not suggesting you just start randomly creating ads to run against each other. No one has the time, energy, or money to just keep throwing random stuff at the wall to see what sticks.

But a few hours' work can help you come up with two similar but distinctive ads, each of which has its plusses and minuses. These can only be tested — then used or improved further — by split testing.

Follow these instructions to run a split test. Then use the results to improve all your ads:

1. **Sign into your AdWords account.**

   Your dashboard appears.

2. **Look for your ad in the upper-left area under the My Ad Campaign tab. Under your ad, click the Create Another Ad link.**

   The Create Another Ad panel appears, as shown in Figure 3-1.

3. **Click the A Variation on My Current Ad radio button.**

   Ignore the other option, A New Ad for a Different Purpose, for now.

   A new area, titled Create an Ad Variation, appears on the same Web page, as shown in Figure 3-2.

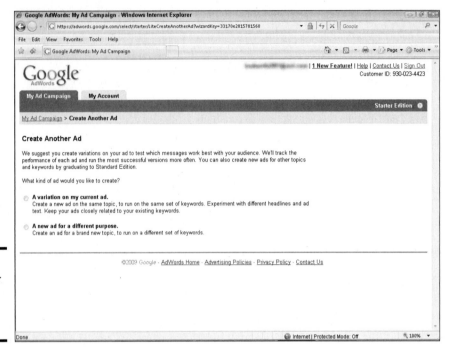

Figure 3-1:
Now's your
chance to
create a
new ad.

Figure 3-2:
Here's
where you
change the
link and the
words.

Using AdWords for testing ideas

How do you test a new idea for a product using AdWords?

Easy enough; create an AdWords ad for the product or service, and see how many clicks it gets.

Where should the clicks go? Simple enough; create an additional page on your site, unconnected to navigation, to serve as a landing page for your test ad. Thank the user for visiting, and consider asking them to send you an e-mail if they'd like to know more about the product

if it launches. (Don't try to sell them anything; they're probably annoyed at unwillingly being part of a test.)

Split tests and idea checking in AdWords are being used every day now, by companies big and small. Best-selling books have arrived at their titles using AdWords.

So now you have a nearly free and very easy way to test your ideas online — and one that sharpens your AdWords skills for your existing products as well.

**Book VI
Chapter 3**

**Selling More with
Google Analysis
Tools**

4. **Change the text of the ad to create the new version. If you also want the new version to direct users to a different landing page, click the Edit link next to the destination link and enter the new URL. To change the displayed link, click the link Edit next to that. When you're done, click the Create Ad button.**

   Often, the same landing page works if you're just making changes to wording to test effectiveness.

   After you click the Create Ad button, your new ad is launched and your dashboard appears. (See the next section.)

    Note the figures — impressions and clicks — for your existing ad before launching the ads together. Otherwise you won't be able to compare results for both ads over an identical time period. (You can avoid this by fine-tuning the reporting period, but you can't know exactly when your new ad actually starts showing, so it's better to subtract the old data.)

Now you just have to sit back and wait for results!

How do you know when you have good results? Certain statistical tests can give you a pretty good idea. A rule of thumb that we've used in the past is that 100 total clicks between the ads is a fairly large number for a relatively brief sampling period — if you stop at exactly 100 clicks, it's easy to calculate percentages. And 100 clicks might only cost you about $10.

Still, 100 clicks usually are only *indicative*, as the statisticians say. For results that are quite likely to be statistically significant, let 1,000 clicks accumulate. This may cost about $100, so make sure your sales machine is up to the task of making the money back. With 1,000 clicks, your results are much more trustworthy statistically — and, if you stop at exactly 1,000 clicks, it's easy to calculate percentages.

Showing More Options in Your Dashboard

Simplicity is great for starting out, but sometimes a bit more complexity can be better.

So it is with the Google AdWords Dashboard, as shown in Figure 3-3. The Dashboard hides, by default, one of the most important settings that AdWords has — and it encourages you to let Google manage this setting for you.

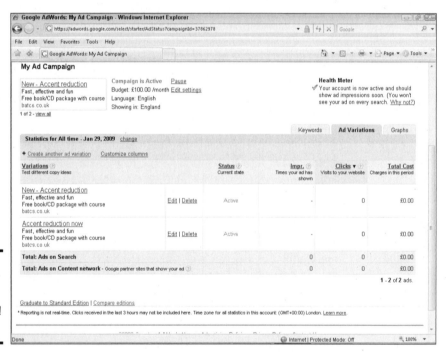

Figure 3-3: On your marks, get set — dash! (board).

This can work fine, or it can lead to very odd results. You must at least understand the settings — including the hidden ones — so you can know what each of them does.

The whole idea of a Dashboard is to allow you to quickly scan the status of something important — your car, your jumbo jet, or your Google AdWords campaign — and quickly, intuitively grasp whether things are going well or poorly. Then you can drill down into the details of any problem areas (or areas that are okay, but could be better) and improve them. Master the settings on your Dashboard — as well as what isn't there — and optimize it to reflect your needs, so it can do its job properly.

Here are the settings that Google does show by default, and a brief explanation of each:

✦ **Status:** Simply whether the ad is active or not. Pay attention to this setting, and don't let your Dashboard display get cluttered with inactive ads. Save the text of any inactive ad in a word processing document or elsewhere if it's valuable, but get the ads off your dashboard.

✦ **Impressions:** This is the number of times your ad has appeared. If someone sees your name several times in various places, it has a slight but possibly helpful branding effect, even if viewers don't click. But mostly, impressions are only valuable to the extent they drive clicks. You can't get clicks without impressions.

✦ **Clicks:** This is the number of clicks you get — your whole reason for doing all this. Clicks are what costs you money. Getting more clicks is the focus of your efforts with Google AdWords. (Getting better results when you do get a click is the job of your Web site, which also needs your attention.)

✦ **Total Cost:** Usually a column like this is the sum or product of other numbers in a table — but the Dashboard doesn't show the cost per click, so you can't derive the cost yourself. You just have to take on faith that Google knows what it's doing.

This is all useful information, but as you go forward, you need more. Here are the three crucial fields you need to keep on top of:

✦ **Click-through rate (CTR):** This is the most important figure in determining the success of your ad campaign, and you need to track it – but it's not shown directly. The click-through rate is simply the number of clicks your ad gets divided by the number of times it's shown, expressed as a percentage. If you get one click in 100 showings — not an awful rate, by the way — that's a 1.00% click-through rate.

✦ **Budget Optimizer on/off:** This option is not even visible in the Dashboard; you have to click the Edit Settings link to see it, as shown in Figure 3-4. In the Standard Edition of Google AdWords, you spend a lot of time worrying about — we mean, adjusting — your cost-per-click. In the Starter Edition, which we're discussing here, it's set for you by Google as it optimizes your campaign. The Budget Optimizer is great for starting, but you should move away from it (and to the Standard Edition) soon after you get started.

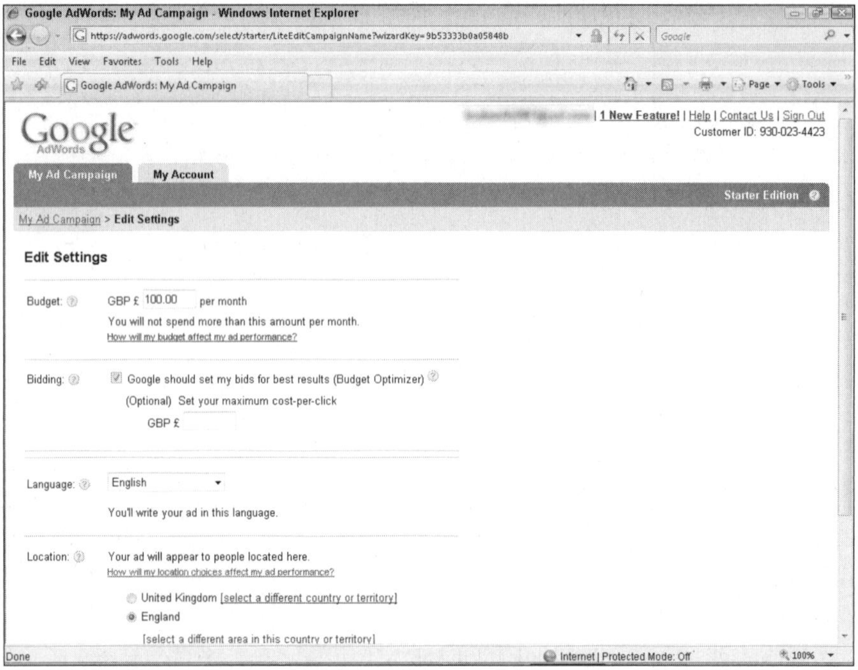

Figure 3-4:
Don't forget
to Edit
Settings.

✦ **Maximum cost-per-click:** Like the Budget Optimizer check box, this option is not visible in the Dashboard, but only after you click the Edit Settings link. This is the most you will spend on a single click. It's optional if Budget Optimizer is turned on — Budget Optimizer optimizes within the cost-per-click limit you set — and required if Budget Optimizer is off.

There are three other fields on the Edit Settings page that you need to keep an eye on:

✦ **Budget:** A small budget might mean few showings of your ad. A large one might mean a large hole in your wallet. Check your spending versus your budget daily to protect yourself.

✦ **Language:** Google AdWords provides the least expensive way imaginable to test your product's appeal in one or more foreign markets, or in different language markets at home (Spanish in the US, French in Canada, Hindi or Arabic in the UK; you'll stand out!). Split test an English-language ad against a different-language one and track the results. It may be worth translating a few Web pages and getting someone bilingual onto your sales staff!

✦ **Location:** This is a huge issue that you should end up spending a lot of time on. You need to begin experimenting with the location to see what effect different levels of targeting have. You have a lot more targeting options in the Standard Edition, so now's the time to begin experimenting.

How Google manages your ads

Google manages your ads in a way that's designed to stretch your budget and maximize both your results and Google's yield. But the specifics of how this works can be opaque and maddening.

You have to totally change your mindset relating to AdWords to understand what Google does with ads. Google wants the highest yield per page shown. That means it wants to put ads near the top with both the highest money per click and the highest chance of getting clicked. It's the product of these two numbers that matters; in particular, a high-paying ad that almost never gets clicked is just about worthless to Google. An attractive, appropriately focused ad that gets a lot of clicks is worth more, even if the cost per click is less.

Google also tries to preserve your budget by rationing your ad showings so you don't run out of displays until the end of the month. This leads to the maddening fact that you often won't see your ad when you do a relevant search, even

if there are few other ads or none at all. Often people try to get around this by setting a high budget, promising themselves to manage it down as the target approaches — then they never do that, so Google gets more per month than you really want it to.

Your precious ad is just grist to the AdWords mill. If it has a high budget and drives clicks at a decent rate, it gets shown — high up and a lot. If not, it gets left off. You, friends, family members, and colleagues who go look for it often won't see it — and neither will customers.

That's why it's important to learn about AdWords and to make needed Web site and business process changes quickly, before you give up from lack of money/profit, sheer frustration, or both. This book is a good taster, but if you like AdWords at all after trying it, move up to *AdWords For Dummies* by Howie Jacobson (Wiley, 2009) and other books, articles, and Web sites that can help you get more out of AdWords.

After you start to understand what kind of click-through rate you're getting, you can start using the Maximum cost-per-click rate if you want to — after all, you may know the most a click is likely to be worth to you. But although we also advocate turning off the Budget Optimizer as soon as you can, you need all the information you can get to make the most of the control you gain — which means you should move to the Standard Edition of Google AdWords at that time or soon after.

Because it's somewhat obscured in the Starter Edition, we have not yet explained a key feature of Google AdWords, and here is a good point to do so. AdWords does not always charge you the maximum cost-per-click you set. Instead, it charges you as little as it can to get the best placement possible.

Let's say there are two ads that could run on a page — yours and one other. The other ad has a maximum cost-per-click of 5¢, and you have a maximum cost-per-click of 10¢.

Google places the other ad second and charges its owner 5¢ — and places your ad first and charges you just over 5¢. This is called the AdWords Discounter. You're only charged the minimum you need to pay for your placement.

Now theoretically that should mean you pay next to nothing when your ad is the only one on a page, as you only have to beat 0¢; but you can actually only be assured that what you pay is somewhat less than your maximum cost per click.

Looking at AdWords Graphs

As you would expect from a dashboard, AdWords produces attractive graphs that can help you manage your account — and it helps you export results to a spreadsheet for further analysis.

When you click the Graphs tab, you see results much like Figure 3-5. (This is after clicking the Change link to show some of the options for changing time periods of the graphs.) The graphs — Clicks, Costs, and Impressions per day — are pretty self-explanatory.

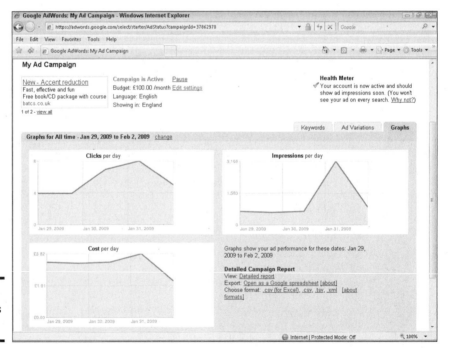

Figure 3-5:
Turn curves
into cash.

They're in the right order in terms of focus, but the wrong order in terms of process. Impressions must happen before clicks, and cost is the result of clicks. So let's discuss them in that order:

✦ **Impressions:** Watch how your impressions vary, first by weekdays versus weekends and then by specific days of the week. This tells you whether your keywords are disproportionately getting searched on at some times rather than others. And yes, it is worth it to, for instance, take down your ads on a weekend if you determine that your sales and profits are less on days when no one's at work to answer the phone — or that it's worth your taking a few calls on the weekends! (Or, alternatively, when someone searching for, say, *limo* is looking for more of a fun-oriented service rather than your business-oriented one.)

✦ **Clicks:** Now look at clicks versus impressions by day. Counter-trends — where the pattern of clicks declines or rises versus the trends in impressions — are interesting, not only for optimizing opportunities from "good" clicks but eliminating "bad" ones that aren't generating business — but are costing you money.

✦ **Cost per day:** Look at your cost per day versus the business you're getting — which is the "missing chart" that you need to generate for comparison. If there are days when costs are low and sales are high, you know what to do!

Changing the time period

You can easily change the time period you're looking at. Just follow these steps:

1. **Click the Change link, to pull down the options for changing the time period.**

2. **To see one of the canned time periods, click the larger pull-down menu and choose a time period, as shown in Figure 3-6. To choose a custom time period, click the smaller pull-down menus, and specify the date range (at least two days). Click Go.**

The choices for the larger pull-down menu are Today; Yesterday; Last 7 days; Last week (Mon-Sun); Last business week (Mon-Fri); This week; Last month; and All time.

When you click Go, the graphs updates.

If you get the persistent error message, "Clicks are unavailable for a period of less than two days," choose the All time option to restore the graphs. Then try different time periods again.

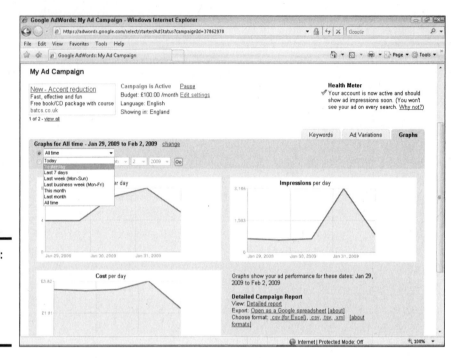

Figure 3-6:
Canned
settings
produce
fresh
results.

3. **To view a detailed report, look in the lower-right area — where the fourth graph would be if there were one — and click the Detailed Report link.**

   A detailed report appears, including a breakdown by keyword, as shown in Figure 3-7. You can also see in the figure that you have options for exporting the report in various formats.

Look at your numbers during different time periods. Although detailed analysis is best done in a spreadsheet — see the next section — you can get a quick feel by using some obvious and potentially counter-intuitive time periods:

✦ **A full week:** Look at data a full week at a time to see differences in individual days and in weekdays versus weekends. Or pull up two weeks at a time; your eye should be pretty good at spotting similarities and differences in the patterns. More than two weeks, and it is hard to see much in the tiny graphs AdWords produces.

✦ **A calendar month:** A calendar month maps to the way you pay many of your bills and gives you a feel for any effect of monthly or bimonthly paydays and so on. Again, if you pull up two full calendar months, you can spot similarities and differences in the patterns rather well.

✦ **A calendar month plus a week before and after:** You can spot monthly trends even better if you review the weeks before and after a given month.

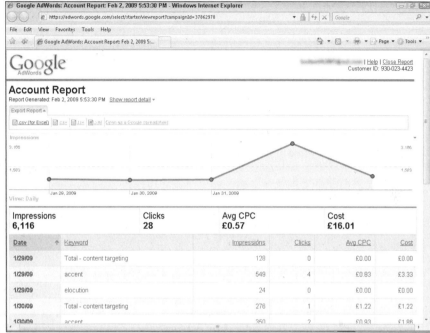

**Book VI
Chapter 3**

Selling More with
Google Analysis
Tools

Figure 3-7:
AdWords'
big report is
impressive
— if your
numbers are
good!

All this is valuable and a great way to spot trends and get ideas. But to really get very far with the data AdWords produces, you need to export your data to a spreadsheet.

The danger of days

The speed with which your ads get put into service varies, as do the habits of people at various times of the day. So it's hard to make much sense of the results you get the day you make a change or the day after.

After some initial experimentation, let your ads run for long enough to get a real sense for trends — a calendar month gives you a good idea, especially if your business is affected by days of the week, changes in the weather, or how close it is to payday for different groups of your customers.

Of course, a full year's data is necessary to get on top of seasonal trends, back to school, and so on, but it may take many months of experimentation before you're ready to let a campaign run with little change for that long.

(Quick) looks can be deceiving

The graphs in the AdWords Dashboard are great for getting a quick first impression or spotting emerging problems. But if you're spending any kind of money at all, they can flatter to deceive — make you think you're more on top of things than you really are. Subtle, but possibly important trends are simply too hard to spot in the simple graphs AdWords produces.

After you get going with your AdWords program, develop the discipline of exporting your numbers to a spreadsheet. Simply click one of the spreadsheet-related links and save the file.

Then combine the newly exported numbers with an ongoing spreadsheet that tracks all your AdWords data. With this spreadsheet you should be able to slice and dice the numbers, producing charts and graphs.

Everyone does different things with spreadsheets — and with business results — but be ready to produce at least the following:

✦ **Daily trends.** Yes, AdWords produces a daily trends graph for you, but it's quite small. You need the ability to produce large, easy-to-read graphs where you can see the individual days and map them to various events in the real world — weekdays and weekends, vacations (yours and your customers'), events and seasonality in your line of business, and so on. Use this to reduce the number of low-sales days and increase the impact of your best days.

✦ **Weekly trends.** Weekly trends cut out a lot of the daily "noise" and give you an idea of how your business is really doing over time. There are only 52 weeks in a year, so weekly trends can help you quickly see how thing are going over the longer term.

✦ **Monthly trends.** If you have a small- to medium-sized business, there's a good chance that your business is changing enough that monthly trends aren't fully comparable. You do need to produce monthly trends for analysis, but in many cases weekly trends are the most useful.

You should be able to produce average sales and profits increases and decreases for each of these time periods. And don't forget to produce two-day, two-week, and two-month graphs so you can quickly compare one period to another.

Producing trendlines

The way the eye sees trends in highly varying curves can be quite deceiving. A technique called linear regression can help; the most popular type uses least squares analysis. It finds the straight line that best fits a given trend.

In Microsoft Excel, the function to use is called TREND. Other spreadsheets may or may not have similar functions. However, some online sites now calculate a least squares line for you. You can then fit this line back onto your own chart by drawing a straight line between the start and end points of the least squares line.

This shows you, for instance, when you might expect gradually increasing sales to reach a given point. Or, less optimistically, when gradually decreasing sales might disappear altogether!

Which reminds us of the point of all this. Avoid "paralysis by analysis" — use the data you gather to help you take practical steps to increase your sales, cut your costs, and build your business.

The futility of stupidity

In the AdWords world, little things can mean a lot. Figure 3-8 shows the results of a search on *AdWords For Dummies*. Can you spot the (admittedly small) mistake? (One of the names has been changed to protect the not-so-innocent.)

If not, look in the lower-right corner. The mistake is within the ad title: Adwords tutorial.

Still don't see it? AdWords uses a nefarious marketing trick beloved of technology companies, the intercap. That's a capital letter in the middle of a word. Truly an unnatural act in English, but very common in marketing.

But some ads don't use the intercap, opting for a lower-case "w". Why? A simple mistake, of course.

But AdWords is all about the relentless pursuit of details. If someone is trying to get you to spend time and money with them to get your details right, shouldn't he be able to get the details right first?

Figure 3-8:
Can you
spot the
error?

Sharpen up those #2 pencils and put on your green accountant's eyeshade
as you plunge into AdWords. Be ready to dot your i's and cross your t's. The
margin between an expensive experiment and successfully building your
business through AdWords is very small indeed.

Introducing Google Analytics

The Starter Edition of AdWords has many advantages. One is the reports
we've discussed. The Standard Edition has many nice features, including the
capability to create custom reports; but it lacks the simple, standard reports
of the Starter Edition.

The Standard Edition also allows you to manage multiple advertising campaigns — definitely necessary if you manage multiple Web sites, but not
such a huge advantage if you only manage one.

What we're trying to say here is that, as long as your spending is fairly low and you're still learning a lot, there's not that much reason to upgrade to the Standard Edition except for one thing: It's only with the Standard Edition that you can access Google Analytics. The home page for Google Analytics is shown in Figure 3-9. It's not an accident that it uses some small type and some big words.

Google Analytics is extremely powerful — and a lot of work. You must understand a few basic concepts and accomplish a few tasks to use Google Analytics successfully:

✦ **Auto-Tagging:** Google goes to the Web page that your AdWords ad links to and tags it so as to pick up reporting information. (Wow!)

✦ **Tracking code:** But Google can't do it all; you have to add tracking code, provided by Google, to some or a lot of your Web site pages.

✦ **Filtering out "friends and family:"** You do not, of course, want to count visits from yourself, colleagues, and employees, and so on in your Google Analytics reports. So you have to enter the IP address — a number like 87.65.43.21 — of every computer used by any one of the visitors you want to eliminate so those computers can be ignored.

✦ **Creating and naming goals and funnels:** A goal might be getting someone to a product page. (A visit from a curious friend, then, would be an "own goal.") A funnel is the series of pages that leads them there. You have to define and name each goal and funnel so you can track the major paths into your key Web pages.

✦ **Data integrity checks:** In case you messed up some of the previously mentioned points, you need to use Google AdWords reports as comparisons to your Analytics data to find out where — and to be sure that you're not counting some of the same traffic twice.

Google Analytics does to your Web site and your AdWords campaign what the doctors do to you when you get a detailed physical: the online equivalent of attaching wires, measuring oxygen in and CO_2 out, and putting perspiration in little pipettes for further analysis. Analytics instruments takes a measure of your Web site — but you have to learn what all the measurements mean.

Figure 3-9:
Be ready
to use this
separately
for each
goal-funnel
combination.

Google Analytics is extremely powerful — but pretty darn complicated. We don't necessarily recommend it until you've thoroughly explored and mastered the features and reports in the Starter Edition, then in the Standard Edition, and now are using a spreadsheet to create some pretty nice custom reports as well. Oh, and we assume you are carefully studying Web site reports and have a pretty good idea how traffic is moving about on your site already.

Howie Jacobson, the author of *AdWords For Dummies* (Wiley, 2009) has kindly lent us a key figure from Google Analytics as our own Figure 3-10. It shows the funnel for a catalog request, a key goal for some Web sites.

We don't want to discourage you from ever using Google Analytics. However, we do want you to understand that it takes time and effort to master, and that you should first master other tools before investing the time and effort needed to get the most out of it.

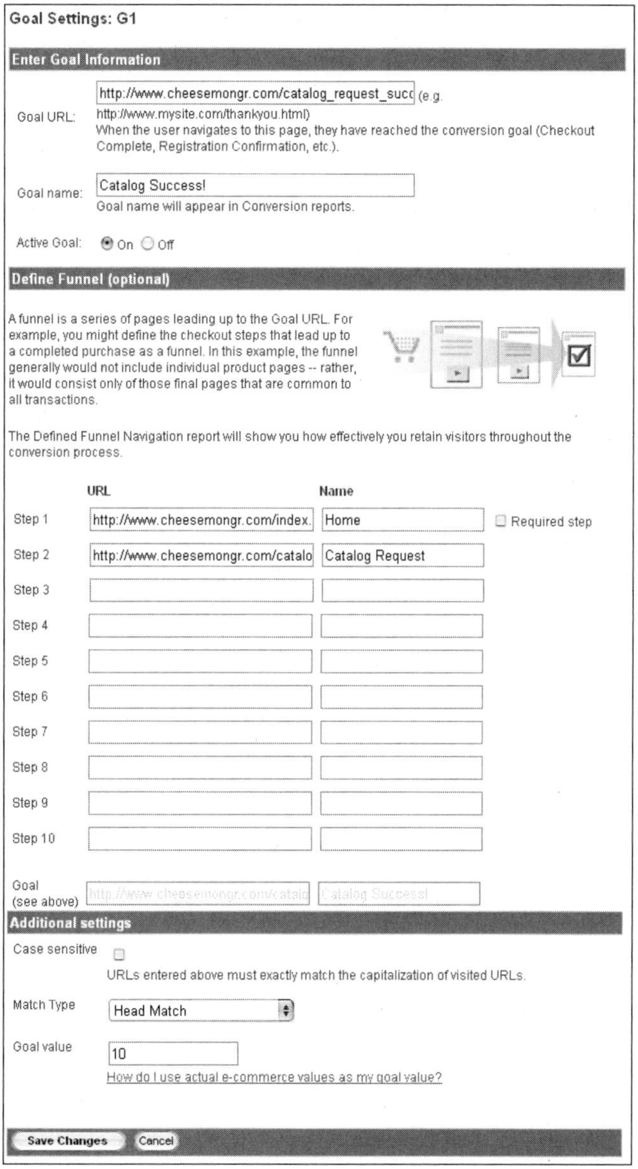

Goal Settings: G1

Enter Goal Information

Goal URL: http://www.cheesemongr.com/catalog_request_succ (e.g.
http://www.mysite.com/thankyou.html)
When the user navigates to this page, they have reached the conversion goal (Checkout
Complete, Registration Confirmation, etc.).

Goal name: Catalog Success!
Goal name will appear in Conversion reports.

Active Goal: ⦿ On ◯ Off

Define Funnel (optional)

A funnel is a series of pages leading up to the Goal URL. For
example, you might define the checkout steps that lead up to
a completed purchase as a funnel. In this example, the funnel
generally would not include individual product pages -- rather,
it would consist only of those final pages that are common to
all transactions.

The Defined Funnel Navigation report will show you how effectively you retain visitors throughout the
conversion process.

	URL	Name	
Step 1	http://www.cheesemongr.com/index.	Home	☐ Required step
Step 2	http://www.cheesemongr.com/catalo	Catalog Request	
Step 3			
Step 4			
Step 5			
Step 6			
Step 7			
Step 8			
Step 9			
Step 10			
Goal (see above)	http://www.cheesemongr.com/catalo	Catalog Success!	

Additional settings

Case sensitive   ☐
URLs entered above must exactly match the capitalization of visited URLs.

Match Type   Head Match ⬍

Goal value   10
How do I use actual e-commerce values as my goal value?

Save Changes   Cancel

Figure 3-10:
Be ready
to do this
separately
for each
goal-funnel
combination.

Book VI
Chapter 3

Selling More with
Google Analysis
Tools

Chapter 4: Maximizing Your Site and Your AdWords Ads

In This Chapter

✔ Understanding customer traffic and how it affects your site

✔ Making sure your site gives users what they're looking for

✔ Targeting your ads with the best timing and location

✔ Increasing traffic to your Web site

*G*oogle AdWords is a perfect complement to the entire set of Google's search functions, Google Apps, and related Google-based capabilities. Other Google-based capabilities allow you to save a great deal of money, get work done more easily and quickly, and get the word out about your business. Google AdWords, however, is the most direct way to make money — taking advantage of the effort you've already invested in all things Google.

A big part of benefitting from Google Search, AdWords, and your Web site — three closely related areas in which you invest time and money — is understanding the different ways Web site traffic does (and in some cases doesn't) benefit you and your business. Some effects are quite subtle; others are very direct indeed. Synching up your Web site with the rest of what you do in your business is vital to your overall success.

When you understand this, you see why increasing traffic to your site — in smart ways — is critical to your success. AdWords is the quick, easy (and potentially expensive) way to do it, but there are other equally important ways as well.

Google AdWords is, first, a great complement to Google Search. In fact, it's a focused and efficient way to come close to doing something millions of businesspeople would love to do, which is to buy places in Google Search results. So looking at how your AdWords ads complement your results in unpaid — *organic* — Google Search is a crucial way to get the best out of both.

Part of the advantage of using AdWords ads instead of directly buying Google Search results is how targeted Google Ads are. You can target your AdWords ads by location, by day and time, in relation to events, and by products. If this sounds like you're going to end up spending all your time targeting your AdWords ads, the truth is that you might — but only because, for some people in some businesses, it's a very rewarding way to spend time.

Understanding Why Traffic Matters

So many companies understand that they need to have a Web site without an understanding of what a Web site can and should do for them. It's a lot like a retailer understanding he needs to have a store without understanding anything about what makes a store work well or poorly.

In fact, what's happened in the real world of retail is that bigger companies, made up of company-owned or franchised stores, have increasingly displaced smaller and even medium-sized companies, putting them, to be blunt, out of business, or at best relegating them to smaller and smaller niches.

Pressure comes from traditional retailers and the online world as well. Amazon.com, shown in Figure 4-1, started out (and is still most famous as) a bookseller. But in recent years, its best-selling category in the crucial Christmas season has been not books but electronics. On-line and off-line retailers in all the categories Amazon now offers — as shown in Figure 4-1 — need to be looking over their shoulders and work to preserve revenues and profits.

Smaller businesses do have advantages: They tend to know their customers, know their type of business well, and know their local areas better than big chains do. But larger businesses have cost advantages and, when they learn how to keep an attractive, productive store, they can then amortize that hard-won (and often expensive) knowledge over a number of properties. The same thing can easily happen online.

In fact, we see this happening today with e-commerce. The bigger and better-known a site is — whether that fame has been gained online, offline, or both — the more likely people are to buy from it online, especially using a credit card. Smaller and lesser-known sites are simply shut out of consideration by many potential customers.

This is part of the reason BATCS doesn't sell its only book, *Get Rid of your Accent*, online directly — but instead points to Amazon and other online and off-line retailers. Rather than leave users agonizing about whether to trust a small site, it removes the option and leaves them focused on buying.

Even if you're not American, the US Census Web site is a fantastic source of market and marketing information and data. With information about 25 million businesses, 100 million households, and about 300 million Americans, not only is there a rich vein of information to study, it's not that hard to calculate some of the key percentages. And there's a great deal of non-census information that you can correlate to census data as well. Visit www.census.gov to start looking; some key statistics about business size in the US are shown in Figure 4-2.

Figure 4-1:
You can find an Amazon breadth of products online.

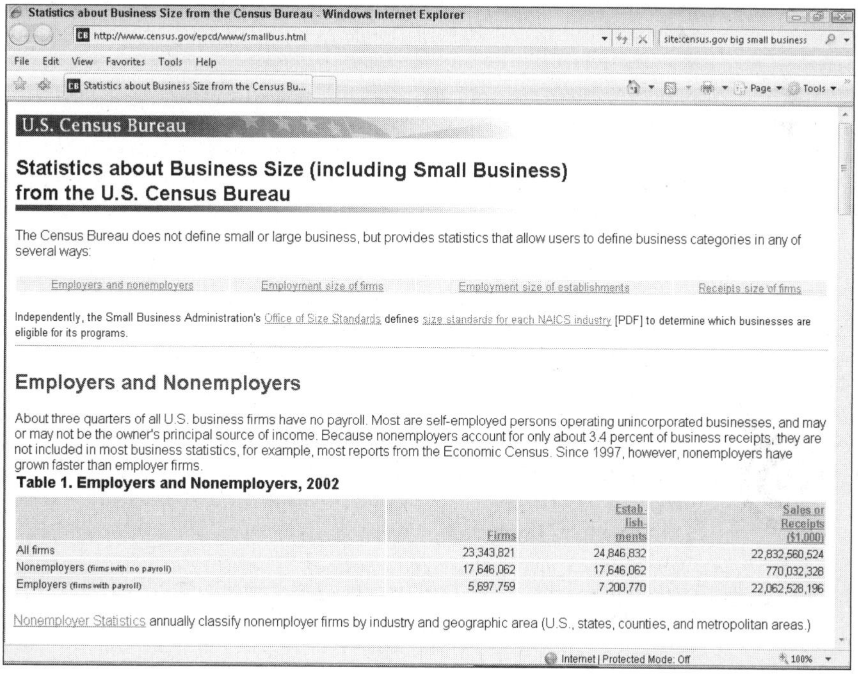

Figure 4-2:
If you're serious about business, start with the US Census.

So it's important that you make the most of your Web site now — even, or especially, if things are going well — so you're ready to make the most money you can today and to face online, real-world, and blended competition tomorrow.

Making Sure Your Site Lives Up to Expectations

There's a lot of guff flying around about what a Web site is for. Most people, particularly the owners and managers of small- and medium-sized businesses, see the Web site as a kind of online brochure. Its appearance seems to be the most important thing about it.

Indeed, many Web site designers — perhaps a majority — are graphic designers, people who know how to make things look good and who have backed into Web site design. They don't necessarily have expertise in what users want from Web sites, how users can most effectively get it, or what businesses need sites to do. Given the tendency we all share to "go with what you know," much of the advice you get about your Web site tends to reflect how it looks rather than what it does.

If you were to follow the user-friendliness advice too literally — that is, to give users exactly what they want — every Web site would have a single button labeled "Send me a million dollars," and would use psychic technology to know where to send the money. Using a related idea, Alex Tew created the Million Dollar Homepage — shown in Figure 4-3. He sold every one of one million pixels on his page to the highest bidder — and made just over a million dollars.

The misapprehension that design matters most had some truth to it in the early days of the Web when people were more impressed that you had a site than by what was in it. They would even click around out of interest to see what was there. But increasingly, as with retail shopping, people are task-oriented: They want to get things done and go to the place where they can most easily do it. You can still create experiences for people online, as you do off-line, but not at the expense of the quick visit.

As with off-line retailers, you also have to judge your site by the company it keeps. As the old saw goes, the top three keys for a successful business are "location, location, location." But whereas a real-world shopper approaches a business from one of a few different directions by road, a typical shopper today comes to you via a search — most often a Google search. Your "location" within organic and paid search results is your priority.

You also need to understand how people use the Web these days. They use it largely as a Web of pages, not a Web of sites. That is, they follow the best path to their goal, whether that path is within a site or across several sites.

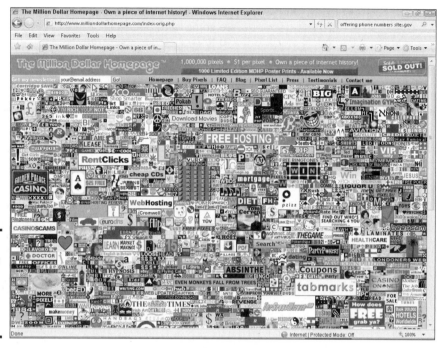

Figure 4-3:
If only every
Web site
made a
million this
easily.

Different people have different uses for your site at different times.

People also have *primary* and *secondary* uses for your site. They may be there to learn about your new product — but they look at your press releases out of interest or to make sure you're "for real." They may be Googling you or one of your company's other employees, but end up looking at your products out of interest — and may even end up buying.

Don't forget, too, that there's a difference between people who are looking to buy *from you* and those who are looking to buy *from whomever meets their need best*. This latter group may or may not know, at the beginning of a Web search, whether you exist; if they find you as the result of a search, your site must reassure and inform them a great deal if it's to initiate a contact or even a sale.

Also remember that one of the primary purposes of a site is to *reassure*. That means it includes all the major functions that a Web site is expected to include, and provides them in a way that's similar to other sites of the same type — and, where it is different, there is a good reason.

Here's a brief checklist of what users look for in any Web site — even if they visit only one page:

✦ **Clean, attractive design:** This is like having a clean store instead of a dirty one. An ugly site or hard to understand site design simply stops people at the front door — they decide not to come in, but click away instead.

✦ **Major functions covered:** People expect one Web site to look pretty much like another one. (When you go into a grocery store, you might ask "Where's the frozen foods aisle?", but not "Is there a frozen foods aisle?") That means your site should clearly display major functions, including Home, Contact, About Us or something similar, product and service descriptions, information for the press, and information about applying for a job. For larger businesses, some kind of public service or similar commitment is somewhere between a plus and an expected feature.

✦ **Contact Us very easy to find:** People who are trying to contact you become very frustrated if this is difficult, and in particular if you hide your phone number — despite the fact that displaying it clearly can send your call volume skyrocketing, with many of the calls not very useful. Even people who are not trying to contact you at the time may want to record your contact information or otherwise be aware of whether you make this information very easily accessible.

The gold standard for contact information these days is to put it on every page — as BATCS does with its business card image — and also have a Contact Us page with the traditional information plus maps, directions, e-mail addresses for specific departments, and so on. A Contact Us form is fine — as long as it doesn't displace the other information, as in the example shown in Figure 4-4. (And yes, the Contact information should include a phone number.)

✦ **A site map:** A site map isn't necessary for sites of ten pages or fewer, but for more pages than that it becomes a very nice feature — and above 50 pages or so it is a strictly necessary one. (See Figure 4-5.)

Including comprehensive contact information

Most Web sites give contact information fairly even-handedly, but this is not really a good idea for many businesses. A key question facing you is: How do you want people buying from you to contact you?

Many businesses are so concerned with avoiding an (often imagined) flood of calls from people with problems, pranksters, and copier salespeople that they hide their contact information, especially their phone numbers. But your Web site, if effectively designed, should be a strong sales tool. How do you want people to buy from you?

Unless you are launching a strongly focused e-commerce site — and that usually takes a lot of money and backing, so don't try that lightly — the main answer is going to be by phone or in person. So you want your key Web site visitors — the strong potential customers — to call you.

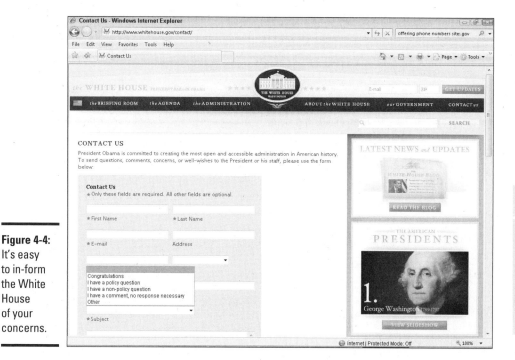

Figure 4-4:
It's easy
to in-form
the White
House
of your
concerns.

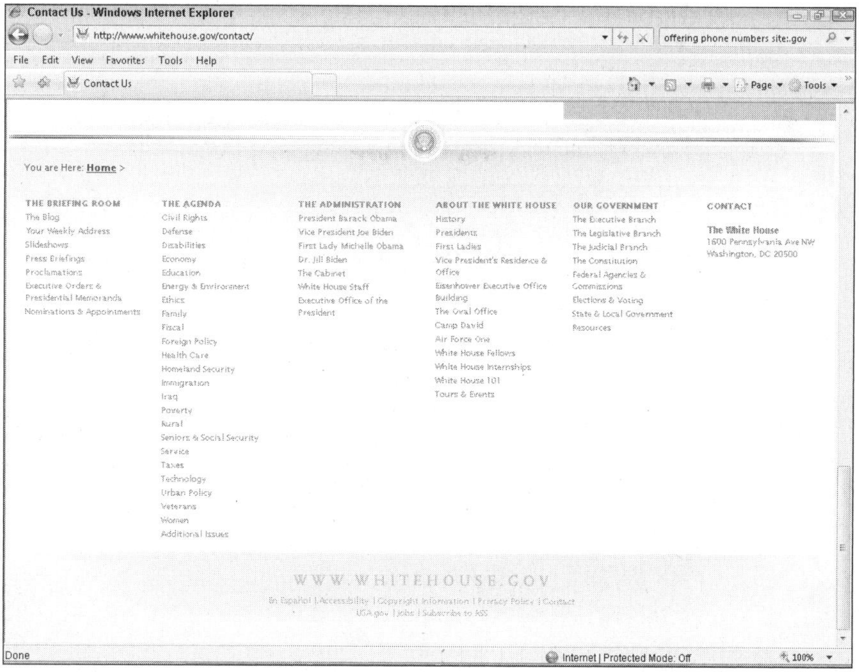

Figure 4-5:
Keeping the
government
in site.

If that means you get a fair number of unwanted calls, so be it. If you make calling you the least bit difficult, the people you discourage are the potential customers, who generally have other options and other things to do — not the people you consider bothersome, who don't.

Most Web sites, in our humble opinion — well, not that humble, we're filling a 900-page book with our ideas — miss a trick here. We think that companies should really think through the phone number issue, including considering the following:

+ **Put the phone number on every page:** It can be prominent — say, in the upper-right corner — or low key, in small text on the bottom of each page. It can be accompanied by your mailing address or not, as you please. Either way, the people you want to call you will really like this.

+ **Include your business hours:** There's nothing that makes someone feel as stupid as calling you expecting an answer and not getting one, so post business hours on your Web site — in the Contact Us section is fine, but you can also do so on every page — and keep to those hours.

+ **Improve your phone message:** We've been stunned to find the number of companies that don't post their business hours on their Web sites, and don't put it on a message on their phones either — so you can't find out when they are open until they are. This is a terrible way to begin your relationship with a by-now-frustrated customer.

+ **Make it easy to get a call-back:** If someone wants you to call him or her, make it easy. This can be as simple as inviting an e-mail from the person including a suggested time when he or she would like you to call. (You can always negotiate a new time if the suggested one is not good for you.)

+ **Consider live chat:** We love live chat features on Web sites. They pleasantly exceed expectations by giving immediate access to information to nerdy people like ourselves who'd rather type than talk. However, you should only do this if you can staff it — not necessarily with an expert, just with someone helpful — at least 80% of the time during business hours and any extended hours you wish to support.

Not every site can, or possibly should, do what the Maryland state government does — which is put the name, department, and phone number of every employee and every department online, as shown in Figure 4-6. For one thing, executive search companies could use the information to try to poach your staff. But from a customer point of view, this is an ideal. Get as close to it as you can.

Adding e-commerce

Going to a full e-commerce site is certainly doable, for anyone determined enough to do it — although the summary offered by the US Department of Commerce might make it seem a bit simpler than it really is. (See Figure 4-7.)

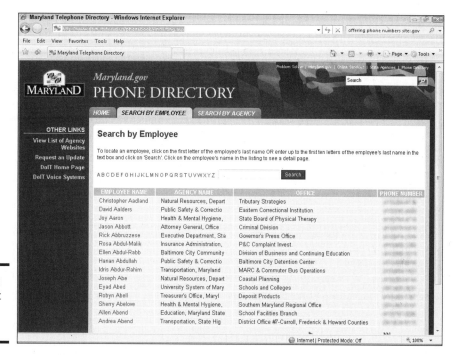

Figure 4-6:
Rikki won't
lose these
numbers.

Figure 4-7:
The US
Depart-
ment of
Commerce
makes
e-commerce
easy.

There are also many process issues that can come up with e-commerce, some of which are mentioned in the following steps. The old medical admonition, "First, do no harm" applies here. Talk to whomever is involved in your current sales effort to discover any concerns about e-commerce. Address them clearly and forthrightly, and consider protecting anyone who might suffer during a transition. (Usually, sales start out slower than you hope — and slower than your existing salespeople or sales partners may fear.)

Beginning online sales step by step may help. As you gradually build up your AdWords expertise, your Web site capabilities, and your understanding of how business really works, you can take steps toward full e-commerce, including any of the following:

✦ **Adding credit card capability:** If you don't already take credit cards, consider doing so. If you take credit cards for other business, add online credit-card capability.

✦ **Simplifying the phone call:** Give customers more and more online information and help them build their orders online. Then have them call for the final step of placing the order. If several callers have the same questions, try to put the answers to those questions into your Web site text to simplify the process, for them and you.

✦ **Supporting re-orders online:** This is the best way for many businesses to start e-commerce. Support re-orders by existing customers online. Customers love this because it makes routine re-orders fast and trouble-free. There's no problem with the customer trusting you or with you trusting them; you can even leave payment out of the process and simply put the order on account.

Having your customers re-order online saves you and them time and money. Consider giving them a small discount for these sales — you may also want to tie it to early payment.

If someone's currently getting a commission for re-orders, consider having the same person get at least most of the same commission if the re-order is online.

All these steps are great moves toward full e-commerce. You can also use them to work out appropriate adjustments in how you work with any current distributors, handle returns and complaints, decide whether salespeople get a share of credit for online sales, and so on.

Comparing Yourself to Your Competition

There's another step you can take which is always a good idea in many different parts of your business, but especially so when you consider using AdWords and e-commerce capability: comparing yourself to your competition.

This relates to an old story about two hikers and a bear. Two hikers are resting by a stream when they see a bear a few hundred yards away across a meadow. One of the hikers sits up and quickly removes his boots, switching them for running shoes. The other hiker says, "That's silly. Even with running shoes, you're not going to outrun a bear." The first hiker says, "I don't have to outrun a bear. I just have to outrun you."

This is similar to your situation with selling online — whether through full e-commerce or not. You don't have to have the perfect Web site or e-commerce capability. You just have to be better than your direct competitors.

Some purchases of products like yours start with a keyword search by people who don't know you or your competition. Others are from people who know you, or your competitor(s), or both. And some start with a visit to your Web site — sometimes involving a check of a competitor's Web site, some not.

So you need to look at your competitive position from a variety of perspectives. One thing to keep in mind here, before investing much in e-commerce, is to "go big, or don't go at all." That is, you have to do it well enough to beat at least some of your competition and get at least some sales, or you might as well wait to make the capability available until it's good enough. (Don't wait too long, though, or you might have trouble catching up.)

If you encourage your customers to buy online from you, they're likely to comparison-shop online while they're at it. Make sure your process and offer are competitive before you start something you may not be able to finish in a positive way.

You can pursue competitive comparisons in many other areas — who offers the best deal in various geographic areas, for different product types, and for different types of customer. You can compare various aspects of your Web site as well.

One of the key features of Google Analytics, described in Chapter 3, is the idea of *funnels* — Web pages that lead the customer, you hope inexorably, from one step of the purchasing process to the next. Compare your funnel to your competitors. It doesn't have to end in an e-commerce sale; a phone call or an appointment made online are other possible results.

Amazon.com is the gold standard for offering an easy to use e-commerce process with lots of extras and special features. Consider including Amazon in your competitive comparisons, even if it is not a direct competitor of yours. And if it is, don't be discouraged; even in the US, where Amazon is strongest, it has less than five per cent of all book sales. Most book sales go elsewhere.

Targeting Google Ads

Now that you've thought some about how to use your site to bring people in, let's look in more detail at how to target your Google AdWords ads to reach the people you want to reach, while saving money that you can use to improve your ads' placement — or for other purposes in your business.

Location, location, location

Earlier, we mentioned the old saw that says the three most important elements in running a business are location, location, and location — and we related it to how people see your business appear in an organic search and Google text ads. But actual physical locations matter a great deal as well.

In Chapter 3, we described how you can use targeting options in the Starter Edition of Google AdWords to narrow the focus of your ad to a particular country or city — for instance, the US, a particular state, or a particular metro area. Now we show you how, in the Standard Edition, you can focus on a variety of different geographical areas.

But before we tackle how, the first question is: Why? Well, that "location, location, location" mantra is hugely important for Google AdWords.

AdWords are already self-adjusting because you only pay for clicks, not for impressions (that is, views of your ads). So anyone who clicks your ad is at least somewhat interested in what you have to offer.

But then the question is, having clicked, how likely is that person to follow through? You need to guesstimate this based on several criteria related to location:

✦ **Distance from you/closeness to competitors:** A pharmacy is highly geographically dependent; people almost always go to the closest one. So it's probably a necessity to run your Google AdWords ad on your turf, pointless to run it on their turf, and worth investigating just where to run it on the contested turf between.

✦ **General idea of *close enough*:** People have a comfort level about how far they'll go for certain kinds of services. Someone in New York is highly unlikely to hire a Web designer based in Boston on the basis of a Google ad; the customer wants to be able to meet.

✦ **Socioeconomic level, age, and so on:** Many products and services appeal disproportionately to certain socioeconomic levels, age groups, and so on. This is somewhat self-correcting at the level of clicks, but you certainly get more wasted clicks from the "wrong" socioeconomic or age groups and fewer from the "right" ones.

The bottom line is that you want to pay for the clicks that are highly likely to follow through and avoid paying for clicks that are highly unlikely to follow through.

BATCS is a good example of this. Offering courses in accent reduction that meet mostly on weekday evenings and being located near a stop on the London Underground, its audience is limited to those willing and able to make the trip after work or after school — in other words, those with access to the Tube, as it's called. So it only makes sense to advertise there.

Some students do come from as far away as Cambridge and Reading, each about half an hour away, but the success rate of clicks from even these fairly nearby areas is lower, and when they do sign up, these students are more difficult to make arrangements with and have poorer attendance. So it's best, if a sufficient number of students can be gotten, to get them from London; and the most effective clicks are the ones that come from, as they say, "within the M25" (the roadway that encircles London).

The best location-based strategy is usually to start with a set of target locations that are the most likely to be your best audience, optimize your AdWords campaign for yield against this audience, and then gradually adjust the target locations to exclude any "dead" areas in the original target zone. You also want to add any "live" areas that are within it. For this kind of strategy, very fine levels of targeting — say, a square block at a time — are potentially useful.

To take advantage of this strategy, you need to upgrade from a Starter Account to a Standard Account. It's not hard to do — you simply click a link in your Starter Account and answer a few questions. But it adds complexity, so you should delay doing this until you need to.

Within a Standard Account, AdWords allows an extraordinary degree of control of the target area for your ads. Let's say you own a bagel shop in Manhattan called Manhattan Best Bagels. AdWords allows you to target a radius around your shop, such as a ten mile radius around the center of Manhattan, as shown in Figure 4-8.

A good starting point for such targeting would be to ask a selection of your customers where they came to your shop from. Targeting customers from the same areas is highly likely to be productive.

Google recommends a radius of at least 10 miles, or 16 kilometers, to drive a useful number of clicks. However, this is going to have very different effects in the city versus the country, and on common search terms (*bagel*) versus highly targeted ones (*bagel-making machinery*). Experiment to find what works for you.

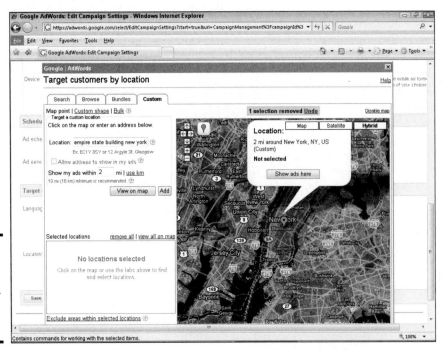

Figure 4-8:
Draw circles around your location for AdWords.

Even more cleverly, AdWords allows you to draw a shape to include and exclude the areas you want. Let's say you wanted to define a larger area including and excluding certain towns. You can do this by drawing a shape to fit.

The shape is built up by clicking spots, one at a time, to surround your targeted area exclusively. To complete the shape, click your beginning point again, and it fills in, as shown in Figure 4-9.

You can include multiple circular areas — defined by a radius — and custom-drawn areas to build up a carefully defined picture of the audience you want to see your ads.

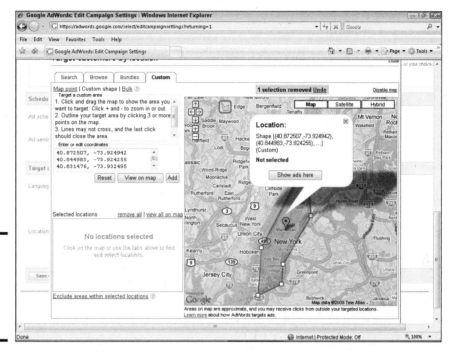

Figure 4-9:
You're not
limited to
circles or
squares
either.

The map-based tools allow you to be a little more precise than reality, though. Google uses terms in a search and the Internet Protocol addresses of searchers to target ads. These locations are often not precise, so there's a fair amount of guesswork in the results.

Timing is everything

Another old saying, "Timing is everything," applies to your Google AdWords ads as well. You can select various days of the week and times of day to run and not run your ads.

Let's say, for instance, that you want to attract more people to your restaurant during its non-busy periods, which (as in many restaurants) are the evenings that aren't Friday and Saturday. In your experience, most bookings for Friday and Saturday come in on Thursday, Friday, and Saturday — when people are planning for, or already into the weekend.

You can schedule your ads to run Sunday through Wednesday. Figure 4-10 shows how the Ad Scheduling area looks after choosing to run the ads all days, then excluding Thursday, Friday, and, as shown in the figure, Saturday. You can also target different hours of the day — for instance, you can target working people when they're at work during the day or when they are off work in the evenings.

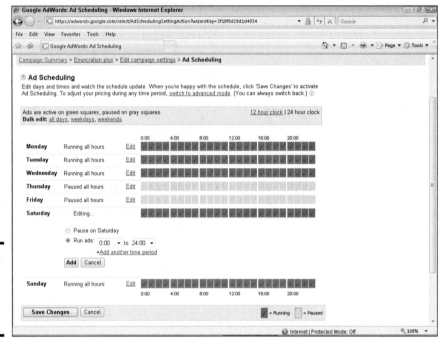

Figure 4-10:
Ad
Scheduling
fine-tunes
time.

This kind of targeting can greatly increase the effectiveness of the clicks you get. But it's a bit trickier than location, because it's still quite possible that your target audience may be searching at various times — they can be hard to pin down.

So use time-based targeting with care. One possibility is to run different ads at complementary times, targeting the content for when your target audience is most likely to be at work or home.

Although you can't completely schedule this, events are another big opportunity. When you know a convention is coming to your area, people in local hotels might be searching for bagels, or a nice restaurant, or even souvenirs. All of these can be targeted with a combination of location-based and timed targeting.

Remember repetition

Remember the value of repetition, as mentioned in Chapter 1. People aren't desperate to buy from you and just waiting to find you once before pulling out their wallets. They often need repeated exposure before they buy from you the first time; after which, it's far more likely that specific later exposures will lead to additional purchases.

So AdWords, organic search results and all your other marketing are working together. The objective is never to reach each potential customer once and only once. It's to make your business part of the environment for your target customers so they encounter you again and again.

Increasing Traffic to Your Site

Google AdWords are certainly likely to drive traffic to your site. And, as you drive traffic with AdWords, you're likely to improve your site to get the most business from your site visitors, including making it more impressive overall.

One example of this is the many articles on the For Dummies site. Those articles accumulate over time, each a potential target for a search, each making the site as a whole more useful, and tying into one or more specific books.

A customer feedback page, like the one on the BATCS site, shown in Figure 4-11, is another example. It's the kind of thing you can't put on your site on Day 1 because you don't have feedback yet. But as you gradually build up this area, as positive comments come in, you make your site more valuable.

So, as your site improves, how do you build up traffic to it — in addition to the powerful, but expensive, AdWords approach?

Real-world marketing is crucial. Putting your URL on business cards, stationery, and signage is a necessity. (Yes, the space at the bottom of your e-mail messages is signage in this sense.)

Getting links is also a necessity. This is easier as your site grows in content and usefulness. Identify sites likely to be used by your target customers. All that work you've done on AdWords begins to pay off here, as you're likely to quickly be able to come up with a list of target sites based on the characteristics you've discovered.

Figure 4-11:
Customer
comments
make great
content.

Some of the sites, such as local directories, may charge for inclusion. Again, your AdWords work gives you a good sense of the value (or not) of specific links.

But the real tough nuts are the unpaid, busy, appropriately focused sites. An article in a local newspaper is golden — not only for the immediate impact, but for the presence on the newspaper's site of the article, you hope forever. As a popular site, with lots of links going into it, links from the newspaper to your site are likely to improve your Google search engine ranking by several places.

You can also advertise the link, borrowing credibility from the source that's linking to you. In BATCS's early days, it included excerpts from newspaper articles that mentioned the general topic of accents and accent reduction. As BATCS got its own specific mentions, these were added to the existing ones. Of course, only the specific mentions of BATCS drive traffic to the site — but all the references add credibility to it.

Book VII

Securing Business Information

Using Postini e-mail security tools

Contents at a Glance

Chapter 1: Is Security Really That Important?

In This Chapter

✔ Understanding the risks of conducting business online

✔ Getting acquainted with online security basics

✔ Planning the security efforts to keep your business safe

*N*obody really has the time to wait for regular mail anymore. It may be good for official documents, large packages, and the occasional holiday card, but today real business is done through e-mail and Web sites. It means everything moves faster, and it gives many more potential customers access to your products or services. However, it also means that you have to be ready for the risks of the new environment. Don't get caught up in any hysteria or paranoia based on what you've heard in news reports, though. It's quite possible to manage your business online and keep your information and finances secure. You just have to take the right steps and be ready for the possibilities.

Being Online Is Risky Business

The best part about shopping on the Internet is that it's always open. If you want to buy anything from a song to a book to a large passenger vehicle, you can go shopping at any time of the day or night. The servers are always up and running, and the Web site is ready to take your requests.

The problem about running a business on the Internet is that the servers are always up and running, and the Web site is always ready to take your business. That means if your information is compromised or bad guys want to break into your servers, they can do it whenever they want, whether you're online, sleeping, or on vacation. Whatever security measures you implement have to take into account that business and crime never sleep. It may sound like a paradox, but you have to keep your Web site locked up at all times to make sure it stays open. You want customers to come in and use your services, but you always want to make sure that your site is secure when they do log on and use it.

When you deal with securing your brick-and-mortar store or even your home, it's fairly simple to make a location safe. You lock the doors, you install a security system, and you trust your neighbors to keep an eye on your place when you're gone. It's a little different when it comes to your online site, however. You're not going to lose a television or have your inventory stolen, but there are still valuables at risk.

Depending on what records you keep online, you might not stand to lose anything. Then again, you might keep valuable information such as human resource records or financial documents on your servers. If that information gets out, both your business and your employees could be compromised. This is the kind of information you want to keep secure at all costs. The easy answer is to just keep all that information offline in a filing cabinet, but that's not always a realistic prospect when it comes to conducting your business. It's your job to make sure this information is secured and protected from unauthorized users.

Unless you've got the technology to implement retinal scans and blood samples for user identification, it's reasonable to believe that you use passwords to access your information. You can make your passwords as long and as complex as possible, or you can use the concept of passphrases (several words strung together) to make guessing or hacking that much more difficult. Whatever you use, though, it's important to keep that information private and secure.

If your password does get out, you've lost the keys to the kingdom. When somebody knows where your information is and what your passwords are, he can get anything you have on your servers. And, if you maintain a Web site, he can guess where your information might be kept. That's why it's important to keep your passwords as secure as possible. After they're out, you are vulnerable until you change them.

Staying Aware of Security

You have a staggering number of choices about where to locate your business data and how you access it from several different locations. You're no longer confined to a bulky desktop computer connected to the Internet by a physical cable, but mobility and convenience come at a price. You always have to be careful where you store your data and how you access it, or you could be looking at a potential security breach.

The bulky desktop I just mentioned may not be that mobile, but it does have a distinct advantage over laptops or smartphones when it comes to security. You're not likely to use that computer on an unsafe wireless network, and you probably won't accidentally leave it in your car, the airport, a restaurant or coffee shop, or other locations where somebody can just walk away with your prized possession.

When you're using a remote computer, it's important that you know how you connect to the Internet. Free and open wireless networks are great for quick and easy access to your information, but you are also sharing that connection with others. Someone could intercept that traffic, either by gaining access to your computer or simply looking over your shoulder. Take precautions to make sure prying eyes of all kinds don't get near your sensitive information.

All the precautions you take don't really make a difference if you don't actually have the laptop or smartphone with you. If you forget the device somewhere, or if it is stolen, you lose control over the data on that computer. Make sure you make it very difficult to get to your data if the unthinkable happens.

Securing Your Computers

There are a few different ways to secure access to your computers. These measures make it difficult for others to gain access to your machines to get the information:

+ **Lock your doors:** It may sound simple, but keeping your computers in secure areas helps you keep the information safe. Keep your computers in private offices and restrict access to the computers to only those who need them. If a thief can't reach the keyboard, it's harder to get the data.

+ **Build a firewall:** If you're at home, most routers and cable modems have a firewall built into them. A *firewall* is a security measure that prevents outside computers from accessing your computers in an unauthorized manner. You may open the firewall at certain points to allow access for certain programs, but always make sure the wall is in place. If you're away from your home router or modem, make sure your computer's firewall is turned on. Windows, Mac OS X, and several open source operating systems all provide firewalls for this purpose — make sure yours is on at all times, even if you're behind a router or modem firewall as well. (See Figure 1-1.)

+ **Keep up on software updates:** Whether you use Windows, Mac or one of the other many operating systems available, realize that none of them is perfect and secure right out of the box. Security threats are always changing and evolving, and the people that make these operating systems are always releasing patches to guard against those security threats.

These updates are released on a regular basis — that is, Microsoft or Apple puts the updates on their servers and notifies the consumer computers that new updates are ready. You can set your computer to either download these updates automatically, or you can manually download and install them. Either way, check these updates regularly and make sure you install them to keep your machine secure.

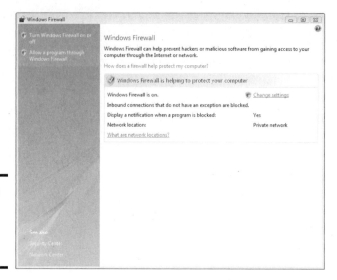

Figure 1-1:
The
Windows
Vista
Firewall.

To check for software updates in Windows Vista, click Start⇨All Programs⇨Windows Update. In Mac OS X, click the Apple icon in the top-left corner and select Software Update from the menu. (See Figure 1-2.)

These updates are usually tested with all sorts of software to make sure they work correctly. However, if you're using highly specialized or scientific software, you might want to check with the manufacturers of your software to see if it will continue working after the patch is installed.

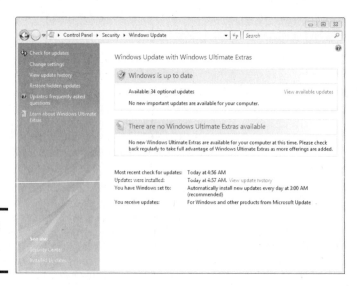

Figure 1-2:
Windows
updates.

✦ **Virus protection:** A good virus protection program keeps your computer safe from the various and sundry threats present on the Internet. You can choose from paid solutions like McAfee and Symantec or free programs like AVG. In either case, install the software and make sure to run frequent updates, just as you would with operating system updates. It's those updates that make sure the software always recognizes threats and helps prevent them. Couple this program with a good malware-buster like Ad-Aware and Spybot, and your computer should remain safe and secure.

✦ **Lock it down:** Laptops and other mobile devices usually have places to insert safety locks. Think of it like an Information-Age–type bike lock. If you have to step away briefly, you have a lock to help keep people honest. And, if possible, don't step away from the laptop or mobile device — take it with you.

Securing Your Passwords

The password is the key to your data — and will be until everybody starts using retinal scans or fingerprints to log into computers (and that day may not be far off). You use passwords to access all manner of information. If somebody gets your password, however, he can get your information and lock you out of your accounts as well. That's why you must keep your passwords secure and private. Here's what you can do to keep your passwords out of the hands of the bad guys:

✦ **Don't use the same password over and over again:** If you use the same password for everything, that means everything can be unlocked with one lucky guess. By using different passwords for different programs, you make it harder for anyone to gain access to all your information at one time. You may lose some access or information with one guessed or compromised password, but you won't lose everything in one fell swoop.

✦ **Make your passwords hard to guess:** Don't use your birthday, your significant other's name, the names of your children, or anything that somebody could easily guess about you. If several people know something about you, that's not the information you should make into a password. If you can remember it, use a random series of letters and numbers.

✦ **Always include letters and numbers:** It's harder to guess a password if it includes several different characters, so make sure you include both letters and numbers in any password you create. You can both include numbers as letters, such as 1 for I or 0 for the letter O, or you can put numbers at the beginning, end, or middle of your word. The more unpredictable your password is, the better it will stand up to guesses.

✦ **Mix uppercase and lowercase:** If you include a combination of upper-case and lowercase letters in your password, it becomes even more unpredictable. Even if the letters are the same, the computer usually recognizes them as different characters, making your password harder to guess.

✦ **Sentence your password:** If your computers or programs allow it, con-sider creating a passphrase instead of a password. Your passphrase becomes exponentially harder to guess if you use a series of words instead of one word. The placement of spaces and the number of words, combined with the steps listed earlier in this section, give you a very secure solution to your security needs.

✦ **Don't write it down:** All these steps don't mean anything if you write down your password and put it under your keyboard or in your laptop case. Writing it down just makes it too easy for anybody else to use. If you do have to write it down, keep it in a secure area and consider using a password protection program that manages your passwords securely, keeping them from prying eyes. Of course, you'll probably end up using a password to secure that program, but that way you only have to remember one.

✦ **Change your password often:** A moving target is the hardest to hit. If you change your password on a regular basis, it becomes harder to guess — even if you have written it down. Set up a regular schedule and change your password to something totally unrelated to your previous password for better security.

An Online Security Primer

Don't be afraid of online security — it can seem overwhelming at first, but everything slows down and seems more reasonable as you understand more about the situation. This section introduces you to the most common ways online security can be breached and how you can avoid those problems. If you just take a few steps, you're already ahead of the pack.

Know your enemy. These possible security problems shouldn't keep you up at night, but they do deserve a little attention. The first step towards addressing your security problems is to understand where they are and why they're a problem in the first place.

Even if you don't know your security threats personally, it's a good idea to know what possible threats you face. The attacks may come from differ-ent people or locations, but they fall into a few common categories. When you identify the categories, you can prevent these attacks from succeeding. These categories include

◆ **Brute force hacking:** Have you ever seen a movie where a hacker sits down, promises to have access to a system within seconds, and delivers the entire contents of a server to whomever they're working for? It's a convenient plot point for the film, but it's nowhere near that easy in real life. Although it is possible to infiltrate private servers and computers like that, it usually requires a lot of lead time and knowledge about the servers before it can happen. And although it's theoretically possible to guess a password, the time involved and the safety measures that block failed multiple attempts make it a slog that's not worth a lot of time or effort.

Most of these attacks are generated by *script kiddies*, or novices who use scripts written by others to try and find their way into servers or computers. They run these scripts and hope for the best. By making sure your computers and servers are patched, you can avoid these threats. Unless somebody is specifically targeting your systems, this isn't going to be a big problem. There are easier ways to get your information than brute force hacking.

◆ **Social engineering:** Instead of brute force hacking, other security threats rely on tricks and deceit via other channels. *Social engineering* involves gaining information from a person and using that information to gain access to computer systems. For example, somebody calls or e-mails another, claims to be from a government agency, and asks them to verify their name, address, and Social Security number. If the caller gains that information, they can use it to gain access to personal information.

The same scenario works for passwords and other electronic information. That's why it's never a good idea to give out your password, especially over an electronic medium like e-mail. You should always keep that information personal and never risk compromising your account. If you think somebody has stolen your password, change it immediately. Never give somebody any personal information unless you're absolutely sure that he is who he says he is.

Testing your security

The previous section gave you some principles to live by when you're establishing your company's security policy. Now it's time to take those principles and put them to practice. Let's assess where you stand right now and what you need to change to make your personal information more secure.

First, look around your office. This applies to wherever you're doing business. That could be as simple as your central office, or it could include all your employees' home offices and mobile computers. Check to see what's around your office and what could present problems. Who has access to your office, and how can you control who gets on your computers? Have users written down their passwords and posted them? (Trust me, everybody looks under the keyboard.) Don't write down your passwords, and certainly don't store them in obvious places.) Make sure that only those who need access to your computers and networks get it, and keep everybody else out.

Now that you've secured everything physically, take a look at your computers themselves. Every computer you use should have the following features enabled and the following programs installed:

+ **User accounts:** All users need their own accounts with their own passwords. No exceptions. Make sure that every computer also has an administrator account with the same password that you and your IT personnel have access to in case of disaster (or a forgotten password).

+ **Separate passwords:** As explained in the previous item, everybody needs to have a different password. Giving everybody a generic password leads to security problems down the road.

+ **Antivirus software:** Every computer needs to have antivirus software installed, and it needs to be updated consistently.

+ **Antimalware software:** Just like the antivirus software, this should be installed and updated consistently.

+ **Admin access:** Unless it's absolutely necessary, normal users should not be administrators on their computers. It's best to restrict such access to a few people.

+ **Firewall:** No matter what operating system you use, make sure its internal firewall software is activated. This helps prevent unauthorized access by those outside of your network.

These features help block unauthorized access to your computers. As long as you remember not to distribute your passwords and personal information, these go a long way towards helping you stay secure.

Even when you hear stories about systems getting hacked or virus getting loaded onto your computers, it's usually because somebody was tricked into downloading and installing the software or virus beforehand. Stay aware, and you should be okay.

It's easy to make all the adjustments necessary to keep your computers safe. It's even easy to lock down laptops with passwords and access restrictions, just in case somebody loses the computer or it gets stolen. Unless you have especially valuable information, the thieves are probably more interested in the computer itself than the information on it. But your business and personal information can also be on smaller (and, therefore, easier to misplace or steal) devices like mobile phones, iPhones, and Blackberries.

These devices don't often have the same security features as your computers, but some of the more advanced smartphones do allow for password protection. If you're going to conduct business on these devices, activate that feature to help keep your information secure. These phones might also have a feature that allows you to erase information from them via a remote command, in case of loss or theft. These features are usually available to larger organizations, but you can check with your service provider to see if you can also utilize these functions.

The easiest way to avoid disaster, though, is to always keep track of your mobile devices and make sure they don't fall into the wrong hands. Restrict the use of these devices to only those who need them, and make sure that they're not used to handle the most sensitive of information. By keeping the number of these devices low and making sure that only those that need them have them, you lessen your risk of exposing your information to the world.

Checking out new and existing employees

The past couple sections have mentioned restricting access to devices and information to only those that need it. Your next step is to establish exactly who those people are. You undoubtedly checked your employees' background and references before you hired them, and you know the jobs they are expected to perform. Use that information in determining who gets access to what information and devices. For example, your IT specialist may need the smartphone and administrator access to all your computers, but it's not likely your receptionist can justify the same level of access. Go over your personnel and make sure they get what they need, but nothing more. This may sound a little harsh, but it helps keep your business information safe and secure.

When you're hiring a new person, go through the same procedures you would with an existing employee, but you may want to consider a probationary access period where you evaluate your new employees before giving them access to the keys to the kingdom. That way, you get to know your new employees for a bit and know that they're going to stick around and honor your IT security policy. And when you have somebody leave, always change any server passwords and disable any accounts he may have had access to in order to prevent him from getting access to your systems after he's left.

Creating a Security Policy for My Site

Before you started your business, you probably had a business plan. That doesn't mean you had everything in place already — you just had a vision of what you wanted your business to accomplish, a list of steps you planned to take to make it to that accomplishment, and an idea of what contingencies you might face and how to deal with them. You're going to do the same thing with your security plan, so keep those steps in mind as you progress through this section. You're adding to your business plan here; it's just a matter of addressing your security needs.

How can a policy protect my business?

It's as simple as the saying "An ounce of prevention is worth a pound of cure." This is where you make yourself ready for problems before they happen and give yourself a list of steps to follow so you don't gloss over any potential problems or, in case of disaster, so you can proceed without panicking.

✦ **Plan for the future:** Keep in mind your current assets and stores of information, but also make you sure you take into account what's coming up and what you might be seeing in the future. Your plan has to grow along with your business. You may only have a few computers and employees right now, but you want to be ready in case you add more locations, employees, mobile devices, and experience similar types of growth.

✦ **Know how to respond:** It's always easier to get somewhere when you have a road map (and you're not too stubborn to use it). A good security policy includes a list of steps to follow in case of a certain event. It guides you through the necessary actions to make sure everything's safe. For example, if you have a computer that becomes infected with a virus, you want to go through the following steps:

1. Disconnect the computer from your network immediately.

2. Remove the virus from the computer, if possible.

3. If your software isn't capable of removing the virus, back up all the important information from the computer and have your IT specialist completely reload the computer.

4. Change the passwords for the accounts on that computer.

5. Before putting information back on the computer, use virus software to scan it and make sure it's not infected.

Having these policies in place beforehand makes everything run more smoothly in case of disaster.

✦ **Change the locks:** Turnover is inevitable in today's business world, and you're probably going to gain and lose employees over the course of your business activities. It's just like a rental house, really — would you let the old tenants keep the keys to the locks after they move out? Because you can't reclaim the passwords, it's easier to change them to deny former employees access. Build transitional steps into your security policy to help you make changes between "tenants" easily and more efficiently.

Key parts of a security policy

Every small business's security policy is going to be different because every small business is different. There are common elements, of course, like not giving out passwords and not posting pictures of your boss's private letters on your MySpace account. However, the fine details are unique to your business, so it's not really possible to set forth a template for your security policy. This section outlines the information that needs to be included in your policy and lets you apply it to your unique situation.

In any case, make sure that you write down the policy and that everybody gets a copy. A security policy is only good if everybody knows and plays by the rules. Otherwise, you're stuck with a good idea and no action to back it up.

Here are the main points to consider:

✦ **Who gets access?** The short answer is "Only those that need it." Specifically, you need to outline every position in your business and decide what information and access that employee needs. For example, everybody may get his own e-mail account and Google Apps homepage, but only you and your IT specialist get to be administrators for the site. For your computers, you can give everybody accounts, but only certain people need to be administrators.

Certain software requires administrator access to run properly. If you have employees who need that software, they must be administrators. You can still minimize the danger by restricting that software to certain computers or requiring that they use their computers only on the company's private network.

✦ **How do they access it?** Your security policy should include approved locations for access to information and what devices employees can use to look at that information. For example, you can specify that your employees can access their calendars from anywhere, but that they cannot log on to your server anywhere but in the office. It might be a little inconvenient, but it helps keep your information safe and secure.

✦ **Changing passwords:** You don't have to require those involved in your business to change their passwords every day, but they should change them on a regular basis. This might be more often if they work on remote locations or use mobile devices and laptops, or it might be less often if they only work on desktop computers in your main office. Still, a regular schedule for password changes is necessary. Consider a change every three or four months (more if you're mobile), and change passwords immediately if you feel any might have been stolen or compromised.

✦ **Offline versus online data:** It's pretty easy to restrict access to offline data — buy a safe, put the data in it, lock it away, and you're good. After information has been placed online, it's theoretically possible for anybody to get on your network and gain access to it. It's not always probable, and somebody would probably have to know what he's looking for to get it, but it's still possible. If you're sure that there's no need to have the information online (your employees' Social Security numbers, for example), don't put it up there. It's easier to prevent access in the first place than it is to get information back after it's been illegally accessed.

Enforcing the security policy

Establishing your policy is only the first step. You also need to follow through and check to see that the policy is enacted and working. It's up to you and your IT staff (which may be one and the same) to actively pursue and enforce your policy and make sure that it's followed through in all cases. Otherwise, there are holes in your wall that could be used to get access to your information.

Remain vigilant. This is where you get to play security guard for your computer system. Check every computer and make sure the virus and malware program updates have been completed. Look over your online documents and make sure they don't contain information that shouldn't be shared or online at all. Check access on your computer accounts and make sure employees have only what they need. Keep an up-to-date inventory on your laptops and mobile devices. If you know what's going on at all times, it minimizes the chances of problems down the road.

Don't forget passwords. Depending on your operating systems, if you log in as an administrator you can force users to change their password the next time they log in. You can also do the same thing with Google Apps by logging in as an administrator and taking the following steps:

1. **Click the User Accounts tab in the Google Apps administrator section.**

2. **Click the name of the user you want to administrate.**

3. **Check the box shown in Figure 1-3 to force a password change the next time the user logs in.**

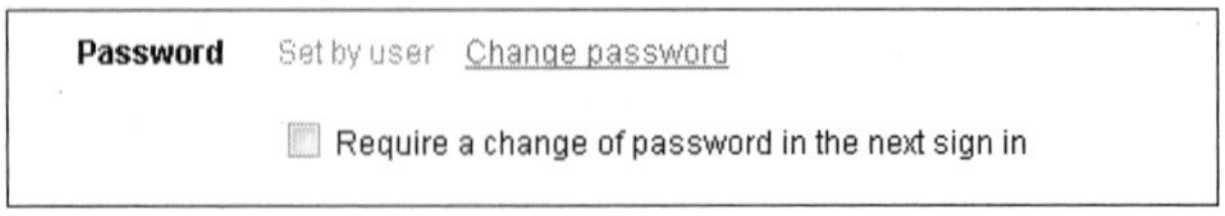

Figure 1-3:
Forcing a
password
change
in Google
Apps.

Password	Set by user	Change password
	☐ Require a change of password in the next sign in	

You can do this for every user in your Google Apps domain. This helps you enforce the password change, even if your users ignore the policy.

It's your business, so you should have access to all the online information for your domain. Feel free to browse these documents and make sure that they fall in line with your security policies. If you've been keeping up with your virus program updates and changing your passwords, it shouldn't be easy to gain access to these documents. Still, somebody could accidentally send out these documents and give others unintentional access to sensitive information. Take a look to make sure that everything that is online should be online.

Keeping the policy updated

As your business grows (or as your old computers die), you need to change your security policy. For example, you may need to scrap an old machine that you're replacing with a new computer, but you want to know what to do with the hard drive of the old one. Or you may be adding a new series of mobile devices with access to your Google Apps domain. Change your policy to adapt to your new needs.

Don't be afraid to re-evaluate your security needs as you grow or shrink, and keep in mind what your most important needs are. After you've identified those needs, you can apply them to new devices and functions. Always keep security in mind first and then adapt your practices to your new situation.

If you've added any new computers, networking equipment (like a wireless router), or other devices, make sure those are addressed in your security policy. For example, take your recently added wireless router. You want to restrict who has access to that network, how often the password for your network is changed, and so on. Write this down and put it in the policy.

If you've added any new employees or any different locations, you also need to account for them in your security policy. Your main goal should be keeping all your information safe and secure at all times. Keep that in mind as you make your changes.

There's no shame in calling in outside help for this project. You're dealing with your business, after all. If you're not an expert on all matters IT already, get somebody who is to help you draft and maintain your security policy.

Chapter 2: Securing E-Mail

In This Chapter

✔ Understanding how e-mail gets to you

✔ Understanding where e-mail can get you into trouble

✔ Avoiding phishing scams

✔ Stopping the buildup of spam

✔ Securing your e-mail traffic

E-mail has worked itself into the fabric of everyday life (which includes your business, naturally), so it's important that you be able to use it securely. Every business transaction you can think of can probably be carried out via e-mail. Its ease of use and capability to operate on a variety of media makes it an easy choice. But e-mail comes with its own set of problems and rules, so be aware of those problems and make sure your e-mails stay safe and secure. That's what this chapter is all about.

Understanding How E-Mail Works

Before you address the potential problems of using e-mail, you need to understand how you send and receive these messages, and how those messages make their way over the Internet to their intended locations. It's a little more complicated than a series of tubes, but you should be able to get the hang of it easily.

Up to this point, you may have been a regular user of e-mail but you may never have known exactly what goes on behind the scenes. You write your message, you type in the recipient's e-mail address (or click Reply All and hope for the best), and then click Send. The e-mail eventually gets to where it needs to go (you could time it by phoning the recipient and checking on it, I suppose, but that's a little too geeky), or it gets lost for some reason and you have to resend it. Here's where you look under the hood briefly and see what's going on.

Sending an e-mail is a pretty simple process. A user creates a message and clicks Send, which causes the e-mail client (either a Webmail client or a program installed on the computer) to pass along the message to the outgoing e-mail server. If it's a Webmail server, the settings are already determined by the service. If it's a client installed on the computer, those settings are manually entered by either the person using the computer or the IT staff. That server then notifies the server that hosts the recipient's e-mail address (the second part of the e-mail address, like gmail.com) that a message exists. It then transmits that message to the server.

After the receiving server has been notified of the new message, it holds that message until that user logs into the account (again, either on a Webmail client or on a computer's e-mail client). Depending on the e-mail protocol, that message is then downloaded to the client or synched with the server and the client. After the message is read, it can be archived, deleted, or filed in another e-mail folder on the computer or the server.

This process is fairly quick, but dangers exist. There are still places along the chain of events where your information can be accessible to others. These locations include the following:

+ When the message is sent from the computer to the outgoing mail server.

+ With the e-mail server holding the message until the user logs in.

+ When the message is downloaded from the server to the user's account.

It's uncommon for e-mail to be intercepted between servers because information is passed along the Internet in several small packets of information that are later reassembled when they all arrive at their intended destination. The highest risk of a message being intercepted is at the time it is being sent or when it is received.

Protecting My E-Mail Server

Your actual server is probably pretty well protected, especially if you're using Gmail or the Google Apps mail function. It's part of a large network that is securely placed in remote locations, and it's backed up regularly as part of a normal security process. Again, the places where problems arise are those where your system and the mail servers interact. Think of it as the joints on either end of a long pipe. There are steps you can take to make your interactions more secure, and they involve protecting those joints.

Using secure connections

If you've ever used online banking or another service where your communications with the server have to be *encrypted*, or hidden with code to make sure they can't be intercepted, you may have noticed that the beginning of the Web address was *https://* instead of *http://*. That last "s" indicates that your interactions through the Web browser are secure. If you're using the Webmail version of Gmail or the Google Apps mail account, these encrypted connections are set up automatically.

If you're using an e-mail client to access your Gmail or Google Apps mail account, you still have to use an encrypted connection to access your mail. As shown in Figure 2-1, you have set the ports and types of encryption to access Google's mail services.

Figure 2-1:
Encrypting
your e-mail
connection.

o Incoming server must be 993, and must use SSL encryption.
o Outgoing server can use 587, TLS encryption.

These secure connections keep your passwords and e-mail encrypted, and thus safe from prying eyes. Make sure you hide your screen if you're sending e-mail in public, though.

If you notice that the http:// has returned when you're logged into your account, manually add the *s* after *http* and press Return. This forces your Webmail account to return to a secure connection. Gmail automatically sends and receives login information over a secure tunnel, but this step forces all traffic to go over a secure channel as well.

Using mobile and wireless devices

After you've taken a device off of your network and put it on a mobile or wireless connection, you've added a security risk. It's possible for these connections to be intercepted more easily than connections made over a physical network. However, you can take steps to make sure your information remains secure:

✦ **Use a VPN connection:** The virtual private network connection creates a secure tunnel between your computer and your server and encrypts traffic, keeping your information private. Consult your IT specialist on setting up a VPN connection or buy one from a private service.

✦ **Use a secure wireless service that requires a password or pre-shared key, available from the network's operator.**

✦ **Don't connect to free, open networks to access sensitive information.**

✦ **Turn off all sharing of folders and files when you use a public wireless network.**

✦ **Stay away from services that advertise free wireless in public areas.** These are often ad-hoc or peer-to-peer networks that connect your computer to another computer making your information vulnerable.

It's always better to be safe than sorry, so stay away from wireless networks you don't trust. A few dollars spent to access a known, secure network is better than losing your secure information in search of a free network.

Avoiding Phishermen

This section has nothing to do with the actual process of catching fish or following the exploits of a Vermont-based jam band. Instead, we're talking about the process of extracting personal information from others via e-mail. It's similar to *fishing* for information, and it's spelled with a *ph* because . . . well, it's different on the Internet.

Phishing is the use of a combination of social engineering and fake Web sites to gather personal information. For example, a phisher sends an e-mail purporting to be from a bank, asking for the recipients to send their account information and passwords or PIN numbers to verify their accounts. The recipient clicks a link, enters his information on a page that looks a little like the bank's Web site, and submits the form. The phisher then takes the information and uses it to take the money out of the recipient's account.

Even if the site looks like the main Web site of the bank, you can still identify phishing Web sites if the Web address differs from the address of the bank's main Web site. Most reputable banks and other institutions don't require that kind of information be sent by e-mail in any case. If it feels wrong, call the bank or service and make sure the e-mail is legitimate before sending any information over e-mail.

Any information that you wouldn't feel comfortable giving out to a complete stranger shouldn't be included in an e-mail. That includes

✦ Your Social Security number

✦ Your bank account information

✦ Any passwords or PIN numbers

✦ Any other personal information that could be used to help steal your identity

If you do choose to use this information on the Internet, make sure it is done *only* over a secure connection on a Web site you've accessed via an official address and not an e-mail link.

Dealing with Spam

I'm no nutritionist, believe me, but it's a fairly safe statement that too much Spam, either the canned version or the e-mail version, isn't good for you. Let's stick to the electronic variety for now. *Spam* is the nickname given to the myriad of e-mails that arrive in your e-mail accounts daily, advertising all sorts of services and products with spurious claims and terrible grammar. They can range from harmless to quite dangerous. It's best to know how spam works so you can avoid the nasty aftertaste.

You probably notice spam more for the sheer number of messages you receive than anything else. Spam never arrives in slow trickles — it carries with it the force of numbers. This affects your e-mail servers in a couple of ways:

✦ **It clogs the servers:** If you're forced to carry too many things while you're walking, you move slower and eventually stop under the force of the weight. A car or truck can carry more, but even those vehicles can only carry so much. Similarly, e-mail servers can handle only so much weight (in this case, numbers of e-mails). If your servers are getting a lot of spam, you may notice a slowness in getting your e-mail, and too much spam can actually slow your servers to a halt.

✦ **It clogs your accounts:** When the spam inevitably trickles into the individual e-mail accounts, it becomes the equivalent of junk mail. Except that you don't usually receive 200 pieces of junk mail in your mailbox each and every day. Because spam is much cheaper to send out than advertising circulars, you're likely to get more of it. Because virtually all e-mail accounts have storage quotas assigned to them, this much spam can eventually stop up your account and prevent you from receiving new e-mails. So you have to go in and keep emptying your account of the spam or else there's no more room for the good stuff. Still, that's a lot of trouble, and there are more elegant solutions to your problem.

You can't just delete it

As easily accessible as your e-mail is these days, it's not practical for you to monitor all your accounts at all times to make sure they stay clear of spam. Your time is probably too valuable for that, and there are better ways to clear your accounts. Think of these methods like the lint trap in a clothes dryer — they act to keep fluffy nonsense from causing you trouble down the road:

✦ **Using filters:** The first option you have to deal with spam is using an e-mail filter. Gmail and Google Apps mail provide a couple of different options for filters. The first is a general catch-all folder marked Spam that's present in all e-mail accounts, as shown in Figure 2-2.

Figure 2-2:
Gmail's
Spam folder.

Compose Mail
Inbox (4)
Starred ☆
Chats 💬
Sent Mail
Drafts
All Mail
Spam
Trash

Google has seen a lot of spam, and it has created a smart folder based on experience that automatically directs messages that are probably spam to that folder. You never have to see the messages in your inbox, and you just deal with the messages you want to view. Google constantly updates their spam records and definitions, so this kind of protection should continue to be effective as long you continue to use the account.

You can also set up more specific filters, should you desire. Look at the links next to the search window in Gmail and click the Create filter link to see the screen shown in Figure 2-3.

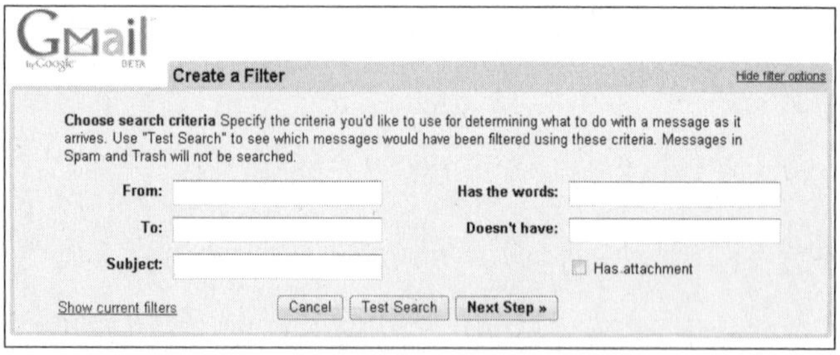

Figure 2-3:
Creating a
filter.

GMail
by Google   BETA

Create a Filter   Hide filter options

Choose search criteria Specify the criteria you'd like to use for determining what to do with a message as it arrives. Use "Test Search" to see which messages would have been filtered using these criteria. Messages in Spam and Trash will not be searched.

From:	Has the words:
To:	Doesn't have:
Subject:	☐ Has attachment

Show current filters   Cancel   Test Search   Next Step »

This is where you can target specific e-mail addresses, subject lines, or message content. Any e-mail messages that meet the conditions set by this filter can be sorted out in a variety of ways. For example, let's enter a common spam subject in the Has The Words field and click the Next Step button to see the screen shown in Figure 2-4.

Here's where you decide what happens to the offending messages. Choose whatever action you want to perform (in this case, we're sending the messages straight to junk mail) and click Create Filter. That filter continues to operate until you delete it.

Figure 2-4:
Sending
your e-mail
through the
filter.

You may have guessed that you can do more with filters than just get rid of spam. That's just what we're using them for here, but you can also automatically set up labels for specific clients or subjects as well. Play with the filters and set up your own organizational structure.

✦ **Checking your nets:** So why doesn't the spam just get deleted, never to be seen again? Well, nothing is perfect, and sometimes spam filters can get a little aggressive. You might see messages that are perfectly legitimate caught up in the traps, and you have to go back in and rescue them. That's why there are folders for spam and not an instant death. Gmail usually retains spam in the folders for 30 days, after which it deletes it automatically. It's a good idea to check these folders once a week or so to make sure you're not losing anything important. More than likely, you won't miss anything. Still, there are messages that you want to receive that will end up in there. Commonly, these include:

- Newsletters

- Advertisements you signed up to receive

- Automated notices of things like password changes to your online accounts

- Messages with typos or mistakes in the subject line

Just give the spam folders a cursory check every so often to make sure you're not losing anything, and you should be fine.

✦ **Updating your filters:** You may notice as you continue using your Gmail or Google Apps mail accounts that you need to refine your filters. Either they're not doing a good enough job, or they're taking too much good mail out with the bad. Click the Show Current Filters link (shown in Figure 2-4) to see what filters you currently have in effect. If you want to modify the rules of the filter, click the Edit link next to the filter and re-enter your new terms. If you want to just rid yourself of the filter altogether, click the Delete link.

**Book VII
Chapter 2**

Securing E-Mail

How spam can hurt

Most spam you receive is harmless advertising. It may clog your inbox, but by itself it's relatively harmless. However, sometimes spam carries with it some more sinister motives, and the sheer volume of spam can cause problems as well. You have to be aware of what's going in and out of your folders to be sure you don't lose anything important.

Not all spam messages are phishing attempts, but they are out there. Be careful that you don't accidentally get caught up in one of these schemes. Again, you should never give out any information in an e-mail that you wouldn't be comfortable telling a stranger.

There's a link in the spam folder that allows you to instantly rid yourself of the contents. It's a satisfying feeling to click it and watch all the spam instantly disappear, but it can also come with a nagging feeling that you just eliminated something important. If you receive a huge amount of spam in your folder, the law of averages dictates that eventually, a real messages will get swept out as well. It's all well and good to eliminate the spam, but always check first to make sure you're not getting rid of necessary information.

Introducing Google Postini E-Mail Security Tools

When you use Google Apps e-mail services, you have the option of enabling a series of tools provided by a Google-owned company called Postini. Think of these services as reinforcements — you might be able to get by on your own with the tools we've already looked at, but Postini gives you a great deal of backup. Postini provides a multitude of tools to help you manage and secure your e-mail services, and the vast majority of them are available with any Google Apps account. Remember, it's in the interests of Google and Postini to keep your servers clean as well. Less clutter around the Internet means better performance for everybody involved.

Postini offers two different groups of tools to your Google Apps account:

✦ *Message Security* enables you to sort out the potentially harmful messages from your normal business e-mail.

✦ *Message Discovery* allows you to review e-mail even after you've deleted it and gives you a secure archiving system for your important communications.

Think of message security as a bouncer and message discovery as a safety net. Between the two, you'll be able to manage your e-mail safely and securely.

Blocking spam

Postini adds another layer of protection between spam and your account. It filters your messages at three levels:

+ Incoming mail goes through a filter, keeping your incoming communications safe.

+ Outgoing mail also goes through a filter, preventing any security threats that somehow start with you. Remember, increased safety benefits everybody.

+ Internal e-mails go through both filters, so your business's private communications remain doubly secure.

This spam is filtered into different folders, so you can review any blocked messages and make sure that you're getting your important information. This protection is in addition to the spam folder and filter tools already available through Google Apps mail accounts, so you're seeing additional protection for every e-mail message that you send or receive.

Vaccinating e-mail viruses

Every computer and device you use should have antivirus protection on it at all times. However, Postini places an additional level of security on the server side that actually prevents viruses from reaching your computer, before they could even think of challenging your antivirus program. In this layer of protection, Postini provides two distinct advantages:

+ **Quarantine:** It's not surrounded by a plastic tent and guarded by armed soldiers, but the concept remains the same. E-mails that carry a virus payload are held here in safety so you can check them out. If they're infected, you can delete them before they ever get a chance to be active. Because this happens on the server side of the e-mail exchange, you never have to worry about your computer being harmed. You can also let the person who sent the message know that it came with a virus or other infection.

+ **Updated virus protection:** Keeping your system clear of viruses depends on your programs knowing how to identify them in the first place. Postini constantly updates its services with the latest definitions (the equivalent of wanted posters for viruses) so the service knows what to look for and what to remove from the flow of e-mails to your system. You don't have to worry about performing the updates yourself, as you might have to do with your antivirus software on your computer. This happens automatically, so you're always covered.

**Book VII
Chapter 2**

Securing E-Mail

Filtering messages

Depending on how your business handles e-mail, you might want to set up different rules on how e-mail is distributed. For example, if you want to make sure e-mails of a certain nature (such as sexually explicit material) never reach your users, you can filter out based on certain words and have those e-mails go into the junk mail folders.

Each user has a series of folders attached to their Postini account, including the following:

+ Junk

+ Viruses

+ Delivered

+ Trash

+ Archive

Depending on how your e-mail administrator has enabled your Postini settings, messages can end up in any of these folders.

You can set Postini to perform several different actions on e-mail messages, depending on factors like the following:

+ Size

+ Attachment types

+ Subject

+ Message content

+ Subject line

+ Sender's e-mail address

After you've identified the filters you want to put in place, Postini gives you the option of deleting the messages entirely, sending them to quarantine, giving them the express treatment to a certain mailbox, or other options.

Make your rules are as specific as possible. Making an overly broad rule means sweeping a great deal of e-mail out with the messages you want to control. Monitor your quarantines and folders to evaluate the effectiveness of your rules and modify them accordingly.

Archiving messages

You don't always have the option of deleting e-mails to clear out your accounts. Depending on your business, you might be required to keep certain e-mail communications around for legal reasons, or you might just want to clean up your inboxes and retain the e-mail for future use. Postini is able to archive these messages and make them available just in case. This could be a lifesaver, whether you need them for a court date or just a quick reference months after the fact.

After you've activated Postini, the archiving functions are in effect. You can set the amount of time an e-mail stays in the archive, but it usually enters the archive after about a half-hour after a user on your domain receives it.

Postini provides a full-featured service that allows you to search for e-mail in your domain's archives based on a variety of terms. You can find messages based on your search terms and exclude other e-mails so that you get only what you need. This saves you the time of pouring through every e-mail just to find the one message you're looking for.

If you've signed up for the Premiere version of Google Apps, Postini has some additional options for you. You get more control over how your e-mail is filtered, and you also get the capability to retrieve deleted e-mails up to 90 days after they've been deleted. No more losing important information through a couple hasty clicks. Google Apps Premiere administrators can also view all e-mail in their domain in one location, making it easier to search e-mail and modify filtering rules.

Installing Postini

The administrator for your Google Apps site has to install Postini before any of these features become active, so let's take a look at how to get the service up and running. Just follow these steps:

1. **Log into your Google Apps dashboard at `http://google.com/a`.**

Next set up SMTP.

SMTP stands for Simple Mail Transfer Protocol, and it's really only "simple" if you already understand it. Luckily, you don't have to understand it to get your Google Apps domain working with Postini. You'll just be entering the appropriate information to make your domain and the service link up and begin filtering your e-mail.

2. **After you've logged into your domain dashboard, click the Add More Services link and then click the Add It Now link under the Policy Management and Message Recovery by Postini heading.**

   This takes you back to the dashboard.

3. **Click the Policy Management and Message Recovery by Postini link.**

4. **Review the terms of the service and click the check box and the I Agree button to register your domain with Postini.**

   This could take a little bit of time, but you get an e-mail when the process is completed and you're ready to proceed to the next step.

   After Postini has made initial contact with your domain, you have to make some additional settings. You receive an e-mail letting you know that you're ready to proceed, and when you log into your Google Apps dashboard, you see the screen shown in Figure 2-5.

Figure 2-5: Proceeding with Postini Installation.

This step makes Postini integrate with your *Domain Name Server* (DNS) records and your *mail exchange* (MX) settings. Postini needs to change these settings so all e-mail going to your domain flows first through Postini's services and then gets to you.

5. **Click the Continue Activation button shown in Figure 2-5 to get directions on changing your MX settings.**

   Google Apps gives you different directions depending on what host you're using for your domain name. In the example shown in Figure 2-6, the domain host is GoDaddy. Yours may differ — if you don't think you're getting the correct information, click the Learn How To Find Your Domain Host link to find the best instructions.

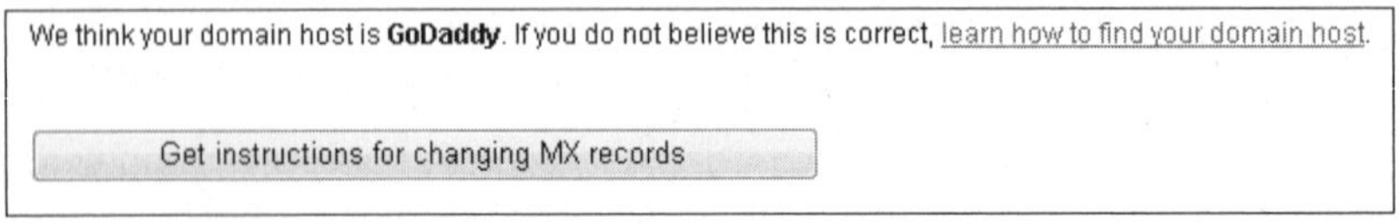

Figure 2-6: Getting your MX instructions.

6. **In a separate browser window, log into your domain host and follow the instructions for adding your e-mail services to the Postini service.**

   Again, instructions will differ from host to host, but you'll be adding information that looks like the following to your MX records:

   • YOURDOMAINNAME.S7A1.PSMTP.COM

   • YOURDOMAINNAME.S7A2.PSMTP.COM

   • YOURDOMAINNAME.S7B1.PSMTP.COM

   • YOURDOMAINNAME.S7B2.PSMTP.COM

7. **After you've put this information in your MX records, go back to the Google Apps browser window and click the I Have Changed My MX Records button shown in Figure 2-7.**

   These changes could take a little bit of time to take effect. If your records show a message saying that changes are pending, just be patient.

Figure 2-7:
Finishing
up your MX
records
change.

When you have logged in to your domain host and changed your MX records, click on "I have changed my MX records" to have Google check on your MX records.

[I have changed my MX records]

When you're done, Google Apps takes you back to your domain dashboard, where you see a message like the one shown in Figure 2-8. It takes time — possibly up to 48 hours — before Postini is configured. Sit back, relax, and enjoy a cup of your favorite beverage. You have to wait until the process is done before you can make use of Postini's features. When it's ready for use, you see the message shown in Figure 2-9 on your domain's dashboard.

Figure 2-8:
Waiting for
your Postini
records to
take effect.

☑ **Message Security and Discovery** by Postini - Updating...
We are checking MX records for your domain. This may take 48 hours to complete.
View instructions again

Figure 2-9:
A fully
configured
and ready
Postini
service.

☑ **Message Security and Discovery** by Postini - Active
Set up email security policies and recover archived messages.
Message Security and Discovery console 🗗

Managing E-Mail Accounts with Postini

After you've gotten Postini configured for your domain, you have a link on
your dashboard allowing you to log in and review your settings. All your
accounts are automatically enrolled in the service at the time of activation,
and you get the default settings for the service set for those accounts. Now's
when you log in and customize Postini to your individual needs.

Click the link shown in Figure 2-9 to log into your Postini control panel. You
see the screen shown in Figure 2-10. To view the settings for your entire
domain, click the System Administration link. For the folders associated only
with your individual e-mail account, click the Message Center link.

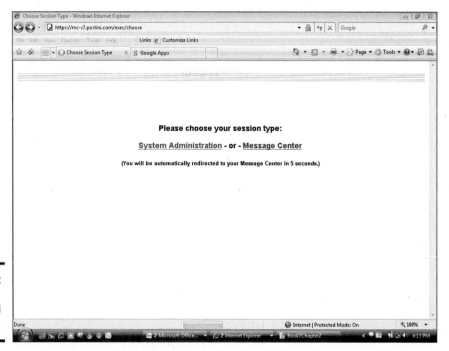

Figure 2-10:
Choosing
your Postini
destination.

Choose the System Administration link to see the screen shown in Figure 2-11. This is the dashboard for managing your entire Postini service.

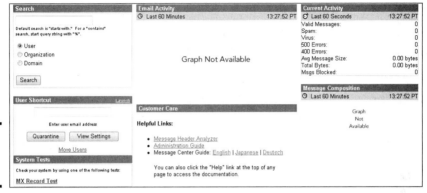

Figure 2-11:
Your Postini
Dashboard.

All the accounts on your Google Apps domain are automatically included in your Postini service. Thereafter, any accounts you add to your Google Apps domain with an e-mail account are included as well, following a delay of no more than half an hour.

At the activation of your Postini account, you get two organizations set up under your domain. Account Administrators have the ability to use the System Administration dashboard, while users see only the folders associated with their account. As an administrator, you can modify the settings for an entire organization or specific users. You can also create different sub-organizations and move users around to create different rules for different groups of users.

To see the organizations associated with your domain, click the Orgs and Users tab at the top of your dashboard to see a screen like the one shown in Figure 2-12.

**Book VII
Chapter 2**

Securing E-Mail

Figure 2-12:
Organiza-
tions within
your Postini
Dashboard.

You can set policies based on the entire domain and each organization below that, or you can select individual users and manage their settings on a one-on-one basis.

Using the Postini Center

Now that you've gotten your Postini service configured and taken a brief look at the hierarchy of Postini's groups, it's time to actually make some changes to your security settings. This section covers both new and existing organizations and users, and it shows you how to customize your settings based on your needs. When you're finished, you have a well-tuned security filter for your e-mail.

In your Postini dashboard, select the organization you want to modify from the drop-down menu at the top of the screen. You can also click the Orgs and Users tab at the top of the screen and choose the organization you want to work on from there as well. You see a screen like the one shown in Figure 2-13.

Figure 2-13: Setting your Postini organization rules.

Any settings you make to these organizations are made to all users in that organization and any sub-organizations that you create from that point on. Existing sub-organizations will need individual attention, however.

Inbound services

This section applies to all e-mail coming into your system. Change these settings to affect how Postini handles e-mail that arrives on your server and where it sends these messages (if it doesn't delete them outright). The current settings for each filter are shown next to the icon. The available settings are as follows:

✦ **Spam Filtering:** Click this icon to modify how you handle spam coming into your domain. This section includes a blatant spam blocker (BSB) that can immediately delete messages that are fairly certain to be spam, or it can bounce it back to its original sender or put the message in quarantine. It can also dispose of messages that lack basic information like a From: address and messages that might be spam, but that aren't picked up by the BSB. You can choose actions and locations for all these depending on how severe you want to be with your spam.

If you're unsure of whether you're missing important messages, it's best to go light on the spam protection unless you're absolutely being buried in junk mail. It's also best to redirect spam to quarantines for review if it's not totally blatant. As you learn more about the spam you're receiving, you can ratchet up the controls to a more comfortable level.

✦ **Virus Blocking:** This section determines what happens to messages determined to be carrying a virus. These messages are usually more easy to determine than spam messages, so you can feel better about deleting them immediately. You can also choose to have the virus stripped from the message before it's delivered as well. Click that icon to change your settings.

✦ **Attachment Manager:** This section determines how to handle messages that contain large attachments. You may want to regulate the attachments that come through your e-mail system for a few reasons:

- Large attachments can clog up your servers and slow down your work.

- You don't want your users clogging their computers with large attachments.

- You don't want certain file types coming into your system.

- You don't want your users trading potentially illegal files, like pirated music or movies.

Click the Attachment Manager icon to see a more complete review of your settings, as shown in Figure 2-14. You are automatically taken to the View tab for your attachment filters.

Click the Edit link at the top of the screen to change how all your filters act. You can turn all the filters on or off, set a global address for any redirection of messages, allow mail from approved senders to bypass your filters, and choose the message sent back to those sending the offending messages. Click Save when you're satisfied with your settings.

Click the Filters link to actually change the rules for any attachments. You see the screen shown in Figure 2-15.

Inbound Attachment Manager - [ryanstestdomain.com] Account Administrators   ▸View   Edit   Filters

Filters messages based on the size or type of attachments. Filters apply to this organization and new sub-orgs you add. You can copy filters to existing sub-orgs.

Filter Type	Disposition	Settings
Message Size		**Status**
20 MB	Bounce	On
Scanning Options		**Quarantine Redirect Account**
Inside Compressed	On	ryan@ryanstestdomain.com
Binary Scanning	Off	**Approved Senders**
		Off
Custom File Types		**Bounce Message**
- none specified -	Approve	ERROR 582
- none specified -	Bounce	The file attached violates our
- none specified -	User Quarantine	email policy
- none specified -	Quarantine Redirect	
- none specified -	BCC-Quarantine	
System Threats		
Executables	Ignore	
Compressed Files		
Encrypted	Ignore	
Unencrypted	Ignore	
Productivity		
Office Documents	Ignore	
Multimedia	Ignore	
Music and Sound	Ignore	
Images	Ignore	

Figure 2-14:
Attachment Settings in Postini.

Scanning Options   ☑ Scan inside compressed file types
                        ☐ Enable binary scanning

Order	Type	
1	**Message Size**	Bounce messages larger than the specified size, which includes both the attachment and the body/header.
		Bounce 20 MB (1-300)
2	**Custom File Types**	Enter file types to filter as exceptions to subsequent filters, or that aren't handled by those filters. Do not precede file types with a period. Separate multiple entries with comma and space. For example: vcf, txt, gif
		Approve
		Bounce
		User Quarantine
		Quarantine Redirect
		BCC-Quarantine
3	**System Threats**	Filter file types that threaten security (click links to see included types). Selecting Ignore passes messages to the next filter. Selecting User Quarantine allows users to deliver filtered messages from their quarantines.
		Executables Ignore ▼
		Compressed Files
		Encrypted Ignore ▼
		Unencrypted Ignore ▼
4	**Productivity**	Filter file types to enforce corporate email policies (click links to see included types). Selecting Ignore delivers messages with no filtering. Selecting User Quarantine allows users to deliver filtered messages from their quarantines.
		Office Documents Ignore ▼
		Multimedia Ignore ▼

Figure 2-15:
Attachment Filters in Postini.

Here's where you can choose to pass certain documents through and push others into different areas, or delete them immediately. Your choices for each setting include:

- *Ignore:* This setting passes the message along to the next filter.

- *Bounce:* This setting sends the e-mail back to the sender with a preset message.

- *User Quarantine:* This setting pushes the e-mail to the user's quarantine folder.

- *Quarantine Redirect:* This setting moves the message to another quarantine folder without notifying the user.

- *BCC-Quarantine:* This setting copies it to a quarantine and sends it along the filtering process, where it might reach the user's mailbox.

- *Approve:* This setting stops the filtering process and moves it to the user's inbox.

You can modify these settings for different file types or all forms of a file like office documents or multimedia files. When you're satisfied with your filter settings, click Save to put them into effect.

✦ **Content Manager:** This function filters messages based on content. Click the Content Manager icon to see the screen shown in Figure 2-16.

Figure 2-16: Content Manager in Postini.

You see two sample filters set up for Social Security and credit card numbers. This is where you can determine what content makes it through your servers and where it gets redirected, if necessary. To create your own content filters, click the Add Custom Filter link in the middle-left portion of the Content Manager page to see the screen shown in Figure 2-17.

You are asked to give the filter a name and turn the filter on. You also get three conditions to apply with the filter. You determine whether the messages can match any of the conditions or if it must match all of them.

Your filter conditions address the following aspects:

- *Location:* Where the information you want to filter is located in the message.

- *Filter Type:* Whether the filter affects messages with the specified information, without the specified information, or acts on other conditions. Use this section to make the rule as precise as possible.

- *Information:* The actual information that is acted on. For example, if you want to filter out certain words, this is where you place the words.

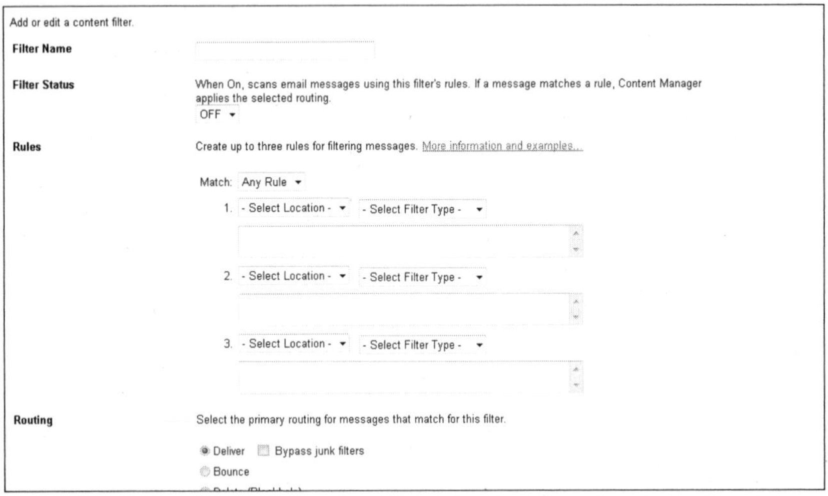

Figure 2-17:
Creating
a custom
Content
Manager
filter.

For example, if you want to send messages with certain keywords in the body back to the sender, you select Subject for the location, Contains Text for the Filter Type, and the text you want to affect in the Information field. Then click the Bounce radio button under Routing (your other choices include Deliver, Deliver and Bypass Junk Filters, or Delete). Click the Add Quarantine Address if you want to also deliver the message to a quarantine account in addition to its normal destination.

✦ **Message Limits:** Click this icon to regulate how many e-mails your users can receive per day. There are also links in this section that determine what happens to e-mail coming to your domain without a valid e-mail address (the first part of the e-mail address is incorrect) and the size of the e-mail (managed under Attachment Manager). Click the icon to see the screen shown in Figure 2-18.

This filter probably won't be of much use to you — there's really no valid reason to restrict the number of e-mails you receive when the other filters can be more precise and restrict the messages based on better qualifications than just number alone. Still, if this needs to be an option for you, it's available.

✦ **Sender Lists:** This section addresses specific users. If you want to make sure e-mails from certain people come through without being filtered, you add their addresses to the Approved Senders list. If you want to block a specific user, add that name to the Blocked Senders list. Click the Sender Lists icon to see the screen shown in Figure 2-19.

You can add specific e-mail addresses or an overall domain. Just type in the information and click Add. You can also select domains or e-mail addresses already on a list and click Remove to take them off of the list.

✦ **Industry Heuristics:** This section applies only to those in the financial or legal industries where e-mail regulations require that more information be received and retained. Click the icon to see the screen shown in Figure 2-20.

Depending on your legal requirements, you can let messages slide by where they'd otherwise be sent to a spam quarantine. You can choose to also ignore this filter or automatically pass them to the inbox. Finally, you can send e-mail from trusted outgoing mail servers automatically to your inboxes. Click Save to make your choices final.

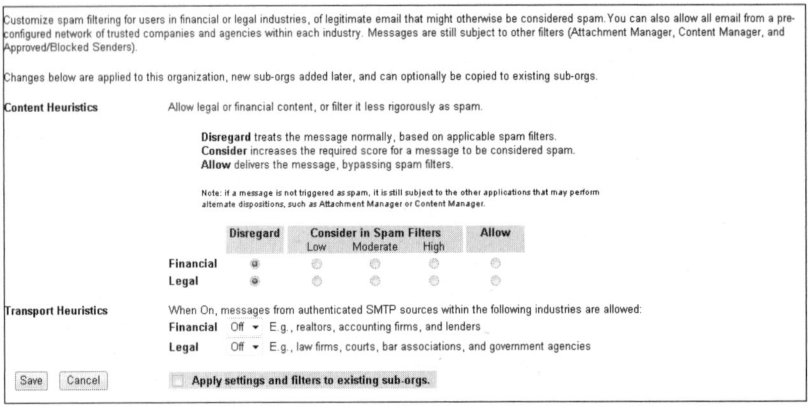

Customize spam filtering for users in financial or legal industries, of legitimate email that might otherwise be considered spam. You can also allow all email from a pre-configured network of trusted companies and agencies within each industry. Messages are still subject to other filters (Attachment Manager, Content Manager, and Approved/Blocked Senders).

Changes below are applied to this organization, new sub-orgs added later, and can optionally be copied to existing sub-orgs.

Content Heuristics   Allow legal or financial content, or filter it less rigorously as spam.

Disregard treats the message normally, based on applicable spam filters.
Consider increases the required score for a message to be considered spam.
Allow delivers the message, bypassing spam filters.

Note: If a message is not triggered as spam, it is still subject to the other applications that may perform alternate dispositions, such as Attachment Manager or Content Manager.

| | Disregard | Consider in Spam Filters | | | Allow |
		Low	Moderate	High	
Financial	⦿	○	○	○	○
Legal	⦿	○	○	○	○

Transport Heuristics   When On, messages from authenticated SMTP sources within the following industries are allowed:
Financial   Off ▾   E.g., realtors, accounting firms, and lenders
Legal   Off ▾   E.g., law firms, courts, bar associations, and government agencies

[Save] [Cancel]   ☐ **Apply settings and filters to existing sub-orgs.**

Figure 2-20:
Industry
Heuristics in
Postini.

Outbound services

Outbound services are applied to all of the e-mail originating from your mail servers. This helps you regulate the spread of any viruses from your accounts if they do manage to get infected, and it also keeps any content you don't want to leave your servers from doing so. These controls may look similar to some of the functions in the inbound services, but pay attention — the actual controls are a bit different.

The available settings are as follows:

✦ **Virus Blocking:** This function helps you prevent any viruses that may have infected your system from spreading any further. Click the icon to see the screen shown in Figure 2-21.

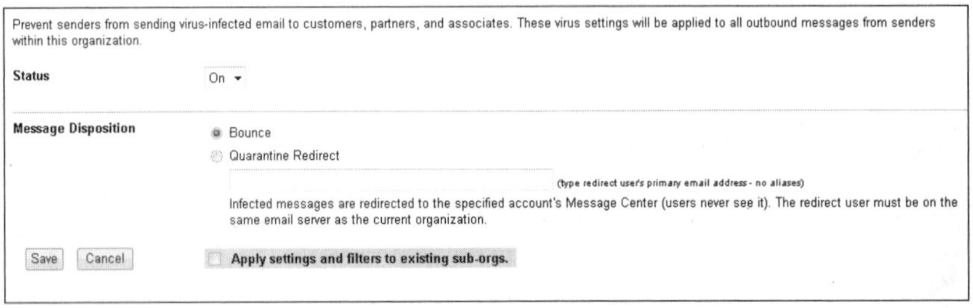

Prevent senders from sending virus-infected email to customers, partners, and associates. These virus settings will be applied to all outbound messages from senders within this organization.

Status   On ▾

Message Disposition   ⦿ Bounce
○ Quarantine Redirect
_____
(type redirect user's primary email address - no aliases)
Infected messages are redirected to the specified account's Message Center (users never see it). The redirect user must be on the same email server as the current organization.

[Save] [Cancel]   ☐ **Apply settings and filters to existing sub-orgs.**

Figure 2-21:
Outbound
virus
blocking in
Postini.

The controls are simple here. You can choose to enable or disable the protection, and you can choose whether the message is bounced back to the offending user or sent to a quarantine folder. The choice of where the message ends up is your choice, but you should always leave this protection engaged.

✦ **Attachment Manager:** This feature looks exactly like its inbound coun-terpart — it just affects the messages leaving your servers as opposed to coming in. Otherwise, you choose the filters in exactly the same way as you would with the inbound filters. Depending on how you want to regulate your e-mail, it's probably a good idea to make these settings the same as your incoming settings, just for the sake of consistency.

✦ **Content Manager:** Again, this feature is exactly the same as the inbound content manager, but it affects the e-mail leaving your servers. Use this feature to restrict what information leaves your servers. If you're dealing with private or confidential information, this is place to restrict its flow.

✦ **Compliance Footer:** This function adds a small message to the end of every e-mail that leaves your servers. This is especially important if you want to let all recipients know that they're dealing with sensitive information or messages that should be kept private and confidential. You've probably seen this kind of message before, and you can click the Compliance Footer icon to see the screen shown in Figure 2-22 and add your own.

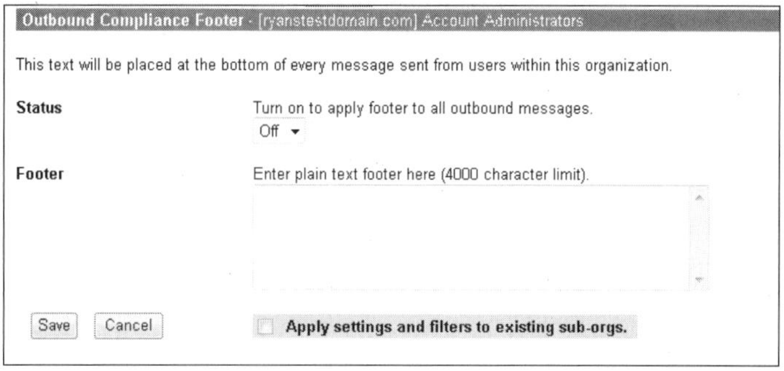

**Book VII
Chapter 2**

Securing E-Mail

Figure 2-22:
Compliance
Footers in
Postini.

Outbound Compliance Footer · [ryanstestdomain.com] Account Administrators

This text will be placed at the bottom of every message sent from users within this organization.

Status   Turn on to apply footer to all outbound messages.
              Off ▾

Footer   Enter plain text footer here (4000 character limit).

[Save] [Cancel]   ☐ **Apply settings and filters to existing sub-orgs.**

To turn on the footers, click the drop-down menu under Status and change it to On. Then type in your footer and click Save. After it's acti-vated, this message is added to all outgoing messages on your servers.

Depending on your type of business, your legal specialists may have some information to put in your footer already. Check with them and use their advice in creating your footer.

Organization settings

These icons govern how Postini interacts with your overall domain. Some of these settings require some attention from you, whereas others don't need any action unless something goes wrong. Look through these items briefly and see if they'll be of any help for you.

The available settings are as follows:

+ **System Tests:** This feature makes sure that your settings are correct and that mail is going through the Postini service correctly. If you suspect something is wrong, click the icon and run the test to make sure everything is okay. If you set up your initial DNS and MX settings correctly, though, you shouldn't have to deal with this function.

+ **General Settings:** This section contains the overall information for your domain. You shouldn't have to change any information here except for the time zone (which is set by default on Greenwich Mean Time) and whether you want e-mail sent to a non-existent user on your domain bounced back.

+ **DNS Instructions:** This feature lists the instructions to set up your MX records. If you've done this correctly, you shouldn't worry about this section. Just refer back to it if you change domain hosts.

+ **User Access:** After you've instituted mail settings for your domain, they're applied to all users in that domain. However, you may choose to allow users to change the settings for their specific accounts. Click the User Access icon to see the screen shown in Figure 2-23.

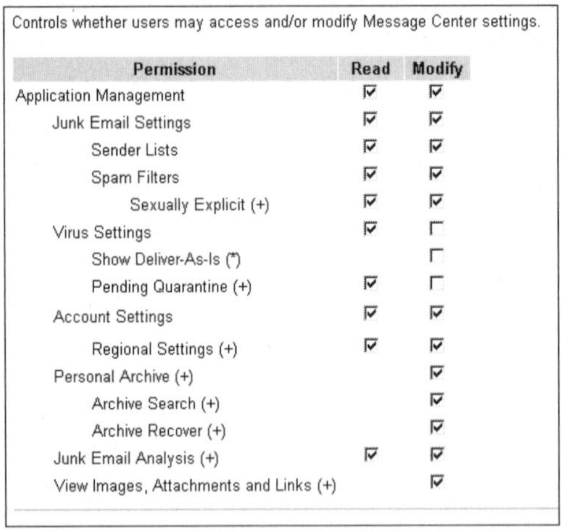

Figure 2-23:
User
Access
settings in
Postini.

Controls whether users may access and/or modify Message Center settings.

Permission	Read	Modify
Application Management	✔	✔
Junk Email Settings	✔	✔
Sender Lists	✔	✔
Spam Filters	✔	✔
Sexually Explicit (+)	✔	✔
Virus Settings	✔	☐
Show Deliver-As-Is (*)		☐
Pending Quarantine (+)	✔	☐
Account Settings	✔	✔
Regional Settings (+)	✔	✔
Personal Archive (+)		✔
Archive Search (+)		✔
Archive Recover (+)		✔
Junk Email Analysis (+)	✔	✔
View Images, Attachments and Links (+)		✔

The Read check boxes allow users to be aware of the policies instituted on their accounts, and the Modify check boxes determine whether the user can change those policies. If you want your settings to be consistent across the board, you should deny the users access to these settings — it'll make life easier for everybody involved.

✦ **Default User:** This setting is the model for all new users in your domain, and you can tweak security settings a little more individually than you can with the more global settings we've addressed up to this point. Click the Default User icon to see the screen shown in Figure 2-24.

Figure 2-24:
Default User settings in Postini.

The icons shown in Figure 2-24 are similar to the global functions, so you should feel comfortable working with them after reading through the earlier parts of this chapter. The main difference is in the Spam Filtering settings. Click the icon to show the screen in Figure 2-25.

Figure 2-25:
Individual User Spam Filter settings in Postini.

You can set how aggressive you want the spam filters to be on certain types of messages. Select the appropriate level and click Save when you're finished.

If you or the user in question notice too many legitimate messages going into the spam filter, back off on the levels in this section.

✦ **Notifications:** This section outlines messages that are automatically sent to users when certain incidents occur. These incidents include

- Welcoming a new user.

- An e-mail containing a virus.

- Early detection of spam.

- Your first spam message.

- Any spam message thereafter.

- Suspension of the user.

- Activation of the Attachment Manager, either incoming or outgoing.

Not all these messages apply to Google Apps users, and others won't really fit into your administrative plan. If you do decide to use these functions, click the Notifications icon, select the message you want to create, and type in the message. Click Save when you're done. These messages go only to those who are part of your Google Apps domain.

✦ **Branding:** Click the Branding icon to see the screen shown in Figure 2-26. This allows you to change the color scheme of the Message Center and upload a company icon, should you desire.

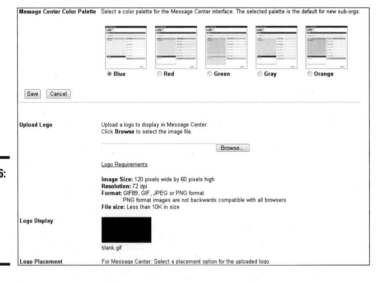

Figure 2-26: Branding the Message Center in Postini.

This won't really affect the function on the Message Center (which we take a look at later in this chapter in the section called "Using the Postini Message Center"), but it will help you integrate the Message Center into your overall corporate look. Select the scheme you want to use and decide if you want to upload a graphic — follow the directions shown in Figure 2-26 if you choose to upload one. Click Save when you're finished to finalize your options.

✦ **Archiving:** This function determines whether you archive your e-mail. You may be mandated to keep messages for a certain amount of time depending on the legal requirements for your type of business, and it's a good idea to archive in any case. That way, you can keep track of old communications if necessary without clogging your users' inboxes. Click the Archiving icon to see the screen shown in Figure 2-27.

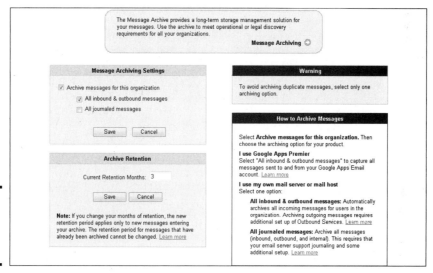

Figure 2-27:
Archiving
e-mail in
Postini.

The settings shown in Figure 2-27 should be good enough for most businesses. These settings apply to all users in your domain at the time of activation — messages deleted before then won't be recoverable. If you're a Premiere user, you can also search through the archives for deleted items within 90 days for all the users in your domain.

To search through the archives, click the Message Archiving link shown in Figure 2-27. You see the screen shown in Figure 2-28.

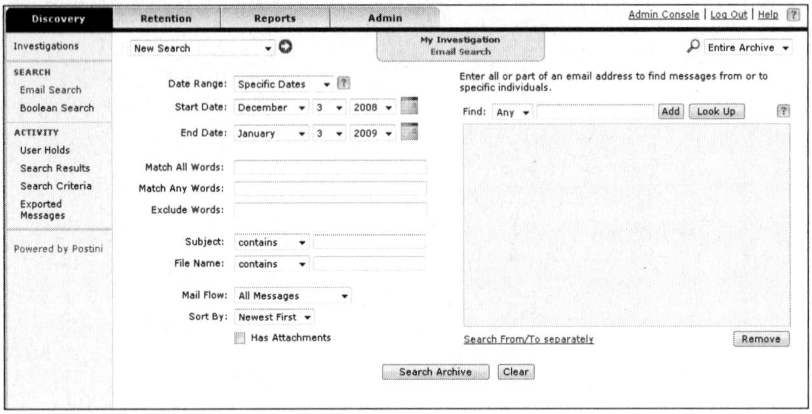

Figure 2-28:
Looking
through
your Postini
archives.

Choose whether you want to use an e-mail-oriented search or a Boolean search (if you're not familiar with those terms, stick with the e-mail-oriented search) and click that link in the left column shown in Figure 2-28. Enter the search terms you want to use, included dates, content, and any attached files or subject lines. Make the search as specific as possible to reduce the time you'll spend searching through the archives. When you're finished, click the Search Archive button to get your results.

Depending on what you find, you can take several actions outlined in the left column. These actions include

- Placing a hold on all e-mails to and from a certain user.

- Saving your search criteria.

- Modifying your saved search criteria.

- Exporting messages to your desktop.

These functions are important if you're holding on to e-mail for legal reasons, but otherwise you shouldn't have to make much use of them.

Your archives automatically purge messages older than your retention time if you desire. If you want to stop purging messages, click the Retention tab at the top of the screen in Figure 2-28 and click the Turn Auto-Purge Off button. You have to manually remove items from the archive if you choose to Auto-Purge, or else you'll eventually run out of room. Given the amount of space Google Apps gives you for your mail accounts, this probably won't be a huge concern. Still, it's something to be aware of.

The Reports tab at the top of the screen shown in Figure 2-28 shows you information on the amount of e-mail in your domain, reports on your monthly e-mail use, displays what information has been purged, and shows audits on certain users. This information is probably more than you want to know, but it's available if you need it. For example, you can see which user has the most e-mail traffic or stored information in case you need to make room on your servers. The Admin tab allows you to restrict what information administrators can look for. This won't affect the normal operation of your domain, so you shouldn't have to change any functions here.

Using the Postini Message Center

Depending on the settings you created for your Postini users, they may be able to view their Postini junk mail and quarantine folders. If you've enabled these functions, users can point their browsers to http://login. postini.com/a/yourdomainhere.com (replacing yourdomainhere. com with your individual domain name, of course) and log in. They are presented with the screen shown in Figure 2-29.

Figure 2-29: The Postini Message Center.

**Book VII
Chapter 2**

Securing E-Mail

Tabbing through your e-mail

The tabs shown in Figure 2-29 are fairly self-explanatory:

✦ **Junk:** This folder shows e-mail that's been identified by Postini as spam.

✦ **Viruses:** This folder displays any messages that have been quarantined due to virus.

✦ **Delivered:** This shows delivered messages that have been filtered through Postini.

✦ **Trash:** Depending on your settings, this folder displays trashed messages retained through Postini.

✦ **Archive:** This tab allows you to search through your account's archives, as shown in Figure 2-30. Type your terms and click Search Archives to find the results.

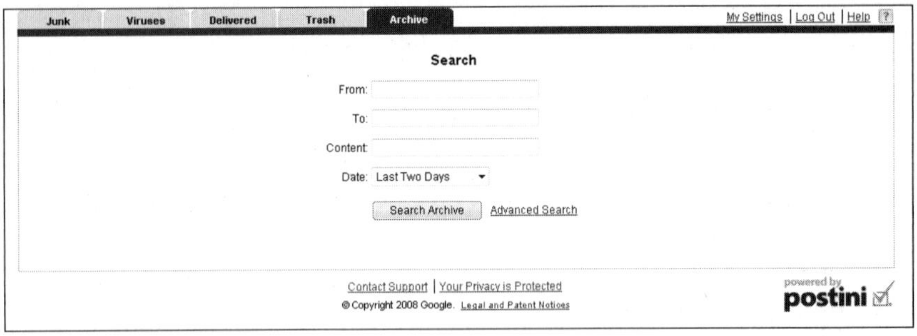

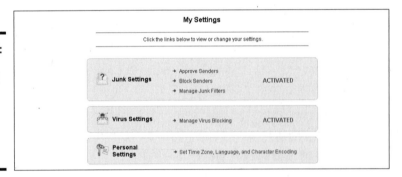

Figure 2-30:
Searching
your
archives.

Managing your e-mail account

Although each account is governed by the global settings for your domain, Postini allows individuals to alter their own mail settings as well (provided you've allowed that access in the global settings). Click the My Settings link shown in the top-right corner of Figure 2-29 to see the screen shown in Figure 2-31.

Figure 2-31:
Changing
your e-mail
account
settings in
Postini's
Message
Center.

The settings here are not as complete as the ones in the Admin Center, but it still gives the user a little control:

+ **Approve Senders:** Click the Approve Senders link to see the screen shown in Figure 2-32. You can enter the addresses, domains, and mailing lists you want delivered directly to your inbox by typing them in the appropriate field and clicking the appropriate Update button.

+ **Block Senders:** Click the Block Senders link in Figure 2-31 to see the screen shown in Figure 2-33. From here you can update your blocked senders and domains in the same way you do your approved senders list.

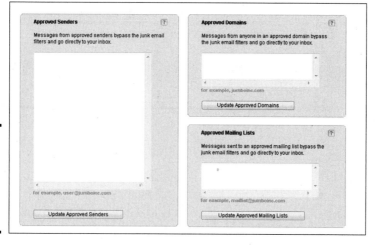

Figure 2-32:
Approving
senders,
domains,
and mailing
lists.

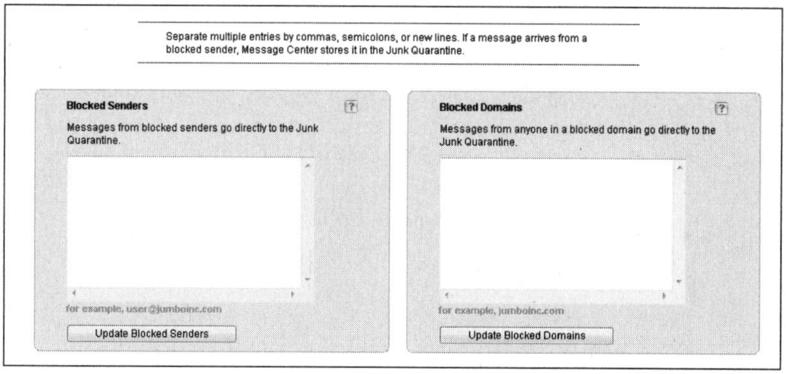

Figure 2-33:
Blocking
senders and
domains.

✦ **Manage Junk Filters:** Click the Manage Junk Filters link in Figure 2-31 and then click the Show Categories filter to see the screen shown in Figure 2-34.

Depending on your global settings, you can turn the junk mail filter on and off by clicking the Activated link. You can also click the Overall Junk Filter drop-down menu to change the filter's aggressiveness from Lenient to Very Aggressive, and you can increase the aggressiveness on certain subject matter from the default level. Click Save Settings when you're done to put your settings into effect.

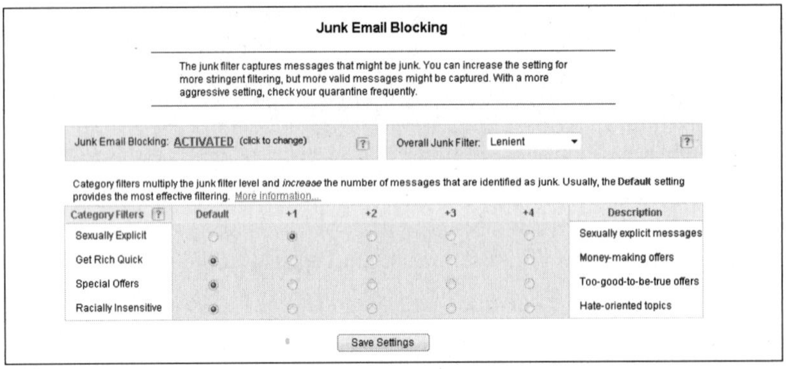

Figure 2-34:
Managing
your
account's
junk e-mail
filters.

✦ **Manage Virus Blocking:** By default, users can't change the settings for this feature, and it's not a good idea to allow them to disable virus blocking in any case. Administrators can let users view the setting, but it's not a good idea to let them modify.

✦ **Personal Settings:** Clicking this link allows you to change the settings for you time zone and language, as shown in Figure 2-35. Click the settings most appropriate to you and click Save Settings. You can also click Restore Defaults to put everything back to where it was.

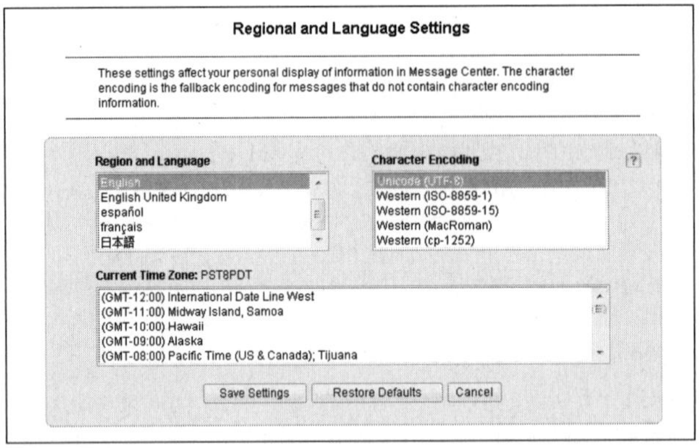

Figure 2-35:
Personal
settings
in the
Message
Center.

Chapter 3: Avoiding Web and IM Security Risks

In This Chapter

✔ Knowing the risks of connecting to the Web

✔ Understand what can get out through instant messaging

✔ Deciding the best way to protect yourself

*I*f you're dealing with Google, you come in contact with a great deal of what's available on the Internet. In addition to the services it provides, Google is connected to a mind-boggling amount of information hosted on others sites. More than likely, you won't have a problem with any of the sites you encounter. You may find some utterly useless information, of course, but nothing harmful. Still, threats to your computers and your network are out there, and you need to be aware of where these threats might be. Google has some protection options available, but it's better to avoid those threats in the first place.

Identifying Web Security Risks

Most of the security risks you face on the Internet rely on trickery and deceit to lure you into their traps. Brute force hacking takes too much time, and it's not guaranteed to work. It's far easier for a malicious program to trick you into providing sensitive information. The following are examples of this kind of trickery:

✦ **Malicious sites:** A malicious site doesn't have to look evil or dangerous. In fact, if it did look dangerous, it wouldn't be effective: You'd be less likely to access the site to begin with. When you load the information in a browser, however, you also load a payload that will try to get information. This payload can include a virus, a keylogger program that records and transmits everything you type, a phishing scam (as examined in Chapter 2 in this book), or other threats.

+ **Spyware:** That browser toolbar or game you downloaded onto your computer may be perfectly harmless, or it may install programs you don't even know about. Spyware tracks your browser activity and other computer functions and transmits these to another source. It can also be the source of popup ads or programs that move files onto your computer without your knowledge. You may only notice a slower computer, or you may notice programs you can't delete or remove. You may have to entirely reload your computer, depending on what software you've accidentally downloaded.

Unless you're absolutely sure of the source of your program, it's best not to install it on your computer. If it introduces security risks, the time and effort you spend to clean out an infected computer are worth more than that game.

+ **Viruses:** The term *virus* is applied to a host of malicious programs that can infect your computer and perform a multitude of actions, all designed to either take over your computer or spread to other machines. A more accurate term is *malware*, meaning software that actively attacks your system. Malware comes in a variety of flavors:

  • *Viruses* require transmission through an e-mail or instant message.

  • *Worms* can copy and transmit themselves across networks without the need for something to carry them.

  • *Trojan horses* install themselves on computer and wait for a command from a remote source.

Depending on what you download, malware can take control of your computer to attack others and spread the virus, destroy information, or take another malicious action. It's because of programs like this that you need to make sure your antivirus programs are active and up to date.

Focusing on Web Security

Now that you know what's out there, you can work on prevention. There are many ways to approach your security needs, and they range from individual measures to business-wide solutions. First, let's take a look at your needs.

If your employees or colleagues need to do a great deal of Web research or access multiple sites, it's important for them to get that access without a great deal of hassle. There's nothing more frustrating than trying to access a site you need to work with but finding that your access is blocked. This is where measures like antivirus software and safe searching become important.

The answer is simple, right? All your problems are solved if your employees and colleagues surf the Web only for what's necessary for business. Although that's an easy answer, it's not necessarily the most realistic. The people in your company will probably go to sites like Amazon.com, celebrity gossip sites, or others of this type — relatively harmless sites that, although they waste a little time, don't present a threat to your computer and network security.

The problems arise when employees surf to sites that cause those threats, and you have a couple of choices at this point. You can either try to block that surfing to begin with, or you can keep your security measures up to date and hope that's enough to protect you. It depends on your budget and your control over your computer systems.

Choosing a Web Security Provider

If you've determined that you need to control the Web sites your employees or colleagues access on company computers, your next step is deciding what kind of Web security you want to install. It could be as easy as turning on certain controls already present on the computers, or it could require some outside support. What's the best way to go about it? Take a look at the information in this section and decide for yourself.

If you're a small business, chances are you don't deal with too much sensitive information. Your financial records are probably not posted on the Web for everybody to see, but even if they were, this wouldn't be a huge loss. On the other hand, if you work in the healthcare industry or you track extremely sensitive information, you may need to take more countermeasures when it comes to your data. If you have any question about the sensitivity of your data, check with a legal expert to see exactly what you need to do.

Depending on the service you choose, a Web security provider can do several things:

+ Block access to certain sites.

+ Prevent the download of malicious software.

+ Monitor and create reports on Web traffic.

+ Prevent unauthorized access to your sensitive information.

This is where you decide what your needs (and your budget) demands are. If you're just trying to restrict access to some Web sites, you can probably achieve that through your operating system's functions. If you require more help, it's time to look at a separate program.

Outsourcing Web security

Many firms out there (including Google itself) can offer services like server security, virtual private network (VPN) connections, Web traffic management, and more. Because this is their stock-in-trade, you're likely to get excellent service with these companies.

However, these services can be expensive, and they usually rely on a subscription service to make their money, as opposed to a one-time purchase. That means it's something you need to budget for now and in the future. Allowing access to outside companies may also present a problem to entities that host sensitive information on their systems. That's not to say that all outside companies will try and steal your information, but the possibility does exist. You want to make sure you go with a well-known and trusted provider if you do decide to take this step.

Bringing Web security in-house

When you bring your service in-house, you get complete control over the situation. You know who has access to your information at all times, and you can make all the choices you want when it comes to your policies. If you need to retain control, this is the option for you.

However, that control means that you (or somebody inside your company) has to study the software and policies, maybe beginning from scratch. It also means that you have to be constantly vigilant about your security — nobody else is going to do it for you. If you have the time and energy to devote to this, in-house Web security could be the way to go for you. Otherwise, it might be worth spending the extra money to have somebody do it for you.

Letting Google Protect Your Web Site

In Chapter 2 of this minibook, we look at what Google's Postini services can do for e-mail security. Also when users of its search service are about to access a potentially malicious site, Google warns them before they actually load the site into their browsers. Google also offers additional security to businesses who want more protection from viruses, malware, spyware, and other threats. It can also filter and control the kind of Web sites your company's computers can access. This kind of service isn't cheap, but it could provide you with the control and security you need.

Google and Postini combine to provide Google Web Security for the Enterprise to those who use Google Apps Premier and are willing to pay an extra fee for this type of management. At the time of this writing, the service costs $36 per user per year, with a minimum of 50 users. If your business is smaller than that, you probably won't have need of this program. If you do, however, this service could help you protect your computers and network effectively.

As noted before, Google's search services warn you when you're about to access a potentially malicious site. However, if you're not accessing the site through the search services, Google Web Security can still insulate you from harm. The service tracks these sites based on the site's reputation, the type of code it tries to install, and other factors. Google can analyze and remove potential threats from malicious sites before they reach your computer as well as stop any downloads of spyware.

Several types of programs can be used to spy on your computers and your network. Spyware can install itself and transmit your data to outside sources. Keyloggers can track everything you type, including passwords, and send this to another location outside of your network. And viruses or other malware can attack your systems and inflict all kinds of damage. Google Web Security can identify these threats and stop them before they arrive on your computers. That doesn't mean that you no longer need to install antivirus software on your computers, but it does give you an additional layer of protection against outside attackers. Google can also extend this protection to your computers even when you're off of your network, which gives you protection against others sharing whatever network you use on the road.

Google's search function offers SafeSearch, which filters content based on sexual explicitness and other factors. When searching on Google, click the Search Preferences link shown in Figure 3-1 to bring up the search preferences page.

Book VII
Chapter 3

Avoiding Web and IM Security Risks

Figure 3-1:
Search
preferences
for Google.

		Advanced Search
		Search Preferences
Google Search	I'm Feeling Lucky	Language Tools

Scroll down the page until you see the screen shown in Figure 3-2. You can choose strict, moderate, or no filter on your searches.

Figure 3-2:
Google's
SafeSearch
settings.

SafeSearch Filtering | Google's SafeSearch blocks web pages containing explicit sexual content from appearing in search results.
- Use strict filtering (Filter both explicit text and explicit images)
- Use moderate filtering (Filter explicit images only - default behavior)
- Do not filter my search results.

Again, this applies only to searches conducted through Google. Google Web Security extends that protection to all facets of your Web searching.

Just because the site you're looking at is generally okay doesn't mean that everything on it is safe. Web filtering blocks certain content from reaching your computer, no matter which site it's located on. You can alter the setting to exactly what you need, depending on what you want to block.

Google Web Security can also block certain content entirely, based on site and code reputation. Because Google thrives on harvested information, you can be sure that just about anything that comes over your browser is identified and acted upon accordingly.

Identifying Instant Messaging Security Risks

Instant messaging is one of the most popular and prevalent methods of communicating on the Internet, and it's not just the province of chatty teens or bored office workers. You can IM anything from a quick note to an entire file or document via one of any IM services, including Google Talk (shown in Figure 3-3).

Figure 3-3:
Google Talk.

As useful as it is, instant messaging can represent a security risk, both from what's sent from your computers to what's sent to you.

Obviously, the purpose of instant messaging is to communicate information in short, quick bursts. You don't have to wait for a response as you do with e-mail because you have a direct link to the person you're talking to. The problem is that, like personal phone calls, this kind of communication can reduce an employee's productivity. It can also mean the inadvertent loss of company secrets. One errant chat or message later, your trade secrets have accidentally been revealed to an outside source. It's certainly worth your time to take a look at how your employees and colleagues use IM services.

Words can hurt a business

When an employee is chatting with her family or friends, there's not much risk of something happening that could endanger your business. More than likely, it's a perfectly harmless conversation. But what if you use instant messaging services to communicate to your customers?

Just because it's in a chat window doesn't mean it's not official business. IM services represent a communication channel from you to your clients and customers, the same as a phone call or an e-mail. What's said over a chat window should be considered official business, and your employees (and you) face the same legal restrictions and liabilities as you do with any other communication.

You'd expect your employees and colleagues to maintain a professional and businesslike demeanor over any other method of communication, including IM. Expect to handle this communication as you would any other conversation to a similar client or customer.

Instant messaging security primer

Instant messaging is a direct link between two or more persons communicating in real time. Most instant messaging services can also transmit everything from pictures and documents to music and movies, making it a potentially hazardous method of communication. It's important to understand what happens during instant messaging and how you can keep yourself and your business safe.

Instant messaging services are usually restricted to known friends and family members via an e-mail address or other identifier. If that ID isn't publically known, you're not likely to get messages from unknown senders. That doesn't mean it's not possible, though. And it's those unknown senders that present the problem. That person might just be interested in your services, or he could be trying to send malware over the chat line. Knowing who you're talking to and keeping your antivirus and spyware programs updated makes a huge difference here.

Normal business hours don't mean much to those connected to the Internet. Today's users may expect support at unusual hours, and it may be in your financial interests to provide that support. However, that means that you need to make sure your security is in effect at all times and that you can have access to conversations that take place past "normal" business hours.

The ease of transferring files and documents is great for getting something to somebody quickly, but it also represents a great danger. That direct connection means that somebody has a direct connection to your computer and can send anything he wants to. The recipient usually has to accept the file, but that one click can mean that any manner of malware could come to your computer and network. This is where the common sense of the IM user has to combine with your antivirus protection to keep your systems from becoming infected.

If you're interested in what your employees are chatting about, most IM services log chats, and you can check those. Google Talk even saves chats to your Gmail and Google Apps mail accounts by default, so you can track them through Postini. If you have Google Web Services for the Enterprise, that extra layer of protection can help protect you through content filtering and virus protection. However, that solution may be cost-prohibitive for you and may require more users than you have. In any case, if you're using IM at work, you need to make sure you have the following in place:

✦ A written policy that informs your employees what the acceptable use of IM at work is and what they can and cannot discuss.

✦ Antivirus software that's updated religiously.

✦ The capability to check chat logs.

Be sure to review your policies regularly and keep up to date on what your employees are doing and how you may need to change their behavior.

Book VIII
Getting Noticed with Gadgets

"So, you want to work for the best browser company in the world? Well, let me get you a job application. Let's see...where are they? Shoot! I can never find anything around here!"

Contents at a Glance

Chapter 1: Introduction to Google Gadgets

In This Chapter

✓ Taking a look at the available Google Gadgets

✓ Assembling the gadgets into your own personal creation

✓ Making gadgets work for you

✓ Putting Google on your desktop

Google's capability to supply and configure information is what makes it the dominant force on the Internet that it is. In addition to the search functions and applications Google provides, it offers the ability to customize and tweak that information and these services into exactly what the user wants. This information isn't just available on Google's standard home page, though. Google offers information and functionality through a series of small programs called *gadgets*, which users can discover, modify, and embed in their own home pages and elsewhere. Better still, these users can create their own gadgets and spread them to the home pages of other users.

Exploring the Gadget Directory

Whether you're using an individual account or a Google Apps domain start page, you have an impressive selection of Google Gadgets available to you. These gadgets can be installed anywhere on your page just by dragging and dropping, and you can arrange them into different tabs as you want. First, though, let's take a look at what's available in the main directory.

The Gadget directory may look a little different, depending on whether you access it through iGoogle or Google Apps. Still, the same gadgets are available to either view. Click the Add Stuff link on the homepage of either service to see the screens shown in Figures 1-1 and 1-2. You can also point your browser to `http://google.com/ig/directory` to see what's available.

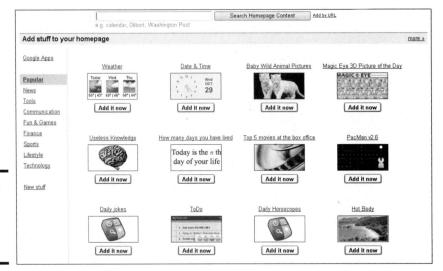

Figure 1-1:
Google
Gadgets
in Google
Apps.

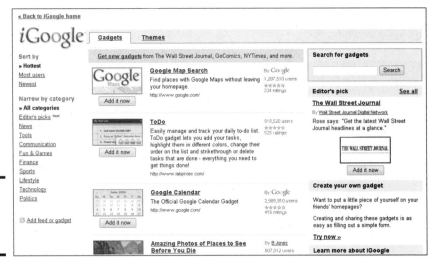

Figure 1-2:
Google
Gadgets in
iGoogle.

The categories of gadgets hint at the possibilities of what's available in the directory, and you can search for additional gadgets on whatever topic you want (would you expect any different from Google?) by entering a few keywords in the Search for Gadgets field and clicking Search.

Both Google and third-party developers are constantly adding gadgets to Google's directory, so it's best to check back on a regular basis and see what's available.

Click one of the categories to see a list of what's generally available for that topic. For instance, Figure 1-3 shows what's new and available in the world of finance for Google Gadgets.

You can also search the directory by keyword, as shown in Figure 1-4 (can you guess what the search keywords were?). If you're interested in searching for gadgets that only apply to certain topics, click the category first and then enter your search terms. Your search will be further restricted, and you can find what you're looking for much more quickly.

Figure 1-3: Financial Google Gadgets.

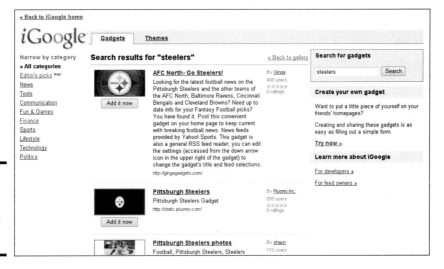

Figure 1-4: Searching for Google Gadgets by keywords.

Whenever you do find the gadget you're looking for, click the Add It Now button under the gadget (shown in Figure 1-5) to put it on your main homepage. After it appears there, you can move it around as you see fit.

Figure 1-5:
Adding a
Google
Gadget
to your
homepage.

Interacting with the iGoogle Homepage

Google wants iGoogle to be your homepage whenever you open a browser. It gives you a customized portal filled with all the information you could want. It's like a totally customizable car dashboard, or a newspaper with just the information you want and no glossy circulars. As your homepage, it's the first thing you'll see whenever you open a browser, and that means you'd like your gadget to be on that desktop whenever anybody looks at it. If you can get that placement, you can make your information seen over and over again. Any updates or changes are automatically pushed out to all your users.

In short, you want to use it because it's a cheap, easy, and consistent way to get to the people you want to reach.

The iGoogle homepage is probably the most common way people view and interact with the Google Gadgets they find and install from the Gadget Directory. The applications work the same on Google Apps homepages, but far more people use individual Google accounts than Google Apps accounts. Therefore, you have to understand how the iGoogle page functions so you can work with gadgets yourself and make your own gadgets work for others.

Before you sign up for iGoogle, all you see is the normal Google homepage when you go to http://google.com, as shown in Figure 1-6. However, note the two links in the upper-right corner. Clicking the sign-in link gives you the screen shown in Figure 1-6, and clicking the iGoogle link leads to the iGoogle page shown in Figure 1-7.

Either way, there's a link to sign in or create an account for iGoogle. First-time users get an invitation to create their home pages, as shown in Figure 1-8.

Figure 1-6:
Signing in to Google.

Figure 1-7:
The generic iGoogle homepage.

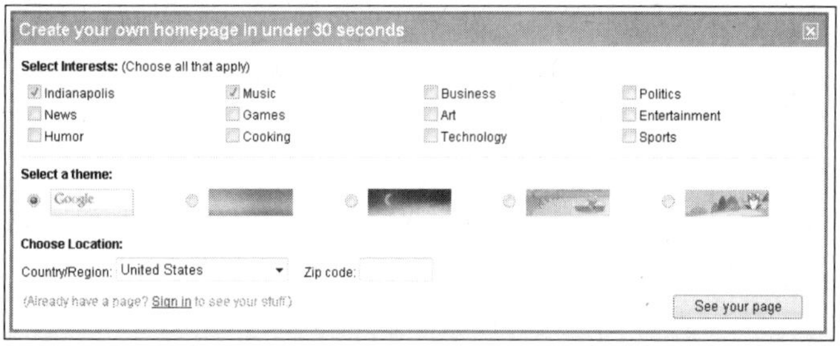

Figure 1-8:
Creating the home page.

After you've entered the information, click the See Your Page button to see the screen shown in Figure 1-9. If you've already signed up for a Google account, this page is saved and accessible from any computer you use. Just sign in, and your homepage is there. If you don't have a Google account yet, this homepage shows up until you clear the cookies out of your browser. It won't be accessible from any other computer.

Given that a Google account is free, it's a good idea to sign up to keep your homepage intact wherever you are. Google Apps accounts also hold their homepages wherever you sign in.

**Book VIII
Chapter 1**

Introduction to
Google Gadgets

Figure 1-9:
Your new
iGoogle
homepage.

After your page is created, there are a few basic ways to customize it. The most common choices are as follows:

✦ **Themes:** The default iGoogle homepage looks a lot like the pages Google creates for itself. It's got a white background, bright colors, and clearly defined borders. That's great if you want to keep it, but Google has plenty of other options available for you, if you wish. Click the Themes for Causes link or the Change Theme from Classic link to see the available themes.

At the time of this writing, iGoogle provides a standard set of themes along with specially designed artist themes and themes that help support a charitable cause. No matter which section you choose, you see a list of themes like the one shown in Figure 1-10.

Just click the Add It Now button to add the theme to your homepage. You can always change it to a different theme later, whether you see a new theme that you like or if you're just ready for a change.

✦ **Tabs and pages:** By default, iGoogle sets up your homepage with one tab and all of the gadgets placed under that tab on the page. If you start building up a wealth of useful gadgets, though, you may find yourself scrolling up and down your homepage just to get the information. Trust me, that gets very annoying very quickly. However, Google enables you to manage several different tabs within your homepage — just a click, and you've got an entire different set of gadgets ready for your use.

Look for the arrow next to the home tab and click it. In the resulting menu, you have the option of adding, sharing, or editing the tab. After you've added more tabs, you also have the option of deleting tabs.

Clicking the Edit This Tab link brings up the screen shown in Figure 1-11. You can change the name of the tab here, or you can share or delete any of the gadgets currently in your tabs line-up.

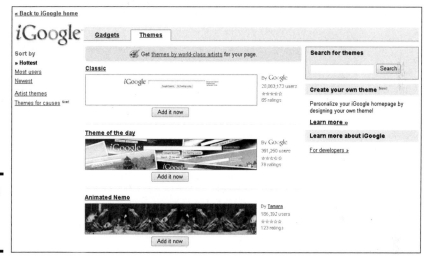

Figure 1-10:
Available
iGoogle
themes.

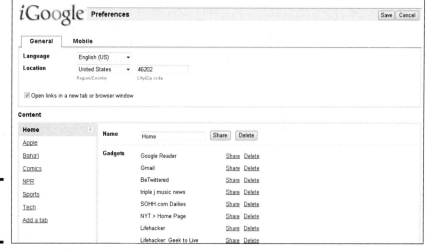

Figure 1-11:
Editing tabs
in iGoogle.

**Book VIII
Chapter 1**

**Introduction to
Google Gadgets**

Clicking the Share This Tab link allows you to send the tab and its associated gadgets to anybody else, although they need an iGoogle account to take full advantage of these gadgets. If she accepts the invitation, that tab is included on her homepage as well. If you're sharing a series of gadgets that could make your normal business activities a little easier, this is a great way of sending them off to friends or coworkers. Take a look at the screen in Figure 1-12 to see an example.

Figure 1-12:
Sharing
your iGoogle
tabs.

You can also add and delete tabs. Click the Add a Tab link to name the tab and, if you choose, have Google add a series of gadgets to your tab based on the name you give it. Type the name, make your selection in the check box for adding gadgets, and click OK, as shown in Figure 1-13.

To delete a tab, just click the Delete Tab link and click OK to confirm your decision.

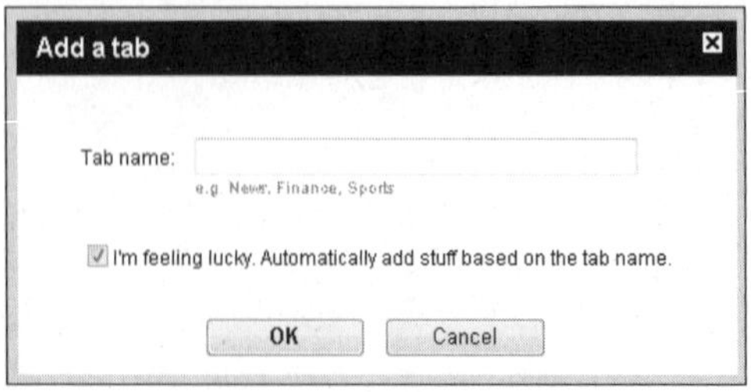

Figure 1-13:
Adding an
iGoogle tab.

Keeping Informed with Google Desktop

If you're interacting with a Web browser, iGoogle gives you everything you need from whatever computer you're using. However, most people have a main computer, or at least one that they use more than others. Google makes a package of software for that computer that allows you to access Google Gadgets (and just about everything else on your computer) without opening up a browser window. Google Desktop puts a sidebar on your computer that uses Google Gadgets to keep you informed, and it also lets you search and access just about everything on your computer.

Installing Google Desktop

Navigate to `http://desktop.google.com` and click the appropriate link for your operating system, as shown in Figure 1-14. Follow the directions to install Google Desktop on your system.

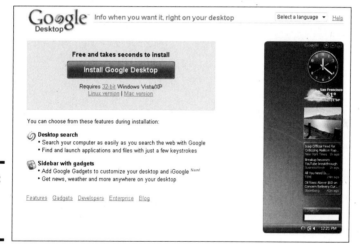

Figure 1-14: Installing Google Desktop.

After you've installed the Desktop software, you see a sidebar on the right side of your screen and, on Windows systems, a small icon in the bottom-right corner of your screen. In the screen shown in Figure 1-15, the Google Desktop icon shows up at the left side of the notification area, below the Google Desktop sidebar.

Google throws in a default series of gadgets, and you can change them to whatever you want. There is significantly less space than on the iGoogle desktop, so you're going to have to be a little judicious in choosing which gadgets make the cut.

Figure 1-15:
Google
Desktop's
sidebar and
icon.

News, e-mail, and chat gadgets are always a good place to start. These services change quickly and stay useful no matter what happens.

Google Desktop also includes a small search window at the bottom of the sidebar. Google Desktop indexes the content of your computer and makes it available when you search for anything on your system. Depending on how you set up Google Desktop, you can also have it search additional locations or other computers. Let's take a look at Google Desktop's search and then continue on to the other Google Gadgets.

Searching from Google Desktop

From the moment you install Google Desktop, the program is taking an inventory of everything on your computer, from programs to files to Web searches. After it's done, you can type search terms into the bottom gadget on your sidebar and get a list of matching results. It's a lifesaver when you're looking for missing invoices, contact lists, or business letters.

To set which items are indexed in this search, click the Google Desktop icon and select Options, which brings up the screen shown in Figure 1-16. Under the Desktop Search tab, select the files you want indexed, install any search plug-ins you want to integrate with other programs (like Mozilla's Firefox Web browser), add additional locations to the search, and decide where you want your feeds stored and whether they're encrypted.

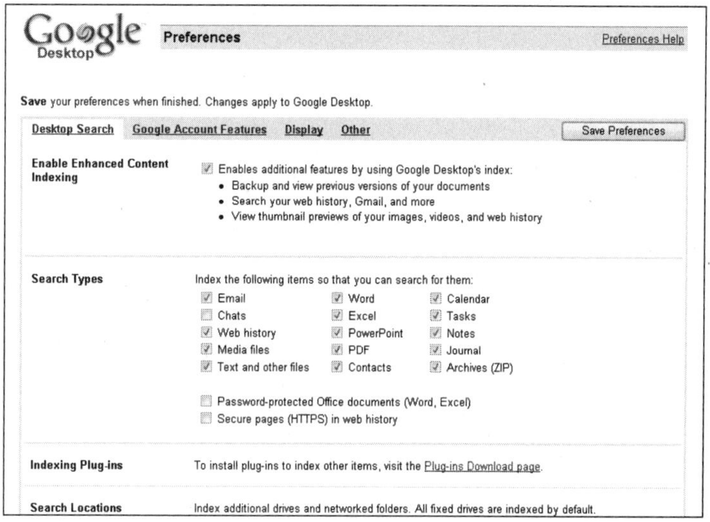

Figure 1-16:
Desktop
Search
options.

When you're satisfied with the index settings, click the Save Preferences button at the top of the page to put your choices into effect.

Under the Google Account Features tab, you can select whether your Gmail account and other computers are indexed as well. To search across computers, you have to name your computer and select whether indexes of documents, Web searches, both, or neither are transmitted to Google's servers for use across multiple systems. Again, after you've made your choices, click the Save Preferences button to make your decision final.

Click the Display tab to choose how to view your Google Desktop. Your choices are as follows:

✦ The Quick Search box is called when you press the Ctrl key twice on your keyboard. Type your search information and press Return to start the search.

✦ Quick Search displays results in your search bar as you type.

**Book VIII
Chapter 1**

**Introduction to
Google Gadgets**

✦ Choose to display Google Desktop as a sidebar, a desktop bar (either floating or locked), or not at all.

✦ Choose whether your gadgets are shown as icons and text, icon only, or not at all.

The Other tab determines whether you share anonymous data about how you use Google Desktop and whether your search results are checked against a list of unsafe or malicious sites. As described before, click the Save Preferences button to make your choices final.

When you're finished, just type the search terms into the search window to get your results. You see a list like the one shown in Figure 1-17.

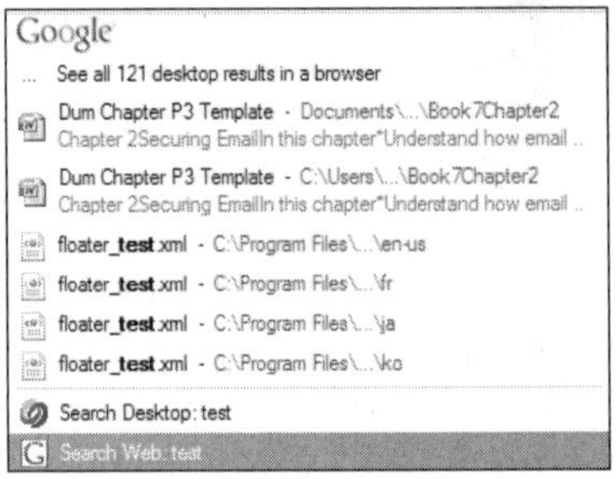

Figure 1-17:
Search
results in
Google
Desktop.

> Google
>
> ... See all 121 desktop results in a browser
>
> Dum Chapter P3 Template - Documents\...\Book 7Chapter2
> Chapter 2Securing Emailin this chapter"Understand how email ...
>
> Dum Chapter P3 Template - C:\Users\...\Book 7Chapter2
> Chapter 2Securing Emailin this chapter"Understand how email ...
>
> floater_**test**.xml - C:\Program Files\...\en-us
>
> floater_**test**.xml - C:\Program Files\...\fr
>
> floater_**test**.xml - C:\Program Files\...\ja
>
> floater_**test**.xml - C:\Program Files\...\ko
>
> Search Desktop: test
>
> Search Web: test

Click on the entry you want, and off you go.

If you want faster results from a smaller subset of documents, limit your search types in the Google Desktop Options menu. If you limit your searches to only your business folders, you get quicker and more defined results.

Using Gadgets in the sidebar

The gadgets used in the Google Desktop sidebar are similar to the ones used in the desktops for iGoogle and any Google Apps accounts. The selection isn't as great, but it can still give you some useful information. More important, you can use sidebar gadgets to monitor your Google account information, including Gmail and Google Talk.

The sidebar comes with a few preset gadgets, including news, weather, and some other items (depending on what you've signed up for with your Google account). If you want to add more gadgets to your sidebar, click the plus sign at the top of the sidebar shown in Figure 1-15. You see a screen like the one shown in Figure 1-18.

Figure 1-18:
Adding new gadgets to the Google Desktop sidebar.

After you find the gadget you're looking for, move your cursor over it and click Add. The gadget appears at the top of your sidebar, and from there you can drag-and-drop it anywhere in the sidebar. Depending on the properties of the gadget, you can also right-click on it and consider more options. For example, you can use the location of the weather gadget or edit the feeds shown in the Web clips.

Again, all these options are dependent on the type and properties of the gadget. Right-click and play around with the options to see what is possible.

The Google Desktop sidebar also has a menu option, accessible by clicking the downward-facing arrow at the top of the screen shown in Figure 1-15. From there, you can add more gadgets, configure and set your gadget options, or choose the position of your Google Desktop sidebar, as follows:

✦ **Sidebar:** This option places the sidebar as shown in Figure 1-15.

✦ **Deskbar:** This option places the sidebar as a toolbar at the bottom of the screen.

✦ **Floating Deskbar:** This option creates a toolbar that you can position at any point on your desktop.

✦ **Auto-Hide:** This option hides the sidebar unless you click a gadgets icon at the bottom of your screen or press Shift twice.

**Book VIII
Chapter 1**

**Introduction to
Google Gadgets**

✦ **Always on Top:** This option stakes out some permanent real estate for the sidebar, pushing everything else on the screen aside. If you've got a widescreen computer, this might be a good option for you.

✦ **Dock Sidebar:** This option moves the sidebar either to the left of the screen or to the right.

✦ **Font Size:** This option lets you choose the default font size, a larger option, or a smaller option.

Play around with the options and see which works best for you. You can find a setup that works for you.

Uncovering the Secrets to Creating Viral Gadgets

So other than convenience and usefulness, why bother with Google Desktop, iGoogle, and Google Gadgets? They're useful tools, but how can they help your business? The answer is that anybody can create Google Gadgets, including you, and you can use them to help promote your business.

Given the amount of gadgets available for Google users, you have to make your gadget stand out among the others. That doesn't mean that you have to conquer the world, though. Keep a few things in mind when designing your gadget to make it as useful as possible:

✦ **You're not conquering the world:** The world is filled with all sorts of people with all sorts of different interests, and it's impossible to please all of them at the same time. Trying to design your gadget to be all things to all people means you're destined to be disappointed. Don't try to be all-inclusive — pick your idea and stick with it. Make it work for your business and your customers.

✦ **Know your audience:** If you're a small business, you've probably gotten to know your customers fairly well. You can set aside items each one might want. You know their preferences, likes, and dislikes. Use that same kind of knowledge when you're writing your gadgets. Target your most loyal customers when you create the gadget — chances are more users like them are out there, and your gadget will help them as well.

✦ **Get people talking:** Viral marketing depends on word-of-mouth recommendations, so you have to make sure people want to talk about your gadget. Pass along word of your gadget to your customers, and encourage them to pass the word along as well. Your goal is to have everybody passing around word about your gadget and business. After people know of your existence, you can talk to them about using your business.

✦ **Make it useful:** Virtual pet rocks might be cute, but they're not very useful, and people will pass them up quickly to add something more useful to their desktops or sidebar. People won't waste real estate on useless items, so it's up to you to make it work for them. If you make a gadget simple but useful, more people are likely to use the gadget and pass it on to others.

✦ **Change your information often:** If nothing ever changes about your gadget, why do people need to go back and look at it? Make sure that your gadget remains useful by refreshing your content often and keeping it interesting. New and different items always capture attention, and you'll have a larger audience because of it.

Now that you've taken a look at the theory behind making gadgets, you can move on to actually creating your gadgets. That information is presented in Chapter 2 of this minibook, entitled "Creating Your First Google Gadgets."

Chapter 2: Creating Your First Google Gadgets

In This Chapter

✔ Understanding what goes into making a gadget

✔ Building a simple gadget with Google's tools

✔ Taking your gadgets to a higher level

*O*ne of the biggest advantages of using Google's services is all the information you can share. The Google Gadgets you use on your iGoogle or Google Apps desktop are made possible by Google, but they've more than likely been built by developers outside the company, either for profit or just for the fun of it. You also have the opportunity to build your own gadgets, even if you've never coded a program before in your life. From the most basic gadgets to an advanced piece of Web-based wonder, Google provides the tools to make it possible.

Why You Should Make Your Own Gadgets

If you've taken a look at the Google Gadgets available online, it may seem a little daunting to try to produce something else to throw into the pool. There are all kinds of gadgets covering all kinds of needs, from news readers to movie times to e-mail and calendar gadgets to photo frames. So why should you attempt to make your own gadgets? Here are some possible reasons:

✦ **To publicize your business:** These gadgets can potentially end up on the desktops and sidebars of many, many users. If you run a business, those are a lot of potential customers. If you make your gadget useful and get it in front of the eyes of those potential customers, you stand to earn yourself quite a bit more business.

✦ **To reward your loyal customers:** You don't want to go around giving 50-percent-off coupons to everybody who patronizes your business, but such incentives can help keep your regulars happy and encourage their return. Happy customers mean more business, which probably means more happiness for you as well. Use your gadgets to make these offers available to your loyal customers without throwing the gates open for everybody.

✦ **To get people talking:** Those happy customers we talked about in the last paragraph aren't silent statues. When you reward them, they're likely to tell others about what you've done. It's the difference between a random customer picking your product up in a store and ten customers heading into the store specifically for your product, telling their friends, family, and the cashier about it, and then showing it off after they get home. All of your business marketing efforts don't have to come from you — that's the foundation of viral marketing. Good business practices and good products couple with the immediacy of Google's information to give you a lot more customers.

✦ **To stay connected:** A Google Gadget on your customer's desktop means you have a direct line of communication to your customers, and you can keep them in the loop at all times. If you change your hours, add some services or products, and need to make some other notifications, you can just change some information on the gadget and you're ready to go. It's easier than making a bunch of phone calls, cheaper than sending junk mail, and less likely to get caught in a spam filter than e-mail.

Understanding the Building Blocks of a Google Gadget

Unfortunately, you can't just draw a small box around some text on your computer, save it, and make a Google Gadget. It takes a little more effort to put one of these little programs together. It's not hard, but you (or somebody working for you) has to know a little about programming for the Internet to get it to work.

XML

XML, which stands for *eXtensible Markup Language* is basically a series of tags Google Gadgets uses to actually define the gadget itself. All the functionality of the code is contained within these tags, which tells Google's various desktops that they're dealing with a gadget and instructs them to act appropriately.

You don't have to have an extensive knowledge of XML in order to create a Google Gadget. In fact, Google provides an example of the XML needed to create a gadget in its help section at `http://code.google.com/apis/gadgets/docs/legacy/gs.html`. It is shown here:

```
<?xml version="1.0" encoding="UTF-8" ?>
<Module>
    <ModulePrefs title="hello word example"
    title_url="http://example.com"
    description="a test gadget"
    author_e-mail="test@example.com"
```

```
      screenshot="http://example.com/example.png"
      thumbnail="http://example.com/thumb.png" />
  <Content type="html">
  <![CDATA[
  Hello, world!
  ]]>
</Content>
</Module>
```

All you have to do is change the sample information to your own information, type in whatever text you want to include in your gadget, save it as a file with the extension .xml, and upload it to either your server, a Google Pages account, or publish it to the iGoogle directory using the Google Gadget Editor (described later in this chapter). Your gadget is up and running!

Google specifies more attributes that you can (and probably should) include in your gadget at the preceding link, but these are the attributes that apply to every gadget that goes online. Depending on the type of gadget you're coding, there might be other attributes you'll want. Don't worry — the link includes plenty of examples and samples of code you can use to create your widget.

HTML

The XML gadget we just took a look at is functional, but it's pretty plain-looking. In fact, it's just plain black text on a white background. If you take a look at the other Google Gadgets available for your desktops, they're probably quite a bit better looking. That's where HTML comes in.

HTML stands for *Hypertext Markup Language*, and it represents the basic building blocks of the Internet. Every Web page you view has HTML as its foundation. Its primary job is to describe how the pages look and are laid out. Think of your text as the main message of the page, and the HTML as the instructions for how the text will look. This is a simplified description, but the point is that HTML affects the appearance of the text.

There's simply far too much to HTML to describe how it makes your widget appear the way you want it to, but the good news is that it's not that hard to learn (you might even consider a resource like *HTML For Dummies*, published by Wiley Publishing). With just a little effort, you can make your gadget look quite presentable to the public.

JavaScript

If you're interested in a little more advanced Web programming, you can also include JavaScript in your gadget. This scripting language doesn't have any relation to the programming language Java (or coffee, either), but JavaScript allows you to write scripts that can interact with the user, including anything from small games to saving information from online forms. JavaScript allows you to add some interactive elements to your gadgets, making for a more personalized experience for the user, You can choose options from drop-down menus or customize the look of the gadget. However, JavaScript does require some more advanced programming knowledge, so it's best left to somebody who has that knowledge to do it for you (unless you already know JavaScript, of course).

Writing Google Gadgets

All you need to write Google Gadgets is a text editor (not a word processor) and a public server. You do all the writing in the text editor (like Vista's Notepad, Mac's TextEdit, or any number of plain text editors), then save the gadget with the extension `.xml`, and upload it to your server. From there, it can be embedded in Web pages or submitted to iGoogle or Google Desktop.

To submit your gadget, go to `http://www.google.com/ig/submit`, read over the user agreement, review the requirements, and enter the URL of the uploaded gadget. (See Figure 2-1.)

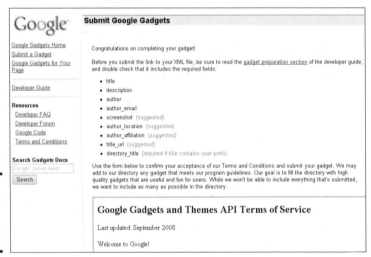

Figure 2-1:
Submitting
your gadget
to Google.

Unless you're very familiar with HTML and JavaScript, writing and submitting a custom Google Gadget can be a frustrating experience. Be prepared to spend some time learning about these languages if you're going to develop gadgets as a serious part of your business.

Using the Google Gadget Editor

If you're developing Google Gadgets for iGoogle or Google Apps desktops, Google provides a WYSIWYG (what-you-see-is-what-you-get) editor for these gadgets at `http://code.google.com/apis/gadgets/docs/legacy/gs.html`. It enables you to both type in your text and see the results of what you're typing before you publish it for use. You can even save your in-progress work and come back to it later when you're signed in to your Google account.

Point your browser to the preceding link and scroll down the page until you see the screen shown in Figure 2-2.

Figure 2-2:
The Google
Gadget
editor.

The links at the top of the screen show examples of gadgets that you can use to study for your own knowledge or customize for your own use. The two tabs just below those links switch between the code view and the preview of the actual gadget. The text to the right of the actual code view gives the name of the gadget you're working on, and the drop-down menu at the left of the screen controls how you save and call up your gadgets.

The screen shown in Figure 2-2 shows the example for a horoscope gadget, and it includes only a brief amount of the actual text that goes into the gadget — the actual code is 1,151 lines long. However, you can click the Preview tab to see the gadget itself, as shown in Figure 2-3.

**Book VIII
Chapter 2**

**Creating Your First
Google Gadgets**

Figure 2-3:
Previewing
the Google
Gadget.

You can flip back and forth frequently to make sure your work is correct and the gadget is performing the way you want it to. You can even interact with the gadget, to make sure the gadget responds correctly to your commands.

The drop-down menu gives you control over how you open, save, and publish your gadgets.

The commands in that menu affect your gadgets in various ways:

✦ **New:** This command opens one of the test or example gadgets shown above the Google Gadget Editor. You can also use the links to pull up that gadget directly.

✦ **Open:** If you're signed into your Google account, you can use this command to open any gadgets you've saved to your personal store.

✦ **Open From URL:** This command opens a gadget from a remote location. Remember, though, that it can't save the gadget back to your server. You have to copy the code and upload it manually.

✦ **Save:** This saves any changes to the code you've made on gadgets saved under your Google account.

✦ **Save As:** This saves any gadget you're working on to your Google account under a new name.

✦ **Rename:** This command allows you to rename a currently saved gadget.

✦ **Upload:** This command takes an XML file from your computer, uploads it to your Google account, and gives it a name, as shown in Figure 2-4. Click Browse to find the file, type in the name, and click Upload to put the file on your account.

Figure 2-4:
Uploading
a file to
the Google
Gadget
Editor.

✦ **Publish:** This command stores the gadget and allows you to send it to your iGoogle page, publish it for public use, or embed it into a Web page.

✦ **Delete:** This command deletes any saved gadget.

When you publish your gadget, Google checks your code and points out any errors, as shown in Figure 2-5.

Figure 2-5:
Validating
your Google
Gadget.

Fix the errors shown in your code and then try publishing it again until you get the message shown in Figure 2-6.

Figure 2-6:
Publishing
your Google
Gadget.

The first link gives the exact location of your Google Gadget. If you choose to publish the gadget to your iGoogle page, click the second link to view the screen shown in Figure 2-7. Click the Add To Google button to finalize your decision and move the gadget around as you choose.

Figure 2-7:
Adding your gadget to iGoogle.

Clicking the third link to publish your gadget to the iGoogle directory brings up the screen shown in Figure 2-1. Again, follow all the instructions and make sure your gadget fits Google's regulations before you submit it. If you want to embed your gadget in a Web page (such as your own page) or make the code available for others to embed in their blogs, click the fourth link to see the screen shown in Figure 2-8.

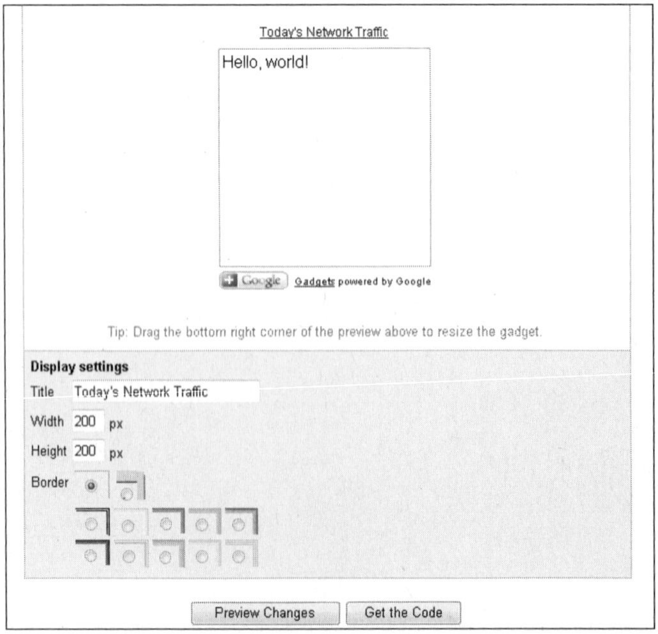

Figure 2-8:
Embedding your gadget in a Web page.

From here, you can change the title of the gadget, change the size of the gadget, and choose a border for the entire gadget if you wish. All changes are shown as they're made, so you know what you're getting before you send the code on to your Web site. When you're satisfied, click the Get Code button to see the text shown in Figure 2-9 just below the Get Code button.

Copy all the text from the window and paste it into the appropriate section on your Web site to display the gadget on your Web page. You can also make the code available to others to post on their Web pages.

Figure 2-9:
Copying
the code of
your Google
Gadget.

Copy and paste the HTML below to include this gadget on your webpage.

```
<script src="http://www.gmodules.com/ig/ifr?url=http://hosting.gmodules.co
```

Making Your Own Gadgets — Even Easier

If you want a decent looking gadget and don't mind choosing from a few pre-made templates, you can always use iGoogle to craft one of seven choices and distribute those options to your colleagues and customers. These only work with iGoogle homepages, and you have to have an iGoogle account to create them. Still, you should be able to get some mileage out of these choices.

Point your browser to `http://www.google.com/ig/gmchoices` and take a look at the choices shown in Figure 2-10.

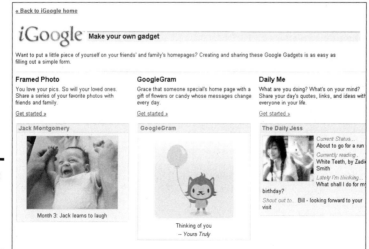

Figure 2-10:
Making
your own
gadgets in
iGoogle.

The available templates include the following possibilities:

✦ **Framed Photo:** This gadget allows you to add photos, captions, and backgrounds to create a gadget-based photo album. Just enter the URLs of your online photos to link them to the gadget.

✦ **GoogleGram:** This gadget allows you to choose a gift, add up to seven days of messages, and sign you in to GoogleGram.

✦ **Daily Me:** This gadget allows you to create some custom fields, add a photo, and share daily updates about your life.

✦ **Freeform:** This gadget allows you to enter an image, some text, and some layout options to create a customizable gadget.

✦ **YouTube Channel:** This gadget gathers your favorite URLs of YouTube videos into a distributable gadget.

✦ **Personal List:** This gadget lets you add list items and change some background options.

✦ **Countdown:** This gadget counts down to a certain date, and you add the date, title, background color, and other information.

No matter what the gadget, all are built in a similar fashion. Here are the necessary steps:

1. **Choose the gadget you want to build.**

2. **Click the Get Started link under the gadget you want to build.**

3. **Fill in the blanks, as shown in Figure 2-11.**

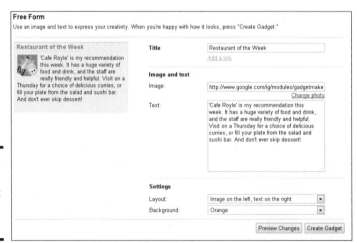

Figure 2-11: Creating your gadget from a template.

4. **Upload any photos as necessary, as shown in Figure 2-12.**

You can choose from Picasa Web photo albums, other URLs, or files on your computer.

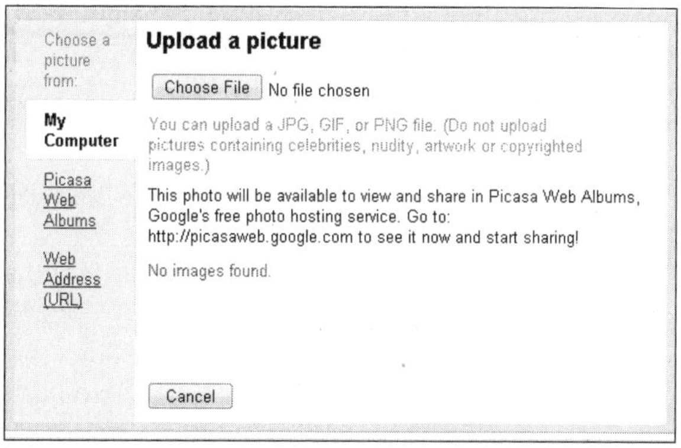

Figure 2-12:
Uploading
a photo to
your gadget.

5. **Click the Preview Changes button to see how your changes have affected the gadget.**

6. **Click Create Gadget to put the gadget on your home page.**

You can also e-mail it to others, as shown in Figure 2-13.

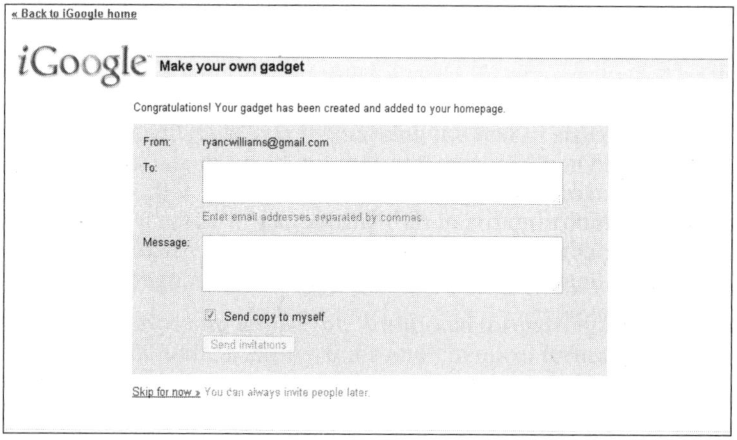

Figure 2-13:
Sharing
your gadget
with others.

To change your gadget, click the menu icon in the upper-right corner. From here, you have a few choices, as shown in Figure 2-14.

About this gadget

Created: Friday, January 23, 2009
Last changed: Friday, January 23, 2009

Created by:
                                    Edit
Description provided by the author:
                                    Edit

Manage your gadget

Invite viewers

Publishing options

Update gadget

Figure 2-14:
Changing
your gadget.

Click the Edit links to change your name and description. Click the Invite Viewers link to e-mail it to others, and click the Publishing Options link to choose whether you keep the gadget private or publish it to the iGoogle directory. Click Update Gadget to put all the changes you've made into effect. Just above the screen shown in Figure 2-14, you see the Edit link, which you can click to change the information in the gadget. You can click Delete to remove it entirely.

Your options are severely limited compared to the Google Gadget Editor or hand-coding your gadget, but using this method means you produce a decent-looking gadget with a minimum of effort, and you can make any updates necessary from your iGoogle page.

Chapter 3: Creating Applications for Social Networks

In This Chapter

✔ **Integrating your business with social networks**

✔ **Understanding OpenSocial**

✔ **Creating your OpenSocial applications**

There are so many useful programs and services available on the Internet that it's usually not a problem finding a program that does something you want. The problem arises when you try to get that program to work with another program. Programmers can be jealous about their code and not want to share it with others, making it difficult for programs to work together. And, even when the code is shared, it's difficult to make everything work together if the programs are not written that way from the start. A shared standard is so important because it enables programs to work together. And that's where OpenSocial comes in.

Introduction to OpenSocial

OpenSocial is the name given to a common *application programming interface,* or *API,* that programmers use to write applications that work across several different social networks and hosted services. It allows applications written for one social network to pull data from different sources, share information across these platforms, and work on different platforms if necessary. That means that applications written using the OpenSocial API can work on

- ✦ MySpace
- ✦ Ning
- ✦ LinkedIn
- ✦ imeem
- ✦ Salesforce.com
- ✦ orkut
- ✦ Six Apart (blogging software that includes Movable Type and TypePad)

These are some of the more popular applications, but OpenSocial allows you to share your programs across more than those listed. A complete list is available at `http://code.google.com/apis/opensocial/whoisusingit.html`, and that list is always changing and expanding.

If you're planning on creating applications that link your iGoogle home page or Google Apps desktop gadgets to other platforms (for example, a gadget that links from iGoogle to your existing MySpace profile or TypePad blog), OpenSocial can help you make that possible. The common standards set through the API make it possible for all these platforms to share information and gadgets. That means all the platforms stay linked, and you (and your customers) can place applications on any preferred platform without issue.

Where Does Your OpenSocial App Work?

OpenSocial gadgets are just like the gadgets created in Chapter 2 of this book because they can be hosted on your own server or in Google's online gadget cache. From there, you can submit and publish them in the same manner as the other gadgets. The main difference is that OpenSocial gadgets use a different API than the one created and used for iGoogle and Google Apps desktops. That API is referred to as the "legacy" API.

You should note that any OpenSocial gadgets you make in the Google Gadget editor might not function properly in preview mode. The Google Gadget editor has yet to be updated beyond the legacy API at the time of this writing, so the terms used in the OpenSocial API might not work correctly. Bear this in mind while you're coding. It's a good idea to decide before you begin whether the gadget you're creating will be for OpenSocial or for the various Google desktops. You can then use the appropriate tools.

After your gadget is written (using the XML, HTML, and Javascript languages referred to in Chapter 2), it can be used in all OpenSocial platforms in just about any Web browser and operating system. That's what makes OpenSocial such an important standard. You can reach just about anybody with a desktop computer, laptop, or smartphone with the gadget you create, increasing your audience and making it possible to spread your message as widely as possible.

Can You Do It Yourself?

The short answer is "yes, absolutely!" But there's a big "if" there, too. Those with knowledge of XML, HTML, and Javascript can put together their own gadgets, publish them on their own servers or store them on Google, and spread the word about their new OpenSocial applications far and wide. The question is: How much knowledge do you need?

Take a look at the screen shown in Figure 3-1. You can reach this screen by pointing your browser to `http://code.google.com/apis/opensocial/`. It's got just about everything you need to get started with the OpenSocial API.

Figure 3-1: The OpenSocial API.

This site lists documents and articles relating to OpenSocial, a frequently-answered-questions list, a blog relaying new developments in OpenSocial, and a community of supporters and developers for OpenSocial. With these tools, you should be able to find any information you need to put together your application and perform the inevitable troubleshooting. All you need to do is review the information, understand the API, write your code, and publish your application.

However, all of that information is really dependent on that knowledge of the languages we mentioned a couple paragraphs ago. Unless you have an in-depth knowledge of the languages used to create these gadgets and you understand the function of the API, you're not in a position to write your own OpenSocial application without putting in a lot of time learning and practicing your programming skills. This is the time to call in reinforcements — find a programmer who can write the code for you.

That doesn't mean that you have to give up the entire development process, though. You can still provide the design and intent of the application and work with the developer through the programming process.

You can still be involved in the initial brainstorming process, and you are a part of the unwritten last step of process — testing. After the first draft of the application is written, it has to be constantly revised and tested to make sure it functions without major issues. Only then can you publish it for others to use.

Chapter 4: Google Chrome and Gears

In This Chapter

✔ **Installing Chrome and Gears on your computer**

✔ **Finding out what makes Chrome different**

✔ **Working offline with Gears**

Google is essentially a Web-based company — almost everything it does is directed at your web browser and built around networked computers, servers, and software hosted at remote locations. In one respect, this makes it an invaluable resource. You can access it from any computer with an Internet connection, and you don't have to worry about losing your online data if your computer ever bites the dust. However, it also limits you if you're not connected to the Internet. Even with the plethora of connectivity options you have to get online, sometimes you just find yourself without an Internet connection. You do have some backup options, though, and they involve software written by Google and stored on your computer and other Web sites. Google has its own Web browser in Chrome, and it uses a program called Gears to help your Web browser access Google-based information even when you're away from the Internet.

Using Google's Machinery

Google uses very mechanical-sounding names to describe the two pieces of software examined in this chapter. You're already familiar with the functionality of Chrome if you've used a Web browser, but you've probably not seen a Gears function, although it is working in the background when you use certain software and Web sites. Before any of that happens, though, you have to install the software on your computer.

Installing Chrome

If you already have a favorite Web browser, you don't have to install Chrome. That's really all the program does, and you can function perfectly well without it. However, Chrome does perform some functions differently from other Web browsers, and you may notice a difference in speed between Chrome and other browsers. If you choose to install it (you can always uninstall it afterwards if you don't like it), point your browser to `http://google.com/chrome` to see the screen shown in Figure 4-1.

Figure 4-1: Installing Chrome.

At the time of this writing, Google's Chrome is only compatible with Windows XP with Service Pack 2 and Windows Vista. Mac and Linux users are expected to get it eventually, but development is ongoing.

Click the Download Google Chrome button, and click the Accept and Install button on the next screen to begin the installation process. Chrome attempts to import bookmarks and other information from Internet Explorer, and it starts up from there.

Installing Gears

Gears is compatible with several different browsers and operating systems, so you're able to use it in more places than you can use Chrome. In addition, it comes preloaded with every Chrome installation, so you don't have to worry about installing it if you're already using Chrome as your Web browser. Point your browser of choice to `http://gears.google.com` to see the screen shown in Figure 4-2.

Figure 4-2:
Installing
Gears
on your
computer.

Click the Install Gears button and click the Agree and Download button on the next page to begin the installation. Follow the instructions from here to install Gears on your computer, and it is ready to interface with compatible Web sites.

What Is Chrome?

Web browsers define how you interact with the Internet, and each one works in generally the same fashion. They interpret the data received from a remote server and organize it into a recognizable Web page. The difference between browsers lies in the way each organizes the information and in the special features each includes. This section takes a look at what makes Chrome different from other browsers. The biggest differences are as follows:

✦ **The homepage:** Most browsers are set by default to a homepage that opens whenever you begin a new browser window. You can also set certain browsers to open different tabs when they first open, giving you access to several different pages in the same browser — you just have to click the tab to move to the next page. Chrome, on the other hand, starts out automatically on a list of your most visited Web sites, as shown in Figure 4-3.

All you have to do is click on the thumbnail to open the page. If you use tabs in your browser, each tab opens with those thumbnails on the page. These thumbnails update dynamically, so any page you start using more than others shows up in the list, and the lesser-used pages drop out.

✦ **The address line is also a search box:** Instead of navigating to Google to search for information or moving over to a separate search window in the browser, you can type what you're looking for in the address line. You are presented with popular results and the choice to search for additional information on Google. This does save you some time.

Figure 4-3:
Starting out
in Chrome.

✦ **Drag-and-drop tabs:** If you want to take a tab out of the browser window and make it into its own window, just click and hold on the tab and drag it out of the window. You can now close the original window and keep the other window open. This can be helpful if Chrome ever crashes, because only the tab that's having problems stops functioning. Other tabs and windows continue to work.

✦ **Safe and anonymous browsing:** Chrome automatically warns you if you try to access a site that could possibly contain malicious programs, viruses, or similar threats. Google searches automatically do this, but with Chrome, you get that kind of security no matter where you go.

You can also use the browser in *incognito mode*, which allows you to access Web sites without leaving a trace on your computer. (See Figure 4-4.) That means that your browsing history doesn't keep track of this visit, and your computer won't retain any cookies or other information from that site. Using this function won't be helpful if you want to keep track of where you've been or you want to retain information for future visits, but it can be helpful if you're using another computer and you don't want to leave your information on it (or you don't want others leaving their information on your machine).

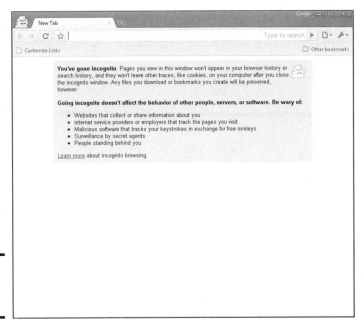

Google

Figure 4-4:
Going
incognito.

These features are where Google Chrome differs most from other Web browsers, but some features are still similar. You can always feel free to keep multiple browsers on your computer (if you're creating Web sites, it's a necessity if you use different browsers for testing). The intriguing thing about Chrome is that Google constantly redefines and redevelops its software, so that means that avid users of Google's service will likely notice more and more benefits from using the browser with Google's associated software. Because it's all coming from the same place, it's likely to work together in more advanced ways than other browsers would.

What Is Gears?

You don't have to see the gears in a machine to know that they're working. They provide the inner movement that makes the larger machine function. Google Gears functions in the same way — you don't actually work with Gears, but they make it possible for you to use other programs while you're not connected to a network.

In order to use Gears, both the Web site you're accessing and your computer must have it installed. It's a two-way street, because Gears takes information from the Web site and stores it locally on your computer. That means you can work with the information wherever you are and sync it up to the site when you reconnect to the network.

Google applications that use Gears include

✦ Google Docs

✦ Gmail

✦ Google Reader

✦ YouTube

✦ Mobile Picasa photo galleries

Sites like MySpace, Zoho, and Remember The Milk also support some use of Gears in their functionality, depending on what the sites actually do.

When you access a site that uses Gears, you are asked if you want to use its functionality with your computer. For example, in Google Reader, you get the message shown in Figure 4-5 when you click the small green Gears icon in the top-right corner of your screen.

Figure 4-5:
Enabling
Gears.

Click the check box and then the Allow button to make Gears work with your computer and the Web site. You are notified that Gears is downloading content from the Web to your computer.

You are now able to view the content from this page even if you're not connected to the network. This information stays on your computer until you re-sync it with the network.

How to Make Chrome and Gears Work for You

You can conduct your business without Gears and Chrome, but these tools can make it a little easier to function and give you some peace of mind. The following list explains how these two programs can help your business:

+ **Accessibility:** If you need to take documents or articles on the road with you, Gears allows you to store the information on your computer. You can read or view them anywhere and then get new information when you're connected up to a network again. This is probably of most use to laptop users, who could find themselves without access to networks in their travels.

+ **Security:** If your workers frequently browse the Web, Chrome's security features could potentially block problems with malicious Web sites. It's no replacement for good antivirus and anti-malware programs, but it does give you a little more help in your searches.

+ **Compatibility:** Gears works with several different browsers and platforms, and development for Chrome on Mac and Linux continues. No matter what system you use, the convenience of Google programs is available to you.

Chapter 5: Going Mobile with Google

In This Chapter

✓ Putting Google on your mobile device

✓ Choosing the mobile Google applications for you

✓ Integrating mobile Google with your business

You don't have to stay in one place to maintain your Internet connection anymore. With wi-fi and 3G data networks, you can access your e-mail and data from just about anywhere you can put up an antenna. That's why Google has developed applications for you to use on the go. Your mobile devices might not be as powerful as your home computer, but the capability to read Google Documents or use Google Maps on the road can be priceless if you need it. And Google gives it all away for free to a multitude of devices.

Accessing Mobile Google

Basically, if you can access the Internet on it, you can use Google. It may not look the same as it would on your nice, wide screen at home, but the functionality is basically the same. Google has a customized version of its site that runs on mobile browsers, tailored to work with smaller screens and different keyboards. Smartphones, like the iPhone and the Blackberry, can also download small applications that run on the phone and access Google services.

Point your browser to `http://m.google.com` to take a look at what mobile services Google has to offer. If you're accessing it from a desktop or laptop, you see the site shown in Figure 5-1. The site presents a list of all the mobile devices Google has created software for.

Figure 5-1:
Accessing
mobile
Google
applications
from your
computer.

Choose the device you use from the list shown in Figure 5-1 and click the icon to see the screen shown in Figure 5-2.

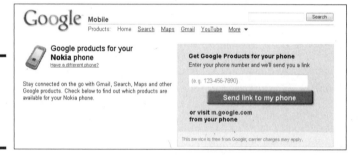

Figure 5-2:
Accessing
mobile
Google
software.

If you type your mobile number into the text field and click Send Link To My Phone, Google sends you an SMS (otherwise known as text) message with a link to access Google software.

Depending on your cell plan, you may be charged more for each text message you receive or for Internet data usage. Make sure you're not going to run up an out-of-control bill when you use Google services. This might be the time to consider that unlimited data usage plan.

If you access the mobile Google site from your mobile device, you see the version of the site tailored for smaller screens and direct connections. An example taken from the iPhone is shown in Figure 5-3. Your version of the site may differ from device to device, but you still get the same basic information.

Figure 5-3:
Google's
mobile
site on the
iPhone.

Each of the icons shown in Figure 5-3 accesses a different Google service. To access these services, you have to sign in with your Google account (which could be a trial, depending on your keyboard), but after you're signed in, you should have access to everything.

If you have a Google Apps account, the mobile Google site accesses that as well. Click the button shown at the bottom of Figure 5-3 to configure the mobile site for Google Apps. Enter your domain name and click Go, as shown in Figure 5-4.

Figure 5-4:
Configuring
Google's
mobile site
for Google
Apps.

The site shows you the applications available for your Apps domain at this point, as shown in Figure 5-5. Click the icon and enter your username and password to use the applications.

Figure 5-5:
Google
Apps for
the mobile
Google site.

Most mobile devices can send and receive data over cellular networks, whether they're the commonly used networks or more advanced 3G networks. In addition, many mobile devices are equipped with wi-fi connections that allow you to use "hot spots" to access the Internet wirelessly. Remember, you're accessing the Internet here, so it's always better to have the fastest connection possible, especially if you're going to transfer large quantities of data.

If you plan to do a lot of work with mobile Google, it might be wise to invest in an unlimited data plan. The smallest bytes can add up by the end of the month. Be aware of how much you're using the data functions, because you end up paying for it somehow.

Using the Google Mobile App

Blackberry and iPhone users can also download an application to run directly off of their phones without accessing a Web browser. iPhone users can download it at the App Store, and Blackberry users can download it from `http://m.google.com/mail`. This application combines several of the different Google services in one area.

The Google Mobile App is divided up into three sections, accessible from the three icons at the bottom of the screen shown in Figure 5-6:

✦ **Search:** The first icon is dedicated to search functions, either by text or by typing. You can type in your search terms at the top of the screen or speak your terms into the phone.

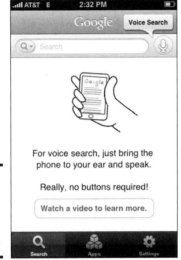

Figure 5-6: Searching with the Google Mobile App.

✦ **Apps:** The second icon brings up all the available applications for mobile Google users. Notice that both individual Google accounts and Google Apps domains are available, as shown in Figure 5-7. Just click the icon of your choice, and the Web browser pops up with the appropriate service. Remember, you have to sign in the first time, but you have access after that.

✦ **Settings:** The last icon takes you to the settings screen, as shown in Figure 5-8. Here's where you specify how Google Mobile App shows you information and what you want to see when you first start the program. The available menus are as follows:

• *Start Screen:* The first menu lets you select whether you start on the Apps screen, your last used application, or the search window (with or without keyboard).

• *Searchable Items:* This menu lets you toggle whether you can search through your contacts, previous searches, Web sites, and suggested sites.

• *SafeSearch:* This menu toggles SafeSearch on or off.

Book VIII Chapter 5

Going Mobile with Google

- *VoiceSearch:* This menu toggles VoiceSearch on or off.

- *Domain:* You can configure your Google Apps domain with this menu.

- *Screen Rotation:* This last menu turns screen rotation on or off, depending on your device.

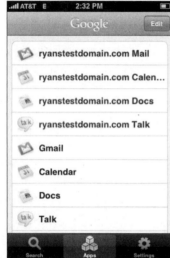

Figure 5-7:
Applications in the Google Mobile App.

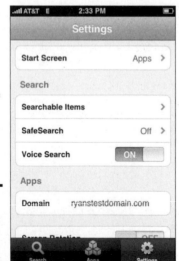

Figure 5-8:
Setting up your Google Mobile App.

Using Google Gears on mobile devices

If you're using Windows Mobile 5 or 6, you can use Gears to take information with you even when you're not connected to a network. Just navigate to `http://gears.google.com` and download Gears to your device. When you're done, you'll be able to work with Gears-enabled sites just as you would on a desktop or laptop computer.

Exploring Google's Mobile Applications

The vast majority of Google's applications can be used on mobile devices as well. They may not look the same, but you still get similar functionality from them. However, depending on the device, you may notice additional features that aren't available on your computer. For example, Google Maps on an iPhone works with a built-in GPS device to show both your route and how close you are to your final destination in real time.

Here are a few favorites:

✦ **Gmail:** This function brings up a simplified version of Gmail on your browser. You are able to send and receive e-mail, delete or archive read mail, and move messages from folder to folder.

✦ **Search:** Just as on the main Google site, you can search from this application for all the information you might require. If you've set up an individual Google account, your saved search preferences are accessible from here as well.

✦ **Maps:** With this application, you can either find locations on the map or create directions from your current location to your destination. GPS-enabled devices can track your current position as well, letting you know exactly how far you have to go before you arrive.

✦ **YouTube:** Ever been stuck trying to describe a particularly funny or memorable video to your friends, only to end up disappointed when they just don't get it? Now can avoid that hassle and just show them the video directly. Some mobile devices might not be able to show all the videos available from the channel, but you should be able to get most of what you're looking for. Just be sure you're using wi-fi or a 3G data connection when you try to play the videos — otherwise, you're going to be disappointed with the video playback, and you friends still won't get the point.

✦ **SMS:** If it's more convenient for you to use text messages to send in Google queries, just type your question in and send it to 46645 (GOOGL). You receive your answer in a follow-up text from Google. Again, this incurs charges for text messages, so use a browser if it's available because it's cheaper.

✦ **Talk:** After you've signed in, Google Talk presents a list of your contacts and the status of their availability. Click the contact you want and type your message in the available text window. Click Send, and it's just like you're sending instant messages at home.

✦ **Calendar:** All your Google Calendar information is viewable from this application in list view, so you see only scheduled appointments from here. There's also a small text field at the bottom of the screen for adding appointments, like "Get haircut on February 17th." The mobile Google Calendar application is still in beta development at the time of this writing, so the views and features are still subject to change.

You can even send an *SMS message* (the proper name for a text message) to GVENT to add events to your calendar or get upcoming events sent directly to your phone. To register your phone for this feature, follow these steps:

1. *Sign in to Google Calendar.*

2. *Click Settings and select Mobile Setup.*

3. *Enter your country and phone number.*

4. *Check to make sure your carrier is supported by clicking the What Carriers Are Supported? link.*

5. *Click the Send Verification Code button.*

6. *Type the code you receive on the phone into the Verification Code field and click Finish Setup.*

After your phone is registered, send your events to GVENT via SMS and you'll get your event on your calendar.

✦ **News:** Accessing the application shows the front page of your virtual newspaper, listing the latest stories and a brief preview of each. Click the Sections button to bring up different subject areas, such as Word, Nation, Sports, Technology, and more. When you click an individual section, you see the stories for that topic. Click the name of a story to read the entire article.

✦ **Photos:** After you sign in to this application, you are able to view your Picasa Web account. This includes individual photos and any Web albums.

✦ **Blogger:** If you have a Blogger site, you can use this application to sign in and work with your site directly from your mobile device. This includes posting, editing, and viewing your blog entries.

✦ **Reader:** This mobile application lets you read all the feeds you've gathered into your Google Reader account. You can sort your feeds by tag or individual feed, and you can click each feed to read the full article.

✦ **Docs:** The mobile Google Docs applications don't allow you to edit the documents on your mobile device, but you are able to read their contents without issue.

✦ **GOOG-411:** When you tap this icon, you are given a link to a phone number that you can call to access GOOG-411 services. The service connects you to local businesses and services from there.

✦ **iGoogle:** The mobile version of iGoogle won't show you the same layout as your desktop or laptop browser, but you can access the gadgets you've embedded on your homepage. Remember that, depending on the gadget, you might not get the same functionality depending on the mobile device you use. This application primarily works with text- and feed-based gadgets.

Making Google's Mobile Applications Work for Your Business

You've already seen how Google's services can help your business in general. On the road, Google's information can be invaluable. The following list is just a sample of what you can do with a mobile device and a little help from Google:

✦ Check your Gmail, get the address you need, and find your customer's location on Google Maps.

✦ Stay in touch with the latest financial developments using Google News or your Google Reader account.

✦ Review your important documents on Google Docs and make sure you have your numbers right before you start negotiating your deal.

✦ You're on a business trip and your car breaks down. Use GOOG-411 to get a tow truck and mechanic on the case.

✦ Update your company's blog through the Blogger update and let everybody else know what you're up to.

Remember that you need a fast Internet connection to make most of these services work for you. Google's services integrate all your information and needs for you, whether you're at home or on the road.

**Book VIII
Chapter 5**

**Going Mobile
with Google**

Index

Numerics

F

G

H

1

K

keyword-extension combination, 311–312
keywords
  choosing for AdWords ads, 535–538
  distributing on site, 347–348
  identifying, 175
  locations as, 294, 342, 344
  names as
    business, 190, 294, 342, 344, 359
    owner, 294, 369
    personal, 342, 344
    principal, 190, 342, 344–345
    product, 190, 294, 342, 344
    service, 190, 342, 344
  searching Google Gadgets directory
    by, 667
  tags, 181
  using to create site map
    BATCS, 353–354
    creating draft of site, 354–357
    overview, 349–352
kiting, domain name, 308–309

L

languages
  Google Custom Search Engine, 197
  Google Search, 143
laptop computers
  Gmail, 36
  running Google Apps on, 10
  security, 611–613
lawsuits, 295–296, 305
layout
  Google Coupons, 246
  integrating maps into Web site, 227
legacy APIs, 694
Length field, Google Product Search, 278
Line tool, Google Maps, 231–233
lines, adding to maps, 232–233
Link button, Google Sites, 376
Link field, Google Product Search, 278

link networks, 189
Link to This Page link, Google Maps, 245
links
  Add a Tab, iGoogle, 672
  Admin Help Forum, Google Apps, 28
  All Products By, Google Product
    Search, 277
  blogs, 180
  broken, 386
  Choose from contacts, Google Sites, 370
  Data Feed, Google Base, 263–264
  Date, Usage Rights, Numeric Range, and
    More, Google Advanced Search,
    145, 160
  Delete Tab, iGoogle, 672
  Edit This Tab, iGoogle, 671
  focus on, 157
  Get Directions, Google Maps, 213, 228
  Google Search, 186–189
  headers and footers, adding to, 124–126
  Help, Google Apps, 28
  From Here, Google Maps, 228
  To Here, Google Maps, 228
  internal, 153, 387–391
  Link to This Page, Google Maps, 245
  Manage This Domain, Google Apps, 37
  maps, adding to, 223–224
  multiple, 227
  My Sites, Google Sites, 120
  overuse of keywords, 186
  overview, 383–387
  PageRank, 153
  within pages, 387–391
  permalinks, 386
  Post a Single Item, Google Product
    Search, 270–271
  Products, Google Base, 251–252
  Remove This, Google Product Search, 271
  Search Nearby, Google Maps, 229
  Send, Google Maps, 228
  Send to Friend, Google Maps, 245
  Services, Google Base, 252
  Share This Tab, iGoogle, 672
  Show Search Options, Google Docs, 86

Q

R

U

Notes

Notes

Notes

Notes

Notes

Notes

BUSINESS, CAREERS & PERSONAL FINANCE

Accounting For Dummies, 4th Edition*
978-0-470-24600-9

Bookkeeping Workbook For Dummies†
978-0-470-16983-4

Commodities For Dummies
978-0-470-04928-0

Doing Business in China For Dummies
978-0-470-04929-7

E-Mail Marketing For Dummies
978-0-470-19087-6

Job Interviews For Dummies, 3rd Edition*†
978-0-470-17748-8

Personal Finance Workbook For Dummies*†
978-0-470-09933-9

Real Estate License Exams For Dummies
978-0-7645-7623-2

Six Sigma For Dummies
978-0-7645-6798-8

Small Business Kit For Dummies, 2nd Edition*†
978-0-7645-5984-6

Telephone Sales For Dummies
978-0-470-16836-3

BUSINESS PRODUCTIVITY & MICROSOFT OFFICE

Access 2007 For Dummies
978-0-470-03649-5

Excel 2007 For Dummies
978-0-470-03737-9

Office 2007 For Dummies
978-0-470-00923-9

Outlook 2007 For Dummies
978-0-470-03830-7

PowerPoint 2007 For Dummies
978-0-470-04059-1

Project 2007 For Dummies
978-0-470-03651-8

QuickBooks 2008 For Dummies
978-0-470-18470-7

Quicken 2008 For Dummies
978-0-470-17473-9

Salesforce.com For Dummies, 2nd Edition
978-0-470-04893-1

Word 2007 For Dummies
978-0-470-03658-7

EDUCATION, HISTORY, REFERENCE & TEST PREPARATION

African American History For Dummies
978-0-7645-5469-8

Algebra For Dummies
978-0-7645-5325-7

Algebra Workbook For Dummies
978-0-7645-8467-1

Art History For Dummies
978-0-470-09910-0

ASVAB For Dummies, 2nd Edition
978-0-470-10671-6

British Military History For Dummies
978-0-470-03213-8

Calculus For Dummies
978-0-7645-2498-1

Canadian History For Dummies, 2nd Edition
978-0-470-83656-9

Geometry Workbook For Dummies
978-0-471-79940-5

The SAT I For Dummies, 6th Edition
978-0-7645-7193-0

Series 7 Exam For Dummies
978-0-470-09932-2

World History For Dummies
978-0-7645-5242-7

FOOD, HOME, GARDEN, HOBBIES & HOME

Bridge For Dummies, 2nd Edition
978-0-471-92426-5

Coin Collecting For Dummies, 2nd Edition
978-0-470-22275-1

Cooking Basics For Dummies, 3rd Edition
978-0-7645-7206-7

Drawing For Dummies
978-0-7645-5476-6

Etiquette For Dummies, 2nd Edition
978-0-470-10672-3

Gardening Basics For Dummies*†
978-0-470-03749-2

Knitting Patterns For Dummies
978-0-470-04556-5

Living Gluten-Free For Dummies†
978-0-471-77383-2

Painting Do-It-Yourself For Dummies
978-0-470-17533-0

HEALTH, SELF HELP, PARENTING & PETS

Anger Management For Dummies
978-0-470-03715-7

Anxiety & Depression Workbook For Dummies
978-0-7645-9793-0

Dieting For Dummies, 2nd Edition
978-0-7645-4149-0

Dog Training For Dummies, 2nd Edition
978-0-7645-8418-3

Horseback Riding For Dummies
978-0-470-09719-9

Infertility For Dummies†
978-0-470-11518-3

Meditation For Dummies with CD-ROM, 2nd Edition
978-0-471-77774-8

Post-Traumatic Stress Disorder For Dummies
978-0-470-04922-8

Puppies For Dummies, 2nd Edition
978-0-470-03717-1

Thyroid For Dummies, 2nd Edition†
978-0-471-78755-6

Type 1 Diabetes For Dummies*†
978-0-470-17811-9

* Separate Canadian edition also available
† Separate U.K. edition also available

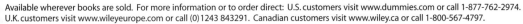
Available wherever books are sold. For more information or to order direct: U.S. customers visit www.dummies.com or call 1-877-762-2974.
U.K. customers visit www.wileyeurope.com or call (0)1243 843291. Canadian customers visit www.wiley.ca or call 1-800-567-4797.

WILEY

INTERNET & DIGITAL MEDIA

AdWords For Dummies
978-0-470-15252-2

Blogging For Dummies, 2nd Edition
978-0-470-23017-6

Digital Photography All-in-One Desk Reference For Dummies, 3rd Edition
978-0-470-03743-0

Digital Photography For Dummies, 5th Edition
978-0-7645-9802-9

Digital SLR Cameras & Photography For Dummies, 2nd Edition
978-0-470-14927-0

eBay Business All-in-One Desk Reference For Dummies
978-0-7645-8438-1

eBay For Dummies, 5th Edition*
978-0-470-04529-9

eBay Listings That Sell For Dummies
978-0-471-78912-3

Facebook For Dummies
978-0-470-26273-3

The Internet For Dummies, 11th Edition
978-0-470-12174-0

Investing Online For Dummies, 5th Edition
978-0-7645-8456-5

iPod & iTunes For Dummies, 5th Edition
978-0-470-17474-6

MySpace For Dummies
978-0-470-09529-4

Podcasting For Dummies
978-0-471-74898-4

Search Engine Optimization For Dummies, 2nd Edition
978-0-471-97998-2

Second Life For Dummies
978-0-470-18025-9

Starting an eBay Business For Dummies 3rd Edition†
978-0-470-14924-9

GRAPHICS, DESIGN & WEB DEVELOPMENT

Adobe Creative Suite 3 Design Premium All-in-One Desk Reference For Dummies
978-0-470-11724-8

Adobe Web Suite CS3 All-in-One Desk Reference For Dummies
978-0-470-12099-6

AutoCAD 2008 For Dummies
978-0-470-11650-0

Building a Web Site For Dummies, 3rd Edition
978-0-470-14928-7

Creating Web Pages All-in-One Desk Reference For Dummies, 3rd Edition
978-0-470-09629-1

Creating Web Pages For Dummies, 8th Edition
978-0-470-08030-6

Dreamweaver CS3 For Dummies
978-0-470-11490-2

Flash CS3 For Dummies
978-0-470-12100-9

Google SketchUp For Dummies
978-0-470-13744-4

InDesign CS3 For Dummies
978-0-470-11865-8

Photoshop CS3 All-in-One Desk Reference For Dummies
978-0-470-11195-6

Photoshop CS3 For Dummies
978-0-470-11193-2

Photoshop Elements 5 For Dummies
978-0-470-09810-3

SolidWorks For Dummies
978-0-7645-9555-4

Visio 2007 For Dummies
978-0-470-08983-5

Web Design For Dummies, 2nd Edition
978-0-471-78117-2

Web Sites Do-It-Yourself For Dummies
978-0-470-16903-2

Web Stores Do-It-Yourself For Dummies
978-0-470-17443-2

LANGUAGES, RELIGION & SPIRITUALITY

Arabic For Dummies
978-0-471-77270-5

Chinese For Dummies, Audio Set
978-0-470-12766-7

French For Dummies
978-0-7645-5193-2

German For Dummies
978-0-7645-5195-6

Hebrew For Dummies
978-0-7645-5489-6

Ingles Para Dummies
978-0-7645-5427-8

Italian For Dummies, Audio Set
978-0-470-09586-7

Italian Verbs For Dummies
978-0-471-77389-4

Japanese For Dummies
978-0-7645-5429-2

Latin For Dummies
978-0-7645-5431-5

Portuguese For Dummies
978-0-471-78738-9

Russian For Dummies
978-0-471-78001-4

Spanish Phrases For Dummies
978-0-7645-7204-3

Spanish For Dummies
978-0-7645-5194-9

Spanish For Dummies, Audio Set
978-0-470-09585-0

The Bible For Dummies
978-0-7645-5296-0

Catholicism For Dummies
978-0-7645-5391-2

The Historical Jesus For Dummies
978-0-470-16785-4

Islam For Dummies
978-0-7645-5503-9

Spirituality For Dummies, 2nd Edition
978-0-470-19142-2

NETWORKING AND PROGRAMMING

ASP.NET 3.5 For Dummies
978-0-470-19592-5

C# 2008 For Dummies
978-0-470-19109-5

Hacking For Dummies, 2nd Edition
978-0-470-05235-8

Home Networking For Dummies, 4th Edition
978-0-470-11806-1

Java For Dummies, 4th Edition
978-0-470-08716-9

Microsoft® SQL Server™ 2008 All-in-One Desk Reference For Dummies
978-0-470-17954-3

Networking All-in-One Desk Reference For Dummies, 2nd Edition
978-0-7645-9939-2

Networking For Dummies, 8th Edition
978-0-470-05620-2

SharePoint 2007 For Dummies
978-0-470-09941-4

Wireless Home Networking For Dummies, 2nd Edition
978-0-471-74940-0